D0208026

THE PAPERS OF

WOODROW WILSON

VOLUME 17

1907-1908

SPONSORED BY THE WOODROW WILSON
FOUNDATION
AND PRINCETON UNIVERSITY

THE PAPERS OF
WOODROW WILSON

ARTHUR S. LINK, *EDITOR*

DAVID W. HIRST AND JOHN E. LITTLE

ASSOCIATE EDITORS

JOHN M. MULDER, *ASSISTANT EDITOR*

JEAN MACLACHLAN AND SYLVIA ELVIN FONTIJN

CONTRIBUTING EDITORS

M. HALSEY THOMAS, *CONSULTING EDITOR*

Volume 17 · 1907-1908

PRINCETON, NEW JERSEY

PRINCETON UNIVERSITY PRESS

1974

L.C. Card 66-10880
I.S.B.N. 0-691-04621-2

Printed in the United States of America
by Princeton University Press
Princeton, New Jersey

EDITORIAL ADVISORY COMMITTEE

INTRODUCTION

AT the beginning of this volume, we find Wilson in Bermuda, on the first visit to that "lotus land" to which he would retreat again and again for rest and restoration. Amid the swirl of social life he meets Mary Allen Hulbert Peck of Pittsfield, Massachusetts. Their friendship, which would be productive of a long and intimate correspondence, was spontaneous and would grow warmer as the months passed.

Returning home in early February 1907, Wilson delivers a major series of lectures on American constitutional government at Columbia University, is active on the alumni and lecture circuit, and is as usual engrossed in the day-to-day administration of university affairs. He confers and corresponds frequently with Ralph Adams Cram, the new supervising architect of the university, about plans for the future development of the campus and buildings; intervenes decisively to persuade Henry van Dyke to withdraw his resignation from the Princeton faculty; carries forward his plans to enlarge the facilities and staff of the scientific departments; and becomes involved in the first stage of a controversy with Andrew F. West over the location of a residential graduate college, West favoring an off-campus site, Wilson insisting that the graduate college should be the energizing center of university life.

In his most important action to date as President of Princeton University, Wilson on June 10, 1907, presents to the Board of Trustees his "Report on the Social Coordination of the University," proposing the construction of quadrangles in which all undergraduates would live and eat and the absorption of the upperclass eating clubs into the quadrangles. The trustees, impressed by Wilson's argument that the quadrangle plan was necessary to end the gulf between undergraduate social and intellectual life, adopt his report with only one dissenting vote and authorize him to proceed to mature the plan.

The report, published in the *Princeton Alumni Weekly* in mid-June, sets off bitter opposition from alumni and several influential faculty members. Retreating to the Adirondacks, Wilson pleads for reasonable discussion and patiently tries to still the fast growing storm of criticism. On October 17, 1907, despite strong faculty support for Wilson, the trustees yield to what is by this time overwhelming alumni opinion and with only one negative vote withdraw their approval from the quadrangle plan. They say at the same time, some of them tongue-in-cheek, that Wilson was free to continue to advocate the proposal before the entire Princeton community. Downhearted and humiliated, Wilson begins to write a letter of resignation; but he sets it aside before completing it, in large measure because of loyalty to his friends on the Board of Trustees and faculty.

Meanwhile, taking suggestions that he was good presidential timber more seriously than he ever admitted to friends, Wilson thrusts himself forward in the role of public spokesman and leader, seeking to encourage a new group of disinterested public men, "men with definite programmes, but not tied to parties and not dismayed if parties will not at once take up the measures which they advocate"–independent men who would fight in season and out of season for militant ideals until parties and the nation rallied to their cause. In magazine articles and in speeches at Jamestown, Virginia, Memphis, Nashville, Cleveland, and Indianapolis, he inveighs against too much reliance upon government and, above all, governmental supervision of business which, he warns, can only lead to public ownership and socialism. "Governmental supervision," he concludes, "will not free us or moralize us; it will in the long run enslave us and demoralize us." In addition, the government, instead of striking at corporations and great combinations through fines and dissolution, thus disorganizing the business of the country, should moralize business by finding the individuals responsible for corporate misdeeds and punishing them. Privately, Wilson prepares a "Credo" for a small group of conservative New York Democrats who were presumably interested in him as the Democratic presidential nominee in 1908, and in a letter that would later be published, much to his embarrassment, Wilson wrote that it would be well if William Jennings Bryan could be "knocked once and for all into a cocked hat."

The strain of overwork and the quadrangle controversy takes its toll in December 1907 when Wilson suffers a new stroke that benumbs his right shoulder and arm for many months. He leaves for a second visit to Bermuda in late January and returns to Princeton on February 27, apparently restored to full vigor and health.

Readers are again reminded that *The Papers of Woodrow Wilson* is a continuing series; that persons, institutions, and events that figure prominently in earlier volumes are not re-identified in subsequent ones; and that the Index to each volume gives cross references to fullest earlier identifications. We also reiterate that we print texts *verbatim et literatim*, repairing words and phrases in square brackets only when necessary for clarity or ease of reading; and that we make silent corrections only of obvious typographical errors in typed copies.

We are grateful to Russell M. Smith of the Manuscript Division of the Library of Congress and J. Owen Grundy, City Historian of the Jersey City Public Library, for continuing invaluable assistance; to Lewis Bateman for editorial help; and to Marjorie Sirlouis for deciphering Wilson's shorthand.

THE EDITORS

Princeton, New Jersey
July 24, 1973

CONTENTS

ILLUSTRATIONS

Following page 354

TEXT ILLUSTRATIONS

ABBREVIATIONS

AL	autograph letter
ALI	autograph letter initialed
ALS	autograph letter(s) signed
CC MS	carbon copy of manuscript
CC T	carbon copy typed
CCL	carbon copy of letter
CCR	carbon copy of report
EAW	Ellen Axson Wilson
hw	handwriting, handwritten
hw MS	handwritten manuscript
MS	manuscript
T	typed
T MS	typed manuscript
TC	typed copy
TC MS	typed copy of manuscript
TCL	typed copy of letter
TL	typed letter
TLS	typed letter signed
TR	typed report
TRS	typed report signed
TS	typed signed
WW	Woodrow Wilson
WWhw	Woodrow Wilson handwriting, handwritten
WWhw MS	Woodrow Wilson handwritten manuscript
WWsh	Woodrow Wilson shorthand
WWsh MS	Woodrow Wilson shorthand manuscript
WWshL	Woodrow Wilson shorthand letter
WWT	Woodrow Wilson typed, typewritten
WWT MS	Woodrow Wilson typed manuscript
WWTCL	Woodrow Wilson typed copy of letter
WWTLS	Woodrow Wilson typed letter signed

ABBREVIATIONS FOR COLLECTIONS AND LIBRARIES

Following the National Union Catalog
of the Library of Congress

CSmH	Henry E. Huntington Library, San Marino
CtY	Yale University, New Haven
CtY-D	Yale University, Divinity School
DLC	Library of Congress
IU	University of Illinois, Urbana
LNHT	Tulane University, New Orleans
MH	Harvard University, Cambridge
MHi	Massachusetts Historical Society, Boston
MdBJ	Johns Hopkins University, Baltimore

NRU	University of Rochester
NcU	University of North Carolina, Chapel Hill
NjP	Princeton University, Princeton
RSB Coll., DLC	Ray Stannard Baker Collection of Wilsoniana, Library of Congress
TNJ	Joint University Libraries, Nashville
TxHR	Rice University, Houston
UA, NjP	University Archives, Princeton University
WC, NjP	Woodrow Wilson Collection, Princeton University
WP, DLC	Woodrow Wilson Papers, Library of Congress
WU	University of Wisconsin, Madison
WWP, UA, NjP	Woodrow Wilson Papers, University Archives, Princeton University

SYMBOLS

[Jan. 26, 1907]	publication date of a published writing; also date of document when date is not part of text
[[March 18, 1907]]	delivery date of a speech if publication date differs
[*c. July 31, 1907*]	composition date when publication date differs
⟨and executing⟩	matter deleted from document by Wilson and restored by editors

THE PAPERS OF

WOODROW WILSON

VOLUME 17

1907-1908

THE PAPERS OF
WOODROW WILSON

To Ellen Axson Wilson

My own darling, Hamilton, Bermuda, 14 January, 1907

It is three days before this letter can go, but my heart is so full of you that I simply *must* talk to you at once for heartsease. I have sent my cable,[1] but that single code word seems to have done next to nothing to relieve my loneliness. What do you say to a letter in the form of a diary?

It is mid-June here, warm and soft and languid, the white limestone houses and white streets shining intensely in the vivid sun and everybody in summer garb. It is as if the quaint and quiet place, set off here by itself to dream, were invaded, a bit to its own surprise, by a swarm of Americans, fresh from a summer resort and unacquainted with any kind of serious living,—an odd place in which to write of government![2] Nations and all big affairs of whatever kind seem here remote and theoretical. What have *we* to do with such things on this little island far out at sea?

Though we started in a chill nor'easter, laden with rain, it turned out no great matter. The sea behaved very decently and our craft was as steady as any reasonable voyager could demand. She rolled provokingly in the Gulf Stream after two o'clock the first night out and, without waiting for that, I departed from my usual custom and was quite actively seasick about early bedtime; but one decided attack cleared me of all uncomfortable humours and for the rest of the voyage I was perfectly comfortable. It was clearly a case of nerves, and rest cured it. The second day out was delightful, and we arrived here this morning in charming weather. We sighted land about daybreak and were at the hotel[3] by a few minutes after nine. One comes in at the back door of the islands to get to Hamilton, rounding them on the northwest and turning almost completely about through tortuous

1 It is missing.

2 Wilson had gone to Bermuda not only for a vacation, but also to work on his forthcoming Blumenthal lectures at Columbia University, about which see his correspondence with Nicholas Murray Butler printed in Vol. 16.

3 The Hotel Hamilton.

channels till the pretty bay is found which runs in towards the north and east.

The hotel is plain but very comfortable and I am quite satisfied with the room they have given me. It has the plainness and airiness of a summer-resort hotel. I have not had a meal here yet: that will be the real test of how I shall fare.

The ship's company, if the truth must be told, were most uninteresting. Young David Reed,[4] of Pittsburgh, his wife and sister[5] were on board and afforded me pleasant companionship (he is Judge Reed's[6] son), and I scraped acquaintance with a very interesting Episcopal dominie, one Mr. Reazor,[7] from Orange, a man with both culture and wit. The rest I left severely alone. It is distinctly hard luck when a passenger list of one hundred and seventy-five yields not a single pretty woman,—nor a married pretty one either!

My things are all out of my baggage and placed for my stay and to-morrow I shall settle down to my routine of study and loafing. Jack Patton[8] turned up at the ship landing and has been most attentive and polite: has put me up at the Yacht Club,[9] informed the Governor[10] of my arrival, and generally interfered with my quiet and freedom of mind. One must be thankful even for unwelcome attentions meant in generous kindness.

A Princeton man stopped me on the street just now: I dare say there will be a number of them turning up. I ought to have raised a beard before starting! This lantern jaw of mine is unmistakable.

Ah, my precious one, how unspeakably I long for you. There is really no offsetting by any means I have yet discovered the loneliness of being separated from you. I can amuse myself and fill my days with this diversion or that and keep my spirits alive and in a way have a good time, but there is always the pain that you are not here, that I am cut off from those sweet influences of love and tenderness which are as necessary to my heart as air is to my lungs, and which, alas! I so constantly breathe with as little apparent appreciation! However foolish and selfish and exacting I am, I nevertheless live by means of what my darling

[4] David Aiken Reed, Princeton 1900, lawyer of Pittsburgh.

[5] Adèle Wilcox Reed and Katharine Reed.

[6] James Hay Reed, member of the prominent Pittsburgh law firm of Knox and Reed, who had received the LL.D. from Princeton in 1902.

[7] The Rev. Frank Burrows Reazor, rector of St. Mark's Episcopal Church of West Orange, N. J.

[8] John MacMillan Stevenson Patton, Princeton 1898, son of Francis Landey Patton and lawyer of Hamilton, Bermuda.

[9] That is, he put Wilson's name up for a guest membership.

[10] Lieutenant General Sir Robert MacGregor Stewart.

gives me and could know neither health nor peace nor joy if she did not give them. They are the breath of my life, and my love for her, however ill I show it, is compounded of everything that is best and happiest and deepest in me. I love her with my mind, my heart, my tastes, my fancy. May God always bless you, my sweet, sweet darling, and grant that I may not often again be obliged to starve my heart with absence from you! Good-bye till to-morrow.

Tuesday, 15 Jan'y, 1907.

Before I forget it, I must tell you a joke on me, and on you. As I was about to get aboard the ship at New York the officer who examined my ticket said, "You've been down with us before, haven't you?" "No," I said. "Somehow your name is very familiar," he said, "I seem to remember it." "Oh," said a steward standing by. "You have seen it in the magazines,–things by Mrs. Woodrow Wilson"[11] (he put the name in our order). Isn't that delightful, that my name should become known to the vulgar through that woman! It almost relieved the gloom of my going off!

I can now report that the table of the hotel is very good indeed. I had taken it for granted that most of our food would come from the islands themselves, but it seems not: almost everything, the very fruit itself, is brought from "the States." There is not even native water. There are no springs, the islands being of coral formation, and wells yield only brackish water. But it rains at least a little (not enough to spoil anything or to interfere with one's pleasure) every day, and we wet our whistles and bathe in rain water. There are strictly enforced local laws about roofs, for the water's sake. The roofs, like the houses they cover, are of limestone, layers of thin stone being used as tiles would be, and every roof is immaculate with whitewash, as the walls also are. One gets at every turn a delightful sense of cleanliness. There is no mud (the soil is too pourous) and apparently no dust either. Tremendous winds sometimes sweep the islands and most of the houses are of but a single story, tucked in some protecting corner. All sorts of half tropical vines cover their walls and flowers fill the little door yards in profusion, the exquisite shell rose predominating. The air seems to me just like what we had at Palm Beach, the air of neither spring, summer, winter or autumn, but

[11] Nancy Mann Waddel Woodrow, former wife of Wilson's first cousin, James Wilson Woodrow. She wrote for many popular magazines, using the pen name of "Mrs. Wilson Woodrow." See n. 1 to J. W. Woodrow to WW, July 29, 1897, printed as an Enclosure with EAW to WW, Aug. 3, 1897, Vol. 10, and J. W. Woodrow to WW, July 24, 1901, Vol. 12.

a breath pure and singular, full of life and yet soft and caressing. It is delicious.

I have not been about much. My day has been this: In the morning work,—getting the second of my Columbia lectures in shape.[12] The first I formulated one evening while you were in Philadelphia; in the afternoon a loaf and talk with some acquaintances here in the hotel and a loaf and talk with some acquaintances at the Princess Hotel down by the water, followed by a delightful stroll in the waning light; and in the evening the amusement, as long as it was amusing, of looking on at a hop given here at our hotel,—the first of the season.

My morning work was interrupted by a call from a Philadelphia newspaper man who wanted to interview me in spite of all evasions (what an amateur I am!) but whom I may be able to dissuade from publishing anything by making real friends with him. Poor fellow, he is suffering with consumption and is here to nurse his life. That made me wax in his hands. But what a disappointment not to have escaped such things even for the time being!

The sunset last evening was exquisite. The colour effects are never brilliant here, it seems, but such soft blues and greens and greys and pinks I have seldom seen, or such tenderness and harmony of colour everywhere. It made the evening very pensive. It was as if the soft airs we breathed had got into the colour scheme of the sky. There was nothing to quicken the senses, but everything to disturb one with sweet thoughts of all persons and places loved and longed for. Such evenings are likely to make me more your lover than ever, if that were possible: their sweetness and tenderness and lovely purity seem to me like a poetical interpretation of the dear one I love most in all the world.

The hop was not as lively or as picturesque as it might have been had the present British ministry not been Liberals, economisers, and Little Englanders. They have withdrawn some five thousand troops from the islands, leaving only one regiment of infantry and one detachment (or whatever such units of the service may be called) of artil[l]ery, and preferring Halifax as a naval station, so that, instead of a fleet, we have only a single vessels [vessel] to supply us with officers.

By the way, dearest, do not suppose that we are anywhere near Jamaica or within the region of the disturbances taking place there.[13] We are six hundred miles out at sea, and are in the lati-

12 He was making brief typed outlines of his Blumenthal lectures. These dated outlines are in WP, DLC.

13 A severe earthquake shook the island of Jamaica on the afternoon of January 14, 1907. Much of the town of Kingston was destroyed either by the shock or

tude of Charleston. We have felt neither storm nor any other disturbance. The news of what is happening at Jamaica has just reached us.

I find a very strong feeling of strangeness on me here, but it is a soothing feeling. The remoteness of the place gives me, what I always so much benefit by, an offing from which I can see my ordinary tasks and involvements in their natural proportions, objectively, not subjectively; and such a view restores my poise and judgment; so that the change is already working a wholesome effect upon my spirits. I feel our separation like a constant pain, but I can be a more satisfactory lover and companion no less because of the restored balance of spirits. Ah, my darling, love, love, love me,—as I love you, and see me, as I am,—always your own lover and chum.

Wednesday, 16 Jan'y, '07.

Our morning shower lasted longer than usual, and made work by my open window easy and placid. There was nothing to tempt one out and the thoughts ran quiet and at command. The second lecture is outlined. I only fear that it has more in it than can be adequately said in an hour, and I do not suppose they will wish more than an hour's eloquence at one time.

There is a piece of business I forgot to leave suggestions about, dearest. Letters will come from D. T. Day[14] and others about my acting as Director of Juries and Awards at the Jamestown Exposition,—describing what and how much I would be expected to do. My own judgment says Do not risk the effects of the work and responsibility, but I do not wish to be selfish and unserviceable. Please read the letters and judge dispassionately for yourself, and reply accordingly, in my name, saying that I am away and have requested you to do so.[15] I wish you would do the same for all the matters that Close[16] finds in my mail and brings to your attention.

---

by the resulting fire. The loss of life was ultimately estimated at between 700 and 800, the injured at 1,000, and property damage at over £2,000,000. See *The Annual Register: A Review of Public Events at Home and Abroad, For the Year* 1907, New Series (London, 1908), pp. 465-67, and "Chronicle of Events," in *ibid.*, p. 2.

14 David Talbot Day, Chief of the Mining and Mineral Resources Division of the United States Geological Survey and honorary Commissioner of Mining for the Jamestown Exposition.

15 See G. T. Shepperd to H. St. G. Tucker, Jan. 1, 1907, printed as an Enclosure with H. St. G. Tucker to WW, Jan. 1, 1907, Vol. 16.

16 Gilbert Fairchild Close, Princeton 1903. On staff of the *Princeton Alumni Weekly*, 1903-1906; with the First National Bank of Scranton, Pa., June-November 1906; Secretary to Wilson, November 1906 to June 1910 and later at the Paris Peace Conference.

This afternoon I went and watched part of a baseball game between this hotel and the Princess Hotel teams, made up indiscriminately of guests and employees; but I soon tired of the poor playing and went off for a walk, the first real tramp I have taken here. I had myself ferried across the harbour to a little settlement opposite called Paget, and from there walked home round about the upper end of the bay, pleased and entertained at every step by the interesting lanes and homes and green corners. There is hardly a single site suitable for building upon anywhere about the bay that is not built upon, and, although every house has at least a garden and the bigger houses more or less elaborate grounds about them, place nestles close to place in the most interesting and unexpected manner. Climbing and descending steps lead up or down to charming houses, half English, half Spanish in style and appearance, and everything shows clean in its coral stone. Walls are built out of what comes from the cel[l]ar and the yards are paved with the same shining lime. Little crooked lanes run at will among the labarynths of gardens, shaded with short stunted firs or dug straight through the coral, with sheer grey walls on either side made of the hills themselves. Hamilton itself looks like a sort of combination, in the style and posture of its houses, of the oldest parts of Charleston or St. Augustine,–the gables to the street and entrances through high walls, hiding gardens or latticed porches,–and a close-built village by Lake Como. The colour and form of the houses and the odd little buildings standing with their feet in the bay, close by stone landing places, as if intended for some unguessable water use and yet looking like closed-in "summer houses," remind me constantly of the places we touched at on Como as we went to Bellagio;[17] and yet as one wanders about he is aware of something everywhere which is much more familiar than anything in Italy is to us, and the only place he can remember getting the same impressions are Charleston and St. Augustine. The pillars rising high above the walls at the gate openings or placed at regular intervals as if to carry an open railing and yet carrying none, are so like what one sees on the back streets in Charleston where gardens stretch at length; and yet they are like Spanish garden walls in pictures, too. I shall try to bring you good photographs; I have not found any yet except big ones unsuitable for putting in letters.

Alas, when the *Bermudian* leaves us to-morrow how desolate it will make me feel,–our only link with home cut for eight days. Her red funnels down at the landing, in full view from my win-

[17] When they made a tour of Great Britain and the Continent in 1903.

dow, have been a great comfort to me these three days. I shall see her off in the morning with an intolerable regret and longing: she will be going where my heart is! I cannot add anything to this letter to-morrow because the mail closes at eight in the morning. So I must say good night and good-bye now. How I hope that our sweet, sweet baby is getting well fast and with no further touch of anxiety for you.[18] Give love without measure to all, but especially to her. My heart longs for her. She would thrive so in this peace, and would so love this singular, fascinating land!

Give yourself no concern about me, my darling. I am perfectly well, and already the quiet and peace of the place have entered into me to heal my spirits and make every nerve in me seem sound. If only I had you I could wish to stay without limit. How we could love and think of each other here! It almost breaks my heart to think that these quiet hours are not to bring you to me along with there [their] other healing. You are all the world to me. In stress and in peace I am happy when I turn to you. I cannot be happy here because I cannot turn to you; but I can, in these days apart, get a sort of happiness which is itself very deep and sweet by knowing my own heart and knowing its love for you, my darling, my incomparable darling. May God bless and keep you for Your own Woodrow

WWTLS (WC, NjP).

[18] Eleanor, who was recuperating from an operation for the removal of tubercular glands in her throat.

George Brinton McClellan Harvey to Stockton Axson

Dear Mr. Axson, [New York] Jan. 16. [1907]

I have read the letters[1] with much interest and return them herewith.

The deliberate suppression in the face of Mr. Wilson's explicit request was shameful,[2] especially when supplemented by gross distortion to serve a personal purpose, and to my mind wholly deprived the culprits of any claim to consideration they may have had.[3]

But I agree with you as to the unwisdom of your giving out the letter at this time, anyway.

It seems well to let the hen set. Persons who resort to such tactics generally fetch adequate reprobation upon their own heads.

Their scheme of course was to take advantage of the mere fact of a letter having been written to misstate the contents and spring a quick caucus yesterday. You may have observed that a cog got into the wheel.[4]

I see no occasion now for a conference. If one should arise, I will wire you. Sincerely Yours, George Harvey

ALS (WP, DLC).

[1] He referred to the correspondence between Wilson and Charles C. Black of January 11 and 12, 1907, printed in Volume 16, in which Wilson had withdrawn his name from the New Jersey senatorial contest. There is considerable correspondence and discussion about his possible candidacy in Volume 16. Wilson had asked Axson to act as his agent in the senatorial affair during his absence in Bermuda.

[2] Wilson had concluded his letter of withdrawal of January 11, 1907, with the words: "I think it would be well for you to publish this letter." However, according to a report in the *Newark Evening News*, January 18, 1907, Black had given this letter to Assemblyman Archibald S. Alexander, one of the managers of the reform candidate, Edwin A. Stevens of Hudson County. Alexander had declined to make the letter public, although he had readily acknowledged its existence and the fact of Wilson's withdrawal. Obviously, Alexander, as Harvey suspected, was seeking to keep the contents of Wilson's letter secret as long as possible because Wilson had not directly endorsed Stevens.

[3] He was referring to a circular letter, made public on January 14, from Black and other Stevens supporters to the thirty-seven Democratic senators and assemblymen, which said that Stevens was the only bona fide Democratic candidate and added: "The baneful influence of gum-shoe candidacies was dispelled, but the selection now of any other person for this honor would immediately give life to the charge that we sail under false colors. . . . Again and again we have declared for the submission of candidacies for the United States Senate to the people. The nomination now of any other man, or of a stalking horse, means party stultification." The authors were obviously alluding to Wilson.

[4] The Stevens forces failed to "spring a quick caucus" on January 15 because a majority of the members favored a later, open caucus in the hope of finding a candidate more broadly acceptable than Stevens, who had little support outside Hudson County. *Newark Evening News*, Jan. 16, 1907. The caucus was finally held on January 22; Wilson's letter had been published on the previous day.

To Ellen Axson Wilson

My precious darling, Bermuda, 22 January, 1907

We had not expected to have a chance to send letters till the Bermudian sailed again, on the twenty-eighth; but a notice in the hotel office says, "Mail for New York closes Wednesday, January 23rd. at 10 A.M.," and, although we see no steamer yet in port to carry it, I cannot miss the opportunity to write to my darling. No doubt it is some slow freight steamer which will not beat the Bermudian in by more than a day or two; but, no matter! it gives me a chance to ease my heart.

And, to tell the truth, it needs easing! It fairly aches with love of you and with homesickness. It is not a case like those Dr. Coit[1] described, either: it is not only when I sit down to write a letter and let my thoughts dwell on you and all the sweet things I have at home that my heart grows like lead. I am having a really peaceful and most enjoyable time here, and feel already that I shall come back renewed in every kind of strength, but it seems to me that I never before felt to the full my dependence on you or so acutely missed the sweet and helpful influences with which you daily surround me. Sometimes when I am at home for long periods together and have no thoughts but such as you share from hour to hour for weeks together I get to taking you for granted as a sort of part of my own individuality and so do not consciously realize, do not stop to make you realize what my heart has in you, my incomparable darling! I cannot in any other way account for the suffering I cause you. When I am away,—especially when I am thus hopelessly away,—no voice, no letters, no news of you from any quarter, no means of going to you or of your coming to me,—my feeling for you dominates my thought day and night; an intolerable longing takes hold of me, which I restrain from overwhelming me only by a great and continuous effort of the will! Ah, my darling, my darling! how I wish you *knew*! How I wish my love availed! It is as deep and pure and whole as ever any lover or husband felt. Life has opened everything to me, and I know you for my perfect wife and sweetheart. May God show it to you, through your own heart, if I cannot, and so take away the only bar there is in the world to my complete restoration to vital strength and happiness. There is not the slightest implication of any fault on your part, my precious one, in that last sentence: I simply do not know any other way of telling you so adequately what you mean to me. You are the translation for me of love and happiness! The dear old simple formula is the only best one,—"I love you with all my heart"!

It was such a delight and relief to get the cablegram[2] saying that our precious Nen. was improving rapidly. You know I have had no letter from home yet, though it is eleven days since I left Princeton, nor can have until Friday, which will be two weeks. It is my first experience of the kind and is hard to bear.

I have made fast friends with the young Reeds of whom I spoke in my last letter. They are thoroughly nice and seem fond of me, so I go about with them everywhere. We have no plans of seeing things without each other. All morning I ordinarily work at my Columbia lectures, and then in the afternoon we walk or drive, though two mornings we have spent on the water, one sailing, the other in a tug which took us out to the reefs, where, in shallow water, in glass-bottom boats we saw all the interesting coral and sponge growths at the bottom of the sea. The island seems to be entirely coral. By-the-way I have feared all week that you were uneasy lest we should share in the earth's disturbances at Jamaica. We are farther from Jamaica than we are from New York, and this island has the best of histories so far as disturbances of this sort are concerned, and is some twelve hundred miles from Kingston. It has been ideal weather ever since we landed, the thermometer ranging from sixty-seven to eighty-two, our windows always open, and soft influences like those of early September about us all the time. Roses are in every garden and line the walks under my window in great profusion. They are to be had at the florists at twopence a dozen! Every walk and drive opens new beauties. Indeed the whole island with its perfect drives, its cosey homes, all set in gardens, its clear skies, and its delightful outlooks on the sea upon either side is like one great garden set for pleasure. My work goes easily and very well; my health is good enough to satisfy the most exacting doctor, and, if I only had my darling here, I could be at ease in heart as well as in body. No place could suit better the purposes of this little vacation. Perhaps when I get my letters on Friday even this strain of separation will be a little lightened.

God bless you, my darling. I love you! I love you! I love you! I wish I could say it a thousand times into your ear, holding you to my heart. Love to my dear, dear Margaret and Nellie, and to Madge[3] and Stock. I will write again of course at every chance.

Your own Woodrow

I find that the steamer which is to take this is the Ponce, which sailed from Porto Rico, broke her shaft at sea, and was lost for over a week. She was finally towed in here, has been repaired in dry dock, and sails to-morrow.

WWTLS (WC, NjP).

1 The Editors have been unable to identify him.

2 This cablegram and all of Mrs. Wilson's letters to her husband during this Bermuda trip are missing.

3 Margaret Randolph Axson, Mrs. Wilson's sister.

George Brinton McClellan Harvey to Stockton Axson

Dear Mr. Axson, [New York] Wednesday [Jan. 23, 1907]

I see no occasion for doing or saying anything at all. Mr. Wilson said his say and that is all there [is] of it. Even G. Cleveland or K[ing]. Edward can't actually prevent people voting for him against his expressed wish. Up in Vermont they are still voting for A. Jackson.[1]

Yours George Harvey

ALS (WP, DLC).

1 In spite of Wilson's request that his name not be considered for the United States Senate, he was nominated in the Democratic legislative caucus on January 22, 1907, and received fifteen votes. He continued to receive considerable support in subsequent votes in the joint session of the New Jersey legislature. See n. 1 to WW to C. C. Black, Jan. 11, 1907, printed as an Enclosure with WW to C. C. Black, Jan. 11, 1907, Vol. 16.

From Sir William Mather

My dear President [London] Jany 25th/07

I am sending by this mail a roll containing the drawing to scale of the Sun Dial[1] to enable you to judge of the dimensions & general appearance of it. Of course it is not a finished drawing for effect. The motto on the line of the date 1581 is, *in full*, "Est Deo gratia." The letters on the original are destroyed other than those you see. But the President of Corpus Christi College[2] who takes the keenest interest in the reproduction for Princeton has searched the library & found complete records of this famous dial with all the mottoes complete (which will be faithfully copied) & also drawings, crude but clear, showing the steps &c. as you will see it. This is a fortunate discovery. There are in all 30 dials! I have employed the most capable opticians to set out the figures & probably you will hear from them about the precise latitude of the spot you have selected. You know this old dial was overthrown, I fancy in Cromwell's days, & suffered much.

The pelican will be *heraldic* in design so you must not compare it with the ornithologically correct bird. There is a Latin motto on each of the 4 faces N. S. E. West.

I wish you would kindly let me know what inscription & arms you would like in behalf of Princeton & select the place from the drawing, then forward me a true sketch for the sculptor to work from.

I met with some lines the other day which I think may please you as an inscription on the base as follows:

"Loyalty is e'er the same
Whether it win or lose the game,
True as the Dial to the Sun,
Although it be not shined upon."
(Hudibras)

For the famous Princeton "teams" this seems to hit off the right spirit, & also for loyalty to truth & the Alma Mater.

There will be a bronze tablet let into the stone in some corner setting forth the fact of the origin of the Dial at Corpus Christi Oxford.

I hope the new year will bring to you perfect health & the wealth of success in your noble work. Also we wish for Mrs. Wilson & your charming girls every happiness.

Very sincerely yours W. Mather

ALS (WWP, UA, NjP).

1 That is, a copy of the Turnbull sun dial at Corpus Christi College in Oxford.

Mather was presenting the copy to Princeton University. For further information about this gift, see H. I. Triggs to WW, Oct. 26, 1906, ns. 2 and 3, Vol. 16.

[2] Thomas Case, Waynflete Professor of Moral and Metaphysical Philosophy and President of Corpus Christi College.

To Ellen Axson Wilson

My precious darling, Hamilton, Bermuda, 26 January, 1907.

I can't tell you how my heart leaped with delight when my letters were handed me yesterday,—letters from the dear girlies, from Jack and from Mrs. Hibben, but the only one my heart waited and panted for was yours. Ah! my sweetheart, my Eileen, what sweet, sweet letters you write, with how many cadences of love singing through them, and how this precious letter of yesterday has refreshed me! My incomparable darling, how my heart nestles and clings to you! You are part of my very consciousness of life. I know by the way life seems to ebb in me when day after day goes by without sound of your voice or touch of your hand. You are life and hope and peace to me.

I am having a fight with myself to keep from going back on this steamer on Monday. The company here seems to come and go with the succession of steamers. Almost everyone whom I know or care to know in the hotel is to go back home on Monday, and the crowd this ste[a]mer brought,—probably to go back when I do,—does not attract me in the least. I do not know that I shall try to make a new set of acquaintances amongst them. My chief friends, as I have told you, have been the young Reeds, from Pittsburgh,—young David Reed of '00 (son of Judge Reed), his wife (they have been married four years), and his sister. We are together all the time that I am not in my room writing,—ride together, walk together, loaf together,—in the evenings drawing into our little circle most of the attractive people of the inn. They are really delightful in their youth and naturalness. He is witty and full of good sense and the girls (they are hardly more) are most sweet and attractive. It has really been a great good fortune to meet them, and they seem very sweetly attached to me,—sought me out, indeed, and annexed me from the outset. They have been almost like affectionate children to me. After they go, on Monday, I shall probably be more or less in George Patton's[1] hands, who arrived yesterday. Jack Patton's well meant plans for me seem to have come to nothing. The Governor's secretary[2] did *not* call on me and I have been left at peace. If the Governor at all resembles the unspeakable Swettenham[3] in character or point of view, I hope I shall be spared the humiliation of meeting him. I saw all the passengers land from the Bermudian. Miss Armstrong[4] looks extremely well, and says that the voyage down was delightful. She is staying with friends here, and I shall call on her soon. I happen to have a card of introduction to the people she is to be with.

Our excursions have now covered practically the whole length and breadth of the islands. They are hardly more than twenty-five miles fr. end to end. Innumerable by-ways, quaint and secluded as anything in the old world, yet await exploration, and I shall make them the objects of my walks next week; but the highways have become familiar. The roads are excellent. One of our pleasantest expeditions was taken one afternoon on hired bicycles. The vehicles one hires here, including the bicycles, seem quite new and are in excellent condition, so that it is a pleasure to ride on them. One has to pay rather high prices for everything, but he gets the worth of his money in quality.

Undoubtedly all this is doing me a vast deal of good. I have practically been in the open air all the time. My window is open close beside me while I write,—is never closed, indeed,—and when I am not writing I am out in the open. I feel a very great access of refreshment and poise. One would stagnate if he stayed here too long, but every moment of a vacation stay seems to bring peace and renewal. If I only had my darling! If I only had you, mavourneen!

I have made outlines (all I intended to make) for four of my Columbia lectures, with a good deal of satisfaction with the results (I had made one at home before I came) and see no reason why I should not finish the remaining three, with a good deal of ease and deliberation, before I sail. Work seems to go readily and without excitement, as it is possible to do all things here. What do you say, love, shall we come here next winter together, and have a new honeymoon? I dream of it all the time. I should feel almost comforted if I could *count* on such a delight close at hand. What a haven of peace it is. I try *not* to make it a place of self-examination. Therein I differ from *other* saints of other generations! I try to be as irresponsible as possible, and so renew my youth. I can at times forget everything and everybody in Princeton except you and the children. Don't divulge the secret. It does not involve any disloyalty to my dear friends: I could not do without them for long. It is only that this land of repose and enchantment seems for the time being to strip me of all but the essential elements of my life and consciousness, and give me the sort of renewal that comes from a return to fundamental principles. Ah, darling, I love you, and by the next steamer I am coming to you! My heart is with you all the time and is altogether yours.

Your own Woodrow

WWTLS (WC, NjP).

[1] George Stevenson Patton, Professor of Moral Philosophy at Princeton.

[2] Capt. L. C. Soltau-Symons, 3rd Warwickshire Regiment, Aide-de-Camp to the Governor.

[3] Sir Alexander Swettenham, Governor of Jamaica. Following the earthquake in Jamaica on January 14, 1907, American warships were dispatched from Cuba to render assistance in the disaster area. Rear Admiral Charles Henry Davis sent parties ashore at Kingston on January 17 to assist in clearing debris and guard the United States consulate. He informed Governor Swettenham of his action in a note which somewhat injudiciously indicated his belief that the Jamaican authorities were not equal to coping with the situation. Swettenham replied on January 18 in a letter couched in highly sarcastic language, which declared that no assistance was needed and requested Davis to re-embark all his men. Davis complied, and the warships departed from Jamaica on January 19.

The incident led to much unfavorable comment in both the United States and Great Britain. The British government disavowed Swettenham's conduct and instructed him to express his regret. The Governor complied and soon afterward retired from the British colonial service. See the *New York Times*, Jan. 21, 1907, and *The Annual Register . . . For the Year 1907*, pp. 466-67.

[4] Perhaps Anne Armstrong, who lived with the Rev. and Mrs. William Park Armstrong at 8 Library Place. Armstrong was Professor of New Testament Literature and Exegesis at Princeton Theological Seminary.

To John Grier Hibben

My dear Jack, Hamilton, Bermuda, 26 January, 1907.

Thank you with all my heart for your letter. It would be hard for me to tell you,–I fear I never can by word of mouth,–how your thoughtfulness and love touch and delight me. Your letter contained just the things I wanted to hear,–just the items of news, and, above all, just the assurances of being thought of and missed and loved. It gave me the feeling, just the feeling that makes me happiest, that I was *needed*,–needed for pleasure as well as for business.

Heaven send that Junius's optimistic expectations about his uncle may be fulfilled.[1] From what I had heard of Mr. J. P. M. I had supposed that he was a man of such instant decision that he never "took under consideration" anything he intended to do. And yet I have had the feeling that he hardly *could* utterly turn down such a man as Mr. Cadwalader or Cleve Dodge.[2] It is delightful that Mr. [Stephen Squires] Palmer is pursuing his ideas with reference to stirring up the Pynes. If they are all like Momo,[3] perhaps they will act for sheer love of peace, for the sake of being let alone by so plain-spoken and irrepressible a person as Mr. Palmer!

I cannot honestly pretend to any regret at old Mr. Frothingham's death.[4] Of course I have a very deep and genuine sympathy with Mrs. Frothingham and Miss Jessie.[5] To them it will not seem like the relief, the release from bondage, it is, but only like a terrible, irreparable bereavement. None the less, it will mean freedom and, if Mrs. Frothingham lives, a normal life in years to come. When we have had time ourselves perhaps we can think of the old codger with more leniency than I can now manage. I was greatly amused by Ellen's account of the effect of the article in the Press[6] on you while you thought that Marvin[7] had written it. If I could now think anything that Dr. Warfield[8] did extraordinary, I would think it only less incredible and discreditable, intellectually, that Dr. Warfield had written it. It's a braw world my lads! If I had been at home, I should have wished to be as late at the funeral as dear old Ormond[9] was. Do treasure all the entertaining things in your memory till I get back; I should hate to miss them.

Ellen's letter brought me the sad news of the death of my uncle, Dr. James Woodrow.[10] No doubt she had told you of it. That takes away the last of that generation in my family, on both sides of the house,–except a sister of my father's whom I have never seen.[11] It takes away, besides, one of the noblest men I ever knew. A man of many small failings, I am glad, for my own comfort, to remember, but a man made to love (in the quiet, self-contained Scottish fashion, but very, very deeply, none the less) and to be loved, and gifted in an extraordinary degree with the powers that make a great thinker and a great man of science. He followed duty to obscure places and kept himself in mere faithfulness from the eye of fame; but his friends and intimates knew him for a man who might have placed his name among the great names of our men of learning. It pleases me to think of the gracious and helpful influences he has brought into the lives of many generations of students, and not least into the life of a nephew who never told him how much he owed to him.

I am feeling very well. I took a fifteen mile bicycle ride the other afternoon with no consequences (besides great pleasure) except tired knees. One can rent excellent wheels here very reasonably (it's almost the only thing that is cheap) and the roads are excellent,–made of rock on the rock by convicts whose time was nothing. Indeed all vehicles here are noticeably good, and the horses fat and well groomed. There is only one automobile in Bermuda, and that, I was delighted to learn, broke down almost immediately after arriving here. There was not a mechanic on the island, it is said, who could mend it, and so it remains happily out of commission.

I have spent all the time when I was not writing with the young Reeds of Pittsburgh: Judge Reed's son David of '00, his wife and sister. They annexed me on the boat and seem really to like my being with them constantly. They are almost like affectionate children to me, and have made my enjoyments brighter by their presence. Young Reed himself is a fellow of real wit and a great deal of sound intelligence and information, and the two young ladies are very sweet and charming. I shall miss them dreadfully when they sail on Monday. The new boatload, that came yesterday, does not seem to contain many persons whom I should like to make comrades of. These young people, bless them, have done me a real service.

Good-bye, my dear fellow. The boat that follows the one that brings this will bring me,—and happy, very happy I shall be to get back to friends and work!

With warmest love,

Your devoted friend, Woodrow

WWTLS (WP, DLC).

[1] Junius Spencer Morgan, Associate Librarian, who hoped to secure a large gift to Princeton from his uncle, J. Pierpont Morgan.

[2] Wilson himself was overly optimistic. J. P. Morgan made no gift to Princeton at this time.

[3] Moses Taylor Pyne.

[4] Arthur Lincoln Frothingham, Sr., who died at the age of eighty-two on January 13, 1907.

[5] Jessie Peabody Frothingham (Mrs. A. L., Sr.) and her daughter, also named Jessie.

[6] Wilson referred to a lengthy obituary of Frothingham in the *Princeton Press*, Jan. 19, 1907. Highly eulogistic, the article placed special emphasis on Frothingham's conservative theological views, with which the writer obviously agreed.

[7] Walter Taylor Marvin, Preceptor in Philosophy at Princeton.

[8] The Rev. Dr. Benjamin Breckinridge Warfield, Princeton 1871, Professor of Didactic and Polemic Theology at Princeton Theological Seminary.

[9] Alexander Thomas Ormond, McCosh Professor of Philosophy at Princeton.

[10] In Columbia, S. C., on January 17, 1907.

[11] A. Elizabeth Wilson Begges of Cleveland, Ohio.

To Charles Williston McAlpin

My dear McAlpin, Hamilton, Bermuda, 26 January, 1907.

Will you not record in the minutes of the last meeting of the Board the following as the committee appointed to consider my unpublished report?[1] The committee was to consist of seven, with myself as chairman, which I interpret to mean that my name is to count as one of the seven.

Woodrow Wilson, chairman,
M. Taylor Pyne,
Bayard Henry (I think he was the mover)
Cleveland H. Dodge
David B. Jones
Melancthon W. Jacobus,
Robert Garrett.

Please arrange the names in order of seniority as they stand in the catalogue; and be kind enough to notify the men of their appointment.

The sailing of the next boat to the one which is to carry me home wakes me up to business.

I am faring here most happily. The vacation is proving a great success. I shall come back with a renewed appitite for everything there is to do.

Please give my warm regards to Mrs. McAlpin, and tell everybody that I am well and hearty.

Affectionately Yours Woodrow Wilson

WWTLS (McAlpin File, UA, NjP).

[1] That is, his supplementary report to the Board of Trustees printed at Dec. 13, 1906, Vol. 16, in which he discussed the problem of the upperclass eating clubs at Princeton and proposed his quadrangle plan as a solution.

From Robert Garrett, with Enclosure

My dear President Wilson: Baltimore, January 26th, 1907.

After considering anxiously for some time the question of the future developments on our campus I have come to the conclusion that I would have to present my views upon it to the Chairman of the Committee on Grounds and Buildings in some definite way. I am therefore sending him a letter upon the subject. I should like to have you know exactly how I have presented it to him and to that end I beg to enclose to you herewith a copy of the letter.

I trust you will accept it in the spirit in which it was written, namely, not one of controversy or of ill feeling, but one that is prompted solely by an earnest zeal for the welfare of Princeton.

With best regards,

Very sincerely yours, Robert Garrett

TLS (WP, DLC).

ENCLOSURE

Robert Garrett to Archibald Douglas Russell

My dear Sir: Baltimore, January 26th, 1907.

For some years I have been contemplating with great chagrin the architectural mistakes on our campus. May I attempt to lay my views before you as the newly appointed Chairman of the Committee on Grounds and Buildings, in the hope that my suggestions may be of help in remedying them? I have from time to time attempted to focus the attention of a few of the Trustees upon them, but without apparent result. I desire now to mention them more or less in detail, and to put in writing my position upon the whole subject.

While Princeton has been making remarkable progress, under the leadership of President Wilson, in the more vital concerns of the University, the architectural development has been allowed to drift on in a haphazard way. At almost every step we are making glaring blunders. It is true that no recent error is so great as that of the School of Science,—a photograph of which is used I believe in New Haven to show students of architecture what to avoid in design,—but Patton Hall is decidedly inferior, and the materials of Seventy-nine and of McCosh Halls, though excellent in themselves, are wholly unsuited to their surroundings. These examples may suffice to illustrate my point. In general I may add that we seem to have gotten into the deplorable habit of employing a new architect and using a new style of architecture and a new material for every new building that is erected.

This matter was forcibly brought to my attention for the first time by an architect who is not a Princeton man, but who is drawn toward her by strong ties, an[d] who, I may add, has no axe whatever to grind. He is fond of Princeton and used to go there frequently, but his interest has been measurably chilled by the architectural enormities that have been committed. Since that time I have observed things more carefully and have discussed the subject with a number of people, and I have come to the conclusion that a different method should be adopted or else I for one would feel compelled to withdraw my financial support from the University. I cannot knowingly aid in continuing the present plan, or lack of plan.

The subject is especially urgent just now in view of the fact that the new building for the Graduate School must soon be erected and also in view of the reports concerning certain other large buildings that may be given to the University in the near future.

I realize that to devise an adequate plan to carry out the views that I am endeavoring to express is not an easy matter, but surely much more difficult problems have been successfully met within the last few years.

May I be allowed to suggest that our committee hold a special meeting to consider this subject and that the Board of Trustees at their March meeting be asked for authority to proceed along lines that the committee may specify more or less definitely. In general I may suggest also that permission be sought to employ a commission of three or five of the ablest architects that can be secured, one of whom should be an expert landscape architect, and that they be required to examine, report in detail and make recommendations concerning all plans for buildings and their sites and other developments or changes that are to be made in the campus. Further than this, a comprehensive plan should be made concerning the probable developments of the next ten years or more and settling once and for all what style of architecture should prevail and what material or materials should be used.

It may be urged that this would be a costly undertaking, but I desire to urge in reply that this would be a small thing as compared with the ultimate cost to the University in reputation and support if a better plan is not devised.

To show my earnestness in this matter I will offer the sum of $5000 to go toward the preparing of the plan and the employment of the architects. If more is needed during the next twelve months I believe I shall be able to furnish a like amount in addition.

I trust that you will bring this letter before the Board at the March meeting. If what I have written should offend anyone in our committee or in the Board, I shall be very glad to offer an apology. I have merely attempted to speak frankly and forcibly in order that prompt action may be taken upon a subject which I think is of pressing importance to the University.

I shall be glad to confer with you at any time upon this matter.

Yours very sincerely, (signed) Robert Garrett.

P.S. I am sending a copy of this letter to President Wilson.

TCL (WP, DLC).

An Announcement

[Jan. 26, 1907]

Church Services.
January 27th, 1907. . . .

ST. ANDREWS.[1]

Morning Service at 10 o'clock.

President Woodrow Wilson, LL.D., Princeton University, N J, will give an address in the evening at 7:30, especially to the young people.

Printed in the Hamilton, Bermuda, *Royal Gazette*, Jan. 26, 1907.

1 St. Andrew's Presbyterian Church in Hamilton, Bermuda, built in 1843.

To Ellen Axson Wilson

My own Eileen, Hamilton, Bermuda, 27 January, 1907.

Just a little note this morning to tell you of the probable time of my home coming. I was so full of thoughts of you when I was writing yesterday that I forgot that I ought to conclude with a a few lines about myself.

The boats have to leave with the tide here, the inner harbour being very shallow; they leave, therefore, at different hours. I find that my boat, on the seventh of Feby, will leave at about one in the afternoon, and that, leaving at that time her captain will expect to be at his dock in New York at about eleven or twelve o'clock on Saturday, the ninth.

My heart leaps to think of it. No doubt I ought to stay and complete my cure, but I shall not have a really light heart until my face is turned towards my darling again. My heart is turned towards her all the time.

I am well, and shall always be happy so long as you love me.

Your own, Woodrow

WWTLS (WC, NjP).

Notes for a Sermon

Hamilton church (Bermuda) Jan'y 27, 1907.

II Corinthians, iii., 17. *"Where the Spirit of the Lord is, there is liberty."*

Universal desire for liberty.

False conception of liberty as freedom from restraint, from trammels of all sorts.

Right conception of it, as perfect adjustment to the governing laws of life, like physical liberty, which is perfect adjustment to the laws of nature.

Liberty of the spirit is perfect adjustment to the laws of God.

Various sorts of spiritual bondage,—to habit, disposition, passion, repulsion.

The exaltation of *Self.*

More miseries involved than those of the mind.

The mind the chemist of the body, the body the laboratory.

We are spirit: only spirit abides. Great spirits rule us from their urns.

The Spirit of God? How revealed?

In providence

In the revelation through *Christ* of the law of love and self-sacrifice.

When a man comes to himself.

27 Jan'y '07[1]

WWT MS (WP, DLC).

[1] Wilson's composition date. The local newspaper, the Hamilton *Royal Gazette*, did not print a report of this address or sermon.

From Dan Fellows Platt[1]

My dear Mr. Wilson: Englewood [N. J.], Jan 27 1907

I went to Trenton last week to see how Democracy would comport herself. I found a condition that confirmed my preconceptions and I feel, as a Princeton man and a Democrat, that I ought to say something to you on the subject.

In the first place, the minority nominee for U. S. Senator is supposed to be given a certain amount of prestige. This prestige Jim Smith[2] does not want to go to Stevens. Stevens is a clean fellow, who cannot be handled by Smith, and he is seeking office from New Jersey. Smith is using your name to kill Stevens and, in spite of your letter, he will continue to use it to force the compromise candidacy of Martine[3] or to make the Stevens men support you. You are the only one who can prevent it. Of course there are others who are ready to jump in and work for you as soon as your name is mentioned—witness the emissary of your friend Colonel Harvey, with whom I had a good talk at Trenton—but those are poor friends who imagine that you need any such prestige as a minority nomination might give. There is only one step higher that you can take and I feel that it is going to be taken;—but a fight to beat a clean man, through the successful use of your name, is one thing; the unanimous tribute of a nomination is another. Your name ought not to be handled by such a man as Smith. It detracts from your present high office.

Another and disagreeable feature is the fight that is being made on you by organized labor. Did you notice how Kleinert[4] (elected leader by grace of Smith) and several others passed on the first vote and did not vote for you till the reading of the law that compels all to vote? Their action was a sop to the labor committee that was present.

With this preface, in the name of Democracy, I want to ask a favor. Letters of refusal are all very well but a talk straight from the shoulder is better. The Democrats will probably go into caucus on Tuesday morning—they certainly will if you ask it of Kleinert,—and it would be a great thing if you could go before that caucus and speak to those Democrats of their splendid opportunity to stand for clean and upright methods by complimenting with their votes a man who *has* stood for them. He is being bitterly fought by the incubus that is weighing down New Jersey's Democracy. If he is beaten, Smith will know it [is] in his power to also beat the good measures which the people of the state want to have passed,—measures not so much in the line of radical legislation as those which tend to deprive the bosses of power—some of the Colby projects,[5] for example. The Democrats have a splendid opportunity to put such measures through the Assembly and up to the Senate, but to do it they must stand united and free from Public Service control. You are the one man who can tell them so. At the same time it would be a fine opportunity to put yourself squarely on record with regard to the labor question. I know you too well to believe that the laboring classes have anything but your warmest sympathies and that what you have said in criticism of labor unions applies only to those features which permit of evil, if carried too far. I thank the Lord for the Labor Trust, which, in these days of the Tariff is the only trust that can successfully tackle our monopolies and obtain, for one portion of the community, at least, some measure of fair treatment.

If you can find time to do this for Democracy, it will give new hope to those of us who are fighting for good government in our state. Are vested interests always to find it easy to purchase control at Trenton? We Democrats can at least *fight* for something different. To-day the fight for prestige is not your fight, it is not Stevens' fight, it is Jim Smith's fight! Will you help him if you can prevent it?

Yours sincerely Dan Fellows Platt, '95.

The Assembly sits Monday night. Should you decide to act, a word by telephone to the State House to Assemblyman Alexander[6] (Stevens' nephew) would prevent his opposing a caucus for Tuesday. Kleinert is a very good fellow.

ALS (WP, DLC).

1 Princeton 1895, former lawyer, gentleman scholar, and Mayor of Englewood, 1904-1906.

2 Former United States Senator James Smith, Jr., head of the Democratic machine of Essex County.

3 James Edgar Martine of Plainfield, who did in fact receive virtually a solid Democratic vote for the senatorship in the final ballot on February 5, 1907. See n. 1 to WW to C. C. Black, Jan. 11, 1907, printed as an Enclosure with WW to C. C. Black, Jan. 11, 1907, Vol. 16.

4 Abram Klenert, lawyer of Paterson and Democratic assemblyman from Passaic County.

5 He referred to Everett Colby, state senator from Essex County and leader of the progressive Republicans in New Jersey, whose projects for political reform included direct primaries, the direct election of United States senators, and civil service reform.

6 That is, Archibald Stevens Alexander, assemblyman from Hudson County.

To Ellen Axson Wilson

Hamilton, Bermuda,
My own precious darling, 30 January, 1907.

Another chance to send you a little message! A steamer for Halifax to-morrow which will carry mail for New York. It's round about, but anything is better than not talking to my pet at all.

Everything goes smoothly and happily with me,—when I do not allow myself to miss you too much. To-day and yesterday we have had some of Bermuda's *winter* weather,—rain and chill winds out of the east, the thermometer down to about 66 degrees; but it is so mild an affair compared with our discomforts that it has not disturbed me at all. I have had a fine time to-day sleeping. After my work this forenoon I took a little snooze preparatory to lunch, and this afternoon I slept from about three until twenty minutes of seven. I am sleepy all the time. Being in Bermuda is like being at sea all the time, without any uncomfortable motion. It is not above a mile to salt water in any direction and one is bathed all the while in airs blown off the wide spaces of the sea. How I wish my darling could feel it. I am having an additional summer vacation, and having it where I love to be,—at sea!

I have a confession to make: I made an address last Sunday evening! I really had not the heart to decline. The little Presbyterian church here is a tiny, struggling affair, the pastor a rather pathetic old gentleman,[1] with a winning Scottish tongue withal, and I did not know how to get out of it,—although it made me very unhappy, as a religious address always does. I never saw a place with so many churches as this island has, and a separate set for the negroes!

On Monday night I dined with the mayor of the town, Mr. James,[2] at a fascinating place a little way from town, and saw for the first time the inside of one of these quaint and delightful houses, unlike anything I ever saw, either in architecture or in interior plan. Mr. James's house is more than a hundred and fifty years old, and the grounds about it are among the most beautiful here. Mr. and Mrs. James, besides, are most interesting. She is really remarkable in intelligence and because of her discriminating interest in things really worth while.

George Patton, too, has been showing me interiors, taking me among some of his relatives and friends. Tell dear Nen [Eleanor] that I saw Winifred Block[3] the other day, and that she made the most affectionate inquiries after her. The Blocks live quite near at hand, and I am to take tea with them to-morrow afternoon. The only drawback is, that Mrs. Block is so deaf that is [it] is necessary to almost touch her ear with one's lips to make her hear. To-morrow I am to lunch out, too, to meet the Chief Justice of the island,[4] who has, by the way, just returned home from a visit to the United States, and to the Pattons at Princeton. He was rather pleased, it seems, with the "dull" weather "in the States" because it rested his eyes from the perpetual glare of the sun here upon the shining white streets and houses.

I am a little lonely since the last boat left. It took away practically everybody I knew. There is almost nobody left to keep my thoughts off from missing you, my Eileen. But my work prospers better. I have finished outlines for all my Columbia lectures but one, and so have time to study for that, the most difficult of all. It is on a theme, "Party Government in the United States," which I have never elaborated in my thought before, and so requires a good deal of reading and digesting. It is all the more interesting on that account. It will be a great relief to have these outlines thought out and ready to be filled from week to week as the lectures are actually delivered.

I can only conjecture when this letter will reach you,—possibly Tuesday or Wednesday: and then it will be only three or four days before I follow it! I shall come back infinitely refreshed by my outing. I am deeply conscious of the good it has done me, of the way in which it has taken the strain off and given me a quiet mind, after the somewhat too strenuous business and anxiety which followed our home coming in October. Those three months contained more than their due share of upsetting things, and Bermuda is just the place in which to recover one's peace and perspective. Next time you shall come with me, and then it will be perfect. Ah, how deep I should sink into this peace (peace of body and of mind) if only my darling were at my side, and moved with me, with her delightful power of enjoyment, amidst these enchanting gardens and by-ways! There can be no perfect cure to my spirits without you, my sweet, incomparable darling. May God keep and bless you always, and show me the way to make you happy in the love of Your own Woodrow

Love without measure to our dear ones.
Love to the Hibbens

WWTLS (WC, NjP).

[1] The Rev. Dr. Andrew Burrows, pastor of St. Andrew's Presbyterian Church in Hamilton, whose salary in 1907 was £18-15-0.

[2] William T. James, Mayor of Hamilton, 1906-1908.

[3] Winifred Bluck, daughter of Arthur William Bluck, prominent merchant and politician of Hamilton and Mayor of the city from 1913 to 1933, and Mary Everest Outerbridge Bluck. The Blucks had at least three daughters.

[4] Henry Cowper Gollan, Chief Justice of Bermuda since 1904.

Notes for a Sermon

Paget Presbyterian church,[1] Bermuda, 3 February, 1907.

II Corinthians, III., 6. "For the letter killeth, but the spirit giveth life." Parallel passage, John VI., 63. "It is the spirit that quickeneth; the flesh profiteth nothing: the words that I speak unto you, they are spirit, and they are life."

We are too apt to think of duty, not as an enterprise or an expansion of our faculties, but as a routine, not heeding the warning of the text, "we are unprofitable servants: we have done that which was our duty to do."

There is life only where there is growth: and there is no growth so long as we stick in the letter of our instructions or our examples.

- The unhappy formality of morals.
- The mistaken emphasis of one virtue. A ribbon for each virtue?
- Spiritual initiative.
- The adaptation of duty to environment and opportunity.
  - The wisdom and duty of each case consist in the the [*sic*] circumstances of that case.

The "spirit" spoken of in the text undoubtedly the spirit of love, which is the spirit of Christ. The spirit which translates all law into privilege.

How does Love give Life?
By satisfaction of inborn instincts.
By release of faculties otherwise pent up or dwarfed
By the functional expansion of the soul itself.
By the revelation of opportunity.
Character, not an original, but a by-product.
By enlargement of view.[2]

WWT MS (WP, DLC).

[1] There was no Presbyterian church in Paget. Wilson meant Christ Church in the adjacent parish, Warwick. Christ Church, founded about 1620, is the oldest Presbyterian church outside Great Britain. The present church structure was built in 1719. Dr. Francis Landey Patton often preached in it when vacationing in Bermuda. Esther K. Law, "Christ Church, Warwick, 1719-1969," *Bermuda Historical Quarterly*, XXVI (Summer 1969), 51, states that Wilson preached in Christ Church.

[2] The Hamilton *Royal Gazette* did not print a report of this sermon.

From William Henry Roberts[1]

Dear Dr. Wilson: Philadelphia, Pa. February 4th, 1907.

Permit me very kindly to draw attention to certain statements which appear on page 47 of the Catalogue of Princeton University. These are as follows: "Convinced of the futility of awaiting united Synodical action, and of the evils which would arise from the supervision of a church judicatory, they determined upon independent though concerted action. They sought a charter for the founding of a College in New Jersey, without assistance from either Synod, which was 'probably neither sought nor desired.' "

I should like to have the evidence that the ministers named on page 47 of the Catalogue believed that any evils would arise from the supervision of a church judicatory. So far as I have been able to understand the period in which these brethren lived, the two influences which affected them in connection with the securing of a charter, were, the futility of awaiting united synodical action and the impossibility of securing a charter in the name of the Presbyterian Church. The latter reason operated not only as to the College of New Jersey, but also as to other institutions.

I should like also to have evidence for the statement that the clergymen named probably neither sought nor desired assistance from either Synod for the founding of a College. The Minutes of the Synod of New York are in my possession as Stated Clerk of the General Assembly. They have been recently reprinted by me in the volume entitled "Records of the Presbyterian Church,"[2] and show intimate connections between the College and Synod.

I should hope that the sentence quoted might be changed to read somewhat as follows: "Convinced of the futility of awaiting united synodical action, and recognizing the unfavorable ecclesiastical situation in England, they sought by independent action a charter for the founding of a College in New Jersey. In this they were aided by members of both Synods. Later the Synod of New York, upon petition by the Trustees of the College, rendered valuable assistance to the young institution.["][3]

Yours very truly, Wm. H. Roberts

TLS (WP, DLC).

[1] Stated Clerk of the General Assembly of the Presbyterian Church in the U.S.A.

[2] William Henry Roberts (ed.), *Records of the Presbyterian Church, U.S.A.* (Philadelphia, 1904).

[3] The passages in question had first appeared in the university catalogue of 1902-1903. Roberts' letter apparently prompted the university administration to make a careful reconsideration of the first three pages of the section of the catalogue entitled "History and Government of the University." In the catalogue for 1907-1908, the material in these pages was drastically revised and condensed to half its previous length. The paragraph containing the statements to which Roberts objected was one of several omitted altogether. Compare the *Catalogue of Princeton University . . . 1906-1907* (Princeton, N. J., 1906), pp. 45-47, and the *Catalogue of Princeton University . . . 1907-1908* (Princeton, N. J., 1907), pp. 45-46.

To Mary Allen Hulbert Peck[1]

My dear Mrs. Peck, Hamilton, 6 Feb'y, 1907

I do not like to go away without saying good-bye. Last evening I only said good night. It was with the keenest disappointment that I found you not at home this afternoon. It is not often that I can have the privilege of meeting anyone whom I can so entirely admire and enjoy, and I take the liberty of writing you this little note to thank you for the pleasure you have given me, and to express again the hope that some happy turn of fortune may give me the opportunity of meeting you again.

With sincere regard,

Very truly Yours, Woodrow Wilson

ALS (WP, DLC).

[1] Born in Grand Rapids, Michigan, May 26, 1862, the daughter of Charles Sterling Allen and Anjenett Holcomb Allen, she grew up in Grand Rapids and in Duluth, Minnesota, where her family subsequently moved. She married Thomas Harbach Hulbert, a mining engineer of Duluth, in 1883. This marriage was apparently quite happy and produced her only child, Allen Schoolcraft Hulbert, born in 1888. Thomas Hulbert died in 1889 as the indirect result of an injury which had occurred some two years before.

On December 29, 1890, Mrs. Hulbert married Thomas Dowse Peck, president of a woolen manufacturing company in Pittsfield, Massachusetts. This marriage seems to have been somewhat unsuccessful from the beginning, and by the early 1900's Mrs. Peck was becoming increasingly estranged from her husband. They agreed to a separation in late 1909 or early 1910 and on July 9, 1912, secured a divorce. Mrs. Peck then resumed the legal surname of Hulbert, which she used for the rest of her life.

She visited Bermuda for the first time in 1892 and spent a portion of many winters there until 1913. In 1909 she moved from Pittsfield to New York and later lived for a time in Nantucket. In July 1915 she went to live with her son in Los Angeles. Around 1920 she and her son returned to New York. She spent the last years of her life in Westport, Connecticut, and died on December 17, 1939.

Mary Allen Hulbert was widely traveled, well read, and an accomplished amateur pianist. She tried her hand at many occupations after her divorce. She published a cookbook, *Treasures of a Hundred Cooks: A Collection of Distinctive Recipes for Lovers of Good Food* (New York and London, 1927), and an anecdotal autobiography, *The Story of Mrs. Peck: An Autobiography of Mary Allen Hulbert* (New York, 1933).

The acquaintance between Wilson and Mrs. Peck, begun during his first visit to Bermuda in 1907, ripened into a warm friendship on his second trip to the island in 1908. The present letter marks the beginning of a long and intimate correspondence which lasted until 1915 and is a source of great importance for the study of the life, thought, and personality of Woodrow Wilson. Mrs. Hulbert told her side of the story of their friendship in the autobiography mentioned above and in numerous magazine articles published after Wilson's death, most notably in a series of ten articles in the weekly magazine *Liberty* that appeared from December 20, 1924, to February 21, 1925.

From Gamaliel Bradford

My dear Mr. Wilson, Boston Feb. 6th 1907

The above slip is not new.[1] I have seen the suggestion a number of times, and think I have also seen your rejection of it. I write to beg you earnestly, as a duty of patriotism, not to do so again, but at least to await passively the moving of the waters.

I do not see why your name is not quite as appropriate and available as was that of Judge Parker.[2] It would be a new, and presumably a very popular, as it would be a desirable thing, to have a University President as candidate, as a change from politicians and generals. It has been my firm conviction since the Spanish war, that the salvation of this republic depends upon escaping from the hand which now rules at Washington; I believe there was then, and is more evidently now, a fixed determination to involve this country in a series of foreign wars, which must result either in an overthrow of the State governments, and the establishment of a centralized military despotism, or else in civil wars of which 1861 was only a beginning.

The only man now in sight on the other side as a candidate, is Mr. Bryan. But beside the fact that he does not in the slightest degree comprehend the situation, being wholly given up to socialistic details, two previous defeats would insure a third. The only chance is to put up somebody strong enough to take away the nomination. Judge Parker did this, and might have been elected, if he had not acted like a log of wood. A few patriotic utterances, and appeals to the people would have done much.

Your position, your book, and your personal standing all offer the requisite elements. It would be very easy to arouse an enthusiasm which would command the nomination, and with the changed situation, and the widespread discontent, election would be by no means impossible.

I do not raise the question whether this course would be agreeable to you. When the cause of the country is at stake, you are not the man to flinch. You are not bound to raise a finger to promote it. But if the call comes, I solemnly appeal to you not to put aside or reject it, but humbly to bow in submission.

Prayerfully yours Gamaliel Bradford

ALS (WP, DLC).

[1] Probably a clipping of an editorial suggesting Wilson for the presidency of the United States. It is missing.

[2] Alton Brooks Parker, unsuccessful Democratic presidential nominee in 1904.

To Robert Bridges

My dear Bobby: Princeton, N. J. February 11th, 1907.

Alas and alas! I have promised the evening of March 1st to the Rutgers alumni.[1] It goes very, very hard to miss the Isham dinner,[2] but there is no help for it. Please give Billy my love and explain the matter to him.

Always affectionately yours, Woodrow Wilson

TLS (WC, NjP).

[1] Wilson spoke on March 1, 1907, to the Rutgers College Alumni Association of New York at the Hotel Manhattan in New York. A brief report in the *New York Tribune*, March 2, 1907, quoted Wilson as saying that "a liberal education should lead to an interest in civic affairs."

[2] About the Isham dinners, see WW to EAW, May 6, 1886, n. 1, Vol. 5.

To Dumont Clarke, Jr.,[1] with Enclosure

My dear Mr. Clarke: Princeton, N. J. February 11th, 1907.

I am very much interested to hear of your purpose of visiting the pope, and shall hope to get an account of it from you yourself when you get back. It gives me real pleasure to comply with your request for a letter of introduction. I wish you every sort of pleasure and profit from your trip.

Very sincerely yours, Woodrow Wilson

[1] Princeton 1905, Secretary of the Philadelphian Society (about which see n. 1 to the news item printed at Nov. 1, 1890, Vol. 7) from June 1905 through October 1906. Clarke was about to embark on a lengthy Mediterranean cruise to recover his health after a nervous breakdown.

E N C L O S U R E

To Pius X

Honored Father: Princeton, N. J. February 11th, 1907.

I have the pleasure of introducing to you Mr. Dumont Clarke, Jr., for some time connected with Princeton University in ways which earned for him our highest respect and esteem.

Sincerely, Woodrow Wilson
President, Princeton University.

TLS (WC, NjP).

To Benjamin Wistar Morris III

My dear Mr. Morris: Princeton, N. J. February 12th, 1907.

Under the influence of the steam heat in our class room[1] in '79 Hall, the panels of the new wainscotting are showing a tendency to loosen, and the joints of the wainscotting are showing a tendency to open. Might it not be well to call the attention of the men who put this wood-work in to the matter, so that they may suggest or take steps to check it?

Allow me to thank you for the handsome photograph of the room, and to say how glad I am that the prospects are favorable for a continuation of the building on Brokaw Field.[2]

Very sincerely yours, Woodrow Wilson

TLS (WC, NjP).

1 That is, the President's Room in the tower of Seventy-Nine Hall.

2 New dormitories planned as extensions to Patton Hall, about which there is much correspondence and other documentation in Vol. 16.

To Gamaliel Bradford

My dear Mr. Bradford: Princeton, N. J. February 12th, 1907.

I have just come back from a little trip to Bermuda, to find your kind letter of February 6th lying on my table. I greatly appreciate it, as I need not tell you.

I have been too long a student of the practical processes of our politics to think at all seriously of the suggestion that I might be nominated by the Democratic party for the Presidency. You were misinformed when told that I had expressed an unwillingness to be considered, for I had not said anything about it, except perhaps in the way of pleasantry.

Without the least affectation I can say that I do not feel myself qualified for the post. I feel with you that if such a thing came to a man in the guise of duty, there would be no escaping it in conscience, but things of this sort have never yet happened, and I can only say in reply to your kind words in the matter that it is a delight to me to know that you think that I could be of real service to the country.

With warm regard and appreciation,

Sincerely yours, Woodrow Wilson

TLS (MHi).

A Fragment of a Letter from Ellen Axson Wilson to Anna Harris

[Princeton, N. J., Feb. 12, 1907]

music. Jessie and Nell have none at all but share my fondness for "art." Jessie has no time for it at college but Nell is specializing in it. She is at "St. Mary's," the old "church school" at Raleigh N. C. of which Rose Anderson's husband, Dr. [McNeely] Dubose, is the rector. Of course it was that fact which largely determined my sending her there, for it is like having her with another mother. Dr. Dubose has been raising the standards and has now two good college years and as Nell did not want a full college course that made a happy compromise. She is such a "mother girl" that she could not bear the idea of being away from home four whole years, but she is having a beautiful time at Raleigh. She is of a very ardent, "southern" temperament and "adores" the warm-hearted girl friends she has made in the south. Everyone says that there is something extraordinarily *vivid* and fascinating about her personality.

We have recently been through a terrible ordeal with her, but she is perfectly well again now. On the day after Christmas I took her in to Phila. to be operated on for tubercular glands in the neck and it turned out to be a frightfully severe case. They had actually to cut 1½ inches of her jugular vein, and of course for some time her life "hung by a thread" as the surgeon said. It was *awful*,–yet already she is *blooming* with health, and leaves on Thursday for school. The trouble, severe as it was, seems to have been altogether local, for during the last two months before the operation though it was growing fast she actually *gained* 8 lbs., weighing 143 lbs. I know that this will interest you because I remember your Lizzie had some similar trouble. Jessie also had the operation five years ago, hers too being quite serious. I was at the hospital with her for that purpose when my darling boy[1] was married,–and the only tear the brave child ever shed about it was from distress that she would "keep Mama from going to the wedding"! Nellie's first severe attack of it was two years ago when she had a high fever with it for a month. She was very ill,—a trained nurse in the house, when my boy was drowned. Stockton was at the same time very ill with nervous prostration and acute melancholia at a Phila. hospital. I had to go down before the funeral to break the news to him fearing the effect of the shock. Truly sorrows "come not single spies." In that one year[2] Jessie had diphtheria, Margaret nervous collapse, Nellie tubercular glands, Madge severe malarial fever in Italy; Woodrow was operated on for hernia in New York and had phlebitis after it, so that he was ill for months, Stockton was almost hopelessly ill the whole year, and I lost my darling boy and his little family. But such a summing up savors too much of self-pity,—a contemptible vice. I have very much to be thankful for even in the matter of health, for the children are all well and have excellent constitutions, and I think I can say, for perhaps the first time in twenty years, that Stockton too is *well*!—well and happy. And as usual, whether well or ill, he is doing *superb* work in the University; he is simply the idol of the students who vote him almost every year "the favourite professor." He is equally adored by the *women*! young and old, for his charming personality and his wonderful lectures on Eng. literature. Madge, of course, has her home with me and is a *beautiful*, charming girl, of an ultra southern type, that makes her very dangerous up here! But she is intensely critical of men, and so hard to please that I fear she will never find the right one! She went through college and spent year before last abroad largely studying in Italy; she is really very clever though with her soft indolent ways and flower face she does not advertise the fact. I think she writes charmingly and I am trying to stimulate her ambitions in that line for I think she needs some stronger interest in her life than she has. I have this fall fitted up for her a cosy little "den" in the tower, which looks south and west over a beautiful country and ought to give her an inspiration. It is very charming, with its low book shelves, soft-toned Persian rugs, draperies, &c.

Woodrow returned on Saturday from a month's stay in Bermuda which he enjoyed extremely, finding it wonderfully restful and sweet. His description of it sounds like a setting for a fairy tale. You know he almost had a very serious breakdown in June, due entirely to over-work; he was first condemned to six months vacation but he improved so very rapidly during the summer that the doctors consented to his resuming work in the autumn on condition that he broke the long strain of the college year by a midwinter holiday. He is very well again now and the doctors say he really has a wonderful constitution. But when one does ten years work in four, as all agree has been his case, some things *must* happen! As all the educational world declares he has really created in those four years "a new Princeton." It is marvellous that so much could be done in so short a time both in invigorating and developing the college,—in raising the standards of scholarship and morals,—and also in raising *money*! Of the $12,500,000 which he said was wanted four years ago, he has already $6,500,000; and as the "Evening Post" said with pleasant malice "he has ruined what was universally admitted to be the most agreeable and aristocratic country club in America by transforming it into an institution of learning." And as for development we had fifty new professors last year and ten more this year; a superb body of men they are too. These are all new foundations for the purpose (most of them) of putting into operation his darling scheme, "the preceptorial system," which they say is to revolutionize American educational standards. But alas! I fear he will never have time to *write* any more—and that hurts. But I am to have a reception and dance here tonight and I suppose I should stop writing and rest awhile.

AL (WC, NjP).

[1] Her brother, the late Edward William Axson.

[2] She meant the year from April 1904 to April 1905.

From the Diary of William Starr Myers

Tues. Feb. 12 [1907].

Bitter cold—thermometer 3 to 6° below zero, I hear, & I had to start my Soph. history classes in #8 Dickinson at 8 & 9 o'clock periods! In evening to a reception and dance at Pres. Wilson's, and a delightful time.

Bound diary (W. S. Myers Papers, NjP).

To Robert Garrett

My dear Mr. Garrett: Princeton, N. J. February 13th, 1907.

. . . Allow me also to acknowledge receipt of the copy of your letter to Mr. A. D. Russell about the systematic physical development of the campus. You know how heartily I sympathize with the main purpose you have in view. I feel very strongly that we must first formulate the lines upon which we mean to develop the life of the University before we can do anything thoroughly systematic on the physical side, which must of necessity be only an expression of that life.[1] But I am working hard to form for myself and realize by common counsel with others the ideas upon which we must act. I presented a portion of them at the last meeting of the Board.

Always cordially and sincerely yours,

Woodrow Wilson

TLS (Selected Corr. of R. Garrett, NjP).

[1] He was of course here referring to his quadrangle plan.

To Archibald Douglas Russell

My dear Mr. Russell: [Princeton, N. J.] February 13th, 1907.

I am sincerely sorry that I did not know of the meeting of the Committee on Grounds and Buildings until I had made an appointment to dine tomorrow evening with the Philadelphia alumni. I made this engagement with them before I left for Bermuda.

I think that there can be no debate as to the desirability of making the most systematic and carefully considered plans for the development of the campus, so that the haphazard or, rather, unsystematic choice of sites may be avoided and the buildings may be suitably related to each other, both in position and style. We have such splendid possibilities of situation here, that it is unquestionably our duty to make the most of them.

But the material development of the University can be nothing more than the expression of its life. What we mean to do, in other words, must necessarily determine the character, the position, and the relations of our buildings to each other. It would be very unwise, in my opinion, to put ourselves in the hands of any commission of architects, except for the purpose of getting from them suggestions as to the way in which our ideas for the University's growth should be expressed in stone and mortar and in landscape arrangement.

We have had so much to do during the last four years by way of reconstructing the University as it is, that we have not had time to form systematic plans of development, and I am clear in the judgment that such systematic plans, I mean the ideas to be carried out, must be carefully and thoroughly debated and agreed upon before an architectural commission can be of any service to us. What I would suggest, therefore, is this: That the committee move slowly in this matter, and that their first object be to secure advice as to the placing of the buildings already planned for: that for the rest we push forward as rapidly as possible the development of our ideas for the future life of the University, and that so soon as these ideas are formulated and agreed upon to our common satisfaction, we seek the advice of architects of the highest reputation, with regard to the landscape and architectural questions involved. We shall then know what buildings we shall need in our generation, whether it is desirable that they should be grouped or separated, what their relative position should be to each other and with regard to their distances from the center of the campus life, and all the other similar questions which must necessarily form a basis of the task we would propose to a commission of architects.

I take it for granted that the committee will give this matter the discussion, not of one meeting but of several, and I shall take pleasure in consulting with the committee at every possible juncture. The questions involved are questions of a sort which immediately concern my own responsibilities.

Very sincerely yours, [Woodrow Wilson]

CCL (WWP, UA, NjP).

To Benjamin Wistar Morris III

My dear Mr. Morris: Princeton, N. J. February 14th, 1907.

So far as I now know, I shall be at home from Tuesday noon to Friday afternoon next week, and if you will let me know when to expect you I will be pleased to confer with you about the wainscotting.

The springing in the panels seems to be chiefly behind the radiators. I spoke to Mr. Lakow's foreman about the probable effect of the heat, but he seemed to expect no trouble from it. One or two of the doors also have shown some tendency to lose their shape. None of the trouble is serious, but I thought that it had better be taken in hand before it became so.

Unhappily, the arrangements with regard to continuing the buildings on Brokaw Field are not in shape to enable us to say definitely, go ahead, but you may be sure that we will let you know at the earliest possible moment.

With much regard,

Sincerely yours, Woodrow Wilson

TLS (WC, NjP).

Notes for an Address

Philadelphia Alumni, 14 Feby. 1907

Ideals: A training at once *liberal* (i.e. looking out on the general field of knowledge) and *fundamental* (i.e. kept near the general, universal elements of knowledge)

Means: Pure literature
Pure philosophy
Pure science
History and politics

Above: Surrounding the central core of undergraduates, personally taught and united in close community, with as various an apparatus of experimental and original study as possible—our connection with the world of progress.

For the undergraduates themselves, the definite, determinate bodies of knowledge,—around them, the curious and alluring tracts of exploration and discovery

Our plans and hopes for scientific study
Research
Graduate instruction

Princeton will keep ideals clear.

WWhw MS (WP, DLC).

Two News Reports of an Address to Princeton Alumni in Philadelphia

[Feb. 15, 1907]

RICH GIFT FOR PRINCETON
WILL MAKE IT WORLD POWER

President Wilson, at Alumni Dinner, Announces
Bequest, Soon to be Made, Will Regenerate University—
Source a Mystery

Princeton University is on the verge of becoming the greatest seat of learning and college of research in the world. From a source concealed from the public the university is about to receive a large bequest. The sum will soon become available. It is to be used to increase the equipment of the college, and to add to the staff and send men into a broad, unlimited field of research.

President Woodrow Wilson made this announcement during the address at the dinner given in Horticultural Hall last night, before the members of the Princeton Club and the alumni of the university. When requested to go into further details as to the source of the fund, President Wilson said that the time is premature.

"Had this dinner been delayed a few weeks," he continued, "I might have been in a position to state in more definite terms just what this bequest is. I will say that it is not from one individual. It is so large that it will allow us to enter into researches on an almost unlimited scale. Our forces and equipment will be brought up to perfection, and I believe Princeton will rank as the first institution of learning in the world."[1]

Although pressed for further details, President Wilson refused to tell the source of the bequest.

The rest of his address was devoted to the present educational problem. He deplored the fact that the large colleges are expending so much of their energies in turning out graduates with literary tendencies. He advocated more courses in mechanics and a broader education generally.

About 300 graduates of Princeton attended the dinner. They were enthusiastic over the announcement of President Wilson, and after his address it was the one topic of the evening.

Printed in the Philadelphia *North American*, Feb. 15, 1907.

[1] Wilson had in mind the gifts already promised by Stephen Squires Palmer, David Benton Jones, Thomas Davies Jones, and Sarah Hoadley (Mrs. William Earl) Dodge for the building, equipment, and endowment of what would become Palmer Physical Laboratory, to house the Physics Department, and Guyot Hall, to house the Departments of Biology and Geology. He also had high hopes of obtaining large grants from other individuals and foundations for the general endowment of the scientific program at Princeton. See, e.g., WW *et al.* to the President and Trustees of the General Education Board, March 6, 1907.

◊

PRINCETON TO GET BIG GIFT OF MONEY

Dr. Wilson Hints at Donation at Club Banquet.

HIS WORDS ARE CHEERED

President of the University Says That Great Improvements Will Now Be Made Possible.

Hints of great extensions in the general work and the equipment of Princeton University, which will be made possible by a large gift to the institution, were dropped by Dr. Woodrow Wilson, president of the university, last night in an address at the annual banquet of the Princeton Club of Philadephia in Horticultural Hall. The announcement electrified his hearers, who gave cheer after cheer.

"I can only speak indefinitely at this time," said Dr. Wilson. "But if this banquet had come a few weeks later I would have been at liberty to tell you that Princeton is on the eve of a great advance. It will be particularly in the line of scientific research. I cannot say anything more now except that the gift which makes this possible comes from no [single] individual." . . .

Doctor Wilson made an eloquent plea for education on liberal lines. He said that many men miss the whole point of life by never learning to properly use their minds.

"Literature is the art of sincere expression," he said. "When men find out that the words that live and endure for ages do so because they breathe out the very soul of the author, then they no longer sneer at books. Education opens up these things to men."

Doctor Wilson declared that too many of the schools of the country have been tied to the factories; that they are turning out only technical men. "Take care of the men and they will take care of the industries," he said. "Train their minds on broad lines. Mechanical experts do not discover the secrets of nature. It is those who have been trained to think."

As the speaker sat down the guests sprang to their feet and joined in the inspiring words of "Old Nassau." . . .

Printed in the Philadelphia *Public Ledger*, Feb. 15, 1907.

From John Allan Wyeth[1]

Dear Sir: New York City. February 15, 1907.

I am sending you under separate cover two catalogues of the New York Polyclinic Medical School and Hospital. This institution I founded in 1881, and it was opened in 1882. It was the first post-graduate medical school in America.

It has been successful in that we have given practical bed-side and laboratory instruction to about 12,000 physicians, chiefly from the United States and Canada, but some from all parts of the earth. We own in fee simple the property and equipment in 34th Street. Its medical staff is a veteran body, thoroughly organized. It is a public institution, chartered, controlled by a board of trustees of public spirited men, well-known in this community.

My object in writing this is in the thought that your university might consider the enlargment of the scope of its work by the development of a medical department of Princeton University. If at any time this should occur to you, and you should desire to confer with me upon the subject, I shall be glad to come to Princeton or meet you at some time convenient to ourselves when you may be in New York.

You may recall that at the Southern Society Dinner,[2] just as you were on the eve of leaving for Bermuda, I told you I was very desirous of having you meet Mr. Wm. M. Laffan, of the "New York Sun." Mr. Laffan has said that he would be very glad to meet and know you personally. He is not only one of the biggest brained men in journalism and exercises a powerful influence in public affairs, but being a graduate of a medical college (University of Dublin) he has always been deeply interested in medical affairs and is moreover a trustee of the New York Polyclinic.

I am just now leaving for Florida for a two weeks vacation, but hope very much that I may see you upon my return.

Sincerely yours, John A Wyeth.

TLS (WP, DLC).

1 Originally from Alabama, he was a noted surgeon, author of books and articles on medicine and other subjects, and president of numerous medical societies, including the American Medical Association.

2 A news report of this affair is printed at Dec. 15, 1906, Vol. 16.

From Harold Griffith Murray

Dear Dr. Wilson, New York February 18th, 1907

Thank you for your letter of the 12th instant, also for your speech at the Philadelphia dinner last week. I listened to it with a great deal of interest.

Enclosed is a list of those who were graduated prior to 1870 and whose financial condition will make it possible for them to give to the University generously if they are so inclined. If you can let me know the result of this correspondence, I will appreciate it very much. I keep in my office a tabulated account of the attitude of each alumnus toward the Committee of Fifty Fund.

Yours very truly, H. G. Murray Sec'y

TLS (WP, DLC). Enc.: typed list of Princeton alumni.

Henry Burling Thompson to Cleveland Hoadley Dodge

Dear Cleve: Wilmington, Del. 2d Mo., 18th, 1907.

You once told me that I wrote too many letters, but I propose again to brave your indignation, and give you my opinion of the Princeton Club matter, as I believe you are on the Committee to report on President Wilson's Report.

I agree absolutely with the President in his statement of conditions and the harm likely to result from continuing the present system, but I was unable to follow him in his conclusions as to curing the evil. Possibly, on closer examination of his scheme I should think better of it.

To be brief,—the trouble is two-fold.

First,—The men who do not get into Clubs are disappointed, and leave Princeton,—in most instances, at least,—not friends of the Institution.

Second,—A period of tremendous unrest is developed in the Sophomore year by the students' desire to secure a Club.

Now, at least, one cure for the first trouble would be to arrange to take the entire Senior and Junior classes into Clubs. The situation to-day is as follows:

The catalogue shows 533 students in the Senior and Junior classes. The "Bric-a-Brac" shows 404 Seniors and Juniors in the Clubs; in other words, 75.5 per cent of the upper classes are Club members; and it would be quite possible, with the present thirteen Clubs,—with the possible exception of two,—to so arrange it that the entire Senior and Junior classes could be comfortably accommodated. I base this statement on the following table:

	Present Membership.	*Additions.*
Ivy,—	26,	14,
Cottage,—	29,	11,
Tiger,—	26,	14,
Cap & Gown,—	31,	9,
Colonial,—	31,	9,
Elm,—	32,	8,
Cannon,—	37,	3,
Campus,—	33,	7,
Quadrangle,—	22,	18,
Charter,—	39,	1,
Tower,—	31,	9,
Terrace,—	36,	4,
Key & Seal,—	31,	9,
	404,	116,—

a total of 520.

It seems ridiculous that Ivy, Cottage and Tiger, with their expensive and commodious Club Houses, should not accommodate as many as Charter and Terrace, with their smaller plants.

Now, if it could be arranged among the Club Presidents,—for I believe this is a matter entirely outside the powers of the Trustees and Faculty,—that there should be some agreement by which the limits of Club membership should be brought to forty (40),—

which number some of the newer Clubs have virtually reached,—it would dispose of, for the present, the entire membership of the upper classes.

You will immediately say—"How would you take care of the increase?" Of necessity, it would require probably more Clubs, or an enlarged membership among the present lot.

I believe the graduates who control the upper class Clubs would be in sympathy with this scheme.

How to meet the second objection is a more difficult problem, but I believe that it would mitigate the evil if the Sophomores could be treated in the same way as the Freshmen, and put in Commons, and the Sophomore Clubs abolished. I should assume that the Faculty had sufficient power to make this change. Sophomore Commons involve expense, but expense has been met before. Yours very sincerely, Henry B Thompson

TLS (WP, DLC).

A News Report of an Address to Princeton Alumni in Baltimore

[Feb. 19, 1907]

PRINCETON FUND A MYTH

President Wilson Settles Rumor At Alumni Banquet.

President Woodrow Wilson, of Princeton, last night settled effectively the persistent rumors to the effect that the university had received, or was about to receive an immense endowment fund, which would place at its disposal more money than possessed by any other institution of the world for original research and extension of courses. But so far from being gloomy over the fact that the report erroneously sent out from Philadelphia where he spoke a few nights ago to the alumni association of that city was not true, Dr. Wilson held it up to Princeton men as a subject of congratulation.

The occasion was the twenty-first annual dinner of the Princeton Alumni Association of Maryland, which was held in the hall of the Arundel Club, Charles and Eager streets. Seventy loyal sons of Old Nassau had gathered to listen to the message of progress to be delivered by the head of their beloved alma mater, and the best elements of almost every sphere of activity in the State was represented at the banquet board.

The old Princetonians cheered the vigorous speech of their president to the echo. When he said that no man was big enough to stamp upon the university by a princely gift his name as the virtual director of its destinies, the enthusiasm manifested was almost unbounded.

Dr. Wilson made a strong plea for university growth along safe and conservative lines that will give to the undergraduate the most liberal education obtainable everywhere, and he deplored the great growth of the elective system in American institutions of learning. He also explained and championed to the alumni the new preceptorial system recently introduced at the university, by which the faculty is able to keep in touch with the real work that is being pursued by the undergraduate body without having to wait for the final examinations to determine the place an individual holds in the undergraduate world. Dr. Wilson said, in part:

"In the city of Philadelphia there are employed as representatives of the press men of vivid imaginings, and some that attended a recent banquet at which I was a speaker in that city reported me as saying something that I did not say.

"There has been no recent enormous gift to Princeton. I have no knowledge of one that is to be made. I do not believe in a university growing by leaps and bounds. Princeton stands for the growth of original research—but it is a growth. It is not to be accomplished by the making of munificent gifts. Such a growth would not be healthy. Princeton is growing just as any other healthy and living thing grows.

"I am not at all certain that I want any one person to take possession of Princeton by giving her a sum so great that his name will always be associated with her. No man that I know is big enough.

"The most important business of Princeton is the giving of degrees, but we have to be heartless about it, for a national university can give degrees only to persons of national reputation.

"The character of the work is higher and the men are taking to it admirably. There were fewer casualties than usual at the mid-year's examination."

Dr. Wilson spoke of the fact that a good many of the instructors live in dormitories, and coming into close contact with the students stimulated them to better work.

"We are, for the most part, opposed to the elective system," he continued. "College spirit is inversely [related] to the elective system. Where there are most electives there is least college spirit. Too many electives destroy communal interest and make the men self-centered.

"The object of education is not to make a living. The object of life is enlightening, not the making of money. We want liberally educated men.

"A man who can be happy in the dark in quiet self-communion is a very fortunate man. I believe any intelligent, educated man can make a living. Any fool can do that. But it is not every man who can make it bring him real pleasure and comfort. Anyone can purchase preoccupation of a sort.

"Pure philosophy, pure literature, pure science and history will give a man a broad outlook on life, and all these elements can be put in a college curriculum.

"You must surround the region of ascertained knowledge with regions to be discovered, areas of adventure. We must fill processes of advanced research to make the college course vital. This is what Princeton stands for and what Princeton is going to do. A general impression has got abroad that if you want to go where men know what they are doing you must go to Princeton. We aim to get the best teachers in the country. We really do know more than the undergraduates we are teaching, and that is why we tell them what to study, instead of asking them what they want.

"Other universities have spread out like a flood, but Princeton is advancing between firm and well-defined banks, generating great power.

"The most splendid example of Princeton spirit was the response of the undergraduate body to the preceptorial system, realizing that this thing is a Princeton thing and studying with a real zest.

"I don't care by what process, but if you get wholesome moral and intellectual forces you can go to your grave with the knowledge that you have done something for your fellow-men."

Printed in the Baltimore *Sun*, Feb. 19, 1907; some editorial headings omitted.

A News Item

[Feb. 19, 1907]

PRESIDENT WILSON'S ENGAGEMENTS.

President Woodrow Wilson '79 is announced to lecture on the Blumenthal Foundation at Columbia University during the months of March and April.

This course comprises eight lectures, one on each Friday afternoon, with the exception of Good Friday. The general topic is "The Government of the United States," and the subject of each lecture, in order of delivery, is: (1) "The Nature of Constitutional Government"; (2) "Place of the Government of the United States in Constitutional Development"; (3) "The President of the United States"; (4) "The Senate"; (5) "The House of Representatives"; (6) "The Judiciary"; (7) "The States under the Federal Government," and (8) "Party Government of the United States."[1] On February 18 President Wilson is to speak at the alumni reunion in Baltimore, and on April 2 will speak at the alumni dinner in Pittsburg.[2]

Printed in the *Daily Princetonian*, Feb. 19, 1907.

[1] Wilson delivered the first lecture on March 1, the second on March 8, the third on March 15, the fourth on March 22, the fifth on April 12, the sixth on April 19, the seventh on April 25, and the eighth on April 26. In the Wilson Papers, there are the following materials relating to these lectures: (1) a WWhw outline of topics; (2) random WWhw notes; (3) WWT outlines; (4) WWsh drafts of press releases for each lecture; and (5) transcripts of the lectures made by an unknown stenographic reporter. These transcripts will not be printed, since Wilson revised them substantially for publication as *Constitutional Government in the United States* (New York, 1908), the complete text of which will be printed in Vol. 18.

[2] A news report of Wilson's address to the Pittsburgh alumni is printed at April 3, 1907.

From John Howell Westcott

Dear Woodrow: Princeton University Feb. 19. 1907

I believe I will venture to recommend that Prentice be allowed to go to California. The benefit to the college will probably be greater than any harm that may result from his going. But I do not wish to insist upon this view, if on further reflection, you feel that the arguments on the other side ought to prevail. You are responsible for all the departments & your field of observation is broader than mine. Do not feel bound by what you said to me this afternoon. But telephone me or drop me a line if you wish me to tell Prentice of an altered decision. You may prefer to tell him yourself.[1]

About naming a professor I am still greatly perplexed. Suppose we get Capps.[2] Then we have 4 professors in Greek + ½ Stuart, & in Latin ½ West, ½ Stuart & what is left of me. The latter seems very little. I can't get myself interested in study, or in any real piece of work.[3] David Magie has my graduate course for this term—arranged so when I was expected to go abroad. It doesn't seem now as if I should ever take it back again, or ever feel capable of bracing up & doing anything but just the routine of old familiar teaching, as low down in the curriculum as possible—& standing about keeping the younger teachers in order & working together, as they are now doing very well—a sort of intellectual coxswain, while the rest are doing the rowing. No doubt that is a useful, though humble function. If I hadn't the children I would clear out now, & stay away till I felt like doing some good work; but as it is, it's better to stay & fight it out on this line as well as I can. But our Latin side seems wofully weak at the top. It is relatively more in need of strengthening than the Greek side. All this is to explain my indecision & delay in beginning any decisive action, not to ventilate my own troubles. They are unfortunately relevant in so far as they affect the department.

Ever yours J. H. W.

ALI (WWP, UA, NjP).

1 Wilson apparently decided not to accept Westcott's recommendation. In any event, Prentice remained at Princeton.

2 Edward Capps, Professor of Greek at the University of Chicago. For additional biographical information on Capps, see Wilson's Annual Report to the Board of Trustees printed at Dec. 13, 1907.

3 Westcott had been suffering depression since his wife's death on September 6, 1905.

To Cleveland Hoadley Dodge

My dear Cleve: Princeton, N. J. February 20th, 1907.

Thank you for sending me Thompson's letter.[1]

Certainly he understands the situation on one side, but he clearly does not understand it on the other. It is easy enough to suggest that all juniors and seniors be taken into the clubs, but inasmuch as they are social organizations based upon a choice of companions, the suggestion is clearly impracticable.

I think, too, that a sophomore commons would be a great mistake and a great danger.

It becomes clearer to me every day that I made the mistake, in reporting to the Board, of putting my own plans only on one and that not the most important ground of desirability to be considered.[2] When the committee meets,[3] I shall lay the matter before them in an entirely different light.[4]

I would like, by the way, to have your suggestion as to when the committee should be called together. I think we need not have more than one meeting before the next meeting of the Board, because this is a matter which ought not to be pressed to an immediate conclusion, and we ought to get the permission of the Board to debate it very much at length.

Always affectionately yours, Woodrow Wilson

TLS (WC, NjP).

1 That is, H. B. Thompson to C. H. Dodge, Feb. 18, 1907.

2 In his supplementary report, he had emphasized the undemocratic nature and snobbishness of the clubs.

3 It met on March 9, 1907.

4 As documents in this volume will later disclose, Wilson avoided the social issues for a time and advocated the quadrangle plan on the ground that it was essential to the academic and intellectual reorganization and development of the university.

To Mary Allen Hulbert Peck

My dear Mrs. Peck, Princeton, N. J. 20 Feby. 1907.

One has no right to whet another's appetite for Walter Bagehot without supplying the means of gratifying it. I am, therefore, indulging myself in the pleasure of sending you his essays, which I am sure you will enjoy with as much zest as anyone I know.

I am sending, too, a little volume of my own essays. I beg that you will not put them at the cruel disadvantage of being read at the same time that you have the flavour of Bagehot on your palate. I send them only that you may know me a little better.

With warm regard,

Sincerely Yours, Woodrow Wilson.

TCL (WC, NjP).

To Moses Taylor Pyne

My dear Momo: [Princeton, N. J.] February 21st, 1907.

I of course had an interview with Norris[1] and arranged to have the outrageous misrepresentation of the Philadelphia reporters corrected.[2] I suppose one is helpless against outrages of this sort, but I do not know when I have been so chagrinned or angered. So far as I can make out, it was a deliberate lie out of the whole cloth.

I am very sorry that I cannot be at the meeting of the Committee on Grounds and Buildings. I carefully explained to Bunn[3] when I could be present, but he seems to have misunderstood.

Always affectionately yours, [Woodrow Wilson]

CCL (WWP, UA, NjP).

1 Edwin Mark Norris, Princeton 1895, Editor of the *Princeton Alumni Weekly.*

2 Norris printed the following statement: "President Wilson's address at the recent annual dinner of the Princeton Club of Philadelphia has been misquoted by some of the newspapers in such an extraordinary manner that we take this first opportunity of placing before the alumni of Princeton the substance of the President's speech on that occasion. He announced that Princeton was on the eve of important developments in the field of scientific study and original investigation; that now that the University had established solid methods of undergraduate instruction, it was her duty to develop along lines of graduate study; that is [it] was the immediate purpose of the University to add to its facilities for scientific study and research, and that we were confidently expecting to get the means to do this on a somewhat liberal scale." *Princeton Alumni Weekly*, VII (Feb. 23, 1907), 331.

3 Henry Conrad Bunn, Curator of Grounds and Buildings.

From Cleveland Hoadley Dodge

My dear Mr. President: New York February 21, 1907.

Many thanks for your good letter of yesterday.

I agree with you as to the impracticability of forcing the clubs to take all the upper class men, but it is evident that they have room for many more than they take now and I should think they could gradually be induced to enlarge their membership and practically take in all of the men who would care to join the clubs. Harry Thompson is going to be in Princeton tonight or tomorrow, and you may run across him, and if you do I wish you would have a little talk with him about the matter.

Regarding a meeting of the Committee, I should think it would be well to hold it shortly before the Trustees' meeting. I hope to come down about the 10th of March to spend two weeks at my house in Princeton,[1] and perhaps the best time would be the day before, or the Saturday before the Trustees' meeting, if that would suit you. . . . Very sincerely yours, C. H. Dodge

TLS (WP, DLC).

[1] At 24 Bayard Lane.

Notes for an Address[1]

Hill School, Pottstown, 22 Feby. 1907.

Discretion

Sober youth of Washington

His hard school of Life

Companionship of older men: equality of the woods and of practical affairs.

His early discretion—efficiency.

Our own long school days of *irresponsibility*

Companionship only with those of our own age: consequent postponement of prudence & efficiency

What is Discretion?

Good judgment,—practical discernment

Thoughtful observation

The wisdom of kindness and accommodation

Efficiency—in work as in play.

The Age of discretion

When we perceive what we are in the world for.

The age of usefulness, not only, but also

The age of zest and happiness

WWhw MS (WP, DLC).

[1] A brief news report of this address is printed at Feb. 26, 1907.

From Mary Allen Hulbert Peck

Dear Dr. Wilson, Inwood,[1] Paget [Bermuda]. Feb. 25 [1907]

Your kind thought of me has touched me more than I can express. If I had not feared that to a busy man it might seem like mawkish sentimentality I would have written in answer to your note of goodbye to tell you what knowing you has meant to me.

I wish a greater gift of expression were mine but I am sure however bunglingly I put it you will understand what I wish to say. It is always a privilege to know a truly great and good man—and because you are that—and more—I want you to know that you gave me strength and courage in a moment when my spirit faltered and the struggle seemed not worth while. Your very presence shames all thoughts of cowardice and is an inspiration for good. And so—I am going on with renewed courage and some little hope that I am not wholly unworthy since you have found some good in me.

The books have not yet come but I am promising myself much pleasure in reading them and you must forgive me if I say I am somewhat prejudiced in favor of the author of the essays!

With deepest and warmest gratitude & regard

Sincerely yours Mary Allen Peck.

ALS (WP, DLC).

[1] Inwood in Paget East is one of the oldest and most famous houses in Bermuda. Built in 1700 by Francis Jones, it remained in the Jones family until 1915, when it was sold to Harriett Smither of Pittsfield, Mass. Inwood has a vast lawn, a formal garden, a rose garden, stables, a two-story servants' house, and a tennis court. Hudson Strode, *The Story of Bermuda* (New York, 1932), pp. 292-96.

A News Item About an Address at the Hill School

[Feb. 26, 1907]

PRES. WILSON'S ADDRESS.

On the morning of February 22, Dr. Woodrow Wilson, President of Princeton University, delivered an address in the gymnasium to the fellows of the school. His subject was "Discretion," as brought out by Washington and as it should be displayed by the older students of our present preparatory schools and our present preparatory schools [*sic*] and colleges. He received a cordial welcome and was heartily applauded.

Printed in the Pottstown, Pa., *Hill School News*, Feb. 26, 1907.

To Moses Taylor Pyne

My dear Momo: [Princeton, N. J.] February 28th, 1907.

Enclosed you will find the brief I undertook to prepare for the General Education Board.[1] I sincerely hope that it will prove to be what you desire, but I hope that you and Dodge will feel at liberty to pull it about in any way you see fit.

If there is any further way in which I can be of assistance, please call on me with the utmost freedom. I suggest that you and Dodge also sign the paper.

Always affectionately yours, [Woodrow Wilson]

CCL (WWP, UA, NjP).

[1] This draft—a TLS in WP, DLC—was heavily emended by Wilson, Pyne, and Dodge and is not printed. There is also a WWsh draft of it in WP, DLC. The letter sent to the General Education Board, a foundation established by John D. Rockefeller for the promotion of education in the United States, is printed at March 6, 1907.

To Robert Garrett

My dear Mr. Garrett: Princeton, N. J. February 28th, 1907.

The Committee of the Board of Trustees of Princeton University to consider the report made by the President of the University at the last meeting of the Board, will meet in the President's Office in '79 Hall, Princeton, at 8 o'clock on the evening of Saturday, March 9th, 1907.

Very sincerely yours, Woodrow Wilson

TLS (Selected Corr. of R. Garrett, NjP).

An Historical Article for Boys

[c. March 1, 1907]

THE SOUTHERN COLONIST

It is now three hundred years since the first permanent English settlement was made in America, at Jamestown in Virginia. We begin to feel our youth as a nation drop away and the touch of antiquity come upon us as we become conscious of this august span of three centuries that lies between us and our nativity, a long tale of years that carries us back to the age of Shakespeare and almost to the "spacious times of great Elizabeth"; and we turn with a deep and serious curiosity to recall those far-away small beginnings of great affairs. It is a very significant thing we are about to celebrate by the waters of the James and the Chesapeake, the first waters into which English keels brought settlers who were to begin an empire in America.

In studying the origins of America we have habitually devoted too much attention to the Puritan settlers in New England, too little to the men who settled in Virginia and built a great commonwealth in the South. Not only did they come before the Puritan settlers and begin before all other Englishmen the work of making homes and establishing states in America, but they were also much more typically English in all their ways and standards, and set up communities which, without peculiar features of their own, transferred English life to America.

The men who first settled New England were men picked out of a particular class and party, the party which had set its heart upon purifying the church both in doctrine and in practice, upon bringing it to the simple beliefs and reformed practices of Calvin: merchants from the smaller towns; villagers who had drawn together before they had left England to establish the life and practice they preferred; ministers trained, most of them, at Cambridge, where the new doctrines of the Reformation had chiefly taken hold, and who had set at defiance the discipline of the church in their own creed and worship. It was their boast and pleasure to say that God had "sifted a whole nation" to send them out to America, and the process of sifting had left all Englishmen of ordinary opinions and ways of living behind. Naturally only men of their own kind and their own beliefs followed them to America in the years succeeding, and New England was for a long age not a place where you could find England transplanted, but a place where Englishmen of a special faith and practice had set up communities of their own kind and after their own liking. Virginia, on the other hand, was a frontier fragment of England itself.

Neither New England nor Virginia, indeed, if the truth must be plainly told, was the source from which things typically American came. The "middle colonies" of New York and Pennsylvania and New Jersey were the first characteristic bits of America. America is not English, although it speaks the tongue of England,—with a difference!—and has received from its first generations of settlers and builders the English forms and traditions of government. It is a people mixed of many races, and has compounded its life out of elements taken from all parts of the European world; and the mixture of races and conditions and origins which is characteristically American was first witnessed in New York and along the Delaware, where Dutch and Swedes and Germans and English first united to make a common life for themselves. The expansion of America has been the expansion of their life rather than the expansion of the lives of Virginians or New Englanders.

The very first settlers brought over to Virginia were certainly not "sifted." They were mixed of every kind, except the steady and the serviceable. Men who were prosperous and who had work to their minds at home naturally stayed where they were, and had no inclination to make the doubtful adventure of going to America. It was for the most part men out of work, or unfit for it, who chose to go in that first day, when the whole enterprise was new and doubtful; and not so much men from the quiet countrysides as idlers and adventurers from the unquiet cities.

Many of them were men of good blood enough, but with no patrimony, no occupation, no steady disciplined habit of any kind, too often "unruly gallants packed thither by their friends to escape ill destinies," and it went hard for a year or two to make successful colonists out of such stuff. But capable men were in charge of the enterprise, there were steady heads a few among the many unsteady, and when once the colony had got a real foothold, settlers of a very different character began to come over, until the stream presently became a stream of average, sober, hardheaded Englishmen, a fair sample of the people they had left behind. Before any Puritan had made a home for himself in New England, the men of Virginia had set up a new England for themselves upon the James River, had their own little parliament, and could show the beginnings of a commonwealth where English custom and English law had taken root in vigorous fashion.

The very year they got their parliament (1619) a Dutch man-of-war came into the river and sold them twenty negroes to be slaves, but it was many a long year before other slaves were brought, and the life of the colony grew to its characteristic features before any custom of slavery settled upon it to modify it.

Of course the life of the colonists could not be exactly what it had been in England, for Virginia was not England—a land long ago cleared of its greater tracts of forests, full of quiet fields and broad acres of grain and soft grass for the cattle; towns with busy marketplaces here and there, and everywhere along the many travelled roads villages clustered about some country house or gathered at some crossing of the ways.

The only highways in Virginia were the streams: the broad waters of the James itself and of the great bay below by the capes at the sea were the chief ways of quick movement and communication. For the rest, there were only bridle-paths through the forests, for long only foot-paths; for horses were not soon brought over, and those who did not travel by boat from place to place on the water went afoot through the shadowed wilderness. It was slow work making clearings in the thick-set forests, and when the trees were at last felled, their heavy stumps stood in the way of the plow for many a weary year before there was time enough or labor enough to take them out and get finally rid of them.

Every man who chose a place for his home and a piece of land to clear for his crops or the pasture of his cattle took care, if it were possible, to secure a frontage on the great river or on some navigable stream that ran into it. He built his own wharf and ship's landing, if he could afford it, and the ships that came in from oversea, if they brought any considerable part of their cargo for him, made fast at his very doors to put their freight ashore. Few stuffs for clothing, few articles for domestic use were made there in the scattered homes and tiny settlements, for the settlers did not collect in towns as the New Englanders did; almost everything except the food they ate, the timber and bricks they used for their houses, and the simple implements they could fashion at their blacksmiths' forges or at the carpenter's bench was fetched out of England by the slow, infrequent ships which plied back and forth to Bristol or Plymouth or London.

It was a rustic yeomanry that grew up there on the long reaches of the quiet river. Here and there was an estate bigger than the rest, a "plantation" of broad acres, whose owner lived like a rustic country gentleman—although not quite as a country gentleman would live "at home" in England, for the conveniences of that rough country were few and accumulated very slowly, as the means to obtain them accumulated.

Like Englishmen in the old country in everything, the Virginians dearly loved and instinctively honored men and women of good blood and gentle breeding. The easy natural intercourse of their small settlements excluded pretension, made punctilious ceremony ridiculous and out of the question; but there were the ships moving to and fro across the ocean like shuttles weaving the fabric of life in England into the fabric of life in Virginia, bringing out upon each voyage not only the clothes the Virginians were to wear and the fashions according to which they were to wear them, not only books and plows and utensils and uncounted articles of personal and domestic use, but thoughts also and the whole atmosphere of affairs as Englishmen saw them across the seas, and life in the Virginian plantations was like a copy of life in England drawn in very simple lines on the rough surface of the wilderness.

A little capital grew up at Jamestown, which was certainly not to be compared even with the smallest county market town at home, but which became the center of fashionable life, as it was the center of politics in the colony, and there in the "season," while the legislature of the colony sat, the House of Burgesses which had been set up first in 1619, there was not a little gaiety and show of gallant manners and innocent intrigue.

There the governor had his "palace," and the governor, good or bad, whether a man sent because of his worth and capacity, or merely some court favorite sent off to be at a safe distance from the intrigues and temptations of the great court at London, was the spokesman and representative of the crown, to which the average Virginian looked with a great deal of simple respect and even reverence.

The government of the colony was patterned as nearly as might be after the government at home. When the colony grew sufficiently to be divided into counties, each county had its lieutenant, whose duties and authority were like those of a Lord Lieutenant in England; its sheriff, like the sheriff of an English county; its justices, who, like the justices in England, constituted its "commission of the peace," administered the law in all ordinary cases, and determined all the ordinary administrative business of the county.

The Church of England was the church of Virginia, and the vestry and churchwardens of each parish looked after the poor and acted in most matters as vestries and churchwardens in England did in the regulation of local affairs. All the chief officers of the county were appointed by the governor in Virginia, as the officers of the English county were appointed by the king, and the "burgesses" of the little parliament of the colony which sat from time to time at Jamestown were as critical of what the governor did or omitted to do as the great Parliament at Westminster of what the king, his master, did or neglected. There was often keen zest in the politics of the colony, and opinion surged in waves of which the governor had to be heedful.

The singular thing was that although these scattered colonists in Virginia led an easy and expansive life, were not drawn together into towns where debate and agitation were naturally bred by the daily contact of minds, as the New Englanders were, did not strive for separate principles and practices of their own, but accepted what they had had at home, both in matters affecting their worship and in matters affecting their government with quiet contentment, as if they were to be accepted like the operations of nature and the seasons, they were as jealous of their rights and as particular to insist upon them as the New Englanders themselves.

The very separateness of their lives from the close democratic contacts of town and village seemed to breed in them a certain individual dignity, a certain stubbornness and pride of independence, which made them the more quick to resent imposition of any illegal assertion of authority. They imported their fashions and their clothes from London, and their ideas concerning the ordinary affairs of life, and were very assiduous to practise what they understood to be the manners of the court; but they had none of the court's subserviency, and seemed to breathe a certain infection of liberty from the free air of the forests which they had made their home—where they were willing to obey all reasonable laws, but were determined not to be put upon by any usurpation or any unjust use even of legitimate authority.

It is beginnings of this kind that we are about to celebrate at Jamestown. A scant fragment of pitiful ruin and a few cracked gravestones are all that remain of Jamestown, where English dominion in America was first set up. But we do not need the material form of that old life to preserve the memory of the gallant thing that was done in Virginia by the men who founded the Old Dominion. Without fret, without rebellion, without conscious purpose to separate themselves or make a new polity as well as a new England on this side of the sea, they devised a placid freedom for themselves which was like a demonstration of what English principles and English ways of life and government would be if reduced to their essential elements, separated from the artificial conditions of old sophisticated monarchies, and planted in the sweet air of remote forests, where men live simply, think clearly, and purpose frankly the things their legitimate interests demand.

Here they made a cradle for liberty, and it grew, not like a child of institutions, but like a child of nature. The lives of the Virginian colonists were strangely contrasted in almost every outward form and practice with the lives of the New England colonists, but when it came to the making of the nation and the safeguarding of political rights and natural privileges, they stood with their kinsmen of New England like brothers of the same breeding, and showed America the way to successful and honorable revolution.[1]

Printed in *The Youth's Companion*, LXXXI (April 18, 1907), 184-85.

[1] There is a WWsh draft of this essay in WP, DLC.

From Melancthon Williams Jacobus

Hartford, Conn.,
My dear President Wilson: March 1st, 1907.

I return you herewith the copy of your supplementary report, for the loan of which I am sincerely thankful.

I can easily understand that the first meeting of the Committee will need to have the time taken up in an illumining talk from you as to what the problem really is and what you wish the Committee to do in presenting it to the Board.

The more I study the matter, the more interested in it I grow, and feel that it is going to take hold of the essential question of the continued existence of the American college. In the changes which have been taking place in the advanced standard of work done by the secondary schools and the decreased standard of work required for the Arts Degree, the time is rapidly approaching when a first-class scholar from Lawrenceville might, by selecting his University, pass from a secondary school to his post graduate studies without much if any time spent in the intermediate discipline of the college.

I do not know that I would seriously object to this—only it is interesting, and if we can establish on our campus a method of life among the college classes which will meet this development and master it to the best results, Princeton will again have shown its right to lead the new way in American education.

Unless you have some other appointment for the evening of Wednesday the 13th of March, I will assign 8:00 o'clock of that evening for the next meeting of the Curriculum Committee, and send out notices accordingly.

I am hoping to bring Mrs. Jacobus with me to the Inn on Wednesday to remain until Friday, on her way back from Atlantic City.

Kindly let me know if the proposed time for the Curriculum Committee will be convenient to you.

With kind regards,

Yours very sincerely, M. W. Jacobus

P.S. Since writing the above I have received your call for the Honorary Degrees Committee at the above hour suggested for the Curriculum Committee. Would 4:30 on afternoon of March 13 or some hour on Thursday forenoon be suitable? Please select the hour best suited to the work which will come before the Com. I will arrange to get up from Atlantic City in time

M W J.

TLS (WP, DLC).

From Robert Garrett

My dear President Wilson: [Baltimore] March 2nd, 1907.

Probably you will remember that some years ago you gave two informal talks before a club of about twelve Baltimore men. The first one was at my home here. The second time we went to Princeton to meet you.

The members of the club have now asked me to request you to meet with us a third time. We would of course go to Princeton for the purpose unless you could and should prefer to come here. A date that would be convenient to us is Thursday, March 28th, and the time, either in the afternoon or about eight o'clock in the evening. It would perhaps be held at your old house on Library Place[1] in case you say that Princeton will be more convenient.

We should like to hear you discuss some one, or several political questions of the present time, or perhaps some question concerning higher education in America. These subjects however are of course merely suggestions on our part. We do not wish, for a moment, to put any restrictions upon you.

I earnestly hope that you will be able and willing to comply with our request.

Very sincerely yours, [Robert Garrett]

CCL (Selected Corr. of R. Garrett, NjP).

1 Which Robert Garrett and his brother, John Work Garrett, had purchased in 1902.

From the Diary of William Starr Myers

Sat. Mch 2 [1907].

Departmental meeting at the "Inn" in evening. Pres. Wilson read a fine paper on Sir Henry Maine,[1] and afterwards an informal talk on the "Preceptorial System" followed by a conference in which most of us joined. What a wonderful man "Woodrow" is—fine voice, wonderful flow of language, and a superb and stimulative scholarship to back it.

1 It is printed at Feb. 25, 1898, Vol. 10, and was published as "A Lawyer with a Style," *Atlantic Monthly*, LXXXII (Sept. 1898), 363-74.

A News Item

[March 4, 1907]

DR. HENRY VAN DYKE '73 RESIGNS FROM THE UNIVERSITY FACULTY.

Dr. Henry van Dyke '73 has tendered to President Wilson his resignation from the University faculty. His connection with the

University extends over a period of eight years, during which time he has occupied the position of Murray Professor of English Literature. It is supposed that Dr. van Dyke wishes to be free to prosecute his literary work.

Printed in the *Daily Princetonian*, March 4, 1907.

From Edith Gittings Reid

[Baltimore, c. March 5, 1907]

Alas! that a Cross[1] should come between you & me—and a "Dicky" one at that! I remain in spite of all, however, your affectionate and faithful friend Edith G. Reid

I intend however to bawl out the Cross! It won't do—is not to be borne.

ALS (WP, DLC).

1 She was referring to Richard Kelso Cross, Princeton 1863, a Baltimore lawyer with whom Wilson had stayed when he addressed the Princeton Alumni Association of Maryland in Baltimore.

Henry van Dyke to Stockton Axson

My dear Axson Boston March 5, 1907.

I telegraphed you an answer to the dispatch from the Princeton Faculty[1] which I found in the Preachers Room at Harvard[2] this morning. Tonight, coming back to my resting-place here, I find your very kind message from the English Department.[3] Will you thank my colleagues from me most heartily? By all this, and by Prest Wilson's visit last night I am surprised, overwhelmed, shaken—so that it is difficult to express my feelings coherently. I felt most deeply Wilson's visit, and the personal kindness of his words. But for his own sake, being of more value to the university than any other man, or ten men, he ought not to have made that journey. Tell him that my letter is in his hands personally,[4]—the right place,—and that it is safe there until I have thought over all that he said to me,—the whole situation, the feeling and wishes of the students, my duty and possibilities of usefulness for the future,—then I will write him in a word what to do with the letter. I am in much perplexity. This trip to Palestine[5] seemed like an "almost Providential" (Duffield) invitation to

'fold my tent like an Arab
And silently steal away.'

But instead of that I am face to face with the most [?] and insistent kind of a problem of responsibility. Believe me, my one wish is to do the right thing, the best thing, for Princeton and the boys.[6] Faithfully Yours Henry van Dyke

ALS (WP, DLC).

[1] The faculty resolution imploring van Dyke to withdraw his resignation is printed in the *Daily Princetonian*, March 5, 1907.

[2] Van Dyke was serving for a brief time as University Preacher at Harvard University.

[3] The English Department's resolution is printed in the *Daily Princetonian*, March 6, 1907.

[4] His letter of resignation, which is missing. Wilson probably returned it to van Dyke.

[5] He was about to leave for a three-month riding trip in Palestine. An article about this trip appeared in the *Daily Princetonian*, Nov. 7, 1907.

[6] Van Dyke announced his decision to remain at Princeton in H. van Dyke to WW, March 13, 1907.

Woodrow Wilson *et al.* to the President and Trustees of the General Education Board

Gentlemen: Princeton, N. J. March 6th, 1907.

We take the liberty of submitting to you a request for your assistance in giving efficiency to our work at Princeton, which we earnestly hope may commend itself to you and receive your favorable consideration. For the purpose of making clear the financial conditions upon which the request is based, we submit with it, as exhibits, (1) the Report of the President of Princeton University for the year 1906, to which you will find the Report of the Treasurer of the University for that year appended, and (2) the budget of the University for the year 1906-7, comprising (a) a list of investments and estimated income, and (b) an estimate of expenses.

Our request is that you assist Princeton by granting $600,000 to enable her to support and develop her means of instruction in science in the manner now made absolutely necessary by the character and stage of her development. Friends of the University have promised $1,200,000 for the erection and maintenance of modern buildings for the natural sciences and for physics, each of which will cost at least $400,000 and each of which will require at least the interest on $200,000 for its maintenance. But the Trustees of the University do not feel that they are warranted in erecting and equipping such buildings until they are sure of sufficient funds by way of endowment to enable them to support and recruit their teaching force in a way commensurate with what they would seem to be undertaking by such an addition to their plant. Their confident belief is that if they could be sure of a grant of $600,000 from your Board, they could obtain an equal sum of $600,000 from individual friends of the University, and so secure the endowment of $1,200,000 which they believe to be the minimum safe foundation for what they wish to accomplish,—what they feel bound to undertake in view of the traditions and present growth and needs of the University. A few words will explain the situation and the necessities.

For the past four years the President and Trustees of Princeton have been engaged in making sound, so far as they could, every branch of instruction attempted in the University. They have revised and given consistency to the courses of instruction; they have made the tests of the work done precise and effective; they have eliminated from their public announcements everything which they could not actually undertake to do; above all, they have reorganized in a quite revolutionary way the methods of instruction in the University, by adding more than sixty men to its faculty, whose duty and function it should be to teach their several subjects of study to small groups of undergraduates with whom they should be in constant and intimate contact and with whom they should undertake independent reading rather than a mere review of lectures and classroom instruction. The men who were in the faculty of the University before these additions were made have adopted the same methods of intimate instruction, substituting private conferences with small groups of pupils for a certain number of their more formal exercises. And the results have been as gratifying as they have been extraordinary. The new methods of instruction have not only made study a daily habit, but they have given it interest and vitality.

But it has been possible to make such additions to the faculty of the University only by using annually sums of money which represent the interest on at least three million dollars; and these methods of instruction have proved most feasible in the reading courses; the languages, philosophy, art, history and political science, economics. The scientific side of the University has remained relatively undeveloped. The cost of the new system of instruction is carried for the present by annual subscriptions from alumni and other friends of the University, pledged for a period of five years from 1905; but the Trustees of the University feel morally bound to support and perpetuate it, and because they feel that three million dollars is the utmost sum they can at present look to the habitual friends and supporters of the University to supply, we are obliged to turn to others, from whom we have not hitherto asked aid, to find the means to enable us to do what is equally imperative for the efficient work of the University, namely, make equally solid provision for instruction in science.

Recent years have witnessed considerable additions to our facilities for teaching chemistry, but our equipment for physics and for the natural sciences has remained practically the same for the past twenty-five years, the years during which the greatest advancements in these branches of instruction have been witnessed. It is for that reason that we have need now of so considerable a sum of money to enable us to do our duty by our students. We have not tried to do more than we could do in science with our existing equipment, but we have done all the while much too little. Our scientific instruction has so far gone without any but the slenderest endowment, and the general funds of the University, already charged with more than fifty thousand dollars annually for its maintenance, can be stretched no further. We earnestly seek your aid in a situation of real exigency in the history of the University.

For the Board of Trustees:
[Woodrow Wilson
M. Taylor Pyne
Cleveland H. Dodge]

CCL (WWP, UA, NjP).

To Robert Garrett

My dear Mr. Garrett: Princeton, N. J. March 6th, 1907.

It will give me sincere pleasure to give an informal address before your club on the evening of March 28th. I shall have to ask them to be very lenient in their judgment of the address, for I simply have not time to prepare anything such as I would prefer to give, but I should like to speak on The Extension of the Powers of the Federal Government.[1]

Always cordially and sincerely yours,

Woodrow Wilson

TLS (Selected Corr. of R. Garrett, NjP).

[1] Wilson undoubtedly used the text of his third Blumenthal lecture on the President of the United States. He spoke to Garrett's club in Princeton.

To Henry Jones Ford

My dear Mr. Ford: Princeton, N. J. March 6th, 1907.

I would need no prompting to offer you a place upon our faculty here, if there were any place to offer, but unhappily the very lines you most want to follow in your teaching are covered here by as many teachers as our funds permit us to employ. I shall not cease to hope that some day you may be associated with us here. And in the meantime I am very much obliged to you for your letter and your outline of lectures.[1]

Always cordially and sincerely yours, Woodrow Wilson

TLS (L. W. Smith Coll., Morristown, N. J., National Historical Park).

[1] Ford's letter and enclosure are missing.

From Cleveland Hoadley Dodge

Dear Mr President New York. March 6th 1907

Momo is in Trenton today & I suppose I will not see your new draft of brief until tomorrow

I write to tell you that Mr Buttrick (Sec. of Board)[1] just called me up to ask when we would send brief in—that he was going away tonight & would see us Monday—& that delay would make no difference.

I asked him as to the advisability of your seeing Dr Gates[2] & he advised strongly *against* your doing so. Therefore there will be no need of your coming up earlier on Friday for that purpose.

He delighted my soul by adding that he had talked with Dr Gates about the matter & that they are *both* in favor of doing something for Princeton but how much & on what terms they could not decide until they study our brief & report.

He did not think it necessary for us to approach any of the individual members of the Board. I imagine that the recommendations of Gates & Buttrick *go* & I feel more hopeful of our getting something from the Board, than I have at any time

Of course if you want to see us on Friday we are at your disposal

I go to Dodge Lodge[3] Friday PM to stay I hope two weeks.

Affy yrs C H Dodge

ALS (WP, DLC).

[1] The Rev. Dr. Wallace Buttrick, Executive Secretary of the General Education Board.

[2] Frederick Taylor Gates, Chairman of the General Education Board and manager of many of the philanthropic activities of John D. Rockefeller.

[3] That is, Dodge's house at 24 Bayard Lane in Princeton.

From Robert Hunter Fitzhugh

Lexington, Ky.

My very dear Doctor Wilson: March 8th, 1907.

Your letter bearing your usual annual gift to my Negro Orphan work, and so full of heart and inspiration, has just come to add brightness to another day of life's opportunities.

It is the spirit that quickeneth after all, and in that your letter abounded.

I am, my dear Doctor, very thankful to you.

Last night, around the blazing fireside, my somewhat literary and teacher family were discussing with great interest and admiration the new (social) method of imparting knowledge recently introduced by you at Princeton; and they all agreed that it was surprising that a method which so beautifully, and successfully obtained in all judiciously brought-up domestic families had not long ago been adopted by the universities. Hurrah for old Virginia, God bless her!

With high & warm regard,

Very truly yours, R. H. Fitzhugh

ALS (WP, DLC).

To John Van Antwerp MacMurray

My dear Mr. MacMurray: Princeton, N. J. March 9th, 1907.

I am sincerely glad to hear that you are to have an immediate opportunity to win an appointment in the diplomatic service.[1] I very heartily wish you entire success and a desirable appointment.[2] It will always be a very pleasant thing for me to remember, if it should turn out that I had been of real service to you.

Cordially and sincerely yours, Woodrow Wilson

TLS (J. V. A. MacMurray Papers, NjP).

1 MacMurray's letter is missing.

2 MacMurray was appointed Secretary of Legation and Consul General at Bangkok, Siam, on May 10, 1907.

From John Adams Wilson

My dear Woodrow: Franklin, Pa. March 9th. 1907

Have secured one of the Boxes for Matinee performance of Triangle Club, and want you for my guest, not only for the performance but during your stay in Pittsburg.[1] I shall secure rooms at the Schenley. You can see your other Pittsburg friends any old time but we do not see enough of each other, or at least I do not see enough of you.

I think Ida, and Kathleen,[2] will go down for the performance. Hope you are all well and happy. I am just getting ready for a trip West, and then turn right around and go to Philadelphia, and

New York. I shall be at the Waldorf, about Wednesday, or Thursday, of next week.

With love to you all from all of us here

Affectionately yours Jno. A. Wilson

TLS (WP, DLC).

[1] When Wilson was to speak to the Pittsburgh alumni on April 2. The Triangle Club show was "The Mummy Monarch."

[2] His wife, Ida Gordon Wilson, and daughter, Kathleen Gordon Wilson.

From John Allan Wyeth

My dear Mr. Wilson: [New York] March 9th, 1907.

I am very much pleased in looking forward to an acquaintanceship between you and my friend, Mr. William Laffan. He wants to know you, and said to me this morning that had he known you were delivering the lecture at Columbia which was noticed in "The Sun" this morning,[1] that he would have had the lecture printed in full; it seems to me that these lectures should be placed before the people.

There is another old acquaintance of mine here in New York, a Virginian, who by extraordinary ability has made himself a power in the nation, Mr. Thomas F. Ryan. Do you happen to know him? If you care to meet him with Mr. Laffan, I am sure he would be glad to accept such an invitation from me, if he is able to get out of his room; he has been housed for quite a while from the effects of Grip, but I know he would come if it were possible.

Will you please let me know if either of the following dates will suit your convenience:

March 13, 14, 15, 21 or 22.

Mr. Laffan goes abroad, I think, on the 23rd.

Sincerely yours, John A Wyeth

TLS (WP, DLC).

[1] A news report about Wilson's second Blumenthal lecture on the place of the government of the United States in constitutional development.

To Edgar Odell Lovett

Princeton, N. J.

My dear Professor Lovett: March 11th, 1907.

Here is a letter which I wish you would read.[1] I need not tell you that there is no man in the Princeton faculty I have more counted on to remain part of us, both in action and in inspiration, than yourself; but I feel bound, when a thing like this turns up, to present it to the man who seems to me best fitted, and let him say whether he wants to be considered or not. Apparently it might be made an opportunity to do a very great service to the South.

Always affectionately yours, Woodrow Wilson

TLS (E. O. Lovett Papers, TxHR).

[1] E. Raphael and J. E. McAshan to WW, Jan. 10, 1907, Vol. 16, asking Wilson to nominate a candidate for the presidency of the Rice Institute then being organized in Houston.

From John Allan Wyeth

244 Lexington Avenue

My dear Mr. Wilson: [New York, N.Y. c. March 12, 1907]

Our little dinner is for the evening of Friday, March 15. Mr. Laffan, Mr. Ryan, you and I will compose the party and the dinner is to be entirely private, at Delmonico's, at 7.30 P.M. Mrs. Wyeth[1] and I expect you to spend the night with us at this address.

Mr. Ryan has been ill and confined to his room for some time, but said he would make an extra effort to be with us on this occasion, as he was very anxious to become acquainted with you.

Sincerely yours, John A Wyeth

My home is just two doors north of 34th St. W.

TLS (WP, DLC).

[1] Florence Nightingale Sims Wyeth.

To Andrew Fleming West

My dear Professor West: Princeton, N. J. March 13th, 1907.

I am sincerely sorry I cannot be with you tonight. I am prevented from coming by a meeting of one of the committees of the Board of Trustees. It would give me great pleasure to join in your tribute to Dr. van Dyke, and to say to him again how entirely we have our hearts set on his remaining in Princeton. Please give him my warm regards.

Always cordially and sincerely yours,

Woodrow Wilson

TLS (WC, NjP).

From Edgar Odell Lovett

Princeton, New Jersey
My dear President Wilson: 13th March, 1907.

I cannot tell you how hard it is for me to say to you that I shall be compelled to consider the matter of which you wrote if the opportunity presents itself. Your recommendation will mean a call, but I am not going to face the situation until it is upon me. In the meantime you must not question my loyalty—you will not—for you know what faith I have had in your plans for Princeton, you know with what loyal pride I have done my modest part in your administration, you know, too, how boisterously I have rejoiced over the things that you are bringing to pass in this place. I am deeply touched by your letter. For reasons that are sacred I broke into tears over it. I thank you for the expression of confidence and good-will which it contains, and with most affectionate regards I beg to remain

Faithfully yours, Edgar O. Lovett

TLS (WP, DLC).

From Henry van Dyke

My dear Wilson, Princeton, N. J. March 13. 1907.

It may be informal and irregular to withdraw a letter while it is "on the way," but the wishes of friends count for more than the rules of etiquette. The Trustees will forgive any apparent informality, I am sure, if I withdraw my resignation, which is in your hands, before it reaches them. This way of doing it is the best way, because you wish it, for the first reason; and, for the second, because my views have been changed by the things which you and other friends have said to me with such kindness and courtesy.

It will be possible, I hope, to keep on with my writing and at the same time to render a hearty service, under your administration, to Princeton. And this I will gladly do.

Faithfully Yours Henry van Dyke

ALS (WP, DLC).

Henry van Dyke to the President, Faculty, Alumni, and Students of Princeton University

Gentlemen: Princeton, N. J. March 13th 1907.

You have overwhelmed me by the warm and earnest way in which you all have urged me to reconsider my purpose of withdrawing from the University to devote my time entirely to other work. Your friendly words and actions have altered my feelings and changed my mind. It will not be necessary to trouble the Trustees to consider my resignation. If you say that Princeton wants and needs me, I stay, and do my best to serve her.

Faithfully Yours, Henry van Dyke.

ALS (Trustees' Papers, UA, NjP).

Henry Burchard Fine to the Board of Trustees' Committee on Morals and Discipline

Gentlemen: PRINCETON UNIVERSITY, MARCH 14, 1907.

Since the time of my last report the Faculty has dismissed one student from college finally on the ground that his reputation among his fellow students for dishonesty was such that he could not properly be allowed to remain in Princeton. The evidence in the case was brought to me by classmates and associates of the student, and was of a kind to leave no room for doubt that he had been repeatedly guilty of lying, stealing, and getting money under false pretenses. Another student has been suspended for a month because of neglect of his college duties, and at its next meeting the Faculty will be asked to suspend another for the same period for allowing a friend to hand in a chapel card for him—the penalty being made no heavier because of the student's frankness in confessing to what he had done, when by deceit he might have escaped punishment altogether. There have been a number of suspensions for chapel absence, but I have no other serious cases of discipline to report.

The Sunday chapel rule adopted last June has proved very effective. The chapel is well filled every Sunday morning and is often crowded. It is an interesting fact that most of our Episcopal students prefer to attend the chapel service rather than the service at Trinity Church, now that their attendance is marked at the church as well as at the chapel.

The number of men dropped at the end of the first term because of failure in their studies was but 58 as against 71 last year and the year before. They were distributed as follows among the several departments and classes:

	Seniors	Juniors	Sophomores	Freshmen	Specials (of all departments)
A.B.	1	1	4	3	
B.S.	0	1	7	9	
Litt.B.	1	1			
C.E.	3	5	4	5	13
	5	8	15	17	13

The corresponding totals for last year were Seniors 5, Juniors 5, Sophomores 21, Freshmen 35, Specials 5. Hence there has been a slight increase—from 5 to 8—in the number of Juniors to come under the rule, a marked increase—from 5 to 13—in the number of Specials, a considerable decrease—from 21 to 15—in the number of Sophomores, and a decrease of more than half —from 35 to 17—in the number of Freshmen.

The increase in the number of Specials is readily accounted for. Of the 58 men dropped all told, 14 had been dropped previously and 5 were men admitted last fall without examination from other colleges, and the 13 dropped Specials belong almost entirely to these two classes of students. I may say in passing that there were in college last term 86 men who had been dropped at some time previously. Of these 72 passed their mid-year examinations successfully[,] 14 of them qualifying for their degrees.

The marked decrease in the number of dropped Sophomores is very gratifying. But the most striking and encouraging fact of all is the unprecedentedly small number of failures among the Freshmen. It shows a marked improvement in the quality and preparation of our entering students, and that they are becoming quick to learn the necessity of industry on their arrival here. We expected that this class, of which 65% entered with not more than one condition each, would attain to an unusually high average of scholarship in its college work, and we have not been disappointed. But, on the other hand, 35 of the Freshmen made so poor a showing in their entrance examinations that they were merely admitted on trial. Only 2 of these 35 men have been dropped. This of course indicates that entrance examinations are not an infallible test of a student's preparation. But when taken in connection with the fact that the total number of Freshmen failures is so small, it also indicates that the individual attention which our students are receiving under the preceptorial system is enabling inadequately prepared but serious men to succeed where they used to fail, and is putting an end to the period of demoralization which in the past has overtaken the less serious men of so many classes in the first term of Freshman year.

I may add that these 17 dropped students constitute almost the entire loss which the Freshman class has suffered since entrance. In previous years it has happened that a few students have left college just before the examinations for fear of failure. I have heard of no such cases this year. Two men included in the 17 left before the examinations, but they were at the time debarred in enough subjects to drop them.

Of the classes which entered in 1903 and 1904, 17% were dropped in Freshman year; of the class which entered last year 12-⅔% were dropped; while, if the same ratio be maintained this year as in previous years between the number dropped in June and February, the present Freshman class will lose not more than 8%.

The preceptorial system was effective from the very start in its main purpose—the promotion of the cause of learning among our undergraduates in general. The results of the present examinations encourage one to believe that the most careless of our students, who at first offered some resistance to the new system with its requirement of work in term time, are beginning to respond to its influence.

Respectfully submitted,

[H. B. Fine] Dean of the Faculty.

CCR (Trustees' Papers, UA, NjP).

A Resolution[1]

[c. March 14, 1907]

RESOLVED, That the Board has learned with the deepest gratification that Dr. Henry van Dyke is to remain in the faculty of the University. Dr. van Dyke's services in the English Department have been of the most unique and distinguished sort, showing him a teacher of the most unusual quality, lifting his subject to a high plane of admirable exposition in his lectures not only, but also communicating to his pupils alike in lecture and in intimate conference an enthusiasm such as only the best teachers have the gift of imparting; and his services to his Department have conferred upon the University as a whole the benefit of an influence of the highest refinement, touched with the most chastened ideals. His loss would have been irreparable.[2]

T MS (Trustees' Papers, UA, NjP).

[1] There is a WWsh draft of this resolution in WP, DLC.

[2] This resolution was adopted and spread on the Minutes of the Board of Trustees for the meeting of March 14, 1907. It was also printed in the *Princeton Alumni Weekly*, VII (March 16, 1907), 280.

From the Minutes of the Board of Trustees of Princeton University

[March 14, 1907]

The Trustees of Princeton University met in stated session in the Trustees' Room in the Chancellor Green Library, Princeton, New Jersey, at eleven o'clock on Thursday morning March 14, 1907.

The President of the University in the chair.

The meeting was opened with prayer by Dr. Stewart . . . .

Mr. Russell, Chairman of the Committee on Grounds and Buildings, reported. The report was accepted, its recommendations adopted and is as follows:

Princeton, N. J., March 14th, 1907.

To

THE PRESIDENT AND BOARD OF TRUSTEES,
Princeton University,
Princeton, New Jersey.

Gentlemen:

I beg to report the following for the Department of Grounds and Buildings since the last meeting, December, 1906: . . .

CONSULTING ARCHITECT. At the last meeting of the Committee on motion of President Wilson, it was voted to recommend to the Board that, in order to secure at every point of development, well-considered plans for the placing, and architecture of buildings, the University secure the services of a Consulting Architect, who should be consulted with regard to each site selected, and with regard to the development of a general plan for the development of the campus; and that the Committee on Grounds and Buildings be authorized to select the architect for this function.[1]

The purpose of the Committee in this action was not to put into the hands of such an architect the actual preparation of plans for buildings but to have his constant supervision and advice regarding the work of the architects actively employed, and regarding the physical relation of the buildings to each other in the general material development of the University. This was thought the best way to secure artistic unity, and harmony, and to avoid haphazard, unsystematic action. . . .

Respectfully submitted,

(Signed) Arch. D. Russell, Chairman. . . .

REPORT OF THE COMMITTEE TO CONSIDER SUPPLEMENTARY REPORT OF THE PRESIDENT

The President of the University reported orally from the Committee to Consider the Supplementary Report of the President made at the meeting of the Board held December 13, 1906. . . .

"Minutes of the Trustees of Princeton University, June 1901-Jan. 1908," bound minute book (UA, NjP).

[1] As the documents will soon reveal, the committee chose Ralph Adams Cram of the firm of Cram, Goodhue and Ferguson, with offices in Boston and New York.

To Edith Gittings Reid

My dear Friend, [New York] 15 March, 1907

That very Cross note you wrote me a week or two ago would have been answered long before this if I had been a free agent. Why any sane man who wishes *some* of the reasonable delights of life,–friendships, for example,–should ever allow himself to be made a college president I can understand only because I know at least one case in which the victim had no notion what he was getting into! I literally have not had *time* to write. The trip to Baltimore was all business and was cut as short as possible because of other business. I could not enjoy anybody, and felt as if I were only making a convenience of the poor Crosses. If you knew how often with what feelings of deep affection and deprivation I think of you, you would be content, at least with *that*, and would think of me always as a friend imprisoned in a task!

Always

Faithfully and affectionately Yours, Woodrow Wilson

ALS (WC, NjP).

From James Bryce

My dear President Washington Mar. 16/07

I was extremely sorry to hear you had been unwell and trust you are now all right again

Thank you heartily for the honour you proposed to give me of a Princeton honorary degree[.] I wish very much I could have come to your Commencement

But if I can leave Washington at all at that time I am bound to be at Chicago & St. Louis from the 10th to the 20th, so it is out of my power to be with you, which I am all the more sorry for because we have so delightful a memory of Princeton, and because I would have liked to talk to you on divers matters, including one on which I see some remarks by you in to-day's newspaper, the tendency to increase the powers of the Central Government.[1] It is a matter much in the thoughts of whoever studies and watches the changes which necessarily pass even on a Rigid Constitution.

With our kindest regards to Mrs. Wilson

Always truly yours James Bryce

ALS (WP, DLC).

[1] He was referring to Wilson's third Blumenthal lecture on the President of the United States.

A Tribute

[March 17, 1907]

GROVER CLEVELAND, MAN OF INTEGRITY

Mr. Cleveland's seventieth birthday, which will occur to-morrow, ought to bring him deep satisfaction. He holds a very enviable place in the esteem of his fellow-countrymen, and he has won it by no adventitious means. His moral courage, his integrity, his deep patriotic purpose, his great capacity and achievement in affairs every candid man in the country now recognizes and applauds. He has come since his retirement from the Presidency into an extraordinary popularity, which he took no pains to gain but which is his because he did take pains to deserve it, by temporarily sacrificing it to considerations of duty and honor. The confidence and deep admiration of his fellow-citizens the country over rests upon their recognition of the fact that he did not yield to clamor or temporary opinion in the administration of any of the high offices he has filled, but in every situation did his duty as he saw it, and was willing to abide the consequences. He brought hatred and obloquy upon himself in order to abide by his convictions and keep the country firm in the path which he deemed right, and so won in due time what he had not sought —the applause and affection of the great people he served.

The American people do not willingly misjudge or knowingly do injustice to their public men. Their judgments are in the long run both generous and just; it is the happy circumstance of Mr. Cleveland's life that he has lived to see the "long run," which has corrected judgments for a little while harsh and unfair. Popular opinion was sure to correct itself soon in the case of such a man. Slow, cautious, circumspect men, the mass of the people, the majority even of thoughtful and well-informed men, are tardy in doing justice to: such men have often to wait for the judgment of a subsequent generation to be set right in the general assessment. But bold, downright, straightforward men get their verdict promptly. Politicians seem very slow to learn the lesson, and slower still to comprehend the significance of it, but the American people love nothing so much as candor, energy, and fearless action. They dote upon the bold man whose individuality and energy dominate a situation and threaten timid men with nervous prostration.

Surely by this time we have had abundant proof of this. Our people have the true sporting instinct to an extraordinary degree. They love to see the confused field of politics swept by a striking personality. If they can only believe in the essential soundness and integrity of his character, they would rather have their President aggressive to the point of recklessness than see the prudent calculations of political managers prevail: and they unquestionably esteem Mr. Cleveland more highly than they would otherwise have done because of the imprudent willfulness which they have seen his successor display. They know now that while they love boldness and are weary of time-serving mediocrity, they would feel much safer if boldness were tempered with good judgment and striking leadership planned along wisely calculated lines. A President who insists upon his own way is in any case interesting, but he is most satisfactory and most serviceable when he chooses his way with an old-fashioned conscience with regard to the law and the long consequences.

And so a great many men of both parties have recently longed for the safe courage and thoughtful audacity of a man like Mr. Cleveland. If there be any other man like Mr. Cleveland. The rich variety of our democratic life produces many men of many minds, and it would seem that it produces more individuals than types. Our more striking Presidents have not been typical men. Washington and Jefferson and Jackson and Lincoln and Cleveland were not types—we should be a stronger nation if they were. Each of these men was individual and unique in his way, differing, no doubt, in greatness, but alike in the striking contrast they presented to the men around them. It is this that makes them difficult to assess. Just because they must be taken as individuals and judged in the sort of isolation that belongs to them, there are no general standards by which to measure them. It is interesting to note that only one of the five that I have named was bred in any formal school of preparation for the task that lay ahead of him, and Jefferson, the only exception, is less singular, less an individual, and more nearly a type than the other four. Each bred himself by a quiet domination of his fortunes and his opportunities.

Mr. Cleveland's moral training consisted in a very definite sense of moral responsibility bred in him from the first in his childhood and youth. His intellectual training he gave himself after his school days, and it was a true instinct that led him to the study and practice of law. In that profession his mind got the definite data of rule and application which it naturally craved —a mind disinclined to theory, very firm and definite in its operation upon facts, intolerant of too great refinement, but admirable in the application of principles, a broad, effective, decisive, comprehending mind, fit always for affairs and action. His training in politics was of the same kind. He was never a member of any political body whose duties were legislative and deliberative; his political duties were always executive, he dealt not so much with programmes as with concrete and tangible conditions, the very stuff of life and occasion. Whether as District Attorney, as Sheriff, as Mayor, as Governor, or as President, his outlook was always upon action, upon the application, the execution of laws and the actual operation of the principles prescribed by law. No doubt he was sometimes too impatient of the difficulties and hesitations and compromises of law-making bodies, never having known in any intimate and personal way the conditions which limit their efficiency and hamper their action, but it was the wholesome impatience of the practical man in a workday world, where things must be done, and ought to be done handsomely, difficulties or no difficulties. He gave tonic counsel, and stimulated even when he irritated.

Moreover, in everything he uttered there was striking, fearless candor, such a sturdy manliness, so refreshing an impression of a man who went straight for his mark and made no timid calculations of self-interest, that he quite inevitably caught the eye and fancy of the country, and for the first time in thirty years supplied the Democratic Party with a Presidential candidate with whom it could decisively win. The country desired a change of party in the administration of its affairs, as it had proved in 1879[1] by its choice of Mr. Tilden, but it desired this particular Democratic man a little more than it desired the Democratic

[1] This is a printer's error. In his manuscript copy, Wilson wrote "1876."

Party; and it desired him unquestionably because he seemed likely to bring into National politics the same refreshing qualities he had brought into local politics at Buffalo and at Albany.

Mr. Cleveland's two terms of office as President, separated by Mr. Harrison's single term, fell within a period of singular doubts and mutations in our politics (1885-1897,) when the definite lines which had separated our parties in the days of the civil war and in the troubled years of reconstruction which followed were breaking away and becoming obscure, and both parties were shifting their accustomed ground in the face of new circumstances and new problems. Economic questions were uppermost; the material development of the country, which has reached such astounding proportions in the last decade, was making apace. Questions of capital and labor and of currency, which were old enough in essence, were assuming new forms and new dimensions under the influence of the rapid development of manufactures and of the mining industries, and rapid changes in the supply of the precious metals; and politicians were manoeuvring for advantageous position in the struggle for votes, rather than for any consistent or intelligent interpretation of the principles for which their respective parties had been thought to stand. In the midst of the shifting scene Mr. Cleveland presently came to seem the only fixed point. He alone stood firm and gave definite utterance to principles intelligible to all. "Courage, directness, good sense, public spirit, as if without thought of consequences either to himself or to his party, made him at once a man whom all the country marked" as a point in its affairs which did not shift or change.

He was a man of strong party convictions; he believed, as all practical men must, that party organizations are an indispensable means of action and control in the politics of a self-governing democratic people; more than that, he saw, as all thoughtful men see, that party is more than a means for organizing victory at the polls—that it is a means, a vital means, of uniting men of the same views and temper in affairs for the accomplishment of common ends, an indispensable means of subordinating varieties of individual opinion to the pursuit of common principles and large objects of policy. He never pretended to be independent of party, always avowed himself a party man, and sought to work his purposes out through those who were of the same political faith and affiliation as he. But he had stronger and more definite party prepossessions, it turned out, than many of his fellow-partisans; while he sat still they had changed; they grew more and more restive under his leadership; more and more chafed under his stubborn insistence on the views with which he had set out; more and more resented his efforts to keep legislation to the paths of his preference, and by the end of his second term were ready to break with him altogether. He seemed at last a man without a party.

It was said that he insisted on his own views without tact, that he ruthlessly wounded the sensibilities of his fellow-Democrats in the House and Senate, at one time trying to manage them and at another refusing to parley with them at all. But such charges and irritations were but symptoms of the deep differences within the Democratic ranks, which his unpliant firmness brought to sharp revelation. The same ferment and disorder, as if of disruption, were becoming evident in the Republican Party as well as in the Democratic. It was one of the almost chance happenings of politics that as the Presidential campaign of 1896 approached, the Republican Party did not espouse the policy of the free coinage of silver instead of the Democrats; it was hardly more than the inborn instinct of opposition between the two parties that prevented both of them from espousing it. The one was as willing as the other to play to the supposed popular wish in the matter, regardless of well-grounded principles of finance, and only its long-practiced discipline and habit of union, the discipline and habit of a party trained to the exercise of power, prevented the Republican Party from falling to pieces in factions. Mr. Cleveland consented to be left by a party which had shifted from the immemorial ground of Democratic principle and practice in matters of finance.

His isolation led to the painful results which always follow such breaches. He retired from office amid a storm of obloquy and misrepresentation; but time has brought about its healing and its revenges. The misrepresentation has not cleared entirely away; it could not in a single generation, when once such fires of passionate feeling had been kindled, but it is no longer a mist in the eyes of the people. Their old admiration for the man, their old confidence in his utter honesty and integrity, their love for his downright utterances and clear sense of right, their belief in his homely wisdom, have returned with an added force and enthusiasm, because of their consciousness of the deep injustice they had for a while done him in their own misinformed thought. He is hailed wherever he goes with as eager a welcome and with a keen zest for what he has to say as is the more piquant Chief Magistrate himself.

The position he now enjoys in the estimation of the country is evidenced in a very significant way by the confidence everywhere felt that his trusteeship of the controlling shares of the Equitable Life Assurance Society and his Presidency of the association recently formed of the chief administrative officers of the greater life insurance companies will clear the management of those companies of questionable practices, and that the interests of the policy holders will be conscientiously looked after and the use of insurance funds carefully safeguarded. What Mr. Cleveland brings to the management of such matters is old-fashioned simple honesty and the administration of all fiduciary business by men who do not seek to line their own pockets; and that, the country feels, is the only effective cure for the abominable abuses it has seen brought to light in these last extraordinary years of revelation.[2] Business ability and clear-eyed integrity are his invaluable contributions to steadying the nerves and restoring the confidence of the country.

Whatever may be Mr. Cleveland's own reflections on his seventieth birthday, his countrymen are entitled to feel a deep pride in what such an anniversary brings to light, the ultimate triumph of character and principle, of native ability without adventitious aid, in a free Republic. We are not hopelessly sophisticated when a man such as this can become our chief citizen. Wealth is not everything when wealth without his aid and correction would fall into hopeless disrepute. Fame still sits serene in her temple, and crowns only those with a stainless crown who come to her with a pure heart and clean hands. The Nation still assesses its public men by moral standards as old as the human conscience, and will not be deceived by any charlatan.[3]

Printed in the *New York Times*, magazine section, March 17, 1907.

[2] About the insurance scandals and Cleveland's role as a trustee of the Equitable stock, see WW *et al.* to J. J. McCook and C. B. Alexander, Dec. 29, 1905, n. 1, Vol. 16.

[3] There is a WWsh draft of this essay, dated March 7, 1907, in WP, DLC, and a carbon copy of the typescript in WC, NjP.

A Reply to a Toast, "John C. Calhoun"[1]

[[March 18, 1907]]

Those who remember only the latter part of Calhoun's life, and associate him with the fateful influences which brought on the Civil War will discern very little of the true proportions and character of the man. The early and latter parts of his career

[1] This speech was given at the first annual dinner of the South Carolina Society of New York City at the Waldorf-Astoria Hotel on March 18, 1907, the birthday of John C. Calhoun. Among the numerous other speakers were the just-retired Secretary of the Treasury, Leslie Mortier Shaw, and the Rev. Dr. Newell Dwight Hillis, pastor of the Plymouth Congregational Church of Brooklyn.

are in marked contrast with each other and disclose the two sides of a strong nature that saw nothing by halves. Throughout all the earlier part of his career he stood with the men who, like Henry Clay, were pushing the nation forward to the expansion of its resources and of its powers, aggressive in the field of international affairs, eager for every policy that would make for increase of commerce or industry or territory in domestic affairs, men of hope and enterprise under whose hands every promising enterprise flourished. When in his later days, he turned about to check much that he had hitherto lent a hand to promote it was at the call of his own people and in the interest of safeguards which seemed to him essential to safeguarding our very system of government. When tariff legislation seemed to him to be pushed to the point where it seemed certain to make one region of the country rich at the expense of another, he threw himself passionately against it. When measure after measure was proposed whose object was to limit the area of slavery and put the South forever in the minority in the once carefully maintained balance of the states in the Senate, he saw what such changes forebode and fought for the maintenance of the equilibrium which seemed to him the only safeguard against revolution. In the first days we saw the ardent lover of progress, in the last the equally ardent defender of the old harmonies and understandings.

Whatever we may think concerning the actual questions involved,—questions now so long settled that all heat of controversy has gone out of them,—it is plain that Calhoun's life as a whole presents the two sides that every question of American politics must first or last present: on the one hand progress, the eager rush of affairs of national life, impatient of obstacles, even obstacles of law, on the other old understandings, old harmonies, the influence of the structure of law meant to restrain and keep all things within bounds.

There is now, happily, no longer any "peculiar institution" to be safeguarded, no radical social or economic contrast between one region of the country and another to be regarded at every turn of national policy, but it is interesting to note how often progress is pushed to such a speed and urged by such means that the peace of the country is threatened, its interests thrown into discard,—interesting to note how often we have to moderate our speed and more or less our policies by checking them.

Our trouble at the present moment is that tariffs and all special means of stimulation have been pushed too far and too fast, to the destruction of the balance and harmony in the social and economic development of the country. We are obliged to stop, take account of cause and effect, note the license and the reckless use of questionable opportunities we have permitted ourselves, acknowledge that we have lost our heads in our pursuit of wealth and material power, our very sense of right and wrong, in our eagerness to succeed and accumulate.

A moment of deep self-distrust, or, rather, distrust of each other, has come upon us. We are disconcerted and demoralized, beyond measure disgusted, and therefore sadly in need of such counsel as shall seek to restore old balances and harmonies and moderations of action. Having lost wise self-possession in our too eager progress, we are in danger of losing it in our efforts to reform, in danger of becoming hysterical in remedy, as we have been reckless in self-seeking. Mr. Calhoun sought to save the old system in which he had been bred: it is our task to save the new system in which we supposed that we had set up at last a just and equal civil order. It is no question now of the clash of competing interests or competing social systems between section and section but a question of purging the whole system of our life of noxious influences and acting for the general welfare.

Undoubtedly we must put reform into the hands of its friends, not in the hands of those who are merely the frightened and repentant participants in the things that have been going wrong; but we must see to it that the processes of reform are moderate and self-possessed, by putting its prosecution in the hands of those who are free from the follies of haste and panic and radical experiment. Systems of the law are a tangled and complicated matter at best and so a radical experiment is more apt to increase the trouble than to remedy it.

Look what has happened directly and frankly in the face. We have stimulated material progress in every way that we could think of; and by material progress we have meant industry upon a great scale,—mining, manufactures, and commerce. Legislation of almost any kind could be had for the asking whose object was understood to be the encouragement of wealth-producing enterprises. The chief instrument of stimulation has been the tariff. By this means it was sought to give to every sort of organized industry some special protection of law, some particular artificial advantage which would make it easier for those who undertook it to thrive and make money, than for those whose vocations the law had left to a hard struggle of survival of the fittest and most capable. Congress became the general foster-mother,—and that in a country whose rich and almost boundless natural resources made such fosterage absolutely unnecessary beyond the initial point where such industries had once been assisted to get on their feet as against foreign competition.

Until recent years the momentum thus induced seemed to threaten nothing. Those who were favored grew rich, but they did not grow rich so fast as to lose all sense of responsibility or of moderation in the use of their wealth for their own ends, and the whole country seemed to grow rich also by their influence. But at last everything moved with a rush, by leaps and bounds. Upon colossal success followed colossal organization. Those who had built up great businesses chiefly upon the special opportunities and advantages offered them by legislation found a way to increase the scale of their success by combining with their chief rivals. Great organizations crowded out small rivals, and a colossal series of manipulations followed. A spirit of madness for success upon a great scale seized upon those who actually conducted the great businesses and knew how to make them pay; a madness for money seized upon those who undertook their manipulation. We ought to discriminate between the two classes. Practical and legitimate enterprise is almost always sober, beneficial, and wholesome. The money-madness which has made us so uneasy is characteristic chiefly of those who deal with our great industries and industrial enterprises on paper, not in fact; characteristic of the manipulators and organizers, not of the workers.

We have reaped the legitimate fruit of our legislation. We created special privileges, contrary to the whole spirit of our polity, and those who were most astute and capable in taking advantage of them have grown so great in power that we wonder if we are equal to restraining them.

Law in a free state should have as its chief object the maintenance of equality of conditions and opportunities. We forgot that principle and have put our equality in jeopardy. We have, by our own forgetfulness of the true principles of legislation, destroyed the balance, the harmony, the one-time generous co-operation of our national life, have created classes and put colossal interests at clash with one another. These changes of our own blind contriving have carried us so far that we are actually invited to alter the balance of our whole constitutional system to set matters right. We are invited to push government into every experimental function in order to correct the vagaries of development we foster but do not understand.

It will take a steady hand and clear head to go to the root of the disease, but to the root we should go, and in order to be ready to perform the operation we should steady our hands and clear our heads. It is clear to me, in the first place, that we ought not to punish prosperous men for having accumulated the wealth we invited them to accumulate. I believe in income and inheritance taxes as means for raising revenue. They are not only perfectly legitimate, but also desirable, because they place the burden of taxation where it can best and most easily be borne. But I do not believe in such taxes, or in any taxes, as a mere means of penalizing the rich, whom we have invited to get their wealth under the fosterage of the government. We do not need income and inheritance taxes as a means of revenue, because the tariff and other existing federal taxes yield revenue in abundance for all reasonable federal spending, and the tariff is the chief source of the privileges which have built up vast fortunes by special advantages. The root of inequality is not in the wealth, but in special favors granted by such legislation as the extravagant tariff legislation which has been put upon our statute books since the war between the states.

Remedies should be slow and moderate and based, not upon superficial symptoms but upon a calm and thorough study of the facts. What we chiefly need is a genuine purpose of reform and sufficient self-possession to undertake it. The genuine purpose cannot come from friends and beneficiaries of legislation of fosterage and privilege: it must come from those who are not its friends but its convinced and earnest opponents. I speak, not of individuals but of parties. But the process of reform must be guided and informed by those who understand the danger of drastic and radical change, who know the folly of rash experiments, who love harmony and adjustment and the right condition of interests more than they love their own striking programs. We must get over our hysteria and regain our self-possession before we can obtain statesmanlike and wholesome reform.

The mere reform of the tariff is not sufficient, it is not even an intelligent, programme. The tariff is by no means the whole root of the difficulty, and is slow to change. It cannot be reformed in a twelvemonth, nor in four twelvemonths. Every correction must be a process of adjustment, of prudent rearrangement. No true statesman can wish to upset the industrial organization and habit of the country by radical or sweeping measures of change.

Moreover, we must be careful to deal frankly and without favor with class privileges of all kinds. We speak too exclusively of the capitalistic class. There is another as formidable an enemy to equality and freedom of opportunity as it, and that is the class formed by the labor organizations and leaders of the country—a class representing only a small minority of the laboring men of the country, quite as monopolistic in spirit as the capitalists and quite as apt to corrupt and ruin our industries by their monopoly. If we are to restore the purity of our law and the freedom of our life we must see to it that no class whatever is given artificial privileges or advantages. What we need is not a square deal, but no deal at all—an old-fashioned equality and harmony of conditions—a purged business and a purged law.

And the present machinery of our federal system is adequate for the task, when once we come to an understanding as to what it is we desire. The federal government shall not be hindered in the exercise of its full powers: no wise man will stand in the way of any wholesome increase of the power of the federal government which can be got by legitimate interpretation from the ancient sentences of the Constitution. But every wise man who feels the true spirit of the American system will see that the vitality of the States is the vitality of the country; that their several powers are as important to the free self-adjustment of the communities of the land of infinite variety as are the powers of the federal government itself; that their atrophy is the emasculation of our political capacity, our conscience, and sense of duty in self-government.

March 13/1907[2]

Transcript of WWsh MS (WP, DLC) with additions in italics from a portion of the text printed in the *New York Times*, March 19, 1907.

[2] Wilson's composition date of his shorthand draft.

George Corning Fraser[1] to Henry Burchard Fine

My dear Dean Fine: New York. March 18, 1907.

At a Special Meeting of the Board of Governors of The University Cottage Club of Princeton, New Jersey, held this day, the following preambles and resolutions were unanimously adopted:

> "WHEREAS in the opinion of the Board of Governors of THE UNIVERSITY COTTAGE CLUB OF PRINCETON, NEW JERSEY, the Princeton University Inter-Club Treaty heretofore, and, as recently amended,[2] now in force has utterly failed to, and does not satisfactorily provide for the conduct of elections from the Sophomore Class, and the prevailing conditions in respect of such elections tend to destroy the traditions of, and the social intercourse between the Undergraduates to the great detriment of the University at large; and

"WHEREAS it appears from a preliminary report of the Sub-Committee of this Board, appointed to investigate and report upon the Inter-Club Treaty situation, that the recent amendments of the Inter-Club Treaty were, in the cases of many of the signatory Clubs, adopted solely at the instance of their respective Undergraduate memberships and cannot therefore be taken as evidencing the sentiments of the Graduate Boards of such Clubs, and that prior to the adoption of such Amendments certain members of the University Faculty were called into conference by the Inter-Club Committee and that no statement regarding the matters under consideration by them has so far been obtained from the Faculty members referred to; and

"WHEREAS it is important and desirable that this Board receive as speedily as may be the fullest information and expressions of views concerning the Inter-Club Treaty situation in general to guide its future actions with reference thereto,

"NOW THEREFORE BE IT

"1. RESOLVED that the preliminary report of the Sub-Committee of this Board, made at this Meeting, be accepted and that such Sub-Committee be, and hereby is continued and instructed to submit in writing a final report to the Chairman.

"2. RESOLVED that the Chairman be and hereby is directed to request, through the Dean of Princeton University, a statement from the members of the Faculty who attended the conference mentioned in the preamble to these resolutions, with respect to the situation then disclosed, and an expression of their views as to how the present evils incident to Club elections can be eradicated.

"3. RESOLVED that the Chairman be and hereby is directed to call a Special Meeting of this Board forthwith upon receipt by him from the Sub-Committee of this Board and the Members of the Faculty, of the report and statement called for by the last preceding resolutions."

Pursuant to the directions contained in the foregoing resolution numbered "2," I beg to request an expression or expressions, from the members of the Faculty referred to, concerning the present Inter-Club situation.

Our Board is convinced that some very radical action must be taken to remedy the conditions adverted to in the minutes quoted, but, realizing the importance of deliberation, desires the fullest information on the subject. Any suggestions which members of the Faculty may care to make will, you may be assured, receive our earnest consideration and be highly appreciated.

Believe me, with esteem,

Faithfully yours, G. C. Fraser[3]

TLS (WP, DLC).

1 Princeton 1893, lawyer of New York.

2 An "Inter-Club Treaty" to regulate the election of sophomores to the upperclass eating clubs had been in effect since 1903, although it had been revised several times in the interim. The principal objective of the treaty was to eliminate electioneering and bargaining for admission to clubs among sophomores and even freshmen. The treaty forbade club members to approach underclassmen in regard to prospective club membership or to inform them of their election to a club before a specified date in the second term of the academic year. The treaty included elaborate form letters of notification of election and for acceptance or refusal of the same, and required the accepted member to pledge his honor as a gentleman that he had neither solicited membership nor been solicited for membership and that, as a club member, he in turn would not solicit underclassmen. The treaty also provided for the establishment of an Inter-Club Committee to enforce its provisions.

The revision of the treaty printed in the *Daily Princetonian* on March 11, 1907, attempted to tighten control of elections still further by providing that all contact between a particular club and the sophomore class was to be "rigidly limited" to two representatives of the club and three sophomores selected by the club to form a "section" of prospective members.

For the treaty as it stood before March 11, 1907, see the *Daily Princetonian*, Oct. 18, 1906. For a general discussion of the club system, elections to the clubs, and the treaty, see Henry W. Bragdon, *Woodrow Wilson: The Academic Years* (Cambridge, Mass., 1967), pp. 317-18, 469 ns. 19 and 20.

3 For Wilson's reply, see WW to G. C. Fraser, April 16, 1907.

From John Haughton Coney

My dear Mr. President Princeton March 19, 07

May I offer my hearty thanks for your speech to the South Carolinians? If it could be considered merely as a personal achievement in the art of expression—a gift of tongues renewed in our very sight—congratulations might suffice. But because it is the most convincing demonstration which has come to my notice in many a long day, that the race of statesmen is not yet extinct among us, I can do nothing less than make acknowledgment of service splendidly rendered.

Gratefully yours John H. Coney

ALS (WP, DLC).

From Joseph Hill Dawson[1]

Dear Sir: Baltimore, Mch. 19. 1907.

Please pardon the intrusion of an entire stranger but I think it is pleasant for all of us to know that our views meet with the approval of others and hence I wish to say that not only do I agree with you in the conclusions you expressed at the South Carolina dinner but that with truthfulness you might have gone further.

There seem to be times when the reasoning of our whole lives is thrown overboard and our hard-earned convictions are ignored. The result is hysteria, constitution-smashing &c &c and a return to our unreliable impulses and a loss of all sense of proportion and a complete obsession by a few ideas without the apparent capacity or willingness to consider the grievous and undeserved ills that may befall the innocent in the pursuit of the guilty. In other words there is a failure to follow to it's logical end, and disastrous end, the practical working of an entirely sound idea. An idea may be good but it does not follow that it is expedient. So let us continue to fight the evils that exist but not at the risk of producing a worse state of affairs than we are trying to remedy.

With apologies I am, Very truly, J. H. Dawson

TLS (WP, DLC).

[1] Lawyer of Baltimore; he was a member of the Princeton Class of 1885 who had not been graduated.

To Edwin Anderson Alderman

[Princeton, N. J.]

My dear President Alderman: March 20th, 1907.

I beg that you will pardon my apparent discourtesy in not replying sooner to your letter of February 25th.[1] The fact is that I have been through a season of rush, such as seldom comes upon me, and have been during that time been [*sic*] constantly drawn away from home, so that my correspondence has fallen into arrears.

It would go very hard with us, I can assure you, to lose Professor [Augustus] Trowbridge, and I must say that I hope if you turn toward him you will find it impossible to persuade him to leave us. But I am bound to say that he has made a most favorable impression upon us, and seems to me to be a man who would worthily fill even the great position you have in mind. I am sure that if I were a physicist I should consider it a great honor to succeed Professor Smith.[2]

Sincerely yours, [Woodrow Wilson]

CCL (WWP, UA, NjP).

[1] It is missing.

[2] Francis Henry Smith, Professor of Natural Philosophy at the University of Virginia, 1853-1907. Trowbridge remained at Princeton.

From Henry Russell Spencer

Dear Sir: Princeton, N. J. March 20, 1907.

As I informed you some days ago, I have been invited to return to Ohio State University at the end of this academic year, as professor of American History and Political Science. I have concluded to accept this proposition, and therefore respectfully request release.

Permit me to express my extreme reluctance to sever the connection with Princeton, which I have found so agreeable and profitable. The new opportunity which presents itself, however, seems to be that which I should have desired after several years here, and it does not seem wise to let it pass.

I am

Yours with sincere respect, Henry Russell Spencer.

ALS (WP, DLC).

A News Report

[March 20, 1907]

NEW CAMPUS ATTRACTION

In the Form of a copy of Turnbull Sun-dial
Presented by Sir William Mather.

The Trustees of the University have recently accepted a very handsome gift from Sir William Mather, M.P. It consists of a copy of the famous Turnbull sun-dial at Corpus Christi College, Oxford, and will be a great addition to the campus. The exact place where it will be put has not yet been decided upon, but its beauty and value assure it a prominent position.

The original sun-dial was built in the quadrangle of Corpus Christi College in 1605[1] by Charles Turnbull, a fellow of the University of Oxford. The original consists of a stone column eighteen inches in diameter and nine feet high, resting upon a square base. This column is surmounted by a square stone, on the four sides of which are carved the armorial bearings of the University of Oxford, King Henry VII, Cardinal Wolsey, the founder of the University, and Hugh Oldam, who was closely associated with him in that work. This stone is in turn surmounted by a large ball, on which is perched a pelican, the emblem of Cardinal Wolsey. The Princeton copy will be placed on a series of bases, the bottom one being fourteen feet square. When completed, the dial will be over twenty-four feet high.

Sir William Mather, M.P., who has made this valuable donation, has been active during his whole public life in educational work. Besides being a member of Parliament, he is at present a governor of Owens College and Victoria University, large English institutions. He is also chairman of the Froebel Educational Institute of London. Some years ago he visited America on behalf of the Royal Committee on Technical Education, and has since been greatly interested in the larger American universities. His gift, enhancing as it will the beauty of the campus, will be deeply appreciated by all Princeton men.

Printed in the *Daily Princetonian,* March 20, 1907.

[1] It was built, actually, in 1581.

From Emanuel Raphael

My dear Sir: Houston, Texas March 21st, 1907.

I have your valued favor of the 13th of March,[1] and have taken the matter up with my committee. Your strong recommendation of Prof. Edgar O. Lovett, has induced us to extend to him an invitation to visit the City of Houston, in order to become personally acquainted with the members of our Board and look over the grounds, and we have written such a letter to him this date.

In the meantime, we would like to hear from you a little more about him in the way of a sketch touching his nativity, age, married or single, and an outline of his work up to the present time.[2] As to other matters connected with this gentleman, we shall have to be the judges.

I desire to thank you for the interest you have taken in our affairs, and to assure you that same is very much appreciated.

Sincerely yours, E. Raphael Secretary.

TLS (WP, DLC).

[1] Wilson's letter to Raphael is missing in the Rice Institute Papers in TxHR.

[2] Wilson's reply to this letter is also missing in the Rice Institute Papers.

From Walter Maxwell Adriance

My dear President Wilson, Princeton, N. J. March 23, 1907.

I was very glad to receive your letter, and wish in reply to assure you that it will give me great pleasure to remain at Princeton.

I am sorry if you were under any embarassment on account of my not having made it sufficiently clear that I really desired reappointment. Understanding as I did, at the time of my appointment last June, that nothing had been promised me here beyond the first year, I have of course taken some steps in the direction of securing some other position in case you had not been able to retain me. But nothing definite had as yet come of those efforts.

For this reason, but even more because I am thoroughly enjoying the work here, and am a most enthusiastic believer in the Preceptorial System, I did very earnestly desire reappointment. And Mrs. Adriance[1] was perhaps even more anxious than I that we might remain in Princeton. If my letter to you was colorless, it was because I did not feel that the intensity of our desire to remain should be made a factor in your decision.

Thanking you very sincerely for your letter, I am

Faithfully yours, Walter M. Adriance.

TLS (WP, DLC).

[1] Helen Campbell Adriance.

From Grover Cleveland

My dear President Wilson Princeton March 24, 1907

Luckily I blush crimson as I attempt to express my grateful appreciation of the generous things you said of me on my seventieth birthday. I fear you have embellished beyond my desert the unattractive mile post I have just passed; but at the age of seventy perhaps one may be excused if he seeks to overcome his scruples of modesty by crediting the affectionate utterances of friends and neighbors against the heavy account of advancing years.

So putting aside all affectation I thank you from the bottom of my old but still warm heart.

One thing more I want to say to you: There are matters in what you wrote of me–concerning motives and intents–which I supposed no one knew but myself. And I am wondering how you found them out. Yours faithfully Grover Cleveland

ALS (WP, DLC).

From Edward Wright Sheldon

My dear Woodrow: [New York] March 24, 1907.

Since seeing you at Princeton and having fresh evidence of the great burden which the manifold needs of the university impose, I have several times found myself wishing not only that your house labors might be temporarily lightened, but also that the added pressure of outside work might be curtailed. I can guess the difficulty it must be to say No when you can do what is asked so commandingly, but with all that you have gone through in the last eighteen months, and with the heavy demands of the future, I do not unreservedly enjoy seeing you adding distinction to the curriculum of Mr. Nicholas Murray Butler's institution or responding to most of the other requests for edification and inspiration. It is *facilis descensus*, the path of overwork, so please forgive [me] for speaking of something which is close to my heart and cannot but cause me embryonic apprehension.

Believe me, as ever,

Yours most sincerely Edward W. Sheldon.

ALS (WP, DLC).

From John Allan Wyeth

My dear Mr Wilson [New York] March 24th, 1907

The night of our dinner you may recall that my friend Mr Laffan spoke of a letter he had ventured to write to Judge Parker in which he stated his views in regard to a platform or an expression of principles, but owing to circumstances had not sent.

I asked him to let me see it. It was at his country place & it was only today that he had an opportunity of going there to look it up. It is of such a nature that after reading I asked him if I might submit it to you, to which he readily assented. He added moreover that he would like to see you again.

I would like to have you read this letter and if you are not coming to the city by Tuesday or Wednesday I will send it out to you. Laffan sails Thursday for several months abroad. He is in great distress over the situation & wants advice & help. If you care to telephone me at any time on any subject I wd suggest one thirty p.m. as I am always in & near the telephone at that hour.

My number is 4194, Madison Square.

We were delighted to have had you at our home & hope you may often come to visit us.

Sincerely Yrs John A Wyeth

ALS (WP, DLC).

From Sir William Mather

My dear President Wilson [London] March 24/07

In view of the fact that the Sun-Dial will be shipped so as to arrive at New York early in May, all going well, I hope the foundations will be finished about that time, in which case the erection could be completed before your Commencement week.

It has occurred to me that you may be pleased to have my friend Mr. Bryce the British Ambassador to unveil it. The occasion would be fitting & his presence & speech at Princeton as an Oxford scholar & former Professor would be singularly gratifying I think to the Faculty & Alumni as well as profitable to the graduates.

In anticipation of your possible agreement in this view, I am written [writing] to Mr. Bryce praying him to undertake the unveiling of the Monument *should you invite him to Princeton.* It would be a great pleasure to many here to know that our Ambassador was to pay his first visit to your University.

I intend to send out a competent man to erect the Dial.

I beg you to convey to Mrs. Wilson & your daughters our kindest regards, and hoping that your health is fully restored I am

Very sincerely yours W. Mather

ALS (WWP, UA, NjP).

To Edward Capps

[Princeton, N. J.]

My dear Professor Capps: March 25th, 1907.

I have been so hurried from one thing to another since you were here, that I have not had time to write and tell you how much we enjoyed your visit or how much we hope that you will be willing to exchange Chicago for Princeton.

We are very much in earnest, as you know, in what we have undertaken to do and to stand for in Classics, and we need the help and counsel of the best men in the country. I write to ask if I may not have the privilege of nominating you to the Board of Trustees as Professor of Classics, at a salary of $5000 a year. This is our maximum salary,—a maximum which we have been able to offer, I am sorry to say, to very few even of our best men. It is, I believe, a salary upon which one can live in Princeton without too anxious management, and besides the salary we should be able to offer you attractive work and a very warm welcome.

With sincere regard,

Cordially yours, [Woodrow Wilson]

CCL (WWP, UA, NjP).

From Robert Erskine Ely[1]

Dear Sir: New York, March 25, 1907.

It is in the highest degree desirable that the ms. copy of the address you are to make before the National Arbitration and Peace Congress[2] be sent to me by Friday of this week, the 29th. The American Manager of Reuter's Agency wishes to send to Europe to be published in all of the newspapers of Great Britain and the Continent, the more important speeches delivered at the Congress. He would like to send these speeches in full, where practicable, rather than an abstract of them.

The Associated Press is also making preparations to send to eight hundred newspapers of this country very full reports of the Congress, and for this purpose also the mss. of speeches is desired. You will greatly increase the larger influence of the Congress in this country and abroad, if you will be so kind as to make a very special effort to comply with the request to send me the ms. of your speech, as soon as possible.[3]

I take pleasure in sending herewith a copy of a "Peace Primer," and a news article from the "Independent."[4] Should you require any further literature on the subject of arbitration and peace I shall be happy to forward it to you immediately, if it can possibly be obtained.

Again thanking you for your appreciation of the immense importance of this Congress, I am,

Very truly yours, Robert Erskine Ely

Postscript: The meeting at which we are expecting you to speak will be held on Tuesday evening, April 16th, at Carnegie Hall. Inasmuch as there are to be several speakers it seems to the committee desirable that each speaker should make an address not exceeding twelve to fifteen minutes in length. The committee do not wish to set an arbitrary time limit to an address, which would make it unsatisfactory to both the audience and the speaker, but we feel it very important that no session of the Congress should be unduly prolonged.

TLS (WP, DLC).

1 Director of the League for Political Education of New York and Secretary of the Executive Committee of the National Arbitration and Peace Congress, about which see the following note.

2 The National Arbitration and Peace Congress was organized under the auspices of the American Peace Society of Boston and the New York Peace Society. Andrew Carnegie accepted the presidency of the Congress, and the lengthy list of vice presidents included Andrew D. White, Seth Low, Alton B. Parker, Samuel Gompers, Charles Evans Hughes, William Jennings Bryan, and all members of President Roosevelt's Cabinet except Secretary of State Elihu Root. The Executive Committee and the General Committee included many other notable Americans among their members. Woodrow Wilson was a member of the General

Committee, as were some of his close friends and associates such as Cleveland H. Dodge, Elgin R. L. Gould, Henry van Dyke, John Bates Clark, and Bliss Perry.

Invitations to send delegates to the conference were sent to some 30,000 business organizations, labor unions, farmers' organizations, churches and other religious organizations, peace societies, ethical, reform, and philanthropic societies, colleges and universities, learned societies, members of Congress, governors, mayors, and so on. Some 10,000 delegates were appointed, of whom 1,253 from thirty-nine states and territories actually registered at the headquarters of the Congress.

The Congress was held at Carnegie Hall and at other locations in New York from April 14 through April 17, 1907. It was intended to express American support for, and arouse the interest of the American people in, the second international conference which was to meet at The Hague in June 1907. The Congress passed a number of resolutions which, among other things, urged The Hague Conference to become a permanent body with regular meetings, to draft a general treaty of arbitration, and to consider the reduction of armaments. The Congress was widely publicized both in the United States and abroad. See *Proceedings of the National Arbitration and Peace Congress, New York, April 14th to 17th, 1907* (New York, 1907).

3 As subsequent correspondence will disclose, Wilson chose not to participate.

4 Lucia Ames Mead, *A Primer of the Peace Movement* (n. p., 1905), and a reprint of Hamilton Holt, "The Approaching National Peace and Arbitration Congress," New York *Independent*, LXII (March 14, 1907), 614-16.

From John Allan Wyeth

My dear Mr. Wilson: New York City, March 26, 1907.

I have just received your letter of March 25. I join in the regret that you will be unable to see Mr. Laffan before he sails.

I enclose to you a letter which Mr. Laffan requests me to keep closely within ourselves; you may return it to me, and I will hold it for him until he comes back from Europe.

In my opinion, our friend and those in interest with him are in something of a panic; they seem to think that the forces which have heretofore contributed to the prosperity of the country and its assured safety have been brought near to bondage, if not already enchained. They are seemingly beating the bushes for some Moses to lead them into a land of promise.

I believe that our two friends[1] were deeply impressed with the idea that you are able to exert an important influence in this crisis.

With kindest wishes in which this family joins with me,

Ever sincerely yours, John A Wyeth

TLS (WP, DLC).

1 That is, William M. Laffan and Thomas Fortune Ryan.

To Mary Allen Hulbert Peck

My dear Mrs. Peck, Princeton, N. J. 27 March, 1907

Pray excuse this official stationery. I have carelessly allowed myself to run out of all other kinds,—no doubt because I so seldom have even a chance quarter of a hour in which to write private letters,—and I must seize the opportunity when it comes.

Your kind letter about the books gave me singular pleasure, and, though I have not answered it, I have carried it in my mind. It has done much to keep me in heart amidst much unrewarding toil. For it was deeply delightful to me to be bidden by you to believe that my friendship had given you pleasure not only but some subtle help also. I do not know how it happened except that you must have seen how immediately I descried and enjoyed the fine things in your own nature. I do not see how anyone could miss them; but perhaps there was an instinctive sympathy between us which made you display them with unusual pleasure to yourself. It makes me feel very humble to be told that I seemed to you strong and fine. I am not aware of any fineness except recognizing and admiring fineness in others and admiring it and enjoying it wholly—and certainly you gave me leave to see things in you which made me wholly glad. If I had the same effect on you, I can only wonder and be grateful

I know that you will love the Bagehot—and I hope that you will not forget that you have a real friend in

Yours in truest respect and admiration

Woodrow Wilson

ALS (WP, DLC).

To Edward Wright Sheldon

My dear Ed., Princeton, N. J. 27 March, 1907

Thank you most heartily for your letter. Your solicitude for me not only pleased and heartened me, it touched me deeply.

I can assure you I *try* to take care of myself. A certain amount of lecturing I *must* do every year, because every year I run a little into debt, and that is the easiest way to pay it off (hence the Columbia lectures, for example); but that does not go very hard. Work does not exhaust me. What wears is responsibility minus resources to make Princeton what she should be. The resources will come in time, however, and perhaps that anxiety will be lightened.

I have reached the end of my speaking engagements now—except Columbia and an alumni dinner at Pittsburgh

Your letter was a comfort and a tonic.

Affectionately Yours, Woodrow Wilson

ALS (WC, NjP).

To Andrew Carnegie

My dear Mr. Carnegie: Princeton, N. J. March 27th, 1907.

You will remember that when we had the pleasure of seeing Mrs. Carnegie and you in the autumn, you were kind enough to give us the hope that we might expect a visit from you when spring came.

I know that the date of your leaving the country must be approaching, and I write for both Mrs. Wilson and myself to beg that you will not disappoint us and that you will give us the very great pleasure of having you here sometime before you sail. We should wish to have it as late as possible, in order that you may see Princeton in her spring beauty, but we beg to leave the selection of the date entirely to yourselves. We hope, moreover, that you will make the visit as long as possible.

There are no dates on my own calendar for the latter part of April that would conflict, except Fridays, and there are no conflicting dates in May at all.

With warm regard,

Sincerely yours, Woodrow Wilson

TLS (A. Carnegie Papers, DLC).

From Cleveland Hoadley Dodge

Dear Mr President New York. March 28th 1907

On the whole I am fairly well pleased. Dr Gates positively told me the other day that it would be impossible for them to give us over 150M & in fact that is all the subcommittee recommended. Mr Buttrick told me today that at first the whole Board was opposed to giving anything to Princeton, when Dr Gates got up & spoke so effectively about the great influence of the Princeton system in raising the standards & ideals of education, claiming that the General Ed. Board was an *educational* & not a charity Board &c &c that the members of the Board spoke up & said if that was true 150M was not enough. If they had had the money they would have given us 500M, but restricted as they are, they insisted on Dr Gates making it 200M. I have had a talk with Dr Gates & seen Mr Geo Foster Peabody who both spoke in the warmest way of what we are doing at Princeton & whilst I regret it isn't more I am very happy that they gave us anything. We have at least made our position felt & as Dr Gates said there is nothing to prevent the Board helping us further in the future[.] They will give us all the time we want to secure the additional

600M & we will be forced to raise that amount at least & have a strong leverage to help us in our appeal

Of course now is a bad time to go for money,[1] but I think we ought to use this opportunity to strike high, when things are hot & later in the year if money matters improve we should make a strong effort to raise a large sum for general endowment at least a million in addition to the 600M or possibly 1400M making $2000000.00 in all.

Anyhow it's bully fun & the finest sport I know

I have lots more to tell you & hope to see you in the near future.

Forgive this unburdening of my soul & cheer up—things I hope are coming our way & everything is emphasizing the fact that Woodrow Wilson is sans exception the leading figure in Education in the world today. Ever affly C. H. Dodge

One thing more—We must not hesitate to go ahead & get the strong new men we need & furthermore we ought to figure out at once our duty to our present fine men & give them their just due if possible. In that way we will have the right incentive & leverage to ask for all we need CHD

ALS (WP, DLC).

[1] The beginnings of a business recession gradually became apparent early in 1907. There was a sharp drop on the New York Stock Exchange on March 14, and stock prices fell rapidly and steadily from that point on for many months. In September, industrial production began to slump also, and a number of banks and industrial firms went bankrupt. A currency panic was set off when the Knickerbocker Trust Company of New York was forced to close its doors on October 23, 1907. A degree of financial stability was achieved in late October and November through the cooperative efforts of the Roosevelt administration and a group of New York bankers headed by J. P. Morgan. The downward trend in the economy had ended by January 1908, and the panic was over.

From Ralph Adams Cram

My dear Sir: Boston March 28 1907

I have received notice of my appointment as Supervising Architect to Princeton University with a very deep sense of the honour done me and with an equal appreciation of the great responsibility placed upon me through my acceptance of such a position.

That I should become connected with Princeton rather than with any other of the great Universities, is a matter of singular satisfaction. The standards of education, the methods of instruction and, if you will permit me to say this, the personality of the President, all appeal to me more strongly than in any other instance, while the architectural standards set particularly by Cope & Stewardson are in my opinion the highest of any

University in America. For all these reasons I congratulate myself on the quite unexpected honour that has been done me.

I am anxious to come to Princeton at the earliest moment in order that I may meet you, Sir, look over the situation, and familiarize myself with the conditions, actual and prospective. If it will suit your convenience I shall therefore come to Princeton on the afternoon of Wednesday, April third, going directly to the Inn, where I shall spend the night, returning to New York on Thursday in season to catch the midnight train for Boston. As I have engagements, for both Tuesday and Friday of that week, I must make this first visit somewhat brief, but it will only be a preliminary visit, and for this the time should be sufficient.

If this arrangement is not satisfactory to you I trust you will not hesitate to tell me, as I desire to accomodate myself to your wishes in every respect.

I am Sir, Very Sincerely Yrs., R A Cram

ALS (WP, DLC).

To Ralph Adams Cram

My dear Mr. Cram: [Princeton, N. J.] March 29th, 1907.

I am very much gratified by your kind letter of March 28th, and am sincerely delighted that you are willing to give us the benefit of your advice in the physical development of the University. I look forward with great pleasure to the association, and to the personal relationships into which it will bring us.

I am sorry to say that I am obliged to be in Pittsburgh next week, and cannot reach home before Thursday the fourth. Would it be possible for you to arrange a visit to Princeton on the following week? I expect to be in Princeton throughout that week, except on Friday.

If this suggestion does not fit in with your engagements, I hope you will let me know at what other time it will be convenient for you to come. My out of town engagements are now decreasing, and it is not likely that we shall hit upon another conflict.

With warm appreciation of your letter,

Cordially and sincerely yours, [Woodrow Wilson]

CCL (WWP, UA, NjP).

To Andrew Carnegie

My dear Mr. Carnegie: Princeton, N. J. March 29th, 1907.

I am deeply gratified by your kind letter of yesterday,[1] and can assure you that it is with the keenest regret that I find myself so bound by previous engagements from which I cannot honorably be released, that it would not be possible for me to be in New York during the Peace Congress before Wednesday evening.

I note your kind suggestion that I might be put on the list of speakers for the banquet which is to conclude the Congress, but the provisional programme which Mr. Ely has sent me this morning, shows the list of speakers already so long as to tax the attention and patience of an after-dinner audience. I do not feel that my name ought to be added or that I could speak with any profit or advantage, if I felt that the maximum impression had already been made by the other speakers already invited.

My heart is altogether with this Congress, and I wish most unaffectedly that I could be of service in promoting its objects. It would be very delightful for me to be present at the concluding banquet, but I know by sad experience how futile a long list of speakers is. I keenly regret that I did not know of the arrangements of the Congress soon enough to avoid previous engagements.

Mrs. Wilson and I warmly appreciate your kind words of invitation, and hope that it will not be long before we see Mrs. Carnegie and you at Princeton.

Always cordially and faithfully yours,

Woodrow Wilson

TLS (A. Carnegie Papers, DLC).

[1] It is missing.

A News Report of a Dedicatory Address in Princeton

[March 30, 1907]

DEDICATION SERVICE.

NEW CHAPEL OF FIRST CHURCH.

The services of dedication of the new chapel and Sunday schools rooms of the First Presbyterian Church[1] were held on Wednesday evening [March 27]. The chapel was crowded to its utmost capacity. . . .

Address by President Woodrow Wilson.

In this address President Wilson sketched the intimate early connection existing between the college and the congregation of the First Church. He said it was significant that in the entire history of the relations between the college and this church it was never alluded to in the minutes of the Board of Trustees otherwise than as the congregation. The early presidents of the college were the ministers of the congregation. This arrangement was not discontinued owing to any loss of interest in the congregation by the college, but because the administrative duties of that office so occupied the time of its presidents that they were unable to minister unto the congregation also. A very cordial relationship between college and congregation had continued during all the intervening years.

The tendency of the age is to make of the church a mere social organization. The same tendency is toward making the college a body of studies, instead of a discipline. The true aim of a college is the discipline of the mind, not the imparting merely of information. And so the power of the church lies in its spiritual teaching and authority. To this high view the First Church in its history has been steadfast. In these days of doubt and spiritual unrest men have turned to the Catholic Church, seeking a haven of peace. He thought one reason for this lay in the fact that, despite errors in her teachings, that church had been steadfast in holding fast the Oracles of God.[2]

Printed in the *Princeton Press*, March 30, 1907.

[1] About this new chapel and Sunday School facility, see the news item printed at May 10, 1905, Vol. 16.

[2] Other participants in this dedicatory service were Paul van Dyke; the Rev. Sylvester W. Beach, pastor of the First Church; the Rev. Dr. William Brenton Greene, Jr., Stuart Professor of Apologetics and Christian Ethics at Princeton Theological Seminary; the Rev. Dr. Francis Landey Patton, President of Princeton Theological Seminary; and the Rev. William Irwin Campbell, pastor of the Second Presbyterian Church of Princeton. For a later commentary on Wilson's remarks, see F. N. Willson to WW, July 4, 1907.

To Cleveland Hoadley Dodge

My dear Cleve, Princeton, N. J. 30 March, 1907.

Your letters are always an unmixed pleasure to me. They contain a true flavour of yourself and act as a tonic upon me. I am always in full heart after I have read them!

I agree with you that the action of the General Education Board is full of encouragement: that we have distinctly scored and ought to be in good heart to get the $600 000. I rejoice, too, in what you say about what we must think of at once by way of just compensation to our best men. I will lay a statement before you as soon as possible.

I am off on Monday night for the alumni dinner in Pittsburgh, and hope to be at home again on the forenoon of Thursday. I hope we shall see each other soon after that.

Most affectionately Yours, Woodrow Wilson

WWTLS (WC, NjP).

From Ralph Adams Cram

My dear Sir, Boston March 30 1907

I beg to acknowledge the receipt of your letter of March twenty ninth. I shall be very glad to change the date of my visit to Princeton to the week of April seventh. I will write you next week just what day I can come. I shall try to make it Wednesday as before.

Very sincerely yours R A Cram

ALS (WP, DLC).

From Edgar Bronson Tolman[1]

Chicago Ill. Mar. 30th, '07

The Iroquois Club will celebrate Jefferson's birthday with a banquet April twentieth next and earnestly requests you to address the meeting on some topic of true Jeffersonian democracy to be settled by you[2]

Edgar B. Tolman, Prest., Iroquois Club.

T telegram (WP, DLC).

1 Prominent lawyer of Chicago.

2 Wilson's reply is missing, but he did not accept the invitation.

A News Report of an Address to Princeton Alumni in Pittsburgh

[April 3, 1907]

TIGER YOWLS! PRINCETON BOYS TAKE CITY BY STORM; GIVE PLAY, THEN DINNER; WOODROW WILSON HERE

What with the presentation of a play at the Nixon,[1] the giving of a dinner at the Schenley and with President Woodrow Wilson on hand to deliver an address, Princeton and Princetonians pretty nearly took Pittsburg by storm yesterday afternoon and last night. Society graced the show, men of note were at the dinner and the alumni generally had the time of their lives. All of which was due to the Triangle Club, about seventy-five strong.

President Wilson of Princeton University was the lion of the banquet. When introduced by Judge Nathaniel Ewing to respond to the toast "The Hegemony of Princeton" he was greeted by a vociferous "locomotive" yell, and when he had finished it was repeated enthusiastically.

He declared Princeton was rapidly assuming a position similar to that of the Nation itself, only on a smaller scale. By recent changes in its manner of government it is developing statesmanship among its students and is becoming more worthy of the trust of the country. Nothing, he said, is so useless as mere information as it is understanding that counts and the proper interpretation of human nature.

An institution, such as Princeton is now striving to be, that exercises the strength of its mind in its own affairs is better, he said, than one that merely supplies information, as the former is trying to get at the true philosophy of education. "The number of men who know things that are not so," he said, "is appalling." Those who believe because some transactions are crooked all are crooked are the kind of men who supply material for a revolution.

"A socialist nation is one that has lost its balance of mind," declared the speaker. He added that leadership in the educational field would preface leadership in public and political life, as those who give their minds to money making professions do not enlighten their minds. Such vocations give them no concern of any care save their own. If the youth of the country have been neglected it is no wonder there is a lack of leaders among its men.

Princeton is attempting to find out what are the elements of modern learning. Having found these elements of modern thought it seeks to saturate the mind of modern youths with them. Modern science, literature, philosophy and history put one in a condition to understand life, and "unless you have found your own way how can you point out the way to others?"

"There is a statesmanship of letters, a disengagement of mind, an effort to stand in one place where the world may be seen without prejudice. Such is the purpose of the modern university. It is not a place where beacons burn that shed their light over the pathway of mankind."[2]

Printed in the *Pittsburg Dispatch*, April 3, 1907; some editorial headings omitted.

1 The Triangle show, "The Mummy Monarch."

2 This last sentence is garbled. Wilson undoubtedly said: "Is it not a place where beacons burn that shed their light over the pathway of mankind?"

From Robert Garrett

My dear Mr. Wilson: [Baltimore] April 8, 1907.

I have been considering of late a proposition that has been made by Mr. William H. Buckler[1] of Baltimore to attempt the excavation of the city of Sardis. If we can secure the necessary papers for this purpose from Constantinople, Buckler and I will have general supervision of the work and will see that the expenses are met.

It would probably be a great help to us in securing the permission to excavate there, and the control of the site, if we could be supported or endorsed in substantial form by Princeton and the Johns Hopkins (with which Buckler is connected). Do you think under the circumstances it would be wise to give such support, and could you do so, or would it be necessary to bring the matter before the Board of Trustees in June?

With best regards,

Very sincerely yours, [Robert Garrett]

CCL (Selected Corr. of R. Garrett, NjP).

[1] William Hepburn Buckler, lawyer and gentleman scholar of Baltimore.

To John Heman Converse

My dear Mr. Converse: [Princeton, N. J.] April 10th, 1907.

You may have noticed in the papers that the General Education Board, which is spending the income of the large endowment for education given by Mr. Rockefeller, recently voted to Princeton the sum of $200,000 as a contribution to a sum of $2,000,000 to be raised for the University. Of the sum of $2,000,000 there is an additional amount of $1,200,000 in sight, for scientific equipment. This leaves $600,000 to be raised, and I am taking the liberty of writing to ask if I could see you on the afternoon of any one of the first three days of next week, to talk the matter over with you.

I find that nothing goes so hard with me as the necessary business of seeking money to support the work of the University, and I think it eminently unfair to seek an interview for the purpose of asking for money, without candidly saying what my errand is.

I know how generous you are, but I wish to assure you that I do not come to impose on your generosity, but to explain to you a very interesting and hopeful situation, in order that if it seems to you possible, it may also seem to you desirable to help us to a development which I believe will be of consequence not only to us, but to the country.[1]

Hoping that you are very well, and with warmest regards,

Sincerely yours, [Woodrow Wilson]

CCL (WWP, UA, NjP).

[1] There is no record of any contribution by Converse.

From Robert Garrett

My dear President Wilson: [Baltimore] April 10th, 1907.

Some weeks I wrote to you concerning Andrew Mills, Jr.[1] of the class of 1897 who had applied for a Bachelors degree. Soon after my letter was sent I saw you in Princeton and you told me, I believe, that the papers concerning the matter would be turned over to the proper faculty committee so that the case might be investigated and reported upon to the Trustees, provided they should find that Mills ought to receive the degree.

I write now to ask what is the present status of the matter, and whether or not, supposing and hoping that favorable action will be taken, the Trustees could pass upon it and the degree could be granted at Commencement. I trust it will not burden you to let me have this information.[2]

Sincerely yours, [Robert Garrett]

CCL (Selected Corr. of R. Garrett, NjP).

[1] At this time in the investment banking business in New York.

[2] See WW to R. Garrett, April 13, 1907.

From Henry Smith Pritchett

Dear President Wilson: New York April 10, 1907.

Mr. Carnegie has had, since the beginning of the Carnegie Foundation, some thought of adding to the work of our Foundation some additional machinery through which insurance might be furnished to all teachers at cost, including teachers in high schools and elementary schools as well as teachers in higher institutions of learning.

At present, the insurance companies sell insurance far above its actual cost. Since the agitation last year in New York, there has been some improvement effected by the diminution of agents' commissions and a corresponding increase in the dividends returned to the policy holder, but the improvement is small.

Furthermore, not only is insurance sold for much more than its worth, but agents rarely sell a straight life policy to one seeking insurance unless they are forced to do so, because the commissions on such policies are less than on the more expensive forms. In consequence, the insured is almost always persuaded to buy an expensive form of insurance rather than straight life insurance.

A third fault of the present system is that persons of modest means find it difficult to carry policies after they cease to earn a fair livelihood. In consequence, a large proportion of policies are surrendered when the holders are between sixty-five and seventy years of age.

A system of insurance under which an endowment furnished the cost of operating expenses and which, therefore, furnished the insurance at cost would save to the policy holder somewhere between 12% and 25% of the cost of insurance and in addition furnish this at such rate that the insurance would be fully paid at the age of sixty-five, which is the time at which professors are supposed to retire.

I should be glad to know whether, in your judgment, it would be a wise thing to establish an agency for furnishing to teachers insurance at cost and whether this could be best accomplished through the Carnegie Foundation for the Advancement of Teaching or by a separate organization. I hope to have an answer to these questions at your earliest convenience.[1]

I am Very sincerely yours, Henry S. Pritchett.

TLS (WP, DLC).

[1] As it turned out, a system of life insurance for teachers was not set up until the establishment of the Teachers Insurance and Annuity Association of America in 1917. See A. Carnegie to WW, April 14, 1905, n. 3, Vol. 16.

To Charles Francis Adams

My dear Mr. Adams: Princeton, N. J. April 11th, 1907.

Allow me to thank you very sincerely for your thoughtful kindness in sending me your Phi Beta Kappa addresses.[1] I was already familiar with them, but am glad to have them in this permanent shape.

Perhaps you do not know that before we established the Preceptorial System at Princeton we undertook a revision of our course of study, which put it upon a systematic basis and seems to us to have corrected the serious evils of the free elective system. This compacted course, together with our new method of instruction, has really wrought remarkable changes, and we sincerely believe that we are on the way to a very much sounder condition of affairs, so far as Princeton is concerned.[2]

With much regard,

Sincerely yours, Woodrow Wilson

TLS (photostat in RSB Coll., DLC).

1 Charles Francis Adams, *Three Phi Beta Kappa Addresses* (Boston and New York, 1907). This book is in the Wilson Library, DLC.

2 Wilson's remarks were inspired by the third address, "Some Modern College Tendencies," originally delivered at Columbia University on June 12, 1906. In it, Adams attacked the free elective system and advocated a curriculum designed to develop the imaginative, reasoning, and observing faculties of the mind and more intimate relationships between teachers and students. In footnotes and a "Supplementary Note" at the end of the address, he commented favorably upon Princeton's preceptorial system as a step in the right direction but expressed doubt about its ultimate success. Significantly, he also advocated the division of the undergraduates of large institutions such as Harvard into a number of residential colleges in which the intellectual life of the students would center.

From James Bryce

My dear President Washington Ap. 11/07

My regret at being unable to attend your Commencement is intensified by a request I have just had from my old & valued friend Sir Wm Mather that I should take part in the inauguration of the Sun Dial he is presenting to Princeton. However the engagements made long ago requiring me to be elsewhere are quite an insurmountable obstacle.

Further consideration leads me to fear that neither can I count on being able to get so far South as Princeton by Oct. 22. I have requests some of which I must comply with from places in New England & N. New York which would fill the last fortnight of October even if we leave New Hampshire so early as the 22nd

I cherish the hope that before we leave this [city] in June you may happen to be in Washington.

Sincerely yours James Bryce

ALS (WP, DLC).

From Louis Dyer[1]

Dear President Wilson, Oxford April 12 1907

Let me commend to your kindness our distinguished neighbours Mr. Gilbert Murray[2] & Lady Mary Murray.[3]

After lecturing at Harvard and seeing New Haven,—where even in May the Spring is sometimes recalcitrant, I have ventured to promise them real Spring weather at Princeton. In any case I make sure beforehand of a most delightful sojorn in your

University glades. The more so because of the interest that attaches to various new departures in educational methods which you are inaugurating.

Thanking you beforehand for any kindness to these good friends, I remain, Yours sincerely Louis Dyer.

ALS (WP, DLC).

[1] An American gentleman of leisure who lived at Sunbury Lodge in Oxford. See WW to EAW, Aug. 6-7, 1899, n. 1, Vol. 11.

[2] George Gilbert Aimé Murray, at this time Fellow of New College, Oxford. He delivered a series of six lectures at Harvard University in the late spring of 1907. They were published, with additional material, under the title, *The Rise of the Greek Epic: Being a Course of Lectures Delivered at Harvard University* (Oxford, 1907).

[3] Daughter of the 9th Earl of Carlisle.

From Edmund Beecher Wilson[1]

My dear Mr. Wilson: New York, April 12th 1907.

This is the first moment when it has been possible for me to announce my decision to you in regard to the question of coming to Princeton. I regret profoundly that it has become impossible for me [to] come. Your offer was so generous, so kindly and delightfully made, so attractive in other ways, that it has cost me a struggle to decline it. But the protests that came to me from Columbia as soon as I made known the change I had in contemplation were so strong, the action of the president and trustees so immediate and generous, that I was placed in a position where I could not do otherwise than remain. Mr. Butler fully appreciated, I think, the considerations that made the Princeton opportunity so attractive to me; but said at once that from the Columbia point of view it was impossible that I should leave; and it was made morally impossible for me to do so, by the exercise not of a compelling authority but of an extraordinary generosity towards my department and personal work, and the exhibition of a feeling that I valued still more highly and that I could not disregard.

I regret greatly the delay in the development of the department at Princeton that may have been occasioned by the length of time I have taken to consider the matter; but this was unavoidable, owing to the absence of Mr. Butler. I wish to say that if I can be of service to you in any way in the development of the biological work at Princeton, I shall feel it a privilege to have such an opportunity. I hope to have opportunity to see you and Dr. McClure in Princeton next week. In the mean time I thank you most warmly for your kindness in inviting me to join your ranks at Princeton—an invitation that I valued not less on account of the way in which it was given than because of the honor that it conveyed.

I have done my best to keep the whole matter confidential, and hope that no report of it will be spread.

With kind regards I am

Very sincerely yours Edm. B. Wilson

ALS (WP, DLC).

[1] Professor of Zoölogy at Columbia University since 1892.

To Robert Erskine Ely

My dear Mr. Ely: Princeton, N. J. April 13th, 1907.

Certainly some evil genius has been presiding over my relations to the Peace Congress. Though I feel it to be no fault of mine, I do feel that I owe you another expression of my very warm regret that I cannot be of service to the Committee of the Congress.

I went to Pittsburgh the week before last, and came back with a cold so severe that I have been an entire week in bed. As a consequence, my university duties fell very much into arrears, and inasmuch as I was not to be one of the speakers at the banquet on Wednesday evening, as originally planned, I allowed myself to make another engagement for that evening, in order to catch up with some of my work here; and so it has turned out that I cannot even speak at the supplementary banquet, for which you are making such interesting plans.

I am sorry, and very much obliged to you for all your kind urgency.

Cordially and sincerely yours, Woodrow Wilson

TLS (WC, NjP).

To Robert Garrett

My dear Mr. Garrett: Princeton, N. J. April 13, 1907.

Our committees are so overworked that everything moves very slowly, and the case of Mr. Andrew Mills, Jr., has not yet been advanced to any sort of conclusion. But I will try to push it forward at once, and in any case it will be possible to decide it either affirmatively or negatively at the Commencement meeting of the Board.[1]

I do not think that it would be necessary for the Board of Trustees to act in the interesting matter you bring to my attention in your letter of April 8th. If you and Mr. Buckler should undertake the excavation of the city of Sardis, I would be very glad indeed to give you the entire approval and backing of the University as a means of obtaining the privileges you desire, and I am sure that I should have the hearty approval of every member of the Board in doing so. The work seems to me of extraordinary interest and importance, and it is very delightful to know that you should be thinking of undertaking it. It will be in the interest of scholarship everywhere. If you will let me know your conclusion in the matter, and the form you would like the endorsement of the University to take, I would be glad to act at any time.

Cordially and sincerely yours, Woodrow Wilson

TLS (WC, NjP).

[1] Mills was awarded the B.S. degree in June 1909.

To Harry Augustus Garfield

My dear Professor Garfield: Princeton, N. J. April 13th, 1907.

Will it be convenient for you to meet Professor Fine, Professor [Paul] van Dyke and me on Monday evening at half past eight, in my office at '79 Hall, for a discussion of some interclub matters? I sincerely hope that it will.

Very truly yours, Woodrow Wilson

TLS (H. A. Garfield Papers, DLC).

To Sir William Mather

My dear Sir William: [Princeton, N. J.] April 15th, 1907.

I wonder if you will be ashamed of us, or merely amused to learn that, like other corporations, we have moved so slowly and so inexpertly in the matter of the sun-dial, that I fear it will not be possible to complete it by Commencement.

In the first place, we could not decide upon a site, and our efforts to decide that question led to nothing less than taking up the whole plan of our future physical development of the college grounds and the appointment of an advising architect, who has just begun to exercise his functions. We still await his advice as to where the sun-dial shall be placed.

I need not tell you that our differences on the subject have been of the most amicable sort, but they have of course led to innumerable delays. I have corresponded with the Treasury Department, and have their assurance that the materials for the sun-dial will be admitted free of duty, as works of art.

We have tried in vain to get Mr. Bryce for our Commencement, primarily to receive an honorary degree, and his inability to be here has disappointed us very much indeed.

It is just possible that the sun-dial may still be erected in time for our Commencement, but I fear not. If this is not possible, we shall plan for a formal unveiling early next autumn. We wish most warmly that it may turn out to be possible for you to come and unveil it yourself. Whatever our plans may turn out to be, you shall be promptly informed. And my all-embracing excuse for not having written to you more than once before is that which I have already given, namely, that our action has been inevitably halted in the matter. I can only pray that you will forgive us, and I am sure that I need not tell you that our delays have not been due to any lack of enthusiastic appreciation, but rather, if anything, to the contrary cause, our interest in having it placed as perfectly as possible.

Mrs. Wilson and my daughters join me in warm regards to Lady Mather, your daughters and yourself.

Cordially and sincerely yours, [Woodrow Wilson]

CCL (WWP, UA, NjP).

To Cleveland Hoadley Dodge

My dear Cleve: Princeton, N. J. April 15th, 1907.

Whenever I have an idea, I feel like handing it on to you for what it is worth.

Is there not some channel through which we could get at Mr. John L. Kennedy,[1] in order to ask him to give us the missing $500,000, and is it not worth while to try him, even in spite of all past discouraging circumstances? If I can personally be of any service in the matter, of course I shall be delighted to do anything you suggest.

Always affectionately yours, Woodrow Wilson

TLS (WC, NjP).

[1] Wilson meant John Stewart Kennedy, Scottish born banker and philanthropist of New York. He later left nearly $4,000,000 to Columbia University.

From Henry Burling Thompson

Wilmington, Del.
Dear President Wilson: 4th Mo., 15th, 1907.

I met Harry Osborn[1] at dinner on Thursday night last, and talked over with him the question of Professor Wilson leaving Columbia for Princeton. Harry's position must be one of neutrality, but he told Wilson, at their original conversation on this question, that his first duty was to Columbia. At the same time, I feel very sure that he is still loyal to his first love, and would not object to seeing Wilson at the head of our Biological Department. Of course, it is absolutely out of the question for him to say this. He, however, did advise me that he thought it would be best for some one to see Wilson in the early future and restate the question to him and urge his acceptance of our offer.

I believe that Momo Pyne was to see you and tell you this, at the same time, I thought, in the event of the message miscarrying, I had better give it to you as above.

I was annoyed, in view of your letter to me, to find that the Committee for the Delaware Princeton Dinner stated in their announcement that you expect to be present. It was simply a stupid error on their part, as your letter had been forwarded to them, but apparently was not understood by the entire Committee. I regret extremely that you cannot be with us.

Very sincerely yours, Henry B Thompson

TLS (WP, DLC).

[1] Henry Fairfield Osborn, Princeton 1877; Da Costa Professor of Zoölogy at Columbia; former Professor of Comparative Anatomy at Princeton; and Curator since 1891 of Vertebrate Palaeontology at the American Museum of Natural History.

To George Corning Fraser

My dear Mr. Fraser: Princeton, N. J. April 16th, 1907.

I hope that you will pardon our long delay in replying to the inquiries of the sub-committee of the Board of Governors of the University Cottage Club with regard to the faculty's views concerning the present interclub situation. It was a matter of too much importance to be hurried, but we can answer now, after very mature consideration.

Last evening Dean Fine, Mr. Garfield, Mr. Paul van Dyke and I (the members of the faculty called into consultation by the undergraduates) met and had a final discussion of the matter, and I was requested to say to you:

First, that in our opinion the present treaty as recently amended is an indispensable modus vivendi. We think that it would be very detrimental to the interests of the University not to accept it for the present and act under it with the most scrupulous care.

But, secondly, we do not regard it as a satisfactory permanent arrangement. It legalizes a condition of affairs, as between the upper and lower classes particularly, which we regard as highly unsatisfactory and artificial. The remedies are not simple. They do not lie in the direction of further amendments to the treaty, nor even in the direction of the maintenance of a treaty of the present sort. They must, we are convinced, be radical in character, and their aim must be to bring the clubs and the whole social life of the undergraduates into organic relations with the University itself.

The means of accomplishing these ends will require a great deal of discussion, to be made clear, sensible and acceptable, and I was requested to say to you that we will push their formulation and discussion forward as fast as possible, and will take the liberty of calling you into conference with us, or of apprising you of our progress, just as soon as we can come to a point where the plans seem to us in a satisfactory shape to be submitted to conference.

Let me add that while the situation is grave, the undergraduates seem to be acting in an excellent spirit and with a desire to serve the best interests of the University, and I believe that all concerned are now in a temper to deal with the matter in a large and statesmanlike way.

Very sincerely yours, [Woodrow Wilson]

CCL (WWP, UA, NjP).

From Robert Garrett

My dear President Wilson: [Baltimore] April 18th, 1907.

Thank you for your letter of the 13th inst. I am very glad you will be able to act in connection with our proposition to secure the right to excavate at Sardis without putting the matter before the Board of Trustees. When the time comes to ask for your endorsement of Mr. Buckler and myself and our plan I shall communicate with you again.[1]

Very sincerely yours, [Robert Garrett]

CCL (Selected Corr. of R. Garrett, NjP).

[1] As it turned out, the excavations at Sardis, carried out under the direction of

Professor Howard Crosby Butler of Princeton, did not begin until 1910 and continued through 1914. The First World War prevented any further work. The magnitude of the undertaking required a much larger group of financial backers than Garrett and Buckler had originally contemplated. Some forty individuals, most of them from the metropolitan area of New York and including many wealthy Princeton alumni, organized themselves as the American Society for the Excavation of Sardis. For the results of the excavations, see Howard Crosby Butler *et al.*, *Publications of the American Society for the Excavation of Sardis* (8 vols. in 10, Leyden, 1916-32).

From Edward Capps

My dear President Wilson: Chicago, April 20, 1907

Professor Westcott, representing you, has given me the information which I desired concerning hours of work, vacations, pension, etc. While I should have been glad to learn that you have at Princeton a regular vacation system, by which all permanent officers enjoy relief from class-room work at fixed intervals in the interest of their own studies, yet I am not disposed to ask for a special arrangement in my own case, in this or in other matters. I should feel more comfortable, I am sure, among my new colleagues, who extend me so cordial a welcome, if I were not the recipient of exceptional privileges, other than those which naturally and properly attach to the kind of work which you expect me to assume.

I have delayed my answer to Professor Westcott's letter, partly because of the distraction of almost continuous conferences with my protesting colleagues, but chiefly that I might have time to formulate a possible plan with reference to Classical Philology. You seem to have surmised, and rightly, that I should find it harder to give up this infant journal than any other single interest here. It is not merely that I have in it a large investment of time and devotion, nor that I have taken on certain financial obligations respecting it, but mainly because it has proved itself so potent a stimulus to all of us, including the whole body of graduate students in the classics both past and present, and that by leaving I should in a measure leave my associates, who are now committed to maintain it, in the lurch. They were unwilling to vote for its establishment, after long months of discussion, until a practicable plan of management had been agreed upon. And the Trustees would not consent to the subsidy until Hale[1] and I, who alone were willing to back the project, had executed a formal obligation, which they now hold, to be responsible for $500 a year for five years. We raised the money by annual subscriptions. As I look over the situation I do not see who of my colleagues who would be willing to take my place as editor could assume the burden and successfully carry it—though they probably do not share this view. But they see that they would be seriously embarassed by my withdrawal, and possibly would be glad to have me keep the laboring oar, even if I were no longer a member of this faculty, under certain conditions.

I am free to say that none of these obligations is of such a kind as to prevent my acceptance of the position you offer me. If you require my answer without further delay I will give it—in the affirmative. But I should be glad to retain my connection with the journal, to relieve my associates of as much of the burden of it as possible, and at the same time to secure for Princeton and her classical department the advantages, which it seems to me cannot be easily estimated, of direct participation in the editorial management of a scholarly journal. Since you have already indicated that you share this general view of the case I will suggest a plan which may prove practicable in the conditions which I foresee here in the immediate future. I have not broached the subject to anyone here except Hendrickson, the chairman of the editorial board, who has accepted a call to Yale.[2]

The financial situation is somewhat complicated. Classical Philology is the property of the University, but morally of the classical faculty, whose desires and interests I would consult in every way. The University grants $1000 a year, the president of the Trustees pledges $500 and Hale and I jointly $500. On the appropriation of "$2000 and the receipts" two journals are maintained, Classical Philology and the Classical Journal, which is the organ of the Classical Association. The receipts consist of payments by the Association of $1.50 for each member, and of general subscriptions. The membership is now about 1100; this year I have planned to bring it up to 2000. From outside subscriptions we now receive about $900, which will be much larger in a few years. The annual budget of the two journals is thus about $4500 at present, Classical Philology contributing to the maintenance of the Classical Journal some $500 a year. The underlying idea, as you have seen, is a tremendous propaganda in favor of the classics, to which the University contributes Classical Philology. The Association was formed with all this in view. What the effect will ultimately be of putting Classical Philology into the hands of a large body of classical teachers in high school and college can only be imagined, but we believe that the possibilities in the direction of sound scholarship and of enlightened teaching are enormous and well worth the sacrifice of time and money. What has been done for the teachers of the Middle West and South[3] should also be done for those of the rest of the country. The Classical Association of New England has just entered into formal relations with us and that of the Middle States and Maryland is likely to desire it. I can see the possibility of bringing in the course of a few years some 5000 teachers into close touch with the large centres of classical influence. The teachers will cooperate readily enough if the large centres will. And Princeton might well be the leader in this movement, with her unsurpassed classical staff and her pronouncement in favor of sound classical training.

Chicago might be induced to share with Princeton the ownership and management of Classical Philology if Princeton would share the financial and editorial burden. Our trustees would not, I think, object and our classical staff might welcome such an arrangement. Princeton's financial contribution would be the same as Chicago's, $1000 at present, and the journal might be edited "by the classical faculties of the University of Chicago and Princeton University," each University to have a managing editor. If Yale would join in this plan, so much the better. Harvard and Cornell have their "Studies" and Hopkins Gildersleeve's journal. Now that Hendrickson is to take Professor Peck's[4] place at Yale he might lay the matter before them if you see anything attractive in the suggestion.

This is the journal situation in brief. As to my engagement at Princeton, I suppose you would expect me to enter upon my duties next October. Unhappily I have arranged to teach here until Sept. 1, and was then expecting to take a vacation of one year, in the hope that I might finish a book long overdue. But I will consult with Professor Westcott about these matters. My only reason for not giving you now my formal acceptance is the thought that I might be in a better position while still a member of this University to negotiate with my associates regarding the journal. But perhaps it would not make any difference. My decision is made.

I trust that you have entirely recovered from your recent indisposition. Very sincerely yours, Edward Capps

TLS (WP, DLC).

[1] William Gardner Hale, Professor and Head of the Department of Latin at the University of Chicago.

[2] George Lincoln Hendrickson, Professor of Latin. He went to Yale in 1908.

[3] At this time Capps was President of the Classical Association of the Middle West and South.

[4] Tracy Peck, Professor of the Latin Language and Literature at Yale, 1880-1908.

A News Item

[April 23, 1907]

FIFTH ANNUAL BANQUET

Of the Press Club Held at The Princeton Inn
Last Evening.

The fifth annual banquet of the University Press Club, which was held at The Princeton Inn last evening, was the most successful ever given by this organization. Covers were laid for about thirty-five persons, including members of the club and invited guests. . . .

President Woodrow Wilson '79 expressed his appreciation of the care the Press Club exercises in the reports of matters connected with the University. He said that he felt greater security in speaking in Princeton than anywhere else.

The newspaper should be a mirror of public events and opinion. The world is always new to those who will look upon it as such; the ignorant man does not realize how much he has to learn. The greatest scholars are men who realize how little they really know, and appreciate how much they have yet to learn. The university man, above all others, should avoid a sophisticated attitude toward the world.

Printed in the *Daily Princetonian*, April 23, 1907.

To Henry Smith Pritchett

[Princeton, N. J.]

My dear President Pritchett: April 24th, 1907.

May I not beg that you will read the enclosed letter, and consider its contents confidential, inasmuch as I really have no right to show it? Professor Joseph A[lexander]. Leighton, the husband of the writer[1] of the letter, is Professor of Philosophy and Chaplain at Hobart College.

Through some disarrangement of my papers, I cannot put my hand on the list of accepted institutions, but I think I am not mistaken in my recollection that Hobart is on that list. If it is, it seems to me that circumstances such as those detailed in Mrs. Leighton's letter are wholly inconsistent with its remaining on that list. That the Bishop of Western New York[2] should have the right to remove the Professor of Philosophy on the ground of his liberal theological views seems to me to be the most intimate and dangerous kind of denominational control, and there can evidently be no doubt about the circumstances.[3]

If you will kindly keep this letter on [in] your private files, I should like to talk the matter over with you when I see you.

Always cordially and faithfully yours,

[Woodrow Wilson]

CCL (WWP, UA, NjP).

[1] Victoria Elizabeth Paul Leighton.

[2] The Rt. Rev. William David Walker.

[3] Nothing substantial can be discovered about this episode. Leighton had recently testified on behalf of an Episcopal clergyman convicted of heresy because he denied the divinity of Christ; he had also published *Jesus Christ and the Civilization of To-Day* (New York and London, 1907), a book of decidedly liberal theological views. If Bishop Walker attempted to remove Leighton from his professorship at Hobart, he did not succeed, for Leighton remained at that college until he was called to Ohio State University in 1910.

To Edward Capps

[Princeton, N. J.]

My dear Professor Capps: April 24th, 1907.

Your letter of the 20th reached me yesterday, and I wish to tell you at once with what deep pleasure and satisfaction I received the news that you had made up your mind to come to us. You may be sure of the very heartiest kind of welcome, and I hope that our labors together will be delightful and rewarding.

I write today, not only to express my deep pleasure, but to say that I have very little doubt that we could enter the arrangement you suggest for the publication of "Classical Philology." I am writing today to the chairman of our Finance Committee about the possibility of guaranteeing one thousand dollars a year for its support, and hope to be able to send you his reply within a day or two. The plan that you suggest seems to me both feasible and desirable. I should certainly be sincerely rejoiced to have our Classical Department connected with the enterprise.

With warm regards,

Sincerely yours, [Woodrow Wilson]

CCL (WWP, UA, NjP).

To Moses Taylor Pyne

My dear Momo: [Princeton, N. J.] April 24th, 1907.

It looks now as if Professor Capps, the distinguished classical scholar of Chicago University whom we have been so anxious to get, will come to us. The only matter which seems to clog his decision concerns the journal called "Classical Philology," which he edits for the Classical Department of Chicago University. He is anxious to retain his connection with the journal, and we are anxious to get hold of it for our Classical Department. Apparently we cannot honorably propose to take it away from Chicago University, which established it, but I think it would be feasible to share the editorship of it with Chicago University and to keep it in Capps's hands (which would practically make it emanate from Princeton), if we can subsidize it to the extent of one thousand dollars a year.

I hope that you will think that it is possible for us to do this. To get Capps and an organ of classical study at the same time would confirm us in our leadership in that department, and put one more department where we want all departments of the University to be,—at the very front, not only in scholarship, but in influence and leadership.

I have told Professor Capps that I would refer this matter to you, and let him know whether the thing was feasible.

Just for the sake of showing you how we have recently been in fact withdrawing money from the Classical Department and giving you a basis of calculation for its restoration, let me call your attention to the fact that Cameron, Packard and Orris have all been subtracted from its staff of professors and that their salaries when at the full aggregated $9,400. I am going to propose at the next meeting of the Finance Committee a net increase in the expenditure for the department of $6,700. This will include $5000 for Professor Capps and $1700 for promotions and additions in the minor part of the staff; so that to undertake the classical journal would seem to come within the old figures for the professorial staff of the department.

Always affectionately yours, [Woodrow Wilson]

CCL (WWP, UA, NjP).

From Robert Garrett

My dear Mr. Wilson: Baltimore April 25 [1907].

We are all very much pleased that you are going to try to come to my wedding[1] and we are disappointed that Mrs. Wilson will not be with us.

I am writing now to say that I hope you will not come,—much as I should like to have you,—if in order to do so you will have to make a great effort, or, in other words, to rush down to Baltimore and hurry back to Princeton on the first train you can get. I understand that you expect to come on the morning of the wedding. I suppose you are aware that one cannot leave Princeton in the morning and get to Baltimore before twelve o'clock.

If you should not come I hope that Miss Johnson and I will both see you in Princeton in June.

Very sincerely yours, Robert Garrett.

ALS (WP, DLC).

[1] Garrett married Katharine Barker Johnson of Baltimore on May 1, 1907.

From Ralph Adams Cram

My dear Dr. Wilson: Boston, April 25, 1907.

I have been giving a good deal of time since I had the pleasure of seeing you in Princeton, to a preliminary study of the situation, and I am sending you today three very rough block plans, which may serve to indicate the way matters look to me at the start.[1] You will understand, of course, that these are really intended only for your own consideration, and I am sending them in the hope that one or other of them may contain elements which seem to justify further study in the same direction.

As you will see, they are all hardly more than modifications of your own plan which was, it appears to me, an attempt to carry out precisely the principles that seem to me to be fundamental.

As I look at it, the solution of the whole problem is the enclosing of a certain central space by a practically solid mass of buildings, one opening from this central space being left toward the southerly view. Around this central area, which is the general focus of activity of the whole University, should come, on the right, residential quads, each isolated as far as possible from the other, each complete in itself; and on the left similar quads devoted to religious, educational, scientific, and academic purposes.

Now it happens that while mistakes have been made at Princeton, some of them very serious, still there is almost nothing that prevents such a working out of the problem. There are, of course, several buildings which are so bad in design that ultimately they will have to go, though it may be fifty years before this needs to be accomplished. There are some that are rather badly placed and there are one or two which are so bad architecturally and so unfortunately placed that, in any general scheme of working out, they must be eliminated and at the earliest convenient mo-

[1] They are missing.

ment. The worst offender in this direction is Dodd [Dod] Hall. I cannot reconcile myself to this building in any respect. In Schemes A. and B., I have shown it entirely eliminated. In Scheme C, it might, perhaps, be moved back forty feet forming temporarily one of the walls of the projected "Five Quad," but this would be only a temporary expedient, for the building is so bad architecturally, it cannot possibly be worked into any consistent scheme.

I should like to write a careful report, taking up every building and considering it architecturally, administratively, and from the standpoint of its location, but it is unnecessary to do this, of course, at the present time when we are merely discussing preliminary schemes. Of course I can see no way in which Witherspoon Hall, Alexander Hall, and Marquand Chapel and perhaps Brown Hall can ever be made to harmonize with a scheme of the beauty and majesty indicated by Blair and Little Halls, still I recognize the fact that these are permanent, at all events for the next fifty years. In Scheme C., for instance, Brown Hall would cease to be an offence and the Art Museum would disappear entirely. Witherspoon can be, in a measure, re-cast, by cutting off its terminating ineptitudes, and Alexander can be well hidden by future structures. So far as these buildings are concerned, therefore, it does not seem to me wise even to consider their elimination. Fortunately their several situations are such that we can go ahead with a good scheme of development, ignoring them for the time being, conscious always that they have been mercifully placed so that they will not militate against the working out of a great scheme.

I think of the two schemes I send you (A. and B. being really two versions of the same scheme) C. is in certain ways the best. It gives you five residential quads in place of the three you had counted on in your own plan and it makes these residential quads better in general dimensions, I think, than those you suggested, which would be rather too large for good effect, as is proved by the ineffective quad of Christ Church, Oxford; in C, also we get the future chapel in a commanding and effective position and should not have to destroy the old Marquand Chapel, which could be left for the future to deal with. I rather like the big open area shown around the site of Dodd Hall on plans A. and B., and we lose a good deal of this in C. through the construction of Five Quad and the quad opposite. Nevertheless, this latter arrangement would give you an additional residential quad and would block out Brown Hall from the general view, which is important. Of course you will see that the two plans could be combined and even with the Chapel on the site indicated in C., you could go on with the big campus shown in A. and B. Another good thing in plan C. is, I think, the driving road which enters from University Place between One and Two Quads, passes around in front of Alexander, enters the campus, divides in front of the terrace between Clio and Whig Halls, one branch going straight to Elm Drive, the other continuing to the entrance to McCosh Walk, then returning until it meets the existing road in front of Dickinson Hall, where it divides again, one line going to Washington Street, the other to Nassau. This would give a valuable driving road through the most interesting parts of the group and would give you one of those very delightful effects you get in Oxford and Cambridge, namely, streets flanked on either side by collegiate buildings.

As for the two laboratories now contemplated, I am quite of your opinion that the Chemical Laboratory should run along Nassau Street as you indicated, connecting with the present Science Hall. I cannot quite bring myself to like the proposed site for the Physical Laboratory beyond 79 Hall. It seems to me very far away from the Science group, and I do not quite like the idea of tacking laboratory buildings onto a dormitory conceived in such a small scale as happens in the case of 79 Hall. I should like to tentatively suggest the possibility of putting the Physical Laboratory where shown on Scheme C, letting it form two sides of the projected quad of which McCosh Hall forms the third side. You might then get other recitation halls around the quad marked A. on Plan C., while the present site of the Chemical and Civil Engineering Laboratories might be given to future engineering buildings, biological laboratories filling in the angle made by Washington Street and Williams Street, marked B. on Plan C. This would bring all your scientific buildings into one great Science group, and Dickinson Hall might be retained for the time being as part of this Science group. I am not at all sure that this proposed site would satisfy the physical department, but I should like to suggest it for your consideration.

I should be very glad to know if the general ideas expressed in these rough sketches appeal to you at all. It might be well for me to come to Princeton quite soon and discuss them with you, even at the present unformed stage, and I think I could get to Princeton early next week if you desired me to do so.

It is quite impossible for me to express the interest this whole project has created in my mind. I confess, it is driving office matters quite out of my head for the time being and it already seems to me of far greater importance and significance than does West Point itself.[2] Very sincerely yours, R A Cram.

TLS (WP, DLC).

[2] In 1903, Cram, Goodhue and Ferguson had won a competition for designs for the rebuilding of the campus of the United States Military Academy. This project occupied much of the firm's time for the next decade.

From Michael J. O'Toole[1]

Dear Sir: Wilkes Barre [Pa.] April 25 1907

In a recent conversation with Col. F. J. Fitzsimmons of Scranton he suggested to me the advisability of you becoming the candidate of the Democratic party for President. In line with our discussion of the subject I prepared and published the inclosed editorial article in the Wilkes-Barre News,[2] of which I am editor, I sent a copy of the article to my friend Col. J[ames]. M[cClurg]. Guffey of Pittsburg, Democratic national committee member from this state. I feel that the editorial in question covers the ground and gives many good reasons why you should be at the disposal of the Democracy of the nation. I hesitate to trespass on your time but if you have any comment to make on the same or suggestions to offer I would be pleased to receive the same, either in confidence or for publication as you may indicate. Believe me— Yours very Truly M. J O Toole

ALS (WP, DLC).

[1] Editor of the *Wilkes-Barre News*.

[2] "Presidential Timber," *Wilkes-Barre News*, April 25, 1907.

From Nicholas Murray Butler

Dear President Wilson: New York April 26, 1907

A glance at my calendar reminds me that your brilliant series of lectures on "Party Government in the United States" comes to an end to-day. I want to send you this word of personal thanks and appreciation for the distinguished service that you have rendered, not alone to Columbia University but to the cause of sound and clear thinking on political subjects. I only hope that the extra exertion has not told unfavorably upon your health and strength. We shall all look forward with keen interest to the early publication by the Press of the lectures in permanent form. All of the details will be arranged for you by Secretary Keppel.[1]

Faithfully yours, Nicholas Murray Butler

TLS (WP, DLC).

[1] Frederick Paul Keppel, Secretary of Columbia University.

From Anson Phelps Stokes, Jr.

[New Haven, Conn.]

My dear President Wilson: April 26, 1907.

I would be under great obligations to you if you would be kind enough to let me know the names of any preachers who have made an especially marked impression upon the Princeton students during the past year or two. I have already most of the preachers arranged for next year as after a good many years experience we have found about fifteen men who can always be relied upon to preach simple, straightforward, strong sermons. I think, however, that you have some preachers who have never been to Yale and I would be glad of an independent expression of opinion from you. If I can reciprocate by helping you in any way from my Yale experience, I shall of course be delighted.

Sincerely yours, Anson Phelps Stokes Jr

TLS (Stokes Letterbooks, Archives, CtY).

From Bliss Perry

My dear Wilson, Boston April 27, 1907.

I am in a begging mood today, and I hope that this letter may find you in an uncommonly benevolent frame of mind. We are going to print a semi-centennial number of the Atlantic next November. Mr. Howells, Mr. Norton, Mr. J. T. Trowbridge, and other early contributors are to write upon special topics connected with the history of the magazine.[1] I am anxious to secure in addition to these more purely reminiscent papers a group of short articles suggested by the words "Literature, Science, Art and Politics," which were formerly printed upon the cover of the magazine. The difference in outlook between 1857 and 1907 in each of these departments of activity is very striking. President Pritchett has promised to write upon the outlook for science in America as a good observer might have seen it in 1857 compared with the present assessment of scientific progress as it seems to a competent observer of today.[2] Colonel Higginson will write upon the American literary horizon of 1857 as compared with that of 1907.[3] There will be a similar paper upon American art.[4] You would be, naturally, my first choice for a paper on the American political situation of 1857 as contrasted with the outlook in American politics today. It seems to me that of the four papers this one on politics affords the most fascinating material in the picturesque contrasts which it suggests. You know all about the state of the country in 1857, and certainly you know more about

1907 than you will want to confess in a magazine article. The article would fairly write itself if you would only undertake it. If there are any phases of the present political situation about which you do not care to commit yourself as early as November, you can play up 1857 as strongly as you please. Five or six Atlantic pages would be enough if you did not find the leisure and inclination to write more. We should expect to pay an honorarium of three hundred dollars, and the copy ought to be in our hands not later than August 1st in view of the special preparations which we are making for this number of the magazine.

I know something of the responsibilities which you are now carrying, and I have really hesitated before suggesting any addition to your burdens. My desire to see that November number as brilliant a one as we can possibly make it tempts me, however, to ask you if you cannot possibly find time between now and August 1st to prepare the paper I have suggested. If I had free access to your "barrel" of lecture notes and after-dinner addresses, I could put together precisely the article we want. In other words, you have already written the article. It is simply a question of copying it off for us. Pray tell me that you will do so![5]

Sincerely yours, Bliss Perry

P.S. Mrs. Wilson will be interested to know that Mrs. Perry and the children[6] reached home safely last Monday. They had a rough voyage, but are so happy to be home again that they have already forgotten their troubles.

TLS (WP, DLC).

1 William Dean Howells, "Recollections of an Atlantic Editorship." *Atlantic Monthly*, c (Nov. 1907), 594-606; Charles Eliot Norton, "The Launching of the Magazine," *ibid.*, pp. 579-81; John Townsend Trowbridge, "An Early Contributor's Recollections," *ibid.*, pp. 582-93; and Arthur Gilman, "Atlantic Dinners and Diners," *ibid.*, pp. 646-57.

2 Henry Smith Pritchett, "Science (1857-1907)," *ibid.*, pp. 613-25.

3 Thomas Wentworth Higginson, "Literature (1857-1907)," *ibid.*, pp. 606-12.

4 Hamilton Wright Mabie, "Art (1857-1907)," *ibid.*, pp. 625-35.

5 Wilson accepted, contributing "Politics (1857-1907)." It is printed at July 31, 1907.

6 Annie Bliss Perry and their children, Constance Goodnough, Margaret Smedley, and Arthur Bliss Perry.

To Edward Capps

[Princeton, N. J.]

My dear Professor Capps: April 29th, 1907.

I am happy to report that, as I anticipated, the Finance Committee of our Board of Trustees is willing to guarantee a subsidy of one thousand dollars a year to Classical Philology, and you may feel at entire liberty to negotiate for a partnership on that basis. I sincerely hope that it may be arranged with entire satisfaction to the Classical Department at Chicago, for I should not like to feel that I was actually stealing from them.

In haste, and with renewed assurances of my very deep pleasure that you are coming,

Cordially and faithfully yours, [Woodrow Wilson]

CCL (WWP, UA, NjP).

To Adrian Hoffman Joline

My dear Mr. Joline: Princeton, N. J. April 29th, 1907.

Thank you very much for sending me your address at Parsons, Kan., before the Board of Directors of the Missouri, Kansas & Texas Railway Company.[1] I have read it with relish and entire agreement. Would that we could do something, at once dignified and effective, to knock Mr. Bryan once for all into a cocked hat!.

Cordially and sincerely yours, Woodrow Wilson.

Printed in the *New York Times*, Jan. 8, 1912.

1 Joline was at this time President and Chairman of the Board of Directors of the railroad. In his speech at the annual meeting of the board on April 4, 1907, he had bitterly assailed the outcries against railroads by politicians and public opinion alike. He specifically attacked William Jennings Bryan's proposal for governmental ownership of railroads. In addition, he defended overcapitalization of the railroads on the ground of *caveat emptor* and declared that it would be the policy of his railroad to oppose by all legitimate means the enactment of laws injurious to the railroad's interest and to contest such laws, if enacted, in the courts. He would, however, obey all laws ultimately declared to be valid "even if it leads to insolvency and a receiver." Joline's speech is reproduced in full in John Forsyth Joline, Jr., "A Footnote to the Campaign of 1912. The Joline Letter. . . . ," MS in NjP. For a summary of the content of Joline's speech as well as a discussion of the use made of Wilson's letter to Joline during the Democratic preconvention presidential campaign of 1912, see Arthur S. Link, *Wilson: The Road to the White House* (Princeton, N. J., 1947), pp. 352-57.

To Andrew Carnegie

My dear Mr. Carnegie: Princeton, N. J. April 30th, 1907.

Thank you for your thoughtful courtesy in sending me a copy of your address on Ezra Cornell.[1] I shall look forward with the greatest interest to reading it.

Always cordially and faithfully yours,

Woodrow Wilson

TLS (A. Carnegie Papers, DLC).

1 Andrew Carnegie, *Ezra Cornell: An Address to the Students of Cornell University on Ezra Cornell Centennial Day, April Twenty-Sixth, 1907* (New York, n. d.).

To Anson Phelps Stokes, Jr., with Enclosure

My dear Mr. Stokes: Princeton, N. J. April 30th, 1907.

We have not been fortunate enough to find a great many preachers who can give our men the kind of sermons that seem the only kind worth while, but I take pleasure in sending you our list—the list to which we have gradually settled. I dare say most of them will be duplicates of your own, and I should be very much obliged to you indeed if you would let me know what names you have that we have not.

Very sincerely yours, Woodrow Wilson

TLS (A. P. Stokes, Jr., Papers, Archives, CtY).

ENCLOSURE

UNIVERSITY PREACHERS.

The Rev. Dr. William R. Richards,[1] 14 East 37th Street, New York City.

Professor Henry van Dyke, Princeton, N. J.

The Rev. Dr. Francis Landey Patton, Princeton, N. J.

Professor Paul van Dyke, Princeton, N. J.

Dean Wilford L. Robbins,[2] 1 Chelsea Square, New York City.

The Rev. Dr. Hugh Black, Union Theological Seminary, New York City.

The Rev. Father James O. H[S]. Huntington, Holy Cross House, West Park, N. Y.

The Rev. Dr. Endicott Peabody, Groton School, Groton, Mass.

The Rev. Ambrose W. Vernon, Hanover, N. H.

The Rev. Willis H. Butler,[3] Northampton, Mass.

The Rev. Dr. James G. K. McClure, McCormick Theological Seminary, Chicago.

The Rev. Dr. William Douglas Mackenzie, Hartford Theological Seminary, Hartford, Conn.

The Rev. Dr. W. Robson Notman,[4] 446 Chestnut Street, Chicago.

President W. H. P. Faunce, Brown University.

The Rev. Dr. J. Sparhawk Jones, 1814 Pine Street, Philadelphia.

The Rev. Dr. Charles Cuthbert Hall, Union Theological Seminary, New York.

The Rev. Henry S. Coffin, (Madison Avenue Church), 36 East 62nd St., New York.

The Rev. Dr. William McEwan, 636 S. Negley Ave., Pittsburgh.

The Right Rev. Ethelbert Talbot, Bishop of Central Pennsylvania, South Bethlehem, Pa.

T MS (A. P. Stokes, Jr., Papers, Archives, CtY).

[1] The Rev. Dr. William Rogers Richards, pastor of the Brick Presbyterian Church, New York.

[2] The Rev. Dr. Wilford Lash Robbins, Dean of the General Theological Seminary, New York.

[3] The Rev. Willis Howard Butler, Princeton 1895, pastor of the Edwards Congregational Church, Northampton, Mass.

[4] The Rev. Dr. William Robson Notman, pastor of the Fourth Presbyterian Church, Chicago.

From Sir William Mather

My dear President Wilson, [London] April 30th 1907

Your letter of the 15 Inst was most welcome for I was feeling somewhat confused concerning the course best to pursue under the circumstances. Mr Henry has written me also about the "battle of sites" and the undeveloped state of the grounds.

Meanwhile I had wired him that the Dial would be shipped & man to erect sent on 9th May, since which cable has arrived from Mr Henry "Dont send man await letter." The letter has reached me today, and I find that your view as to the doubtful possibility of erecting Dial for Commencement is confirmed. But as you say —"It is just possible that the Sun-Dial may still be erected in time for Commencement," I have resolved to let it go forward though substituting the 17th May for the 9th as before arranged. The delivery will be made in Philadelphia direct from the Thames, London, to avoid railway journeying as much as possible; and as I presume Phila is your nearest port & the Pennsylvania railway connects each end of distance between you the delivery should be safely effected. We may presume therefore that the whole thing (in several heavy parts) will be on your ground before end of May if you so order it. I shall send you Bills of Lading & particulars in advance so that you can instruct shipping agents at the port of arrival as you desire.

I am glad to learn that your Treasury has allowed admission free of duty as the sum would be very considerable in the usual way, apart from the unpleasant feeling of having a gift of goodwill taxed for revenue by the recipient!

As to the man to erect he will of course not come out as I proposed. You will therefore have to determine whether you will confide the erection (which must be very carefully done) to your own builders, or whether you will employ a man from the Sculptors here, Farmer & Brindley, for the purpose when you are quite ready. I think it most probable that there may be a man of *that Firm in America* through the Summer or Autumn months carrying out work there for F. & B. who do quite a large business in the States. . . .

Now as to Mr Bryce, he has written me at length regretting the fact that your invitation only came after he accepted a function elsewhere. He writes "It would have given me the livliest pleasure to present your Sun-Dial to Princeton, but unluckily before they invited me to go to their Commencement there and receive an honorary degree I had promised to go to another far distant University on the same day. I must look to visit it some other time." Now, should you postpone the unveiling to Commemoration day I respectfully suggest that you should tell Mr Bryce *at once*, for I am sure he would much enjoy the function & also please you all with a good address &c. I hope this will work out right.

You will have time before "Commemoration" anyhow to make everything quite perfect & I would rather the unveiling were deferred than that Mr Bryce should be absent. He knows the old Dial well, for it stands in the quad of Corpus Christi within a stone-throw of Bryce's old rooms at Oriel.

I was at Oxford last Saturday to make sure of the last touch being right. President Case of the College showed me a very interesting old book 300 yrs old beautifully printed in *manuscript* describing the Dial &. I shall have it photographed & bound to send copies to you for distribution at the unveiling.

I think you might erect the Dial with the aid of a good local working sculptor to directions which Farmer & Brindley could send, if it should happen that no man of the firm is in the States when you are ready.

I hope you are now quite well & also Mrs. Wilson & your daughters. My wife and girls join in affectionate regards to you all. It is a pity we cannot come out this year but we are always looking out for the opportunity in the near future.

Very Sincerely Yours W. Mather

ALS (WWP, UA, NjP).

From Anson Phelps Stokes, Jr.

My dear President Wilson, [New Haven, Conn.] May 1, 1907.

I beg to acknowledge receipt of your kind letter of April 30th, with list of Princeton's preachers enclosed. There are seven men on the list who have never been to Yale, and I should highly appreciate it if you could find time to send me a word or two with reference to their capacity to interest young men; Professor Paul van Dyke, Father Huntington, Mr. Butler, Dr. Notman, Dr. Jones, Dr. McEwan, and Bishop Talbot. May I ask whether Father Huntington conducts the service in academic robe? I know, of course, of his power as a preacher. He used to be a favorite at St. Paul's School when I was there.

As to our Yale preachers, I am sending you a list of those for this year as they appear in the University catalogue. I am glad to add a word or two about some of the men whom we have found especially helpful.

Dean Hodges,[1] of Cambridge, is always helpful. He has no great power but has a capacity to put spiritual truth in a simple, straightforward way.

President Rhees,[2] of Rochester, was a most acceptable preacher this year.

Dr. Lyman Abbott always interests our men.

Rev. George A. Gordon, of Boston,[3] combines clearcut thought with great earnestness, more than almost anyone that I know of in this country.

Mr. John R. Mott and Mr. Robert E. Speer are among the preachers whom the students most like. Mott is very vigorous and strong; Speer you must know all about, as he is a Princeton graduate. He is not as broad as most of our preachers, and he is a little bit too personal in his remarks about morality and sin to suit some but he is undoubtedly one of our most helpful preachers.

Bishop McDowell[4] is the strongest Methodist that we have been able to find after much effort. He is most acceptable.

President [Henry Churchill] King of Oberlin is a fairly strong preacher.

Professor Palmer, of Harvard University,[5] is a most interesting and finished preacher, a little beyond the Freshmen and Sophomores but very helpful to the older men.

Rev. Mr. Dawson, of Taunton, Mass.,[6] has a rather unattractive personality but he is considered by most of the students an unusually strong preacher; although somewhat of an evangelist by occupation, his appeal is to the mind and will entirely, not to the feelings.

Three younger men who are good are Rev. Mr. Potter, of Hartford,[7] Rev. Mr. Sanderson, of Hartford,[8] and Rev. Mr. Tweedy of Bridgeport.[9] The last named is perhaps somewhat too brilliant, but they are all earnest and helpful.

If I can be of any further service to you in this matter, please do not hesitate to let me know.

Sincerely yours, Anson Phelps Stokes Jr

TLS (Stokes Letterbooks, Archives, CtY).

1 The Rev. Dr. George Hodges, Dean of the Episcopal Theological School, Cambridge, Mass.

2 The Rev. Dr. Benjamin Rush Rhees, President of the University of Rochester.

[3] The Rev. Dr. George Angier Gordon, pastor of the Old South Church, Boston.

[4] The Rev. Dr. William Fraser McDowell, Bishop of the Methodist Episcopal Church, resident in Chicago.

[5] George Herbert Palmer, Alford Professor of Natural Religion, Moral Philosophy, and Civil Polity at Harvard University.

[6] The Rev. Dr. William James Dawson, English-born evangelical minister and author, who had migrated to the United States in 1905 and was at this time living in Taunton, Mass.

[7] The Rev. Rockwell Harmon Potter, pastor of the First Church of Christ, Hartford.

[8] There was no minister named Sanderson located in Hartford at this time. Perhaps Stokes was thinking of Edward Frederick Sanderson, who had been graduated from Hartford Theological Seminary in 1899 and was at this time pastor of the Central Congregational Church of Providence, R. I.

[9] The Rev. Henry Hallam Tweedy, pastor of the South Congregational Church, Bridgeport, Conn.

To Anson Phelps Stokes, Jr.

My dear Mr. Stokes: Princeton, N. J. May 3rd, 1907.

I am sincerely obliged to you for your letter of May 1st. It will be most helpful to me in enlarging our list of preachers.

I am very glad indeed to tell you briefly what I think of the men about whom you ask.

Professor Paul van Dyke has not the literary art of his brother, Dr. Henry van Dyke, nor has he the same finished delivery, but he preaches with the greatest earnestness and fills his sermons with matter of the greatest pertinence and interest, so that he always holds the attention of the men and is accounted one of our most acceptable preachers.

Father Huntington does not preach in academic costume, but in his own dress. His chief characteristic is simplicity. He is always warm with fine feeling, and seems to get at the men through his effect upon their imaginations as much as through his simple and earnest counsel. He is most acceptable to our undergraduates.

Mr. Butler is one of our own graduates. His preaching is irregular in merit, but never falls below a high level and sometimes is exceptionally spirited and interesting. He writes his sermons, and they bear evidence of great thoughtfulness and of not a little insight, besides being couched in excellent form.

Dr. Notman comes from the other side of the water. He is in no sense a master of the phrase. The details of his sermons do not satisfy one, but somehow in the bulk each sermon of his seems to lift you to a fine and impressive view, and I consider him an important element in our variety.

Dr. Jones is, from the point of view of form and thought, the finest sermonizer in the country, judged by my own taste. His delivery is not good, and unless the acoustic properties of your chapel are excellent, there would be some danger of his not being heard by a portion of the congregation.

Dr. McEwan is a great big-natured, wholesome man, who speaks the truth without art and yet with the force of a very interesting personality.

Bishop Talbot is the original of Mr. Owen Wister's Western Bishop,[1] and has the physical size and geniality and simplicity which make him tell in the mass, though his preaching has no particular intellectual quality.

Hoping that I have said enough to give you light on these men, and trusting that you will call on me for further information whenever you choose,

Always cordially and sincerely yours,

Woodrow Wilson

TLS (A. P. Stokes, Jr., Papers, Archives, CtY).

[1] About Bishop Talbot and Owen Wister, see EAW to WW, May 4, 1903, n. 3, Vol. 14.

From Edward Capps

My dear Mr. Wilson: Chicago, May 3, 1907.

I gratefully acknowledge the action of the Finance Committee of your Board of Trustees in expressing willingness to guarantee a subsidy of $1000 to Classical Philology if such an arrangement should prove satisfactory to the Classical Department of the University of Chicago. The situation here is slowly defining itself, and in the course of the summer I feel sure that some arrangement may be made which will prove satisfactory to all. It will take some time to get Professor Hale's opinion, since he is now in Rome.

I fear that in my last letter to you I did not take into consideration fully your convenience and desire regarding the proposal of my name to your Trustees. I meant to leave you perfectly free to act in the matter whenever it seemed best to you. It is understood here that I am going to leave.

Assuring you of my deep appreciation of the cordial welcome which you extend to me, and with the hope that I shall be able to render to Princeton the service which you expect of me, I am,

Cordially yours, Edward Capps

TLS (WP, DLC).

To Hopson Owen Murfee

My dear Mr. Murfee: Princeton, N. J., May 4th, 1907.

I am almost ashamed to send you the enclosed, because I promised it to you so very long ago, for the book of which you spoke.[1] I dare say that you have long ago despaired of receiving it and have long ago made up the book without it.[2] I am only giving my conscience a belated satisfaction in sending it to you and asking you to do what you please with it.

There are all sorts of excuses, of illness, of the distractions of business, of absorption in difficult tasks, which I might plead, but they would be mere excuses. I could, if I had been watchful of the opportunity, have written this long ago, but alternately forgot and neglected it. I can only ask you generously to forgive me.

Always cordially and sincerely yours,

Woodrow Wilson

TCL (RSB Coll., DLC).

[1] See H. O. Murfee to WW, Jan. 12 and 18 and March 12 and 18, 1906, all in Vol. 16.

[2] In fact, Murfee never succeeded in completing the book.

An Essay

[c. May 4, 1907]

EDUCATION AND DEMOCRACY

The reasons why the mass of people should be provided with education in a republic, whose successful maintenance depends upon the intelligence of its ordinary citizens, are patent enough and have often been pointed out with great force and eloquence. But the arguments for popular education under our forms of government have generally been arguments for elementary education, the only education that can reasonably or successfully be extended to the masses of the people, not arguments for that sort of education which carries the pupil forward to more definite training and the more advanced stage of intellectual development. And yet the arguments for secondary schools and for colleges, as a means of supporting and fertilizing democracy, are as interesting and conclusive as those which we have time out of mind accepted with regard to elementary education and the common schools.

The fact that state universities, sustained by general taxation, have been established and maintained upon a liberal scale in almost every state of the Union, except those which already possessed some ancient private foundation which made the creation of such a university at the public expense unnecessary, is evidence enough that opinion everywhere recognizes the need for higher education as a public need, and that tax payers are willing to pay for it, though fully aware that only a small minority can avail themselves of it. But the use made of state universities makes it at least questionable whether they are really maintained in the interest of higher education. They are strictly, some of them even narrowly, utilitarian in their objects and their standard of utility is economic, not intellectual or spiritual. They are chiefly intended to give young men and young women a training for the professions: for law, for medicine, for teaching, for agricultural work, for engineering, for handicrafts, and for the technical processes of manufacture. The greater part of their funds is used to provide instruction in technical branches,—in the several kinds of engineering and in scientific farming. Even their more general, less technical, instruction in the sciences is thought of rather as a foundation for the practical applications of science in manufactures and in the practical arts, than as a discipline whose object is intellectual and spiritual development. They are not much resorted to by those who seek study for its own effects, without immediate regard to money-making callings.

It is education of a different kind and pursued with other objects that I should like to see set in its true relation to democracy. The case for the university is the same as the case for the preparatory school, as I see it. After the common school, what do you want? I do not mean what does the individual want, but what does the community want that understands its own true interests? I grant the answer cannot be got without some ultimate standard of utility. But there are many standards of utility, and some are far higher than others and less superficial, going to the very heart of things that deeply concern us. We are in danger of impoverishing our national life by having but one standard of utility, namely the standard of practical efficiency. Our life is full of difficult practical tasks; they multiply with the years; each man's livelihood seems more and more to depend upon an expert mastery of them; and we have been slowly shaping all our education to the single end of producing skillful workers and efficient industry.

Undoubtedly a great part of our education must be devoted to that purpose. For the majority of men education must be very practical in its objects; and the objects sought must be immediate —the objects which directly connect themselves with self-support, that self-support which is in our day easy only for the man who has a trained eye and hand, a ready knowledge of the methods and material of his work. But the inevitable result of such training is complete immersion in particular tasks and interests. The man or woman whose mind is consciously centered upon a practical calling throughout school and college days is sure to be immersed in thought and sympathy in that undertaking and to look at all the rest of the world from the point of view of a particular occupation. The country is impoverished if all these youths must take, and be narrowed by, such schooling. That is undoubtedly the way to get efficiency, but it is not the way to get enlightenment, and the nation needs light as well as force.

Indeed, enlightenment is the ideal end of education, and no nation can long resist the debasement of mere materialism, which does not produce thousands of men who seek enlightenment and scores of institutions whose aim and ideal it is to supply it. A great many men must have broad views and a comprehensive grasp upon life, if a great policy is to be kept free and liberal, and without taint.

Undoubtedly what is called practical education is needed for the maintenance and development of the modern nation, and multitudes of schools of applied science must supply it, supply it in its best and most serviceable form; but the modern nation perhaps more than any other, and the free nation most of all, with its tasks of impartial legislation, and its nice adjustment between public power and private privilege, needs for its political maintenance and development schools of liberal learning, whose function shall be, not economic efficiency, but intellectual liberalization. Two kinds of education we must have. Of the majority of youths we must make skilled mechanics,—mechanics of the hand and mechanics of the brain: masters of some particular skill or technical occupation. To the minority, to as many as can afford it, we must give the equipment of those who are more than mechanics, and who are free for the larger uses of society. These two kinds of education are not sharply distinguished, as if separated by any chasm of contrast; in their foundations, on the contrary, they overlap. But their objects and their ideals are different.

Both sorts of education must be grounded in the same fundamentals, that is, in the great primary truths of science and of the human mind, which are common to all right thinking and intelligent action, but the one is "technical," and the other "liberal." That is "technical" which confines its view to the practice of some particular art, profession or trade; that is "liberal" which looks abroad over the general field of human knowledge, thought or action, which frees the mind from the trammels of a particular body of knowledge and creates it a citizen of a larger world, in which bodies of knowledge can be seen in their general relation to men and to one another. A liberal training is in a sense more democratic than a technical, because it makes a mind free to go this way or that, to change its path and discriminate its opportunities. It is the statesmanship of intellectual equipment. Its object is not primarily knowledge, but the relation of the faculties, the introduction of the mind to a comprehensive understanding of the modern world.

What are the elements of the modern world, from an educational point of view? What is necessary for its comprehension? In the first place, it is a world of exact science applied; a world in which knowledge is exploited as never before, made use of to the utmost: knowledge of the processes of nature, of the geology of the globe, or the properties and uses of the soil, of the social and economic condition of men in every part of the world, of the quality of minerals, coals and woods, of their kind and the uses to which they can be put,—it is knowledge of every kind that can be brought into play to swell the wealth or facilitate the trade of each nation and of the world. Every kind of knowledge is eagerly sought, because every kind of knowledge can be made to yield some tangible profit.

By the same token, it is a world of extensive enterprise. No industry, no trade keeps to its old boundaries or proportions. The whole world is drawn into a common market, and commerce and manufacture have become forms of statesmanship by which the needs, the tastes, the prejudices, the economic and social possibilities of the whole globe must be studied and taken advantage of. Not only is nation set against nation in rivalry for political or economic advantage, but also merchant against merchant, manufacturer against manufacturer, farmer against farmer, miner against miner: the outlook and interest of every producer is international, and he must know the world in order to use it.

And yet this new world in which exact science is applied and knowledge used upon a vast scale has no new breed of men in it. The men who pile wealth upon knowledge, draw enterprise together in great corporate organizations, send their agents abroad to take possession of foreign markets, and weave an international network of gain and power, are not different from the men of other generations when enterprise was local, undertakings not corporate but individual, business a thing of neighborhoods and not of nations. They are men of the same passions, loves, cupidities; the same innocences to be deceived, the same shrewdness to observe their interest, very foolish and yet touched with nobility, very full of business and yet in love with ease. Their traits are to be seen written in all literature, set forth in all experience, in one much as in another. They are no products of the age in which they are so extravagantly magnifying themselves. The masquerade has changed, but not the man.

Above all, it is a world of vast combinations. Men no longer undertake their enterprises singly, or upon the capital of a few. They draw together in great combinations, corporations, trusts, unions, associations, for economy of organization and abundance of resources, striving to shut out as much as possible individual rivalries, and obtain the irresistible energy and efficiency of harmony and cooperation. Their voluntary combinations force government into the same field. If the individuals combine, government must seek to regulate not individuals but combinations; must lay itself alongside the complex structure of industry and multiply its functions, in order to adjust law to the change. Since trade ignores national boundaries and the manufacturer insists on having the world as a market, the flag of his nation must follow him, and the doors of the nations which are closed against him must be battered down. Concessions obtained by financiers must be safeguarded by ministers of state, even if the sovereignty of unwilling nations be outraged in the process. Colonies must be obtained or planted, in order that no useful corner of the world may be overlooked or left unused. Peace itself becomes a matter of conference and international combination. Cooperation is the law of all action in the modern world.

It is evident that technical and professional teaching, and the study of science in its specific applications, touch only the little interior pieces of such a world, and that its greater wholes are as important to be understood as its clear-cut segments. If you are to be bred in such a world and to handle its elements with abiding success beyond the limits of a single locality, you must know men as well as fact, and be able to look far afield. The applied science upon which manufactures and mining and engineering depend cannot stand still in a world so quick with energy and boundless ambitions, and the only foundations of its increase are the foundations of pure science, the studies of men bent upon knowing all there is to be known of nature, whether they can use it for their profit or not. You cannot use markets unless you can use men, and you cannot use men if you have kept yourself bound close to the learning of a single kind of skill and know nothing of them. Pure science, history, literature, philosophy, and the language in which men have to speak, these are the sources whence you shall know the world in which you live,—know it in its long measurement, in its past life as well as its present,—hear its voices of passion and perceive its visions of itself; and these are the sources by which liberal learning sits, inviting students to look there, in those springs, into the mirror of the world.

Nowhere is the task of coordination more imperative than in a democracy of free and various life, in a democracy where individual energy is so extraordinarily developed as it is with us, and where each man turns eagerly to a special task. And coordinations of thought are as important as coordinations of organization. Government is as important as industry,—not only the thing we formally call government, but also the government of right thinking, of clear thoughtful planning of minds trained to see things in wholes and combinations, divorced from special interests and released upon the general field of thought and observation. A great body of liberally trained men and women is the balance wheel of a free industrial nation.

If this be true, there is no part of the great field of education which a democracy can afford to leave uncultivated. The great law of vitality in a republic is the law of self-preparation: and so great and of such supreme importance in the field of government in the broad sense in which I have used the word—the field of guidance and coordination, of correct, comprehensive thinking—that it is of special significance whether many or only a few enter it. An equipped and efficient liberal training is the true gate of entrance to every kind of oversight and planning and management. Every captain of modern enterprise must have it, whether he gets it in the school of life, or more quickly when he is more teachable, in the classrooms of the University. The argument for liberal training is not an argument for scholars, but an argument for democratic variety and strength.[1]

TC MS (RSB Coll., DLC).

[1] There is an undated WWsh draft of this essay in WP, DLC.

From Anson Phelps Stokes, Jr.

My dear President Wilson, [New Haven, Conn.] May 4, 1907.

I am under real obligations to you for your important letter of May 3rd with reference to University preachers.

Faithfully yours, Anson Phelps Stokes Jr per B.

TLS (Stokes Letterbooks, Archives, CtY).

Ellen Axson Wilson to Anna Harris

My dear Anna Princeton May 5 1907

Your dear letter came yesterday and I should have written you immediately but for the fact that I was giving a dining and the hour was drawing very near. It is about the *afghan* that I am writing in such haste, dear! Alas! alas! it did not come! This is the first I have heard of it. If it is really lost I shall be simply broken-hearted! and Mr. Wilson too is *truly* distressed. To think of all that lovely work of your dear mother's,–*gone*! It is maddening. But in spite of all the time lost it may still be traced; they do not *sell* things that have miscarried at express offices for a year, I am told. I have made enquiries and learn that the tracing must be done from *your* end. It certainly did not reach this office,–so the officials say. Do tell your mother, dear, that I thank her with all my heart; it is indeed impossible for me to say how deeply we do appreciate it, how much we are *both* touched that she should do all that lovely work for us. And it would be (no! *will* be, for I am sure it will be found yet!) the greatest comfort to Mr. Wilson, –will supply him with a luxury that he has never in his life possessed.

Now I should *love* to follow this letter and make that spring visit with which you tempt me! But I haven't even time to *enumerate* the many duties that render it impossible! If I could write down all I have to do and to plan for and to superintend–to "carry through" in various directions between now & the 12th of June, I am sure you would be left gasping. For one item, "social functions,"–there are six formal dinners of from eighteen guests down to ten; a formal, course, luncheon to the 24 trustees, (there are four of those luncheons every year) the University preacher to be entertained from Sat. to Monday every week and men invited to meet him, guests in the house much of the time, casual visitors to Princeton,–foreign or domestic,–liable to come in to a meal at any time and two receptions, one to five hundred guests at commencement and one of 150 guests to the class of '97. That is, to my darling boys class-mates, who will be back this commencement for their tenth anniversary. Rather strenuous! isn't it? And this has been going on all the year, beginning with the annual Freshman reception,–500 guests,–and a large dance for Margaret; it is her first year "out." Fortunately I am never in the least excited or worried by any of it, but I must keep rather steadily at the helm.

Another interruption–so I must close in the greatest haste or lose a mail. Am glad to hear about Penn Harvey[1] & shall invite him promptly to dinner. Do write me *soon* again, dear. Do you realize that you did not tell me *anything* about *yourself* in that charming letter. You have my *deepest* sympathy in your dear Lizzie's long illness. I am *so* glad that you can report improvement. My love to her, your mother & all. Believe me, dear Anna, as ever Fondly yours, Ellen A. Wilson.

ALS (WC, NjP).

[1] A member of the junior class at Princeton from Pensacola, Fla., whose father, Henry Harvey, had apparently lived or worked in Rome, Ga., at one time.

To Andrew Fleming West

My dear Professor West: Princeton, N. J. May 6th, 1907.

I think it very important that we should confer at once about all matters affecting the Graduate School, and I hope that you will let me see you tomorrow morning at eleven o'clock.[1]

Will you not be kind enough at the same time to remind me of the necessity of setting a date for the meeting of the Committee on the Course of Study?

Always sincerely yours, Woodrow Wilson

TLS (UA, NjP).

[1] According to West's account, Wilson during this meeting said that it would embarrass him if West made a recommendation concerning the site of the proposed Graduate College at the meeting of the trustees' Committee on the Graduate School on May 31. West insisted that he was bound to make a recommendation, whereupon Wilson requested him to submit his report in writing to him for presentation to the committee. Andrew F. West, "A Narrative of the Graduate College of Princeton University . . ." (mimeographed copy in NjP), pp. 31-32. West's report is printed at May 13, 1907.

To Clarence Poe[1]

My dear Sir: Princeton, N. J. May 6th, 1907.

Allow me to apologize most sincerely for having kept you waiting so long for a reply to your kind letter of April 23rd.[2] I have delayed, not out of neglect, but in the hope that I might find it possible to accept the invitation for the night of October 18th, which your letter so cordially conveys. It would be particularly pleasant and gratifying to me if I could do so, but I find that the intervening months are to be so filled with duties of the most imperative kind, both professional and literary, that it would be simply folly for me to add another engagement to those I have already undertaken.

Pray express to the Executive Committee of the Association my very warm appreciation of the honor they have done me, and my most unaffected regret that it proves impossible for me to accept the invitation.

Very sincerely yours, Woodrow Wilson

TLS (in possession of Clarence Poe).

[1] Clarence Hamilton Poe, who soon dropped his middle name, editor and chief owner of the Raleigh, N. C., *Progressive Farmer*.

[2] Poe's letter, inviting Wilson to address the annual meeting of the North Carolina State Literary and Historical Association, is missing. Poe was at this time Secretary-Treasurer of the organization.

To Edward Capps

My dear Professor Capps: [Princeton, N. J.] May 7th, 1907.

I am sincerely obliged to you for your letter of May 3rd. I understood you to mean in your previous letters that I was at liberty to present your name to our Board, but I am glad to have this explicit permission.

I am very much pleased to know that you think that satisfactory arrangements with regard to "Classical Philology" can probably be made, and I hope that if there is anything you wish me to consider in the matter, you will feel free to write at any time to me or to Westcott.

Always cordially and faithfully yours,

[Woodrow Wilson]

CCL (WWP, UA, NjP).

Notes for an Address

Philadelphian Soc'y— 9 May, 1907

College Man in Public Life

Not a "*profession*" in the U. S.

Rather, *a universal duty* to take part in political action.

Involves time, attention, sacrifice of private convenience and interest.

Necessity for independent conviction and for Leadership.

Such conviction must be got from the long view

Chiefly by the college man and in college

A disturbed and doubting generation

Conservative classes less organic than the radical and in need of systematic suggestion

Insight—study—high ideals.

WWhw MS (WP, DLC).

A News Report of a Talk to the Philadelphian Society

[May 10, 1907]

MURRAY HALL MEETING ADDRESSED
BY PRESIDENT WILSON.

President Woodrow Wilson '79 delivered a very interesting and instructive address on "The College Man in Public Life" at the regular mid-week meeting of the Philadelphian Society in Murray Hall last evening.

President Wilson said that the trouble with the country at present lies in the fact that the majority of brainy men are leading private lives, whereas they should be putting themselves forward in the public affairs of the country. For never was there such a time when men with clean-cut, well-thought-out principles were needed to step forward and demand the leadership, not for their own selfish interests, but for the good of the world. Nor has any man a better chance to do this great good than the college man of to-day. For it is he who is given a deep insight into the real questions of the times and is enabled to see clearly what he owes to his Master when he is sent out into the world to do His work. For a college man must realize four things: first, that he owes his life to Christ; second, that he owes his life to the world; third, that he owes it to the world to understand its affairs, and fourth, that he owes it to the world to explain its affairs to others.

Printed in the *Daily Princetonian*, May 10, 1907.

To Sir William Mather

My dear Sir William: [Princeton, N. J.] May 13th, 1907.

Allow me to acknowledge with much appreciation your letter of April 30th. I am very much pleased that the parts of the dial are coming forward at once, and think that the arrangements you have made to have them shipped direct from the Thames to Philadelphia are in every way excellent. They will suit our convenience perfectly.

We have at last, with the advice of our Consulting Architect, fixed upon a site for the dial,[1] and shall begin preparing the foundations just so soon as the leveling of the ground of the site (which turned out to be necessary) can be completed.

We had ourselves thought very promptly of inviting Mr. Bryce to be present on our Commemoration Day, October 22nd, to unveil the dial, and I wrote to him some time ago making the suggestion, but have been again disappointed. He has made engagements for the autumn also, which barred his acceptance for that date. Unhappily, that is the only date besides Commencement on which under the laws of the college we can confer honorary degrees, and we should very much like, when we do get hold of Mr. Bryce, to confer a degree upon him. For the time being I am very much at sea, therefore, what to do. Perhaps by unanimous resolution of our Board we can make use of another date, and I will bring the matter up at the next meeting of the Trustees, in the hope that we may come at some satisfactory solution.

It is a genuine disappointment to all of us that we cannot have you. That would make the whole thing perfect.

Mrs. Wilson and my daughters join me in affectionate regards to Lady Mather, your daughters and yourself.

With warm regard,

Sincerely yours, [Woodrow Wilson]

CCL (WWP, UA, NjP).

[1] In the courtyard north of McCosh Hall. A photograph of the sun dial appears in the illustration section.

From Ralph Adams Cram

My dear Dr. Wilson, Boston, May 13, 1907.

I have been giving a good deal of study to the question of the arrangement of the Scientific Buildings and have worked out a new scheme which seems to me to promise the best of all. I enclose in this a rough tracing for your consideration.[1] I began by developing the other plan, the one we talked over in Princeton, and it worked out perfectly well, but the objection to it was that the group of buildings "sidled" down the hill, that is, the main axis of the ultimate group was parallel to the rather steep grades, instead of across them. I therefore worked out this second scheme, which, as you will see, provides for a big group of buildings with the main quadrangle opening directly to the south and so arranged that the whole thing can terrace down to the level of the future gardens. The effect of this would be, I think, far more beautiful than the other scheme, and you will notice that the new laboratories can be built at once in such a way that they will interfere even less with the Infirmary than would the other scheme, while the southerly view from the Infirmary is left entirely open.

I am to meet Hardenbergh[2] on Wednesday morning and talk with him about his plans and at that time I shall take on both schemes to show to him and see what he has to say, first, about the two general arrangements; second as to whether his plan can be reversed after the fashion we spoke of in Princeton.

While it is a small matter, perhaps, the new scheme for the arrangement of the laboratories would be much more effective architecturally for the long period that must elapse before these laboratories are extended, than would the other arrangement, which left matters rather at ragged ends, the two laboratories having somewhat the effect of floating in the air, whereas now they will occupy a fine architectural position, the Physical Laboratory tying in with 79 Dormitory, the Biological Laboratory closing the side of Washington Street, and the two quite shutting off all view of the objectionable Infirmary from the Street.

If there is any insuperable objection to this new plan, I should be very glad if you would telephone me at my office in New York Wednesday morning before 11 o'clock, at which hour I am to see Hardenbergh and go over the plans.

Very truly yours, R A Cram.

TLS (WP, DLC).

[1] The enclosure is a tissue tracing in which Palmer Physical Laboratory was placed near its present location, and the biological and geological building, later named Guyot Hall, ran along Washington Street in a southerly direction, with a small wing pointing westward.

[2] Henry Janeway Hardenbergh of New York, who was the architect for Palmer Physical Laboratory.

Andrew Fleming West to the Board of Trustees' Committee on the Graduate School

Gentlemen: PRINCETON UNIVERSITY May 13th., 1907.

By request of President Wilson I have put in his hands for presentation to your Committee my recommendations regarding the site of the Graduate College.[1]

I I beg to recommend that Merwick, the site of eleven acres now used for the Graduate House, be selected as the site of the Graduate College.

II In order to provide ample room for the complete development of the Graduate College, I also beg to recommend that an option be secured on the adjacent property [Stanworth] of Professor Sloane, which contains seventeen acres.

My reasons are as follows:

1. *This site is admirably suited to the purposes of the Graduate College.*

[1] Wilson read this report to the trustees' Committee on the Graduate School when it met on May 31, 1907.

It is a highly-developed beautiful place, with plenty of fine trees,—many of them planted fifty years ago. It is near the campus and yet sufficiently retired to ensure the residential separation of the graduate from the undergraduate students. Without this much separation—but no more—the proper life of the Graduate College cannot be successfully developed. The experience of the last two years has made this perfectly clear.

The site is now within eight minutes' walk of the campus. It can be brought within five minutes, and can also be brought more visibly into relation with the campus by opening an avenue of approach through the rear of the properties of Professor Henry van Dyke and Professor Libbey, thus reducing the walking distance to 1350 feet—a quarter of a mile. This is almost the same as the walking distance from Nassau Hall to the '79 Dormitory or from the University Library to University Hall. Along this avenue of approach there would be good places for professors' houses—one of several incidental advantages of choosing this site.

The site has been tested in a preliminary way for two years. If there is any disadvantage in it as a site for the Graduate College, the test of use has failed to reveal it. Both Professor Butler and myself, who have had the closest and most constant intimacy with the life of our students at Merwick can testify to this, and the attachment of the students to the site as being uniquely fitted for their graduate life is enthusiastic and unanimous.

The site has special advantages for attracting the donors on whom we must depend to complete the endowments and buildings of the Graduate College. If Thompson College, the first of these buildings, is placed there and is as fine architecturally as Merwick is scenically, such a sample of our intentions will help to complete our plans. I know no other obtainable site of which this is true in any such degree.

As an important incidental consideration I may mention that it is also well placed for handling the specially difficult problem of domestic service. The trouble in handling this question in our upper-class clubs is aggravated by the fact that the clubs are situated so close to the street. Our experience at Merwick has proved that the servants of the Graduate College cannot be well managed unless they live in residence and are kept a little apart from the town. Our present servants stay around the place. Being a little way from the town and finding plenty of room on the place, they have become attached to it. They do not roam the streets or hang around the saloons. We know the difficulties our upperclass clubs have in these matters—the servants handing out provisions to their friends outside and doing other undesirable things. That this does not happen at Merwick is one reason why the food bills are moderate and the servants respectable.

2. *The site is suitable from the point of view of the general interests of the University.*

We are all agreed that the proposed Graduate College is not only a most valuable thing in itself, but is also necessary to the University as a whole, as the safeguard and consummation of the system of education for which Princeton stands. In regard to the harmonious relation of this important part to the University as a whole, there are three factors which need to be considered. They are the administrative, the scholastic and the residential.

On the administrative side the control of the President and Trustees is legally and morally complete. It is also operatively complete, provided the Graduate College is not placed beyond easy administrative reach or in surroundings where it will tend to develop in the direction of separation. No such danger can arise from selecting for the Graduate College a site as close and convenient to the campus as Merwick is.

On the scholastic side there can be no separateness, because the graduate students have and are to have their classes and exercises in the class-rooms, seminaries, libraries, laboratories and observatories on the central campus where the undergraduate exercises are held. This fact remains fixed, no matter where in Princeton the graduate students have their rooms, meals and social life. If the University desired to have it otherwise, the cost of making special provision for this purpose would be prohibitory.

On the residential side there is one and only one disadvantage in selecting Merwick. It is not so situated that the buildings will be in close, inevitable daily sight of the mass of undergraduates. I wish there were some suitable and obtainable site where the Graduate College could be placed without serious peril to its life and where it would also be persistently visible to all our undergraduates every day. But to get the good result we desire in this way, we must actually have a real Graduate College, exhibiting its own true life as well as its site and buildings, if the effect we desire the undergraduates to experience is to be produced. To sacrifice or risk the true life of the Graduate College is too great a price to pay for the sake of making its site and buildings constantly visible to the eyes of our undergraduates,—desirable as that is for their sakes.

To place the Graduate College on the central campus, or immediately next to it, close to the clubs and surrounded by the general rush of the athletic, social, sight-seeing and miscellaneous undergraduate diversions is, in my judgment, to make the task of developing the true life of the Graduate College almost if not quite impossible. And this is particularly true when we have so few genuinely graduate students of the type we desire to form the nucleus of our Graduate College—amid our twelve hundred undergraduates. It might be different, if we already possessed a strongly developed Graduate College, with a formed tradition behind it. Even then there would be a risk, and yet a risk that might be taken. But such a risk is too great to be taken in *starting* the Graduate College.

If the College is placed at Merwick, although it will not be visible except as persons walk somewhere near it, it will not be hidden. I do not want it placed where undergraduates cannot conveniently see or cannot conveniently get at it, but just enough aside to save it. And much can be done to help its visibility. A great tower can be placed at the head of the avenue of approach. There would be plenty of glimpses of the buildings amid the lawns and trees, both from the avenue of approach and along Bayard Lane. Wherever the College is placed in Princeton, it is sure to be one of the sights of Princeton and a favorite place for undergraduates to show their friends. Then, too, undergraduates can be invited from time to time, as a sort of privilege, to come and dine—as is done now in a limited way at Merwick with good results. Much more of this can be done as the College grows.

3. *No other available site is free from great disadvantages.* The only other site which is suggested is the so-called Olden Tract. This is bounded by Washington Road, Prospect Avenue, Charlton Street and William Street. It is composed of several properties and includes in all 9-½ acres. The particular field in it belonging to Mrs. Olden[2] has 3-½ acres. It is a fine piece of land, prominently situated and immediately adjacent to the campus. If the Graduate College is placed there it will be constantly visible to the undergraduates as they pass it on their way to and from the Clubs and the games.

But, whatever the advantages, the objections to the Olden Tract seem to me very serious:

a. The whole area is 9-½ acres, as against 11 at Merwick, with 17 more added if Professor Sloane's place is acquired,—thus making 28 acres in all. If the Olden Tract is secured entire, the Graduate College is limited to 9-½ acres for the indefinite

[2] This land seems to have been held in the name of Miss Susan W. Olden of 44 Washington St.

future. It will be impossible to get more, except at great expense, because the tract is practically surrounded on all sides by four streets lined with buildings, which would have to be bought at high prices and then removed or destroyed.

b. It is not certain that the whole tract can be acquired. If it can be, it must be done piecemeal at great expense, and with many delays. The University now owns the part where Professors Brackett and Lovett live,[3] and I suppose can get soon two of the small lots on William Street. Mrs. Chamberlain's[4] property could no doubt be purchased—but probably not for some time. But this is all. The eight other pieces, held by five owners, comprise the greater part of the tract. There is some reason to believe that one of them will not sell. If they all sell, the expense involved will be not only the cost of the land and existing buildings, but the destruction or removal of all the buildings, moving out two professors, making a new Working Observatory, and generally improving the property. To do this would entail much delay and will cost more than Merwick and Professor Sloane's place combined.

In the meantime, if Thompson College is erected on such parts of the Olden Tract as the University has and can get soon, we shall not even then be in position to show more than a partially acquired site to any persons whom we hope to induce to furnish the large sums needed to complete the endowments and buildings. The general effect would not be that of a great plan, revealed in part by the extent, completeness and highly developed character of a site already acquired and ready to be put to use, but of arrested and fragmentary development.

4. *It is important that, if at all possible, the choice of a site should be made now.*

The tendency of Princeton real estate has been upward for at least ten years. Good sites are getting fewer and more expensive. The prompt possession of a proper site will not only enable the University to locate Thompson College, but to adopt a plan for all the buildings of the Graduate College. Possession of such a site and plan of buildings will materially help in securing the endowments and buildings needed. It seems to me that the long time we have had to delay is over, and that the right time for action has come.

Respectfully submitted, Andrew F. West

TLS (WWP, UA, NjP).

[3] At 4 Prospect Ave. and 16 Prospect Ave., respectively.

[4] Mary Hale (Mrs. William M.) Chamberlain, who lived at 26 Prospect Ave.

To Ralph Adams Cram

My dear Mr. Cram: [Princeton, N. J.] May 15, 1907.

Thank you for your letter of May 13th, with the enclosed sketch of a scheme for the new laboratories. The arrangement strikes me most favorably and as a decided improvement on what you first thought of, for the reasons you yourself indicate.

I am afraid that the upper Northeast corner of the physical laboratory invades Prospect Garden, which is (legally) pre-empted ground, but I dare say a little adjustment would avoid that.

I have only this to suggest about the biological laboratory. It is to be devoted to both biology and geology, but the biological men imperatively need a North light for their work. I dare say that could be secured by putting their rooms in the wing of the building which you have indicated as running off about West by South from the long piece of the laboratory lying upon Washington Road, but this would be a matter which would require discussion with Parrish and Schroeder, the architects of the building.[1]

It is very delightful to see order coming out of, not chaos, but doubt.

Always cordially and sincerely yours,

[Woodrow Wilson]

CCL (WWP, UA, NjP).

[1] See C. H. Dodge to WW, Dec. 19, 1906, n. 4, Vol. 16.

From David Benton Jones

My Dear Doctor: Chicago May 15th, 1907.

I tried to see you before leaving Princeton, as I had a very interesting talk with Dean Fine and a shorter one with Professor Hibben regarding the club situation.

I found the Dean, if anything, more impressed than you are that some radical solution will have to be found of existing conditions. He has all the zeal of a late convert. Mr. Hibben has travelled far enough to recognize the situation as a difficulty of the first order. You therefore have two very substantial supporters in the Faculty and, from my talks with them, I do not believe you need hesitate to confer with them freely. Of the Dean, I am certain.

The fact is, that for some time a considerable portion of the under graduate body has looked upon Princeton University as simply an academic and an artistic background for the club life that is now such a prominent feature of the place. If this situation is not remedied, the clubs will exercise a dominating influence over university life. Should this come about and become publicly known, it will, of course, end all hope of any considerable financial support coming to Princeton, as no one will care to merely fill in the background for club life as it now exists. The clubs will therefore strangle the university unless some radical modification is devised and applied.

If you were able to say to the Committee when it meets in early June that the Dean and Mr. Hibben were in full accord with you as to the absolute necessity of finding an early remedy for the present situation, you would, I think, find the Committee much more disposed to regard the situation as not only very serious, but very urgent. If the Board can be fully informed as to the evils of the present condition of things, they will, I think with great unanimity insist that some remedy must be found and that without much delay, even though the remedy may seem very radical or even revolutionary.

Very sincerely yours, David B. Jones

Please do not regard this as calling for any reply whatever. I am only anxious that you should be able to bring a "body of opinion" to bear on the Committee. Some members simply don't know & some are Club men first and University men second.

TLS (WP, DLC).

From Martin Jerome Keogh

My dear President Wilson: New Rochelle, May 16th 1907.

I am sure you have seen in the New York papers as well as in the papers throughout the country the wonderful success of our People's Forum.

We all remember with infinite pleasure and gratitude how splendidly you contributed to its success by your great address two Winter's ago.[1]

It will be some pleasure and I hope some reward to you to know that the most unanimous and insistent demand is made upon us by men of all kinds of opinion and station in life, to invite you to again address the Forum next Winter.

After your last address, for months and months, your opinions and arguments were discussed at the working men's clubs and in the press editorials and by letter, and your timely address in my judgment did a vast amount of good.

Will you delight us all again by consenting to address the Forum some Sunday afternoon next Winter, between December 1st and March, that may be convenient to you, on any living subject of the day that you may choose?

I promise you a reception that will do you good, and in some degree at least reward you for the sacrifice you make.

Of course next Autumn we can arrange the date definitely. All I wish to know now is that you will promise to come, and approximately the month when you can do so.[2]

With kindest regards, I remain,

Very faithfully yours, Martin J. Keogh

TLS (WP, DLC).

[1] A news report of this address is printed at Feb. 27, 1905, Vol. 16.

[2] Wilson was unable to accept this invitation.

To James Burrill Angell

[Princeton, N. J.]

My dear Professor Angell: May 17, 1907.

A great rush of engagements as the college year draws to a close has prevented my reading and answering your letter of May 2nd.[1] I beg that you will pardon the delay.

I have read your letters to President Pritchett and his replies with great attention and interest. I think that the question with regard to the admission of State universities to the benefits of the Carnegie Foundation is practically a closed question, because of action taken at their last meeting by the Trustees of the Foundation; and while I admit that there are two big sides to the matter, I cannot help believing that the action of the trustees was wise. I fear that if we were to act upon your suggestion and extend the benefits of the Foundation to the State universities for a definite number of years, with the statement that at the close of that period the states would be expected to establish their own pension systems, the device would be wholly ineffectual because the withdrawal of the benefits would not be taken seriously until it came, and then all sorts of pressure would be brought to bear for its continuance. It would only postpone the inevitable day when the states must take care of the professors in their own universities. They will not do so until it is seen that those professors are at a distinct disadvantage as compared with the men in privately endowed institutions, and it does not seem to me possible for any private foundation to provide for all the universities of the country.

I say this, of course, without meaning to put the action entirely on the ground I have been arguing. Dr. Pritchett has stated the grounds upon which the Board acted, with entire accuracy, and I think has stated them very well.

The question has perplexed and distressed us, but we sincerely believe that we have acted in the interest of the whole country in taking the position we have taken, and I have reason to believe that Mr. Carnegie is gratified by the decision.

We often think of you here with the greatest pleasure and interest, and as often regret that you did not see your way clear to come to Princeton.[2]

Mrs. Wilson joins me in warm regards to Mrs. Angell and yourself. Sincerely yours, [Woodrow Wilson]

CCL (WWP, UA, NjP).

[1] It is missing.

[2] A mysterious reference.

Two Letters from Ralph Adams Cram

My dear Dr. Wilson: Boston, May 17, 1907.

On returning from New York, I find your letter of May 13, in which you sanction the general principles of the last scheme for arranging the Scientific Buildings. I am very glad this scheme appeals to you, as it seems to me far better than the original plan.

Yesterday in New York, I had a most satisfactory interview with Mr. Hardenbergh and Messrs. Parrish and Schroeder. I anticipate no difficulty whatever, so far as our personal and professional relations are concerned. I took on large scale plans showing the general arrangement of this scheme and found, to my gratification, that the plans Mr. Hardenbergh had under way, and the ideas of Messrs. Parrish & Schoeoder, adapted themselves perfectly to this layout. The only radical change is involved in the reversal of Mr. Hardenbergh's scheme. He heartily approves the idea of this reversal and neither he nor I could see any reason, so far as we could judge, which would lead the Professors most directly interested to object to this change.

One considerable difference between the plan I had worked out and those now being studied by the architects lies in the fact that the authorities have considered necessary much wider buildings than I had judged would be necessary, working wholly on the basis of the sketch plans I received from yourself. Instead of the units of the several buildings and the group of buildings being 36 ft. wide, they must range from 58 ft. to 65 ft., in other words, the plans desired by the Professors involve rooms on both sides of a central corridor, instead of rooms on one side with a corridor lighted along the other, as I had hoped might be the case. This change does not militate against the carrying out of this scheme of the Scientific group, but it makes necessary a complete readjustment of the masses, and I am now engaged on this and will send you the results in the shape of block plans at the earliest possible moment. These block plans I shall send also to Mr. Hardenbergh and Messrs. Parrish and Schroeder for their consideration.

In the case of the Biological Building, I found that the special thing required which governed the dimensions of the building was one great museum from 55 Ft. to 60 ft. wide over all and 350 ft. long. This can be provided for perfectly well, in fact it is somewhat extraordinary that the scheme I had worked out should be so completely on the lines of the desires of the Professors and the sketch plans already prepared by the architects.

I told both the firms that I had recommended brick instead of stone for the walls of the building and in both cases this idea seemed to appeal to them very strongly.

May I suggest that you direct Mr. Bunn to send both firms of architects photographs of Blair and Little Halls. I think these will prove of extreme use to them as indicating the general type of architecture you have in view. It would also, I am sure, be a great convenience to them if they could have the large scale topographical surveys of this portion of the ground. Sheet 8, would, I think, be all they need.

Within a few days, I shall hope to be able to send you block plans of this Scientific group, together with a general plan, thoroughly revised, of the scheme for the entire group of buildings at a scale of 100 ft. to the inch.

Very truly yours, R A Cram.

My Dear Dr. Wilson: Boston. May 18, 1907.

I am sending you today, the very rough tracing showing how the Scientific buildings will block out, now that I have obtained dimensions, etc. from the architects.[1] As I wrote you yesterday, Hardenbergh's plan is worked out in considerable detail and I have shown it exactly as it stands, on this sketch plan, only reversing it. The width and length of the Biology building is also fixed, apparently. It seems to me that your suggestion that the Geology Department occupy the wing of the second building is admirable, and you can obtain special entrances from the court. I shall send you a larger scale working out, of this group, within a few days.

Yours very truly, R A Cram.

TLS (WP, DLC).

[1] This tracing is missing.

To Moses Taylor Pyne

My dear Momo: [Princeton, N. J.] 20 May, 1907.

I return the enclosed papers. I think there are so many things to be considered with regard to filling the vacancy in the Board[1] that the more slowly we move the less we are likely to have to regret.

I think that in view of the promises we made to Professor Richardson when he came to Princeton, we really have no honorable choice but to assume as much of the necessary expense for his apparatus as possible. $4000 was the sum which he was originally told he could spend.

I wish I might have an early opportunity to tell you how extraordinary a find Richardson has proved to be. I think that taken all in all he is quite the most valuable acquisition we have made, and everything makes me hope that he may be made to feel comfortable and unhampered here.

As for the additional mechanic, I have known for some time that that was necessary, but was hoping to postpone the thing until the new physical laboratory was built. Part of the calculations for maintaining it already include two skilled mechanics, so that the expense, which I dare say is absolutely necessary, for an additional mechanic in our present shop would be only temporary and would come to an end when the laboratory was finished.

It is distressing how expenses accumulate, but these are certainly among the most legitimate and necessary.

Always faithfully and affectionately yours,

[Woodrow Wilson]

CCL (WWP, UA, NjP).

[1] The vacancy was created by the death of the Rev. Samuel Bayard Dod, Princeton 1857, who died in South Orange, N. J., on April 19, 1907. He had been a Life Trustee since 1882.

To Ralph Adams Cram

My dear Mr. Cram: [Princeton, N. J.] May 20th, 1907.

Allow me to acknowledge with appreciation your letters of May 17th and May 18th. I am very much gratified to know that you have established such satisfactory relationships with Mr. Hardenbergh and Messrs. Parrish and Schroeder. I think the reconsidered sketch for the combined masses of the two laboratories and their probable extensions most excellent and satisfactory. I suppose it was just a mistake of the draftsman to mark the portion of the projected natural history museum and laboratory which runs approximately North and South, Biology, and the one which runs approximately East and West, Geology. It should of course be the other way.

I am asking the Curator of Grounds and Buildings to send both firms of architects working on these plans the photographs and surveys you suggest, and hope that he will have them in their hands in a few days.

It is delightful to have matters moving so definitely and so satisfactorily. The Committee on Grounds and Buildings of our Board is to meet on Saturday next, and I will of course immediately lay your suggestions before them.

Always cordially and sincerely yours,

[Woodrow Wilson]

CCL (WWP, UA, NjP).

To Robert Price[1]

My dear Dr. Price: [Princeton, N. J.] May 21st, 1907.

Allow me to acknowledge the receipt of your letter of May 17th, and to say that nothing could gratify me more than to find that I could be in some degree of service to you. I shall take pleasure in representing your case to the Executive Committee of the Carnegie Foundation in the way in which I think you would wish it represented, and I shall be profoundly grateful if it should turn out that we can provide a retiring allowance for you upon some exceptional basis.

It was delightful to hear from you again, and to know of your continued health and welfare. Please accept my warmest assurances of regard.

Cordially and sincerely yours, [Woodrow Wilson]

CCL (WWP, UA, NjP).

1 The Rev. Dr. Robert Price, Professor of History and English Literature at Southwestern Presbyterian University, 1882-85, and Professor of General and Ecclesiastical History at the same institution, 1885-1912. He was an old friend and former colleague of Joseph Ruggles Wilson.

To Neander Montgomery Woods[1]

[Princeton, N. J.]

My dear Chancellor Woods: May 21st, 1907.

Allow me to acknowledge the receipt of your letter of May 17th. It will give me real pleasure to consult with my colleagues of the Executive Committee of the Carnegie Foundation with regard to a retiring allowance for Dr. Price. It would be extremely gratifying to me if I could be of service to Dr. Price, and you may be sure that I will represent his case as strongly as possible.

I feel quite sure that the committee will feel that the connection of the Southwestern Presbyterian University with the governing bodies of the church is too intimate to allow of the university's being put upon the accepted list of the Foundation, but this does not prevent us, if it should prove possible, from providing for Dr. Price upon an exceptional basis.

With much regard,

Sincerely yours, [Woodrow Wilson]

CCL (WWP, UA, NjP).

[1] The Rev. Dr. Neander Montgomery Woods, Chancellor of Southwestern Presbyterian University.

To Henry Smith Pritchett

[Princeton, N. J.]

My dear President Pritchett: May 21st, 1907.

Will you not be kind enough to let me file the enclosed letters with you, so that we may take them up with any other memoranda you may have, at the next meeting of our Executive Committee?

I know Dr. Price very well, and know him to be one of the noblest men among all the Southern teachers. It would be extremely gratifying to me if, after discussing the matter, we could feel ourselves justified in placing him upon our exceptional list. Certainly in length and character of service he is abundantly entitled to consideration.[1]

Always faithfully yours, [Woodrow Wilson]

CCL (WWP, UA, NjP).

[1] Dr. Price did not receive a Carnegie pension.

To Andrew Fleming West

My dear Professor West: Princeton, N. J. May 21st, 1907.

At the next meeting of the Association of Colleges and Preparatory Schools of the Middle States and Maryland, a committee is to report on the establishment of a college entrance examination board for its territory, and there is a general desire to have the question of entrance to college by certificate discussed at the same time.

The meeting of the association takes place in the fall, and I am writing to ask if you would be willing to present to the association a brief paper on "Admission to College by Certificate." I think if the arguments against the plan were stated cogently and briefly, we might bring the association to some definite declaration of opinion. The plan suggested would involve another paper in the affirmative, by some well-recognized schoolmaster.

I hope that you will be able to do this. I have the misfortune to be the President of the association for the current year.

Cordially and sincerely yours, Woodrow Wilson

TLS (UA, NjP).

From Moses Taylor Pyne

My dear Woodrow: New York, May 21st, 1907.

I have your letter regarding Richardson and will try and work the matter out in some way which will be satisfactory.

I also meant to speak to you the other day about Prof. McCay. He has been here a great many years without vacation, and, I think, is beginning to feel that he is getting a little rusty. If we could make some arrangement by which next year, or the year after, he could have a year in Germany, it might be advantageous to the University and to him, both. He has not spoken to me about the matter and does not know anything about it, but I simply bring it up to call your attention to it.[1]

Very sincerely yours, M. Taylor Pyne

TLS (WP, DLC).

[1] McCay did not receive a leave of absence during Wilson's presidency of Princeton.

To Andrew Fleming West

My dear Professor West: Princeton, N. J. May 23rd, 1907.

I am sincerely sorry that you are to be out of town on the evening of June 3rd, but I am afraid the Committee on the Course of Study had better be called notwithstanding. The matter for which it is to meet is after all largely a matter of routine.

I would be obliged if you would always include me in notices regarding meetings of the [faculty] Committee on the Graduate School. I received no notice of the last meeting. It so often happens that I have matters to submit to the committees, that it is very inconvenient when I do not receive notices and have an opportunity to attend.

Always faithfully yours, Woodrow Wilson

TLS (UA, NjP).

From Ralph Adams Cram

Sir: Boston, May 23, 1907.

I have the honour to submit herewith a scheme for the location of the proposed Physical and Biological Laboratories. As I wrote you personally, this scheme is a modification of the plan tentatively agreed upon at our last conference in Princeton. I think, however, it possesses several elements of superiority over this first plan, while it has the merit of meeting the wishes of the architect for the Physical Laboratory and of the architects for the Biological Laboratory. The original plan provided for a courtyard grouping, this court opening on Washington Street. A careful study of the contours served to show that such an arrangement was awkward, and to convince me that the ultimate group of Scientific Buildings should be ranged around a quadrangle which should drop down on the line of the grade and should open out toward the south. Such an arrangement will mean the least interference with the existing grades and will, I believe, give a more effective and practical arrangement.

Another great advantage which this plan possesses over the first is that it removes the buildings about to be erected as far as possible from the present Infirmary. It is understood, I believe, that this Infirmary can only be considered as a temporary building, but it is also admitted that it would be unwise at present to consider the question of removing this Infirmary and constructing another at great expense on some other site. The position I recommend for the Physical and Biological Laboratories is, therefore, just as far from the Infirmary at every point as the land will permit and there is no reason why this Infirmary should not remain as it is until it becomes necessary to extend the Scientific group or until funds are available for the construction of a more satisfactory type of building.

I have submitted this tentative plan, both to Mr. Hardenbergh and to Messrs. Parrish & Schroeder. Mr. Hardenberg has already worked out his floor plans in considerable detail and was able to give me exact dimensions. It so happens that his building adapts itself perfectly to the present plan, except that it will be necessary to reverse the general arrangement, placing the front to the north and near 79 Dormitory, rather than to the south near the Infirmary, as he had originally intended. I am not aware of any reasons which would stand in the way of this reversal of the plan and the result will be that the Physical Laboratory will front at once, as it should, on the open space between the President's house, McCosh Hall and 79 Dormitory, instead of fronting, as would otherwise have been the case, directly on the Infirmary. The dimensions of the Physical Laboratory as shown on the plans I send you are those determined upon by Mr. Hardenbergh as the best for the proposed building.

In the case of the Biological and Geological Building, Messrs. Parrish & Schroeder have prepared no sketch plans, as they had not been advised of the location of the building. I have ascertained from them, however, that a structure of the dimensions and shape I have shown will meet their requirements satisfactorily.

Another point in favour of this arrangement is, I think, that while ultimately a consistent group of buildings will be obtained, at present the two Scientific Buildings will be separated and therefore each architect will be at liberty to carry out his ideas more or less independently of the other.

I recommend that in the case of the Biological and Geological Laboratories, thoroughfares be provided at the levels shown. In one case a foot-path that passes from Washington Street at the existing grade of the Infirmary and continues to exit points from two different places in the main academic group; in the other case a driveway and foot-path, also running from Washington Street substantially on the lines of the present drive and entering the main academic group at a point near the present northerly end of Patton Hall.

The gardens, which I understand will be necessary in connection with the Biological and Geological building, will occupy the level meadows to the south. Portions of these may be considered as "show" gardens and would lie directly south of the main axis of the group of buildings, being entered from the circle at the foot of the court-yard steps. The working garden will be nearest Washington Street and quite hidden from the public portions of the University.

In accordance with your recommendation, I have shown the site of the future Mechanical Engineering Building as being that on the left of Washington Street opposite the northerly portion of the Biological and Geological building. This position seems to me admirable, both architecturally and from an administrative standpoint.

For many reasons, it seems to me that it would be very desirable to fix upon brick as the principal building material of these Scientific buildings, the trimmings being either or [of] limestone, white terra cotta or concrete stone. 79 Dormitory fixes a type at this point and in my opinion the effect is extremely beautiful. It seems to me that considerable variety in material and colour is desirable in the case of so large a group of buildings as this of Princeton, and by fixing on brick as the building material for the Scientific group, we shall obtain at this point a very effective piece of colour that will differentiate itself sufficiently from the more monumental work immediately surrounding the Campus.

I have sent blueprints of these drawings to both Mr. Hardenbergh and Messrs. Parrish & Schroeder, and should be very glad if the Trustees would advise them if the scheme meets with their approval or not. If it does, then it would be possible for both firms to proceed at once with the completion of the working drawings.

Very respectfully yours,

R A Cram, Supervising Architect.

TLS (WP, DLC).

To Ralph Adams Cram

My dear Mr. Cram: [Princeton, N. J.] May 24th, 1907.

Allow me to thank you most sincerely for your report of May 23rd, with regard to the location of the proposed physical and biological laboratories. Our Committee on Grounds and Buildings meets tomorrow, and I will lay your report before them with the confident expectation that they will approve it, as I do. It seems to me excellent, and I think will commend itself to everyone.

The plans to accompany your letter have not arrived this morning, but I take it for granted that they will reach me before tomorrow.

In haste, with warm regards,

Sincerely yours, [Woodrow Wilson]

CCL (WWP, UA, NjP).

To Robert Garrett

My dear Mr. Garrett: Princeton, N. J. May 27th, 1907.

The committee to consider the Supplementary Report of the President of the University will meet at Princeton, in the President's Office in '79 Hall, at 8.30 on Thursday evening, June 6th, and I sincerely hope that you will be able to be present. I shall have a definite action to suggest to the committee.

Faithfully yours, Woodrow Wilson

TLS (Selected Corr. of R. Garrett, NjP).

From John Hays Hammond[1]

Dear President Wilson, New York May 27. 1907.

I write to ask if you will kindly send me one of your photographs. I would like to see it hung in my study among the photographs of some of my other distinguished friends, such as Ex-President Cleveland, Count Witte, President Diaz, Secretary Olney, Secretary Taft, and the late Secretary Hay. I would be obliged if you would write on the photograph that you have presented it to me and sign your name.

We will be leaving shortly for our summer home at Gloucester, Mass., and it will be our pleasure to have Mrs. Wilson and yourself make us a visit there during the summer, if it fits in with your plans.

My wife joins me in sending you our regards, and hoping that we may see you before long. I am

Yours very truly, John Hays Hammond

ALS (WP, DLC).

[1] Professor of Mining Engineering at Yale University. He was also involved in various international mining ventures and employed as consultant to the Venture Corp. of London and the Guggenheim Exploration Co. of New York.

From Cleveland Hoadley Dodge

Dear Mr. President: New York. May 28, 1907.

I have yours of yesterday and hope I will be able to get down to Princeton for Thursday evening, the 6th.

Very sincerely yours, C H Dodge

TLS (WP, DLC).

From Andrew Fleming West

Dear Wilson: Princeton, N. J. May 28, 1907.

I should have answered your note of May 21st. sooner. I am willing to prepare a brief paper on the question of Admission to College by Certificate as you desire, and to present it to the meeting of the colleges of the Middle States and Maryland in the Autumn. I am of course opposed to any general plan of admission by certificate from schools and shall take that position. I do not, however, think the position should be taken so sweepingly as to exclude the possibility of exception when special cause can be shown for constituting such an exception. For instance, I believe it would be greatly to the benefit of Princeton University and of the Lawrenceville School, in view of the peculiarly intimate relations they hold to each other, to admit to our Freshman class without examination all Lawrenceville boys who have satisfactorily completed their school course giving full time to all the subjects we require for admission, and passing these subjects satisfactorily in the school. But I should not want to see exceptions made to our general rule requiring *college* examinations for entrance, save in a peculiar instance like Lawrenceville.

Ever yours, Andrew F. West

TLS (WP, DLC).

From Ralph Adams Cram

My dear Dr. Wilson: Boston, May 28, 1907.

I was much gratified at receiving your letter of May 24, in which you expressed your approval of the scheme for the two laboratories. I hope the large scale blueprint reached you in time for the meeting of the Committee on Grounds and Buildings on Saturday and that it may have received their approval also.[1] I shall be very anxious to hear as to their attitude in the matter and whether it will be possible for the two architects to go ahead on these lines. I have just heard from Hardenbergh that the scheme meets with his most enthusiastic approval.

Very sincerely yours, R A Cram.

TLS (WP, DLC).

1 The Editors have been unable to find this blueprint.

From John Howell Westcott, with Enclosure

Dear Woodrow: Princeton University May 29. 1907.

In the multiplicity of greater affairs I trust you will remember our conversation relative to Rankin's hardship in the matter of his room rent.[1] While we are speaking of Rankin, I wish to record my impression of the extraordinary success, judging by the examination, which he has had in teaching freshman Latin XIII, an unpromising B.S. division. I feel that this is an unmistakable evidence of his value as a teacher, and that he deserves a higher estimate than some have been disposed to accord him.

I report an anonymous gift of $1200, two years salary for a special fellowship in classics. I was directed to name the fellow, & to pay the money to him directly, in order that he might get the benefit of interest accruing from the first moment. I appointed Jones, (C. H.), our instructor, who will go to Halle & take his degree; & I paid the money over to him, & took his receipt. It only remains to report the matter to the Trustees, & to print Jones's name in the next catalogue as fellow, and not as instructor. We hope to have him return to us as preceptor. No one in the department has had a more striking success in his work than Jones, & we shall miss him sorely, while he is away.[2]

Yours faithfully, J. H. Westcott

Mr. Harmon[3] accepted by cable within a few hours. The list is now complete. The college owes me $2.80.

I have mislaid Prof. Abbott's[4] address, but I will ask Capps again for it.

ALS (WWP, UA, NjP).

1 Edwin Moore Rankin, Preceptor in Classics, who roomed at 43 Seventy-Nine Hall. For biographical information, see Wilson's Annual Report to the Board of Trustees printed at Dec. 14, 1905, Vol. 16.

2 Charles Hodge Jones, Princeton 1900, at this time Instructor in Classics. He left Princeton at the end of the academic year 1906-1907 and pursued graduate study at the University of Halle. He returned to Princeton in 1909 as Preceptor in Classics.

3 Austin Morris Harmon. For biographical information, see Wilson's Annual Report to the Board of Trustees printed at Dec. 13, 1907.

4 Frank Frost Abbott, Professor of Latin at the University of Chicago and known for his work on Cicero, Tacitus, and Roman political institutions. He became Professor of Classics at Princeton in 1908.

ENCLOSURE

A Memorandum

[May 29, 1907]

Confidential.

[Andrew Runni] Anderson—excellent scholar, will probably make his mark. General sentiment of professors rather unfavorable to his remaining for a second term. Seems to lack tact, is rather obstinate & inflexible, can't size up a personal situation. Is probably not popular with pupils[1]

[John William] Basore—Very quiet, hard to "get a line" on him—modest & scholarly, refined & courteous. Everybody likes him. Probably a little lacking in force. Some call him "Grandfather."[2]

[Donald] Cameron—Somewhat uncouth—not much liked by pupils—is a slow worker. But colleagues probably like him better as time goes on. Has some excellent practical, shrewd suggestions to make now & then. Probably better not engage him more than a year after term expires.[3]

[Harold Ripley] Hastings—Much liked—has sweet disposition, lacks maturity. Should probably go at end of his term & take his degree somewhere.[4]

[George Dwight] Kellogg—May be regarded as a success, makes somewhat the same kind of impression on pupils as Carter did, in less degree.[5]

[Donald Alexander] MacRae—a little too old, has family—will never acquire the Princeton character; good drillmaster for preceptees, but, I judge, not an interesting or inspiring teacher. Professors seem to think he'd better go at end of his time. Has good scholarship for a schoolmaster, not the kind for college work. Is a Canadian & a little rustic.[6]

[David] Magie [Jr.]—I can't give a criticism—he's my "favorite son." It would do him good to be head of a department among strangers for a while. But I could hardly do without him.[7]

[Edwin Moore] Rankin—I spoke of him in another connection as a faithful & successful teacher. He makes pupils work, willy nilly; they are not excessively fond of him, but they respect him thoroughly. I should hate to lose him, he's so reliable in every sense. But I think he would be happier in another place. He can't quite hit the note of Princeton life, owing to a certain lack of humour.[8]

As to [Duane Reed] Stuart & [LaRue] Van Hook, we have just settled their cases.[9]

It is a fine body of men. There are no failures, & some brilliant successes. I believe, from all I can hear, that Anderson and MacRae might do better elsewhere; that Hastings should go & take his degree after a year. Cameron will probably be on the look out for a place & we shall let him go. If you speak to any this summer, I should think these were the ones, especially the first two.

I omitted [Fred Leroy] Hutson: he stands very high in the general opinion. We should certainly wish to re-engage him for the unexpired year of his contract. You remember we postponed the year.[10] Barret is engaged for the year of Hutson's absence, & takes his salary $1500.

I have engaged as preceptors for one year at $1500 each

1 Dr. Leroy C. Barret { Wash. & Lee / J. H. U. }

2. Mr. Austin M. Harmon { Williams 19? / School at Rome }

and as instructors for one year at $1000 each.

3. Mr. Paul Nixon. { Wesleyan 1904, Rhodes Scholar of Conn. / Balliol Coll. Oxford }

4. Mr. W. A. Fleet Jr. { U. of Va. 1904? Rhodes Scholar of Va. / Magdalen Coll. Oxford / Christian name not given }

5. Mr. Herbert Pierrepont Houghton { Amherst AB 1901 / to be Ph.D. of J.H.U. 1907. / Descendant of Jonathan Edwards in 6th generation. }

6. Dr Harry B. Van Deventer.[11] Yale AB & Ph.D.

These six take the places of four, viz: Stuart, promoted; Hutson, on leave of absence; Jones, made a fellow; [Walter Woodburn] Hyde, term expired.

Insert Capps—strike out [Jesse Benedict] Carter[12] & [Hamilton Ford] Allen[13] on Faculty list for 1907-8 Catalogue.

Hw memorandum (WWP, UA, NjP).

1 Anderson was retained until 1909, when he resigned to go to Northwestern University.

2 Basore remained at Princeton and was promoted to Associate Professor in 1921.

3 Cameron was retained until 1909, when he resigned to become Professor of Classics at Boston University.

4 Hastings in fact remained at Princeton until 1909, when he resigned to go to the University of Wisconsin to continue graduate study.

5 Kellogg stayed until 1911, when he left to assume a teaching position at Union College in Schenectady, N. Y.

6 MacRae stayed until 1909, when he went into secondary school work.

7 Magie was promoted to Professor of Classics in 1911.

8 Rankin remained a Preceptor in Classics until 1911, when he resigned to become Professor of Greek at Lafayette College.

[9] Stuart was promoted to Professor of Classics in June 1907; Van Hook was retained until 1910, when he went to Barnard College.

[10] Hutson resigned in 1907 to finish his doctorate at the University of Chicago. He returned to Princeton in 1908 as Preceptor in Classics and became Registrar of the university in 1919.

[11] For more precise information about Barret, Nixon, Fleet, Houghton, and Van Deventer, see Wilson's Annual Report to the Board of Trustees printed at Dec. 13, 1907.

[12] Who had been on leave since 1905. He finally severed his connection with Princeton in 1907 to become Director of the American School of Classical Studies in Rome.

[13] He had taken Carter's place from 1905 to 1907. In the latter year he became Associate in Classics at the University of Illinois.

From Edwin William Pahlow[1]

Dear President Wilson, Oxford, May 29/07.

Although my name is quite unknown to you, perhaps you will consider it sufficient introduction if I tell you that I write at Professor [Winthrop More] Daniels' request. I am a student of history; and at Prof. [Thomas Marc] Parrott's solicitation, I went up to London today to meet Prof. Daniels. We had a conference, at the end of which he urged me to call on you as soon as possible after my return to America, if I should find myself in the neighborhood of Princeton. As it will be necessary for me to run down to New York some time in June or July, I can arrange my affairs so as to come to that place whenever you find it most convenient to see me. I shall land in Boston about June 18th, where my address will be c/o Hon. Charles F. Brown, 835 Exchange Building.

Respectfully yours, Edwin W. Pahlow.

At Prof. Daniels suggestion, I have asked Professors Turner and Haskins to write to you.[2] E W.P.

ALS (WWP, UA, NjP).

[1] Litt.B., University of Wisconsin, 1899; M.A., Harvard University, 1901; at this time en route to the United States after a year of research and study at the University of Munich. He was appointed Instructor in History, Politics, and Economics for 1907-1908 and promoted to the rank of Preceptor in 1908.

[2] See C. H. Haskins to WW, June 10, 1907, and F. J. Turner to WW, June 14, 1907.

To the Board of Trustees' Committee on the Graduate School[1]

GENTLEMEN: [Princeton, N. J.] May, 1907 [c. May 30, 1907].

I take pleasure in presenting to the Committee Dean West's paper upon the question of the choice of a site for the Graduate

[1] Wilson read this letter to the Committee on the Graduate School when it met on May 31, 1907.

College,[2] and also in reading to the Committee the representations of the students resident at Merwick on the same subject,[3] because they seem to me to state with unusual force and adequacy,—no doubt because with enthusiasm,—the arguments for placing the College at a distance from the present grounds of the University, in the very beautiful park now occupied by Merwick. I do not wonder that two years of residence at Merwick have created a deep attachment to the place. Its charm justifies the attachment. I have been very much impressed by the arguments of these papers: if I could agree with their ideals of academic seclusion and could separate the Graduate College from the organic problems of the University as a whole, I think I should have been convinced by them.

But I cannot separate it in consideration from the life of the University as a whole. Perhaps it is not reasonable to expect any but the President and Trustees of the University, whose responsibility is whole and indivisible, to look at its parts only as parts, and at none singly and for its own sake; and I do not wonder that, with his natural concentration upon the interests of the school he has conceived, Dean West should have formed wrong impressions. Geographical separation from the body of the University has already created in the Graduate School a sense of administrative as well as social seclusion which, slight as it is and probably unconscious, is noticeable, and of course undesirable. It could, no doubt, be overcome, but, because it is natural from the situation of the place, it would have to be overcome with conscious effort. It is the inevitable consciousness of separateness: and that is a consciousness which would naturally grow as the Graduate College itself grew to proportions which would give it a great and complex individuality of its own.

Separation is not a question of distances in a town so small as Princeton and so definitely constituted in its life and prepossessions: it is a question of situation entirely. Sites very near the university campus are psychologically separated from the University as sharply as if they lay remote, by Lover's Lane. To turn into Mercer Street or into Bayard Lane, or even into Chamber's Street, is to leave the vicinity of the University. Undergraduates will pay high prices for rooms on University Place while better rooms at half the price go begging a stone's throw off in Mercer Street. I would not deprive the Graduate College of seclusion: I know that seclusion is of its essence as we have conceived it. But

2 That is, A. F. West to the Board of Trustees' Committee on the Graduate School, May 13, 1907.

3 M. S. Burt *et al.* to the Committee on the Graduate School, March 13, 1907, TLS (WWP, UA, NjP).

seclusion is not a matter of geographical separation; it is a matter of construction, as every college in Oxford attests. A quad. that opens straight on the crowded street may be as secluded as if it were flanked by the spaces of a park set upon the outskirts of the town: indeed it is the common comment of every visitor to Oxford that the seclusion is in some subtle way enhanced and emphasized and given an additional charm, a stronger hold on the imagination, by the fact that just without the wall is the thronging thoroughfare. The gardens that lie beyond, to be reached only through quiet quads, and lying safe within their sheltering walls, have an air of privacy and of privileged enjoyment you will never find in any country garden which has only the privacy of remoteness. The effect of this imaginative seclusion upon the mind and fancy of the undergraduate,–the effect of passing every day by secluded places which he would seem almost to touch and yet was expected neither to invade nor to use uninvited,–would be incomparably deeper than that of any seclusion he took casual note of on his walks abroad or conducted friends to the edge of the village to wonder at. Dean West is mistaken in his psychology.

I have, therefore, the gratification of knowing that in leading the Committee to a very different conclusion with regard to its site I am not in danger of taking away from the Graduate School even so much as an added element of charm: that I am, on the contrary, proposing to give it the true charm and seclusion of an Oxford college with its private gardens, rather than that of a gentleman's country residence with its open park and pleasure grounds; and that I am, moreover, recalling Dean West to his own original and better conception of this great instrumentality of our intellectual growth when I declare it to be my clear and mature conviction that it should, at whatever cost of trouble or of money, be placed upon the property which faces the end of McCosh Walk and lies at the heart of our university life.[4]

I should do this even if it were at the expense of a little added charm and privacy; for it is not merely a question of taste and preference, or merely a question concerning the development of a graduate college. It has wider and more important aspects than appear in any representations that have yet been made to you.

We are about to attempt nothing less than the social coördination of the University, a thing more hopeful and of deeper consequence than anything we have hitherto turned our counsels to. We shall have left our teaching without rootage or atmosphere if we leave the University at loose ends in its social structure as it is now; if we do not go on to make the increasing intimacies of

[4] That is, the Olden tract across Washington Street from McCosh Walk.

teacher and pupil, already to be seen in the daily conference, intimacies also of friendship and companionship, the intimacies of a common life. Our work will have been in vain if the processes of disintegration and of distorted social ambition now so noticeable amongst us are not checked and remedied by some radical change which will unite classes and studies by the effectual nexus of life itself. The most liberalizing and the most informing influences of education are created by the intimate conversation of men of different studies and at different stages of advancement. We have had partial proof of this in the intercourse at Merwick and at the Bachelors Club,[5] but we have nowhere any example of it in our undergraduate life.

The social organizations formed by our undergraduates have been formed with no intellectual purposes or ideals of any kind at their foundation, and have developed an exclusively social tradition, delightful but empty of serious content. And the social struggles which have arisen out of the desire to belong to them have resulted in cutting the lower classes sharply off from the upper classes not only but also from each other, by a process of segregation which seems as inevitable as it is extraordinary and unfortunate. It is the common conviction amongst us, a conviction shared by all thoughtful undergraduates, especially by those who have sought to combat the evils of the system, that the present social organization of undergraduate life is impossible of wholesome maintenance or even of successful reformation on its present lines. We are ready,—ready in opinion as well as in purpose,—to do whatever may prove to be necessary to reintegrate our social life and to coördinate it with the intellectual impulses which have brought us to the brink of real achievement.

There need be no fear, therefore, that in placing the Graduate College at the geographical heart of the University we shall be endangering its *morale* by putting it into close neighborhood to demoralizing club influences. The influence of the clubs will not continue to be demoralizing. Their life will unquestionably be tied in some effectual manner into the general life of the University; and nothing will so steady and invigorate the process of transformation as the close neighborhood, the unmistakeable example, and the daily influence of the Graduate College. My hopes and my chief administrative plans for the University would be injured and deranged at their very heart were the Graduate College to be put at any remove whatever from such a central

5 An eating club at 80 University Place founded in 1901, to which belonged junior members of the faculty, graduate students, and resident graduates in Princeton. The members took their meals at the club, and some members had rooms there. It was disbanded in 1937.

site. I count upon it as a model and cause of intellectual and social changes of the deepest and most significant kind. It is upon the model and by means of the inspiration of such a College, with its dignified, stimulating, and happy life, that, in my judgment, the University is to be made over into a body academic, vital and of universal example in America. When the initial change is once wrought,—the task of our generation,—additional quadrangles for graduate residence may be put almost where you will; but this first American example of true graduate intercourse and development must be undertaken at the spot where it will best serve for the regeneration of the whole body: the body which we can, by its influence and example, make the abiding model of American university life.

Our life has broadened to new aspects since the Graduate College was conceived, and the new features and forces which mark its renewal all draw it in spirit and in kind towards the Graduate College itself. Our academic life is all some day to be of a kind in its method and purpose, but it is not yet: it is only finding its way to unity. There has never been a time, therefore, and there never can be a time again when the administrative and psychological arguments for placing this College at the geographical heart of the campus were so obvious or so imperative.[6]

[Woodrow Wilson]

CCL (WWP, UA, NjP).

[6] There is a WWsh draft and a WWT draft of this letter, both dated May 1907, in WWP, UA, NjP.

To Ralph Adams Cram

My dear Mr. Cram: [Princeton, N. J.] May 30th, 1907.

Allow me to acknowledge the receipt of your letter of May 28th, and to say that at the meeting of the Committee on Grounds and Buildings of our Board, held on Saturday last, the plan as outlined in your letter and indicated in your drawings was approved in every particular. Your letter was spread upon the minutes of the board as the minute of their action.

It is very gratifying to know that Mr. Hardenbergh has concurred in the plan so entirely.

It is still necessary that the Board of Trustees confirm the action of its committee, but we feel that it is perfectly safe, in the meantime, for the architects to go ahead on the lines indicated in your plans. I think the outcome in every way very gratifying.

Very sincerely yours, [Woodrow Wilson]

CCL (WWP, UA, NjP).

From Coleman Peace Brown[1]

Dear Sir, Princeton, N. J. May 31st, 1907.

I have been in Princeton about a week and have been following very carefully the general trend of events and have been gathering all the information possible from every available source relative to the present state of affairs respecting Upper Class Clubs. I feel that I have to hand an adequate solution of the whole problem. A solution which will solve the present difficulties and one which will be in line with whatever policy you may have in mind regarding the future. At least it will not be at variance with any future solving of the problem. It relates in fact to the taking in of sophomores in the clubs. The present crisis demands something definite and although last year such a solution was regarded as ill omened and was accepted by nobody, every person with whom I have talked since I have been here (I should say twenty five in number including faculty members[,] seniors and juniors) have come around to my view. I feel that the solution is sane and logical and healthful in every way and I feel sure that although you may not agree with me[,] yet if you knew the facts and the present trend of undergraduate sentiment perhaps such information as I have to hand would aid you at any rate. I was going to leave town Sunday but if I can be of any assistance and if you would desire to hear me and I am most anxious to tell you what I know, I will gladly wait over till you have the opportunity. If you think well of the plan I will see to it that it goes through which I think it will do. However, I am unwilling to take any steps that may be at variance with anything you have in mind. If I can help I would care to. If you do not agree with the step I will certainly do nothing further but will leave it as it stands. Trusting that I may be fortunate enough to be able to see you and hoping that you may be able to give me a brief moment or two from days which I know are already filled with engagements[,] I beg to remain

Most sincerely and obediently yours,

Coleman P. Brown.

ALS (WP, DLC).

1 Princeton 1905, draftsman for the J. G. Brill Co., car builders of Philadelphia.

From Ralph Adams Cram

My dear Dr. Wilson Boston June 1st, 1907

I am deeply gratified at the action of the Committee in the matter of the Scientific buildings. I will send a "fair copy" of the plan to be posted in the proper position on the big map Mr. Bunn has put up in the office.

I have now acted as Supervising Architect for three months and I think I ought to take up the matter of my compensation. May I deal directly with you in the matter or shall I refer it to Mr. Russell? Very sincerely yours, R A Cram.

ALS (WP, DLC).

Harold Griffith Murray to Cleveland Hoadley Dodge

Sir: New York June 1st, 1907.

The following is a report of the Committee of Fifty for the fiscal year to June 1st.

In my report to you June 5th, 1906, I stated that the total income for the fiscal year ending July 31, 1906, was $102,000. inclusive of interest on sums paid into endowment, and that in the first, or endowment form, we had secured in pledges $500,000. of which $135,000. had been paid in. Since this report the Committee has received additional pledges in the *endowment form* advancing the total amount received under this form of subscription to $605,125. of which there has been paid in, $185,000. The balance, $420,125. is drawing interest at 5% according to the terms of the pledge.

In pledges, under the *term form*, the income for the present year to date is $109,218. This, with the interest on $185,000. paid in from the endowment form at 4½%, $8,325. gives a total income of $117,543. By the end of the present fiscal year, July 31st, it is hoped and expected that this amount will equal $120,000. While this latter sum is no greater than that raised by the Committee of Fifty last year, it must be remembered that $20,000. of the amount was contributed by a few to pay off the balance of the deficit which this Committee was unable to raise, while this year the same amount is made up by small contributions from several hundred of the Alumni.

At a meeting of the Committee of Fifty held in Princeton October 17th, 1906, it was unanimously decided to re-organize the Committee on the basis of class representation, that more efficient cooperation might be afforded the Secretary than was possible by the original committee. With this end in view, a committee consisting of the President of the University, Dr. Wilson, the Chairman of the Committee of Fifty, Mr. Cleveland H. Dodge; Mr. C. C. Cuyler, '79; and Mr. A. C. Imbrie, '95[1] were appointed to select the members to compose the new Committee, with the result that the present Committee of Fifty is composed of a representative from each Class from 1870 to 1906, inclusive, with ten members "at large."

ALUMNI DORMITORY.

The plan for erecting a dormitory to the South of "Patton Hall" and East of "Brokaw Field" by various classes desiring to make memorial gifts under the same plan as pursued in the erection of "Patton Hall," has made little progress during the past year. Twelve months ago it was hoped that by this time the dormitory would be well under way. Owing to the lack of funds on the part of various classes, matters have been delayed, but it is expected by next Spring there will be no difficulty in erecting at least ten entries. Neither time nor trouble has been spared by this Committee to expedite matters, but the majority of class officers are unwilling to bind the classes which they represent until a sufficient sum has been raised to ensure the erection of an entry, and an extension of time has been asked for until next Spring, with the idea at this period there will be no further hitches in the financing.

The Trustees, of the Alumni Fund have agreed to devote their principal sum, some $36,000. to the erection of two entries in this dormitory.

THE PRESS BUREAU

During the past year arrangements were concluded with the managers of the Alumni Weekly, through which there will be published three times in each Academic year, a short but complete review of all important matters pertaining to the University since the previous issue. The numbers of the Weekly containing these reviews will be sent to every Alumnus and former student of Princeton, free of charge. By this plan, the Alumni will be kept informed of all matters of special interest pertaining to the University and educated in the needs of Princeton, and what she is accomplishing.

I would suggest that each one of these special issues of the Weekly contain, hereafter, a condensed, but comprehensive review of a Department of the University, written by its head, so that gradually the alumni may be put in touch with, and thoroughly understand each Department, its aims and methods.

During the past year eight articles, written by graduates, descriptive of the leading academic features of the University, appeared in the Newark Evening News. Through the courtesy of that paper, they have been re-published in booklet form by the

Committee of Fifty,[2] and have been distributed free, to the Alumni and friends of Princeton. Some eight hundred of these have been sent to Libraries of the principal Preparatory Schools throughout the United States, and to the libraries of the leading Universities in this Country and abroad.

In addition, this Committee has purchased and handsomely framed one hundred pictures of the recently made photograph of Princeton Campus, and sent them to the leading Preparatory Schools.

In my report made to you last June, I mapped out a scheme for the conducting of a "Press Bureau," through which from time to time, general articles of interest relative to the University might be sent to the daily newspapers throughout the Country.

It was the intention to have these articles dignified in tone, and in no way tend to advertise the University in an unseemly manner, but rather to disseminate Academic and Scientific information so as to reflect credit on the University. In the early Fall, the "Press Bureau" sent forth several articles which were given considerable publicity throughout the Country, but owing to our inability to secure a proper correspondent in Princeton, the matter is for the time in abeyance. Undoubtedly in the Fall, we shall be able to find some one who will be able to fill the position acceptably.

During the past year, the office of the Secretary of the Committee has become a bureau of general information, and considerable correspondence has been held with Alumni and others who have desired information on various matters pertaining to the University. . . .

Respectfully, H. G. Murray Secretary.

TLS (Trustees' Papers, UA, NjP).

[1] Andrew Clerk Imbrie, Princeton 1895, at this time treasurer of Abbey & Imbrie of New York, which manufactured fishing tackle. He was elected an Alumni Trustee in June 1907 to succeed Nathaniel Ewing.

[2] *Princeton University, Some Characteristic Features* (n.p., 1906).

To Ralph Adams Cram

My dear Mr. Cram: [Princeton, N. J.] June 3rd, 1907.

I have yours of June 1st. I have never undertaken the business side of anything in connection with the University, and beg that you will write with regard to the money arrangements to Mr. Archibald D. Russell.

We find ourselves growing a little uneasy lest the exterior of Mr. Hardenbergh's building should be something that would distress us, and I am wondering whether you have tackled him on that side yet or not. I should be very much relieved to hear that he was proving amenable to suggestions, and even to coaching, in the matter of the exterior appearance of the building.

I think you would be gratified if you could know the universal satisfaction that is felt that your advice is constantly available.

Always cordially yours, [Woodrow Wilson]

CCL (WWP, UA, NjP).

From Edward Capps

University of Chicago,

My dear President Wilson: June 4, '07

A letter from Professor Hale, who is in Rome, just received makes it clear to me that he would be unwilling to entertain any proposal at the present time for the joint ownership and management by Princeton and Chicago of Classical Philology, and without his full and free consent I should not desire it, much as I cling to the journal. Professor Shorey[1] is of the same mind, though the rest of the editors would welcome the arrangement, I think. If it ever comes about it will be only after Hale and Shorey are tired of it or after they have failed to secure a renewal of the subsidy.

I write you the moment I am sure of this state of affairs in order that the appropriation which your Board granted may no longer be held for that purpose—unless you would prefer to consider the establishment of another journal, which in my opinion would be impracticable at the present time. The investment of the money in Abbott would yield far better dividends to Princeton.

With cordial regards, I am

Very sincerely yours, Edward Capps

TLS (WP, DLC).

[1] Paul Shorey, Professor of Greek at the University of Chicago, known for his work on Plato and Horace.

From Ralph Adams Cram

My dear Dr. Wilson: Boston, June 4, 1907.

Permit me to thank you for your very kind letter of June 3. I will take up the financial question with Mr. Russell as you suggest.[1]

As for the exterior of Mr. Hardenbergh's design, I confess I am far less apprehensive than before I saw his first studies. He expresses an intense interest in this particular type of work and seems to be going ahead on very conservative, though somewhat dry lines. I find him most amenable, not only to suggestions, but to criticisms. I am trying to arrange to come to Princeton the end of this week, as I very much wish to see you, and beside I want to see Mr. Pyne before he sails for Europe. I am somewhat vague as to what I shall be able to do, however, as Mr. Goodhue's[2] mother[3] is at the point of death, and this morning I get word that one of my sisters-in-law is threatened with appendicitis, in which case it would be necessary for Mrs. Cram[4] to go on to Philadelphia at once, and the situation is further complicated by the fact that we are today moving out into the country, and if Mrs. Cram has to leave I cannot see how I can get away at the same time, as in the new country place, I should have to stay and look after an invalid mother-in-law and two small children. I hope, however, that matters will so develop that I can be in Princeton either Friday or Saturday of this week.

Very truly yours, R A Cram. Supervising Architect.

TLS (WP, DLC).

[1] By action of the Board of Trustees on June 10, 1907, Cram was paid $5,000 for his first year of service as consulting architect. He was to be paid from $1,200 to $1,500 per annum thereafter.

[2] His partner, Bertram Grosvenor Goodhue.

[3] Helen Grosvenor Eldredge Goodhue.

[4] Elizabeth Carrington Read Cram.

From John Lambert Cadwalader

Personal

My dear Mr. President: New York, June 4, 1907.

I was exceedingly sorry to be unable to get to Professor West's meeting the other day.[1] Every now and then I get knocked over—a sort of nervous exhaustion, I think—and I was unable to be out that day.

I wanted also to be there to say a word as to the vacancy in the Board. I hope that will not be filled this June, and give us time to turn. I have felt for some time, and have expressed it to you, that Stephen Palmer would be a very useful trustee at Princeton. I think his capacity for affairs would entitle him to the place, entirely apart from his interest in the University and his desire to do something serious for it; at the same time, I rather feel that at the moment, when he is doing something important—say now at this time—it might be an inopportune moment to elect him as a trustee. Perhaps later it might work out all right. I am sure that if he were on the Board considerable benefits would accrue to the University, although I am perfectly aware that no person ought to be elected a trustee for any such reason alone. Perhaps in the autumn it would do.[2]

I feel also that [David Benton] Jones' connection with the University ought not to be severed at the end of his service as alumni trustee. I do not know his exact feeling on the subject, but *I* have had a notion that it would tend somewhat to depreciate the office of alumni trustee if it was deemed to be a sort of temporary appointment from which people might be appointed to be life members; in other words, I have felt that the alumni trustees out [ought] to serve out their terms, and that, while they should not be limited to strictly one term, after a reasonable time they might well retire. I think Jones a most useful man for the Board and I should hope that in some way his connection with the University would be continued. He has expressed a determination not to be again a candidate for alumni trustee.[3]

I am sure you will pardon these suggestions; they are not intended to be officious, but are from my large interest in whatever concerns the University.

On one or two occasions we have had a committee to which the vacancies in the Board were referred for suggestions. Of course if we continue that indefinitely we would practically take away from the Board the power of appointment and confer it upon the committee, and the Board might object to that in cases where only one vacancy existed.

I am very sorry to be away at the next meeting of the Board, but I am compelled to go to Canada this year and must get some woods and some fresh air.

Believe me, with my best wishes for the summer,

Yours faithfully, John L. Cadwalader

I suppose following the example of the Prest. of the U.S. (attending to all affairs—everywhere) that when you are elected Prest. of the U.S. that you will not feel obliged to retire as Prest. but will be able to spend Sundays in Princeton and still run the University. J. L C.

TLS (WP, DLC).

[1] That is, the meeting of the Committee on the Graduate School on May 31.

[2] Palmer was elected a Life Trustee in April 1908.

[3] Jones persevered in his determination and left the Board of Trustees when his term as Alumni Trustee expired in June 1908.

A Report to the Board of Trustees of Princeton University

[c. June 6, 1907]

REPORT on the SOCIAL COORDINATION of the UNIVERSITY.

June, 1907.

GENTLEMEN of the BOARD OF TRUSTEES: Your Committee, appointed to consider the recent report of the President of the University on the social conditions now affecting the academic spirit and intellectual growth of the University,[1] have been led to believe that a great problem of reorganization confronts us whose immediate solution is necessary to the health and progress of Princeton both as a teaching body and as a social body. Moreover, radical as the processes of solution may prove to be, they are happy to believe that there never was a time when such processes could be undertaken with less fear of serious friction or factious opposition. The social conditions to which we shall call your attention would no doubt have disclosed themselves in any case, but they are more emphasized in existing circumstances than they would otherwise have been, because of the contrast they present to recent changes in the University in other respects and the peculiar obstacles they put in the way of carrying our present plans to a satisfactory completion. Fortunately the recent innovations, because of the manifest improvement they have wrought, have put the whole university body in a wholesome humour of reform and have made all well-considered changes, devised and executed by frank common counsel, much easier of accomplishment.

We have witnessed in the last few years the creation of a new Princeton, as the result,—the astonishingly prompt result,—of our attempt to give the University a vital, spontaneous intellectual life,—not a life of pedants and grinds or of youngsters held inexorably to formal tasks, but a life of young men led by many influences to read and think for themselves along great lines of study, emancipated from school methods and stimulated to use their minds outside the class room. We realized that, for all its subtle charm and beguiling air of academic distinction, Princeton, so far as her undergraduates were concerned, had come to be merely a delightful place of residence, where young men, for the most part happily occupied by other things, were made to perform certain academic tasks; that, although we demanded at stated times a certain part of the attention of our pupils for

[1] That is, Wilson's supplementary report to the Board of Trustees printed at Dec. 13, 1906, Vol. 16.

intellectual things, their life and consciousness were for the rest wholly unacademic and detached from the interests which in theory were the all-important interests of the place. For a great majority of them residence here meant a happy life of comradeship and sport interrupted by the grind of perfunctory "lessons" and examinations, to which they attended rather because of the fear of being cut off from the life than because they were seriously engaged in getting the training which would fit their faculties and their spirits for the tasks of the world which they knew they must face after their happy freedom was over.

Undoubtedly, if we would give Princeton the highest distinction and that academic leadership in the country which she may now so easily gain, we must study at every turn the means by which to lift her intellectual life and achievements out of mediocrity not only, but also into such an order of naturalness and energy and distinction as shall make her by reason of her way of success a conspicuous model and example. There is no true intellectual life for the undergraduate in the mere faithful performance of set tasks, no matter how eagerly or with what concentration he devote himself to them, if between tasks his mind be emptied of the interest they have created and his life run entirely free of their influence. There must somehow be brought about an interpenetration of his experience inside the class room and conference and his experience outside academic exercises, where men register their interests by what they do and say and let their minds have play upon. A college without sport and without a great deal of irresponsible boyish disengagement from serious talk and thoughtful effort no one can desire who understands the real economies and needs of the mind. The more wholesome sport and thoughtless fun the better both the work and the intimate comradeships upon which intellectual endeavor depends for energy and enlargement. But leisure and study ought not to be separated in air-tight compartments. Leisure ought to be enriched and diversified by the interests which study creates. In the midst of play there ought to be a constant consciousness of what the place means and must be made to stand for,—a place of thoughtful, manly, disinterested men, disciples of university ideals.

When we introduced the preceptorial system we made the greatest strategic move in that direction that has been made in the whole history of American universities. By it we meant to say that the intellectual life of a college did not consist of attendance upon class exercises or of preparation for recitations, but consisted, rather, of constant contact with study and

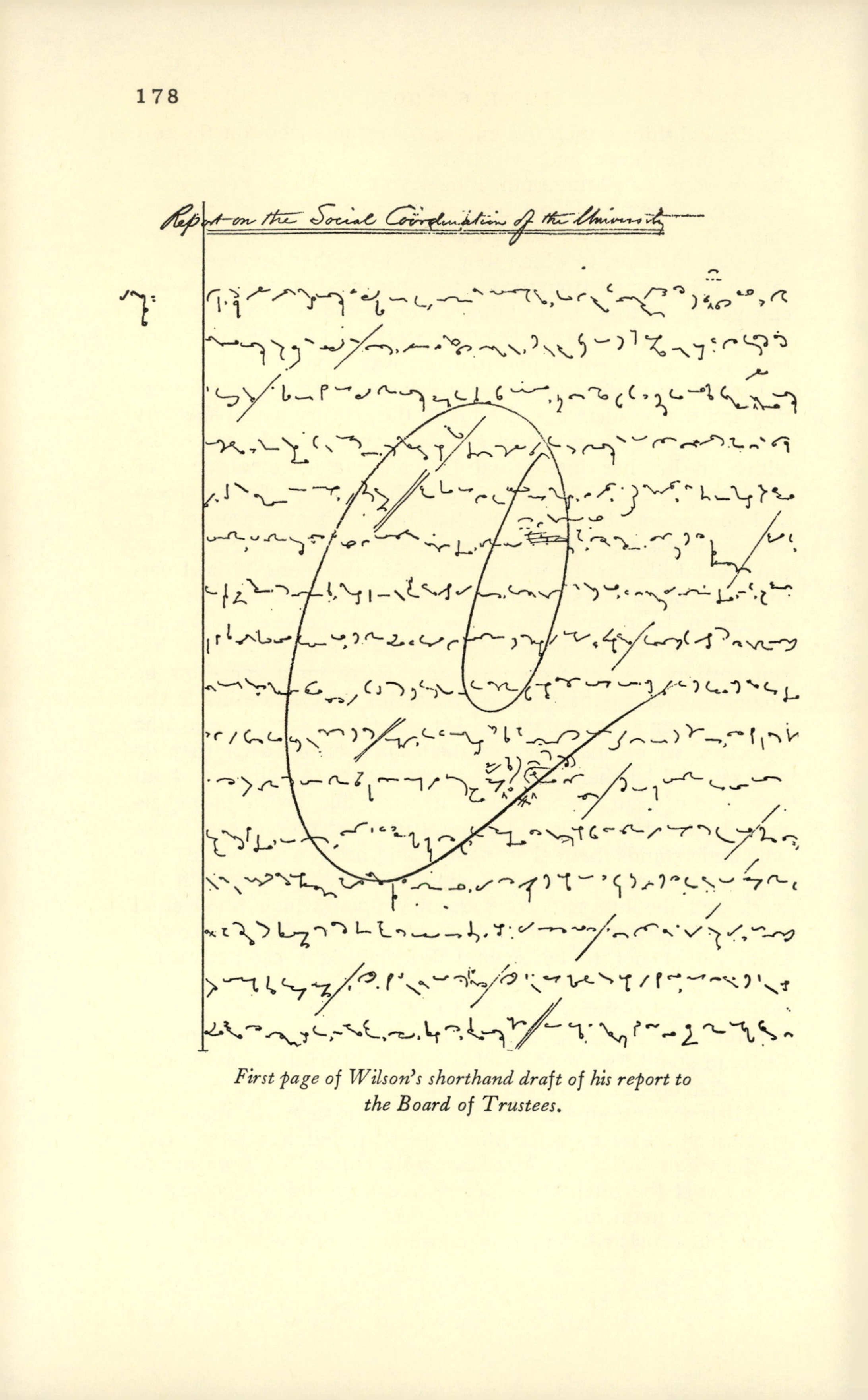

Report on the Social Coördination of the University

First page of Wilson's shorthand draft of his report to the Board of Trustees.

REPORT on the SOCIAL COORDINATION of the UNIVERSITY. June, 1907.

GENTLEMEN of the BOARD of TRUSTEES: Your Committee, appointed to consider the recent report of the President of the University on the social conditions now affecting the academic spirit and intellectual growth of the University, have been led to believe that a great problem of social reorganization confronts us whose immediate solution is necessary to the health and progress of Princeton both as a teaching body and as a social body. Moreover, radical as the processes of solution may prove to be, they are happy to believe that there never was a time when such processes could be undertaken with less fear of serious friction or factious opposition. The social conditions to which we shall call your attention would no doubt have disclosed themselves in any case, but they are more emphasized in existing circumstances than they would otherwise have been, because of the contrast they present to recent changes ~~of~~ in the University in other respects and the peculiar obstacles they put in the way of carrying our present plans ~~for the University~~ to a satisfactory completion. ~~At the same time, happily, our~~ Fortunately, the recent ~~changes~~ innovations, because of the manifest improvements they have wrought, have put the whole university body in a wholesome humour of reform and have made all well-considered changes, devised and executed ~~taken~~ by frank common counsel, much easier of accomplishment.

We have witnessed in the last few years the creation of a new Princeton, as the result,—the astonishingly prompt result,—of our attempt to give the University a vital, spontaneous intellectual life,—not a life of pedants and grinds or of youngsters held inexorably to formal tasks, but a life of young men led by many influences to read and think for themselves along great lines of study, emancipated from school methods and stimulated to use their minds outside the class room. We realized that, for all its subtle charm and beguiling air of academic distinction, Princeton, so far as her undergraduates were concerned, had come to be merely a ~~place of~~ delightful place of residence, where young men, for the most part happily occupied by other things, were made to perform certain academic tasks; that, although we ~~claimed~~ demanded at stated times a certain part of the attention of our pupils for intellectual things, their life and consciousness were for the rest wholly unacademic and detached from the interests which in theory were the all-important interests of the place. For a great majority of them residence here meant a happy life of comradeship and sport interrupted by the grind of perfunctory "lessons" and examinations, to which they attended rather because of the fear of being cut off from the life than because they were seriously engaged in getting ~~a~~ the training which would fit their faculties and their spirits for the tasks of the world which they knew they must face after their happy freedom was over.

Undoubtedly, if we would give Princeton the highest distinction and that academic leadership in the country which she may now so easily gain, we must study at every turn the means by which to lift her intellectual life and achievements out of mediocrity not only, but also into such an order of naturalness and

First page of Wilson's typed draft of his report on the Social Coordination of the University.

the intimate association of teacher and pupil outside the class room, where the tradition of lectures and recitations was forgotten, rejected, and a thoroughly natural and human relationship, the relationship of fellow students, substituted. And that meaning has at once been made evident to the whole country. The contrast with the old order of things is most marked in the case of the intercourse of undergraduates with those preceptors who invite them often to their houses or who live in the same dormitories with them. A natural and easy social relationship, an informal, frequent exchange of calls, the easy, unconstrained talks of ordinary comradeship make study itself seem a thing natural and human, a thing not so much of formal exaction under rules as of the vital contact of minds. It is, by intention and in actual fact, a widening of the atmosphere of study to seem a natural medium of life and serious enjoyment.

But the new process, vital as it is in itself, suited as it is to the object we have had in view, may be checked and even nullified by hostile or unfavorable influences. Our new methods of study require as their soil and indispensable environment a new social coördination,—a coördination which will not only make sure of a constant and natural intercourse between teacher and pupil, but also knit the student body itself together in some truly organic way which will ensure vital intellectual and academic contacts, the comradeships of a common life with common ends. Your Committee is of the opinion that this can best be done by combining the undergraduates in residential groups,—groups so made up that the forms and conditions under which each man in residence lives may as far as possible be the forms and conditions which are common to all.

Princeton has not since the earliest years of her development been in any full sense a residential college. She provides her students with lodgings, but with nothing else; and not all of them with that. And even the buildings in which she lodges them have never as yet been drawn together into such geographical relations as might be expected to bring their occupants into natural groups of association. They form no closed units, suggesting intimate associations; there are no common rooms; lodgings are assigned by lot, and close neighbours may never know each other. Our social life for generations together has formed itself around the boarding house and club tables. Men have associated themselves with congenial groups of companions to eat together, and, when no sufficiently comfortable boarding house could be found, have rented or built quarters of their own in which they could command their own comforts and their own bill of fare in pleasing independence.

The outcome in our own day has been the development of the upper-class clubs with their attractive club houses, in each of which there are not only dining rooms and kitchens and servants' quarters, but also well-appointed common rooms, libraries, billiard rooms, smoking rooms, private dining rooms for parties, and sleeping rooms for visitors. The members of the Freshman and Sophomore classes are not admitted to membership in these clubs; but the Sophomores maintain clubs of their own upon a more simple scale in rented houses; and in providing, as we have recently provided, eating places for the Freshmen, instead of organizing a commons for the whole class, as economy and ordinary usage would have suggested, we have felt obliged to provide a large number of separate dining rooms in which they could distribute themselves in groups as inchoate clubs, and to set aside for each group which thus formed itself a separate common room in addition, to which the members of the group could resort after meals to smoke and spend a pleasant half hour of diversion together. And that is our social organization. The dormitories are mere sleeping places and places for study, or for the briefer social calls that break the busy hours of the evening.

The evident peculiarity of this life is that it severs the social from the intellectual interests of the place, and does not, with its scattered clubs and divided classes, make us up into a community even on the social side. The vital units are the club units. They divide all four classes into segments and sharply separate the classes as wholes from one another during the two earlier years of the undergraduate course, when characters are being formed and points of view established. Their organization is entirely outside university action; has no organic connection whatever with anything academic; produces interests which absorb the attention and the energy of the best undergraduates as of all others, and yet nowhere interpenetrates the associations which arise out of study, carries no flavour with it which it might not as well have in any other town or in any other similar environment.

It absorbs the attention and all the planning faculties of the undergraduates because all social ambitions turn upon it. It would be difficult to exaggerate the importance in the life of the undergraduate of the question whether at the end of his Sophomore year he is going to be taken into one of the upper-class clubs. His thought is constantly fixed upon that object throughout the first two years of his university course with a great intensity and uneasiness whenever he thinks either of his social standing, his comradeships, or his general social consideration among his fellows. The clubs do not take in all the members of the Junior and Senior classes. About one-third are left out in the elections; and their lot is little less than deplorable. They feel that they cannot continue to associate on terms of intimacy with friends who have been elected into the clubs, for fear they will be thought to be seeking to make favour with them and obtain a belated invitation to join; and, even when many of them as individuals are not disappointed at having been passed by, they must seek their comradeships with other classmates who are very much disappointed and who feel their isolation with a good deal of bitterness. It is difficult for them to arrange for comfortable eating places; and the places at which they do board are only too much like caves of Adullam. They go forward to their graduation almost like men who are in the University and yet not of it. Often they are cheerful and steadfast enough; individuals here and there are sometimes quite indifferent to their comparative isolation, being absorbed in their books or in the task of earning the money necessary to pay their college expenses, but as a class their position is most trying, and most discreditable to our university democracy. It often happens that men who fail of election into one of the clubs at the end of the Sophomore year leave the University and go to some other college or abandon altogether the idea of completing their university course.

There is a great deal of admirable solidarity still in our undergraduate life. The "Princeton Spirit" of which we so often speak, and which is so strong and excellent a force in everything that affects either the life or the fortunes of the University, has impelled the leading spirits among the undergraduates to strive with the utmost loyalty to keep the upper-class clubs from becoming factional centres and dividing the undergraduate body into cliques which would prefer the interests of their clubs to the interests of the University as a whole. They have felt that the upper-class clubs differed very radically, and very much for the better, from the fraternities which have cut the undergraduate body of other colleges into segments and factions, because they include only Juniors and Seniors in their membership and leave the Sophomores and Freshmen undivided, to acquire the democratic habit and united feeling of the place. So soon as the practice threatened to grow up of seeking out attractive and especially desirable under-classmen and pledging them in advance to accept elections into particular upper-class clubs, a treaty of the most stringent character was entered into by the clubs which sought to make it an act of personal dishonour on the part of any upper-classman who was a member of a club even to cultivate relations of personal intimacy with under-classmen for fear such ends might be in view. That treaty has again and again been violated, and again and again renewed, in stricter and stricter form, until, in its present shape, as now pending for readoption, it practically seeks to fix an impassable gulf between the upper and lower classes in order that such attempts and suspicions may be altogether avoided.

It even goes further. It attempts to minimize the personal and social intercourse between Sophomores and Freshmen, and so segregates the Sophomores entirely. Because the Sophomores, since they cannot be sought or solicited as prospective candidates for membership in upper-class clubs, which are the natural goal of their social ambition, associate themselves in groups to seek admission,—not openly or avowedly, but none the less systematically and effectively. That is the recognized object of the Sophomore clubs. It is equally well known, and indeed matter of course, that the groups of Freshmen who form their separate clubs in the several dining rooms in which the Freshmen now eat are formed with a view to being taken at the end of the year into the different Sophomore organizations or "followings" (the so-called "hat-lines" described in the President's report), and so making their way, in turn, into the upper-class clubs, where all roads of social preferment in the University end. The makers of the latest inter-club treaty endeavour, in the terms of the document they have just drawn up, to minimize and in part control that tendency also, by regulating in some degree the personal and social intercourse between Freshmen and Sophomores, over whom the clubs, the parties to the treaty, clearly have no jurisdiction whatever.

Two very significant and very undesirable, and even dangerous, things have thus come about: the two lower classes, who need above all things the forming and guiding influence of the upper classes, have been almost completely segregated, and the very influences which seemed to render their segregation necessary from the point of view of the clubmen have brought about the very result their segregation was meant to prevent,—that is, they have cut them up into groups and cliques whose social ambitions give them separate and rival interests quite distinct from, plainly hostile to, the interests of the University as a whole.

No one seems to expect such treaties to be kept. A majority will always respect and obey them, as laws to which they have voluntarily submitted themselves; but a minority will always break and ignore them,—with more or less indulgent condemnation from the majority. For it is universally admitted that they are in restraint of human nature: that there is, of course, nothing intrinsically dishonourable in the desire of an upper-classman to secure some friend in the lower class for his own club, and that the natural rivalry of the upper-class clubs, at any rate for the picked men of the lower classes, will frequently lead individuals to break through the artificial restraints of the treaty, no matter what pledges are exacted of them or of their clubs as organizations. In brief, the social ambitions created by the existing system of club life are too strong for individual honour; and treaties in restraint of natural impulses, even if obeyed, do not prevent the social divisions among the Freshmen and Sophomores which it is their main purpose to prevent. And all the while, treaties notwithstanding, the several groups formed by the Freshmen and Sophomores, if not in effect detached sections of the upper-class clubs, are at any rate their satellites and attend them most observantly.

Along with the steadily increasing concentration of the attention of the undergraduates upon the social question and the centering of all social ambitions upon the upper-class clubs has gone a very noticeable, a very rapid, increase in the luxury of the upper-class houses. The two oldest clubs[2] now have houses of extraordinary elegance and luxury of appointment and five other clubs are maturing plans for replacing their present comfortable structures with buildings which will rival the others in beauty, spaciousness, and comfort. The University, which gives life to those clubs and constitutes their ostensible *raison d'etre*, seems in danger of becoming, if the present tendencies of undergraduate organization are allowed to work out their logical results, only an artistic setting and background for life on Prospect Avenue. That life, as it becomes more and more elaborate, will become more and more absorbing, and university interests will fall more and more into the background. The interest of the lower classes will more and more centre upon it and the energies of the upper classes will be more and more engrossed by it. The vital life of the place will be outside the University and in large part independent of it.

These tendencies have not been obvious until the last year or two. Though for a long time apparent enough on close observation, they seemed until lately to be without formidable momen-

2 Ivy Club, founded in 1879, and University Cottage Club, founded in 1886.

tum and quite controllable by the conservative influences of the place. But now the undergraduates themselves clearly perceive them and are uneasily aware that they are rapidly getting beyond their control. Before the establishment of the preceptorial system, with its necessary corollary of the intimate association of teacher and pupil,—the coördination of the undergraduate life with the teaching of the University,—these things were not so near the heart of our plans and hopes for Princeton's intellectual development and academic revitalization. But now they are of the essence of everything we are striving for, whether on the undergraduate or on the graduate side of the University's work, and we are bound to consider the means by which to effect an immediate reintegration of our academic life.

Your Committee is of the opinion that the only adequate means of accomplishing this is the grouping of the undergraduates in residential quadrangles, each with its common dining hall, its common room for intercourse and diversion, and its resident master and preceptors; where members of all four of the classes shall be associated in a sort of family life, not merely as neighbors in the dormitories but also as comrades at meals and in many daily activities,—the upper classes ruling and forming the lower, and all in constant association with members of the Faculty fitted to act in sympathetic coöperation with them in the management of their common life. In brief, your Committee is of the opinion that the only way in which the social life of the undergraduates can be prevented from fatally disordering, and perhaps even strangling, the academic life of the University is by the actual absorption of the social life into the academic.

This is not the scheme of the English colleges. Those colleges have separate autonomy. Each separately undertakes the instruction of the undergraduates resident within it. The plan we propose involves only a convenient residential division of the University as a social body. It does not involve its division, or the alteration of its past academic life, in any other respect whatever. It is a plan to substitute for the present segregation of the classes a reunion of the classes, and for the present division of the University into small social segments, which constantly tend to war with one another and to cut the University into factions, larger segments, or, rather, vital groups, which could not possibly develop like rivalries and cliques and which would be permeated by their very organization and environment by the soberer influences of the place,—groups which would constitute the best possible *media* for the transmission of such impulses as we are now counting on to transform Princeton entirely. It is a choice between one sort of social transformation and another; and this is clearly the time when the choice must be made.

The effect of this plan upon the upper-class clubs would be either their abolition or their absorption. The withdrawal of the greater part of the Juniors and Seniors from the life of the proposed residential quads would of course be out of the question. A separate club life for them would rob the whole plan of its vitality, and is not to be thought of. But the history of the upper-class clubs has been most honourable and useful. They have served the University in a period of transition, when no plans were thought of for its coördination, as perhaps no other instrumentalities could have served it. Their abolition ought not to be thought of if their adaptation to the new order of things can be effected. It would be a violent breach of historical continuity and out of tone with the traditions and standards of growth which have hitherto kept Princeton intact as an organic whole. Fortunately, if we should be happy enough to secure their coöperation, it will be quite possible to develop them into smaller residential quads as part of the University itself: and this, in the opinion of your Committee, would be the happiest possible solution of the difficulty, giving to clubs which are now in danger of embarrassing and even profoundly demoralizing the life of the University a role of singular distinction and public spirit in its organic development, and affording the country at large a new example of Princeton's capacity to lead the way in matters of organization which are now puzzling the authorities of all our larger universities. We can lead in social example, as we are already leading in teaching example. And our alumni and undergraduates will, as usual, be our partners in the enterprise.

Your committee, therefore, recommend that the President of the University be authorized to take such steps as may seem wisest for maturing ⟨and executing⟩ this general plan, and for seeking the coöperation and counsel of the upper-class clubs in its ⟨execution⟩ elaboration; and that this Committee be continued to consult with the President from time to time as the matter may take shape and as he may require further counsel and advice, and to mature detailed plans for the future consideration of this Board so soon as such plans can be perfected by common counsel among all concerned.

Respectfully submitted, Woodrow Wilson, Chairman[3]

TRS (Trustees' Papers, UA, NjP).

[3] There is a heavily emended WWT draft of this report in WP, DLC. There are also a WWhw outline and a WWsh draft, both undated, of this report in WC, NjP.

From Franklin Murphy, Jr.[1]

My dear Dr. Wilson: Newark, New Jersey June 7th, 1907.

I have been away for a few days and find your note and memorandum concerning Clubs,[2] on my return. I shall be at our annual meeting at the Tiger Inn to night and I will read the memorandum to the members present.

I feel a good deal of concern about the future of the Clubs at Princeton. They have reached a point where they assume an importance in the life of the undergraduates which is very much exaggerated. The tendency seems to be for the worse instead of for the better and I think that something radical will have to be done ultimately. It is not yet clear to me that your solution is the proper one and yet it may be. I haven't had time to reach a conclusion as yet. I want to bring one fact to your attention and that is the financial situation. Some of the Clubs own their property and have no debt. Most of them however have a debt of considerable importance. The interest and sinking fund are taken care of by a system of graduate dues, payable a certain number of years after graduation and helped out by the initiation fees. Unless the income from these two sources is maintained we could not get money for the interest and the mortgages would be foreclosed. I should be very glad to do anything that I thought would best serve the interest of the University, even if it meant the abolition of the present Club system. I should be glad at any time to take up the matter further with you by correspondence or in person and I shall be glad to let you know the sentiment of the Tiger Inn if I can obtain such an expression at the meeting tonight.

Yours sincerely, Franklin Murphy

TLS (WP, DLC).

1 Princeton 1895, President of the Board of Governors of Tiger Inn and Vice President of the Murphy Varnish Co. of Newark.

2 This memorandum, which Wilson sent to the presidents of the various clubs about June 3, is included in the news release printed at June 10, 1907. In WP, DLC, there is a WWsh draft of this memorandum dated May 27, 1907, and an undated WWTS copy.

A Sermon

BACCALAUREATE ADDRESS. 9 June, 1907.

"And be ye not conformed to this world: but be ye transformed by the renewing of your mind, that ye may prove what is that good, and acceptable, and perfect will of God." Rom. XII., 2.

Gentlemen: You are thinking of yourselves as just about to begin life. There is a great deal that is false and merely conventional in the thought. You have been in the midst of life these twenty years and more, and every year has added to the intimacy and the variety of your contact with the persons and the circumstances that lay about you. Particularly since you entered college you must have been aware that earlier trammels and safeguards had fallen away and that you were put upon your mettle as men, to win a place and make a career. What is about to happen to you now will be no sudden or violent thing. The scene will only slowly widen about you, as hitherto.

Of course it is true in respect of most of you that the paths you have trod hitherto have been sheltered and private ways such as thoughtful love has prepared, generation after generation, for the feet of the boys who are to be nurtured and trained for the work of their years of independence and maturity. I pity the man who cannot look back to those delicious sequestered places from which we first saw the world, that dear covert made by mothers' and fathers' love and kept inviolable by all the gentle arts of guardian care. What free spaces there were for play and all light-hearted sport! How generously long those golden days seemed, and with what gracious figures they were filled, of knights and fairies and heroes who seemed our very comrades! How slowly the years moved, and how good it was that they were long and full of dreams!

The years presently quickened their pace, you remember, and when we became schoolboys the world grew more definite about us: there were fewer dreams and more realities. But the paths were still sheltered and delightful. There was no anxious shifting for ourselves: the plan of our days was made for us. They were still free days, made for sport and pleasure. School hours and study only gave zest to play and to all the unchartered liberties of the mind. We did not come upon short days and engrossing tasks and the feeling that work was the veritable master in all things until we got to college; and even there we kept, perhaps kept too long, the spirit of boys, and made the work as much as might be an incident still, and not an occupation.

In a very real sense, therefore, you are at the threshold of the life which is to mean constant and independent endeavor, the actual making of the careers you have been looking forward to; and this is the day, the very sacred day of special counsel, when we ask ourselves what chart and mode of life we have found by which to determine and make safe our course of life henceforth, by which to make sure of hope and courage to sustain us as we break up these dear comradeships, leave a little world that has known us, and severally seek places for ourselves among strangers. The text of Scripture that has seemed to come most directly to meet my thought as I pondered this turning-point in your life is that which is contained in certain words to be found in the second verse of the twelfth chapter of Romans: *"Be ye not conformed to this world: but be ye transformed by the renewing of your mind, that ye may prove what is that good, and acceptable, and perfect will of God."*

It may seem strange and futile counsel to give to a company of young men who are about to go out into the world to ask a living of it,—a chance to serve it, to partake of its life and of its rewards,—to tell them that they must not conform to what they find, must not accept the rules of the life they enter as novices, by permission and not by right, as those who would learn and not as those who would teach. Their advice will neither be asked nor accepted, and they will be laughed at for their pains if they offer it. But the counsel of the words I have quoted is no counsel of presumption. It is a mere counsel of integrity. The 'world' is no fixed thing or order of life that remains unchanged from generation to generation, or even from day to day. Its habit and practice change with every generation that rules it, and your generation is to come, one of these days, upon its years of rule. Have you anything in your hearts which will distinguish you from the common run of men who lose themselves in the mass and never emerge again carrying any light of their own?

"Be ye not conformed to *this* world,"—*this* world that is always changing, that is never sure that it sees any fixed points or stands upon any lasting foundations. You have been given an opportunity to get the offing and perspective of books, of the truths which are of no age but run unbroken and unaltered throughout the changeful life of all the ages. You know the long measurements, the high laws, by which the world's progress has ever been guaged [gauged] and assessed,—laws of sound thinking and pure motive which seem to lie apart in calm regions which passion cannot disturb, into whose pure air wander no mists or confusions or threats of storm. Amidst every altered aspect of time and circumstance the human heart has remained unchanged. No doubt there were simpler ages when the things which now perplex us in hope and conduct seemed very plain. If life confuses us now no doubt it is because we do not see it simply and see it whole. Look back more often and you shall find your vision adjusted for the look ahead.

Reflections like these seem to me to spring naturally to the thought out of the words of Scripture counsel I have read. "Be ye not conformed to this world: but be ye *transformed* by the renewing of your mind,"—by that simplification of motive and of standard which is a return to a sort of youth and naturalness of thought drawn out of those only fountains of perpetual youth, the fountains of just thought and true feeling. At them, and only at them, do you get a veritable and constant renewal of your minds: the refreshment which brings back the taste for all things sweet and primitive in their truth. These fountains have always lain about you, when you were children, when you were growing youths, since you became men with open eyes here in college.

Some of them are *the fountains of learning*, which have here been so accessible to you. If their waters have not tasted pure and sweet to you, with a tang of the wholesome earth that renews all things, it is because you have drunk of them neither often enough or copiously enough to wash the dust of the common road from your palates. Learning is knowledge purged of all that is untested and ephemeral. It is neither the rumour of the street nor the talk of the shop nor the conjecture of the salon. It has been purified and sifted in quiet rooms to which passing fashions of thought do not penetrate. It has passed through mind after mind like water through the untainted depths of the earth, and springs to the places of its revelation, not a thing of the surface, but a thing from within where the sources of thought lie. Men come and go, but these things abide, like the face of the heavens. Age is linked with age by the permanence of the physical universe and the unchanging nature of the human spirit. Hearts are ever the same, whatever the setting of the stage or the plot of the play.

And so the fountains of learning become the fountains of perpetual youth. At them are our minds renewed; at them do we drink of the pure waters undefiled whose sources lie below all circumstance, all accident, all surface temperature or season. After we have tasted of them much of the talk of the day seems like the mere leas [lees] of cheap wine, of the vintage of yesterday. We are renewed by learning in the sense that our minds are, as it were, brought back to the originals and first bases of thought, to direct communion with all that is primitive and permanent and beyond analysis or conjecture: as our manners are renewed, —that is, simplified,—when social convention and all mere fashion falls away in the presence of danger, of sincere, unselfish love, and of all pure passion; as our lungs are renewed by the pure, untainted air of free uplands or by the keen breath of the wind that comes out of the hills. Learning has come into the world, not merely to clear men's eyes and give them mastery over nature and human circumstance, but also to keep them young, never staled, always new, like the stars and the hills and the sea and the vagrant winds, which make nothing of times or occasions but live always in serene freedom from any touch of decay, the sources of their being some high law which we cannot disturb.

But the fountains of learning are not the only fountains of perpetual youth and renewal. There are other springs of the spirit which, like the springs of learning, renew us from age to age in all our spiritual qualities, which hold us to the originals of all that is fresh and enjoyable in the life from which we draw our strength. There are *the fountains of friendship*, copious, free, inexhaustible, confined to no time or region or season. Do we not know them? Do they not abound in this place? Whether we have resorted to the fountains of learning or not, though we may have neglected them in our folly, we have known the refreshment of these other sources of renewal, these sweet fountains of friendship,—have drunk of them almost to intoxication here in this place of comradeships. I hope that we have drunk of them with comprehending hearts, perceiving the true and excellent quality of the sweet waters we quaffed. If pure and taken with pure lips, they will have given us taste of unselfishness and self-sacrifice. That is not true friendship which proceeds merely from the action of a self-pleasing taste, which is nothing more than a self-indulgent pleasure. It is very delightful to consort with companions who gratify our zest for good fellowship, amuse us with gay talk and entertaining jest, walk our own familiar ways of thought and feeling, welcome our coming and never bore us; who, if dull, are dull to our liking, of the quality of dullness that rests and reassures us. But friendship is a much larger, much finer, much deeper thing than this mere relish of good company. It is a great deal more than mere congenial companionship. Let true and deep affection once grip you; let interest and pleasure once deepen into insight and sympathy and a sense of vital kinship of mind and spirit, and the relationship takes on an energy and a poignancy you had not dreamed of in your easy search for pleasure. Spirit leaps to spirit with a new understanding, a new eagerness, a new desire: and then you may make proof whether it be true friendship of [or] not by the quick and certain test whether you love yourself or your friend more at any moment of divided interest.

True friendship is of a royal lineage. It is of the same kith and breeding as loyalty and self-forgetting devotion, and proceeds upon a higher principle even than they. For loyalty may be blind, and friendship must not be; devotion may sacrifice principles of right choice which friendship must guard with an excellent and watchful care. You must act in your friend's interest whether it please him or not: the object of love is to serve, not to win. It is a hard saying, I know;—who shall be pure enough to receive it? There is but one presence in which it can be made plain and acceptable, and that is the presence of Christ, where it may stand revealed in the light of that example which makes all duty to shine with the face of privilege and of exalted joy.

Here are the fountains of real renewal. I suppose that we can speak of our minds as indeed renewed when they are carried back in vivid consciousness to some first and primal standard of thought and duty, to images which seem to issue direct from the God and Father of our spirits, fresh with immediate creation, clear as if they had the light of the first morning upon them,—as those who go back to the very springs of being. It is thus of necessity that our renewal comes through love, through pure motive, through intimate contact with whatever reminds us of what is permanent and forever real, whether we taste it in the fountains of learning, of friendship, or of divine example, the crown alike of friendship and of truth.

To one deep fountain of revelation and renewal few of you, I take it for granted, have had access yet,—I mean the fountain of sorrow, a fountain sweet or bitter according as it is drunk in submission or in rebellion, in love or in resentment and deep dismay. I will not tell you of these waters; if you have not tasted them, it would be futile,—and some of you will understand without word of mine. I can only beg that when they are put to your lips, as they must be, you will drink of them as those who seek renewal and know how to make of sadness a mood of enlightenment and of hope.

You will see that I but go about to elucidate a single theme: that all individual human life is a struggle, when rightly understood and conducted, against yielding to weak accommodation to the changeful, temporary, ephemeral things about us, in order that we may catch that permanent, authentic tone of life which is the voice of the Spirit of God,

> "A presence that disturbs us with the joy
> Of elevated thoughts; a sense sublime
> Of something far more deeply interfused,
> Whose dwelling is the light of setting suns,

And the round ocean and the living air,
And the blue sky, and in the mind of man;
A motion and a spirit that impels
All thinking things, all objects of all thought,
And rolls through all things."[1]

It is not a thing remote, obscure, poetical, but a very real thing, that lives in the consciousness of every one of us. Every thoughtful man, every man not merely of vagrant mind, has been aware, not once, but many times, of some unconquerable spirit that he calls *himself*, which is struggling against being overborne by circumstance, against being forced into conformity with things his heart is not in, things which seem to deaden him and deprive him of his natural independence and integrity, so that his individuality is lost and merged in some common, undistinguishable mass, the nameless multitudes of a world that ceaselessly shifts and alters and is never twice the same. He feels instinctively that the only victory lies in non-conformity. He must adjust himself to these things that come and go and have no base or principle, but he must not be subdued by them or lose his own clear lines of chosen action.

The college man, particularly if, while he studied, he has lived as we live here, where the world is reproduced in small, with its comradeships and rivalries and organizations, its social compulsions and its voluntary efforts of individuals and of societies, is entitled to think that he can distinguish the permanent from the ephemeral, determine what he will ignore, what accept. He should have learned that non-conformity is not antagonism: that he is not undertaking the impossible and ridiculous task of rebuking and reconstructing a world established and independent of him: that what he is attempting is what I may term an influential non-conformity, which adds a new item of force to the world,—adds a man who thinks for himself, a man renewed by fresh contact with the sources and originals of thought and inspiration, and ready to give the world just that occasional thrill of reminder which keeps the breath of progress and of renewal in its nostrils. The world always responds to the impulse when it finds an authentic man, whom it cannot crush or ignore, who speaks always words of his own, and yet who flings no foolish defiance to his generation, is ready for all generous coöperation, is an eager servant of his day and time, not its opponent or critic of destruction,—just a self-respecting, thoughtful, unconquerable human spirit.

[1] From Wordsworth's "Lines Composed a Few Miles Above Tintern Abbey."

"Be ye not conformed to this world: but be ye transformed by the renewal of your mind." This transformation is no apotheosis, it is no changing of men into angels, no transmutation of common flesh into stuff of immortality. It is a transformation effected by the renewing of your minds, a transformation of attitude and motive, of purpose, of point of view. It is the transformation effected in the spirit itself by seeing the world as a work of God, in its largeness and entirety, contained in no single generation, lasting, a thing of spirit, from age to age, from friendship to friendship, from love to love; knit together of human beings, spirits great and small, inspired and paltry, lifted or debased by victory or defeat in a continual struggle to see and receive the truth; a mode of energy serene, augmenting, persistent. Every great thought and principle works its transformation upon the spirits of those who receive it, and a mind renewed is a mind transformed.

Princeton has been a place of transformation for you, whether you willed it to be or not: the question is only in how great a degree you have been transformed. You are not what you were when you came here: you cannot have escaped some wider view of men and of truth and of circumstance and of nature than you had when you came here unformed boys; and for some of you the transformation has been complete. You neither think nor purpose as you did before the processes of our teaching and our life wrought upon you; and now you are about to have occasion to show how vital the process has been. The transformed university man, whose thought and will have been in fact renewed out of the sources of knowledge and of love, is one of the great dynamic forces of the world. We live in an age disturbed, confused, bewildered, afraid of its own forces, in search not merely of its road but even of its direction. There are many voices of counsel, but few voices of vision; there is much excitement and feverish activity, but little concert of thoughtful purpose. We are distressed by our own ungoverned, undirected energies and do many things, but nothing long. It is our duty to find ourselves. It is our privilege to be calm and know that the truth has not changed, that old wisdom is more to be desired than any new nostrum, that we must neither run with the crowd nor deride it, but seek sober counsel for it and for ourselves.

Our true wisdom is in our ideals. Practical judgments shift from age to age, but principles abide, and more stable even than principles are the motives which simplify and ennoble life. That, I suppose, is why the image of Christ has grown, not less, but more distinct in the consciousness of the race since the tragic day in which He died upon the cross. How unlike in every external circumstance was that day to our own; how the world has changed and shifted in every institution and every circumstance since the day when all men were provincials of Rome; and yet there has been no age to which Christ did not seem to belong as truly and intimately as he belonged to the world in which Palestine was property of imperial Rome, and Joseph and Mary obscure subjects of the Caesar. He is the only permanent person of history, the only being who was of no age because he was of all, the only complete and unalterable epitome of what man is and what man would be, a creature of two worlds, the world that changes and the world that changes not: the world where spirit but struggles for recognition and the world in which spirit is released to know its own freedom and perfection. How the task of renewal and transformation is simplified for us by his person and example, so clear to our vision, so easy to be understood, so dear to every right instinct in us,—our divine kinsman, to whom our spirits yearn whenever stirred by pain or hope!

And if Christ is adjusted to all ages he is conformed to none: he is the only true citizen of the world. There is in him constant renewal, the fresh, undying quality that draws always direct from the sources of knowledge and of conduct. He interprets,—only he can perfectly interpret,—our text. His is the non-conformity of the perfect individual, unsophisticated, unstaled, unsubdued. His is the perfect learning distilled into wisdom, the perfect friendship lifted to the utter heights of self-sacrifice, the perfect sorrow steeped in hope which keep his mind and spirit naif, spontaneous, creative, the cause, not the result of circumstance. Not all the hoarded counsel of the world is worth the example of a single person: it is abstract, intangible until incarnated: and here, incarnate, is the man Christ who in his own life and person shows us and all the world "what is that good, and acceptable, and perfect will of God" which would have us see in the face of all knowledge, of all love, of all experience the long lines of light which illuminate the meaning of our lives,—lines that blaze unbroken out of the elder ages that have gone and sweep past us into the mysterious days whither we go, from which, one by one, we draw the veil away. In an ancient place of learning we stand where generations meet and merge, where ages render their common reckoning, and the teaching of a university with regard to the long processes of human life should be the same as the Master's: that every soul that is truly to live must be born again, must come fresh into its own age with the spirit of immortality, which is the spirit of eternal youth, upon it, the brightness of another morning of creation about it, the dayspring from on high. "Be ye not conformed to this world: but be ye transformed by the renewing of your mind: that ye may prove what is that good, and acceptable, and perfect will of God" which is without date or age or end and which gives to every one of us a like immortal youth and liberty and power.

GENTLEMEN OF THE GRADUATING CLASS: I have tried to give you in these parting words, on this solemn day, some glimpse of spiritual things. I hope the words have not been too mystical, too remote from the vocabulary of what we ordinarily think and say. We have gone a happy journey of four years together. Our comradeship has not depended upon an actual personal acquaintance with one another. Nothing happens to Princeton that does not happen to all of us: there is no current of our lives which we do not all feel. We have had much counsel together. Though you hand your function of counsel on today to those who are to succeed you, you must know that you will leave much behind you that is your permanent contribution of love to the growth and wholesomeness of the place. And you can never be spiritually severed from Princeton. Some part of Princeton will always live in you, and it is just that fact which I wish might interpret Princeton to you and, through you, to all the world. This *place*, Princeton, is but a material image that changes from age to age: the real Princeton is a spirit, and goes with you, as it stays with us: the spirit of learning which is always young, and which does not conform to this world; the spirit of friendship which unlocks the secret of loyalty and of self-sacrifice; the spirit which seeks intimate contact with the springs of motive, and which lifts us into the presence of Christ. It is a solemn thing to look one another for the last time in the eyes, to grasp hands and say farewell; but we do not in fact break company if we have indeed been linked in spirit. Be brave; walk with open and uplifted eyes; let neither hardship nor sorrow touch you with dismay. Nothing but our own weakness can taint the integrity of manly candour and simple uprightness. God send you stout hearts in all weather. Our love and our faith shall follow you. We pledge you with all good cheer for the long journey and pray God we shall all meet at home at its end.[2]

T MS (WP, DLC).

2 There is a brief WWhw outline, a WWsh draft, and a WWT draft dated May 12, 1907, of this sermon in WP, DLC. It was published, with a few changes, under the title, *The Free Life* (New York, 1908).

Grover Cleveland to the Board of Trustees of Princeton University

Gentlemen: [Princeton, N. J.] June 10, 1907.

. . . Your Committee[1] are of the opinion that the bequest which under the terms of Mrs. Swann's will is to be applied to the erection of a Graduate College building, will upon the final settlement of the decedent's estate amount to nearly or quite two hundred and fifty thousand dollars, of which about two hundred thousand dollars has already been turned over to the University. By the terms of this bequest a building for the use of the Graduate College is to be erected "as soon as practicable." While it is necessary that this building shall be considered as a distinct structure provided by Mrs. Swann's generosity, it is also necessary that it be considered in relation to a general plan for other buildings which must be added to constitute our completed Graduate College.

The site of this building which your Committee must regard as only the first of an imposing group which in the future will be the home of our Graduate College, and its general plan of construction which must be adjustable to future growth has led your Committee to give careful consideration to these questions of site and plan in connection with the contemplated building. There are, however, such a variety of contingencies and circumstances to be weighed in arriving at such a conclusion as the members of your Committee could regard as the best solution of the problem that your Committee is not prepared at this time to present a definite recommendation touching these matters.

All of which is respectfully submitted,

Grover Cleveland Chairman

TRS (Trustees' Papers, UA, NjP).

[1] The Committee on the Graduate School.

A Resolution

[June 10, 1907]

Resolved: That, in view of the need by the President of the University of a stated rest day in the week, the duty of the correspondence with and the entertainment of the University preachers selected by himself and the responsibility for the conduct of the Sunday services in the Chapel be devolved upon Professor Paul van Dyke of the Faculty and that with the approval of the Finance Committee the sum of Five Hundred dollars ($500) annually be set apart from the General Funds of the University for the expenses so incurred.[1]

Hw MS (Trustees' Papers, UA, NjP).

[1] This resolution, introduced by M. W. Jacobus, was adopted by the Board of Trustees.

From the Minutes of the Board of Trustees of Princeton University

[June 10, 1907]

The Trustees of Princeton University met in stated session in the Trustees' Room in the Chancellor Green Library, Princeton, New Jersey, at eleven o'clock on Monday morning, June 10, 1907.

In the temporary absence of the President of the University Mr. John A. Stewart, the Senior Trustee present, called the meeting to order.

The meeting was opened with prayer by Dr. DeWitt. . . .

The President of the University entered the meeting and took the chair. . . .

The President of the University, Chairman of the Committee on the Supplementary Report of the President, reported as follows: . . .[1]

After reading the report, the President of the University spoke on it[2] and then in view of the nearness of the hour for luncheon it was voted to postpone discussion until half past two o'clock.

REPORT OF COMMITTEE ON SUPPLEMENTARY REPORT AND REMARKS BY PRESIDENT ON REPORT TO BE PUBLISHED

On motion of Mr. John A. Stewart duly seconded it was

RESOLVED, that the President of the University be requested to reduce to writing his remarks on the Report of the Committee on the Supplementary Report of the President and that the Report of the Committee and the remarks by the President be published in the Alumni Weekly. . . .

RECOMMENDATION OF COMMITTEE ON SUPPLEMENTARY REPORT OF PRESIDENT ADOPTED

After a full discussion on the Report of the Committee on the Supplementary Report of the President on motion duly seconded the recommendation of the Committee was adopted.[3]

ADJOURNMENT

The Board then adjourned to meet again at half past nine o'clock on Wednesday morning June 12th.

[1] Here follows the Report on the Social Coordination of the University printed at June 6, 1907.

[2] The gist of Wilson's remarks is printed in the following document.

[3] D. B. Jones to H. van Dyke, July 10, 1907, states that only one member of the board voted against the motion. C. H. McCormick to WW, June 10, 1907, indicates that he was Joseph Bernard Shea.

A News Release

[c. June 10, 1907]

PRESIDENT WILSON'S ADDRESS TO THE BOARD OF TRUSTEES

In presenting the above report, as chairman of the committee, President Wilson spoke, in substance, as follows:

Gentlemen of the Board of Trustees: I have never had occasion, I probably never shall have occasion, to lay a more important matter before you than the proposals contained in this report; and, full as that report is, I feel justified in detaining you to add some explanatory matter of my own.

The plan outlined in the report is not of hasty or recent conception, and its object is not primarily a social reorganization of the University. It is but part,—an indispensable part,—of the purpose we have steadfastly set ourselves to accomplish, namely, the reorganization and revitalization of the University as an academic body, whose objects are not primarily social but intellectual, and whose characteristic work can be accomplished only in organic fashion, without confusion of aims or methods, and without regard to things which are immaterial to the main end in view. I have long foreseen the necessity of thus drawing the undergraduates together in genuinely residential groups in direct association with members of the Faculty, as an indispensable accompaniment and completion of the preceptorial system and of all other measures we have taken to quicken and mature the intellectual life of the University.

The upper-class clubs seem, in the report, to occupy the foreground of the entire picture, and to be somehow at the heart of the circumstances which render a social recoordination of the University necessary; but that is only an accident of our development. What the report proposes would in any case be necessary. It is in itself the best and most thoroughly tested means of drawing the social and intellectual life of any college together which desired to do the things it is our purpose and duty to do for Princeton. The clubs simply happen to stand in the way. They are not consciously doing anything to the detriment of the University. Their spirit, on the contrary, has, throughout the greater part of their existence, been singularly fine. The thoughtful men in them have done everything in their power to prevent factional feeling in the University and a too keen rivalry between the clubs; and the clubs have always been centres of the most loyal feeling for the University. But, in spite of their admirable spirit and of every watchful effort they have made to the contrary, and by a process which neither they nor we could successfully control, a system of social life has grown up in the University by reason of their existence which divides classes, creates artificial groups for social purposes, and renders a wholesome university spirit impossible. Circumstances created, not by design, but by the inevitable operation of human nature, render a radical reorganization of our life imperative, if the main ends for which that life is meant are to be attained.

Intellectual and spiritual development, in the broadest sense of those terms, are the chief and, indeed, the only legitimate aims of university life. Not that sport and social pleasure are to be excluded; they ought, on the contrary, to be given the keener test by being made parts, the natural accompaniments, of a life that is deeply stimulating and interesting. But a university is first of all a place of study, a place in which to acquire a certain mastery in the use of the mind, in which to throw off crudities and gain a habit of thoughtful comprehension which is very different from a knowledge of set "lessons" and a mastery of allotted tasks. This is our chief thought and ideal for Princeton; and if we can in any considerable degree realize it every other good thing will come in its train,—the companionships which stimulate and reward, the fun that clears the head and lightens the spirits, the zest of youth that is the true seed of real manhood. These things come only when a university is made a real community, its companionships academic and steeped in the atmosphere of a life so constituted as to feel all the deeper impulses of the place: a life in which teacher and pupil alike take a natural part in terms of spontaneous intimacy, and in which there is constant matter-of-fact contact between men young and old. Contacts of mind become the common accompaniment of social pleasure in such a community. Such is the purpose of the residential quads; and there is the abundant proof of long experience that they will accomplish it.

Under our present social organization there is a constant, even an increasing, disconnection between the life and the work of the University, between its companionships and its duties; there is an almost entire disconnection of consciousness between its hours and its ideals of pleasure and its hours and ideals of work. The social activities of the place not only have no necessary connection with any of its serious tasks, but are, besides, exceedingly complex and absorbing; do in fact absorb the energies of the most active undergraduates in purely unacademic things. It has become common for Sophomores, as the end of the academic year approaches, to ask the advice of their instructors (now that there is some intimacy of counsel between them) as to which career they shall choose for the remainder of their course, the studious or the social, the life of the student or the life of the clubman,—and that not because there is in the clubs any cynical indifference to study but because the social activities into which their members are naturally and inevitably drawn are very many and very delightful and very engrossing, and study has to take its chance in competition with them.

The last two years have seen influences of this kind increase in strength at an extraordinary rate, and gain a momentum which makes this the imperative time of action. It is clearly evident to anyone who lives in Princeton and intimately touches the life of the place that these influences are now cutting at the root of a thing upon which we depend for the maintenance of some of the best things in our custom and tradition. They are splitting classes into factions, and endangering that class spirit upon which we depend for our self-government and for the transmission of most of the loyal impulses of the University. The "politics" of candidacy for membership in the upper-class clubs not only produce a constant and very demoralizing distraction from university duties in Freshman and Sophomore years and enforce all sorts of questionable actions, putting the sanction of habit upon many understandings which seriously hamper the freedom and the personal development of lads who have good stuff of initiative in them: they cut deeper even than that. Group rivalries break the solidarity of the classes. The younger classes are at no point made conscious of the interests of the University; their whole thought is concentrated upon individual ambitions, upon means of preference, upon combinations to obtain selfish individual ends, and the welfare of the University, as against any particular bad custom which will serve that purpose, is ignored, labour as the upper classmen may to point it out and enforce it. Not only do men in all classes feel that too great absorption in study will involve a virtual disqualification for social preferment: they also feel that the chief objects of their happiness and their ambition are connected with their social affiliations, not with the general interests of the University. They strive against this, when they become Juniors and Seniors, but they do not strive against it successfully; and when they are Freshmen and Sophomores they do not strive against it at all. Men who enter the University after Freshman year are generally thrown out of the running altogether and find themselves in the upper years isolated and lonely, to the still further weakening of the old-time class solidarity. If for nothing else than to keep the classes undivided in spirit, the new quad. divisions would be preferable to the present club divisions. The present system of our life is artificial and unwholesome. Individuals and classes alike must be restored to that feeling of intimate and constant connection with the University as *the University*, as an organic, indivisible thing, their home and their atmosphere, upon which Princeton's strength and prestige depend.

The facts are disputed by no one who knows our undergraduate life as it is now constituted. It is by common consent threatened with the loss of college feeling and of class feeling and it is entirely disconnected from the intellectual purposes of the place in its aims and organization. Debate turns, not upon the facts, but only upon the means and methods of reorganization. The finest evidence of the spirit of Princeton seems to me to lie in the fact that the undergraduates themselves have, during the past year, come to recognize the situation in all its significance and to wish for an entire emancipation from it, by no matter how radical a remedy. The things they have foreseen and dreaded and tried to stave off have come upon them, and they are ready to accept any thoroughgoing reform.

The remedy proposed by the committee whose report I have read is radical, indeed, but not wholly out of line with the organization it is meant to replace. The associations formed in the quads. will be like the associations formed in the clubs; with the elective principle left out, indeed, but with all the opportunities for a natural selection of chums and companions that the larger number in residence will afford; and with an added dignity of association, under resident members of the Faculty, fitted for the association and for the function of leadership and example which will naturally fall to them. The elective principle in the clubs at present amounts to little more than the right to choose groups of men (artificially enough formed, as every body knows) rather than individuals. And, whether the new plan is like the old plan or not, it is not the social side that our thought is dwelling on. We are not seeking to form better clubs, but academic communities. We are making a university, not devising a method of social pleasure. The social life of the quads. will be all-inclusive, and it will serve as the medium for things intellectual.

The question, how the transition from our present social organization to the new organization is to be effected,—with what adjustments, accommodations, measures of transformation,—is now our main subject of debate; and we can enter on that debate with a frankness and confidence in each other which I believe no other university in the world could hope for in an undertaking of such delicacy and magnitude. We have a body of alumni for whom the interests of the University as a whole, as they may be made to see those interests at any moment of action, take precedence over every other consideration, and over every rival sentiment. They are ready to be partners with the undergraduates and ourselves in accomplishing anything that may be necessary to give free and wholesome vigor to the life of the University and to secure to her the fame which she covets and must win,—the fame of distinct intellectual purpose and a clear knowledge of the means by which she proposes to attain them.

I take leave to say that Princeton is the only university in the country which has found itself, which has formulated a clear ideal and deliberately set about the synthesis of plan necessary to realize it. She has set the country an example in the methods of teaching necessary to give a great university the intimacy of contact and the direct efficiency of instruction hitherto supposed to belong only to the small college, and suited to create, besides, something which the small college has seldom known how to create,—a habit and freedom of independent reading which makes a "course" something more than the instruction of a single classroom or a single instructor; and now she must take the next step. She must organize her life in such a way that these contacts between the university and the student shall be stuff of daily habit, and not merely matters of formal appointment; not a thing of the class-room and conference only, but a thing which may touch every hour, any hour, of the day, and fill seasons of leisure and enjoyment with a consciousness of what it is that vitalizes a university and makes it a force in the life of a great nation. Common counsel shall bring us to this consummation, —not without trouble, but without serious conflict of opinion or purpose, as a new exhibition of what love of Princeton can do for her regeneration when her sons set themselves to the task. The labour will be pleasant, and the abiding fame of it will belong to all of us in common.[1]

* * * * * * * *

[1] There is a WWT outline, a WWsh draft, and a WWT draft of this statement in WP, DLC.

In order to complete the record of Commencement with regard to this important matter, we add the memorandum which Dr. Wilson sent to the presidents of the several upper-class clubs, in order to afford them an opportunity to discuss the project at their annual banquets, if they chose to do so, in a form which would be exact and not made up out of oral report. This memorandum, he gave it to be understood, emanated only from him individually and did not when it was issued rest upon any action of the Board of Trustees. Since he sent it out the Trustees have adopted the essential idea and purpose of the plan. The details embodied in the memorandum remain President Wilson's individual suggestions.[2]

MEMORANDUM CONCERNING RESIDENTIAL QUADS.

I am very glad indeed to have an opportunity to explain a plan which, though certainly radical in character, can easily be so misunderstood as to seem much more radical than it is. It is a scheme I have long had in mind as a necessary means of giving Princeton not only social but also academic coordination and of making her new methods of study a vital part of her undergraduate life.

The plan in its briefest terms is this: to draw the undergraduates together into residential quads. in which they shall eat as well as lodge together, and in which they shall, under the presidency of a resident member of the Faculty, regulate their own corporate life by some simple method of self-government. For this purpose it would be necessary to place all future dormitories in such relation to those already erected as to form close geographical units, and to erect in connection with each group a building which shall contain a dining room, kitchen and serving rooms, a handsome common room for social purposes, and rooms for the member of the Faculty who shall preside in the quad. Every undergraduate would be required actually to live in his quad.—that is, to take his meals there as well as lodge there; and the residents of each quad. would be made up as nearly as might be of equal numbers of Seniors, Juniors, Sophomores, and Freshmen: because it is clear to every one that the life of the University can be best regulated and developed only when the under-classmen are in constant association with upper-classmen upon such terms as to be formed and guided by them. The self-government of each group would naturally be vested in the Seniors, or in the Seniors and Juniors, who were members of the quad.

[2] This paragraph is added from the WWT draft just mentioned.

The objects of this arrangement would be (1) to place unmarried members of the Faculty in residence in the quads. in order to bring them into close, habitual, natural association with the undergraduates and so intimately tie the intellectual and social life of the place into one another; (2) to associate the four classes in a genuinely organic manner and make of the University a real social body, to the exclusion of cliques and separate class social organizations; (3) to give the University the kind of common consciousness which apparently comes from the closer sorts of social contact, to be had only outside the classroom, and most easily to be got about a common table, and in the contacts of a common life.

This plan directly affects the upper-class clubs because, under it, it would be necessary to keep the most influential and efficient Seniors and Juniors in residence in the quads. for their government and direction. It would be clearly out of the question to let them eat elsewhere and find their chief interests elsewhere, leaving the quads. to Freshmen and Sophomores and a minority of upperclassmen who would be too few to play any true part of influence or control. The adoption of the plan would obviously make it necessary that the clubs should allow themselves to be absorbed into the University, by the natural process of becoming themselves residential quads., and so retaining their historical identity at the same time that they showed their devotion to the University by an act of supreme self-sacrifice. I cannot imagine a service to the University which would bring more distinction, more éclat throughout the entire university world, or which would give to our present clubs a position of greater interest and importance in the history of academic life in America.

The details of the adjustments which would be necessary I have in large part thought out; but I do not wish to dwell upon them now, simply because I wish them to be subject to change in my own mind. These complicated things cannot be wisely planned or enacted except by slow processes of common counsel; and I should wish the details of such a scheme of transformation to be worked out by the frank conference of all concerned.

But some things seem to me clear. I should hope that, in effecting the transition, each club would vest its property in the hands of a small board of trustees of its own choice who should be charged with administering it for the benefit of the University in association with the present university authorities; and that that board should have important powers of advice or confirmation in respect of the appointment of resident members of the Faculty and the regulations governing the assignment of students to the quad. under its supervision, and with regard to all matters upon which they could retain a hold without embarrassing the uniform government of the University as a whole or the supreme authority of the Trustees of the University itself. And I see no reason why the graduate members of the several clubs might not retain all the privileges they now enjoy in respect of the use of the club property and meals at the club tables on their visits to Princeton. I see no reason why they should ever feel their relations to the clubs at all radically altered because the clubs had in effect become residential colleges.

Moreover, I should hope that it would be borne in mind that this scheme of social and academic coordination, which present conditions in the University seem to render imperatively necessary, is not a plan to prevent club life in Princeton. Club life is based upon social instincts and principles which it would be impossible to eradicate. But these natural instincts and tendencies would, under the new order of things, undoubtedly express themselves in a different way, a much better way than at present, —as they express themselves wherever men of congenial tastes find themselves in need of relaxation. Probably clubs of an entirely different character, not residential, but purely social organizations, would from time to time spring up; and I do not think that the university authorities would be jealous of that, provided such associations were sharply separated both in form and in tradition from the processes which have given us our present social strifes, perplexities, and divisions. No one can now predict just how the new developments would come or just what shapes they would take. Woodrow Wilson.[3]

CC MS (WWP, UA, NjP).

[3] This news release, together with Wilson's Report on the Social Coordination of the University, was published in the *Princeton Alumni Weekly*, VII (June 12, 1907), 606-15.

From Cyrus Hall McCormick

Pennsylvania Special
En Route. June 10, 1907.

Dear Woodrow:

On the train to Philadelphia Mr. Jones and I had a chance to talk with Mr. Shea, and he assures us that he will support in the most loyal way the vote of the trustees.

Now as to the method of presenting this matter, would it not be well for you and such members of the Committee as are available, to have your conference with representative men of the most influential clubs—and in fact all the clubs—next October instead of now.

The main object of my writing is to send you a cordial message on this subject from Mr. Jones and from me, that you may feel that we will do all we can for a united movement on this subject, which now has the backing of the Board as to the general scheme.

Please do not answer this, for we know that you have all that you can do before taking the vacation which any man ought to need very much who has done the work that you have during the last few weeks. I am

Very sincerely yours, Cyrus Hall McCormick

TLS (WP, DLC).

From Ralph Adams Cram

My dear Dr. Wilson: Boston, June 10, 1907.

I find it will be convenient for Mr. Pyne if I come to Princeton for next Friday, and I have, therefore, arranged to do so, when I shall hope to have the pleasure of seeing you.

I shall send you tomorrow a tentative general scheme for the development of the University plan. This is a modification of the first sketch already shown you. I am anxious to obtain, if possible, conditional approval of this scheme on its general lines, in order that I may study the entire plan in detail and at a larger scale. If this general scheme is approved, I propose to study out each section at a scale of 20 ft. to the inch, and as each sheet is finished, have it posted by Mr. Bunn over the corresponding section of the large plan he has placed on the wall of the office next his own department. When all the sections are completed, it will be possible to study the scheme as a whole and reconsider such portions as seem to the University authorities to require such reconsideration.

I have also taken the liberty of asking Mr. Bunn for plans showing the exact size and location of McCosh Hall and of Patton Hall; also, I have asked him if at his convenience he can have all the important trees around the various buildings indicated accurately on the large scale plan. I feel very strongly that the final arrangement of buildings should be considered very carefully in connection with the position of the more beautiful of the trees, as I am extremely averse to wilful destruction of those trees that are beautiful in themselves, or because of their position.

Very truly yours, R A Cram. Supervising Architect.

TLS (WP, DLC).

From Charles Homer Haskins

Dear Dr. Wilson: Cambridge, Mass., June 10, 1907.

One of my old Wisconsin students, Edwin W. Pahlow, writes me that, at Professor Daniels' suggestion, he is a candidate for a possible preceptorship at Princeton. On the whole I believe Pahlow would be a very good man for such work. His preliminiary training before he came to college was not very thorough, a defect which crops out occasionally, and I shall be surer of his intellectual staying power when he has worked out a doctor's thesis, but he has good ability and a good knowledge of history and related subjects. He spent one year after graduation at the University of Wisconsin and three years here, and he has had, at different times, two years in Europe. Two years ago he was one of my assistants in the freshman course in history, and last year he was instructor at Wisconsin. He has been particularly interested in modern European history but he has worked over other fields. I found him a good assistant, not so severe in his standards as [Hiram] Bingham, but getting a good hold of his boys. At Wisconsin he did his work to their satisfaction, and showed particular capacity for administrative duties. He was president of the History Club the last year he was here, and carried it through an uncommonly successful year.

Personally Pahlow is a delightful fellow, and I am very fond of him. He is enthusiastic for his work, he makes warm friends, and he takes a keen personal interest in his students. I should expect him to get on admirably with his men under a system of personal conference. Moreover he has a charming wife,[1] and the two would be welcome members of your community.

Turner can tell you more of Pahlow. He likes him as I do.

Sincerely yours, Charles H. Haskins.

TLS (WWP, UA, NjP).

[1] Gertrude Curtis Brown Pahlow, who later—between 1914 and 1935—published eight novels.

From the Diary of William Starr Myers

Tues. June 11 [1907].

At the alumni luncheon in the gym. at one oclock. We formed in front of Nassau Hall, & marched down to it. The largest number I have ever sat down at table with, must have been 800 or 1000 men. . . .

Notes for an Address

Alumni Lunch '07 11 June, 1907.

A year of achievement and of promise.

I. ACHIEVEMENT: Confirmation of preceptorial system and of our new order of life.

Extraordinary life of hitherto dormant forces.

Princeton has set out on a career of intellectual development which nothing can stay or limit except lack of resources.

II. Promise: Great gifts to science, and what they foretell.

Professor Capps.

Social re-coördination.

The conditions

The plan, sanctioned by the Board of Trustees.

The method: common counsel among all the partners.

III. Standing and Example of Princeton.

A *united body* capable of what no other University would dare to undertake.

Definite Ideals.

Constructive methods.

Synthetic conceptions and processes.

The only university in America that has found itself in an age of doubt and of conflicting counsels.[1]

WWT MS (WP, DLC).

1 There is a brief report of this address in the *Princeton Alumni Weekly*, VII (June 12, 1907), 603.

From James Mauran Rhodes, Jr.[1]

Dear Sir: Philadelphia June 11th, 1907.

Since hearing your circular to the "Ivy Club" on the proposed changes in the makeup of Princeton University last Friday night and discussion since that time by various Alumni, I am desirous of hearing more about it.

The suggestions you make are so radical that I want to give them considerable thought and sincerely trust that others will do likewise. I feel so strongly that conditions existing in the University to-day bear some relation to the general conditions existing all over the country incident to the rapid expansion and acquirement of great fortunes in the last ten years, that a solution of the conditions at Princeton are in a measure a step toward a solution of the larger proposition,–through educating men while young to a more democratic spirit than appears to exist at the present time.

I understand a report was made to the Board of Trustees yesterday by a sub-committee appointed to consider your proposals, and write to ask if this report is to be published and sent to the Alumni, and if not, how can I procure either a copy of it or some statement fully describing the proposed changes.

Hoping my communication will not bother you too much, I beg to remain,

Yours very truly, J. M. Rhodes, Jr., '97

TLS (WP, DLC).

[1] Princeton 1897, at this time a securities broker with Rhodes, Sinkler & Butcher of Philadelphia.

From David Benton Jones

My Dear Doctor: Chicago June 12th, 1907.

I hope that tomorrow will bring you rest and relief from the strain of the last few days. Nothing is now so important as that. The issue has been fully and clearly stated and when the report and your statement are printed, the club men can exercise their teeth upon them and will find more comfort in gnawing at a file than in attempting to bolster up the present social organization of the University. After your comments upon the report, I was most impressed by the very brief and simple statement which Mr. Pyne made. Coming from him with his long and intimate knowledge of the situation and his close personal relations to it, it was overwhelmingly impressive and pathetic to a degree. It showed great courage and strength in a great emergency and it gave me a new insight into the man's real character.

Until you have had a very substantial rest, I hope you will limit your work on this great problem to dictating your comments upon the report and having both printed. I am so confident that the statement of the condition of things is all the argument needed that you need not be at all anxious as to the outcome. You know what I think of the courage it took to present the issue in its present form. When Princeton is re-organized and redeemed, as I hope it will be, one secondary result of importance will be the putting an end to the adoration of the athlete as the supreme emotion of the undergraduate world. This craze can only be eliminated by the substitution of such a life as you hope for for Princeton. It cannot be eliminated by any direct attack as long as the intellectual side is subordinate to the social.

Please do not send even a line of acknowledgment in reply to this letter. I hesitate to break in even to the extent of having you read it. You will need all the endurance you can accumulate during your long vacation to work out this great problem during the coming year. I do not mean by working out that you will be able to put it into full effect, but to formulate the details of the solution. Very sincerely yours, David B. Jones

TLS (WP, DLC).

From Lawrence Crane Woods

My dear Dr. Wilson: Pittsburg, Pa. June 12, 1907.

We were all disappointed that we lost the splendid address you made to us when you were here in April.[1] I was, therefore, delighted to see that you had the full notes of your baccalaureate which I had the great pleasure of hearing Sunday morning. Has this already been printed? If not, is there not some way in which I can get a copy of it? It was one of the most helpful, thoughtful and beautiful baccalaureates that I ever heard. My mother,[2] Rev. Dr. Campbell,[3] Judge Macfarlane, '78,[4] and others would like very much to read it.

Allow me to express the appreciation and gratitude of every Princeton man for the magnificent progress that the University has made in a hundred and one directions since you assumed the presidency. As I went over the campus, saw the new buildings, the restoration of old ones, the exquisite landscape gardening, tree planting, to say nothing of Carnegie Lake, etc., I could see the physical indication of the vital, intellectual forces which are guiding Princeton in such a wonderful way. Time and again I was impressed with not only the amount of money but more particularly the endless thought which must have been expended in every direction, spreading out into the beautification and improvement of the town itself. The best part of it all is to feel that it is based solely on the record of intellectual supremacy, that people are now giving their time and money to Princeton because they know that you are conducting the University on lines which more than justify the expenditure of large capital. From a sentimental devotion to an ideal, you have given us solid reason for our faith in Princeton.

Your last proposal as to the evolution of our club system meets with my hearty endorsement, although I should not express this publicly as I am not an Ivy man and there were no other clubs in existence when I was in college. I am aware, however, of the serious nature of this problem to Princeton and am very glad that you are grappling with it. I have no question but that the outcome will be ultimately satisfactory to everyone, and the wisdom of your solution be fully justified.

I can only regret that I can so feebly express the admiration and pride which I hear echoed on all sides by trustees, faculty, alumni and undergraduates alike as to your administration.

Trusting that you may have a most restful and delightful summer, believe me, always,

Very sincerely yours, Lawrence C Woods

TLS (WP, DLC).

[1] That is, when Wilson spoke to the Princeton Club of Western Pennsylvania on April 2, 1907. A news report of his speech is printed at April 3, 1907.

[2] Ellen Cornelia Crane (Mrs. George) Woods.

[3] The Rev. Dr. William Oliver Campbell, pastor of the Sewickley, Pa., Presbyterian Church.

[4] James Rieman MacFarlane, Princeton 1878, judge of the Court of Common Pleas in Pittsburgh.

To Cyrus Hall McCormick

My dear Cyrus: Princeton, N. J. June 14th, 1907.

Thank you most sincerely for your telegram and letter en route. I had no real doubt that Mr. Shea would be loyal to our decision, but it is greatly reassuring to have it directly from him, and I deeply appreciate your thoughtfulness in telling me of it.

We have a great task before us, but fortunately everybody who knows the facts is convinced of its necessity, and throughout Commencement I have had the most gratifying indications that the alumni will lend us their support in the most loyal way; that all we have to do is to be frank with them in order to carry them with us in a body.

With warmest regard,

Always faithfully yours, Woodrow Wilson

TLS (WP, DLC).

From George Corning Fraser

My dear Dr. Wilson: New York. June 14, 1907.

I understand that a report, embodying the suggestions outlined in your Memorandum sent me under date of the 3d instant, was submitted to the Board of Trustees of the University, at its Meeting this week.

I would be deeply appreciative if you would advise me whether this is a fact and, if so, what action the Board has taken in the matter. Is the report, if any was made, of such a nature that you could properly permit me to see it?

The situation sought to be met is so grave, and the remedy suggested so radical, that I feel justified in troubling you for further information, since you were good enough to present the matter to me in your recent letter.

Faithfully yours, G. C. Fraser

TLS (WP, DLC).

From Frederick Jackson Turner

My dear President Wilson, Madison [Wisc.] June 14, 1907

Mr Edwin Pahlow writes me from Oxford that he is applying for a preceptorship in Princeton, and I am glad to support his application.

Pahlow is a man with scholarly qualities, and is interested in research and is ambitious. He will, in my judgement, do good, but not great, work in research; but his strength is as a good historical and personal influence among undergraduates. He is a charming fellow, and with his wife, during the year he spent with us filling a temporary position, he made a center of undergraduate life that was helpful, and wholesome. He is a reasonably good lecturer but is not so strong in this direction as in his personal contact with young men. His training is adequate and I presume he has given you a full account of himself. His name may indicate a Wisconsin German type, but he is socially gifted and experienced and makes warm friendships among nice people.

I should like to see you give him a position. We have recommended him to fill a vacancy in the University of Oregon, but he would be in more natural surroundings in the east.

With cordial regard

I am Yours ever Frederick J. Turner

ALS (WWP, UA, NjP).

To George Corning Fraser

My dear Mr. Fraser: [Princeton, N. J.] June 15th, 1907.

You are quite right in the information you received. A committee of the Board made a full report on the matter of the social reorganization of the University, and its report was adopted by the Board, authorizing me to go forward with the maturing of the plan which I outlined to you in the memorandum I sent.

The report will, I am glad to say, be published in the next number of The Alumni Weekly, which is to appear in about a week or ten days,[1] and will be accompanied by explanatory matter which the Board requested me to add. This copy of The Weekly will be sent to all the alumni, in order that their information about this exceedingly important matter may be as full as possible.

I shall be very glad if you will write to me after reading the report, to make any suggestions that may occur to you. We shall need common counsel in this matter, to work it out in the proper way. Always cordially and sincerely yours,

[Woodrow Wilson]

CCL (WWP, UA, NjP).

[1] As has been noted earlier, it appeared in the issue dated June 12, 1907, which actually came out about June 24, 1907.

To Frederick Jackson Turner

My dear Turner: Princeton, N. J. June 17th, 1907.

Thank you very much for your letter of June 14th. Mr. Pahlow had written to me, and Haskins has also been kind enough to write about him. I have asked him to see me as soon as possible after his arrival in this country. I am very much interested in what you say about him, and we happen to be in need on [of] additional assistance in his department.

It was a great pleasure to hear from you. I sincerely hope that you are well and that all goes well with you.

Always cordially yours, Woodrow Wilson

TLS (F. J. Turner Papers, CSmH).

From Sir William Mather

London, June 17th, 1907.

Hearty greetings and congratulations to graduating class. Best wishes to assembled alumni. My homage to President, Faculty and Trustees. Long may Old Nassau flourish and become Alma Mater to generations yet unborn.

William Mather, London.

T telegram (WWP, UA, NjP).

To Sir William Mather

My dear Sir William: [Princeton, N. J.] June 18th, 1907.

I came in from a walk yesterday to find your cable lying on my table. It is most delightful that you should remember us in this way, and I wish with all my heart that your message had come while the town was full of alumni. Our Commencement season closed last Wednesday, the twelfth. Probably something misled you as to the date. I am going to ask the editor of our Alumni Weekly to publish your cable, for I know how gratifying it will be to everyone.[1] I am sure that I am speaking for all my colleagues in sending you the warmest greetings and the sincerest thanks.

Having failed in our efforts to get Mr. Bryce, we are now wondering if you would find it possible and pleasant to come over next spring and join in some simple ceremonies connected with the formal giving of the sun-dial. We all of us particularly desire that you should be present on that occasion, and I am sure that the delay would not take away its zest or appropriateness.

Mrs. Wilson and my daughters join me in warmest regards to Lady Mather, your daughters, and yourself.

Always cordially and sincerely yours,

[Woodrow Wilson]

CCL (WWP, UA, NjP).

[1] It was published in the *Princeton Alumni Weekly*, VII (June 12, 1907), 604.

From John Allan Wyeth

My dear Mr. Wilson: [New York] June 18, 1907.

I was glad to know from your letter of recent date that later, when you were resting from your labor, you would take up the matter of Mr. Laffan's letter to Judge Parker, and would elaborate it in your own way.

It has occurred to me that something of this kind might be done, with great benefit to the public, especially if it could be presented through the New York Southern Society. I have the honor to be President this year, and our annual dinner is on the 11th of December, at the Waldorf-Astoria, and I wish very much you could see your way to make our Society the forum from which you could give these conclusions to our whole country.

I should deem it a very great honor, as well as pleasure, to have you speak at my dinner.

We enjoyed the class day exercises very much, and Heaven seemed to be on our side, both in the matter of weather and of winning the ball game.[1]

My big boy[2] comes home for his vacation hale and hearty, full of enthusiasm for Princeton.

Sincerely yours, John A Wyeth

TLS (WP, DLC).

[1] When Princeton defeated Yale 4 to 3 on June 8, 1907.

[2] Marion Sims Wyeth, who had just completed his freshman year at Princeton.

From Franklin Murphy, Jr.

My dear Dr. Wilson: Newark, New Jersey June 18th, 1907.

Please pardon my delay in reporting to you upon the feeling at the Tiger Inn concerning your proposal for the future use of the Clubs. I was away all last week and this is really the first chance I have had to write you.

I read your memorandum to our Club at the annual meeting Friday night and there were about sixty men present. The sentiment was very strongly against your suggestion and a resolution was offered stating that the sentiment of the Club was strongly opposed to the adoption of your suggestion because it seemed to mark the end of class cohesion. After a discussion it was unanimously decided that it was not fair to you to pass such a resolution without an opportunity for further explanation and careful thought but there is no doubt that practically every member present felt it would be a most unfortunate step for Princeton to take. If there is one thing that makes Princeton strong with her alumni it is the class spirit. Boys go there as freshmen and share each other's troubles and by the end of sophomore year become closely attached to each other and that feeling grows and reaches its climax at graduation. From what I have observed it maintains its hold as long as a man lives and to an extent that no other college approaches. Any action that puts the class spirit in peril is alarming to graduates. I have discussed this matter with many men since I received your letter and there has not been a single one who approved of your suggestion and yet I think it is perfectly true that the faith the alumni have in your judgment will assure an unprejudiced consideration when your plan is more fully explained and developed.

Would it be too much trouble to send me another copy of the memorandum? My copy was taken away at our Club meeting and I could not find it again.

Sincerely yours, Franklin Murphy jr.

TLS (WP, DLC).

To Franklin Murphy, Jr.

My dear Mr. Murphy: [Princeton, N. J.] June 20th, 1907.

I thank you sincerely for your letter of June 18th. It is just the kind of letter which will assist to throw light on the very difficult matter we are now handling.

The particular argument against the new scheme to which you yourself attach so much weight and which has been used so prominently in the discussions you have heard shows a very singular thing: namely, how rapidly conditions change at Princeton and how possible it is for the alumni of the University to be quite unaware of the radical things that are happening.

As a matter of fact, nothing is more damaging to the homogeneity and spirit of the classes than what is going on here, and it is one of our deepest convictions that the measures we are seeking to take will do more than anything else could do to prevent the loss of class spirit, which we all value so highly. Under present conditions the feeling of the freshmen and sophomores for the University is being rapidly replaced by a clique feeling and by impulses of social ambition, which are wholly incompatible with the old order of things as you knew them while you were in college. I quite agree with you that class spirit must be maintained as one of the foundations of our self-government and of a great many things which we value profoundly, but I can assure you that it cannot be maintained under the present social organization of the University. Of that we have had abundant and convincing proofs during the last year and a half or two years.

I touch upon this matter in the remarks with which I accompany the report recently adopted by the Board of Trustees, in the forth-coming number of The Alumni Weekly.

Allow me again to thank you for your letter and to express my appreciation of the feeling manifested by your club in postponing all action with regard to this matter until fuller discussion should have brought all its merits to the surface.

Cordially and sincerely yours, [Woodrow Wilson]

CCL (WP, DLC).

From John Howell Westcott

Dear Woodrow: Princeton University June 20, 1907.

I was never more, if as much, surprised in my life as last evening when the letter about my increase of salary came.[1] Of course that much money is very welcome, & the evidence of the appreciation of my services is far more grateful. But it doesn't occur that they are worth so much, & I almost feel as if it were wrong for me to take so much. You have no idea how little my mind has worked these last two years. I've just managed to keep moving under the terrible load of depression & put up a pretty poor bluff for the public view. I seemed to be at work, but its only a fraction of my mind that has been doing anything. And so I feel half dishonest to draw so much salary. I hope other people, at any rate, were equally well treated—some of them deserve it far more. It has always been my luck to be overappreciated.

At any rate, in six years I can be put on the Carnegie pension list. You can easily get a better man for $4000. Just now I wish money was no object—then I could give my salary to Abbott. Having been appraised so high, it would be a satisfaction to serve the college for nothing the rest of my active years, & get him in to help. I am more than ever convinced that he is the best man in the country for us at present.* But I could not feel disappointed that you could not make it possible to get him now. So much has been done, that the year is a memorable one and we must be profoundly thankful for what we have been able to secure. But I shall keep my mind on Abbott. The chance may come again.

I suppose you knew I went to see you & Mrs. Wilson the last day in Princeton. May you both have a satisfactory & happy summer! You must get a good rest. It's no flattery, but sober truth that immense importance attaches to your being well & strong for years to come. All about the country they are manifestly recognizing the unique value of your plan of education, & it must be kept going till it is well established.

Yours ever J. H. Westcott

* I mean, after getting Capps, of course.

ALS (WP, DLC).

[1] His salary was increased from $3,000 to $4,000 per annum.

From Samuel Ross Winans

My dear Dr. Wilson, Princeton June 20 [1907]

May I express to you my very deep appreciation of the Board's action touching salary,[1] of which the Secretary has apprised me.

I congratulate you on being able to effect in this direction what I know you have had at heart—and I trust each year may bring fresh realization of your larger plans,—plans (if you will let me say it) so nobly conceived, and prosecuted with the quiet patience and unshaken determination—which marks great leaders. Very Sincerely Yours S. R. Winans

ALS (WP, DLC).

1 His salary was increased from $4,000 to $4,500 per annum.

From Edwin William Pahlow

Dear President Wilson, Reading, Mass. June 20th/07.

Your cordial note of the 15th awaited me on my arrival in Boston yesterday. As we are staying within a stone's throw of Cambridge, I can easily await your convenience there on the 26th.[1] I shall plan to spend the day in Cambridge, and, if you desire, will try to see you during the morning to make an appointment for later in the day. If you find you cannot spare the time then, I will let you know by telegraph (as you suggested), on what day I shall come to Princeton.

Yours very respectfully Edwin W. Pahlow.

ALS (WWP, UA, NjP).

1 Wilson was to be in Cambridge, Mass., on June 26 to receive the LL.D. from Harvard University and to speak at the afternoon exercises in Memorial Hall. See n. 1 to the address printed at June 26, 1907.

From Henry Burling Thompson

Wilmington, Del.

Dear President Wilson: 6th Mo., 21st, 1907.

I enclose a letter received to-day from Mr. Cram, with copy of my reply to same, and will ask you to let Mr. Cram know as to the exact date at which his salary begins.

Kindly return me his letter and my reply, as I am filing all these letters for Archie Russell's review on his return.

I spent Wednesday night at Riverdale with Cleve Dodge, and he seemed to be entirely satisfied with the way in which the question of the new Biological building has been handled.

This morning I received a letter from Mr. Schroeder, which is encouraging, as he seems to feel that the solution of the problem on the lines laid down is not an impossible one.

Yours very truly, Henry B Thompson

TLS (WP, DLC).

From John Allan Wyeth

My dear Mr. Wilson: [New York] June 21, 1907.

I am very happy to know, not only of your willingness, but that it is probable that you may be with us on the 11th of December.[1]

I shall hope between now and then to have a few minutes with you, in order to submit to you about thirty lines of my convictions of what the Southern man of to-day should represent. . . .

We go to the Adirondacks on July 1st for the Summer, and Mrs. Wyeth, my children and I send our best wishes for you and yours. Sincerely yours, John A Wyeth

TLS (WP, DLC).

[1] As it turned out, Wilson was unable to speak to the Southern Society of New York in December on account of illness.

To Henry Burling Thompson

My dear Mr. Thompson: Princeton, N. J. June 22, 1907.

Thank you for your letter of the 21st. I am writing to Mr. Cram today, to confirm your decision that the year for which his first year's salary is to be paid began the 28th of March.

I am very much pleased to hear what you tell me about Cleve Dodge's feeling concerning the biological building, and Mr. Schroeder's hope that the problem can be solved on the lines laid down at our conference at Pyne's house.

I am looking forward with a great deal of pleasure to seeing you often this summer.[1]

Always cordially and faithfully yours,

Woodrow Wilson

TLS (WC, NjP).

[1] They were both spending their summer vacations in the Adirondacks at St. Hubert's, Essex County, N. Y.

To Ralph Adams Cram

My dear Mr. Cram: [Princeton, N. J.] June 22, 1907.

Mr. H. B. Thompson, the Acting Chairman of our Committee on Grounds and Buildings, has sent me your letter of June 18th. It seems quite clear to me that your first year's service should date from March 28th, unless for the sake of convenience you should prefer to have it from the first of April. The notification from the Secretary concerned only the formal action of the Board with regard to a matter which had already, of course, been settled with you. The Secretary's name, by the way, is Charles W. McAlpin.

Mr. Schroeder seems now to think that he can satisfy the ideas of the biological men without forcing upon us the impossible building which some of them apparently had in mind. I think our last conference at Mr. Pyne's house probably cleared things up.

Always cordially and sincerely yours,

[Woodrow Wilson]

CCL (WWP, UA, NjP).

From William Wirt Phillips[1]

My dear Dr. Wilson New York, N. Y. June 25th 1907

I received your letter addressed to me as President of the Trustees of Cap & Gown and read it to the club at our annual dinner.

It was very seriously and thoroughly discussed at the dinner but it was such a radical change that the opinions of it expressed at that time were, I felt sure, apt to be snap judgements so I have waited some little while before writing you so that I might get the ideas of more men.

We all appreciate the seriousness of the club situation in Princeton today and regret bitterly that it has reached any such acute stage. We know something has to be done and we stand ready to help out in any place which will be for the good of the University—please do not think that C & G. men have reached the point of putting the club ahead of Princeton.

As you probably know, this question is of particular importance to our club at this time as we are just starting to erect a new club house and our Trustees feel that before we go ahead with our plans it would be wise to learn more about your proposed changes in the university life as it effects clubs since it might have some influence upon the construction of our house—as for instance a change in our plans which would make it easy to enlarge the house at a near date if your plan goes into effect.

In view of all these facts the officers of our board, Mr. Schuyler Smith,[2] Mr. Edward Delafield[3] and myself, are exceedingly anxious to talk the matter over with you and would very much appreciate it if you could find time to see us some afternoon after 5.30, or some evening next week if you are still going to be in Princeton. We hate to bother you but this [is] a very serious matter with us and we need advice badly.

Very sincerely yours William W. Phillips

ALS (WP, DLC).

[1] Princeton 1895, Assistant Cashier of Strong, Sturgis & Co., bankers of New York.

[2] Wilson Schuyler Smith, Princeton 1901, securities broker with De Coppett & Doremus of New York.

[3] Edward Coleman Delafield, Princeton 1899, associated with the New Jersey Zinc Co. of New York.

From Leon Michel Levy[1]

Dear Sir, Scranton, Penna. [c. June 25, 1907]

I notice by this morning's press that you contemplate radical changes in the present social system of your university, and lose no time in taking the liberty of addressing a few lines to you on the subject. As a Princetonian of two years' standing, I wish to be one of the first sons of Nassau to congratulate you for your fearlessness and independence in striking at an evil, which was bound in a few years to undermine the beneficial status of a great American college.

I was only at Princeton two years but in that brief period I suffered more social humiliation, and drained the dregs of more class prejudice than ever before or I am thankful to say ever since; and all sir, because of your abominable system of club life. The democracy of Princeton! Faugh! The essence and acme of snobbishness, that's what I found.

Let me state my experience briefly.

As my name shows I am a Jew. Without any undue egotism I can say that I am not of the worst type. My scholastic work at Princeton the first year was very fair. I did second division work throughout in the classics, was poor in mathematics, and was one of the best men in the class in English, both years. (Vide Professors Colwell, Axson & Chambers.[2])

Princeton appealed to me from the start. The beautiful campus and buildings, the spirit, the traditions, the romance all impressed me greatly and my heart swelled and thrilled with pride at the mere thought of being a humble undergraduate at the alma mater of one president and the home of another. I was hazed a great deal, but took it goodnaturedly, with never a thought that prejudice or racial contempt might have inspired some of it.

At home I had never encountered such a thing. In my folly I had vaunted thus: "Let a boy or man act white, let him do unto others as he would be done by, and he'll find no prejudices." Alas for the fond hopes and fallacies of boyhood.

I was rudely awakened at the end of the first year by discovering all of my class mates landed in clubs, while I wandered hopelessly on the outskirts, an Ishmaelite and outcast. True I wore no yellow cap, the badge of disgrace imposed by the simple, brutal mediaeval customs on my forefathers; but the absence of a cap or insignia of any sort branded me as an outsider.

It was a harsh awakening. I am more or less sensitive and the discovery of such depths of cold contempt and icy prejudice cut me to the quick. Sophomore year was worse than the previous one.

Throughout it I was limited to companionship with two kindred spirits, outcasts like myself. True it was that they were both bright, refined young men of good family, ostensibly gentlemen. But they too bore the brand of Cain. Members of the chosen people, as they were, at Princeton they were realizing the irony of this historic title.

Two years was enough. I went to the Pennsylvania Law School, where in three years I made many friends, was accorded every courtesy refused me at Princeton (no fraternity of course, but otherwise proper treatment). My fellow-students treated me like a man and brother. There was no distinction between Jew and Gentile, and when I left Penn it was with the best of feeling towards every one of the seventy men in my class, as well as hundreds of other good fellows I had met.

At Princeton, besides the two fellow exiles heretofore referred to, I can remember exactly two men with whom I contracted a deep and lasting friendship. They were men indeed. One of them an eccentric literary genius, by far the ablest poet in the university; the other your finest debater.[3] Fellows able to gulf and cross the gap of racial hatred which yawns black and gloomy indeed at your democratic and free university.

Think of it. A class of four hundred men! And of that number I am forced to remember the great majority as snobbish, addle-headed young cads, with ambitions centered on upper-class clubs, and their idol not a Calf of Gold, but a calf of sinew with an arm to match.

Democracy of Princeton! Faugh!

When I think of myself, the enthusiastic buoyant lad of nineteen who entered Princeton, full of ideals, happy in the consciousness of living in a free country, in a land of universal equality and realize the jar those tender sensibilities received, why then, President Wilson, it is tremendously difficult for me to think kindly of Princeton.

Of your professors, of the faculty I have none but the kindest feelings. A splendid group of gentlemen, my intercourse with them was always of the most pleasant nature, and the recollection of my class hours particularly those with Professors Axson and Chambers (the latter's special course) will always be to me the oasis in an otherwise arid desert of Princeton memories.

I am proud however to see that in you a strong man has arisen to lead the sons of Princeton forth from the bondage of narrow-mindedness and bigotry into a new atmosphere of tolerance and Twentieth century broadness. That you may succeed in your enterprise is the hearty wish of,

Leon M. Levy, Sometime of the Class of 1905

P.S. While I realize this caution is superfluous; please do not give this communication any publication.

ALS (WP, DLC).

[1] At this time a lawyer in Scranton, Pa. He was for two years a member of the Class of 1905 at Princeton, as a freshman during 1901-1902 and as a special student during 1902-1903. A member of Whig Hall, he won that society's Sophomore Essay Contest in 1903. From 1903 to 1906 he studied law at the University of Pennsylvania, receiving the LL.B. in 1906.

[2] Percy Robert Colwell, then Instructor in English, Stockton Axson, and David Laurance Chambers, then Assistant in English.

[3] He was probably referring to Norman Mattoon Thomas '05.

From Daisy Allen Story[1]

Lawrence Long Island,
June twenty fifth 1907

Dear Sir,

In this morning's paper I have read with great interest of the reforms you propose at Princeton and I wish to express my sincere admiration for this possition [position] you have taken.

I have recently had occasion to talk with one of the Freshmen and have been very much impressed by his experiences.

He has been so fortunate as to make a good club, he is a good student, having graduated at the head of his Prep. School, he was President of his Class in School and is generally considered a popular Boy, so he should be free from prejudice.

He is deeply impressed by the selfish spirit he sees in College. While he has made third group, he tells me he has not done anything like as good work as he is capable of, because he has been distracted by the atmosphere of self seeking policy which seems to pervade the place.

If a student who has been so fortunate as this boy has, can feel this influence strongly—what can be the mental attitude of one less fortunate?

I hope you will pardon me for taking so much of your valuable time, but you seem to have described so exactly the conditions which detract from College life as it now exists, that I cannot refrain from expressing the hope that the splendid policy you have outlined will prevail.

Very sincerely Yours D. A. Story.

ALS (WP, DLC).
[1] Mrs. William Cumming Story, President of the New York City Federation of Women's Clubs.

From Robert Scott Walker[1]

Dear Sir New York. June 25/07

I wish to express my entire accord with your views in regard to the Club Life at Princeton. From my own observations during my son Edward's[2] Course there, I soon became convinced it was a serious evil & very detrimental to the ideals for which Colleges are established & maintained.

I sincerely hope therefore you will persist in your efforts to bring about a much needed reform in this matter, & trust you may have complete success in them. In this way you will render a great service, not only to Princeton, but to the cause of higher education everywhere.

With sincere respect for your independent & courageous stand on this important matter believe me to remain

Very truly yours Robt. S. Walker

P.S. I would like 2 or 3 copies of your circular

ALS (WP, DLC).
[1] A retired broker of New York.
[2] Edward Washburn Walker '07.

President Charles William Eliot's Citation of Wilson for the LL.D. Degree[1]

[[June 26, 1907]]

"Doctors of Laws:

"Woodrow Wilson, Virginian of Scotch-Irish descent, vigorous student and teacher of history, politics, and government, and eminent author on these subjects, President of Princeton University for five years past, years eventful and fortunate indeed for that patriotic and serviceable institution. . . ."

Printed in the *Harvard Graduates Magazine*, XVI (Sept. 1907), 68.

1 Conferred at the Commencement of Harvard University on the morning of June 26, 1907, in Sanders Theatre in Cambridge, Mass. Other recipients of honorary degrees included William Goodell Frost, President of Berea College; George Lyman Kittredge, Professor of English at Harvard; Paul Gavrilovitch Vinogradoff, Corpus Christi Professor of Jurisprudence at Oxford University; Elihu Root, Secretary of State; James Bryce, British Ambassador to the United States; Jean Jules Jusserand, French Ambassador to the United States; and Luigi Amedeo, Prince of Savoy and Duke of Abruzzi, who was in the United States to represent the King of Italy at the opening of the Jamestown Exposition.

An Address at Harvard University[1]

[[June 26, 1907]]

Mr. Toastmaster, Mr. President, and Gentlemen: I will reward you for staying by a very brief speech. After all the distinguished men who have preceded me, you will not wish to hear any more sound doctrine. And yet I should be ashamed to go away from this place without expressing my very deep appreciation of the honor which Harvard has conferred upon me to-day. It has confirmed me, however, in some things that I was inclined to think. I shall have to be very careful about what I say about receiving a degree from Harvard because of the recollection of what I have said in receiving degrees from other universities; but I am confirmed in the conviction that a man is not educated "by degrees,"—that a university is a mere episode in his life; that what a university labels him with is the result of what he endeavors to do; and that when we pride ourselves upon the distinguished rôle of our graduates we should praise the choice of those who chose to come to us, and not ourselves. What we are praising, what every university can justly praise, when speaking of the distinguished rôle of her graduates, is the fertility and the resources, the strength and achievement of American manhood, in the field of letters as well as in the field of affairs.

I feel that Harvard is very catholic to include me on her roll. I cannot help thinking, as I sit here in this hall, that it is dedicated to men who thrashed the men that I most loved. I come from a more ancient Commonwealth than the Commonwealth of Massachusetts, namely, the Commonwealth of Virginia, and I am one of those who are of the seed of that indomitable blood, planted in so many parts of the United States, which makes good fighting stuff,—the Scotch-Irish. The beauty about a Scotch-Irishman is that he not only thinks he is right, but knows he is right. And I have not departed from the faith of my ancestors.

Princeton is not like Harvard, and she does not wish to be. Neither does she wish Harvard to be like Princeton. She believes, as every thoughtful man must believe, that the strength of a democracy is in its variety, and that where there are a great many competing ideals, you are sure that the best ideal will survive the competition. The reason that I remain proud of the men who lost in the struggle of the Civil War is that they didn't consent to be convinced that they were wrong until they were thrashed. Now we at Princeton are in the arena and you at Harvard are in the arena; and, though ideals in the field of mind are not like ideals in the field of politics, while it is not necessary that one should go down and the other survive, I do believe that every ideal flourishes by reason of the opposition made to it. I should very much regret not being able to put myself to the trouble of proving what I believe. As Mr. [Augustine] Birrell once said, "If you really wish me to believe you witty, I must trouble you to make a jest." I may claim a great many things for the Princeton idea; you need not admit them. You may have the philosophical temperament that the old negro had who had recently married and was complaining of the extravagance of his wife. He said, "She's de mos' 'stravagantest woman I ever seed; she wants money in de mawning, an' she wants it in de middle of de day, an' she wants it at night." Some one said, "Well, Rastus, what does she spend it on?" "She ain't spent it on nothin'; I ain't give her none yit." Now you may not favor these things on which I wish to spend an extravagant boast, but I wish you to know what they are.

The Secretary of State has said that the greatest question for this country now, as in the past, is the question of government. And the questions of government with which we are face to face are questions in which our agreement with each other, our solidarity, our discipline of temper, our union in ideals, are more important to us than anything else. I want to say frankly that Harvard seems to me to be doing what all America wants to do,—namely, she is saying to every one, Assess yourself; seek what you want; get what you please. And Princeton is doing for America what she should wish to do. She is seeking to combine men in a common discipline in which the chief term is tradition, in which the chief emphasis is law, in which the chief idea is submission to that discipline which has made men time out of mind, and made them companions in a common social endeavor. Now you may think that she is not using the means to realize that ideal. I will not discuss that with you. I am merely interested to show you that that is her ideal. If you will follow anything that she has done in the past five years,–for that is all I am responsible for,–you will find that it is something the purpose of which is to make of those who teach and of those who are taught a community, something that is intended to make the hours between the last exercise on one day and the first on the next more important than the hours spent in the class-room. And these saturations of a community life, these saturations of mind, these saturations of purpose, this community of ideals, this sense of a common discipline, and a union for a common purpose, is the whole creed of the place which temporarily endures my government.

I see many things about me which resemble what I see in the youth that come under our instruction. I hear very little discussion of law and a great deal of discussion of what we want to do. I hear lads say, "That is not what I want,"–and I hear the country say, "That is not what we want." And if you ask them if they will stop to get what they want by established law, they are too much inclined to say,–"No, we will get it by a shorter route than that,–we will get it by the direct approach of our own desire." We are face to face with a competition between the sense of law and a reckless desire for change.

Now the reason that I would not have Harvard resemble Princeton is that both of these things are necessary. The individual desire for benefit and advantage, the popular desire for change, the impatience of restraint, all of these are evidence of strength and of youth, of a wholesome strength which is the strength of youth. But there should be combined with this that sense of the cordage of custom, that sense of the things which restrain, that sense of a common undertaking upon which we insist at Princeton. It should be exploited by somebody and exploited with an emphasis and a distinctness which shall not escape the attention of the nation. We need men who wish change; but we need that that change should be debated and accomplished under the restraints of established law. These are the two elements so difficult to combine, which America must combine in her schools as well as in her legislatures. For in a democratic country the whole world is a school, and we all learn of each other that discipline of temper which is the chastening of purpose.[2]

Printed in the *Harvard Graduates Magazine*, XVI (Sept. 1907), 85-87.

[1] Wilson spoke at the afternoon exercises held in Memorial Hall. The Commencement exercises of the forenoon, held in the much smaller Sanders Theatre, were limited to those receiving degrees and their parents and friends. The afternoon exercises were attended by many returned Harvard alumni as well as other friends of the university. Charles Joseph Bonaparte, Attorney General of the United States and President of the Harvard Alumni Association, presided. The

speakers were, in order of their appearance, the Prince of Savoy; Charles William Eliot; Curtis Guild, Jr., Governor of Massachusetts; Jean Jules Jusserand; James Bryce; Elihu Root; Woodrow Wilson, and John Davis Long, former Governor of Massachusetts, representing the Harvard Class of 1857 on its semicentennial. See the report of the ceremonies, with full texts of the speeches, in the *Harvard Graduates Magazine*, XVI (Sept. 1907), 69-88.

2 There is a WWhw outline of this address, dated June 26, 1907, in WP, DLC.

From Harry Augustus Garfield

Newstate, Berkshire Co., Mass.,
June 26th 1907.

Dear Wilson,

You see I avail myself of the friendly privilege you held out to me last summer.[1] The events of the past few days make me more than ever inclined to give expression to the regard in which I hold you, for they point sternly to a course which would separate me from Princeton. Dr. Hopkins,[2] the president of Williams has presented his resignation to take effect a year hence. The Trustees have accepted it and elected me his successor "subject to my acceptance." I was called down from my mountain retreat & urged to accept at once, that announcement might be made today at the Alumni dinner. This I have refused to do, although, in view of the unanimity that seems to prevail, I do not see on what ground I can refuse in the end to accept the election. I write you in the midst of the tumult of my feelings, because I wish you to know what is taking place, & to hear it from me & not from another, if, contrary to expectations, the situation becomes known. Please do not give yourself the trouble to answer. I know that you wish me to remain at Princeton. I need no further assurances upon that point. The affectionate regard of my Princeton friends, the position & future of Princeton in the educational field & the delightful life we are now living there are constantly before me & make an appeal which is well-nigh irresistible. I have put aside without a second thought several other proposals to leave Princeton, but I need hardly tell you that a call from Williams comes to me with peculiar force, indeed almost as a command. I shall write you as soon as my decision is reached. Of course I should not think of leaving Princeton before the end of the next college year, unless it would be more convenient for you to have me do so.

With sincerest regards, I remain always,

Cordially & Faithfully Yours, H. A. Garfield.

ALS (WP, DLC).

1 When Wilson, in a letter to Garfield of September 3, 1906, had asked Garfield if he might not call him by his last name.

2 The Rev. Dr. Henry Hopkins, President of Williams College since 1902 and son of Mark Hopkins, president of the same institution from 1836 to 1872.

From Nelson Burr Gaskill[1]

Dear Sir: [Trenton, N. J.] June 26. 1907.

I met last night some Princeton men, graduates like myself, of some years ago, to discuss your projected plan for the salvation of all that is distinctly valuable of the Princeton we knew, otherwise termed the "Social Coordination of the University." I think we were all surprised that the time for action had so soon arrived, astonished at the boldness of the conception and pleased beyond measure by the confident tone with which it was set forth. And so strong is my personal feeling that I am writing you a wholly unnecessary letter of applause and encouragement.

When Doctor McCosh put fraternities under the ban, it seems that he did not foresee how his plans were to be shattered by the development of the upper class clubs which, based as a friend of mine once said, upon "an aristocracy of the stomach," furnished all the ills and none or few of the benefits of the fraternity system. Or it may be that a lack of financial support hampered and prevented a wider action. Certainly the whole system has its origin in the failure of the Princeton boarding house and the search for some thing better by those who could afford to pay for it.

In my time, 92-96, the membership in these clubs composed but a minority of each class but the war was already on. One of my friends was much embittered by his failure of election and a body that had lasted for the first two years under went a very painful readjustment at the opening of Junior year. Class politics split on this rock and friendships broke. And the much vaunted democracy was showing holes and ragged edges. Living as close to Princeton as I have done, I have kept in more or less touch with the movement of undergraduate life, personally and through friends in that body, so that I was not surprised to have a Yale man speak of the harm the clubs were doing to the college spirit. "It has gone from Yale" he said, "and the clubs will kill it at Princeton as the frats have at Yale.["]

I think you will have the hearty support of the older alumni, the men who have carried away with them the spirit of Princeton. As to the men of more recent years, they may feel that heart and treasure have been simultaneously removed but what are they among so many? There may be groans but there will be cheers too, many of them, which is what I have been trying to say. I wish you all success.

Very truly yours, Nelson B. Gaskill.

ALS (WP, DLC).

[1] Princeton 1896, Assistant Attorney General of New Jersey.

From Theodore Whitefield Hunt

Dear Dr, Princeton University 6 26 1907

I have just read, with the greatest interest, your plan as to the coordination of our social and intellectual interests and congratulate you on the high ideals which you are aiming thus to realize. That the result contemplated is desirable and urgent, must be conceded by every right-minded man, and, I believe, that, in its substantive factors, it is feasible. Your presentation of it is eminently temperate and judicious, and, in the best sense, diplomatic. You will, I am sure, have the faculty with you and, in the end, the great majority of the alumni and undergraduates.

From certain quarters, of course, you will expect adverse criticism, but with that Scotch-Irish and Stonewall Jackson courage and persistence which you have inherited and developed, you will succeed.

This plan and that of the preceptorial instruction are enough in themselves to make any administration historic and brilliant. Even should you fail in this new departure, you would fall with your face toward the light.

Trust you will have a restful summer

Cordially T. W. Hunt

ALS (WP, DLC).

From William Berryman Scott

My dear Wilson: Princeton, N. J. June 26th 1907

It is to your kindness, I am sure, that I owe the extremely surprising & equally gratifying announcement from the Secretary of an increase in my salary.[1] Supposing that I had reached the limit, future increases had been entirely despaired of. I appreciate the honour of this action of the Board quite as much as the enlarged income, & that is saying a great deal, for the needs of a family like mine are by no means small. I hope that Sinclair was among the fortunate band.[2]

Needless to say, your scheme of "social reorganization" has interested me profoundly & has gained my instant adhesion. It seems to me, however, that we can effect such a reform only by convincing the graduate members of the clubs that some such change is imperatively needed.

With cordial thanks, I am

Very Sincerely Yours W. B. Scott.

ALS (WP, DLC).

[1] His salary was increased from $4,000 to $4,500 per annum.

[2] William John Sinclair, Instructor in Geology, who did not receive a salary increase in 1907.

From John Conover Ten Eyck[1]

Dear Sir: New York. June 26, 1907.

I beg to express my earnest satisfaction with your suggestions with regard to Club Life at Princeton.

This subject has been a matter of anxious discussion at every meeting of my classmates that has been held in recent years. We have, however, been silent, owing to our confidence in you.

For my own part, I can say truthfully that my love for Princeton is unabated,–if it changes at all, it grows with the passing of time, and yet when I consider sending my sons there, it fills me with anxiety to think of their being either in or out of club life.

Whatever your program may be as finally determined upon, you can doubtless carry it through without my feeble aid, yet I wish the privilege of assuring you that I will not spare any effort that you will permit me to make, in order to hold up your hands in this business.

Yours very truly, Jno. C. Ten Eyck. '75

TLS (WP, DLC).

[1] Princeton 1875, a member of the New York law firm of Ten Eyck, Morris & Hitchcock.

To Melancthon Williams Jacobus

My dear Dr. Jacobus: [Princeton, N. J.] June 27th, 1907.

I find that, having been absorbed in one thing, I very stupidly overlooked some very important business for the Curriculum Committee at Commencement. There are six preceptors whose term of service ran out in June and ought to be renewed. May I have your permission as chairman of the Committee, to report the following men to the Catalogue Committee to be retained on our faculty list, pending the next meeting of the Board of Trustees? At that meeting I will propose their continuance for the terms indicated: Walter M. Adriance, History and Politics, for one year: Edgar Dawson, History and Politics, for three years; William Starr Myers, History and Politics, for two years; Douglas L. Buffum, Modern Languages, three years; George T. Northup, Modern Languages, one year; and Nathaniel E. Griffin, English, one year.

You will be interested to know what cordial endorsement our scheme for the social coordination of the University is receiving from influential people of many kinds. I was at the Harvard Commencement yesterday, and the men up there bade us God-speed with the greatest earnestness, confessing that they had not had the courage to tackle the problem, and saying, of course if you do it, we shall have to do it. A storm is breaking in some quarters, but we have the support of all thoughtful persons.

Mrs. Wilson has wanted to write you ever since Commencement, to express her and my deep sense of relief and gratification at the arrangement made with Paul van Dyke, with regard to the ministers. The promptness and effectiveness of the action quite took our breath away. I cannot help a sneaking feeling that I am avoiding a duty by accepting the arrangement, but it will ease my nerves in a great many ways, and I am deeply grateful for it.

I hope that you are going to get real rest and recreation this summer.

Always faithfully yours, [Woodrow Wilson]

CCL (WWP, UA, NjP).

From Harold Zeiss

Dear Sir: Chicago, June 27, 1907

I take the liberty of addressing this letter to you in the hope that a few observations of a graduate of the class of 1907 may be of some little value.

The individuality of a Freshman is crushed by club distinctions in his own class, and by customs that tend to make all men alike. The Freshmen and Sophomores lose the good moral and intellectual influences of the upper classes. The Freshmen are immediately more or less cut off from each other by their clubs, and their positions in the social life of the college are prematurely fixed, regardless of ability. A man "queers" himself by some little thing Freshman year and is likely to be "down" for the rest of his college course; there is a tendency to cater to riches and social position in the selection of men for Freshmen clubs.

Some men get good experience in the management of club affairs during the four years of college, but for the most part it is worrying and intrigueing that is demoralizing.

In Freshman and Sophomore years, the scheming selfish individual usually gets along, and gives a bad tone to the student leadership throughout the rest of the course. Men of small means are for the most part together. Many men lose the opportunities of associating with the more cultivated. Many others lose the opportunities of broadening and democratizing themselves by sympathetic companionship with all kinds of men. In Sophomore year, all eyes turned to the upper class clubs, the acme of snobbish[ness] and "bootlicking" that results from a system of cliques, is reached. There is a cut throat competition among the upper class clubs to get Sophomores that is demoralizing. In some of the upper class clubs there is a tendency to cater to wealth and social position in the selection of Sophomores. This gives an unwholesome undemocratic atmosphere to the club. The last two years the men are more than ever shut off from each other by the upper class clubs. Some of the clubs are too grand for a democratic Princeton. The club life inevitably keeps men from their studies, and it makes the cost of living unnecessarily high. Aside from the unjust distribution of men in the upper-class clubs, the most distressing feature of the system, is the large number of men in no clubs. These men lose many pleasant opportunities, they are often miserable, and cannot become whole hearted Princeton men.

Sincerely Harold Zeiss[1]

ALS (WP, DLC).

[1] Zeiss was not a member of a club.

From Linsly Rudd Williams[1]

My dear President Wilson: New York, June 27, 1907.

When I heard of the proposed change in the undergraduate life at Princeton, my first thought was that this was very radical. After several days consideration, I felt that these changes were most progressive, and, after free discussion with some of the alumni who are more conversant with the present undergraduate life than I am, and after carefully reading the complete statement in the Alumni Weekly, I am fully convinced that these proposed changes are not only radical and progressive, but absolutely necessary for the welfare of the University.

One learns best from one's own experience, and while reading your report, I saw how closely the description of undergraduate life applied to me as one of the majority who led for four years, "a happy life of comradeship and sport, interrupted by the grind of perfunctory lessons and examinations." During those four years I drifted aimlessly through the College curriculum, electing all manner of subjects and in the last half of my Senior year, so chose my course with what I thought, at the time, consummate skill, that I had no regular college duties after twelve o'clock, and the week was ended by Thursday noon. When I read of the organization of the preceptorial system, I sincerely regretted that I was not an undergraduate to be stimulated to work and to be able to choose appropriate courses under the guidance of my preceptor, which would have been of material advantage to me in my future career. Instead of that, I look back upon the college curriculum of my undergraduate days as a kaleidoscopic collection of neglected opportunities.

Undergraduate life with me was far from serious. Condition and being dropped in Sophomore Year, though fortunately for me reinstated, was nothing more than a joke, but as soon as I became interested in the study of medicine and found my entire environment one of study and serious purpose, without any apparent effort on my part, at the end of four years I could with pleasure admit to myself that I had been a good student, something which I had never dreamed of at college.

While a student at the College of Physicians and Surgeons at Columbia, the major part of the course in the Department of Medicine was didactic. During the past few years this Department has been completely reorganized, so that now lectures play a very minor part, and the bulk of the teaching is given to students in small groups. The course in the third and fourth years being given to 150 students by some 25 different instructors. As an instructor in this department I can see the enormous advantage that this "preceptorial" system has over the older didactic method.

As a member of an Upper Class Club, I was keenly interested in club life and the pleasures thereof, and a few years after graduation was still sufficiently interested to be able to give, for me, a large amount of money toward a new club house. I have realized more and more each year that I take less interest in the club and more interest in Princeton, and that now I would be extremely grateful if the money which I have given toward the club could be given to Princeton, for I have as yet given nothing to Princeton except small contributions to the Class Fund.

When I graduated from Princeton twelve years ago, there were five Upper Class Clubs to which less than one third of the class belonged. Amongst the club members there was not the slightest feeling that there weren't scores of others in the class who would have been desirable as club members, nor did the majority of the class who were not club members, feel that they were unfortunate or neglected. Perhaps the most prominent man in our class was not a club member. I refer to Mr. Imbrie and I do not think that at any time he has regretted that he was not a club member. I am told that the clubs now number fourteen and that from three fourths to four fifths of the Upper Class men belong to them. It was natural that those who are not elected should feel there were some stigma upon them.

I sincerely hope that the scheme presented to the Trustees by your Committee will be carried into effect at an early date. Undoubtedly, there will be considerable opposition from many "club members" among the alumni. But as a graduate member of an Upper Class club, I have written perhaps at too great length, to inform you of the hearty approval that I have for this object and to assure you that I will endeavor to use what little influence I have among the graduates of my own club, to overcome opposition (if there be any) to this essential reorganization of undergraduate life.

Very sincerely yours, Linsly R. Williams.

TLS (WP, DLC).

[1] Princeton 1895; M.D., Columbia University, 1899. At this time he was practicing medicine with Dr. John Seymour Thacher of New York and serving as instructor in the practice of medicine and chief of the Vanderbilt Medical Clinic of the College of Physicians and Surgeons, Columbia University.

To Harry Augustus Garfield

My dear Garfield: Princeton, N. J. June 28th, 1907.

I of course knew it must come some day, but I was hoping that Dr. Hopkins would have some extraordinary lease of life and vigour, and that we should be permitted for a long time to keep the man whom we very much love and value and honor.

I feel that it would be selfish and presumptious on my part to argue against what you may consider a command of duty, but quite apart from my affection for you and the value I attach to your work here, I feel that the influence you have exerted here and would continue to exert has been of peculiar value and has added great force to a place where the traditions of good teaching of politics and of high principles in citizenship have been so persistently maintained. Moreover, I know from experience how taxing and trying the duties of a college president are, and I could wish that your powers might be reserved for that calmer and more intimate sort of work in which the deepest influence lies.

But these are, I dare say, reflections born of selfishness. I did not wish to persuade you. It would delight me if you could see it your duty to decline, but if you accept you may be sure my trust and affection will go with you.

I am delighted that if it must be, it need not be for a year to come.

Faithfully and affectionately yours, Woodrow Wilson

TLS (H. A. Garfield Papers, DLC).

From Daniel Coit Gilman

North East Harbor Maine.

My dear Wilson June 28 [1907]

Rejoice in every honor that you receive & in every service that you render to higher education. You were in good company at Harvard, & I was glad to see in the papers that your name was first on the list. Where ever you go, you are sure to be in the very first ranks & I am proud to sign myself

Your old & faithful friend D. C. Gilman

ALS (WP, DLC).

From Stephen Squires Palmer

My dear Dr. Wilson: New York, June 28, 1907.

We hope to have the plans of the new physical laboratory completed within the next week or ten days, when they will be submitted to you for examination and criticism.

I should be pleased if you will be good enough to advise me at your convenience to what address you desire them forwarded, as I do not know the date you expect to leave Princeton nor where you contemplate spending your vacation. I dislike to encroach upon your well earned rest from details connected with the University, but, as you must appreciate, it is absolutely necessary to get this building under way as soon as possible if it is to be finished and ready for occupancy when the University opens in the autumn of 1908, and this is my only excuse for burdening you at this time about the matter.

I greatly hope that these plans will meet with your approval and that we may have your authority to begin construction by August 1st.

With Kind remembrances, I am, as always,

Very sincerely yours, S S Palmer

TLS (WP, DLC).

From James Bryce

My dear President Ottawa. June 30/07.

To me it has been a great disappointment not to be able to be at your Commencement, & I fear that it is not possible for me to promise to be with you on Oct. 22, because we are to spend our summer & autumn in the White Mts and I have some New England engagements to discharge before I can return to Washington, which in any case would hardly be before the end of Oct. or early in Novr. The chances are therefore that I could not get to Princeton so early as the 22nd. But as Princeton is comparatively near Washington I shall hope to be able to be with you some time there before my duties on this side come to an end, & the sooner I can be with you, the better pleased shall I be. We both remember with the liveliest pleasure our days with you three years ago.[1]

With very kind regards to Mrs. Wilson,

Sincerely yours James Bryce

ALS (WP, DLC).

[1] The Bryces had visited the Wilsons in October 1904. See J. Bryce to WW, Oct. 8, 1904, n. 1, Vol. 15.

From Sir William Mather

My dear President, [London] June 30th/07

Your very kind letter of the 18th Inst. is just to hand.

I am truly sorry that my message was belated. I reckoned from the date on which you held Commencement 2 years ago beginning as I thought on the 14th June and lasting several days.

It will gratify me much to have the message inserted in the Alumni Weekly, if only to show that Princeton means something to me for the rest of my life. I believe it means also great things to come for America North & South. I look to Princeton as the fountain from which will flow a fertilising & purifying stream of young manhood of the highest type, not only of men of high intellectual culture, but of splendid ideals & moral power which will be *felt* and will have to be reckoned with by those who think of self-interest before the honour & welfare of their country.

You speak of "having failed" with Mr Bryce as regards the Sun-dial ceremony? Is this quite settled? I think not. I wrote him not long ago suggesting that he should name to you certain dates, after Commemoration, on which he could visit Princeton. But you might also write him to the same effect; then having agreed on a date you could probably arrange by special resolution of your Trustees and Faculty to confer on him the degree you have twice offered on dates impossible to him, but which under the special resolution might be conferred whenever his visit took place.

Would not this make success doubly sure?

My chief desire is to get Mr Bryce to Princeton, and that he should be invited to address the *under-graduates*. He is most willing, even anxious to visit you. His previous refusals were inevitable because he is called on from all quarters well ahead of time to join in many functions. I feel sure there will be no failure from this cause if you can adopt my suggestion now submitted, with all respect & deference.

You are more than kind in pressing me to come out in the Autumn, or next year. But please consider that it would be not a little embarrassing, and even compromising, if I came to celebrate my own simple deed. I wish to stand outside as the mere instrument in having brought Oxford and Princeton into closer relationship, and Oxford's distinguished Son—our Ambassador—would stand for Oxford herself and all she means to the British race on both sides of the Atlantic. The authorities at Oxford take a great interest in the event of their famous Sun-dial having been transplanted as it were to Princeton, and they will be immensely gratified by the use of the occasion of unveiling the monument at the hands of Mr Bryce.

I should deeply regret the postponement of the event to next year, and my objection to be[ing] present would hold good all the same. So please consider my plan and arrange with Mr Bryce accordingly, for I feel confident that he wishes to do this thing.

With warmest regards to your good self and the members of your family from all of us

Believe me Very Sincerely Yours W. Mather

ALS (WWP, UA, NjP).

To Daniel Coit Gilman

My dear Dr. Gilman: Princeton, N. J. July 1st, 1907.

I very warmly appreciate your kind letter of June 28th. I think you must know how highly I value your approval and friendship, and I want to say that I was more than pleased, I was touched, by your thoughtful kindness in writing to me as you did. I sincerely hope that I shall always prove worthy of such friendship as you have given me.

Cordially and Sincerely yours, Woodrow Wilson

TLS (D. C. Gilman Papers, MdBJ).

To Cleveland Hoadley Dodge

My dear Cleve: Princeton, N. J. July 1st, 1907.

Would you be willing to give me a letter of introduction to Mrs. Sage,[1] which I could use some time this summer, and would you be kind enough to ascertain for me where I should be most likely to find her? I want to ask her for money to carry out our new schemes. I am more deeply convinced every day that those plans must be carried out at once. In the agitation created by the new proposals, things come to the surface every day which confirm me in my belief that that is the only remedy not only, but also reveal in a new and extraordinary way the degree to which the clubs have taken precedence over the University in the thoughts and affections of our recent graduates.

Richardson, the physicist, the other day expressed in a very striking manner his astonishment at the social conditions here, and said that they were such as would strangle any university. He entirely confirms me in my impression that such conditions would be impossible under the system which we are planning to put into operation.

When I was at Harvard the other day, the men I talked with up there were most deeply interested and most warmly congratulatory. Their general sentiment was, "If you do it, we must; and we ought all long ago to have done it." You will notice from the article of John Corbin on Wisconsin University, in the number of The Saturday Evening Post for June 22nd,[2] that President Van Hise of Wisconsin is already about to put a similar plan into operation and has got a grant from the Legislature for the purpose, of $100,000 a year.[3]

The fight is on, and I regard it, not as a fight for the development, but as a fight for the restoration of Princeton. My heart is in it more than it has been in anything else, because it is a scheme of salvation.

With warmest affection,

Faithfully yours, Woodrow Wilson

TLS (WC, NjP).

1 Margaret Olivia Slocum Sage, widow of Russell Sage, the railroad magnate, who had died in 1906. Mrs. Sage supported the work of the Russell Sage Foundation and donated money to various educational and social service organizations. As future documents will reveal, she later gave the money for most of the large dormitory complex known as Holder Hall, as well as for Holder Tower.

2 John Corbin, "Wisconsin: The Utilitarian University," *Saturday Evening Post*, CLXXIX (June 22, 1907), 3-5.

3 The Van Hise plan, initiated by President Charles Richard Van Hise of the University of Wisconsin, was similar in many respects to Wilson's own quadrangle plan. Like Wilson's, it was modeled after the residential colleges of Oxford and Cambridge and envisaged the construction of residence halls, each having a common room, kitchen, dining commons, and dormitory rooms. Also like Wilson's plan, Van Hise's proposal was designed to counteract what he saw as the growing undemocratic divisions within the student body. Van Hise received a pledge from the Wisconsin legislature of $100,000 a year to institute the plan, but enough money was appropriated for the construction of only two buildings. See Merle Curti and Vernon Carstensen, *The University of Wisconsin: A History* (2 vols., Madison, Wisc., 1949), II, 76-77.

To Melancthon Williams Jacobus

My dear Dr. Jacobus: [Princeton, N. J.] July 1st, 1907.

. . . The fight for the quads is on very merrily, and must now be seen through to a finish. I think that in the long run it will be taken soberly and judiciously, though now there is a great deal of wild talk, and amidst the wild talk scores of particulars come to life which show that the situation is even worse than I had supposed, and that the remedy is absolutely imperative. Professor Richardson, whom we have just got from Cambridge, corroborates my impressions of the conditions here and of the adequacy of the remedy, in a way that is most explicit and refreshing.

Hoping that you are to have a restful vacation,

Always cordially and faithfully yours,

[Woodrow Wilson]

CCL (RSB Coll., DLC).

From Joseph Haswell Robinson[1]

My dear President Wilson, White Plains, N. Y. July 1. '07.

Altho for some time I have seen reports in newspapers and periodicals of proposed changes in Princeton life on its "social" side, not until now have I seen the complete report on its exact purpose.

I do not know that the feeling of one graduate can be of any service to you in the matter, but I want at least to please myself by writing you—that after studying the details of the new plan of residential quads, I believe them to be the greatest advance in Princeton life which could be imagined. The actual, *practical*, effect of them cannot but be, eventually, of great value in developing the University feeling of men, in winning a yet more undivided love for Alma Mater from all her sons—but I confess that that is not to me the completest reason for their adoption. "Jeremy" Ormond[2] taught me a most unfortunate love of ideals and principles & theories—and somehow I can't get over my predilections toward these. I believe this step, which I hope will receive the enthusiasm of all Princetonians, old and young, to be the greatest step in the advancing of the *American* ideals, the ways of Democracy, that a College system can take, and that Princeton will be affecting the *national* life for the best, in this step, as nobly & perhaps more fully than in all the long and greatly honorable way in which men of Old Nassau have been leaders in the nation.

With heartiest appreciation of your own fine leadership in this, and the character required to take that leadership, and with good hopes of its success

Faithfully yours, J. H. Robinson, '91.

ALS (WP, DLC).

[1] Princeton 1891, pastor of the Westchester Presbyterian Church of White Plains, N. Y.

[2] That is, Alexander Thomas Ormond.

To Frederic Yates

My dear Mr. Yates: Princeton, N. J. July 2nd, 1907.

It is a real privation to me that I must always be writing you business letters and never the kind I should like to write, pouring out my affectionate regard for you and dwelling upon all the delightful recollections of last summer. I have just heard from Harper,[1] who speaks in the most delightfully enthusiastic terms of the Yates's, as we of course expected. I hope that you will enjoy him as much as he is evidently enjoying you and Mrs. Yates and Mary.

Mrs. Wilson asks me to say that the palette knife came, and that she is delighted with it. We don't quite understand whether the plate of Jessie's photograph is to come, as well as the photographs themselves. Neither plate nor photographs have yet arrived, but of course that is due to the delays of the customs office, or possibly to Mr. Bell's own delays, and we are not the least anxious on that score. I am enclosing a post-office order for one pound, the sum of money in which we are indebted to you. I wish it were as easy to pay the other debts to you, which can never be discharged except as we *are* discharging them, by devoted friendship.

I am still in the midst of business, but hope that leisure moments are at last in sight.

With warmest messages from us all to you all,

Always faithfully yours, Woodrow Wilson

TLS (F. Yates Coll., NjP).

[1] G. M. Harper to WW, June 16, 1907, ALS (WP, DLC).

From Cleveland Hoadley Dodge

My dear Mr. President: New York July 2, 1907.

Many thanks for your delightful letter of yesterday, and I feel very strongly, as you do, about the necessity of carrying through your plans; but I think we both agree that, if we can do it by evolutionary methods rather than by revolutionary methods, it will be better.

As to Mrs. Sage, it is very difficult to know what to advise. I have no definite idea where she is to be this summer, although I suppose she will spend most of her time at her country place on Long Island. It is a question whether it would not be better to wait until fall before approaching her, but I will take pains to ascertain from Mr. De Forest[1] exactly where she is to be and what is the best way of getting at her. You have probably heard the report that she is contemplating the erection of a dormitory at Princeton. I believe she has had nephews there and is quite interested in the University, and it is quite possible that you may be able to interest her deeply in your new plan.

I expect to be away for the rest of this week, but will be here all of the first part of next week, and if you are in town, perhaps we can arrange to lunch together; or you might possibly be willing to come up to Riverdale and spend the night.

Hoping to see you soon, I remain,

Very sincerely yours, C H Dodge

When are you going to Mts

TLS (WP, DLC).

[1] Henry Wheeler De Forest, member of the New York law firm of De Forest Brothers and financial and legal adviser to Mrs. Sage.

From Melancthon Williams Jacobus

My dear President Wilson: Hartford, Conn., July 2d, 1907.

Pardon my delay in replying to your inquiry of the 27th of June, but I was anxious to have the enclosed ready to submit to you when I wrote.

Some days ago there appeared in both the morning and evening papers of Hartford editorials, copies of which I enclose, relating to the new move at Princeton.[1] These editorials seem to be so largely based on imperfect information and to have got so generally the spirit of opposition that I felt there ought to be a reply to them of some character, preferably that of a letter to the Courant, simply in the interests of fair judgment.

I worked out something in this line, making free use of your reports as given in the Commencement number of the Alumni Weekly, and borrowing without remorse the ideas which you have so forcibly incorporated in your communications to the Committee, the Clubs and Board of Trustees. For this I hope you will pardon me and be perfectly frank to pass judgment on what I have written.[2]

In view of the importance of Hartford as a center of New England ideas and New Haven prejudices, nothing should be sent to the paper which is not accurate in respect of facts and worth while in the good it does to the interests of Princeton. If on reading over my letter you think that nothing sufficient will be gained by its publication, please be perfectly free to say so. I have had only the interests of Princeton at heart, and would be most grieved to feel that they had not been conserved in the public printing. If you think that, on the whole, it is worth while to print what has been written, with modifications in the statements, I would be most thankful to have you make them in order that the best good may be done.

Now, as to your request, I am only too glad to grant you formal permission to report the men you name to the Catalogue Committee to be retained on the Faculty list pending the next meeting of the Board of Trustees, and will make note of this fact to be presented to the Committee next fall. . . .

You do not know how relieved I am to know that your Sundays are to be preserved to you as days of rest. It is the least we could do to one whose value to Princeton is quite beyond all calculation.

What you report as having been said to you at the Harvard Commencement is most encouraging. I have talked with some

Yale men here, but they are deeply wrapped up in the conviction that there is no academic democracy quite equal to that which they have in New Haven, and are inclined to look upon everything else as degenerate and behind the times. I fancy that they will wake up soon to the situation which in reality exists on their campus, though they know it not.

I am perfectly resigned to the fight which is now in progress, and only hope that it will be honest and thorough enough to make the result recognized on every hand when it comes. Whatever we can do during the summer to disclose the situation as it exists and make clear the object and end we have in view, will be so much gained for the closer conflict which will ensue upon the re-opening of the academic year.

With kindest regards and best wishes for a thoroughly restful summer, I am

Yours very sincerely, Melancthon W Jacobus

TLS (WP, DLC).

1 These enclosures are missing, but they were clippings of editorials from the *Hartford Times* (the evening newspaper), June 25, 1907, and the Hartford *Courant* (the morning newspaper), June 26, 1907. After describing the quadrangle plan, the *Hartford Times* said that it was "in fact a blow at the individual freedom which students particularly enjoy." The *Courant* said that Wilson had been daydreaming. "He has told his dream," the editorial continued, "and a pretty commotion it is going to make among the Princetonians."

2 See WW to M. W. Jacobus, July 6, 1907.

To Cleveland Hoadley Dodge

My dear Cleve: Princeton, N. J. July 3rd, 1907.

Thank you sincerely for your kind and heartening letter of yesterday. I wish with all my heart that I might be able to see you before I go to the mountains next Monday, but it looks now as if it were going to be impossible. But I really think that something might come out of an interview with Mrs. Sage, and I shall hold myself in readiness to come out of my mountain retreat at any moment for the purpose of seeing her, if you can possibly manage it for me, or rather, not manage it but suggest to me some natural way of making an opportunity.

You may be sure that I believe in evolutionary processes, but money will lubricate the evolution as nothing else will. Indeed, as I look forward to the execution of the scheme, there is nothing but the financial side of it that gives me uneasiness. Everything else, I am sure, will work out as we desire it to work out, after the excitement has passed off and everybody has had his say.

My address in the mountains will be St. Hubert's, Essex County, N. Y. This is in Keene Valley.

Please give my warmest regards to Mrs. Dodge, and believe me,

Always affectionately yours, Woodrow Wilson

TLS (WC, NjP).

From Henry van Dyke

My dear President Wilson: Princeton, N. J. July 3. 1907.

A report in the newspapers leads me to turn to you for authoritative information. Has it been determined to adopt the plan of "residential quads" at Princeton, (including the abolition and absorption of the clubs,) or is it an open question? I do not refer to the details and methods, but to the essential idea and purpose of the plan. Has that been already adopted?

Faithfully Yours Henry van Dyke

ALS (H. van Dyke Papers, NjP).

From Harry Augustus Garfield

Newstate, Berkshire Co., Mass.,

My dear Wilson, July 3, 1907.

I have decided to accept the Williams presidency & am so advising the trustees today. Not until I had posted my letter to you the other day did I appreciate how much I wished to have your sympathetic understanding of what would probably be my decision. Hence I the more appreciated your letter & its expressions of affectionate regard.

The decision is not easy, but I am satisfied that it is as it should be. I am glad that it leaves us another year in Princeton & look forward to it in the hope that the winter may be made to count most of all for the things we have been working for together.

With sincerest regard, I remain,

Very Affectionately Yours, H. A. Garfield.

ALS (WP, DLC).

From George Sibley Johns[1]

My Dear Doctor: St. Louis. Mo. July 3rd, 1907.

I want to congratulate you and the Committee of Trustees on your suggestion and their plan for the democracizing or, as you put it, "social coordination" of Princeton. The speech I made at the alumni luncheon two years ago on the necessity of maintaining equality in the university, and the danger of driving away young men of moderate means and little means by the growing distinctions of wealth and social position, was suggested by the development of the club system and other features which tended to emphasize these distinctions.[2] Your plan is in line with the thought that I tried to convey at that time, and I believe it will have an admirable influence—that it is the one thing needful in American university life. I hope it will prove a great success, and am especially delighted that Princeton takes leadership in this movement. I enclose an editorial comment on the plan which I published last Sunday.[3]

Yours sincerely, Geo S. Johns

TLS (WP, DLC).

1 Princeton 1880, editor of the *St. Louis Post-Dispatch*. He had served with Wilson on the editorial board of the *Princetonian* and had succeeded him as editor of that newspaper in 1879.

2 Johns spoke at the alumni luncheon on June 13, 1905, and "emphasized Princeton's duty to the student of moderate means." *Princeton Alumni Weekly*, v (June 17, 1905), 616.

3 A clipping of an editorial, "A College Democracy," *St. Louis Post-Dispatch*, June 30, 1907.

A News Report of a Celebration at the Jamestown Exposition

[*July 4, 1907*]

CHEER HUGHES AS NEXT PRESIDENT

President Wilson's Speech.

NORFOLK, Va., July 4.—Ten thousand people to-day cheered the declaration that Gov. Charles E. Hughes of New York would be the next President of the United States. The enthusiasm broke loose at the celebration of Independence Day and the reunion of descendants of signers of the Declaration of Independence at the Jamestown Exposition.

Gov. Hughes had an ovation not even second to the one given President Roosevelt on his two visits. For five minutes the crowd wildly cheered Mr. Hughes when he was introduced, waving hundreds of flags. Throughout his speech the Governor was interrupted by cheering that he was unable to silence until the enthusiasm had spent itself.

But it was in the course of the speech of President Woodrow Wilson of Princeton University that the most significant demonstration took place. President Wilson was discussing the greed of trusts, and interpreted [interrupted] his remarks by asking: "What remedy would an aggressive Chief Executive like Hughes apply?"

"He'll bust the trusts—and we're going to make him the next President," came in thundering tones from the rear of the hall. A mighty shout followed. Cheering followed cheering, with cries of "Hughes!" and President Wilson was unable to proceed for ten minutes.

Gov. Hughes throughout the incident sat quietly back of President Wilson. He smiled, but showed no other recognition of the demonstration, and did not reply to the calls, allowing the speaker to proceed.

To-night men who have officiated in all of the big days of the exposition admitted that no other speaker had such a reception from the crowds. . . .

Individual accountability for the acts of corporations, the arrest and imprisonment of corporation heads instead of the fining or dissolution of corporations themselves, is the remedy for the monopolistic tendencies and the unlawful practices of modern industry, urged Woodrow Wilson, President of Princeton University, in an address at the Jamestown Exposition today. . . .

Printed in the *New York Times*, July 5, 1907; some editorial headings omitted.

An Address[1]

[July 4, 1907]

THE AUTHOR AND SIGNERS OF THE DECLARATION OF INDEPENDENCE

It is common to think of the Declaration of Independence as a highly speculative document; but no one can think it so who has read it. It is a strong, rhetorical statement of grievances against the English government. It does indeed open with the assertion that all men are equal and that they have certain inalienable rights, among them the right to life, liberty and the pursuit of happiness. It asserts that governments were instituted to secure these rights, and can derive their just powers only from the consent of the governed; and it solemnly declares that "whenever any government becomes destructive of these ends, it is the right of the people to alter or to abolish it, and to institute a new government, laying its foundations in such prin-

[1] There is a WWhw outline, a WWT outline, and a WWsh draft dated June 29, 1907, of this address in WP, DLC.

ciples, and organizing its powers in such forms, as to them shall seem most likely to effect their safety and happiness." But this would not afford a general theory of government to formulate policies upon. No doubt we are meant to have liberty, but each generation must form its own conception of what liberty is. No doubt we shall always wish to be given leave to pursue happiness as we will, but we are not yet sure where or by what method we shall find it. That we are free to adjust government to these ends we know. But Mr. Jefferson and his colleagues in the Continental Congress prescribed the law of adjustment for no generation but their own. They left us to say whether we thought the government they had set up was founded on "such principles," its powers organized in "such forms" as seemed to us most likely to effect our safety and happiness. They did not attempt to dictate the aims and objects of any generation but their own.

We are justified in looking back with a great satisfaction to the documents which spoke the purposes of the Revolution and formed the government which was to succeed to the authority of king and parliament. They speak the character of the men who drew them as clearly as they speak the circumstances of the times. The fifty-six men who put their names to the Declaration of Independence were not of the sort to meet an acute crisis in affairs with a treatise on government. They were accustomed to the practice of business, and as apt to go straight to their point as any minister over sea. They were of every calling;—men were apt in that day of beginnings to have been of several callings by the time they reached middle life. Lawyers predominated among them, men like James Wilson and John Adams and Edward Rutledge; but there were merchants too, like Robert Morris of Philadelphia and John Hancock of Boston; country gentlemen of large affairs like Benjamin Harrison and Charles Carroll; and physicians, like Benjamin Rush and Lyman Hall. Thomas Jefferson and Benjamin Franklin we cannot classify. Each stands unique and individual, a man supported by genius. And hard-headed Englishmen, like Button Gwinnet of Georgia; and men sure of their rights because they were Irishmen, born with an inclination to assert them, like James Smith and George Taylor, added to the handsome variety; and a man like John Witherspoon, the indomitable President of Princeton, turned statesman to authenticate the teaching he was giving lads like James Madison and Henry Lee, contributed his own flavour of unhesitating directness, both of thought and speech. Only Scotchmen seem able to be formidable at once in philosophy and in fact. The only professional politician among them was Samuel Adams, at home a master of agitation and political organization, but in the Congress quiet enough, a statesman of grievances, not of measures.

The genius of the new republic was expressed among these men as it was expressed eleven years later among the men who framed the Constitution of the United States, by practical capacity, thoughtful indeed and holding at its heart clear-cut, unmistakeable conceptions of what government of free men ought to be, but not fanciful, a thing of action rather than of theory, suited to meet an exigency, not a mere turn in debate. We do not live in times as critical as theirs. We are not engaged in making a nation. But we are engaged in purging and preserving a nation, and an analysis of our duty in the situation in which we stand is in many ways more difficult than that which they attempted, the remedies to be applied left less obvious to our choice. They gave us the nation: we owe them, not empty eulogy, but the sincere flattery of imitation. If we are their descendants either in blood or in spirit, let us distinguish our ancestry from that of others by clear wisdom in counsel and fearless action taken upon plain principle.

No one now needs to be told what the principle of the American Revolution was: it was the principle of individual liberty. Though those men who signed the Declaration of Independence were no theorists but practical statesmen, a very definite conception of what the government of enlightened men ought to be lay back of everything they did, and that conception they held with a passionate conviction. They believed government to be a means by which the individual could realize at once his responsibility and his freedom from unnecessary restraint. Government should guard his rights, but it must not undertake to exercise them for him.

No doubt the most interesting spokesman of that conception was that eminent Virginian, that unique and singular author of the Declaration of Independence. No doubt Thomas Jefferson was an astute politician; no doubt he was a most interesting philosopher; certainly he was a most inscrutable man. It would be impossible to make a consistent picture of him that should include all sides of his varied genius and singular character. He took leave, like all great men of affairs, to be inconsistent and do what circumstances required, approaching the perfection of theory by the tedious indirections of imperfect practice, but the main base of his theories was the base upon which all thoughtful men in his day founded their thinking about politics and intended to found their measures also. He believed consistently and profoundly in the right of the individual to a free opportunity, and in the right of the nation to an unhampered development, and was ready to support every law or arrangement which promised to secure the people against any sort of monopoly in taking part in that development. Moreover, he knew that government was a thing conducted by individuals, men whose weaknesses and passions did not differ from the weaknesses and passions of the men whom they governed; and that government must operate upon individuals whose tangled rights and opportunities no government could look into too curiously or seek to control too intimately without intolerable consequences of paternalism and petty tyranny. Every man who signed the Declaration of Independence believed, as Mr. Jefferson did, that free men had a much more trustworthy capacity in taking care of themselves than any government had ever shown or was ever likely to show, in taking care of them; and upon that belief American government was built.

So far as the Declaration of Independence was a theoretical document, that is its theory. Do we still hold it? Does the doctrine of the Declaration of Independence still live in our principles of action, in the things we do, in the purposes we applaud, in the measures we approve? It is not a question of piety. We are not bound to adhere to the doctrines held by the signers of the Declaration of Independence: we are as free as they were to make and unmake governments. We are not here to worship men or a document. But neither are we here to indulge in a mere rhetorical and uncritical eulogy. Every Fourth of July should be a time for examining our standards, our purposes, for determining afresh what principles, what forms of power we think most likely to effect our safety and happiness. That and that alone is the obligation the Declaration lays upon us. It is no fetish; its words lay no compulsion upon the thought of any free man; but it was drawn by men who thought, and it obliges those who receive its benefits to *think* likewise.

What then do we think of our safety and of our happiness,—of the principles of action and the forms of power we are using to secure them? That we have come to a new age and a new attitude towards questions of government, no one can doubt,—to new definitions of constitutional power, new conceptions of legislative object, new schemes of individual and corporate regulation. Upon what principle of change do we act? Do we act upon definite calculations of purpose, or do we but stumble hesitatingly upon expedients? To what statements of principle would a declaration of our reasons and purposes commit us before the world: to those the signers of the Declaration of Independence would have avowed, or to others very different and not at all novel in the political history of the world? This is not a party question: there is apparently little difference between parties in regard to it. It is a national question,—a question touching the political principles of America. We ought not to hesitate to avow a change, if change there is to be; but we should be ashamed to act in radical fashion and not know that there was a change. Precedent is at least a guide by which to determine our direction.

There is much in our time that would cause men of the principles of Mr. Jefferson the bitterest disappointment. Individual opportunity is not unhampered. The nation has had in every respect an extraordinary material development, but the chief instrumentalities of that development have been at least virtually monopolized, and the people, though they created the opportunity and contributed the labor, have not shared the benefits of that development as they might have shared them. This has not been due to the operation of our institutions; it has been due to the operation of human nature, which is alike under all institutions and which has perhaps had freer play under our institutions than it would have had under any others, as Mr. Jefferson wished that it should have. Moreover, there is no doubt that we shall set all things right; but it is important we should inquire the way and not set them right by methods which may bring new trouble upon us, if the old methods will suffice for our safety and happiness. What were those methods? What was the spirit of the nation at its inception,—in 1776 when the great declaration of its intentions was framed, and in 1787 when it made deliberate choice of its form of government?

There is no difficulty in answering these questions; the answers to them have lain before us since we were children, in every book that spoke of our history or of our character as a nation. Let us use them as a mirror into which to look in order to make test whether we shall recognize our own features, disguised as they are by change of circumstance, in our present habit, as we live.

The most obvious characteristic of the men who gave the nation voice and power was their profound regard for law. That conviction is upon the surface and at the heart of everything they said or did in support of their purpose. They did not fling off from the mother country because they wanted new rights, but because the rights they had time out of mind enjoyed as free men under the laws and constitution of England, and the rights they had been promised as colonists in a new country with a life of its own, had been arbitrarily disregarded and withdrawn, and they knew not what ancient and undoubted liberties and privileges they could count upon. They wanted, not less law nor even better law, but law they could rely upon and live by. Their case was a case for legality, for the established understandings of law, upon which they knew that liberty had immemorially depended. There is no longer any need to debate what liberty really is; the question has been tried out again and again, both in theory and in practice,–in the council chamber and on the field of battle, where the air was calm and where it thrilled with passion,–and by no race more thoroughly than by that from which we derived our law; and we may say that we know. Affairs swing this way and that, sometimes with revolutionary force, as interests wage war for advantage, but we know where the midpoint of perfect poise lies and seek constantly to turn our lines of policy towards it. Liberty consists in the best possible adjustment between the power of the government and the privilege of the individual; and only law can effect that adjustment. Where liberty is, there must be a perfect understanding between the individual and those who would control him; and if either he or they can disregard the understanding, there is license or anarchy. It was in that knowledge that the founders of our government loved the law.

These same men, therefore, who revered law and depended upon its grants and definitions for their security and happiness, were deeply jealous of too much law. It is easy to talk of "society," of "communities," of "the people," but the fact is that these are but names we give to bodies made up of individuals. It is easy also to speak of "governments" as if they were forces set apart from us and above us; but governments also consist of individuals of like nature with ourselves. That is the reason, the very interesting and important reason, which the founders of our government needed not to have explained to whem [them], why control of our affairs by the government and the regulation of our relations to each other by the law are two very different things and lead to sharply contrasted results. The history of liberty in the past, from which we may possibly gather some intimation of its history in the future, has been a history of resistance to too much governmental control and a careful discovery of the best forms and the most prudent degrees of legal regulations; and it is clear that the law which the signers of the Declaration of Independence loved was something which they regarded, not as a body of powers possessed by a government, but as a body of rules regulating the complex game of life, no more favorable to control than was necessary to make it a safeguard of individual privilege and a guarantee of equal rights. Too much law was too much government; and too much government was too little individual privilege,—as too much individual privilege in its turn was selfish license.

Now let us hold this mirror up to ourselves and see if we recognize in it the image of our own minds. In that mirror we see a conception of government which frankly puts the individual in the foreground, thinking of him as the person to be at once protected and heartened to make a free use of himself; the responsible administrator of his own liberties and his own responsibilities; and of government as the umpire; and which depends upon law for nothing else than a clear establishment of the rules of the game. That is hardly our notion. We are indeed in love with law,—more in love with it than were the makers of the government,—but hardly in love with it as a government of mere regulation. For us it is an instrument of reconstruction and control. The individual has eluded us, we seem to say, has merged and hidden himself in corporations and associations, through the intricacies of whose structure we have not time to thread our way in search of him; we will therefore meet the circumstances as we find them, treat him not as an integer but as a fraction, and deal with the association, not with the individual. We will prohibit corporations to do this or to do that, to be this or to be that, and punish them either with fine or with dissolution if they disobey. The morals of business and of law we will frankly accept as corporate morals, and we will not set these corporations, these new individuals of our modern law, to watch and sue one another for infractions of the law: they might combine, and there is no sufficient motive for them to check one another in illegal practices. Neither can we depend upon individuals: they are now too minute and weak. The moralizer and disciplinarian of corporations can in the nature of the case be none other than the government itself, and, because corporations spread from state to state, can be none other than the government of the United States.

It is amusing how we extend this new theory of law into some of the new details of our life,—extend it at any rate in our thinking, if not in our legislation. We hear it suggested on every side, for example, that the true and effective way to stop the driving of automobiles along our highways at excessive rates of speed is to lock up the automobiles themselves whenever the speed laws are violated, so that for a long time at least it may not be used again. I suppose we shall some day see officers of the law arresting electric cars and steam locomotives for the offences which their motormen and engineers have committed, and the faults of men everywhere corrected by locking up their tools. The trouble is that the tools are wanted, and the lives of all of us are inconvenienced if they are taken away. Even the automobile is useful, when used with sanity and caution. And there is exactly the same serious trouble about the way we now deal with our corporations, punishing inanimate things instead of persons. When we fine them, we merely take that much money out of their business,—that is, out of the business of the country,—and put it into the public treasury, where there is generally already a surplus and where it is likely to lie idle. When we dissolve them, we check and hamper legitimate undertakings and embarrass the business of the country much more than we should embarrass it were we to arrest locomotives and impound electric cars, the necessary vehicles of our intercourse. And all the while we know perfectly well that the iniquities we levy fines for were conceived and executed by particular individuals who go unpunished, unchecked even, in the enterprises which have led to the action of the courts. And so from one body of hidden individuals we turn to another, and say, "Go to, we will instruct the government to regulate this thing in place of boards of directors: if necessary, we will instruct the government to transact the business which these corporations have made the government interfere with on account of bad practices. We shall then have honesty: for are not the men who compose the government men of our own choice, our servants for our common business?"

It needs no prophet to predict that too much government lies that way, and nothing but too much government,—and no increased efficiency or improved business to be had in the bargain. And beyond too much government lies the old programme, repeated and repeated again and again every time the like thing has happened: a new struggle for liberty, a new eagerness for emancipation from the law that dictates, into the freedom of the law that umpires. No doubt the old cycle must some time be gone through again; but we ought not to be the people to go through it. We have had too much light: we have furnished the world with doctrines and example in this kind, and we cannot afford to illustrate our own principles by our mistakes after having illustrated them by our successes. Shall we return to our old standards, or shall we attempt arrangements which we know our children will be obliged to reject?

Can we return to our old standards in this strange and altered day, when all the face of circumstances seems changed and nothing remains as it was in the time when the government was hopefully set up? Undoubtedly we can. Not everything is changed: the biggest item of all remains unaltered,–human nature itself; and it is nothing to daunt a free people,–free to think and free to act, that the circumstances in which that old, unalterable nature now expresses itself are so complex and singular. The difficulty of the task is part of its desirability: it is a new enterprise upon which to stretch our powers and make proof of our sanity and strength. It is the task of making a new translation of our morals into the terms of our modern life, where individuality seems for the time being lost in complex organizations, and then making a new translation of our laws to match our new translation of morals. It is the task of finding the individual in the maize [maze] of modern social, commercial and industrial conditions; finding him with the probe of morals and with the probe of law. One really responsible man in jail, one real originator of the schemes and transactions which are contrary to public interest legally lodged in the penitentiary would be worth more than a thousand corporations mulcted in fines, if reform is to be genuine and permanent.

It is only in this way that we can escape socialism. If the individual is lost to our law, he is lost to our politics and to our social structure. If he is merged in the business group, he is merged in the state, the association that includes all others. Unless we can single him out again and make him once more the subject and object of law, we shall have to travel still further upon the road of government regulation which we have already traveled so far, and that road leads to state ownership. We have not even tried to extend the old roads into this vast new area of business and of corporate enterprise, which recent years have seen open up like a new continent of mind and achievement; and until we have tried, we cannot claim legitimate descent from the founders of the government. We have abandoned their principles without even making trial of their efficacy in a new situation.

The elaborate secret manipulations by means of which some of our so-called "financiers" get control of a voting majority of the stock of great railroad or manufacturing companies, in order to effect vast combinations of interest or properties, incidentally destroying the value of some stocks and fictitiously increasing the value of others, involve first or last acts which are in effect sheer thefts, making the property of thousands of stockholders so much waste paper, or arbitrarily decreasing the relative earning capacity of corporations for a share in whose earnings thousands of men and women had paid hard-earned cash; but we have never sought to bring the details of these transactions within the definition of the criminal law. Not to do so is like overlooking the highway robberies of the mediaeval barons. Moreover, it leaves an unjust stain of popular suspicion upon transactions similar to all outward appearance, but conceived in justice and fair-dealing. Every corporation is personally directed either by some one dominant person or by some group of persons, in respect of every essential step in its policy: somebody in particular is responsible for ordering or sanctioning every illegal act committed by its agents or officers; but neither our law of personal damages nor our criminal law has sought to seek the responsible persons out and hold them individually accountable for the acts complained of. It would require a careful hand and a minute knowledge of existing business conditions to draw the law, but statutes could oblige every corporation to make such public analysis of its organization as would enable both private individuals and officers of the law to fix legal responsibility upon the right person. We have never attempted such statutes. We indict corporations themselves, find *them* guilty of illegal practices, fine *them*, and leave the individuals who devise and execute the illegal acts free to discover new evasions and shape the policy of the corporations to practices not yet covered by the prohibitions of law. We complain that directors are too often mere names upon a list and that even when they attend the meetings of the boards to which they belong, they give no real heed to what is done and allow some committee to have its own way unquestioned; and yet the law could easily make them responsible, personally and individually responsible, to any extent it chose for acts which their votes authorized, and could thereby quickly change their nominal participation in the affairs of the corporations they pretend to govern, into real participation and watchful oversight. Let every corporation exactly define the obligations and powers of its directors, and then let the law fix responsibility upon them accordingly.

I need not multiply examples. We know that the vast majority of our business transactions are sound, the vast majority of our business men honest. In order to clear the way of unjust suspicion, give credit where credit is due, condemnation where condemnation; let us set ourselves to work to single out individuals and real personal responsibility, and we shall both lighten the difficulty of government and make a new platform of life. Governmental supervision there must be, but of the kind there has always been in District Attorneys' offices; not the kind that seeks to determine the processes of business, but the kind that brings home to individuals the obligations of the law.

It would be a happy emancipation. We should escape the burden of too much government, and we should regain our self-respect, our self-confidence, our sense of individual integrity; we should think straightway with regard to the moral aspect of conduct, and we should escape perplexities with regard to our political future; we should once more have the exhilarating freedom of governing our own lives, the law standing as umpire, not as master.

By such means we should prove ourselves indeed the spiritual descendants of the signers of the Declaration of Independence. It is fashionable, it is easy, to talk about Jeffersonian principles of government. Men of all kinds and of the most opposite doctrines call themselves by Mr. Jefferson's name; and it must be admitted that it is easy to turn many of Mr. Jefferson's opinions this way or that. But no man's name settles any principle, and Mr. Jefferson was originating no novel doctrine, announcing no discoveries in politics, when he wrote the Declaration of Independence. What it contains is in fact the common-place of political history. There can be no liberty if the individual is not free: there is no such thing as corporate liberty. There is no other possible formula for a free government than this: that the laws must deal with individuals, allowing them to choose their own lives under a definite personal responsibility to a common government set over them; and that government must regulate, not as a superintendent does, but as a judge does; it must safeguard, it must not direct.

These thoughts ought still to linger in the very air of this place. The first English settlers came here while the breath of the "spacious times of great Elizabeth" was still in every man's lungs, and the quickening impulse of enterprise and adventure. The great Tudor queen had known how to deal with mettlesome men: she had given them leave to do what they pleased in the world, if only they would remember always her sovereignty and their allegiance, and deal always with each other's rights as the law commanded. The things which government fostered and sought to manage never throve in America, amongst the French colonists in Canada and the South, and amongst the Dutch and Danes on the North and South Rivers; but the free English energy throve like a thing bred for the wilderness. That breath of individual liberty has never gone out of our lungs. Too much government still suffocates us. We do not respect ourselves as much as fractions, as we do as integers. The future, like the past, is for individual energy and initiative; for men, not for corporations or for governments; and the law that has this ancient principle at its heart is the law that will endure.[2]

T MS (WP, DLC).

[2] This address was printed under the same title in the *North American Review*, CLXXXVI (Sept. 1907), 22-33.

From Frederick Newton Willson

Dear Dr. Wilson: Spring Lake, N. J. July 4, 1907.

There has never, till now, seemed to be any special occasion for my expressing my views as to your policies, although I have been in hearty accord with them so far; but at a time when you are being put in so false a light as to the recent discipline,[1] and when an attempt is evidently being made to use that to arouse a sentiment adverse to your new schemes as to the clubs, and, in addition, the press is endeavoring to make it appear that the Faculty is in some measure disloyal to your plans, I wish to assure you of my belief in the soundness of your ideas and in their ultimate triumph. I shall await with interest the course of the Dean, as to assuming the whole responsibility for the *method* of procedure which is so exasperating the students.

While writing, I may add a word of hearty appreciation of the address you made at the dedication of our new lecture room.[2] Your stand for the maintenance of the spiritual against the encroachments of the secular upon the domain of the church was most timely. It is strange that, since then, encouragement should have been given to the hope that the large audience room of the chapel would be available for presenting dramatic entertainments. I cannot feel that we should strive to ease our consciences as to whatever may be our special indulgence in the matter of the debatable pleasures, by dragging them inside the house of God and seeming to have secured the church's endorsement of them. "Render to Caesar," etc., is a safe principle to go on in everything.

Very sincerely yours, Fred N. Willson.

TLS (WP, DLC).

[1] This disciplinary action is explained in Dean Henry B. Fine's report printed at Oct. 17, 1907.

[2] That is, of the First Presbyterian Church of Princeton. See the news report printed at March 30, 1907.

To Henry van Dyke

My dear Dr. van Dyke: Princeton, N. J. July 5th, 1907.

Thank you for your letter of July 3rd. It was the understanding at the meeting of the Board in June that the essential idea and purpose of the plan for residential quads had been adopted, but that there was a very wide range of choice as to details and methods, and that there was to be the freest possible inquiry how the idea might best be realized by common counsel.

The Board was very decidedly in favor of the essential idea and purpose of the plan, and felt that it would contribute very much to reaching a definite result, if it expressed its judgment to that effect at once.

I am looking forward with the greatest pleasure to being near you, for a time at any rate, this summer, and hope to have many long talks with you on the subject.[1]

Always cordially and faithfully yours,

Woodrow Wilson

TLS (H. van Dyke Papers, NjP).

[1] "Later in the same summer President Wilson and I were together in the Adirondacks, and he expressed very warmly his wish that I would support the Quad Scheme. I told him how sorry I was that I could not do so, because it seemed to me that the proposal to divide the student body into separate colleges after the Oxford model, was not in harmony with the democratic spirit of Princeton, where the unity of the student body in all vital matters had been so notably preserved and illustrated. It would therefore be my duty to do all that I could to defeat the plan, which in my opinion was likely to lead to aristocratic divisions among the students similar to those which existed at Oxford." H. van Dyke to William Allen White, May 17, 1924, CCL (H. van Dyke Papers, NjP).

From Henry van Dyke

My dear President Wilson, Princeton, N. J. July 5th, 1907.

Thank you for your prompt and full letter of July 5th. I feel bound to tell you, personally, of my profound regret at hearing that the essential idea of the plan of residential quads for Princeton must be understood as already adopted. It is the "essential idea" that makes the radical change,—a change which seems to me full of the gravest perils to the life and unity of Princeton. I am sorry that you did not tell me last Spring, when we were talking together, about this most important plan; and still more sorry that there has been no opportunity for general consideration and discussion before the decision was announced. Of course, if the essential idea is adopted, there is little more to be said.

I hope we shall all have a good time together in the Adirondacks this summer. There are some glorious mountain walks there that I should like to take with you. As ever,

Faithfully and cordially Yours Henry van Dyke

ALS (WP, DLC).

To Melancthon Williams Jacobus

My dear Dr. Jacobus: [Princeton, N. J.] July 6th, 1907.

Absence at the Jamestown Exposition, where I had promised to be on the Fourth of July, has delayed my reply to your interesting and important letter of the second. Certainly the tone of the editorials you sent me is very unsatisfactory, and I think that on the whole it would be wise to publish something in explanation of what we are really purposing to do. I think, too, that what you have written will serve the purpose admirably. I have only one suggestion to make. I am particularly anxious that it should be understood that we are not attacking our clubs for what they are and do, for it seems to me that their life and spirit is in every respect excellent, but that our whole point is that their existence leads to social results which stand in the way of a simple organization suitable for intellectual purposes. Perhaps it would be possible for you to add a paragraph to that effect.[1]

All sorts of apparently malicious rumors are afloat, some of which represent me as having attacked the clubs for actual vice and debauchery, though nothing that I have said or thought could possibly be given that color.

Thank you very much for your letter. I appreciate it in every respect very deeply. I leave for the Adirondacks on Monday, the eighth. There my address will be St. Hubert's P. O., Essex Co., N. Y. I should be delighted to hear from you, if you have anything that you wish to suggest or consult me about.

Always cordially and faithfully yours,

[Woodrow Wilson]

CCL (RSB Coll., DLC).

[1] Jacobus, in M. W. Jacobus to the Editor, July 6, 1907, printed in the Hartford *Courant*, July 8, 1907, included the paragraph suggested by Wilson. The quadrangle plan, he wrote, "does not attack the clubs for what they themselves are and do, for their life and spirit are in every respect excellent. What it has in mind is simply the social results to which they lead and which stand in the way

of the intellectual realization of the university life. It does not aim primarily even to reorganize the social life of the university, but rather to revitalize the university as an academic body, whose objects are not dominantly social but intellectual. It is a natural rounding out of the preceptorial system, which would be necessary whether the clubs existed, or not."

From John Allen Holt[1]

Dear Sir: Oak Ridge, N. C. July 6, 1907.

I have just read some of the extracts from your speech delivered at the Jamestown Exposition the fourth of July, which have the right ring; and I am of the opinion that if the Democratic Party should look for a candidate east of the Mississippi, it could place no man at the head of its ticket who would be as likely to win next year as yourself.

Believe me very sincerely and respectfully,

J Allen Holt

TLS (WP, DLC).

[1] Co-Principal of the Oak Ridge, N. C., Institute, a boys' school.

From Ellis Paxson Oberholtzer[1]

Dear Prof Wilson Philadelphia July 6, 1907.

Noting Prof. Garfield's recent appointment in New England I am writing to you to ask whether the successorship at Princeton is still an open question. If it be it occurs to me that you might be interested to know of my disposition to fill such a place at an institution whose services I so highly esteem. I think I was led into my "Referendum in America"[2] by your "Cong Government.". . .

I nourish a desire to take up the History of the U.S. since the war, where McMaster leaves off[3] and I should like to do it in connection with a college chair—and my relations social and other are such that I cannot go very far from Philadelphia.

I fear I do not know how your elective body is composed but I feel satisfied that whatever commendations might be required I could very soon muster for its use. My range of study, information and experience, I believe, covers the field of this professorship. But of course if you have anticipated your wants I will dismiss the subject from my mind.[4]

Sincerely Yours Ellis Paxson Oberholtzer

ALS (WWP, UA, NjP).

[1] Journalist and author, residing in Philadelphia. At this time he was editor of the American Crisis Biographies series published by George W. Jacobs & Co. of Philadelphia, to which he contributed *Abraham Lincoln* (Philadelphia, 1904).

2 *The Referendum in America* (Philadelphia, 1893; revised edns., New York, 1900, 1911). This was his Ph.D. dissertation at the University of Pennsylvania under John Bach McMaster.

3 He did in fact do this and published his history in five volumes as *A History of the United States since the Civil War* (New York, 1917-37).

4 Wilson's reply is missing in the Oberholtzer Papers, PHi, but he undoubtedly did not encourage Oberholtzer.

To Henry van Dyke

My dear Dr. van Dyke: Princeton, N. J. July 8th, 1907.

Thank you very much for your frank letter of July 5th. I hasten to reply to it, because it contains a misapprehension. The essential idea of the new plan has certainly been adopted by the Board of Trustees, but, as I was saying to Paul [van Dyke] the other day, this does not mean that there will not be a full opportunity to discuss it on its merits in the faculty of the University. It goes without saying that if I cannot have the support of the faculty, the plan cannot be carried out. It has all along, therefore, been my intention to bring the matter in some suitable form to the attention of the faculty next year. For reasons which I shall fully explain then, it seemed to be necessary to ask the action of the Board upon the matter immediately, but this does not essentially alter the relation of the faculty to it, at any rate in my own judgment.

We can go fully into this, however, when we see each other in the mountains.

In the meantime, please believe me,

Always faithfully and cordially yours,

Woodrow Wilson

TLS (H. van Dyke Papers, NjP).

From John Grier Hibben

My dear Woodrow On N. Y. Central train. July 8, 1907

I had a few words with Mrs. Wilson as we were parting which enabled me to see that my conversations with her & with you the last few days had failed of the end which I had sought to attain in speaking as frankly and as freely as I have done. It grieves me most deeply to feel that I have wounded you without avail; for Mrs. Wilson told me that I had merely disheartened you for the fight which you only felt more than ever you must wage to the finish without yielding in any respect whatsoever. Now, Woodrow it certainly makes my heart exceedingly heavy as I reflect that the poor but well intended offices of friendship have so miscarried[.] You know that I would never have sought to 'rob you of hope,' as Mrs. Wilson characterized it, unless I had thought that I might at the same time forarm you by forwarning you of the gathering opposition. Were it not for my own convictions as to the dangers which attend this plan as regards the vital interests of Princeton, I would have gladly stood with you shoulder to shoulder against the world. Feeling as I do on that score, the only possibility remaining as a friend was to show you as far as I saw it myself the existing conditions as regards the attitude of the Trustees, Faculty & Alumni to your plan & the manner of its presentation to the Princeton community. I had hoped that you would be willing, not necessarily to change your own point of view, but merely to allow the question to be reopened for more detailed investigation & discussion. Such a suggestion coming from you would have given the impression, and that a true one, of magnanimity. You know that from the beginning of your administration, I have always had an instinct, the instinct of a deep affection, to rush to your side whenever danger, however slight, seemed to threaten. And yet now I have the feeling which I have endeavored vainly to throw off that at this juncture I have gone too far, and have succeeded only in distressing you without helping you in any way whatsoever. I can not allow any time to pass without writing you thus as soon as possible; and expressing my deep regret & sorrow if my too blunt & too frank words have inflicted wounds which have no healing power[.] With love from us all,

Your devoted friend Jack

P.S. Will you kindly show this letter to Mrs. Wilson as I felt she was deeply distressed by the effect of my talks upon you

J. G. H.

ALS (WP, DLC).

From Andrew Clerk Imbrie

Dear Dr. Wilson, University Club [New York] July 8/07

I have been dining here this evening with a half dozen Princeton men, all of whom are active in alumni affairs, and we have spent the evening discussing the question of "Residential Quads." We all feel that we can be of more help to you if certain points which are not quite clear to us may be explained. There seems to be a good deal of misunderstanding as to just what is proposed, even among men who are supposed to be in close touch with Princeton.

So I am writing to ask you if you could dine with ten or twelve of us here at the University Club, any evening this week or next. If so, we shall see that a room is reserved for you, and we shall see that the men who come to the dinner are active workers for Princeton, whose enthusiastic support I feel sure it will be desirable to gain at this particular time.

I hope you will not disappoint us, and that I shall hear from you by letter or telegram saying what evening will be most convenient to you to dine with us.

Yours faithfully Andrew C Imbrie
(18 Vesey St. New York)

ALS (WP, DLC).

From Cleveland Hoadley Dodge

My dear Wilson: New York July 9, 1907.

Thanks for your good letter of the 3d. I am very glad that you have been able to get away to the mountains, and trust you may have a good and thorough rest there. Meanwhile, I will see what we can do about Mrs. Sage, although I very much doubt the advisability of approaching her during the hot weather.

I went with Harry Thompson yesterday afternoon to see the plans for the new Natural History building. The architects have drawn two sets, which are to be sent to the Faculty Committee at Princeton for their consideration, and I think everything will work out very well.

With warm regards,

Very sincerely yours, C. H. Dodge

TLS (WP, DLC).

From Charles Travers Grant[1]

My Dear Sir: Akron, Ohio. July 9th 1907.

The Alumni Weekly of June 12th, carrying the report of the Committee on Social Conditions in Princeton, with your comments thereon, contains the first outward manifestation of an appreciation on the part of those charged with the trust of administering the affairs of the University, of a condition which will soon, if it has not already, so change the character of the institution from what it was fifteen or twenty years ago, that those of us who knew it then, will look upon it as a stranger.

Having left Princeton in the early days of the Club System, I perhaps cannot speak intelligently of that system, and must admit that its apparent success carries with it some evidence of virility. But from my occasional visits there since graduation, I cannot but feel that it is mischievous in principle and contains the elements of destruction of all the best ideals of student social life, as known to those who are now becoming the older graduates, and I bespeak for you and your colleagues the hearty support of the graduate body, in your efforts to remedy this condition, even to the point of eradication of the cause of the disease, if eradication shall become necessary.

This, however, will not be necessary, as the aggregate good sense of the under-graduate body, guided by the advice of those in authority, will, I believe in a short time bring about a realization that what appears as a personal sacrifice to-day, is necessary for the eternal good of the institution. This will more surely result as you offer in lieu thereof a system calculated to satisfy the social yearnings of the young man, without the attendant evils of the present club system.

I am not unaware of the opposition which you are meeting, and will meet in this undertaking, but have no doubt that in the end you will meet with the success which has been yours thus far in the enormous work of your administration.

With best wishes, I remain,

Very truly yours, C. T. Grant.

TLS (WP, DLC).

[1] Princeton 1893, who practiced law in Akron, Ohio, and lived in Cuyahoga Falls, Ohio.

From Arthur Herbert Osborn[1]

Dear Dr. Wilson, New York City July 9, 1907.

Being interested as I naturaly am in the present social condition of Princeton I have taken the liberty to write you and offer a suggestion in regards to the solution of the problem.

It would seem to me from what I read in the Alumni Weekly which was sent to me, that the steps proposed are far *too radical.* The abolition of the upper-class clubs, so distinctive a feature of Princeton, would be, I feel sure, a most unfortunate occurance.

Looking at it from the graduates standpoint, see how it would affect him. Under the present conditions he returns to Princeton for a few days visit, and, if he be a member of a club, he makes his headquarters at his club-house where he may eat and sleep, and meet men he knows, and in short make it a medium whereby he may once more enter into, one might almost say, the undergraduate life. It strikes me as being an ideal system for this reason if no other. It is a sort of second home to him.

On the other, if the clubs be turned into "quads" as suggested, and the clubs abolished, the grad returns to find men living in the house that his energy, time, and money have helped to create. Men living there, concerning whose right to do so he has no opportunity to say *yes* or *no*, while he, to whom, in part at least the house is due, must seek quarters elsewhere wherever he can find room and seek his meals at some town restaurant. This does not seem right to me, and should be reason enough I think, to not even consider the abolition of the clubs.

I have talked to many Princeton men since the "quad" plan was announced and in every case the criticism has been much the same as the one I made, and has aroused, as far as I have been able to observe, much discontent.

As regards the undergraduate standpoint. Cliques and clubs cannot be prevented unless human nature be made over. Our system is certainly way ahead of the fraternities of other universities, and to try and kill the clubs would be only to make them live under cover rather than out in the open.

Undoubtedly there is room for improvement, and it is bound to come if we are patient. It is in this respect that I have made many suggestions in my plan.

In conclusion I would beg to repeat myself in saying that I feel sure, from what I have heard that much serious harm would result from the abolition of the clubs, and Princeton would stagger under a heavy blow. A man cannot help but feel angry when he sees property of which he is at least part owner confiscated. It is contrary to the Constitution of our Country.

On separate paper I respectfully submit a plan over which I have done much thinking and on which I should value your opinion.[2]

Trusting you will understand all I have said in the spirit in which it is written, Believe me

Very sincerely yours, Arthur H. Osborn.

ALS (WP, DLC).

[1] Princeton 1907.

[2] The enclosure is an eight-page, signed, handwritten memorandum entitled "*A Plan* in respect to the *Club Situation* in *Princeton* to-day." It suggested abolishing all underclass clubs and grouping all freshmen and sophomores in quadrangles; the erection of a quadrangle for upperclassmen not elected to clubs; and requiring club members to eat frequently at the underclass quadrangles.

To John Grier Hibben

St. Hubert's, Essex Co., New York.

My dear Jack, 10 July, '07.

I need not tell you how deeply I appreciate your letter written from Albany. I send this reply by the very first post that goes out since we came last evening.

I beg that you will not grieve yourself with thinking that we have in the least degree or particular failed to understand all of the fine purpose and devoted affection that have prompted everything you have said and done. We have interpreted it just as you wished us to interpret it, and you may be sure that not the least shadow of any kind has fallen upon our perfect understanding.

Moreover, you may be sure that your counsel has had a deep effect. Ellen says that you quite misunderstood her when you took what she said to mean that it was more than ever my intention to insist upon my plan "without yielding in any respect whatsoever." She knows how the whole process of our talks have worked upon me: how they have disposed me to look for opportunities for concession, how anxious they have made me to render the utmost justice to the other side and seek amidst common counsel for a path which we can all tread. What I am, of course, not able to yield is the principle of the whole thing, namely, that the club basis of our life (that is, the elective basis) must give place to an organization absolutely controlled, not negatively, but constructively and administratively, by the university authorities. Not to insist on that would be to gain nothing but a temporary lessening of the present evils.

It is true that what you have told me of the attitude of the trustees, the alumni, and the faculty (above all the faculty) has "deprived me of hope." I can only hope that you are mistaken. If what you suppose to be the prevailing sentiment and purpose should turn out to be so indeed, I shall stand isolated and helpless. But before I accept that conclusion I must do everything in my power that is honourable and legitimate,—everything that a gentleman and a lover of our dear alma mater may do,—to convince all upon whom I depend for support of the wisdom and necessity of what I propose. They have most of them made up their minds before hearing me, before two-sided debate, instead of after it. Two-sided debate there shall be, of the frankest and most genuine sort. The Faculty shall know in the autumn, whatever they may now believe to the contrary, that I am ready to put myself in their hands. They may refuse to support me in this matter, and if they do I shall with no bitterness whatever, I hope and believe, accept their decision as a definitive defeat. I say without bitterness because I shall believe that many of them are moved by the same high, unselfish motives that move you, my dear, dear friend. I cannot conceal from you the deep anxiety and sadness that fills me in view of the whole situation. I cannot for the present think of Princeton without a deep pang of realization of what may be the consequences of this agitation; but I should feel a mere contempt for myself should I lose courage or falter: for I never had a clearer sense of duty. I should feel myself faithless and utterly blind to what the performance of my duties as president has brought to light were I to draw back. Mistakes of judgment are, of course, possible even in a measure so deliberately and anxiously conceived as this; and failure is bitter, how bitter it would be impossible to say, for a man convinced of duty as I am; but worse than either, infinitely worse, is it to shirk. To shirk would kill me; to fail need not.

This, my dear Jack, is the whole matter, as I would speak it to my own heart. You have done your duty, and I love and honour you for [it]; I shall try to do mine, and so win your love and respect. You would not wish me to do otherwise. And our friendship, by which I have lived, in which I have drawn some of the most refreshing, most renewing breath of my life, is to be as little affected by our difference of opinion as is everything permanent and of the law of our hearts. Do not, I beg of you, torture yourself in any way about it all. A struggle is ahead of me,—it may be a heartbreaking struggle,—and you cannot stand with me in it; but we can see past all that to the essence of things and shall at every step know each other's love. Will not that suffice?

Most of our party reached the cottage here yesterday afternoon about five o'clock, but Jessie and I did not arrive until almost ten at night. She had been misinformed about connections and I had to drop off and wait for her. I will tell you all about it in my next letter.

The cottage is a very rough affair, but we are accepting it in a holiday spirit, as a good enough camp, and expect to be very happy in it.

We are all well, and all unite in love to Mrs. Hibben and Beth and you. Bless you for the letter and believe the truth,—that everything is all right and as it should be.

Your devoted friend, Woodrow

WWTLS (photostat in WC, NjP).

To Andrew Clerk Imbrie

My dear Mr. Imbrie, St. Hubert's, New York. 10 July, 1907.

I left home for this somewhat remote retreat (we are twenty-four miles from the railway, near Keene Valley) the very day your letter, which has followed me, was written. I am extremely sorry. I have been surprised to find how many misapprehensions about the quadrangle plan were afloat, and think it extremely important, as you do, that they should be corrected by direct counseling together.

If you are willing to send me a list of questions, I will take the greatest pleasure in replying to them as fully and carefully as possible; or, if you think personal conference not only better but necessary in the circumstances, I will come out of the woods and join the little circle of men you speak of as soon as a date can be set. We could arrange that by telegraph; and I beg that you will tell me very frankly what you think best.

Thank you very much for your letter. I appreciated it very much indeed.

With much regard,

Faithfully Yours, Woodrow Wilson

It would take me some thirty-six hours to reach N. Y.

W. W.

WWTLS (photostat in RSB Coll., DLC).

From Andrew Fleming West

My dear Wilson, Princeton July 10 1907

I wish to appeal to you on the one question now uppermost in the minds of Princeton men. The sweeping and unexpected action of the Board of Trustees regarding the residential reorganization of our students—an action taken at your instance and without allowing any opportunity beforehand for hearing the opinion of the Faculty or of other persons properly interested and deeply concerned—has so disheartened me that I have [been] unable to think of anything else or to shake off the feeling of dismay at the troubles ahead of us.

I would have spoken of this to you before you left, instead of waiting to write, had I been able to compose my feelings or to believe that you would care to talk with me on the subject.

Of course I realize that whatever action the President and Trustees take must be accepted and carried into effect—and that this is binding on me as on every other officer of the University. Men in position to know the facts about the action of the Trustees tell me very plainly that the main issue is virtually decided and that the plan in its essentials will "go through." Whether this is so or not, the fact remains that unconstrained discussion of the essentials of the plan by the Faculty is now made utterly impossible. Yet at the risk of any misunderstanding whatsoever, I feel bound to say that not only the thing that has been done, but the manner of doing it, are both wrong—not inexpedient merely—but morally wrong. If my saying so to you and others to whom I have the right to speak is construed as impugning either my loyalty or security, then I must fall back on the teachings learned in childhood and say "We ought to obey God rather than men."

You have been President for five eventful and useful years, and every measure of your administration has had my unwavering adhesion and best efforts—even to the point of sending me to the hospital. I have served Princeton and your administration for something more than salary and office. If the spirit of Princeton is to be killed, I have little interest in the details of the funeral.

It has been hard for me to write this letter, and I want you to know that for writing it I have no more reasons, no less reasons and no other reasons than the critical nature of the whole situation, the hope that an appeal to you will help to straighten matters out, the obligation I owe to let you know where I stand, and our common interest in the welfare of Princeton.

Ever Sincerely Yours Andrew F. West

ALS (WP, DLC).

From Henry Burling Thompson

Wilmington, Del.

My Dear President Wilson: 7th Mo., 10th, 1907.

When in New York on Monday and Tuesday of this week, I held two meetings with reference to the Geological and Biological Building, and the Physical Laboratory.

Cleve Dodge and I met Mr. Schroeder on Monday afternoon, and went over with him in detail the two sets of preliminary sketch plans which he has prepared for the Geological Building.

Plan No. 1 is carried out on the lines suggested at the conference held at Princeton.

Plan No. 2 is an attempt to meet the views of the Biological Faculty Committee.

Plan No. 1 is the better architecturally. Placing the museum on the second floor gives a very much finer museum from a spectacular point of view, and I see no reason why it should not be equally good from the working standpoint.

Plan No. 2 is worked out very well, and is not bad architecturally, but Schroeder has been forced to make the museum with a ceiling 15 feet high, which would preclude putting in any gallery.

As the result of our conference I wrote to Mr. van Ingen,—copy of which letter I enclose with this.

Cleve and I both feel that very little serious work can be done on these plans much before September, for it will be impossible for the members of the various Committees to get together before that date, but I feel now that the matter is in fair shape for a reasonable compromise with our Biological friends.

I met Mr. Palmer, by appointment, at Mr. Hardenbergh's office yesterday morning, and went over the Physical Laboratory plans. I am very much pleased with this building. The elevation is dignified and in good taste. Of course, I have to criticise the interior from the layman's point of view, but it certainly appeals to me as adequate for the needs of this department for many years to come, and evidently is a very well-thought out scheme.

Mr. Palmer is anxious to go ahead and start on his building at the earliest possible date. He has named August 1st, but this will be impossible. He proposes to send the drawings to you, and as soon as we have your final approval, he will make his contracts. He proposes to relieve us of all responsibility in this matter, and will assume all the work himself,—the supervision of it being in the hands of himself and his architect. He also will take care of all the grading, and proposes to turn over to the University a finished building; but before going ahead, he wants us to feel thoroughly satisfied that the building is right, and then let it stand at that.

I understand that the members of the Physics Faculty Committee approve of his scheme; consequently, it will rest with you to give the final say-so.

Very sincerely yours, Henry B Thompson

TLS (WP, DLC). Enc.: H. B. Thompson to Gilbert van Ingen, July 8, 1907, TCL (WP, DLC).

From Albridge Clinton Smith, Jr.[1]

Dear Sir Orange, N. J. July 10 1907

At the request of the Education Committee of this Association,[2] I write for information as to the present status of the plan for the academic & social coordination of the undergraduates at Princeton into quads.

Do you construe the action of the Board of Trustees on June 10th, in adopting the report of your Committee, as printed in the Alumni Weekly of June 12th, as a final adoption of the plan of residential quads at Princeton, or a mere recommendation that the plan be investigated, developed and presented for final adoption at a future meeting of the Board?

Your reply will be greatly appreciated by our Committee

Very truly yours Albridge C Smith Jr. Secretary

ALS (WP, DLC).

1 Princeton 1903, who practiced law with his father, Albridge Clinton Smith, in New York and lived in Orange, N. J.

2 The Princeton Alumni Association of the Oranges, of which he was secretary.

David Benton Jones to Henry van Dyke

My dear Doctor: Chicago July 10th, 1907.

I was delighted to receive your letter of the 5th, to know you are home again and to read what you say of the crisis at Princeton. Your anxiety is not without cause.

If you have seen only the printed references to the situation, you have naturally concluded that it is a case of "reform on the rampage." There may be that element in it, but that the present social organization at the University is in need of reform, or, possibly, of re-organization, is the deliberate conclusion of everyone who has looked closely and deeply into the subject. So far all are agreed.

Those in authority claim, and they make statements that are very convincing, that the present club system is a distinct hindrance to the intellectual development of the two thirds admitted to club life and that it discourages and embitters the lives of most of the excluded one third and that this excluded one third comprises a majority of the best minds and frequently the finest spirits among the students. If the club system results in these two things—that is, in the discouragement of intellectual activity on the part of two thirds and the embitterment of the remaining one third, it is an exceedingly serious situation.

For six months I have urged that the subject be considered by a committee of the Faculty in conjunction with a committee of the recent graduates who are club members. This procedure was objected to for various reasons. A committee of the Board was appointed to consider the matter last December. They made no report at the March meeting and the report made at the June meeting which appeared in the Alumni Weekly is the first formal statement regarding the subject which has been made public. The report which the Committee made to the whole Board was signed by every member and only one member of the Board voted against its acceptance and approval.

I am not sure that I can recall every member of the committee, but Pyne, Dodge, Garrett, Jacobus and myself are on it, with possibly one other. The conclusion of the committee was based more upon the necessity of finding a remedy than upon their affirmative approval of the form of the remedy suggested—that is, the quad. scheme. Dean Fine was present during the long last session of the committee and made statements which convinced every member of the necessity of a remedy.

As you doubtless know, Charles Francis Adams in his three Phi Beta Kappa addresses[1] has developed and urged much the same remedy for the condition of things at Harvard. The essential principle of the quad. scheme is to break up the mass into smaller units. Whether this can be done and still conserve the integrity of the larger university feeling and spirit, no one can tell. At Oxford the units are independent, each college having its own equipment and carrying on its own work in its own way. As you know, the development of scientific work and interest is creating great embarrassments at Oxford and Cambridge by reason of the fact that each college cannot equip itself to do scientific work on its own account, scientific equipment being, of necessity, by reason of its expense and character, distinctly university work.

Whether the quad. system, so far as its social features are concerned, can be successfully transplanted and be made to take root at Princeton, is a matter of prophecy—and I am not a good prophet. Your indictment is very comprehensive and in certain specifications applicable to existing conditions. You say "It seems to me to imperil the unity of our life, the democracy of our spirit, the integrity of the classes, the working of our educational plan and the continued existence of the Princeton spirit." It will interest you to know that this indictment agrees, almost in the arrangement of terms even, with the indictment brought against the present club system.

I still feel that a fuller discussion, more or less open in character, would be wise. One difficulty is that it would not be wise to make public a full statement of the evils of the present club system. This is strongly urged by those in authority and, in my opinion, with a good deal of force.

The committee was continued and the President was authorized to mature the plan suggested. There is some indefinit[e]ness as to just what is meant by the Board's seeming approval of the essential idea and purposes of the report. As I understand it, the "elm" you speak of has been condemned, but has not been cut dowm [down]. I confess to almost as much perplexity as Othello felt. Whether a wider discussion and a deeper inquiry can be had, I do not know. I should be glad to see more team work and less individual initiative and action at Princeton.

I hope you will keep an open mind. When the facts are fully stated, I think you will admit that "mistletoe and crooked branches" are not the only elements to be considered in deciding the fate of the elm which in youth sheltered you and me.

If during the summer I am within reasonable distance of you and you should not regard it as too much of an intrusion, I shall be glad to take something of a journey to go over this matter with you. My anxiety is that the remedy, whatever form it may take, should have the approval and support of the men most intimately associated with the work and life at Princeton itself. Those of us who are out and away must see that Princeton should be more than the mere custodian of delightful traditions and associations. We should be content to know that it is doing the work of the life that now is, even if it results in more sunlight and less shade than in times gone by.

Very sincerely yours, David B. Jones.

One or two sentences in this letter are doubtless out of place as referring to method & procedure, but the report of the committee took its form from the method in part. The fact of my having written you can be spoken of if need be. But I may have gone farther than I should in naming the committee & in the sentences mentioned. I cannot be secretive when such issues are involved. I trust your discretion as to the names & the strictures mentioned. D. B. J.

TLS (H. van Dyke Papers, NjP).

1 Charles Francis Adams, *Three Phi Beta Kappa Addresses* (Boston and New York, 1907).

An Article on the Quadrangle Plan by Henry van Dyke

Princeton, July 10th, 1907.

THE "RESIDENTIAL QUAD" IDEA AT PRINCETON

The announcement, at the end of June, in the newspapers and in the last number of The Alumni Weekly, that Princeton University was to be altered into an organization of "residential quads," or colleges, came as a surprise to the great majority of Princetonians young and old. No proposition of the kind had ever been laid before the faculty for discussion. There had been no opportunity for serious consideration of such a plan among the undergraduates, the graduates or the teachers. We heard through the press, that a committee had been appointed in December to draw up a report on the subject, and that their report on the "social co-ordination of the university" was presented to the Trustees in June, and adopted at the same meeting.

The very serious statements in regard to the Senior and Junior eating-clubs of Princeton which accompanied this announcement in the newspapers also came as a surprise. We knew, of course, that these clubs were not perfect, that they had faults and dangers, that they needed, like all other human institutions, correction, improvement and the inspiration of better motives. But we supposed that they met a real need by supplying students with fairly edible food at a fairly reasonable price, and giving them an opportunity to cultivate the more personal friendships of their upper-class years amid surroundings which, if sometimes too luxurious, were not vicious or degrading. We thought that, in spite of their defects, they would compare favorably, in sobriety, decency, and general good order and fellowship, with student organizations in any college in America, or even with the Oxford colleges. We thought that they had really participated in the intellectual quickening of the university during recent years. It was a surprise to hear that they were so dangerous that it was necessary to abolish them, or to absorb them by transformation into "residential quads" or separate "academic communities."

This remedy, it has been rightly said, would be "radical indeed"; and the announcement in the press that the Trustees had already "adopted the essential idea and purpose of this plan," hardly seemed to invite discussion of the main question. Yet surely on this important main question, affecting the very life of the university, there ought to be liberty for even the humblest son of Princeton to form and to express an honest opinion. It is both loyal and respectful to take it for granted that there has never been any intention to avoid or to restrict this liberty, and that the action which has been taken was of such a nature as to leave the way open for a thorough investigation of the actual conditions and a careful and free discussion of the question whether such a radical remedy is necessary, practicable, or desirable. Simply as a graduate of Princeton, I feel bound in honour to give some proper expression to my grave apprehension and dismay in regard to this new scheme.

It would seem to be a most dangerous proposal to remedy the faults of the clubs by raising them to the Nth power and making them into "residential quads" or "academic communities." Would a group of young men who, instead of merely eating together, spent all their free time together, and lived entirely under one roof within the walls of the same structure, be likely to escape from the spirit of clique and exclusiveness? The name which is given to these proposed quadrangles makes no difference; they would in fact divide the university into distinct colleges. Oxford has developed on that plan, and anyone who really knows Oxford knows that it is not distinguished by the democratic tone or the unity and equality of its life. Is there an "Oxford Spirit" to be compared to the "Princeton Spirit" of to-day? The attachment of the Oxford man is first to the public school in which he was prepared for the university, and then to the college, Balliol, or Magdalen, or Christ Church, in which he lived with his friends. The attachment of the Princeton man is still fundamentally to Princeton; and this attachment is something that is worth keeping. Split the university up, and the Princeton Spirit will be lost among the fagots.

Suppose the members of these "residential quads" are assigned to the different colleges, on their own application or on the application of their parents, according to the scale of the room-rents in the different buildings, or the rates of board at the different tables. The result will inevitably be the creation of "academic communities" within the same university on the basis of money. We already regret the evils that have come, perhaps unavoidably, with the difference in scale of expenditure among students. But these are modified at present by the fact that a man may have a poor room and eat at a good table, or *vice versa*, and that in all our American colleges the most vigorous and interesting part of the life is still an open and common life. Is it advisable to accentuate and intensify the differences among dormitories and eating-tables and clubs by transmogrifying them into distinct communities?

Suppose that the room-rents and the rates of board in these

colleges are made uniform, and that membership in them is placed under the authority of a central executive. A committee, or an officer of the university will then assign men to some particular college by alphabetical selection, or by lot, or by some other method. They will be required to eat and live and play and talk together whether they like each other or not. True, they will be certain to form little companies and associations for themselves within each "quad," but it is hard to see how these associations will be different from, or in spirit superior to, the secret fraternities which used to have an unauthorized existence and an undesirable influence at Princeton. If they are suppressed by the strong hand, if the social companionship and the table intercourse, as well as the scale of living, of the undergraduates are strictly regulated by an absolute central power, then the residential quads will be like "Houses" in a big boarding school, and the student body will feel that it is placed under a system of restraint which impairs self-reliance, and deprives their college-life of that freedom which is a part of the higher education.

A mixture of these two methods, appointment by lot and appointment by request, is a bewildering thought. Could there be two kinds of students or parents, one kind compelled to draw lots, and the other kind permitted to make a choice among the "quads"? Would it not require superhuman qualities to execute such a plan?

The heavy initial cost of such an experiment is a grave objection to it. Money is urgently needed for things that are not of doubtful value. A further addition of professors, strong and leading men, to the teaching force is a great need. The Graduate School, which is essential to the development of the university, has long waited, and now earnestly pleads, for better housing, more liberal support, more opportunity to enlarge and improve its work. We need, and have long needed, one or more handsome, well equipped commons-halls on the campus to supply the students with good food, and perhaps a central club or students' union open to all without compulsion or exclusion. There are many things that Princeton really wants; but these will necessarily have to wait a long time if she sets out on an expensive career of "residential quads."

Another reason for hesitation is the fact that such an experiment will probably be a serious interruption to the real business of the university. These new social alignments, these residential groupings, these combinations and complications of "academic communities" will undoubtedly make a great social turmoil, and perhaps attract much notice in the public press. But that is not precisely what we need just now. What we need is a continuance of steady work in the class room; plenty of industry and energy applied to the efficient operation of the present system; a lot of patient, wise, enthusiastic labor put into the perfecting of the preceptorial plan, which is a promising experiment, still deserving and demanding the most careful attention. It would be a misfortune if the strength of Princeton were diverted at the present moment from that plain, quiet, hard work which is the real secret of university success. The introduction of a new scheme of "residential quads" would be likely to produce first social confusion, and then social stratification.

This after all is the alarming thing about the new scheme. It is full of danger for the unity, for the fellowship of the undergraduate body. With all its indefiniteness on practical points, its "essential idea" is undemocratic, separative, exclusive. It is distinctly an un-American plan. It threatens not only to break up the classes, but also to put the Princeton spirit out of date, by forming permanent, artificial groups of Freshmen, Sophomores, Juniors and Seniors, selected on some undefined principle, and giving to each of these groups a "Master" as well as "a local habitation and a name." It promises rivalries, jealousies, and political complications which will effectually extinguish all that we have of common feeling among the undergraduates. For perilous possibilities the little finger of the quasi-Oxford scheme looks thicker than the loins of the present club system.

Of course no man can prophesy that all of these evils will surely come to pass if the new scheme is adopted. But at least those who love Princeton may well ask whether it is wise to enter now upon such a dangerous and costly enterprise. If the report that the essential idea of the plan (that is, apparently, the "residential quad" idea) has been adopted should prove to be a misapprehension, it will be most fortunate. For then there will be time to discuss, without impropriety, two or three sober questions:

Is it really necessary or prudent to give up the American university organization, under which Princeton has prospered, for something alien and unknown? Is it wise to use a remedy for present evils which may be more dangerous than the disease itself? Is it not highly probable that careful consideration and united discussion would find a democratic and efficient way of dealing with the troubles which have grown around the present club system, without radically transforming the constitution of the university at a single blow?

HENRY VAN DYKE, Class of 1873.

Printed in the *Princeton Alumni Weekly*, VIII (Sept. 25, 1907), 4-7.

To Andrew Fleming West

My dear West: St. Hubert's 11 July, '07

I have just received your letter of the 10th, and have read it with deep distress. I am sorry, very sorry, that you did not say these things to me before I left Princeton. It is only in conversation that misconceptions so deep as yours can be removed.

I can assure you that you are entirely mistaken in saying, or in supposing, "that unconstrained discussion of the essentials of the plan by the Faculty is now made utterly impossible," and that if you had waited, with some confidence in my character, until the autumn, you would have seen how wholly gratuitous and unfounded such a statement is. Certainly there is no plan, or purpose, or possibility of "killing the spirit of Princeton." I really cannot imagine what you mean. You must be speaking out of some extraordinary misconception of the whole idea and purpose.

The plan involves so many elements which lie within the province and authority of the board alone, that it seemed to me imperative that it should first receive the sanction of the trustees. No one who candidly considers its scope and character can fail to see that. But the board intended, as I of course did, that the freest possible discussion should follow; and it is to follow, in order that every element of common counsel may contribute to the final decision.

A frank conference with me would have saved you much of the distress you are now laboring under. At this distance we can only say that a little patience, a little unexcited thinking will bring things, for you and for all others who have misunderstood both its character and its method, into a new light.

Very Sincerely Yours, Woodrow Wilson

Transcript of WWshLS (WP, DLC).

From John Mirza Bennett, Jr.[1]

Dear Sir: San Antonio, Texas. July 11th, 1907.

I have read in the Alumni Weekly, your report to the Trustees about the social condition of the University as affected by the upper class clubs, and I have read with special delight your proposed method of dealing with the situation.

As a member of an upper class club while in Princeton, I want to add my mite to the flood of commendatory letters that I know you are receiving, by offering you my heartiest endorsement.

Yours very truly, J M Bennett, Jr "1900"

TLS (WP, DLC).

[1] Princeton 1900, Assistant Cashier of the National Bank of Commerce in San Antonio, Texas.

From Andrew Clerk Imbrie

Dear Dr Wilson, New York, Jul 13 1907

I have just telegraphed to you that it will be unnecessary for you to make the long journey to New York to discuss "Quads" with the men here. I have talked with several since I received your letter yesterday, and we will write out the questions which have been raised in our various talks, and follow your kind suggestion. I hope to write fully within a week or so. In the meantime I shall make it my chief business to see as many men as possible who have really given the matter thought; so that when I do send you the list of questions, they will cover the difficulties as nearly as can be. The trouble seems to be that there is no one hereabout who is able or willing to discuss the matter authoritatively, and there is everywhere some doubt as to just how far the Trustees are committed to the plan; that is to say, has the Quad idea been offered as a *proposed scheme* or has it been *adopted* as the *policy* of the *University*? In the first case, other plans to correct the club situation may profitably be discussed; but in the second case, we are apparently confined to the consideration of the method by which the plan may best be put into operation. If I could have this point made perfectly clear, it would help me in preparing the longer list of questions which have risen. Many thanks for your kind offer to help us to an understanding.

Yours faithfully Andrew C Imbrie
18 Vesey St.

ALS (WP, DLC).

From Henry Burling Thompson

Wilmington, Del.
Dear President Wilson: 7th Mo., 13th, 1907.

You have doubtless received from Mr. Cram a plan for the grading, drainage, walks, etc. around McCosh Hall.

Mr. Bunn writes me that approximately this work will cost about $5,000.00. I assume this includes the foundation for the Sun Dial.

As far as I know, the Grounds and Buildings Committee made no provision for this object. Properly, it should go against the cost of the building, and I have written to Cleve Dodge, asking him whether we are to so consider it. He is away on a yachting trip, and is not expected back until next Tuesday or Wednesday. If the donors of the building feel that the College ought to assume the charge, would it be proper for me to authorize Bunn to go ahead? Bunn is all ready, and daily expects an answer from me. The work must be done, and I should feel inclined to authorize him to go ahead and let the Finance Committee, at the proper time, take care of us.

I shall present this matter to Bayard Henry on Monday in the same way in which I have presented it to you in this letter, and if both of you approve, I can then authorize Bunn to go ahead.

I shall be in Princeton on the 20th instant, and will be in a position then to go into exact details with Bunn as to just how to proceed.

I regret to have to trouble you with these matters while you are on your vacation, but I should feel that I was exceeding my authority unless I consulted the members of my Committee with whom I can get in touch.

Very sincerely yours, Henry B Thompson

P.S.,–The foundation for the Sun Dial I believe comes to some $1200.00 or $1500.00. This, of course, should be considered as a University expense.

H. B. T.

TLS (WP, DLC).

To Andrew Clerk Imbrie

My dear Mr. Imbrie, St. Hubert's, N. Y., 15 July, 1907.

Thank you for your letter of the thirteenth, which reached me yesterday. There is no chance here to answer a letter on the same day it is received. The single outgoing mail leaves within a few minutes after the single incoming mail is distributed.

It was clearly understood at the meeting of the Board that we were adopting the *principle* or *idea* of the quad. plan as the policy of the University; but, at the same time, it was desired to have the freest possible criticism and discussion on the part of everybody concerned. I am sure that the Board would be perfectly willing to consider any other scheme having the same end in view. They did not mean in any respect to shut their minds, but only to express their purpose.

It is the more important, therefore, to state that purpose with the utmost clearness. It is, to give the University the organization best suited to its intellectual development, its development as a place of serious study. The object of the plan proposed by the Committee was not primarily or even chiefly social; it is academic: aims, that is, at the best *university* organization. Speaking for myself, I may say that it would have been proposed had there been no clubs. There being clubs, clubs in every way worthy of consideration, it is our earnest desire to see them come into the scheme and become an integral historical part of it. I should be very much distressed to have the plan regarded as an attack on the clubs.

I feel that you are rendering a real service to the University in what you are doing to bring out thoughtful and genuine opinion on this fundamental matter, upon which I feel that the whole future of the University depends, and her whole opportunity to set the colleges of the country an imperative example; and I sincerely hope that I may be called upon with the utmost freedom to further all frank and thoroughgoing discussion.

With warmest regards,

Faithfully Yours, Woodrow Wilson

WWTCL (WP, DLC).

To Albridge Clinton Smith, Jr.

My dear Mr. Smith, St. Hubert's, N. Y. 15 July, 1907.

Your letter of the tenth has been forwarded to me here. I regret that any delay in answering it should have been caused by my distance from home.

I construe the action of the Board of Trustees recently taken on the report of the Committee printed in the Alumni Weekly as an adoption of the principle and idea of the proposed quads; but it was the desire of the Board, as it is my own desire, that the whole process of transformation should be matter of common counsel. I am sure that the Board would be glad to consider even alternative plans and proposals, having the same end in view.

The end is not primarily social or even predominantly social, but academic and intellectual. Our hope is to constitute the University in the way best suited to its intellectual aims.

Thanking you for your letter,

Sincerely Yours, Woodrow Wilson.

WWTCL (WP, DLC).

To John Grier Hibben

My dear Jack, St. Hubert's, N. Y., 16 July, 1907.

Thank you very much for letting me see [Walter Augustus] Wyckoff's letter.[1] His enthusiasm is very refreshing, and it was a very generous, characteristic impulse that led you to let me read what he said, evidently so spontaneously.[2]

It is delightful to hear of the fishing and the walks in the woods which are making Princeton seem so far away to you all. I hope with all my heart that the saturation of rest will become more and more complete for each of the dear Hibben's, until every recollection that disturbs is obliterated.

My correspondence keeps the place and its business very vividly before me, but physical separation from it and the calming influence of the woods are restoring my self-possession and, I believe, steadying and clearing my judgment, and a sort of release from strain may come after while, when I get deep into my writing.

We think of you all constantly and with the deepest affection and admiration. Please give my love to Mrs. Hibben and Beth, and think of me always as

Your devoted friend, Woodrow

WWTLS (photostat in WC, NjP).

[1] Hibben's letter, to which this was a reply, is missing.

[2] W. A. Wyckoff to Jenny D. Hibben, July 4, 1907, ALS (WP, DLC). Wyckoff, who had left Princeton before Commencement, was enthusiastic over what he had read about the quadrangle plan in the *Princeton Alumni Weekly*.

To Harry Augustus Garfield

My dear Garfield, St. Hubert's, N. Y., 16 July, 1907.

I congratulate Williams with all my heart, and I know that Princeton's loss is irreparable. I do not know whether to congratulate *you* or not. It is very delightful to serve one's alma mater with all one's powers, but I believe there is no one in the country who can realize more vividly or more fully what you are sacrificing and what exceeding burdens you are assuming than I can. I often long for my old quiet life as student and professor with an intensity that makes me very unhappy. But I am sure that you are answering a call of duty as I did; and I hope that, with your disposition, you will not suffer as much as I have suffered under the burden of painful tasks and misunderstandings,—struggles with one's friends, and a sort of isolation of responsibility the extent of which I had not at all anticipated. I pray with deep affection that you may be blessed in every part of your work, and that some good fortune may often give us touch of one another's mind and heart. We must make diligent use of the year of comradeship that remains to us.

Your affectionate friend, Woodrow Wilson

WWTLS (H. A. Garfield Papers, DLC).

From Andrew Clerk Imbrie

Dear Dr Wilson, New York, Jul 16 1907

I thank you for your letter of yesterday. I hope within the next week or so to send you a memorandum of the various questions which have arisen in our frequent discussions, and I am grateful to you for offering to help us to a clear understanding, especially as you ought to be relieved of such troublesome matters when you are supposed to be enjoying a vacation.

Yours faithfully Andrew C Imbrie

ALS (WP, DLC).

Henry Burling Thompson to Harold Griffith Murray

[Wilmington, Del.]
My dear Murray: 7th Mo., 16th, 1907.

Can you give me any information as to how the Alumni in general are receiving Wilson's new "Quad Idea"? I suppose you have a better chance to get the correct idea of the Princeton sentiment on this question than any other man. Has it affected your work in curtailing subscriptions?

I have been unable to get a line on the sentiment excepting the little I see in the New York papers and the Philadelphia sentiment. Here among the graduates and in Philadelphia it has no friends. I have yet to hear from a man who endorses it.

If you can give me any information on this point I should be glad to hear from you.[1]

Yours very truly, Henry B Thompson

TLS (Thompson Letterpress Books, NjP).

[1] Murray's reply is missing in the H. B. Thompson Papers, NjP.

To Edward Graham Elliott

St. Hubert's, N. Y.,
My dear Elliott: July 17th, 1907.

Upon Daniel's recommendation I have asked Edwin W. Pahlow to act as instructor doing preceptorial duties next year in our Department. I suggested to him that it might be possible to assign him to work with the Juniors, in order that he might not be overwhelmed during his first year by the harded [harder] work with the Seniors. I wonder if you would be willing to write to him at Marblehead Neck, Mass., and give him definite information as to what arrangements can be made for his work.

He has just been studying at Oxford and has had experience in teaching at Wisconsin, his alma mater, and Harvard, so that I think it possible we may make something out of him. The reappointment of Whittlesey and this appointment of Pahlow is my makeshift for substitutes for [Hiram] Bingham and the younger Spencer. If you know of any other crack man whom we could put in as instructor, to earn his spurs, I should be delighted to hear of him.

I sincerely hope that you are finding rest and refreshment somewhere.

With warmest regard,

Faithfully yours, Woodrow Wilson

TLS (WC, NjP).

To Arthur Herbert Osborn

St. Hubert's, N. Y.,
My dear Mr. Osborn: July 17th, 1907.

Allow me to acknowledge the receipt of your letter of July 9th, which with its enclosure has been forwarded to me here. I have read it with a great deal of attention.

I must say that it does not seem to me to meet the difficulties of the case at all, but I have no doubt that I could understand it better if I could have a personal talk with you about it. If you feel so inclined, I should be very glad indeed to see you at Princeton at any time after the term opens, so that we might talk the matter over. It is our desire to go very slowly with this matter and to consider every opinion, and if you would let me know beforehand when you were coming I could arrange it so that we could be sure not to miss one another.

I feel like adding this. The primary object that the Board has in view is not social, indeed that is not its chief object. The object is academic and intellectual. We are seeking the organization best suited to the intellectual development of the University, its development as a place of serious study. I should be distressed to have the plan regarded as in any sense an attack on the clubs. It would have been proposed, even if there had been no clubs, as a desirable method of drawing the undergraduates together in an academic organization, and the clubs are involved in the question only because it is our sincere desire to make them, if they are willing, an historical part of the change.

Very sincerely yours, Woodrow Wilson

TLS (WC, NjP).

To John Mirza Bennett, Jr.

[St. Hubert's, N. Y.]

My dear Mr. Bennett: July 17th, 1907.

I am heartily obliged to you for your kind letter of July 11th. Unhappily there has not been a "flood of commendatory letters" pouring in upon me with regard to our new plans at Princeton, but I cannot help feeling confident that in the long run the tide will turn in that direction. It of course hits very hard to deprive the men most favored of their present club life at college, and I do not wonder that their affection for the clubs at first governs their judgment.

It is very delightful to receive such letters as this of yours, and I thank you for it most cordially. One has to be kept in heart by substantial approval of this kind.

With warm regard,

Cordially and sincerely yours, [Woodrow Wilson]

CCL (WP, DLC).

To Edwin Plimpton Adams

St. Hubert's, N. Y.

My dear Mr. Adams: July 17th, 1907.

I very much regret to learn from Professor Magie that you are thinking of the possibility of accepting a professorship in Colorado college. I want to give myself the pleasure of telling you how much we value you at Princeton and how sincerely I hope that it will be possible for you to see that your advantage lies in sharing our really great prospects in your department. I of course do not wish to persuade you against your own advantage, but I cannot help thinking that the possibilities of Princeton ought to be enough to hold a man whom we value as much as we do you.[1]

With sincere regard,

Very truly yours, Woodrow Wilson

TLS (UA, NjP).

[1] Adams, Assistant Professor of Physics, was promoted to a professorship in 1909 and remained on the Princeton faculty until his retirement in 1943.

From Louis Irving Reichner[1]

Dear Dr. Wilson: Philadelphia, July 17th, 1907

As a Princeton graduate I have been very much interested in the discussion which is now going on in reference to the club question and thought that I might presume to write this letter, embodying a few thoughts which I have on the subject. No doubt the suggestions may be defective, and I express them for what they are worth.

First; let the University buy all the club houses for the amounts expended in their erection and let the occupancy of the various club houses be by assignment of the university, in other words, each year let the various upper class clubs be assigned certain houses for their use and occupancy, in rotation, paying to the university the same sums in the way of dues and cost of board that they would ordinarily pay if they were occupying their own properties.

If there were say five clubs owning club houses, this would give each club the occupancy of what was its own house once in five years and would do away with an argument which is so often used in obtaining members from the lower classes that certain clubs are to be preferred because they have the most expensive houses.

Second; let the club hatbands, neckties and club insignia be abolished, in order that no unconscious influence may be exerted by their display on the part of undergraduates, and let the graduates be asked to discontinue the practice of wearing the distinctive bands or regalia so to speak, upon the occasion of their visits to Princeton.

Third; Let a commons be established for the Freshman class and one for the Sophomore class, in which every member of these respective classes should be required to eat.

Fourth; Let all Freshman and Sophomore clubs and social organizations of any description be abolished and forbidden together with the distinctive hats and regalias now used. Let more class contests be established between all the classes, but more particularly the Freshman and Sophomore classes, as the institution of games in which large numbers could take part would be of benefit in the establishing of class spirit. Rushes under proper supervision and various other forms of rivalry might prove effective along the same line.

The above suggestions, to my mind, might work out a solution, although the problem is a most difficult one and I heartily sympathize with those to whom the solution of it has been delegated.

The adjustment of the upper class clubs to the college life might be helped by the abolition of the basis for the arguments which are used in inducing men to join this or that club. A sophomore no doubt desires first of all to enter that club where the majority of his friends are going, yet on the other hand the whole body of men selected by that club from the sophomore class may have been brought in through a desire to obtain what they think would be prestige, through membership in a club owning a fine property and having a list of prominent graduates.

Again a sophomore might be unconsciously influenced by seeing some well known graduate wearing the regalia of a certain club and in this way his natural selection might become biased.

If the Freshmen and Sophomores are deprived of the chance to form small cliques and if thc class spirit is fostered and strengthened, they will become a more compact body and the habit so to speak, of class spirit, having been strongly formed in the first two years of their course, will be carried along with them in a minor degree during the last two years.

I send you these lines to try and voice a few of the thoughts which I have on the subject and I hope you will consider this letter a purely personal one to yourself.

Yours very truly, L. Irving Reichner

TLS (WP, DLC).

[1] Princeton 1894, attorney of Philadelphia.

From George McLean Harper

Brimmer Head Farm,
Easedale, Grasmere July 18, 1907

Dear Wilson:

Nothing could be more frank, more truthful, or better suited to its purpose than your statement in the *Alumni Weekly* on the Social Co-ordination of the university. As you know, I, like some others possibly, had long hoped that the day for organizing Princeton as a group of subordinate colleges would come in our time, but I found that men to whom I spoke of the matter were singularly slow in grasping the idea. Your proposal is eminently conservative and considerate of existing prejudices, & I trust the alumni will, in due course of time, understand it. When they understand it they will support your efforts. The tone of their comments as reported in the few newspaper clippings which John W[estcott]. & Frank MacDonald[1] have sent me, is altogether boyish & provincial. When I recollect the absorbing & unnatural fascination the Clubs have exerted in the case of several students with whom I was intimate, the morbid jealousy, the perverted sense of loyalty & honor, the sensitiveness to criticism, I am less amazed at the attitude of the young alumni, but am all the more convinced that your proposal should be carried out at any cost. If you succeed in this, you will have done something for higher education in America of even greater importance than introducing the preceptorial system, and of more good consequence to Princeton than even the new course of study. The fundamental argument in favor of a collegiate system is that in small residential colleges the educative influence comes from above, perpendicularly, whereas in a large institution existing in class divisions a man is affected for the most part by others of his own year only,—a horizontal influence. Complicate this with our Club ambitions & distinctions, & you have chaos, with no encouragement to learning or social progress. Do keep in fighting trim. Out of the sincerest personal friendship, no less than out of love for Princeton, I beg you not to let the politicians so much as talk to you, & also not to use your strength making speeches. By a sudden expansion of authority you have now undertaken to educate 7000 alumni, on the subject of education itself. It will be slow work at first, but will have a glorious success, I fondly hope.

We are not only happy, but busy at last. Between desire to see the country thoroughly on foot, & the opportunity to know many pleasant neighbors, we are somewhat distracted. Mr. & Mrs. Yates have been very good to us, & so have many, many others. We had a fine glimpse of the [Winthrop More] Daniels family & a visit from [William Harry] Clemons. Norman Smith & I are to see Ayrshire together.

Please don't think of answering this letter. I only want to assure you of my cordial support in your new undertaking, especially since I hear that it is stupidly misapprehended in some quarters.

With best regards from us all to you & Mrs. Wilson & your daughters, I am

Ever sincerely yours, Geo M. Harper

ALS (WP, DLC).
[1] Francis Charles MacDonald, Princeton 1896, Preceptor in English.

From Walter Augustus Wyckoff

Dear President Wilson, Chester, Nova Scotia 18 July, 1907.

A communication received several days ago from the Board of Trustees through its secretary has brought me information of an increase in salary voted to me by the Board.[1] As I am at a loss as to whom an acknowledgement of this communication is due, I beg leave to make my acknowledgement to you.

My appreciation on grounds of domestic economy of an increase in salary will be readily intelligible to you, for you have taught economics and you are well aware of the significance to men of fixed incomes of the steady rise for the past ten years of the general price level. But I find it difficult to express adequately my appreciation of the action of the Board in view of what I gather of the financial situation of the University. That the Board should have taken this thoughtful action at a time when so many urgent needs are making pressing demands upon the resources of the University is a matter that not only stirs my gratitude but gives me a renewed sense of loyalty and devotion.

I very gladly take advantage of this acknowledgement to add a word with reference to the new proposals for the social coördination of the University.

Leaving Princeton, as I was obliged to, in the middle of commencement week, I had practically no opportunity of discussing the matter with anyone; but I have thought of it a good deal, and your presentation of the plan in the last issue of the Alumni Weekly has helped me much along the road to a personal decision. I can see many serious difficulties in the way of the adoption and operation of the plan; but after all, if a good, workable solution can be found for the problem involved in getting our undergraduates satisfactorily assigned to the various quads, I see no insuperable difficulty in the way of such a newly-organized university life. And I am bound to say that the plan itself seems to me to show clearest insight into our present evils and their consequent dangers, and to be thoroughly harmonious with our recent growth, and to promise, not only the solution of our difficulties, but a most consistent and wholesome development of our university life.

Believe me Yours sincerely, Walter A. Wyckoff.

ALS (WP, DLC).
[1] His salary was increased from $2,500 to $3,000 per annum.

To Louis Irving Reichner

My dear Mr. Reichner: [St. Hubert's, N. Y.] July 20th, 1907.

Allow me to thank you for your letter of July 17th, which I have read with the greatest interest.

I feel like saying in the first place that it seems to me that it is necessary, in order to understand our problem at Princeton, to approach it from the other end. I mean that it is not primarily a question of the clubs, it is a question of finding for the University the social organization which will be most suited to it as a place of study, as a place of intellectual training where it is desirable that the infections of study should be constant. The plan, the general principles of which the Board of Trustees have approved, is one which I would in any case have proposed to them as a necessary completion of what we began in the establishment of the Preceptorial System. We approach the clubs, therefore, in our argument, only in the second place. We are really seeking, not to better the present social organization of the University, but to create a new social organization, and the only thing that stands in the way is the existence of the Upperclass Clubs, for whose history and traditions I have the highest respect. It is just because I respect them that I so earnestly hope that they will consent to become an integral historical part of the great change we are contemplating.

I am convinced that nothing less systematic (I will not say revolutionary, because it is not revolutionary except upon the surface) would effect the changes in the social makeup of the University which we deem indispensable.

I would be very pleased if you would make an engagement to see me in the autumn, in order that I may have the benefit of your criticism of the plan from this point of view. In the meantime, I shall take pleasure in retaining your letter as a memorandum of our starting point. I am sincerely obliged to you for your desire to take a part in the counselling which will be necessary before we work out a satisfactory detail for our plan.

With much regard,

Sincerely yours, [Woodrow Wilson]

CCL (WP, DLC).

From Stephen Squires Palmer

My dear Dr. Wilson: New York, July 23, 1907.

Mr. Hardenbergh will forward to you tomorrow building plans for the physical laboratory, and I bespeak for them your careful consideration.

We have devoted much time and thought in their preparation with the view of developing a building that for practical purposes would be as nearly complete and effective as possible.

Your working force at Princeton has been of the greatest assistance in solving this problem, and in which they are much interested.

Awaiting your further advices, I am, as always, my dear Doctor, Sincerely yours, S S Palmer

TLS (WP, DLC).

From Andrew Clerk Imbrie

Dear Dr. Wilson, New York July 25/07.

Since I received your letter of July 15, (the receipt of which I have already acknowledged) I have talked over the question of "Residential Quadrangles" with a good many Princeton men here in New York. Several of them are influential members of the Boards of Governors of the more prominent upper class clubs. Others were not members of clubs; but all of them are interested in the report of your committee and while at the present time I can find practically no one who is ready to declare himself altogether in favor of the proposition, I think I may say that most of them are disposed to consider the question with an open mind.

However, many questions have arisen in our discussions which I have been unable to answer as I did not become a member of the board until after the meeting at which the report of the committee was discussed. I think that the Alumni should know the names of the committee who reported favorably on the plan. Will you give me their names?

I will appreciate it if you will give me at your convenience, some information upon the following points.

1. What is the proposed method of appointment or election to the several "Quads"? Is it ever to be by the choice of the parent of the student? Under any circumstances will the student himself have a choice in the matter? Or is it to be by faculty appointment? If by faculty appointment what considerations will weigh

with the individual member of the faculty or with the committee upon whom the responsibility will rest? Or are appointments to be made by lot as in the present assignment of rooms? Will the Freshman Commons in University Hall be continued or is it proposed to assign Freshmen to Quads immediately after entering college?

2. As to transfers from one quad to another. Under what circumstances are they to be permitted? Is an effort to be made to make all the Quads as nearly as possible equally desirable? How is the natural tendency for congenial men to group themselves together to be regulated?

3. If there should be in the university too many students to be accommodated in the quads what will become of the surplus? What men will be left out? May a student live in town with his family? If so, what will prevent men *choosing* to live in town if they are assigned to Quads which for one reason or another may be considered undesirable. Is it not conceivable that a number of men if they had the means to do so, might "maintain residences" in their respective Quads and actually live together in town?

4. Are all four classes to have the use of the Common Room in each of the Quads? Are they to sit by classes at meals or is that a matter of detail which may be determined by each Quad for itself? Will a student, by virtue of his membership in the University, have access for social purposes to all Quads?

5. As to the relations of the university with the present upper class clubs. How can the university take over the property of the several clubs for the purpose of making Quads of them? Suppose some or all of the clubs refuse to turn over their property. Is it proposed to forbid undergraduates joining them, and so to force the clubs to do one of three things: either to co-operate with the Quadrangle plan, or to become bankrupt, or to be maintained solely as graduate organizations?

6. If the Ivy Club or the Cottage Club (for instance) should become a Quad is it proposed to give sons or brothers or cousins or "friends" of former Ivy or Cottage men the privilege of entering such Quads?

7. If the Quad plan is put into operation and assuming that the clubs can be persuaded to co-operate with the university, is it proposed to enlarge some or all of the present club buildings or will they (at least temporarily) be severally used as the Commons for particular dormitories on the campus?

8. How is it proposed to begin the system? Are all the dormitories to be altered simultaneously to include dining rooms and Common Rooms? If we are to introduce the system *by*

degrees how is it to be determined who shall join the first Quads? If it is to be done *at one time* what is the estimated cost? Has anybody intimated that the funds for the establishment of the system will be forthcoming or is it expected that the Alumni at large, will contribute as they have already contributed for the establishment of the Preceptorial System?

9. In your letter of July 15, you state that the plan proposed by the committee was not primarily or even chiefly social; that it is academic and aims at the best university organization. You state further that the idea of the Quad plan while adopted by the Board of Trustees as the policy of the university, was nevertheless open to criticism and discussion on the part of everybody concerned. If I am a judge of the present temper of the Alumni, I believe that we cannot over-estimate the difficulty of putting into operation the plan as proposed by the committee in the face of the very serious opposition which we may expect from many thoughtful graduates upon whom we have hitherto depended for enthusiastic support. If a plan can be devised which will make use of the present club organizations and which will at the same time recognize more fully the natural tendency of men to find social relaxation among those who are congenial, a plan which will eradicate or at least minimize the objectionable features of the present club situation and at the same time provide for a more democratic mingling of the members of all classes —do you think that the Board would be likely to consider it? Or, do I understand from your letter that having adopted the Quad principle substantially as outlined in the report of the committee, they are only open to argument upon the question of ways and means; and that the splitting up of the university into small groups from which the elective principle has been barred out, and to which men are more or less arbitrarily assigned, has been finally and definitely adopted as the future organization of Princeton? Yours faithfully, Andrew C Imbrie[1]

TLS (WP, DLC).

[1] This letter and Wilson's reply of July 29, 1907, were printed in the *Princeton Alumni Weekly*, VIII (Sept. 25, 1907), 7-9. The last two sentences in the second paragraph of Imbrie's letter were omitted from the published version.

To Antoinette Cole Comstock

My dear Miss Comstock: St. Hubert's, N. Y., July 26th, 1907.

I am sincerely pleased and complimented that the Keene Valley Country Club should have done me the honor of electing me a member, and I wish most sincerely that it were possible for me to avail myself of their kindness. But we are so far away, and have made plans for so many things that keep us close at home, that it seems as if we could hardly hope to avail ourselves of the advantages of the club.

I hope that you will convey to the Committee on Admissions our very warm appreciation and sincere regret.

Very truly yours, Woodrow Wilson

TLS (WC, NjP).

From Lucius Hopkins Miller

Muskoka Lakes [Ontario]

My dear President Wilson, July 28, 1907.

At the Northfield Conference this summer, Tertius van Dyke,[1] who is to be Philadelphian Society President next year, and George Duff 1907, who is to be General Secretary, went over with me very thoroughly the work for next year. This was especially necessary because, owing to Mr. Dumont Clarke's retirement the work this year became not demoralized but disorganized and the men not so much dispirited as lacking in vigor & initiative.

One of the things that seemed to us all wise to plan for during the coming year was to have a series of special meetings near the beginning of the second term in order to arouse inert Christians and to bring out into a definite position men who might thus be won to active Christianity.

I do not know how you feel about such meetings but I think you sympathize with the feeling we strongly entertain that the natural inertia & indifference of a body of men like ours may be rightly and successfully overcome by special appeal provided the appeal is made by the right men and conducted throughout in a proper manner.

Our own convictions in the matter were strengthened by the unusual success attending similar efforts at Yale of recent years. Each year they try to diagnose their case and whether it be Immorality, or Doubt or need of deeper Consecration, they choose their men accordingly and carry on a strong campaign for a definite object.

We think that *Indifference* is the greatest foe we have to fight at Princeton just now—more than Immorality or Doubt and our idea is to build up a Series around the Central Thought of *Devotion to Jesus Christ*, turning our guns in various directions of course.

Pending your approval of the scheme we have secured the tentative acceptance of Mr. Mott[,] Mr. Speer & Mr. Boyd Edwards[2] for the week March 1-8, which seemed the best time in view of the College Calendar.

If you approve the plan I should like to suggest the advisability of having the Chapel Preachers of March 1st & 8th specially selected and instructed to fit into the thought of the week and it might be wise to extend this to the preachers of preceding and succeeding Sundays.[3]

We hope by personal example & direct effort to engender from the very first of the year a strong spirit of service & interest in their fellows among the members of the Society so that outsiders will feel that the Special Effort in March is not strained but a natural thing resulting from work & interest of foregoing months.

Very truly yours, Lucius Hopkins Miller

ALS (WP, DLC).

[1] Son of Professor Henry van Dyke and a member of the Class of 1908.

[2] John Raleigh Mott, Foreign Secretary and Associate General Secretary of the International Committee of the Y.M.C.A.; Robert Elliott Speer, Princeton 1889, Secretary of the Board of Foreign Missions of the Presbyterian Church in the U.S.A.; and the Rev. Franklin Boyd Edwards, associate pastor of the South Congregational Church of Brooklyn.

[3] See WW to L. H. Miller, Aug. 3, 1907.

To Andrew Clerk Imbrie

My dear Mr. Imbrie: St. Hubert's, N. Y. July 29th, 1907.

I take real pleasure in replying to the questions contained in your letter of July 25th. I would say by way of preface that almost all of them concern matters which the committee of the Board deliberately intended to leave open to discussion. My answers to them, therefore, will be my personal judgments regarding them, subject to such revision as discussion may bring. I have naturally myself thought out these details, and none of the points you raise is therefore new to me.

Lst [1st]. The freshman commons in University Hall would not be continued, but freshmen would be assigned to quads immediately after entering college. It would be best that assignments to the several quads should be made by a committee of the faculty. As a rule, such assignments would be virtually by lot, but I should hope that a very considerable degree of latitude and elasticity would be allowed in the matter. For example, I at present see no conclusive objection to allowing the choice of parents in the matter to have considerable weight. I should think it perfectly permissible to assign boys, for example, to quads in which brothers or near relatives were already living. The only thing to guard against would be any tendency for men of a particular kind to flock to a particular quad, and so give quads over to the occupation of particular "sets."

2nd. As to transfers from one quad to another, I see no serious objection to allowing men in one quad to transfer to another, when that should prove possible by reason of the vacating of rooms, in order to be with special friends, though here again the same thing would have to be guarded against that I have mentioned in the last paragraph. An effort would certainly be made to make all the quads as nearly as possible equally desirable, and the main point of the regulations would certainly be to prevent any one quad or quads coming to seem particularly exclusive or desirable.

3rd. With regard to the possibility of there being too many students to be accommodated in the quads, I would say that it would be necessary to provide accommodation for everybody, if not immediately at any rate as soon as possible, and in the meantime to have men live only in places under some sort of direct supervision by the university authorities, as it were attached to particular quads. I am clear that all men ought to be obliged to live in the University in one or another of the quads, that the growth of a non-residential group or body of students would be highly undesirable, and that it would be necessary to limit the numbers admitted to the University to the accommodations available. I mean, of course, after the initial stages at which we had caught up with our numbers by additional dormitories.

4th. It would be my judgment that only juniors and seniors should have the use of the common rooms in each of the quads; that the way they should sit at meals would be a matter of detail to be determined by each quad for itself; and that every student, by virtue of his membership in the University, would of course have free access at all times to all quads.

5th. As regards the relation of the University to the present Upper-Class Clubs, should the clubs be unwilling to come into the new scheme, it would of course be necessary to forbid undergraduates to join them. This seems on the surface a harsh decision, but I think that it will be evident to anyone who thinks of it, that such a decision is necessarily involved in the adoption of the quad system. If the best men in the University were drawn off to the clubs, the new system would certainly lack both heart and vigor.

6th. If the Ivy Club or the Cottage Club, to take your example, should become a quad, I should certainly hope that sons or brothers of former Ivy or Cottage men might be given the preference in assignments to those quads.

7th. If the quad plan is put into operation, I should think that as a transitional provision it might be best to use the buildings of such of the clubs as were willing to come into the arrangement, as commons for particular dormitories or groups of dormitories on the campus, until the complete arrangements of the system could be made.

8th. Your eighth question opens up what is, of course, the chief difficulty of the whole thing, the ways and means. I do not think that we can expect the alumni at large to defray the cost of establishing the new system. I shall hope that the money for it will all come from some one source, though nothing is at present pledged for it. To establish the system entire and at one time would probably cost $2,000,000. Personally, I do not doubt that the money can be found, but of course, if it cannot, the adoption of the system may have to be postponed. The dormitories will not be altered to include dining rooms and common rooms: it will be necessary to erect buildings containing dining rooms and common rooms, and add them to groups of dormitories. If it is necessary to introduce the system by degrees, a committee of the faculty would have to determine who should join the first quads.

9th. What I meant in my letter of July 15th by saying, "that the plan proposed by the committee was not primarily or even chiefly social; that it is academic and aims at the best university organization," was that the object of it was to embody the life lived by the undergraduates outside the classroom in an organization which should be a university organization and not a congeries of social organizations managed entirely by undergraduates and primarily for social purposes. I am sure that the Board would not only be willing, but glad to discuss any other plan that might be proposed, which had this or substantially this end in view, and I hope that the alumni may presently understand the temper in which we are approaching the whole matter. It is a temper which is as far as possible removed from a desire either to force the pace or to conclude the discussion before it is begun, and it is my very earnest desire that the utmost freedom of suggestion should be exercised. We could not see, in our discussion of this matter, any way of reaching our end which did not involve what the quad system involves, namely, the substitution for what the clubs now supply, of larger residential groups whose membership should not be made up by the process of undergraduate election, and in which the life could be so arranged that, at any rate by the presence of many of its members, the influence of the faculty might constantly be felt. There is no thought, of course, of making these quadrangles like the residential houses of a school, under the authority of masters. They should be in the truest and most extensive sense possible self-governing, and the influence of the resident members of the faculty would be proportionate to their personal gifts and qualities.

You ask for the names of the committee which adopted and submitted the report published in The Alumni Weekly. You are yourself, of course, entitled to know the membership of that committee. It consists, besides myself as chairman, of Mr. Pyne, Mr. Dodge, Dr. Jacobus, Mr. Bayard Henry, Mr. David B. Jones, and Mr. Robert Garrett, and the Dean of the University sat with it. Mr. Henry was unable to be present at the meeting which adopted the report, but voted for its adoption in the Board itself. I realize that a certain amount of odium attaches to proposals as radical as these which the committee made, and I am not sure that the members of the committee would be pleased to be especially saddled with the responsibility which now belongs to the whole Board. I have the feeling that perhaps I ought myself to be the only individual singled out for the brunt of the responsibility. At any rate, I do not feel that I have the liberty to publish the names of the members of the committee. I think that you will see how I feel and how I am placed in the matter, and I am perfectly willing to leave it entirely to your prudence and good sense. I am not expressing this doubt because of anything members of the committee have said to me at any time, but merely out of a disinclination to bring upon them the brunt of affairs which must in any case fall upon myself.[1]

As for myself, I feel that we are here debating, not only a plan, but an opportunity to solve a question common to all the colleges and obtain a leadership which it will not be within our choice to get again within our lifetime. The colleges of the country are looking to us for leadership in this matter, as in others, and if we disappoint them it will be an opportunity irretrievably lost. I have talked this subject over with a great many men from other universities, and I feel convinced that our solution will be accepted as the general solution, if we have strength and courage enough to act upon it.

I have no doubt that it is true, as you say, that in the present temper at any rate of some part of our body of alumni, it would be very difficult to put the plan in its integrity into operation, but we will devote as much time as necessary to the discussion of the matter before acting, and I for one confidently believe that

[1] The foregoing paragraph was omitted when this letter was published in the *Princeton Alumni Weekly*.

the bulk of the alumni will in the long run be willing to do even this radical thing for their alma mater. I believe that all that is necessary is a clear understanding of the facts and a candid coming together in common counsel.

I very much appreciate the fine way in which you are handling this matter, and hope that you will not hesitate to call upon me at any time, even to come to New York if you should deem that necessary.

With warmest regard,

Faithfully yours, [Woodrow Wilson]

CCL (WP, DLC).

From Bayard Henry, with Enclosures

My dear President Wilson: Philadelphia. July 29 1907

Your good letter of 25th inst. was received by me yesterday on my return from Princeton. . . .

I sincerely hope Mr. Bryce will be willing and able to come some time in October or November. Sir William [Mather] seems so earnest that Bryce should make the address, I hope it will be possible for him to do so.

I have just received the enclosed letter from Momo Pyne, which shows how kind Sir William has been to him both in London and in Cambridge. Possibly we may be able to induce Sir William to come over next spring, during May, when we might secure from him an address.

Harry Thompson and I were at Princeton on the 20th and Mr Cram sent word he could be there last Saturday. As Thompson could not go I met Cram and we spent the day together with Mr. Bunn. After the heat of Thursday the cool weather of Saturday made our visit delightful. Mr. Cram was also gratified by the fact that it was the first time he had been in Princeton without the accompaniment of a rain-storm. He approved the plans for walks in McCosh Hall and in the McCosh Quad. Also the location and foundation of the sun dial, of walks along Washington Road and location of Physical Laboratory. We also had conferences with Profs. Scott and Van Ingen concerning plans for Biological Hall. I left Mr. Cram in the afternoon with Prof. Van Ingen and they seemed to be getting together on a plan which will be satisfactory to every one.

As you know, the proposition in relation to colleges and quads at Princeton is being vigorously discussed. Some of the trustees feel the plan was not adopted but the idea merely was approved, provided it met with the approval of all concerned. I have been giving a good deal of thought to the subject, and enclose copy of letter I sent Harry Thompson after the meeting of the Princeton Club in Philadelphia. Since writing it, I have seen a number of Princeton men, and though all, excepting one or two, were of opinion radical changes should be made in relation to clubs, and club life, no one was favorable to "quad" idea, excepting Prof. Ordmond [Ormond], who thought the college plan might be introduced at Princeton. Committees have been appointed by several of the alumni clubs, and I presume by all of the clubs at Princeton, to confer with you, as well as the committee of trustees, in order that there shall be some understanding as to details of the plan proposed.

As, at the best, it will be a number of years before sufficient funds can be obtained to build the necessary dormitories and dining halls and kitchens, and as it is urgent that some steps be taken at an early day in relation to sophomore commons, or sophomore dining halls, and, also, in relation to regulation of club elections, as well as club life, it seems to me we should make it clear that the latter are the present objective points, and that the "quad" and college idea need not be made too prominent at this time, but it is a thing which, if finally approved by all concerned, can be worked up to, while in the meantime the things to be regulated are the elections into the clubs, the club life and the sophomore dining halls, and some provision made for the seniors and juniors who cannot afford or do not care to go into the clubs. If the hat lines[1] and sophomore clubs were abandoned, and if all men who desire to join clubs had their names put up, and if in each club there were two or three members of the faculty elected by the clubs themselves, and the elective committee to the quads consisted of one or two seniors and one or two juniors and one or two graduates, and one or two members of the faculty, and provision made for those not elected, and also some provision made for the sophomores so that they could get decent food in some commons, that would be a long step in the right direction and the "quads" or colleges might follow after, although I fear that any college system which designed to have members of all classes meet together in a dining hall would not work out in a place like Princeton. The great interest which has been manifested in the discussion of the "quad," and college idea, is a most healthy sign of the deep loyalty of the alumni to Princeton, and the certainty of their backing any scheme or plan, which they are of opinion would be for the benefit of the University, to any reasonable amount. I am satisfied funds can be immediately raised for sophomore dining halls and that radical changes can be made in the present club life, but doubt if the large sums needed to erect dining halls, kitchens and new dormitories can be obtained at this time, nor do I believe they would work out satisfactorily even if we had the funds; most of the alumni whom I have met feel that the wisest course is to go step by step, and then only after the most careful consideration and consultation.

Harry Thompson and I have talked over this matter several times since I wrote the letter of which the enclosed is a copy, and he will see you on Wednesday or Thursday of this week.

With very best wishes and hoping you will have a delightful summer I am with regards

Yours sincerely Bayard Henry

TLS (WP, DLC).

1 For a description of the hat lines, see Wilson's supplementary report to the Board of Trustees printed at Dec. 13, 1906, Vol. 16.

E N C L O S U R E I

Bayard Henry to Henry Burling Thompson

My dear Harry: [Philadelphia] July 13 1907

Sorry you could not come up to meeting of Princeton Club. It was a large and representative gathering of the Philadelphia Alumni. Mr. Van Renssalaer[1] presided and after considerable discussion it was unanimously resolved that the president appoint a committee of five men to confer with President Wilson, the Committee of Trustees and with committees from other Alumni Clubs. Speeches were made by a number of men, all of whom admitted there were serious evils connected with the present club life at Princeton, but no one of whom was in favor of the "quad" or College idea. In fact, the meeting, while not disposed to criticize President Wilson, was practically unanimously opposed to the "quad" or college idea. Before the meeting and since I have given a good deal of thought to President Wilson's report, and am satisfied that, while there are evils connected with the college life as it exists at Princeton, it is advisable that other remedies be tried for their elimination rather than the one proposed by President Wilson and adopted by the Trustees.

In view of all the circumstances and the intense opposition which the plan has aroused among the Faculty and the Alumni,

1 Alexander Van Rensselaer, Princeton 1871, president of the Princeton Club of Philadelphia, and an Alumni Trustee.

I fear it was not sufficiently considered by either Faculty or Trustees, nor did the Alumni (to whom we now almost exclusively have to look for future support) know enough of the plan to thoroughly understand it, before it was adopted. The benefits of the plan, if it could all be carried out as suggested, would be great, but the trouble is to put it into operation without ruining the University. In the first place, in order to erect the necessary dining halls and kitchens and join the various "quads" so that they should be various units or entities to be called colleges, would require an expenditure of at least $2,000,000.

Second, even if the $2,000,000 were forthcoming, and the dining halls or refrectories were built, they would not be acceptable to the students. Commons at Harvard and dining halls in other institutions in this country have not been a success, and even at Oxford and Cambridge many men frequently breakfast and dine in their own rooms or in little clubs of their own, and not in the common college dining hall.

In a dining hall for one hundred or more, the seniors or juniors, to say nothing of the sophomores, would not willingly eat at the same table as the freshmen, and you could not make them do it. They would preferably go to some other university, where they could have the right to cho[o]se their own table-companions.

Again, if seniors and juniors would object to eating and living with freshman and sophomores, much more would the freshman and sophomores object to being under the tutelage or guiding eye of instructors and preceptors or dons. They might elect professors, instructors and preceptors into the clubs, but unless they had a choice in regard to the matter, it would not work out any more than the Honor System would, had not the men themselves taken hold of it in the beginning. No matter how eager or earnest a man may be in his studies, he prefers as a rule to spend his eating hours among good fellows and intimate friends, and not be bothered by "intellectual pursuits."

The most difficult thing of all, however, after the securing of the $2,000,000 necessary to erect the buildings, would be to arrange for a satisfactory method of selection of the members of the various quads or colleges. If this is done along intellectual lines, all the brilliant students would be in one college, all the ordinary students in another and all the backward students in another, which would be impossible. If along financial lines, with varying room rentals, all the wealthy students would be in certain colleges, which would produce an intolerable condition of affairs. It is impossible to see how you can arrange for all students paying exactly the same room rent and the same board. In a University, as well as elsewhere in America, men like to be on their own level, or else to be in a position where they can better themselves. They will not be put on a level with those below them. Wilson's idea of uniformity as to food is socialistic and not natural, and if students are to have the same food at so much a week there is no reason why they should not wear the same clothes or a uniform, which would be all right in a military or naval school, but hardly satisfactory in a college or university. If the selection is made along academical lines, the scientific students would be in certain colleges and the classical students in others; making still further divisions, along these lines, one college would have all students devoted to mathematics, another to physics, another to biology and another to the classics, or another to politics and political economy, according to the bent and spirit of the residential professors and instructors. In such a division all the advantages which accrue to a fellow through association with men of different tastes would be lost.

Again, with a class divided into ten or fifteen colleges, there would be no class life and no class spirit, for there would be little to bring the members of the various classes together, and much to separate them. With the class spirit and class association gone, and without welding the men together for protection along class lines, as is done in the freshman and sophomore years, the so-called "Princeton Spirit" would be short-lived, no matter how great the devotion of the Alumni to their Alma Mater.

Another difficulty would be in regard to fellows who were friends at home or at a Prep school, who would wish to continue their close association and friendship in college, and if they could not secure it at Princeton (rooming and eating together) they would go elsewhere. If Princeton were a Government institution and the men were compelled to follow certain lines of studies and have no choice as to what they would pay for rooms or board, it would be different.

Again, if all the students were to pay the same for board and rooms, new dormitories would have to be built and large endowments provided for the aid of those who now cannot afford to pay as much as others, and all plans for fellows working their way through college at Princeton would have to be abandoned.

There would also be serious difficulties in relation to the Faculty. Many of the best men would not care to act as president of a college where the students regulate their college life by some "simple method of self-government." Then too, the older professors and heads of departments who did not live in the "quads" or colleges would be placed in a different position as regards the students; not being on the same intimate relation. This might cause constant complaints as to the inefficiency or disagreeable character of the president of the "quad" or on the other hand it might cause jealousy and friction if the president of a "quad" were too easy-going or became too much attached to certain students and indifferent to others.

It is unfortunate the plan was made public at this time, because of lack of funds to carry it into effect and the practically unanimous opposition of the Alumni and of a large number—if not a majority—of the Faculty. The evils connected with the upper class clubs, the methods of election and their lack of stimulus to intellectual life, should be corrected. Provision should be made so that every man could have an opportunity of entering one club or another, and the clubs should be required to elect a certain number of instructors or preceptors into their number, who (with the graduate members) should take a hand in the regulation of elections to the clubs. There is not much likelihood of the entire plan approved by the Trustees being carried out, but it may lead to reforms which will be beneficial. In President Wilson's report, he says he has considered the difficulties involved, and if so, at the next meeting of the Committee, or at the October meeting of the Trustees, he can explain in detail just how these difficulties are to be overcome. It may be he has in mind someone who intends to provide the necessary funds for the building of dormitories, for the clubs, as well as kitchens and dining halls on the campus, and the new buildings to complete the "quads." If not, and if he has no suggestions as to how these difficulties can be overcome, some steps should be taken to allay the anxieties which the adoption of the plan has provoked among the Faculty, the students and the Alumni, as well as doubts in the minds of boys who thought of entering Princeton.

With best wishes and hoping to see you soon, I am,

Yours sincerely, [Bayard Henry]

CCL (WP, DLC).

E N C L O S U R E I I

Moses Taylor Pyne to Bayard Henry

My dear Bayard Dieppe July 17 1907

Thanks for your letter enclosing clipping from the Outlook which is very sound.[1] I am by no means certain myself that the "quad" system is the best, especially for the Clubs, but I do feel that this agitation will do more than could be done in any other way to remedy the great evil caused by undergraduate selection to the clubs.

I am very sorry that Garfield is going. I have always feared this and appreciate the position he is in. A call of this kind by one's Alma Mater is practically irresistable.

Sir Wm Mather was most kind to us. He called (and Lady Mather) several times[,] asked us to dinner every day and did all he could to make it pleasant for us. We dined quietly with him & his family on Wednesday last and on Friday I went to a dinner where he had the Prime Minister,[2] as well as "Lulu" Harcourt,[3] Winston [Spencer] Churchill, [Hilaire] Belloc, Cherry (the Irish Attorney General)[4] John Bright's son[5] &c which was very pleasant and agreeable. Then we had a good time in Cambridge where every one was most genial and pleasant.

We crossed the Channel and spent last night at Amiens. To-day we came here. It is a much pleasanter place than I had anticipated and we shall stay here a couple of nights and then go on to Rouen. All are well

With kind regards to Mrs Henry believe me

Yours ever M Taylor Pyne

ALS (WP, DLC).

1 After commenting briefly on Wilson's speech at Harvard on June 26, 1907, the editorial in the *Outlook* went on to discuss the Princeton club system and Wilson's quadrangle plan, although without coming to any firm conclusion for or against either the clubs or the quads. See "The College: Two Points of View," New York *Outlook*, LXXXVI (July 6, 1907), 493-95.

2 Sir Henry Campbell-Bannerman.

3 Lewis Harcourt, First Commissioner of Works in Campbell-Bannerman's government.

4 Richard Robert Cherry, Attorney General for Ireland, 1905-1909.

5 Probably John Albert Bright, M.P. for Oldham, the oldest and most prominent of John Bright's three surviving sons.

From James Bryce

My dear President Intervale N. H July 29/07

It is a pleasure to hear from you; and it would be a pleasure to visit Princeton again and join in dedicating Sir W. Mather's Sun Dial.

My plans for Nov. are not yet quite made up, but I will see if it is possible to arrange for a run to Princeton within the first half of Nov. I hope to be back at Washington from Cleveland, O. about the 4th of Nov. Will it do if I suggest a day three weeks or a month beforehand?

This is a beautiful region & we are enjoying rest & fresh air in it. I trust you & Mrs. W. Wilson are also having a good time

With our united kind regards to her,

Always truly yours James Bryce

ALS (WP, DLC).

From Andrew Clerk Imbrie

Dear Dr Wilson, New York, Jul 30 1907

I thank you for your very prompt and full reply to my long list of questions. Perhaps I may bother you again with some points that may still arise in our talks. (I am beginning to fear that you are having a vacation only in *name*!) Next week I am to meet a few men who have shown an especial interest in the discussion.

My purpose in asking the names of the Committee was in order that we could know which members of the Board had gone into the question in detail, and were therefore better able to discuss the matter. Of course I have no wish to embarrass anybody; for my own part, had I been a member of that committee I should prefer that the fact were known. Yet I appreciate your feeling in the matter, and I shall have a copy of your letter made from which the paragraph referring to the names is omitted, so that the answers you have given to my questions may be read by men who are interested.

Again thanking you for your help in our discussion believe me

Faithfully yours Andrew C. Imbrie

ALS (WP, DLC).

Henry Burling Thompson to Moses Taylor Pyne

Dear Momo: [Wilmington, Del.] 7th Mo., 30th, 1907.

. . . The only cloud in the sky is Wilson's "Quad" scheme. Bayard [Henry] is taking this very seriously, and looks for an early dissolution of the Faculty and the University. I am inclined to think things will hold together until the Trustees' meeting in October. All the same, the opposition is deeper, stronger and more bitter than I had anticipated. Looking at it as things are to-day, I think the result of the whole thing will be the cleaning up of the evil conditions that exist in the Clubs, and the quad system dropped for the present. I do not think—as I see the matter now—that we have tackled this thing in the right way. Wilson's eloquence has over-persuaded us.

Bayard and I lunched with West the day we were at Princeton. His attitude, to me, seems almost vindictive. It seems a pity to me that a man of his capacity should have such a silly streak of opposition in him towards the President. I do not know whether the President's attitude towards him is much better; but to an outsider the whole thing seems silly.

I leave here to-morrow for the Ausable Lakes, and my address for the month of August will be "St. Hubert's Post Office, Essex County, New York." My next neighbor will be Woodrow. Henry Van Dyke and Alan Marquand will be near neighbors. I presume the quad system will, at least, be touched upon. I propose to listen and say nothing. I shall reserve my opinion until the Trustees' meeting.

With kind regards to Mrs. Pyne,–I am

yours very sincerely, Henry B Thompson

TLS (Thompson Letterpress Books, NjP).

An Historical Essay

[*c. July 31, 1907*]

POLITICS

(1857-1907)

We are separated from the year 1857 as men of one age are separated from those of another. We live amidst scenes and circumstances to which the events of that day can hardly be made to seem even a prelude. A stupendous civil war and the economic and political reconstruction of a nation have been crowded into the brief space of fifty years,–one era closed and another opened, –and it hardly seems possible that men now living can recollect as the happenings of a single lifetime events which seem to have wrought the effect of a couple of centuries. It was in fact the completion of one great process and the beginning of another. The process by which a nation was created and unified came at last to an end, and a still more fateful process began which was to determine its place and example in the general history of the world. Whether the new century we have entered upon will carry us to the completion of another phase of our life remains to be seen.

So far, a century seems to have been our dramatic unit: one century, the seventeenth, we spent upon the processes of settlement; another, the eighteenth, in clearing the continental spaces we had chosen for our own of all serious rivals, the Spanish, the Dutch, the French, and in making ourselves free of oversight and interference from over sea; a third in constituting a nation, giving it government and homogeneity of life and institutions; and now we have entered upon a fourth century, and are sometimes in doubt what we shall do with it. We have for the nonce no clear purpose or programme. We are finding ourselves in a new age, amidst new questions and new opportunities, and shall have a clear vision of what we are about only when common counsel shall have further steadied and enlightened us.

If assessed by events, the year 1857 was not a year of particular significance. It was rather a year between times, when the sweep of events seemed to pause, and some were tempted to interpret the signs of the times as signs of peace, it seeming on the surface as if old issues were in some sort concluded and a time of settled policy at hand. Men who looked beneath the surface could, of course, see that no peace or settled mode of action could come out of opinions and policies constituted as were the opinions and policies they then saw to be the ruling elements of politics. Such, among others, were the men who founded the *Atlantic Monthly*. And yet it was at least a year quiet and undisturbed enough to afford the historian an opportunity to look about him, and take stock of what had come and was coming. It was a year in which one chapter may close and another open, as if at a pause or turning-point in the narrative.

The year 1856 had witnessed a presidential election, and in March, 1857, Mr. Buchanan became President in the place of Mr. Pierce, Democrat succeeding Democrat; but some significant things had taken place within the Democratic ranks within the four years that had elapsed since Mr. Pierce was elected. In 1848,[1] Mr. Polk, the Democratic candidate, had carried fifteen out of the twenty-six states that then constituted the Union; in 1852 Mr. Pierce had received the electoral votes of every state except Vermont, Massachusetts, Tennessee, and Kentucky; but Mr. Buchanan had received the support of no states outside the South except Pennsylvania, New Jersey, Indiana, and Illinois. His party, from being national, had seemed amidst the new ordering of affairs to become of a sudden little more than sectional, and, in spite of its success and its apparent confidence, seemed touched, as other parties were, with change and decay. The Democratic party had had its easy successes at the last three presidential elections largely because other parties were going to pieces and it held together unbroken and with definite purpose

[1] This error—the statement that Polk ran for President in 1848—also appears in the WWsh draft of this essay which, together with a WWT outline, is in WP, DLC.

with regard to the main issues of the day; but at last its own followers were yielding to the influences of divided opinion, and few besides its southern adherents remained steadfast of purpose.

The slavery question had proved an effectual dissolvent of parties,—not the question of the continued existence of slavery in the Southern States, but the question of the extension of slavery into the regions of settlement where new territories and states were being erected. It seemed a question impossible of definitive settlement until the ceaseless movement of population should come naturally to an end and the spaces of the continent should have been filled in everywhere with communities which had chosen their own order of life. Attempt after attempt had been made to determine it beforehand. The great Ordinance of 1787, contemporaneous with the making of the Constitution itself, had excluded slavery from the broad Northwest Territory which the States had ceded to the Union as a nursery of new commonwealths; the Missouri Compromise had excluded it from so much of the territory embraced within the Louisiana Purchase as lay north of the southern boundary of Missouri extended; and the extensive State of California, a small empire of itself, cut out of the vast territories snatched from Mexico, had been admitted as a State with a constitution of her own making which excluded slavery, thus determining the critical matter for the only portion of that great region with regard to which the movement of population rendered its immediate settlement imperative. Settlers by the tens of thousands had rushed into California upon the discovery of gold. The discovery had been made the very month the treaty of Guadalupe-Hidalgo was signed (February, 1848), and before Congress was ready to legislate for the new possessions, California had become a self-governing community of the familiar frontier pattern, with ruling spirits to whom it was impossible to dictate laws they did not like. The gold-hunters and the tradesmen who went with them neither had slaves nor wanted them, and Congress had no choice but to admit them as a state upon terms of their own making. And the rest of the Mexican cession it left open to be taken care of by the fortunes of settlement and the preference of its first occupants, after the same fashion. Such had been the terms of the famous Compromise of 1850, which also shut the odious slave trade out of the District of Columbia and provided southern slave-owners with a stringent Fugitive Slave Law which enabled them to recover their runaway slaves by simple and effective process through the action of the local officials of the federal government itself. That great Compromise, upon which Mr. Clay had spent the last years of his life and power,—that latest "settlement" of the irrepressible question,—was but six years old when Mr. Buchanan was chosen President.

But each successive handling of the critical matter seemed rather to unsettle than to determine it; and this last attempt to deal with it proved the least conclusive of all,—seemed, indeed, purposely to leave it open with regard at any rate to so much of the Mexican cession as was not included within the boundaries of the new State of California. Mr. Calhoun had explicitly denied the right of the federal government to exclude slaves, the legal property of such settlers as might come from the South, from the territories of the United States, and had declared it as his opinion, and that of all southern men who thought clearly of their rights under the partnership of the Union, that the people of the several territories, wherever situated, whether on the one side or the other of compromise lines, had the constitutional right "to act as they pleased upon the subject of the status of the negro race amongst them, as upon other subjects of internal policy, when they came to form their constitutions," and to apply for admission to the Union as states. The Compromise of 1850 had been framed upon that principle; and that compromise was not four years old, Mr. Calhoun was not four years dead, before the new principle had been enacted into law, to the sweeping away of all former compromises and arrangements.

It had been an astonishing reversal of policy, brought about by a man of surprising vigor and directness, who for a little while seemed the leader of the country. Not Mr. Calhoun only, but Mr. Webster and Mr. Clay were dead; a new generation was on the stage, and its leader, while parties changed, was Stephen A. Douglas, since 1847 one of the senators from Illinois. No man better fitted for confident and aggressive leadership in an age of doubt and confusion could have been found, even in the western country from which he came. He was but forty-one, but had won every step of his way for himself since he came a lad out of Vermont, and knew how to work his will with men and circumstances. His appearance bespoke what he was. He was short of stature, but gave the impression of mass and extraordinary vigor, carrying his square, firmly set head with its mass of dark hair with an alert poise that gave their right bearing to his deep-set eyes and mouth of determined line. His friends dubbed him the Little Giant, with affectionate familiarity; and his opponents found in him a candor that matched his fearlessness, a daring and readiness of wit that were the more formidable in contests before the people because he was a bit coarse-fibred and could be counted on to hold his own in any sort of debate. He had in a certain sense taken Mr. Benton's place in the Senate. His chief interest was in the development of the western country, the new communities constantly making to the westward, which were like the Illinois of his own youth, and carried so much of the vigor and initiative of American life; and he had by natural selection become chairman of the Senate's Committee on Territories. West of Iowa and Missouri stretched the great Platte country all the way to the Rockies, and across it ran the trails which were the highways into the far West. The western Indians had their hunting grounds there upon the plains, and the authorities at Washington had once and again thought of allotting to them an extensive reservation which should secure them in their hunting privileges. Mr. Douglas feared that something of that kind might throw a barrier across the main lines of the westward movement which he watched with such sympathy and interest, and had more than once urged the erection of a territory in the Platte country. In 1854 he had had his will, and had quickened the approach of revolution by the way in which he chose to have it.

His measure, as finally submitted to the Senate, provided for the creation of two territories, one lying immediately to the west of Missouri and to be known as Kansas, and the other, to be known as Nebraska, stretching northward upon the great plains through which the Platte found its way to the Missouri. Both lay north of the southern boundary of Missouri extended, the historic line of the Missouri Compromise, established now these thirty-three years, but Mr. Douglas declared himself impelled by "a proper sense of patriotic duty" to set that compromise aside and to act upon the principle of the later compromise of 1850, legislation which had been framed but the other day to compose the agitation of parties. The bill which he introduced, therefore, explicitly declared the Missouri Compromise "inoperative and void," and left the matter of the extension of slavery into the new territories entirely to the sovereign choice of the people who should occupy them.

Mr. Douglas did not wish to see slavery extended; he was simply taking what seemed to him the straightest way to the settlement of a vexed question which apparently could be settled in no other way. He did not expect the settlers of the new country to accept or desire slavery; he expected them to reject it. But whether they accepted it or rejected it, he thought them the best judges of such a question, affecting their own life and social makeup; and he did not believe that in any case Congress could either successfully or constitutionally determine such a matter beforehand. There were men in the Senate who earnestly opposed what he sought to do: Seward, and Sumner, and Chase, and Fish, and Foote, and Wade were there, the representatives of a new party which had devoted itself to this very task of blocking the extension of slavery; but they did not avail against the confident Democratic majority, which seemed to find a certain exhilaration in having obtained at last a leader who did not propose compromises but was willing to venture the open contests which only actual settlement and the direct action of the people themselves could conclude. It seemed clearly Democratic doctrine, this doctrine of "squatter sovereignty," and they accepted it with a certain zest and sense as of relief.

They must have seen how direct a challenge it was to the rival interests, pro-slavery and anti-slavery, to attempt a conquest of the new territories. Not that there was any question about Nebraska. That lay too far north to be available for the extension into it of the southern system. But that system had got its established foothold already in Missouri, and Kansas lay close neighbor to slave territory within the same parallels of latitude; and so far as her lands were concerned the challenge was accepted,—accepted in a way that held the attention of the whole country. It was a very tragic thing that ensued. Settlers out of the slave-owning states just at hand were naturally the first to enter the new territory, taking their slaves with them; but there presently began a movement of settlers out of the North which was of no ordinary kind. Nothing could have stimulated active opposition to the extension of slavery more than what Mr. Douglas had done. He had notified the country that law was neither here nor there in such a matter; that there was no legislative body that had the authority to say beforehand whether slaves could go with the settlers who entered the new lands of the national domain or not; that the predominance of men who wished slavery or did not wish it—their predominance, not in the nation, but in the territories themselves—must determine the question. In brief, he had made it a question of numbers, a question of conquest, of prevailing majorities on the one side or the other. Kansas therefore began to be peopled as no other territory had been. Settlers were sent there by organized effort. Individuals and societies in the North set themselves to work to find the men and the means to take possession of it, and the new settlers came prepared for anything that might prove to be necessary to establish themselves or their principles in the new territory, whether legal or illegal, understanding that it was not to be a process of law but an act of choice made in any form of fact.

It was an opportunity for desperate men, as well as for peaceful immigrants who wanted homes and came to till the broad, level acres of the prairie; and desperate men availed themselves of it. Kansas became a veritable battlefield. Men stopped at no violence to prevail, and flames of partisan warfare burst forth there which threatened, as every one saw, to spread to the whole Union.

Mr. Douglas's principles were put to the test the very year Mr. Buchanan became President. Until that year the pro-slavery men who had come out of Missouri and the farther South had predominated in numbers in Kansas, and had pressed their advantage with characteristic energy and initiative. Before they had lost their majority by the pouring in of settlers coming faster and faster out of the North, they had called a constitutional convention, and had submitted to the people of the territory an instrument which established slavery by organic law. One of the first things it fell to Mr. Buchanan to do was to submit to Congress their application for admission to the Union as a state under that instrument. But Mr. Douglas would not vote to accept the new state on those terms, and there were men enough of his opinion in the Democratic ranks to exclude it. He knew that, even at the time the constitution which was submitted with the application was in process of being drawn and submitted, the weight of opinion in the territory had shifted, and that when the popular vote upon it was taken the majority of the voters of the territory were against it. Multitudes had refrained from voting upon the question of its acceptance at all, because they had felt that they were being tricked. The instrument was not submitted to them to be accepted or rejected, but to be accepted "with slavery" or "without slavery,"—all other provisions contained in it in any case to go into effect; and it was clear from the text of it that to vote for it "without slavery" would not in fact exclude slavery; because clauses which were quite independent of the organic provision in question threw effective safeguards about the ownership of slaves, which would in all probability in any case indirectly secure it. This was not "squatter sovereignty." Whatever might be said of Mr. Douglas's doctrine, he held it candidly and in all sincerity, and would not consent to deal falsely with it; and at the certain risk of losing the confidence of the southern wing of his party, now its chief and controlling wing, he voted against the admission of Kansas under a pro-slavery constitution, notwithstanding the fact that the President backed it with his recognition as, in form at any rate, the legally expressed wish of the people of the territory.

And so things stood in the year 1857, a very doubtful face upon them,—a vast deal undone that had seemed at least to give definite form and security to the movements of politics, and nothing done by way of new definition or settlement. And then, as if to complete the confusion and destroy even Mr. Douglas's principle of action, came the Dred Scott decision, and the country learned that in the opinion of the Supreme Court of the United States the people of a territory had no more right than Congress to forbid the holding of slaves as chattels within their boundaries. Dred Scott was a negro of Missouri, whose master had taken him first into one of the States from which slavery was excluded by local law, and then into one of the territories from which slavery had been excluded by the congressional legislation of 1820, the famous Missouri Compromise. After his return to Missouri and the death of his master, Scott sought to obtain his freedom on the ground that his temporary residence on free soil had operated to annul his master's rights over him. The court not only decided against him: it went much farther and undertook a systematic exposition of its opinion with regard to the legal status of slavery in national politics. It declared that in its opinion slaves were not citizens within the meaning of the Constitution of the United States, but property, and that neither Congress nor the legislature of a territory—the power of a territorial government being only the power of Congress delegated—could legislate with hostile intent against any species of property belonging to citizens of the United States; that the compromise legislation of 1820 had been *ultra vires* and had no legal effect; and that under our constitutional allotment of powers only states could make valid laws concerning property, whether in slaves or in anything else. The repeal of the compromise measures of 1820 by Mr. Douglas's Kansas-Nebraska Bill of 1854 had not been necessary. They had been legally null from the first. The Dred Scott decision was uttered two days after Mr. Buchanan's inauguration.

As if there were not grounds enough of uneasiness, financial distress was added,—not because of the political fears and disquietude of the time, though they no doubt played their part in disturbing the minds of men of business and clouding their calculations of the future,—but because of the operation of forces familiar enough in financial history. An era of extraordinary enterprise had followed the rapid extension of railways and the successful establishment of steam navigation on the seas, and the discovery of gold in California had added excitement to enterprise when stimulation was not necessary and excitement was very dangerous. It was hard at best to give solidity and prudent limit to industrial and commercial undertakings which sought to keep pace with the growth of a new nation, to follow a people constantly moving everywhere into new lands, spreading their thin and scattered settlements far and near upon the practically unlimited spaces of a great continent. It was a speculative process in any case, based upon necessarily uncertain calculations as to the movement of population and the development of industry. The very railways which facilitated enterprise were themselves hazardous pieces of business, and had been pushed so fast and far through sparsely settled districts as to give those who invested in them scant return for their money, when they gave them any return at all and did not prove utter financial failures, so far as those were concerned who met their first cost. The speculative element in business, necessarily present everywhere, had grown larger and larger until, added to mere waste and bad management and flat dishonesty, there had come an inevitable crash of credit, and in the reaction business was prostrated. The crisis came in the winter which followed the presidential election of 1856, and Mr. Buchanan's term of office began when its effects were freshest and most depressing. It did not wear the features of panic, after the first crash had come, so much as of mere lethargy. Enterprise was at a standstill: the face of all business was dead; men not only did not venture, they did not hope: they were stunned, and the spirit taken out of them.

It was one of the significant signs of the times that no particular political importance was attributed to these financial disturbances. No one sought to make political capital of them. No doubt the uneasiness of the time, the removal of old political foundations by the repeal of the Missouri Compromise, the apparent transformation of the process of settlement into a process of civil war in Kansas, the rising passion of conviction that the contest of parties upon the question of slavery must presently come to some hot issue, contributed to confirm merchants and manufacturers and bankers and transportation companies in the opinion that nothing was safe that depended upon calculations of future advantage; but such matters lay apart from what politicians were chiefly thinking of, seemed to belong among the ordinary interests of the country's every-day life, and not among the extraordinary interests they were called on to handle, interests that loomed bigger and more ominous the more closely they were approached, the more intimately they were dealt with. Nothing financial was for the time being of party significance or interest. It was even possible to revise the tariff without party contest, in the interest of business instead of in the interest of politicians. It seemed to men of all parties that the tariff as it stood contributed to the financial distress of the time. It was steadily drawing into the Treasury a surplus of funds which the government did not use and which it was at that time especially inconvenient to withdraw from circulation. It was agreed, therefore, to put many of the raw materials of manufacture, hitherto taxed, on the free list, and to reduce the general level of duties to twenty-four per cent. Not since the War of 1812 had it been possible to arrange such a matter so amicably, with so little debate, with such immediate concert of action. The interest of parties was evidently withdrawn to other things.

These friendly debates, Mr. Buchanan's decisive majority in the electoral college, and the apparent dispersion of all organized elements of opposition, might give to the year 1857, as we look back to it, a deceptive air of peace. Even the radical views of the Supreme Court in deciding the Dred Scott case, and the uncomfortable matter of determining the right of Kansas to enter the Union with a pro-slavery constitution, might be made to look like the end of a process of change rather than the beginning of things still more radical and doubtful of issue, if one were seeking signs of accommodation and were satisfied to look no deeper than the surface. Undoubtedly 1857 was a year of pause, when the strains of politics were for the moment eased. It seemed a year of peace and settled policy.

It was in fact, however, the pause which precedes concerted and decisive movements of opinion upon matters too critical to form the ordinary subjects of party contest. Parties will join issue as hotly as you please upon any ordinary question of the nation's life, even though the elements of that question cut perilously deep into individual interests and involve radical economic or political changes; but they waver, postpone, and evade when they come within sight of questions which cut as deep and swing through as wide a compass as did that which divided North and South, and seemed to involve the very character and perpetuation of the Union of the States. The Democratic party had held a steady enough course upon the question of slavery. No doubt it was the easier course to maintain,—the course which seemed only a fulfillment of the older understandings of our constitutional system, only a working out of the policy of the country on lines long established and, it might be, inevitable. No doubt, too, the definite principles and undeviating purposes of the Southern men who constituted so important an element of the strength of the party, and who furnished from the ranks of their politicians so many men who had the capacity and the desire to lead, gave the party a leadership and a motive for framing definite programmes which the party of opposition lacked; and in a time of vacillation and doubt the confident party, with a mind of its own, has always the advantage. But, for whatever reason, the Democrats had so far remained for the most part of one mind and purpose, and other parties had gone to pieces. Only within the year had it begun to look as if a party ready to face the Democrats with resolute purpose and determined programme would at last form. The Whig party had finally gone to pieces in the presidential campaign of 1852. It had never been a party to declare its principles very strongly at critical moments or to espouse a cause very definitely in a time of doubt. It had had splendid leaders. The annals of the country have been made illustrious by few greater names than those of Webster and Clay, and their steadfast endeavor to keep the government to clear lines of thoughtful policy it must ever be the pleasure of the historian to praise; but the party had too often gone into presidential campaigns depending upon some mere popular cry, some passing enthusiasm of the people for a particular hero. The only Whig Presidents had been successful soldiers, General Harrison and General Taylor, both of whom died in office, to be succeeded, the one by Mr. Tyler who was not a Whig but a Democrat, the other by Mr. Fillmore who followed the leaders of his party, and counted for little in the formation of policies. Mr. Clay himself had shifted very uneasily from Yes to No in 1844 on the question of the annexation of Texas, when pitted against Mr. Polk, and the confident programme of the Democrats for "the reoccupation of Oregon and the reannexation of Texas," to the great loss of personal prestige; and the "Liberty Party" which then drew discontented Whigs from Mr. Clay's following had found successors in parties which showed more and more powerful as the number of voters grew who found the Whigs without courage or purpose on the chief issue of the day.

It was easy, with the machinery of nominating conventions open to everybody's use, as it had been since General Jackson's day, to bring new parties into the field from season to season, though it was by no means so easy to give them strength and coherency amidst shifting opinion; and independent nominations had more than once diverted votes from the ruling party at critical moments. There was little doubt but that the sixty thousand votes cast for the candidate of the Liberty Party in 1844 had been chiefly drawn from the Whig ranks, and had cost Mr. Clay the election. In 1848 a "Free-Soil" convention had nominated Mr. Van Buren, and a strong faction of Democrats in New York, displeased with the attitude of their party on the question of slavery in the Mexican cession, had followed their example, with the result that the Whig candidate won and the Democrat lost. The opposition to the extension of slavery was strongest among men of Whig connections, but it showed itself also in the Democratic ranks and rendered party calculations most uncertain. Mr. Wilmot, whose proviso against slavery had made such difficulty in the debates on the Mexican cession, was a Democrat, not a Whig, not a professed partisan of the new men of Mr. Seward's creed, who were slowly making their way into Congress. The Free-Soil men held another convention in 1852, when the Whigs went to pieces, and spoke to the country with a ringing platform of "no slave states, no more slave territories, no nationalized slavery, no national legislation for the extradition of slaves," and again made their own nomination for the presidency; but opinion was shifting again; the Compromise of 1850 had disposed voters for the time to let critical matters alone; restless men were turning in other directions, and the Free-Soilers reaped no apparent advantage from the break-up of parties. It was not until Mr. Douglas's Kansas-Nebraska Bill, and the pitiful spectacle of the struggle in Kansas which followed, had drawn men sharply from thought to action, that the Republican party emerged and showed the strength of a party that would last and win its way to power; and even then it felt obliged to compound a singular Free-Soil-Anti-Nebraska-Whig creed and nominate a Democrat for the presidency.

Meantime there had been witnessed an extraordinary diversion in the field of parties. The Know-Nothing party had sprung into sudden importance, with a programme which had nothing to say of slavery one way or the other, but concentrated attention upon the formidable tide of foreigners pouring into the country, because of the famine in Ireland and the political upheavals of 1848 in Europe, and urged upon the country the necessity of safeguarding its institutions against alien influences, of confining its gifts of political office to native Americans, and of regulating very circumspectly the bestowal of the suffrage. Voters turned to this new party as if glad to find some new current for their thoughts, some new interest touched at least with a common patriotism. In the autumn of 1854 the Know-Nothings elected their candidates for the governorship in Massachusetts and Delaware, and sent nearly a hundred members to the House of Representatives. In the autumn of 1855 they carried New Hampshire, Massachusetts, Rhode Island, Connecticut, New York, Kentucky, and California, and fell but little short of winning majorities in six of the Southern States. The House of Representatives which met in December, 1855, was an extraordinary medley of Democrats, Anti-Nebraska men, Free-Soilers, southern pro-slavery Whigs, northern anti-slavery Whigs, Know-Nothings who favored the extension of slavery, and Know-Nothings who opposed it. Nothing was certain of that assembly except that the Democrats had lost their majority in it. Even in 1856, when the elements of opposition began to draw together into the Republican party, there were still in the field a remnant of Whigs and a remnant of Know-Nothings. The four years of another administration were needed for the final formation of parties as they were to enter the conclusive contest of 1860. And so the year 1857 was a year between-times, when the country had not yet consciously drawn away from its past, had not yet consciously entered its revolutionary future.

It was indeed a revolution which ensued. Changes more complete, more pervasive and radical than those which were wrought by the war between the States, by the "Reconstruction" of the southern States, and by all that has followed of social and economic transformation, could hardly be imagined. The nation of 1907 is hardly recognizable, socially, politically, or economically, as the nation of 1857 or of 1860. The generation that wrought that extraordinary revolution left the stage but yesterday. We have all known and familiarly conversed with men who belonged to it and who performed its tremendous tasks. Some of the soldiers who officered the armies of that war of transformation are still among us. But we do not think their thoughts; it requires an effort of the imagination to carry our minds back to the things which are for them the most vital facts and recollections of their lives. Even they are now unconsciously dominated by influences which have lost all flavor of the days they remember. They have come to think our thoughts and see the world as we see it: a nation not made apparently by the forces they handled, but by forces new and of a modern world,—by vast economic alterations and unforeseen growths of enterprise and endeavor; by the opening up of the Orient and the new stir of affairs upon the Pacific; by an unlooked-for war which has drawn us out of our one-time domestic self-absorption into the doubtful and perilous field of international politics; by new influences of opinion and new problems of political organization and of legal regulation. Nothing remains of that older day but the irreparable mischief wrought by the reconstruction of the southern States. That folly has left upon us the burden of a race problem well-nigh insoluble, which even the alchemy of these extraordinary fifty years has not transmuted into stuff of calculable human purpose. That is of the old world; all else is of the new. We see what has gone by only across a gulf of unfamiliar things.

And so we stand in the year 1907 as if in a new age, and look not back but forward. It would perhaps be too fanciful to pretend to find in 1907 a close parallel of circumstances with the far year 1857, which lies so long a half century away from us; but there is this particular feature of resemblance, that this, like that, is a brief season between times, when forces are gathering which we have not clearly analyzed, and tasks are to be performed for which we have not formed definite party combinations. Parties are in partial solution now as then, and for the same reason. The issue of the day is clearly enough defined in our thoughts, as was the issue with regard to the extension of slavery in the thought of all observant men in 1857; but parties have not yet squarely aligned themselves along what must of course be the line of cleavage. It is manifest that we must adjust our legal and political principles to a new set of conditions which involve the whole moral and economic make-up of our national life; but party platforms are not yet clearly differentiated, party programmes are not yet explicit for the voter's choice. Let us hope that we are on the eve of a campaign of sharp definition.

There are many things to define, and yet there is only one thing. It is easy enough to point out the perplexing complexity of our present field of choice in every matter that calls for action. Our new business organization is so different from our old, to which we had adjusted our morals and our economic analyses, that we find ourselves confused when we try to think out its problems. Everything is upon a gigantic scale. The individual is lost in the organization. No man any longer, it would seem, understands the whole of any modern business. Every part of every undertaking demands special knowledge and expert skill. Individuals play their parts in subordination to the organizations which they serve, and we are made to doubt their moral responsibility beyond the limits of the mere tasks they are set to do; and yet the morality of the machine itself we do not know how to formulate. If we cannot formulate its morals, we cannot formulate the legal principles upon which we are to deal with it; for law is only so much of the moral understandings of society, so much of its rules of right and of convenience as it has been possible to reduce to principles plainly suitable for general application without too much doubt or refinement. Our thinkers, whether in the field of morals or in the field of economics, have before them nothing less than the task of translating law and morals into the terms of modern business; and inasmuch as morals cannot be corporate, but must be individual, however ingeniously the individual may seek covert, that task in simple terms comes to this: to find the individual amidst modern circumstances and bring him face to face once more with a clearly defined personal responsibility.

And that is the one thing which the politician, as well as the moralist and the economist, must make up his mind about. It is easy to state the matter in a way that makes it sound very subtle, very philosophical, a thing for the casuist, not for the man of affairs. But it is a plain question for practical men after all. And practical men are very busy just now, in confused and haphazard ways, perhaps, but very energetically, nevertheless, in settling it for better or for worse. We state our problem for statesmen by saying that it is the problem of the control of corporations. Corporations are, of course, only combinations of individuals, but the individuals combined in them have a power in their respective fields, an opportunity of enterprise, which is beyond all precedent in private undertakings and which gives them a sort of public character, if only by reason of their size and scope and the enormous resources they command; some of them seeming, if it were possible, rivals of the government itself in their control over individuals and affairs. Lawyers have always spoken of corporations as artificial persons, but these modern corporations seem in the popular imagination and in the minds of law-makers to be actual persons, the colossal personalities of modern industrial society.

One school of politicians amongst us, one school of lawyers and of law-makers, accepts the prodigy as literal fact, and tries to deal with it as with a person. It is a new doctrine of "squatter sovereignty." Mr. Douglas maintained that those who formed the great corporate bodies of the West which we have called territories could not by any rightful legal principle be dealt with as citizens, but must be suffered corporately to form their lives and practices as they pleased, and then dealt with as states; his modern counterparts tell us that corporations must contrive their ways of business at their pleasure and peril, and that law cannot deal with them as a body of citizens but only as an organized power to be regulated in its entirety and handled as a corporate member of our new national society of corporations. Corporations, we are told, have grown bigger than States, and must take a sort of precedence of them in the new organism of our law, being made participants in a federal system of legal regulation which States cannot negative or tamper with. The only way in which to meet such amazing–I had almost said amusing–ideas, is to meet them as the older doctrine of squatter sovereignty was met: by a flat denial that there is or can be any such thing as corporate morality or a corporate privilege and standing which is lifted out of the realm of ordinary citizenship and individual responsibility. The whole theory is compounded of confused thinking and impossible principles of law; and the political party that explicitly rejects it and substitutes for it plain sense and feasible law will bring health and the exhilaration of comprehensible policy into affairs again.

The present apparent approach of the two great parties of the nation to one another, their apparent agreement upon the chief questions now of significance, is not real, it is only apparent. At any rate it is plain that if it is in fact taking place, it does not truly represent the two great bodies of opinion that exist in the nation. There is a great and apparently growing body of opinion in the country which approves of a radical change in the character of our institutions and the objects of our law, which wishes to see government, and the federal government at that, regulate business. Some men who entertain this wish perceive that it is socialistic, some do not. But of course it is socialistic. Government cannot properly or intelligently regulate business without fully comprehending it in its details as well as in its larger aspects; it cannot comprehend it except through the instrumentality of expert commissions; it cannot use expert commissions long for purposes of regulation without itself by degrees undertaking actually to order and conduct what it began by regulating. We are at present on the high road to government ownership of many sorts, or to some other method of control which will in practice be as complete as actual ownership.

On the other hand, there is a great body of opinion, slow to express itself, sorely perplexed in the presence of modern business conditions, but very powerful and upon the eve of an uprising, which prefers the older and simpler methods of the law, prefers courts to commissions, and believes them, if properly used and adapted, better, more efficacious, in the end more purifying, than the new instrumentalities now being so unthinkingly elaborated. The country is still full of men who retain a deep enthusiasm for the old ideals of individual liberty, sobered and kept within bounds by the equally old definitions of personal responsibility, the ancient safeguards against license; and these men are right in believing that those older principles can be so used as to control modern business and keep government outside the pale of industrial enterprise. The law can deal with transactions instead of with methods of business, and with individuals instead of with corporations. It can reverse the process which creates corporations, and instead of compounding individuals, oblige corporations to analyze their organization and name the individuals responsible for each class of their transactions. The law, both civil and criminal, can clearly enough characterize transactions, can clearly enough determine what their consequences shall be to the individuals who engage in them in a responsible capacity. New definitions in that field are not beyond the knowledge of modern lawyers or the skill of modern law-makers, if they will accept the advice of disinterested lawyers. We shall never moralize society by fining or even dissolving corporations; we shall only inconvenience it. We shall moralize it only when we make up our minds as to what transactions are reprehensible, and bring those transactions home to individuals with the full penalties of the law. That is the other, the greater body of opinion; one or other of the great parties of the nation must sooner or later stand with it, while the other stands with those who burden government with the regulation of business by direct oversight.

Such a season between times as this in which we live demands nothing so imperatively as clear thinking and definite conviction: thinking clear both in its objects and in its details; conviction which can be satisfied only by action. The *Atlantic Monthly* has enjoyed the great distinction of supplying the writing of conviction throughout the deep troubles and perplexities of a half-century of contest and reconstruction; it enters now upon a second half-century which is no less in need of similar tonic. Our very political ideals are now to be decided. We are to keep or lose our place of distinction among the nations, by keeping or losing our faith in the practicability of individual liberty.

Printed in the *Atlantic Monthly*, c (Nov. 1907), 635-46.

An Essay

[*c. Aug. 1, 1907*]

THE PERSONAL FACTOR IN EDUCATION

To say that there can be no vitality in teaching, and no reality, either, unless the teacher himself be vital, is surely to say a very obvious thing. The vigor of all thought and of all learning is in the thinker and the scholar, and in such words, spoken or written, as he can, by some magic, lend his own vitality to.

Undoubtedly there are men who do excellent thinking and yet cannot make the processes clear to others, men who have gathered real treasures of learning and yet must, however generous their impulse, keep them private for mere lack of any power or gift of expression. For some the things that possess and govern their spirits are communicable, for others they are incommunicable. It goes without saying that the former are the only real teachers.

The world must be served; and because it is in need of a multitude of servants, the dull and awkward must be employed along with the apt and capable. There is a vast deal of teaching to be done to draw the young forward to the places their elders are presently to leave, to make good the progress the world has so laboriously attained; and only a teacher here and there will lift the difficult business into the light.

Men and women without a vigor and freshness of mind which they can communicate must be used as well as those who touch their work with a spark of originality and of individual fire, like a spark of life.

Fortunately, there is a great deal of routine in teaching, as in everything else, and in the doing of the routine we can make shift with the teacher who is a bit mechanical and without any power to freshen or illuminate the things to be taught. There is a great deal of mere information to be communicated to the pupil, a great deal of mere drill in which he is to be exercised and disciplined; and very unoriginal teachers will often be serviceable enough in such things.

But education is not, after all, when properly viewed, an affair of filling and furnishing the mind, but a business of informing the spirit; and nothing affects spirit but spirit.

The business of teaching is carried forward with a certain thoroughness and efficacy from generation to generation, and oftentimes with a certain triumph of achievement, because some men of an extraordinary vitality and strength of personality engage in it. The fire that leaps in them kindles the spirits of the young people whose lives they touch. These are the torch-bearers, and upon their life and energy depend the perpetuation and acceptance of the truth, the life of all knowledge.

It is a rare child that is born with an appetite and readiness for learning and that turns to books with a sort of native taste and eagerness. Most of us have had to be awakened to an interest in what the world has thought and done, have had to be held off from play and the natural occupations of a child's day, to which we would have turned had we been left alone, and obliged by the force of another's will, stronger than our own, to fix our attention upon things that lay outside our immediate experience, things done long ago, when the world we live in was only a-making, things thought out concerning ourselves and matters lying all about us which we would never have dreamed of or attempted to originate, and would have gone all our lives without knowledge of had the schoolmaster not forced us to look and see and comprehend. And no one who has ever really learned anything can fail to remember the teachers who thoroughly awakened him and first set his mind aglow with interest and comprehension.

Every schoolboy should read "Tom Brown at Rugby."[1] He will find himself reproduced in Tom or in Harry East or in some one of the delightful boys, jolly or sedate, who crowd those pages. And he will see a great figure there, the figure of the great Arnold of Rugby, the master of the school, its dominating spirit, the man to whom every lad gave reverence and from whom every lad drank a spirit of honor and high purpose and love for the things that satisfy.

He will not know till afterward, when his reading leads him elsewhere, how great a man he has met. Thomas Arnold was great among scholars in the wide field of history, and great among those who gave to the Church of England a statesmanlike vision of what it was to guide a nation and evangelize a world.

But there at Rugby he was great enough, the friend and counselor of boys, their model of what was elevated and just and gracious. They felt every day how stern he was to insist on duty, on tasks well done, and yet how tender to sympathize and how quick to strengthen even a boy at fault, and show him where safety and honor lay.

He was no doubt a great historian, a great churchman, a great citizen because he was the man these lads saw him, a lover of learning and of right living, a lover and counselor of those who were setting out upon the great enterprises of life, which contained for them joy or defeat according as they took or would not take the lessons he taught them, by precept and by example.

Every boy who went from Rugby went touched, he knew not how, by this great spirit, who seemed the spirit of the place itself, and yet also the spirit of all learning and of all reverent thoughts. The annals of our American colleges are rich in ex-

1 Thomas Hughes, *Tom Brown's School Days* (Cambridge, Eng., 1857, many later edns.).

amples of this personal factor in education, this vivification of everything connected with it by reason of the presence of some great spirit whose touch, it would seem, undergraduates could not escape unless they were made of mere insensible clay.

There are four names more frequently mentioned than any others: Eliphalet Nott, Francis Wayland, Mark Hopkins, James McCosh. Each of these notable men was a great personality.

Eliphalet Nott was president of Union College through two generations (1804-1866), and many a man active and useful throughout the strenuous nineteenth century, the formative period of the nation, looked back to him as the man who had given him hope and principle in action.

No man came out of Union College in those days untouched by the influences of that great nature, that shrewd and kindly master of the spirits of young men. Youngsters incorrigible elsewhere found in him a man who at once comprehended and dominated them. He gave them his sympathy and took the pains to understand their troubles,—that seemed instinctive with him, as if all young men's secrets and sins were an open book to him,—but he mastered and commanded them also, and they found through him hope and means of reformation.

He was like a great moral dynamo, an inexhaustible source of moral energy for all who lacked or had lost it. He was the personal friend and counselor of every man in the little college of his day, and no man left those halls ignorant of the duty and destiny he had been put into the world to fulfil. The college was a school for the rectification alike of the mind and of the conscience. Study, when understood as Doctor Nott understood it, became, not a mere set of daily tasks, but a means of life, and the duties of the college shone clear as but the preliminary duties of a whole career.

Not a few of our colleges had teachers and presidents like this man in the simpler days when students were not too numerous to constitute, as it were, a single family of comrades.

Some of our smaller colleges have them yet; here and there a man of this type stands out a notable figure even in the faculty of some great university—a man who is the intimate guide and counselor of his pupils, an inspiration to them in study, a never-to-be-forgotten model in conduct; a man from whom ideals are taken; a man who communicates those finer conceptions of thought and duty which shed light upon all a man's pathway and solace and cheer him at every turn.

It is because of such men that learning keeps its dignity and its fruitful connections with the life of men. Two such men will redeem a whole faculty of plodders; a half-dozen of them will give any university a foremost place of influence in their generation. They are the true knights of education.

Francis Wayland was not of the same type as Eliphalet Nott. His strong nature, direct and full of force in everything, was felt at Brown almost as vividly as Doctor Nott's at Union, by the students individually as well as by the college as a living organization.

He acted upon individuals no less than upon bodies of men. He loved men and counsel. But he was also a great organizer of teaching, a master in the classroom and behind the lecture desk, projecting great subjects upon the comprehension of his pupils by a singular mastery of exposition; busying himself with the preparation of text-books which should serve young minds for introduction into great bodies of thought; keeping his strong shoulder always to the task of systematizing and perfecting the teaching of the great fundamental subjects of instruction.

He served, not Brown alone, but all American schools by his vital example and direct assistance, and was a great serviceable citizen of the republic of learning—his services at the nation's disposal.

Such men make learning a branch of the public service. They display a sort of statesmanship in letters and lift education to universal significance. They are of the same stuff and capacity as great men of business, great organizers of enterprise, great originators of undertakings which have a scope embracing peoples and nations. There is a vitality in them which seems to renew the initiative and energy of a whole generation.

Mark Hopkins, the beloved president of Williams, was more nearly of the type of Doctor Nott, the father and exemplar of his pupils—and yet there was something else in him, which it is difficult for one who never knew or saw him to describe.

Mr. Garfield once said that if you had only a log for a seat, a lad on one end and Mark Hopkins on the other, you would have all the essential elements of a college. Doctor Hopkins was more of a teacher than Doctor Nott was. There was in him the sweetness and the strength of a scholarship that is deeply human, genial, pure, selfish, and yet something also of the serious Puritan strain that made the conscience master of all things.

He preached often of love as the law of life, and it was love, deep, simple, unaffected, which governed his dealings with the men about him. And you felt that there was something else suggested by his tone and presence, something besides that gracious, noble personality, that there was some figure standing behind or beside him to which he was himself obedient—the figure of Christ, no doubt, but of Christ speaking amidst the duties of modern life, speaking of love and forgiveness, but also of tasks to do, a partizan of learning and of all that lifts and disciplines the human spirit, a teacher of life no less than a sacrifice for sins.

In the presence at once of master and servant, you felt the deepest compulsions of the classroom, and knew that you were in a college whose tasks were but a part of life.

The mere tradition of such a life will last a college a generation. It seems the function of such men to inform institutions themselves with a vivid personality. The impulses they impart release ideals from the abstract and transmute them into places and studies. There is no estimating the fertilizing force they exercise upon young minds. Education in their hands is more than learning; it is life itself. And only when learning and life are thus spiritually united are they both lifted to perfection.

James McCosh was my own master in the days when he was transforming Princeton. I can speak of him, not by hearsay merely and by report of what other men felt and learned who came into contact with him, but also out of my own fortunate experience. I shall never cease to be thankful that I came into direct personal association with a man so vital and individual at every point, so easy a master in whatever he undertook.

It added a good deal, no doubt, to the impression Doctor McCosh made upon all whom he dealt with on this side of the water that he was a Scotsman. There was a brusque directness in his manner that at once arrested the attention. An interesting intonation went always with the sentences that came from his lips, redolent with the flavor of the Scottish accent, that gave piquancy to everything he said. There was always some phrase or turn that seemed wholly his own.

But the force that was in him needed nothing accidental to enhance it. He found Princeton a quiet country college and lifted it to a conspicuous place among the most notable institutions of the country, the place to which its age, its traditions, its long history of intelligent development entitled it. He laid the foundations of a genuine university, and his own enthusiasm for learning vivified the whole spirit of the place.

It would be difficult to exaggerate the degree of stimulation he imparted to every element of growth there was in the place, or the reach and significance of the changes, both of method and of organization, brought about at Princeton by his influence.

But these are the things of which the historian of education in America will tell; they are not the things which the men who were undergraduates in the days of his presidency recall and are grateful for.

Every one of them felt that in knowing him they had come into contact with a great man and a great personality. They could never afterward lose the sense of his power, of the singular energy and directness of his nature, of the keen and concentrated ardor with which he sought the things that made for the intellectual and moral advantage and advancement of the men round him and under him.

He was often very absolute and sometimes not a little arbitrary, but only small natures laid that up against him; because every man who had any insight could see with how transparent an honesty he acted and with how high and single a purpose, always for the college, never for himself.

His faults were the faults of his qualities, and his qualities were obviously great qualities; qualities such as belong only to great and vital men; qualities that rule and create. The life of the place seemed to spring from him as its source, and his very oddities seemed to add to the impression of individuality and force.

Such men freshen everything that they touch, and seem creative even when they only adjust and adapt. It would be difficult to overestimate the effect upon young men of coming into immediate personal association with them. Although Princeton grew rapidly in his day, the number of students never became so large that he could not, in one way or another, touch all of them. He dominated them even when they were least willing, and they at least got the clear conviction it was needful they should get, that learning was a thing alive and quick with the power to generate life.

No one can doubt that education would be a thing hopelessly dull and without life and potency were it not for such men as these and many others, a little company of great spirits in each generation.

Nothing can communicate fire but fire itself; nothing can touch spirit but spirit; and there is no vital touch but the individual touch. Men must meet face to face to kindle each other, and must know each other, not in crowds merely, not in lecture-rooms and at formal exercises alone, but also intimately, singly, with a look directly into each other's eyes, and that direct touch of thought which comes when the one fixes his attention upon the other and mind touches mind.

The problem of the great university, where pupils throng thousands strong, is the problem of the separation of teacher and pupil, the problem of crowds and of the loss of this vital contact.

How can even the genius of the born teacher avail to lead and quicken so many? How shall he find the time, where shall he find the place and the opportunity to get intimate access to individuals in so great a multitude?

The English universities solve the problem by their divisions into colleges; or, rather, their division from the first into colleges, in each of which only a comparatively small number of undergraduates can live and study, enabled them to avoid this loss of the teacher among the crowd.

Each college is a little community apart, a little academic family in which there can be daily intimacy between teacher and pupil; and nowhere, probably, in all the academic world, is the contact between the two more natural, more constant, more influential than there.

The masters of Balliol have been the foster-fathers of generation after generation of men who have been awakened to the highest achievements alike of scholarship and of public service in their day.

And nowhere better than in the English colleges can the part which the personality of the teacher plays in education be studied—the deadening effect of intercourse with teachers who make their teaching a mere routine and have no spark either of enthusiasm or of natural energy with which to make themselves potent to the stimulation of the students entrusted to their care, and the quite incalculable stimulation of intimacy with teachers fitted to be guides, eager to be guides, and showing at every step a loving familiarity with fair regions of learning and of science—good companions, good counselors, lovers of young men and of all that quickens and informs their spirits for the work of the world. A great tutor will beget in the men he touches an energy and worth of faculty which go to the very depths of character as well as of achievement.

The personal factor in education is the chief factor. For the young it is necessary, in order that they may get the real zest of learning into their hearts, that learning should live in their presence in the person of some man or woman whom they can love and must admire; whose force touches them to the quick, they scarcely know how, whose example they cannot shake off or forget, whose spoken words they cannot dismiss, whose written words even, although they be seen after many years, when the sound of the voice, the gesture, the glance of the eye have been lost, bring back upon the instant all the old magic like a recreative touch, a rebirth of the very person.

No system of teaching which depends upon methods and not upon persons, or which imagines the possibility of any substitution of the written word for the living person, can work any but mechanical effects. The teacher's own spirit must, with intimate and understanding touch, mold and fashion the spirit of the pupil; there is no other way to hand the immortal stuff of learning on.[2]

Printed in *The Youth's Companion*, LXXXI (Sept. 12, 1907), 423-24; editorial subheadings omitted.

[2] There is a WWsh draft and the last page of Wilson's typescript of this essay in WP, DLC.

From Hamilton Holt

My dear President Wilson: New York, Aug. 1, 1907.

If this report in THE REVIEW OF REVIEWS[1] is at all correct, it seems to me that you are doing as great a thing for Princeton in reforming the societies as you did in establishing the Preceptorial System. The social life in all our American colleges in my opinion is in a pretty bad way. Extravagance, exclusiveness, and a host of other evils almost outweigh the good that is in the system.

Will you not write an article on the subject for THE INDEPENDENT. I am sure it will do a great deal of good, especially in its example to the other universities who seem for the most part afraid to tackle the problem.[2]

Yours very truly, Hamilton Holt Managing Editor.

TLS (WP, DLC).

[1] The enclosure was a clipping of an article, "Dr. Wilson's Plans at Princeton," New York *Review of Reviews*, XXXVI (Aug. 1907), 145. The anonymous author strongly approved of Wilson's quadrangle plan.

[2] Wilson's reply is missing, but he declined the invitation.

From Bliss Perry

My dear Wilson, Boston August 2, 1907.

I cannot tell you how greatly I am pleased with your contribution to the November Atlantic. It is all that I hoped for, and more, and is enough in itself to lend distinction to a number which will not be lacking in that quality.

I am just taking the train for Greensboro [Vt.], where Mrs. Perry and I are planning to have a week or ten days with Westcott and the Hibbens. We are making our headquarters in Williamstown this summer, and everything is going well with us.

I was sorry that I could not see more of you in Cambridge on Commencement week. The allusion to your "serviceable institution" amused me very much, and I wish I could have heard your speech at the dinner. It seems to have delighted everybody. Two or three days afterward I had a letter from a well-known Harvard man saying that he liked that speech so much that he had about made up his mind to send his son to Princeton instead of to the college of his ancestors.

I am asking Messrs. Houghton, Mifflin and Company to send you today the honorarium for the article, and proof will go to you in good season.

With many thanks, and all good wishes,

Faithfully yours, Bliss Perry J.P.

TLS (WP, DLC).

To Lucius Hopkins Miller

St. Hubert's, N. Y.

My dear Professor Miller: August 3rd, 1907.

Your letter of July 28th has reached me here, and I hasten to say in reply that the plans you outline for the Philadelphian Society next year have my entire approval. I think that in the hands of the right persons such meetings as you purpose holding will be extremely useful. I am sorry to say that all the appointments for the University Pulpit at that period are already made. Very possibly, however, we may, as the time approaches, find it feasible to enlist the gentlemen who are to preach at that time in the general plan. I will be very glad to take the matter up with you when we come together again in the autumn.

It was very interesting to see that your letter is dated from the Muskoka Lakes, one of the places I love best and where I have spent three delightful summers, not at The Woodington, but above you at Mr. Snow's place, The Bluff. I sincerely hope that you are having fine weather and are both enjoying the vacation. Mrs. Wilson joins me in warm regards to you both.

Always faithfully yours, Woodrow Wilson

TLS (Selected Corr. of L. H. Miller, NjP).

To Cleveland Hoadley Dodge

My dear Cleve, St. Hubert's, N. Y., 4 August, 1907.

I have been greatly distressed to learn from Harry Thompson, who has just come with his family, that you are being pestered to death about our quad. scheme and are finding it a real burden. Cannot you turn the letters over to me? I am not getting much vacation anyhow and the burden of the thing of rights belongs to me. It makes me sorrier than I can say to know that you are being harrassed. I did not know that you were going to stay in New York and be exposed to the brunt of the thing. Do let me step in to take the thing off your hands if there is any way in which that can be managed.

The task is every way legitimately mine. I feel that I am in reality engaged in nothing less than the most critical work of my whole administration, the work upon which its whole vitality and success depends. Only a very deep conviction to that effect would ever have led me to lay such far reaching plans before the Board. If Princeton cannot be made what we wish her to be in this way I do not know in what way she can. The whole question has for me, therefore, the deepest and most solemn significance, affecting my whole success as president; and I do not grudge any effort or work spent upon it, and beg with all my heart that you will let me come to your relief. I cannot bear to think of your being distressed in this way. I do not believe, my dear fellow, that you can know the affection and gratitude I feel for you.

We are all well; and there is real tonic in this Adirondack air. I hope that you are about to get away and find release and refreshment somewhere.

With all my heart

Faithfully and affectionately, Woodrow Wilson

WWTLS (WC, NjP).

A Credo[1]

6 August, 1907.

My training has been that of the law, and it has been under the influence of that discipline that I have formed my conception of our constitutional system. I recognize the constitution as the formulation and guarantee of our liberty. It is by virtue of the constitution that we are the nation that we are, and I regard any deviation from its true spirit and plain meaning, by ingenious interpretation or otherwise, as a direct blow at the nation's life and integrity.

And, as I regard the constitution as the entirely adequate instrumentality of our national life, so also do I regard the law in

[1] As earlier letters from Dr. John A. Wyeth have disclosed, this statement was prepared at Wyeth's urging for transmission to William M. Laffan.

which I have been trained, the common law received into our system at the Revolution and since expanded by our own practice, as adequate, if interpreted with insight and applied with courage and intelligence, to remedy the wrongs which have corrupted modern business. If it needs amendment and addition, it needs it chiefly on the side of definition, that the novel processes of modern business may be explicitly brought within its ancient terms. Our courts have lost some of their one-time courage and initiative; have grown accustomed to look to statutes for extensions and adaptations of the law; and will doubtless need the aid of legislation in the responsible task that is now laid upon them.

The object of constitutional government is the liberty of the individual. There is no such thing as corporate liberty or corporate morality: only the individual can be free or moral. We need statutes not to regulate the business of the country, but to single out the individual amidst the intricacies of modern industrial organization, and to fix upon particular men the responsibility for particular transactions. Great trusts and combinations are the necessary, because the most convenient and efficient, instrumentalities of modern business; the vast bulk of their transactions are legitimate and honest; their methods are for the most part sound and unobjectionable; but, sheltered by their complex organization, tempted by the opportunities for manipulation afforded by their vast financial operations, and the chances to crush rivals inherent in their immense power, some men engage in transactions which the law should unquestionably prohibit and punish,—transactions no doubt already prohibited and punishable under the law, but not handled with frankness and directness in our modern practice. We shall not remedy the matter by attempting the direct regulation of corporate business through governmental commissions. That way lies the danger of attempting what government is not fitted to do, the danger of governing the people overmuch, and of drawing to public officials duties which too much abridge the freedom of the individual and are sure in the long run to slacken the energy of private enterprise.

Undoubtedly modern business has brought into use transactions novel to our older practice and almost unknown to our present legal definitions, which are in contravention both of good morals and of sound business. Such transactions should be brought within the prohibitions of our law: those which are not essentially criminal in character within the prohibitions of our civil law, as subjecting the individuals who engage in them to heavy damages, those which are essentiall[y] criminal in character, that is, essentially dishonest and inimical to the general morality of the community, within the prohibitions and penalties of the criminal law. But the government should not undertake the direct supervision and regulation of business.

We cannot afford to repeat that fruitless experiment, the experiment of paternalism against which our whole political history has been a brilliant and successful protest. We should only be obliged some day to re-Americanize our government by once more clearing the field of governmental commissions and setting up again the right of the individual to apply his energy as he will and to combine with his fellows with the utmost freedom of contract. Under the constitution of the United States there is secured to us that most precious of all the possessions of a free people, the right of freedom of contract. Destroy that right, and we cease to be a free people. The constitution guarantees to every man the right to sell his labor to whom he pleases for such price as he is willing to accept. In the exercise of that right he must be upheld by the use of every power with which this government is clothed. The men who would abridge or abrogate this right have neither the ideas nor the sentiments needed for the maintenance or for the enjoyment of liberty.

There can be no government set up within this government which is not opposed to this government and which will not, if it be allowed to persist, overthrow and destroy this government. The law was created by the people for all the people, and that any class should assert its exemption from the law is intolerable. Lawlessness, once condoned, becomes itself law, and when the law is divided against itself our form of government is at an end, and is superceded by anarchy or autocracy.

Considerations of this kind apply with especial force to any definition of the duties of the President of the United States. He is the only active officer of the government who is chosen by the whole people. He alone, therefore, speaks for them as a direct representative of the nation. His voice and initiative must in the nature of the case, as the affairs of the nation enlarge and multiply, increase in significance and importance. But they are separated by plain constitutional definitions from the initiative and power of Congress, and the powers of the presidency cannot rightfully be augmented by any encroachment upon the sphere either of Congress or of the courts. The courts stand umpire between individual and individual not only, but also between the individual and the government. Their independence and integrity are the central safeguards of a free government. Any interference with them either by Congress or by the Executive is fatal to the morale of our whole system. The relations of the President and Congress must of necessity be more intimate. They can take counsel together and act in close coöperation without the least violation of the spirit of the constitution. But the courts must act free from either executive suggestion or legislative dictation; and the law-making powers of Congress can be exercised in the true spirit of the constitution only when they are used without suspicion of undue or covert executive influence. The constitution can be obeyed in statesmanlike fashion without either taint or destruction of the immemorial principles of a system of law which has been adequately interpreted by generations of able and enlightened jurists and which no candid man can affect to misunderstand.[2]

WWT and WWhw MS (WP, DLC).

[2] There is a WWsh draft entitled "Credo," of this statement in WP, DLC.

To Bayard Henry

My dear Mr. Henry: St. Hubert's, N. Y. August 6th, 1907.

I find that it may be possible for Mr. Bryce to come to Princeton and take part in the unveiling of the sun-dial about the second or third week in November. He at any rate holds out that hope, and is going to let us know some three or four weeks beforehand. I shall presently write to Sir William Mather and inform him of our probable success. I am sincerely glad that we can meet both our own and his wishes in this matter and can plan for a really distinguished ceremony.

With regard to the quad plans, let me beg that you will not lose heart too early. You must remember that so far the alumni have debated this matter with all the debaters on one side. I have the greatest confidence that when the necessity for the change is explained to them in detail and the plans justified to them by the method in which they are to be executed, they will rally to us with their usual patriotism and enthusiasm. It may be a long process and it may be a slow process to convince them, but it is absolutely necessary to attempt it with courage and patience, because I cannot too seriously assure you that I deem the whole ultimate success of what we have recently attempted and achieved at Princeton dependent on the execution either of this plan or of some other equivalent to it in object and effect. I shall certainly not be inclined to push the process of discussion too fast, and I believe that when the first shock of these radical proposals is passed, we can get for ourselves all the support we need.

I am very much surprised that you should assume that a large portion of the faculty of the University is against this new scheme. I have every reason to believe that you are quite mistaken as to that, and that by the end of another year you will find the elements very much changed in a discussion which now seems confused, largely because there has not yet been an opportunity for full explanations and justifications.

Thank you very much for your frank letter on the subject, and for letting me see your letter to Mr. Thompson and the letter from Momo Pyne.

With much regard,

Always sincerely yours, [Woodrow Wilson]

CCL (WP, DLC).

To Henry Janeway Hardenbergh

St. Hubert's, N. Y.

My dear Mr. Hardenbergh: August 6th, 1907.

I beg that you will pardon my delay in returning the drawings, which I am sending to you today by express. Just after I wrote to you last, Mr. Thompson, the Chairman of our Committee on Grounds and Buildings, arrived, and so many matters that needed to be discussed and settled came up in our first conversation, that we kept the plans for reference. I hope the delay has not caused you any inconvenience.

I notice that you have substituted stone for brick below the water table (you will pardon me if I use architectural terms incorrectly), and it seems to me that it will be of the utmost importance, if stone is used there, to select a stone which will rapidly mellow in color and not form too sharp a contrast with the brick above it. I feel sure that you will agree with me that harsh contrasts in the color scheme of so impressive a building ought carefully to be avoided. My own taste and Mr. Thompson's would prefer brick even there at the base of the building, and stone only for the cut work and trimmings, but if you feel that stone is necessary for any structural reason, we will of course offer no conclusive objection, only begging that the stone chosen be not such as to maintain a sharp contrast. Indiana limestone would of course mellow very rapidly and very satisfactorily, but Indiana limestone does not cut with a rough face, and you seem to have indicated a rough-faced stone in your drawings.

Mr. Thompson and I have very carefully discussed the question of the exact site of the building, and have conferred with

Mr. Bayard Henry, the only other member of our Committee on Grounds and Buildings who is now accessible. It is our unanimous desire that the eastern end of the laboratory should be placed in line with the western wall of that part of '79 Hall which will be nearest to it, and that for several reasons:

In the first place, we think that the building would in that way be more satisfactorily disclosed from the direction of McCosh Walk, the point of view from which its proportions will be best displayed and from which it will be most often seen.

In the second place, we are very anxious to preserve the row of trees which runs along the bank at Washington Road, and to have any building placed there set far enough back to avoid the appearance of being perched up on a retaining wall. It is our wish to retain the bank at Washington Street by a wall, and to run the path which must go there without such change of grade as would disturb the trees, and we think that to place the laboratory as we suggest would greatly enhance the effect which we wish to produce there.

In the third place, we want very much to avoid the monotonous effect of a very long line of buildings running down Washington Road upon the same plane, particularly because the grades there will make it necessary that the line should be a descending line, going down, as it were, by steps. We think that such an effect would be very tiresome and ought to be avoided. The point of view from which this line of buildings will almost always be seen will be from above rather than from below, and it would not meet our objection to place buildings erected below the physical laboratory further in from the road, because by that arrangement they would be lost to the eye of an observer standing at the corner of Prospect Avenue. Another consideration which has influenced our preference is that the laboratory is on so different a scale from Seventy-Nine Hall, that it would seem to us to be best in this way to emphasize its disconnection of face lines or plane with the dormitory.

I hope that you will submit these reasons to Mr. Palmer, as the unanimous opinion of our committee, but that you will say to him at the same time that we are heartily desirous of meeting his own wishes in every possible way, and hope that if this decision does not meet with his approval, he will not hesitate to say so. We are quite willing to defer to any decided preference he may have. Our decision is really a return to your original preference in the matter, I remember, and I therefore assume that it will be agreeable to you. Let me say that I am very much pleased indeed with the drawings, and that it is very delightful to be so near the realization of our hopes with this splendid laboratory. It could not, so far as I can see, be better.

With much regard,

Sincerely yours, [Woodrow Wilson]

CCL (WP, DLC).

From Cleveland Hoadley Dodge

My dear Wilson: New York August 6, 1907.

I cannot tell you how deeply I appreciate your lovely letter of Sunday, which has touched me very much. I am afraid that Harry has given you an exaggerated account of how I have been harassed. To tell you the truth, during a good part of July, nearly every Princeton man I met had something to say, and it was not all encouraging. But now, thank fortune! nearly everybody is out of town, and I am having a good rest from all such trouble. I think the first excitement over the matter has died out, and men are beginning to take a little cooler and more sensible view of the whole matter.

I am getting a few days a week off, on my yacht, but cannot go far, on account of my dear Mother's[1] serious condition. We hope to get up to our camp on the Upper Saranac early in September, when I trust we may be able to run over to St. Hubert's and see all our good friends there before they leave.

I am expecting Bayard Henry to spend Sunday with me, but I shall absolutely prohibit any discussion of the important matter about which he is so greatly disturbed.

I thoroughly agree with you as to the tremendous importance of your scheme, but as we are building for the long future, I think we can afford to go a little slow. I am delighted to know that the Adirondack air is going [doing] you so much good, and I sincerely hope that you will come back to your duties in the fall thoroughly refreshed. You will certainly need all the strength and vigor possible.

With warm regards to all your family,

Yours affectionately, Cleve Dodge

TLS (WP, DLC).

[1] Sarah Hoadley (Mrs. William Earl) Dodge.

To Sir William Mather

My dear Sir William: St. Hubert's, N. Y. August 7th, 1907.

I am very happy to report that it now looks as if we could get Mr. Bryce for some date in the early part of November. He has not named the date, but he has promised to try to find a date when he will be free and when it will be possible for him to come to Princeton, and I now feel a good deal of confidence that he will be able to do so. We are all very much delighted at the prospect and shall look forward to the day with the keenest interest and pleasure. We shall miss you sadly, but perhaps it will save you many blushes not to hear what we will say of you. November is apt to be one of our most beautiful months, when autumn is turning into Indian summer, and a very beautiful and quiet aspect lies upon everything, and we shall hope that the day set will turn out to be one of the most perfect of our autumnal days.

I am very much obliged to you for your very kind letter and for the suggestion which has resulted in this new hope of getting Mr. Bryce. I had feared from what he said that there was no time in the autumn when he could find himself free to come. I very deeply appreciate, too, what you say about Princeton. Such confidence as you express in her future and influence heartens me more than I can say. It is delightful to count you among Princeton's friends.

We are spending a quiet summer in the Adirondack Mountains, where the air is tonic and where the heavy influences of our American summer seldom penetrate. Mrs. Wilson and my daughters join me in messages of warmest regard to Lady Mather, your daughters and yourself, and I am as always,

Cordially yours, [Woodrow Wilson]

CCL (WWP, UA, NjP).

Winthrop More Daniels to John Grier Hibben

My dear Hibben: Princeton, N. J. Fri. Aug. 9. 1907.

Your recent letter came to hand yesterday, and was much appreciated. . . .

I have had several long talks with Axson about the President's proposal, and the President's attitude thereto, or towards any possible modification of it. A. says he has never seen Wilson more stiffly bent and insistent on a project;—and this quite confidentially—that if concessions as to minor details do not gain substantial approval sufficient—after, let us say, a year's time or so—to secure its adoption, he should not be at all surprised at W's resignation. Axson has read this over, and says it should be shaded a trifle, especially in the matter of time—one year.[1] Axson asked W. if he would not be satisfied to think the scheme might be in working order at the end of 5 years' time; upon which W. said he would be greatly disappointed if it were not in operation long before that period had elapsed.

In thinking the matter over, I think the first thing to be clear about is in regard to the manner in which the plan was "sprung" on alumni and Faculty alike. I do not think there is any tenable foundation for making the claim that the Faculty in justice to itself must assert its outraged dignity in some formal way. Paul [van Dyke] and West say that if the Faculty is invited to discuss "details" without being allowed to register opinion on the essential idea, they will protest; and, failing that, will walk out of the Faculty. I believe Henry van Dyke has expressed himself of this mind. This seems to me all rubbish. I don't see that the President is bound first to take the Faculty into his confidence on a matter of this sort. (Even Billy Magie said to me he didn't propose to be the member of any body "that was a *mere Douma*.") And it certainly is a bit ridiculous to imagine West going around holding in his arms the funeral urn of Faculty dignity—"whose holy dust was scattered long ago." . . .

I think the greatest present danger that threatens is the possibility of Wilson's retiring—voluntarily of course,—and I propose to do what I can to render that as unlikely or as impossible as possible, trusting to time and Providence to avert lesser evils. . . .

Yours very sincerely W M Daniels.

ALS (W. Farrand Coll., UA, NjP).

1 Daniels added this sentence in the margin after completing this letter.

To George William Lay[1]

My dear Mr. Lay: St. Hubert's, N. Y. August 12th, 1907.

I owe you a very humble apology for not having replied sooner to your letter of July 2nd.[2] We have not, of course, been so grossly discourteous as really to neglect it, but a series of circumstances, which I very much regret, have unreasonably delayed my reply.

My daughter was unable to answer the question you asked, as to the Greek texts she was expecting to read next year, and laid the matter before her teacher who had prepared her for college. Her teacher promised to write to her fully on the subject, and we have been delaying from week to week to reply to your letter, in the hope that the advice we were expecting from her would come.

But it has not come, and we do not feel justified in waiting for it any longer. I write in my daughter's name, therefore, to beg that you will make your own selection of the texts she is to read, and to assure you that she will be perfectly satisfied with your choice.

With much regret and many apologies,

Sincerely yours, Woodrow Wilson

TLS (G. W. Lay Papers, NcU).

1 The Rev. George William Lay, teacher of Greek at St. Mary's School in Raleigh, N. C., which Eleanor Wilson was attending.

2 It is missing.

From Welling Sickel Katzenbach[1]

My dear Dr. Wilson New York, August 12th, 1907.

As you doubtless are aware there is a great deal of discussion going on among the Alumni, particularly those of us who belong to the younger group, regarding your plans for the introduction of the Quad System.

I would esteem it a great favor if sometime at your convenience you would grant me a personal interview as I should like to talk the matter over with you and learn more about your views on this important proposition.

Hoping that I am not intruding on what should properly be your vacation, and with high esteem, I am

Yours loyally Welling S. Katzenbach '04.

TLS (WP, DLC).

1 Princeton 1904, President of the Board of Trustees of the Quadrangle Club and Secretary of the Charles E. Sholes Co. of New York, manufacturer of chemicals.

To Henry Janeway Hardenbergh

St. Hubert's, N. Y.

My dear Mr. Hardenbergh: August 13th, 1907.

Thank you for your letter[1] with the sketches and blueprints accompanying it. I am returning the prints today, with a larger blueprint showing the plan for future extensions of the laboratories, which has been adopted by the Grounds and Buildings Committee of our Board of Trustees, upon the authority of the Board.

I am very much obliged to you for stating so fully your views with regard to the site of the building, but I must say very frankly, after consulting again with the Chairman of the Committee of the Board, that we think it necessary to adhere to our general plan. There are a great many things to be considered, and we have thought the plan out as a whole and it seems to us that the reasons for it are conclusive.

I should feel very sorry to have you disappointed in any respect about the position of the fine building you are about to erect, and I feel very confident indeed that you will not be. The laboratory is upon a considerably larger scale than Seventy-Nine Hall, has a very considerable frontage on Washington Street, and, standing a hundred feet from Seventy-Nine Hall, will certainly be perfectly disclosed from Prospect Avenue except to persons standing very close to Seventy-Nine Hall, and I think that the fact that it stands a little withdrawn from the road will greatly enhance its dignity, in view of its size. Moreover, I think that you will find that your recollection of the positions of the trees and shrubs which might hide the front of the building from McCosh Walk is not quite accurate. Of course, the little brick magnetic observatory which now stands close to McCosh Hall will be removed, and when it is taken away the only trees of any size whose foliage will break the view will be two standing very close together at the rear of Seventy-Nine Hall. For the rest, the only large trees are some standing in Prospect garden which will undoubtedly screen the western end of the laboratory, but I think you will find that the greater part of the building will be beautifully visible and will make a very fine impression.

I did not mean in my last letter to insist at all upon the base of the laboratory being of brick, but merely to express it as my opinion that the color scheme would be better with brick than with stone. If you and Mr. Cram think that Indiana limestone with sawed face would improve the building architecturally and would eventually tone down to a color which would not offer too harsh a contrast to the brick, I think no member of the committee will have any objection. There is to be a good deal of stone in the building, considering all the corner trimmings, the windows and their mullions, and the work about the entrance door, and I am only afraid of the brick work being subordinated and patchy if so large a body of stone is put in at the base. But, as I say, I am quite willing to leave that to your own and Mr. Cram's artistic judgment.

I feel so confident that the plan now decided upon by the committee with regard to the placing of the building will result to your ultimate satisfaction, that I am looking forward to the prosecution of the work with the greatest interest. I am sure that you will push it as fast as possible. If you should wish me to be at Princeton at the time the foundations are actually staked out, I will very gladly come.

With much regard,

Sincerely yours, [Woodrow Wilson]

CCL (WP, DLC).

[1] It is missing.

From Stephen Squires Palmer

My dear Dr. Wilson: New York, August 13, 1907.

Mr. Hardenbergh has shown me your letter to him as to the plans, also his reply.

I am much pleased that our efforts to develop a building (which is to be in fact a workshop) meets with your approval, and I can assure you that we have devoted much time and thought in working out the details.

This morning Mr. Hardenbergh received a letter from Mr. Cram stating that you and Mr. Thompson had adopted his last suggestion as to the exact location for the laboratory. As there seems to be some slight difference of opinion (in our minds at least) as to the location, and as we all are most desirous of doing what will prove to be for the best interests of the University, both present and future, I think that it might be best if Messrs. Thompson, Cram and Hardenbergh meet you and myself at Princeton and finally settle this matter on the ground. I make this suggestion as you wrote me some time ago that you would come on for that purpose.

As time is fast slipping by, I am most anxious that we begin actual work as early as possible so that the building will be finished and ready for occupancy when the University opens in the autumn of 1908.

In order to save as much time as possible, most of the specifications are now ready to be submitted for tenders, and we will take up this latter matter at once, but no contract will be made until you have settled the points at issue and we have your full permission to proceed.

Thank you for your kind inquiries about my son.[1] I am happy to say that he has fully recovered and is at the office once more.

With kind remembrances, I am, as always, my dear Doctor,

Very sincerely yours, S S Palmer

TLS (WP, DLC) with WWsh notations on verso.
[1] Edgar Palmer, Princeton 1903.

From John Allan Wyeth

My dear Mr Wilson [Lake Placid, N. Y.] Aug 15th, 1907

I was very happy to know you were among the mountains & resting. We are for the summer at Lake Placid Club a few miles away & find it so delightful that the time is slipping away only too rapidly.

Mr Laffan arrives Saturday from Europe & I shall have him read your political "moral law" which in the language of a certain book my parents required me to study "is summarily comprehended in the ten commandments"[1] as expressed (to me) so satisfactorily in your communication.

I am greatly comforted to know our Society is to have you & hear from you then a reiteration of the Franklin maxim "Honesty is the best policy" in politics as well as business. L. Q. C. Lamar changed the phraseology somewhat in saying that "Honesty was better than policy." With best wishes John A Wyeth

Mrs Wyeth & the children ask me to send you their message of good-will.

ALS (WP, DLC).
[1] He was here quoting Question 41 of the Westminster *Shorter Catechism.*

From Bayard Henry

Dear President Wilson: Philadelphia. August 16 1907

It is fine Mr. Bryce will be able to be at the unveiling of the Sun Dial, and I hope that everything will pass off in good style.

As to "quad" plans for Princeton, it is not a matter of losing heart but simply one of judgment, and what will be the best for Princeton. There are serious problems which will have to be met, and changes which will have to be made in connection with the social life at Princeton. From an architectural point of view, however, even if all the clubs were willing (and so far as I know, no one of them is) it would be impossible to erect dormitories in connection with the clubs which would be at all satisfactory. The only way that could be arranged would be for the clubs to sell their properties, and then use the proceeds for building quads, with dormitories, in other places. Dormitories could not be built in the rear of the present buildings with any success. So far as the sentiment of the Faculty, and whether it is favorable to "quad" plan or not, you probably know more about it than I, although I was advised by a number of the professors they were opposed to the plan, and regretted it had not been discussed before it was adopted by the Trustees. I agree with you that it is advisable not to "push the process of discussion too fast" and that either this plan, or some other equivalent one, may in time be adopted. For example, if instead of attempting to convert the clubs into colleges and dormitories and quads, some one could be induced to give a completed quad, with kitchens and dining hall, and the endowment necessary to maintain it, that would be an object lesson, and, if successful, other quads could be built without any radical or sudden changes which might destroy the class lines and seriously injure the University. In the meantime, and until sufficient funds are in hand to make possible the changes deemed desirable, rules will have to be made in relation to the evils now existing in the club elections and club life, the Sophomore clubs and the lack of dining halls for those who cannot be accom[m]odated elsewhere. I see they are having difficulties at Oxford and Cambridge the same as here,[1] but so far as Princeton is concerned we have a more devoted and liberal body of Alumni than any of the English Universities, and can confidently look for hearty support from the Alumni in all matters which will be for the best interest of the University.

With kind regards, and hoping you will have a delightful vacation, I am, Yours sincerely, Bayard Henry

TLS (WP, DLC).

1 Henry was referring to a renewal of agitation for reform of the Universities of Oxford and of Cambridge, which culminated in a proposal in the House of Lords on July 24, 1907, for the appointment of a royal commission "to inquire into the endowment, government, administration, and teaching of the Universities of Oxford and Cambridge and their constituent colleges in order to secure the best use of their resources for the benefit of all classes of the community" (*Parliamentary Debates*, Fourth Series, CLXXVIII [July 11-24, 1907], 1526).

As it turned out, no commission was appointed at this time, but the public discussion of reform continued. One of the key subjects was the relationship of the Oxford and Cambridge colleges to their respective universities as a whole. It was alleged that the colleges dominated the university: the loyalty of students and graduates was to the college rather than the university, the bulk of endowment funds went to the colleges instead of to the university, and the very success of the tutorial system created vested interests which severely hampered the effectiveness of university-wide teaching on the professorial level. It was asserted, moreover, that the great wealth of the richer colleges permitted them to monopolize the best students and that they competed aggressively for entering students. Finally, the great cost of attending the colleges was also frequently criticized, particularly because it restricted the number of students from working-class and middle-class families.

See George Nathaniel Curzon, 1st Marquis Curzon, *Principles and Methods of University Reform* (Oxford, 1909), and Alfred Isaac Tillyard, *A History of University Reform from 1800 A. D. to the Present Time, With Suggestions towards a Complete Scheme for the University of Cambridge* (Cambridge, Eng., 1913). Both of these books were directly inspired by the proposal in July 1907 for a royal commission.

To Stephen Squires Palmer

My dear Mr. Palmer: St. Hubert's, N. Y. August 17th, 1907.

Allow me to acknowledge the receipt of your letter of August 13th. I note that it was written before the arrival of my second letter to Mr. Hardenbergh, sent last Tuesday and containing a blueprint of the lay-out for the two laboratories and their future extensions which has been adopted by the Committee on Grounds and Buildings. That drawing originated in this way: Some five days after he saw you, Mr. Thompson went down to Princeton to look the ground over once more, and himself independently came to the conclusion that it was best, in order to save a line of fine trees and in order not to put a tall building too near the retaining wall which would be necessary on Washington Road, that the physical laboratory should stand further from Washington Road than he had at first thought would be necessary. He therefore asked Mr. Cram to go down to Princeton again and look the ground over once more. This Mr. Cram did, and the drawing of which I sent Mr. Hardenbergh a blueprint is the result. To my mind the plan shows admirable symmetry and seems to justify itself. I am wondering if it has not modified Mr. Hardenbergh's own feeling in the matter, and whether you still think the question of the best site debatable.

If the building is placed one hundred feet from Seventy-Nine Hall, as Mr. Hardenbergh prefers and we all agree it should be, the whole of the easterly face of it will be visible from every part of Prospect Avenue, even if its easterly line be made an extension of the westerly line of Seventy-Nine Hall. Mr. Hardenbergh will find that if the laboratory be placed as we suggest, a line run from its northeastern corner, past the front of Seventy-Nine Hall, will clear Professor Brackett's corner[1] and run to a point almost opposite the gates to McCosh Walk, so that anyone would be able to see the whole eastern face of the building the moment he had crossed the street from McCosh Walk, on his way to Prospect Avenue. So that his fear that the building may not be visible at that side seems to me clearly groundless.

We dare not put this great mass of buildings too near Washington Road at any point, because that road is becoming more and more a highway, and it is not improbable that at some future day it may be necessary to widen it.

Mr. Thompson was away when your letter came, and I was not able to show it to him until yesterday. He has made engagements to go into camp next week, which he feels he cannot break, but he is to leave for home either two weeks from Saturday or two weeks from Monday next, and would be very glad to come to Princeton then for a conference upon the matter, if you still deem it necessary. We are twenty-four miles from a railway, and it would take us three days to go to Princeton and back. But that is neither here nor there, if you desire it. I merely want to make sure that you are still of the same mind after seeing the blueprint to which I have referred and my last letter to Mr. Hardenbergh. I note that you say that the specifications are just being sent out for tenders, and I take for granted that it will not be possible to secure those tenders in less than a couple of weeks. If you will let us know, through Mr. Hardenbergh, the progress of that business, and if you still desire us to discuss the point of site again on the ground, we will of course come down in time for the signing of the contracts, so that every question may be settled, as you very rightly desire, before the contracts go into effect. Mr. Thompson is my near neighbor here, and we are in daily consultation.

Will you not let me say once more how delightful it is to deal with you in these and all other matters, because it is so easy to get quickly and directly to our points?

With warmest regard and the keenest appreciation of what you are so magnificently doing for Princeton.

Always faithfully yours, [Woodrow Wilson]

CCL (WP, DLC).

1 That is, the northeastern corner of Washington Road and Prospect Ave.

From Welling Sickel Katzenbach

My dear Dr. Wilson: New York, August 17th, 1907.

Your favor of the 14th inst. has just reached me, and I thank you particularly for offering to meet me in Albany. However, I do not regard the necessity for an interview so pressing as to warrant my disturbing your vacation plans, also I doubt whether pressure of business would permit me to get up to Albany before the first of the month.

I am going to Jamestown for a couple of weeks the beginning of September and will take pleasure in calling to see you at Princeton on my return.

In the meantime if there are any further developments, I would very much appreciate it if you would keep me posted.

Yours loyally, Welling S Katzenbach.

TLS (WP, DLC).

From Stephen Squires Palmer

My dear Dr. Wilson: New York, August 19, 1907.

Thank you very much for your letter of the 17th instant just at hand.

Mr. Hardenbergh is at the moment at York Harbor, Maine, but is expected at his office tomorrow, or at the latest the following day.

As soon as he returns, I shall take up the subject matter of your letter with him and write you. In the meantime, there is not the slightest reason why either you or Harry Thompson should make any change whatever in your outing arrangements. Incidentally I only wish that I was twenty-four miles from a railroad, telegraph or telephone wire.

Very truly yours, S S Palmer.

TLS (WP, DLC).

From Charles Whitney Darrow,[1] with Enclosure

Dear Sir: Princeton, N. J., August 20, 1907.

I am sending you herewith at the suggestion of Mr. Charles Scribner, a copy of the report which I submitted to the Company. Mr. Scribner thought you might be interested as it contains several recommendations in regard to the University printing and the future relation of the Princeton University Press[2] to the University.

Yours very truly, The Princeton University Press.
C. Whitney Darrow Mgr.

[1] Princeton 1903, Manager of Princeton University Press and Business Manager of the *Princeton Alumni Weekly*.

[2] The idea of establishing a university press at Princeton had been in the minds of several persons, including Edwin M. Norris, editor of the *Princeton Alumni Weekly*, since about 1903. However, it was the young C. Whitney Darrow (he had already stopped using the "Charles" and eventually dropped the "C." altogether) who in 1905 first suggested a practical means of getting the project under way. Darrow believed that the press should begin in a very small way by printing the *Princeton Alumni Weekly* (which it still does to the present day) and then develop slowly. The *Alumni Weekly* was at that time printed by William C. C. Zapf on his job printing press in the basement of his residence at 2 Nassau Street. Darrow persuaded Zapf to sell his equipment and good will for $5,000. Then, through Robert Bridges, Darrow was introduced to Charles Scribner, Princeton 1875, who agreed to give $1,000 toward establishing what was first called the Alumni Press. With Scribner's backing, Darrow soon secured the remaining $4,000 from Moses Taylor Pyne, John David Davis, J. Lionberger Davis, Cornelius C. Cuyler, and the Princeton Bank. Darrow took over the Zapf press in November 1905.

Some two months later, the employees of the Princeton Press went on strike. This plant, located at 30 Nassau Street and owned and operated by Charles S. Robinson, was the largest printing establishment in Princeton. In addition to printing the *Princeton Press*, the town's major newspaper, Robinson's press at this time printed the *Daily Princetonian* and did much of the university's printing work, as well as most of the town's job printing. Robinson was so disturbed by the strike that he decided to sell his plant and informed Darrow of his intention. Darrow persuaded Scribner to contribute $5,000, and the balance of the purchase price of $9,500 was quickly secured. The transfer of property took place in January 1906. By November 1906 all the operations of what was now named the Princeton University Press were located at 30 Nassau Street. Robinson continued to own and edit the *Princeton Press*, which was printed by the new firm for some time. Princeton University Press next acquired all the stock of the Princeton Publishing Company, owner of the *Princeton Alumni Weekly*.

Princeton University Press was incorporated on October 4, 1910, in the State of New Jersey "in the interests of Princeton University, to establish, maintain and operate a printing and publishing plant, for the promotion of education and scholarship, and to serve the University by manufacturing and distributing its publications." The original Board of Trustees consisted of Scribner, Pyne, Parker Douglas Handy, Archibald Douglas Russell, and Clarence Blair Mitchell. Darrow continued as Manager until 1917, when he joined the firm of Charles Scribner's Sons in New York.

Princeton University Press was, and still is, an entity legally separate from the university and was intended from the beginning to be self-supporting. Scribner gave the money to purchase the land and construct and equip a building for Princeton University Press at the corner of William and Charlton Streets. It was completed in 1911 and still houses the editorial and business offices of the Press. Princeton University Press published its first scholarly books in 1912: John Witherspoon, *Lectures on Moral Philosophy*, edited by Varnum Lansing Collins, and Allan Marquand, *Della Robbias in America*.

The generally accepted founding date of 1905 makes Princeton University Press the sixth oldest, continuously functioning university press in North America, following the Johns Hopkins Press (1878), the University of Chicago Press (1891), the University of California Press (1893), Columbia University Press (1893), and the University of Toronto Press (1901). Cornell University and the University of Pennsylvania had established presses in 1869 and 1890, respectively, but they failed and were not re-established until the late 1920's.

See [Charles] Whitney Darrow, *Princeton University Press: An Informal Account . . .* (Princeton, N. J., 1951), and Gene R. Hawes, *To Advance Knowledge: A Handbook on American University Press Publishing* (New York, 1967), pp. 29-40.

E N C L O S U R E

Charles Whitney Darrow to the Stockholders of Princeton University Press

[Princeton, N. J.] August 1, 1907.

I herewith submit the financial report of The Princeton University Press for the fiscal year ending Aug. 1, 1907.

From the date of purchasing the Robinson Press we have been cramped for room and it was impossible to accommodate the Zapf plant which had to be moved to this building on Nov. 1st. Accordingly an arrangement was made whereby Mr. Robinson rebuilt the old electric lighting plant building in the rear of the building we have been occupying. The work on this was completed Jan. 1st, and the rent we pay for the addition is a fixed percentage of the cost of the building, making our entire rent at the present time $784.00, this being but $84.00 more than we paid Mr. Zapf and Mr. Robinson before the addition was built.

Our present lease extends to Aug. 1, 1908, and we have the privilege of renewal year by year for the period of five years at the same annual rental. This addition gives us a complete press-room on the ground floor, besides a stock room and bindery. All machinery is now in this wing of the building, and has both gas engine and motor attachments. The building is fire-proof.

The fourth floor of the old building has been partitioned off into two large rooms; one used for storage, and the other one, in front, is used as The Alumni Weekly editorial office. The third floor is used entirely for composition, and the second floor for office, with the exception of the one room in the rear which is devoted exclusively to poster work.

Last summer a superintendent was engaged to take direct charge of all the manufacturing details, and under him are a foreman of the composing room and a foreman of the press-room, both working foremen.

In the way of work we have done practically all the University and Seminary work with the exception of the University Catalogue. In addition, we are printing all the publications of the American Economic Association, The Princeton Theological Review, The Princeton Alumni Weekly, The Princeton Press, The Daily Princetonian, the Seminary Bulletin, also several books have been turned out, in addition to considerable job work. The only contract work we have lost since organization is the Nassau Literary Magazine.

We have been compelled to work out an entirely new office and shop system to suit the needs of our particular business, which has been very difficult as the business was old and established in its ways and had no system which we could use. After many revisions we now have in use a system which is very complete, and at the same time simple, by which we keep accurate record of all jobs going through the shop, and by which records are kept of the actual cost of each piece of work turned out.

Our books have not been all they should have been, and no one has been directly responsible for them. A new set has been started with the assistance of the auditors and is now in operation, and one clerk in the office will take entire charge of them.

Our present situation is a very complete plant, a suitable building, a very complete office system in good working order and a fair amount of regular work.

Three things are noticeably needed to complete the efficiency of the plant and secure the greatest possible results from the present operating expenses. These are

(1) Style
(2) Clean proofs–intelligently read
(3) More work

(1) By our lacking style I mean that the work does not show character or good taste and the office cannot furnish ideas. To secure the class of work we are best fitted to do it is necessary to turn out work which is artistic and in good taste which suits the subject matter. Our present superintendent,[1] while most faithful and reliable, is most lacking in this qualification, and there is no one else with the time or necessary ability to attend to this.

(2) With the amount of copy we are handling our proof reading has become a serious problem. All proofs have to be read by Mr. Huckin, the superintendent, whose time is more than filled without this work. He has neither the education nor experience necessary to proof reading, and lack of time causes hurry with resulting errors in the proofs which leave our office, and in the case of press proofs many forms have had to be re-run owing to errors. To have work leave our office with obvious errors in punctuation, English, and spelling, even though it is following the copy, works harm to the office whose imprint it bears, while on the other hand customers with a quantity of work go to the office in which they have confidence and where they can get good service.

(3) We have a plant, office, and organization, which, with scarcely any extra expense, can easily handle more than twice the amount of work we are now doing. Instead of employing twelve to fifteen men we could and should, with our present accommodations and expense of management, employ between twenty-five and thirty. Our operating expenses which cannot be lessened and still do the work in hand, are too great in proportion to the amount of work we do.

To remedy these difficulties.

First as to style. This, I feel, will have to be where our growth is most gradual, but at the same time should be taken in hand to some degree at the present time and watched very carefully. We must have a new superintendent. We are paying $1404.00 per year, and to secure a man with the experience and education and other qualifications necessary we must pay at least $2000 per year. We cannot afford this at the present time, nor can we until our work increases considerably. Mr. Huckin is very reliable and faithful, and personally I need the assistance of a man I can rely on absolutely, and I would respectfully suggest that I be empowered to look for such a man during the coming

[1] Charles Huckin.

Woodrow Wilson

James Bryce and Woodrow Wilson at the dedication of the Mather Sundial

McCosh Hall, erected 1906

Cleveland Hoadley Dodge

Melancthon Williams Jacobus

Paul van Dyke

Henry Fairfield Osborn

Hamilton Hotel, Bermuda

Mary Allen Hulbert Peck and Woodrow Wilson
at Shoreby, Paget West, Bermuda

Jessie Woodrow Wilson

year and engage him for the first of next August, provided our increased work warrants the expenditure. Furthermore, we need one most competent pressman and one most competent compositor, men who are worth $20 to $25 per week and who will act as working foremen. Our force at the present time is composed of sober, reliable men, but men without any outside experience in fine work and with absolutely no idea of style. To secure men ourselves to take these positions and place them over men who have held these positions for years requires a superintendent with tact and force, such a man with the practical knowledge to take most strenuous action if the placing of new men and the removing of the old causes trouble with the Union. I do not have enough confidence in the ability of Mr. Huckin to warrant these changes now.

Another step of no less importance, but possible to carry through practically at once, is one which combines the solution of the proof reading problem, together with the solution of the question of style and good form and taste so far as the University is concerned, and also partially answers the question of how to bring the University Press in closer touch with the University. This recommendation, which is not only suggested from our own point of view, but after also consulting the needs and interests of the University, is that a proof-reader be engaged as a regular employee of The Princeton University Press who is educated and has had experience in proof reading. In the second place, after consultation with President Wilson I should suggest that the Company propose to him that he request the head of the English department to appoint a committee of three to make a "Style Book" for distribution in the faculty and among the University officers and the styles therein set down as regards spelling, punctuation, capitalization, abbreviations, etc., to be followed in all University work and office publications and forms in order to secure uniformity, which is now utterly lacking. This book, in the form of a recommendation or report, to be acted upon by the English department, and then submitted to the President for approval who would authorize the printing of this and instruct us to follow its form in all University work. As the next step I would recommend that it be suggested to the President that he appoint a member of the faculty as University editor, such a man having already been suggested who is eminently qualified in experience, good judgment, and interest in the subject. Such a man would supervise the work of our proof-reader so far as the proof reading of the University work is concerned. He would at the start revise all forms, decide on the changes in type, size of page, margins and such incidentals, with the object of making this work uniform and giving it a style peculiar to Princeton University. After such a style had been decided by the University editor this style would be followed thereafter by our proof-reader who would refer to the editor any question which might not have been already covered.

This plan has been suggested to President Wilson, who is very much interested and who will be pleased to consider this on his return if the Company think best to report to him on the subject. On a much larger scale this idea is in operation in the University of Chicago Press. If any of the University departments or the Graduate Schoold [School] should do anything in the way of publishing texts, as has been talked of, this idea of a University editor could be enlarged upon to meet the requirements of the work.

In looking ahead and considering the possibility of work in Princeton we must rely largely upon the growth of the Graduate School, which will doubtless add considerable work for us in printing, and possibly in publishing. There is a certain amount of work in Princeton which is at the present time being done in Trenton and other places, but in most cases it is most undesirable work and a very cheap grade of work on which it is hard for us to figure. The work of the undergraduate organizations amounts to considerable in the course of a year, and during the past year we have had our share. But this class of work cannot be relied upon, in as much as the management or editorial board of each organization changes each year, and they are, as a rule, a very hard class to please, and very often new managers change the place of publication, or of having their work done, rather for the sake of a change than for any benefits they may derive from the change. This class of work is also very poor pay and very often it is impossible to collect any money. The town work is a very small consideration.

Outside of the growth of the University there is one other field which will probably bring results. We have found it possible to compete with New York and Philadelphia printers, and I feel we should secure a considerable amount of business from personal work in New York, which I am hoping to handle during the coming year in connection with work on The Alumni Weekly.

It has been suggested that The University Press be brought in closer touch with the University whereby we could do a more definite work for the University, the Press at the same time reserving its actual independence and be conducted on a strictly business basis. To accomplish this, and at the same time not to interfere with the present organization, two steps have suggested themselves to me.

The first step has already been spoken of—to cooperate with the University in the establishment of a "University Style" and in the appointment of a University editor.

The second step is a financial one whereby the Company would give to the University, either yearly or semi-yearly, whatever percentage of the profits from the business they felt could be taken out of the business at the time, and this money apportioned in some suitable way to the various departments of the University to assist them in printing important bulletins, theses, and other work which they would not be able to print without this help. In this way would our profits return to the University in the same way as if the University owned the Press, and would enable them to do considerable important work they otherwise could not do, while at the same time the organization of The University Press would remain as at present.

This appears to me as accomplishing all we wish to accomplish without transferring the Press to the University, which does not seem to be desirable or practicable for the present at least.

Respectfully submitted,

C. Whitney Darrow Manager.

FINANCIAL STATEMENT

PRINCETON UNIVERSITY PRESS, JULY 30, 1907.

ASSETS.

Accounts Receivable	$3,870.80	
Plant Account	13,336.45	
Cash Balance	1,380.46	
Inventory	1,881.95	$20,469.66

LIABILITIES.

Capital Stock	$16,500.00	
Accounts Payable	649.24	
Assets in excess of Liabilities	3,320.42	$20,469.66

Note—To Assets should be added Unexpired Insurance $102.20

Inventory consists of Stock on hand $1,310.19
and unfinished work 571.76

Plant Account includes Betterments, Cost of Moving, less 10% of original estimated value for depreciation.

THOMPSON & SUMMERFELDT.
Auditors.

TRS (WP, DLC).

From Sir William Mather, with Enclosure

Lyndhurst, Hants.
My dear President Wilson Augt 22d 1907

Your letter of the 7th Augt. gave me great satisfaction & pleasure. It is sure now that Bryce will fix a day, for he wrote most hopefully in that belief a short time ago, since which he has communicated with you. About the date I received your good news, Bryce would receive a letter from me in which I stated that he was indispensable. I have therefore quite concluded that you & he will "fix it up" somewhere about the early part of November.

Trusting to this, I enclose my formal letter presenting the Sun-dial to you on behalf of the University, and accompanied by a detailed description of the Corpus Christi Dial.

I have dated my letter the "*Fourth of July*"—the immortal day, because my gift is to represent the whole-hearted recognition of Englishmen of that great event, which, while severing us outwardly, has united us inwardly forever. You see, I can choose any date for my *formal* presentation, because the Dial was delivered in May or June. I trust you will share my desire that the "Fourth of July" shall appear in the record as the date of the gift, while the unveiling being a separate affair stands by itself.

I have been compelled to decide this matter now, because my letter to you will appear & also the description of the original Dial, as a brochure which I am having specially printed & bound, & of which you will receive copies to distribute on the day of the unveiling to your Trustees & Faculty. It will take considerable time to get this brochure completed, so I have ventured to prepare the contents without delay & send you the matter as it will be printed.[1] Of course, I assume Bryce's presence as assured, & I am sending him by this mail, a copy of what I send you, so that he may understand the whole scheme.

We are in the New Forest—a land of pure delight. We greet you heartily one & all, & hope the "tonic" in the air of Adirondacks may arm you against all bodily ailments.

Very sincerely yrs W. Mather

ALS (WWP, UA, NjP).

[1] For a description of the brochure, see W. Mather to WW, Oct. 20, 1907, n. 1.

E N C L O S U R E

From Sir William Mather

My dear President, London. Fourth of July, 1907.

I ask you to accept on behalf of Princeton a replica of the famous Sun-dial at Corpus Christi College, Oxford, which I have had executed by eminent sculptors in London.

You did me the signal honour in 1905 of inviting me, on behalf of yourself and the Trustees, to attend your Commencement to receive the Honorary degree of Doctor of Laws on that occasion.

I heartily responded to your invitation, and accompanied by Lady Mather and my daughter, spent amongst the assembled Trustees, Faculty, Graduates, Alumni, and their friends, a week of such infinite delight and interest, combined with the highest appreciation of the honour you conferred on me, that I shall ever regard the event as the most gratifying and memorable of my life.

In wandering around the lovely grounds of Princeton, and reading in its buildings its history, commencing with the foundation of the College in British Colonial days, from simple "Old Nassau" to the most recent splendid architectural erections; and further in reading the terms of the Royal Charter which conferred on Princeton the rank of Oxford as to its degree and purpose as a classical University, I conceived the idea of sending over from England on my return some object that should symbolise the connection not only between Oxford and Princeton, but between Great Britain and America.

Under the guidance of the eminent architect Mr. Inigo Triggs, I found the famous Turnbull Sun-dial in the quadrangle of Corpus Christi College, Oxford.

It seemed to me to be a singularly appropriate object, if reproduced in all its dignity and quaint impressiveness, to form a lasting monument in the beautiful Princeton grounds, of the imperishable attachment between the inhabitants of the Old Country and the New, as well as a symbol of the common purpose of Oxford and Princeton in spreading universal knowledge and high ideals of life amongst the youth of either nation from generation to generation as the Sun-dial marks the passing hours.

Alike in origin under British Royal Charters, though differing in dates, and not withstanding the historic evolution which has substituted the glorious and independent American nation for a British Colony, Oxford and Princeton remain united in close allegiance to the spirit of knowledge, culture and human progress.

I trust the noble and singularly interesting column I have sent to you may ever be regarded,—by the continuous stream of young

Americans who for generations to come will derive from their Alma Mater, the highest culture and ideals of life and duty to their country,—as an impressive memorial of the indissoluble bonds which, founded in a common ancestry, will forever preserve Great Britain and America one people in making for the regeneration of mankind by promoting peace, goodwill amongst men, and glory to God in the Highest.

Sun-dials from time immemorial have marked the time for all peoples. I venture to quote the quaint and pr[e]gnant words of Charles Lamb in connection with their uses in past ages:

"What a dead thing is a clock, with its ponderous embowelments of lead or brass, its pert or solemn dulness of communication, compared with the simple altar-like structure and silent heart language of the old Dial! If its business use be superseded by more elaborate inventions, its moral use, its beauty, might have pleaded for its continuance."

The Corpus Christi Sun-dial aptly illustrates this excellent sentiment. The Pelican standing on a terrestrial globe on the summit of the column is symbolical of the spiritual significance of Our Lord's life of sacrifice that future generations might live more nobly and abundantly. For the symbolical meaning of the rest of the column I refer you to the accompanying detailed description.

I should like to record the fact that Dr. Case, the President, and the Fellows of Corpus Christi College, Oxford, graciously granted me permission for the replica to be perfectly carried out under the direction of the architect Mr. Triggs, and offered every possible facility for the work by reference to old manuscripts in the College Library descriptive of the old Dial.

It is a matter of the deepest satisfaction to me that my distinguished friend, His Excellency the Right Honourable James Bryce D.C.L[.,] the British Ambassador in America, will perform the ceremony of unveiling the column and finally presenting it to Princeton. Very Sincerely yours William Mather

TLS (WWP, UA, NjP). Enc.: "Description of the Sun-dial, in the Quadrangle of Corpus Christi College, Oxford," T MS (WWP, UA, NjP).

From Lawrence Crane Woods

Port Carling, Muskoka Lakes, Canada.

My dear Dr. Wilson, August 24th [1907]

Your letter of the nineteenth has been forwarded to me here. Allow me to say at once that to serve you or Princeton in the slightest is only a pleasure to me.

While I judge from your letter that there is no urgency in the matters I write to say that I will be able upon my return to make rather a complete report to you. I knew Mr. [Henry Jones] Ford *personally* as well as by reputation when in Pittsburg. He lived in Sewickley some years ago. Mrs. Woods and I both recall the daughter who mingled with the nicest people. I should suspect that Mr. Ford a newspaper man, moving more or less frequently from city to city[,] was somewhat Bohemian in manner of living. But personally he is a most scholarly and quiet unassuming gentleman. I shall write you fully in a few weeks and meanwhile enclose a letter from our Secretary Mr. Duff[1] who forwarded your letter to me. Duff is a thoughtful level headed fellow whose opinion is valuable and will keep silence.

My brother,[2] who knows Mr Ford and perhaps his family, is now with his family at Lake Placid Club, *Essex Co.* I do not know whether or not that is near you but as I know what a pleasure it would be to them to see you and your family and how much clearer picture you could get of Mr Ford and his family by talking with some one[,] I have taken the liberty of forwarding your letter to him.

I wrote you the other day hoping you were in these regions and I might have the pleasure of seeing you.

I am most deeply interested and frankly *concerned* over the "Quad" proposals. From my correspondence I believe that considerable patient education will be essential to secure the completely *hearty* loyal support of the great body of our very best alumni; those who have been most generous in giving time and money to Princeton.

Believing thoroughly that you are right in your policies I should like to be in as intelligent position as possible to support you in Pittsburg and elsewhere. If you see my brother Edward and feel disposed to do so I should appreciate your talking fully with him who is deeply interested

With most cordial best wishes,

Sincerely, Lawrence C. Woods

ALS (WP, DLC).

1 William M. Duff to L. C. Woods, Aug. 21, 1907, TLS (WP, DLC).

2 Edward Augustus Woods, manager of the Equitable Life Assurance Society agency in Pittsburgh.

From Henry Janeway Hardenbergh

My dear Sir: New York. Aug. 26th, 1907

I have delayed replying to your favor of the 13th inst. as I had in mind to make another visit to Princeton, which was accomplished on Saturday in company with Mr. Palmer, at which time we went over the ground very carefully and thoroughly in company with Mr. Bunn who had set the stakes showing the exact position of the building in accordance with the two schemes.

You will be pleased to learn that we agreed that the site as chosen by you and the Board, would be entirely satisfactory, and for my own part, I am pleased to waive any objection which I may have had at the time of writing. This decision would seem to clear the ground for a start upon the work at a very early date.

My plans and specifications are now virtually ready to be placed in the hands of the Contractors for estimating, and this will be done at once. Mr. Palmer seems anxious to get under way at the earliest moment, and I am wholly in sympathy with him in this matter, in order that as much work as possible can be accomplished before Winter weather retards us in any way.[1]

TL (WP, DLC).

[1] The balance of this letter is missing.

From Stephen Squires Palmer

My dear Dr. Wilson: New York, August 27, 1907.

Referring to my letter of 19th instant, Mr. Hardenbergh and myself were in Princeton on Saturday last. The two lines were staked out and we both agree and accept the line as suggested by Mr. Thompson, of which Mr. Hardenbergh has advised you.

I am still without your permission to commence operations, and wish very much that you would be good enough to authorize me to go ahead with the building. As soon as I have your authority to proceed, I shall sign the contracts and push matters as much as possible.

As it is, I have had a clerk of construction under retainer since August first, and as heretofore written you, we must be up and doing if the building is to be completed and ready for occupancy when the University opens in the Autumn of 1908.

Kindest remembrances to Mrs. Wilson, Harry Thompson and your own good self. Sincerely yours, S S Palmer

TLS (WP, DLC).

From William Belden Reed, Jr.[1]

Dear Sir: White Plains, N. Y. August 27, 1907

At the usual summer meeting of the Board of Governors of the Elm Club held recently, your letter of July 29th to Mr. Imbrie explaining some matters connected with your proposed "quad" system was read with considerable interest. After discussing this matter at some length I was asked, as Chairman of the Board, to write to you the following questions which occurred to different members of the Board as being important and covering points upon which we were ignorant.

I, therefore, submit these questions to you with a request that you answer same at your convenience in order that we may be in possession of as much information as possible regarding this proposed change.

I.—In the event of a change to the "quad" system where would the ownership of the property be vested? Would it be in the University itself? or in the "quad"? which would be the outgrowth of an existing club? Who would assume the fixed charges such as mortgage interest if a mortgage should exist? In the event of the property being vested in the University itself how would the compensation to be received by the existing club be arrived at? In most cases the Alumni, either by subscription ot [or] otherwise, have paid for each property, or the equities in the properties as they now stand, for which they receive the benefits of the clubs as places to return to at Commencement and other times of the year. What would be the supposed position taken by these Alumni, many of whom have subscribed large amounts for the privilege of returning to the Club, either removed entirely, or rendered unattractive by new surroundings? Will the "quad" system be intended to provide shelter for graduates returning at Commencement?

II—What provision would be made for Freshmen between the time of entrance and the time of their being assigned to a "quad" since the present commons is to be abolished?

III—Would it be possible for the present club to maintain a certain amount of its individuality and still become part of the "quad" system?

IV—Is the "quad" system intended to displace the present class spirit working up certain rivalry between the "quads" and thereby taking the place of the clubs in College politics?

V—If members are assigned to certain "quads" according as they elect certain lines os [of] study is it not probable that men so assigned will be socially uncongenial? and if so, will they not segregate along social lines? and if so, what provision is to be made for such social segregation?

VI—If men may be transferred from one "quad" to another, who is to do the transferring and upon whose initiative, and how will it be determined as to where he will be transferred?

VII–Is there to be an initiation fee similar to the one now charged by the clubs? If so, and transfers permitted, to which "quad" does the initiation fee belong?

VIII–Would the assignment of "quads" include the assignment of room-mates? Would men who wish to be room-mates, or "quad" mates have any opportunity to room together?

IX–How would the cost of living in "quads" compare with the present system of Dormitory and Club? What would become of men, such as our now club managers, who cannot afford to pay the board charged by the clubs?

X–If an existing club without a club house of permanent construction went into the "quad" system what provision would be made for building a permanent home when it became necessary, and upon whom would the burden fall?

XI–Is it proposed to take in eventually all of the clubs which now exist? If so, will they be taken in all at the same time? If they are taken in one at a time what is to be a status of those remaining out till along toward the last?

XII–Would Undergraduates be forbidden to join in social organizations similar to the present clubs by being forced to sign an agreement similar to the one now existing covering Greek Letter Fraternities?

XIII–Would the members of "quads" have the choosing of the Faculty member, or members, who is to live with them, or would he, or they, be assigned to the "quad," or "quads"? If one were selected, or assigned, who prooved [proved] uncongenial could he be removed? and by what process?

XIII [XIV]–If the members of any club refuses [refuse] to sanction the merging of their club into a "quad" could, or would, the University authorities prevent a club from electing men upon graduation and run the "quad" as graduate club entirely?

Yours very truly, William B. Reed, Jr.

TLS (WP, DLC).

1 Princeton 1896, Vice-President and Treasurer of the White Plains Construction Co.

From Harry Howard Armstrong[1]

Dear Sir: [Oakmont, Pa.] Aug. 29th, 1907

My position as travelling engineer of our company, since my graduation in 1905, has kept me in touch with many alumnae in this section of the country. Moreover my brother Wm. M. Armstrong 1907 has kept me informed regarding Princeton life during '06 & '07, and in addition to this B. M. Price '04 has kept the Oxford idea before my eyes. He is my next door neighbor. Naturally the purposed quadrangle system holds the center of the platform just now and the general ideas that occupy attention among the alumnae seem to be these:

Princetons people, her alumnae, are most loyal to their alma mater and to each other for the reason that Princeton has instilled traditional ideals in them that are part of their lives. These graduates would like to have more time and opportunity to think over and discuss the quad. system in order that they can better lend aid and advise to their President and the Board of Trustees.

The alumnae I have seen are unanimously in favor of stamping out "club politics" but with the least possible injury to "club social life and spirit"; these latter being the hub in the wheel of Princeton loyalty.

The following questions seem to be in most of the graduates minds regarding the new system: "Will there be sufficient of interest in things intellectual to cement the men together in their own quads if they have no voice in the selection of them?" "A socially uncongenial quad. would ruin it intellectually." "Can poor men attend Princeton with any more or less advantage than formerly?"

"Will the mixing of classes cause Princeton to become (as is Chicago Univ.) a machine shop to turn out students who have few intimate associations or friendships among themselves?" "Will Princeton individuality be lost?"

"Can we raise the money?"

Personally I believe the new system will place Princeton men in the highest and broadest intellectual class, if the social life can be attractively adjusted. If the alumnae have time to consider they will be able assistants.

Yours sincerely

H. Howard Armstrong. Class of 1905

ALS (WP, DLC).

[1] Princeton 1905, engineer with the Pressed Radiator Co. of Pittsburgh.

To Frederic Yates

My dear Yates: St. Hubert's, N. Y. August 30th, 1907.

. . . I cannot tell you how we enjoy the sweet and generous letters that come to us from Mrs. Yates[1] and you or how often and with what deep affection we think of you.

I have been working all summer in the forenoons, putting into shape some lectures which I delivered last spring in New York at Columbia University, and which must now be published. When they are in book form I will send you a copy. They are about the Government of the United States.

This Adirondack region is full of tonic air. I have done almost all of my work out of doors, and think that I am quite fit to go back to my winter's work, which will begin now in two or three weeks.

We caught some glimpses of you through the Harpers' letters, and I need hardly say that they were very charming glimpses. I have been homesick for Rydal all summer and don't see how it is going to be possible for me to keep many summers away from it. All join me in most affectionate messages to all three of you, and I am always

Your sincere friend, Woodrow Wilson

TLS (F. Yates Coll., NjP).
1 These letters are missing.

To William Belden Reed, Jr.

My dear Mr. Reed: St. Hubert's, N. Y. August 31st, 1907.

I am very glad indeed to reply, so far as I can, to the questions contained in your letter of August 27th. Most of your questions refer to matters which have not yet been directly considered by the Board of Trustees, and therefore I can only give you by way of answer my own personal judgment as to how the plans should be carried out.

Assuming that you have a copy of the questions you have asked in your letter, I shall reply to them by number.

1st. In the event of a change to the quad system, it would be my idea that the property of each club that chose to come into the system should be vested in a small Board of Trustees, the majority of whom should be chosen by the present authorities of the club, and who should have the right after a certain period of time to elect their own successors.

Of course, the arrangements in regard to property rights in the case of a quad formed out of a club would be different from the arrangements made in respect of the quads formed by the University itself out of its own property. I hope that it is generally understood that it has been no part of the purpose of the new plan to get control of the club properties. The plan of course would be greatly simplified and its execution greatly facilitated if the University could simply proceed to carry it out by itself, but I have not felt that it would be right to ignore the clubs and not give them a full opportunity to become the partners of the University in this change and thereby retain at any rate their historical continuity. I should hope that the University authorities themselves would assume such fixed charges as mortgage interest, if a mortgage should exist. The answer to the rest of your first question seems to me to be contained in the Memorandum concerning the quads which I sent to the several clubs at Commencement. For fear you have not a copy of this memorandum at hand, I am sending you a copy under another cover for convenience of reference.

2nd. With regard to the provision to be made for freshmen, I should hope that there would be no more time between the date of their entrance and the date of their assignment to a quad than was unavoidable, and that it would be at the most only a few days in the case of men not already assigned before they came to Princeton.

3rd. I should think that under the system of separate trustees which I have suggested, the present clubs could maintain a certain amount of individuality in the development of their property and in their relation to the quad system. That would largely depend upon the way in which the matter was handled.

4th. The quad system is not intended to displace the present class spirit. For my own part, I should do everything possible to maintain the present class spirit. I think that the division into quads would be less likely to weaken that spirit than the present tendencies of our university life.

5th. Members of the University would certainly in no case be assigned to quads according to the lines of study they elected. That would be a great and fundamental mistake. Each quad should, as far as possible, be a small cross-section of the University.

6th. If men are transferred from one quad to another, it should be done under the superintendence of a committee of the faculty and generally upon the initiative of the men who wish to be transferred.

7th. There would be no initiation fee for entrance into the quads.

8th. The assignment to quads would not include the assignment of room-mates. That would be managed by the choice of the men themselves; and I should hope that by a reasonable system of transfers men who wished to be quad-mates could be put together. The only thing to guard against, as I said in my letter to Mr. Imbrie, would be any tendency for a particular set to concentrate upon one quad.

9th. I am confident that the cost of living in the quads would certainly be considerably less than the present cost of dormitory and club life combined. The men, such as our present club managers, who cannot afford to pay the board charged by the clubs could quite certainly be assigned such duties in connection with the administration of the quads as would enable them to earn the difference between what they were able to pay and the cost of the board.

10th. I do not see any way by which an existing club without a club-house could be afforded an opportunity of entering the quad system. But perhaps I do not understand just what you mean by a "club-house of permanent construction."

11th. The clubs taken into the system would certainly have to be taken in all at the same time. I should suppose that some of them would not feel that they had attained a sufficient strength or development to attempt the transformation.

12th. It would certainly be necessary to forbid undergraduates to join social organizations similar to the present clubs, but, as you will see by the closing part of the memorandum to which I have referred, this does not mean that they would be forbidden to join social organizations.

13th. Your thirteenth question also seems to me to be answered in the memorandum. I should hope that the assignment of faculty members to the quads developed from clubs would be made with the full approval of the trustees of the quads, who would be, at first at any rate, representatives of the present club organizations.

14th. I do not see that the University would have any right or power to prevent any one of the present clubs from staying out of the arrangement and constituting itself an exclusively graduate club.

Hoping that these answers will prove what you desire, and that you will not hesitate to put others if the Board of Governors of the Elm Club should be in doubt upon any other points,

With much regard,

Sincerely yours, [Woodrow Wilson]

CCL (WP, DLC).

To Stephen Squires Palmer

My dear Mr. Palmer: St. Hubert's, N. Y. August 31st, 1907.

Thank you very much indeed for your letter of August 27th. I had already heard from Mr. Hardenbergh of your visit to Princeton and of your decision about the position of the building, and received the news with the greatest satisfaction. I think that the position now agreed upon will prove permanently satisfactory and advantageous. I am only sorry that Harry Thompson and I were not there to enjoy the day with you and complete the business.

Things go very slowly in this vacation district, and it has taken me more than twenty-four hours since receiving your letter to find Harry Thompson, who is constantly off on expeditions of one kind or another. I have just seen him this morning, and we very cordially agree of course that the work should go forward at once at your convenience. You are fully authorized to take all the necessary steps and to proceed with the construction of the building. I am delighted to know that Mr. Hardenbergh's plans and specifications are ready for bids, and sincerely hope that nothing will turn up to disappoint you and us with regard to the early beginning of the work.

I cannot help expressing again my profound delight and gratitude that this splendid building is to be erected and that our Physics Department is to be put upon so perfect a footing of efficiency.

I am expecting to be back in Princeton by the eleventh, and hope sincerely that I shall have some early opportunity of seeing you again just for the pleasure of it.

Cordially and faithfully yours, [Woodrow Wilson]

CCL (WP, DLC).

To Royal Meeker

St. Hubert's, N. Y.

My dear Mr. Meeker: September 2nd, 1907.

It is hardly necessary to add anything to the letter which you must by this time have received.

I am very sorry indeed to be obliged to disappoint you in respect of the Bowdoin appointment, but I was very clear in my judgment that I could not in conscience impair the efficiency of our Department by releasing you from your engagement with the University at this time. It is my invariable principle not even to endeavor to retain anyone who does not wish to stay, and any request of this kind made to me before the end of June would certainly have been acquiesced in. But at this period of the year it would be impossible to fill your place, and I should be responsible for allowing the Department to limp painfully through a whole year because of what I fear would be a too weak compliance on my part.

I want to assure you again of the very high esteem in which we hold you at Princeton and of the very high value we place upon your services, and to say that I feel confident that it will be worth your while to remain with us and abide the chances of promotion at Princeton.[1]

Very sincerely yours, [Woodrow Wilson]

CCL (WWP, UA, NjP).

[1] Meeker remained a Preceptor and Assistant Professor at Princeton until 1913, when he was appointed United States Commissioner of Labor Statistics by President Wilson.

To Harry Howard Armstrong

St. Hubert's, N. Y.

My dear Mr. Armstrong: September 3rd, 1907.

Your interesting and important letter of August 29th has been forwarded to me here. I am sincerely interested to learn what you are doing and of the success you are meeting with.

I wish very much that I might have a personal talk with you about our new plans at Princeton; they are so hard to explain satisfactorily in a letter. But I shall take the greatest pleasure in answering any question you may ask with regard to them. I can assure you that no haste will be made in carrying out these plans and that an abundance of time will be allowed for a very full and thorough understanding and discussion of the whole matter before any step is taken. That has been our purpose from the first, and I have been expecting to devote this next winter to discussing the matter with anyone who cares to discuss it with me. You need not fear that the alumni will not be given abundant opportunity to express their views.

My general position in the matter is that it is not possible to build a true university spirit, I mean a true spirit of study and intellectual achievement, on a life which is organized entirely by independent undergraduate action. I agree with you that the present clubs supply something which is extremely valuable, but I think that the University itself could supply the same thing through a quardangle [quadrangle] life which would be a reproduction of club life on a larger scale without the exclusion of the men now practically excluded from university life altogether. I think that a free discussion of this matter can bring us all together.

In reply to your specific questions, I would say that it will not depend entirely upon interest in things intellectual whether the men in the several quadrangles are cemented together. It will depend rather upon a combination of intellectual interests with free self-government. I believe that the feeling of intimate connection with the University itself in the government of the quads, together with the intellectual interests which will center there, will be a most powerful cement. Of course, a certain amount of discretion must be used in the allotment of the men to the several quads, and it would be perfectly possible to see that no quad gained the reputation of being socially uncongenial.

2nd. I should say that poor men could attend Princeton under the new arrangement more easily and with greater advantage than formerly, partly because there will be more ways in which in connection with the administration of the University they can in part pay for their board, and because the men who are under the present arrangement excluded from the clubs because they cannot afford to enter them will have the full advantages of university life and associations.

3rd. I am confident that the mixing of classes in the quads will have no tendency to make Princeton like Chicago or any other university, and that Princeton individuality will be enhanced rather than lost, if the scheme is carried out as I have conceived it.

4th. I think that we can raise the money, not from the alumni, who are already carrying a sufficient burden, but from others who can afford to support it.

I have the greatest confidence that the social side can be arranged to the common satisfaction, and I really do not see any other way by which club politics can be eliminated and Princeton men raised to a leading place among the intellectual influences of the country. If we could add real scholarly attainment to the present splendid manly spirit and capacity at Princeton, we could hold the front rank within a single college generation.

Thanking you most sincerely for your letter,

Always cordially yours, Woodrow Wilson

TLS (WC, NjP).

From William Belden Reed, Jr.

White Plains, N. Y.

My dear Doctor Wilson: September 3, 1907

I acknowledge receipt of yours of August 31st in reply to mine of August 27th and wish to thank you, both personally, and in behalf of the other members of our Board for your prompt and full reply to our questions.

Regarding my tenth question, I probably did not make myself as clear as I should have. By club house of "permanent construction" I meant one of the general character of Ivy, and Cottage; that is, one built of such material as to be of a permanent nature as contrasted with those frame structures which if the club should perpetuate those in any form would some day have to be re-built and probably have to be either brick or stone structure. I wondered on whose shoulders the expense connected with this re-building would fall.

In your reply to my twelfth question you stated that it would be necessary to forbid undergraduates to join social organizations similar to the present clubs, but that they need not be forbidden to join social organizations. What would be the nature of such social organizations that would be permitted to exist under the proposed new regime? Would they be allowed to have club houses and what would be their standing in the College community?

I should like to ask one question for myself and not as an officer of the Club; and that is, how far has the arrangement for this quad system progressed? Is it to be considered as an assurred thing? or is it open for discussion? and should the discussion show a predominance of opinion against it, would it then be dropped? whould [Should] all the clubs decline to become part of this system and the University organize quads on their own account, would the University authorities then keep undergraduates from becoming members of the present clubs?

Again thanking you for your trouble, and regretting having broken into your much needed vacation, I am,

Yours very sincerely, William B. Reed, Jr.

TLS (WP, DLC).

John Grier Hibben to Ellen Axson Wilson

Dear Mrs. Wilson Greensboro [Vt.] Sep 4/07

I reached Greensboro yesterday morning about noon. Jenny had walked over to Greensboro Bend to meet me. It was then raining so furiously that we could not walk back as we had planned, but were compelled to accept the humiliation of a ride in a chance conveyance going our way. As I look back over the week just passed, it seems as though a whole summer had been crowded into a few days. I do not see how I could have accomplished more or have enjoyed myself more completely in every way. You & Woodrow were indeed very kind to enlarge your family circle so as to include me, for I did not feel like an ordinary guest, but as one of you. And that privilege I regard most highly. I hope that my erratic orbit did not cause too many perturbations in your orderly & well regulated household. Will you kindly thank your two excellent & thoughtful housekeepers for their good care of me. I see in my mind future homes which will give a larger scope for their newly acquired experience of this summer. Where they will be, only Ouija knows. I sincerely hope that Woodrow is much better than when I left, & not attempting too much for the remaining days of his vacation. It will be a great pleasure to see you all so soon again in Princeton. With much love to you all, & my warmest regards to Miss Hoyt.[1]

Ever faithfully yours John Grier Hibben

ALS (WP, DLC).

[1] Mary Eloise Hoyt or Florence Stevens Hoyt.

To William Belden Reed, Jr.

St. Hubert's, N. Y.

My dear Mr. Reed: September 6th, 1907.

Allow me to acknowledge the receipt of your letter of September 3rd, and to thank you for the fuller explanation of your tenth question.

I should expect that if a club which had not already built in a permanent style should come into the new arrangement, its quadrangle would be constructed at first in a way that would be in keeping with its present building, and I should confidently expect that within a very few college generations the graduates of the quadrangle would subscribe to put it in permanent form.

As to the new social organizations which are likely to spring up when the quadrangular organization has taken its form, I feel that none of us can predict exactly what shape they will take. They would certainly spring up in some spontaneous and natural manner, and it would be possible to be guided with regard to the question of their development by the circumstances of the quadrangle life. I do not feel that we can predict the process with any degree of certainty or that it is desirable to do so. All that I meant to indicate was that the new plan would certainly not be meant to exclude the natural association of congenial men.

As to the question which you ask for yourself rather than for your club, I would say that it was understood at the last Board meeting that the Board had expressed its approval of the principle of this change, but it was also distinctly understood that it was to be put before the alumni for the fullest discussion, and I can assure you that no definite step will be taken toward the execution of the plan until the fullest opportunity for discussion has been offered, the Trustees being sincerely desirous of being guided as much as possible by the opinion of the alumni. As yet, I do not think that the plan is even thoroughly understood by the alumni. I have not myself yet had an opportunity of explaining it to them or discussing it with them.

If the plan should be carried into execution, it could be executed more easily without the coöperation of the clubs than with it, but I think we are all agreed that it would be a matter of the deepest disappointment if the clubs should disappear and lose their individuality entirely, by not becoming parts of the future life of the University. That was the spirit in which the committee made the suggestions contained in the report, and the spirit in which I made the suggestions contained in the memorandum sent to the clubs.

Allow me to thank you for the candor and fullness of your letters. Sincerely yours, [Woodrow Wilson]

CCL (WP, DLC).

From David Benton Jones

My dear doctor: Chicago September 6, 1907.

Your note of the 4th has just come. I can meet with the committee[1] at any time on sufficient notice to reach Princeton at time appointed. It is so important that a meeting should be held, and if possible a full meeting, I shall consider any date you name as a fixed engagement.

I have not written you during the Summer, and I hope that others have done so in a limited way only, as complete rest is the best thing for the work of the year. I have no preference as to the meeting place. New York or Princeton will suit me.

I have had some very gloomy letters during the Summer, one or two bordering on purple even. What has amazed me most in this matter is to find club members displaying the spirit of labor unions. Blind and deaf to every consideration, except to the continued domination of the clubs. Personal friendship, Princeton's glittering opportunity for almost dramatic leadership in a great work, the blighting of the intellectual interests of many of her best minds and finest spirits count for nothing—loyalty to the clubs, everything.

Will it be wiser, perhaps even necessary, that the committee should invite representatives of the clubs and certain members of the faculty to appear before it and make such statements as they wish to make and to give such answers as they can, to the charges brought against the club system? My own feeling is that this hearing should be granted. They complain of closure without debate of any kind.

The committee should be prepared to give the matter all the time necessary before the Board meets in October. If we meet about the middle of September in case all can come, it will enable us to determine what should be done, and leave time enough to do it before the meeting of the Board October 21st.[2]

Would it be possible to take the club memberships for the past five years and have a table compiled showing how many came from each of the five groupes into which the under-graduates are divided by the committee on examination and standing? This tabulation might not show anything one way or another.[3]

My conviction has been confirmed by everything that I have heard and inquired into during the Summer, that the Clubs, as now organized, must go, or Princeton cease to be an important element in University leadership in this country. I do not know where else the intel[l]ectually ambitious can go, but it will do them but little good to go to Princeton as now constituted. I am, of course, writing to you more frankly than it would be wise to repeat, but it is the way I feel about it.

I hope that the Summer has brought you renewed physical strength and rest of spirit. I hope you will be able to allow the other side to do all the fretting and fuming, and rest your case, that the Clubs, as at present constituted, must go, upon the simple statement that they are a blight upon the work of the institution, if it claims to be an institution of learning.

Very sincerely yours, David B. Jones.

TLS (WP, DLC).

1 That is, the Committee on the Supplementary Report of the President.

2 Actually, the board met on October 17.

3 For such an analysis, see WW to D. B. Jones, Sept. 26, 1907.

To Edwin Boone Craighead[1]

St. Hubert's, N. Y.

My dear President Craighead, 7 September, 1907.

Your kind letter of the second, just received,[2] makes me aware of a serious omission in my reply to your letter inquiring about men suited to succeed Professor Ficklen.[3] I did not realize that you might be asking his successor to come to you at once, and therefore did not say that I could not without upsetting the whole work of a very busy Department let any of the men I named go to you this session, or this university year.

Perhaps you understood that; but, in case you did not, I write these lines. If you could make shift with some temporary arrangement for this academic year, I should think that your chances of making a permanent arrangement that would be satisfactory would be greatly increased.

With much regard,

Sincerely Yours, Woodrow Wilson

WWTLS (LNHT).

[1] President of Tulane University.

[2] It is missing.

[3] This letter from President Craighead is also missing. John Rose Ficklen, Professor of History and Political Science at Tulane, had died on August 2, 1907.

From Joseph R. Wilson, Jr.

My dear brother: Nashville, Tenn. Sept. 7, 1907.

It has been a long time since I last heard from you but I am as much to blame as you, for my letters, like yours, have been few and far between.

I suppose you have returned by this time from your summer vacation wherever that may have been spent and are now preparing for the opening of the fall term. I hope your summer rest has been of great benefit and that you enter upon the arduous duties of the early fall feeling well prepared physically for the coming tasks.

My summer has, most of it, been spent in Nashville. Two weeks early in June I took a brief rest and we three went to Clarksville for the time. Last month Kate and Alice went to Clarksville again while I toiled away here through the summer heat. Fortunately mid-summer is generally a quiet time with the newspapers as well as with all other lines of business, so I had time to recuperate after my daily work. Our health has remained good during the summer and we are prepared for the coming season. Alice has entered school again and Kate is enthusiastic in her church work. Her friendly disposition has enabled her to make a wide circle of friends in Nashville and we are all three well contented in our home, our only regret being that we did not make the move ten years sooner than we did. It has been nearly three years since we came to Nashville and they have, we feel, been the most satisfactory years of our married life.

My work on the Banner is entirely congenial still and due appreciation has been shown by the management from time to time by the assignment of responsible work and more satisfactory salary. I am now assistant to the City Editor and have during the summer done desk work in the office, being thus placed in a position to demonstrate my ability to perform any duties in connection with the editorial or news work of the paper which might be given me. They seem to consider me as a sort of general utility man who can be worked in any position they desire to place me. Unfortunately, perhaps, for the newspaper profession, there are not many men of this character. I do not say this in a boastful spirit, but because I know that you will be interested in learning that I am making a success of my work. A new morning daily was recently started here, ["]The Tennessean," and they made me two flattering offers, one being the news editorship which, in rank, is next to that of managing editor. I did not favor the night work, however, and decided to remain with the Banner in whose financial stability I have entire confidence rather than to go with a paper which might not out-grow its swaddling clothes.

I have heard nothing of sister Annie for fully six months and would be glad to have her address so that I may renew at least an occasional correspondence. Please give me this information.

We are looking forward to your coming south early in November and certainly expect our usual visit from you enroute.[1] Would it not be possible for sister Ellie to come with you this time? I have received a pressing invitation to attend the Memphis meeting of the Princeton Alumni and hope to be able to make my arrangements to attend. I can get the necessary railroad transportation and the cost of the trip would therefore be nominal. The only obstacle I apprehend is the fact that Kate's oldest single brother, George [Wilson], who is now a civil engineer in Philadelphia, is to be married at Clarksville this fall, and the date may make it impossible for me to make both trips. You will stop here so if I should go to Clarksville and not to Memphis I would not thereby miss seeing you.

Please fine [find] time to write me soon and tell me all about yourself and yours. Kate joins me in much love to you all.

Your aff. brother, Joseph

TLS (WP, DLC).

[1] Wilson arrived in Memphis on November 8, 1907, to deliver several speeches there, including one to the Princeton Alumni Association of Tennessee on November 9. He arrived in Nashville on November 10 and stayed with Joseph R. Wilson, Jr., and his family until November 13. See the news reports printed in this volume between Nov. 8 and Nov. 12, 1907.

From Lawrence Crane Woods

My dear Dr. Wilson: Pittsburg, Sept. 9, 1907.

I appreciate your letter of the 30th ult. which reached me in Pittsburg, where I returned a week ago. From time to time I will secure further information which I hope will enable you to obtain quite a comprehensive view of Mr. Ford.

I am very sorry that I cannot have the pleasure of seeing you. As I wrote to Mr. [Robert Edwards] Annin the other day, I think it is exceedingly important that during the early fall now the whole situation among the alumni should be handled with the greatest delicacy and tact. Everyone of us who loves Princeton should be very temperate in his remarks, and should refuse to form or express any opinion until he is sure it is an intelligent one. I think it is fortunate the summer vacation came in so that the graduates and undergraduates had an opportunity to cool off before they were given any opportunity of expressing themselves, because, (without wishing to discourage you in the least, which I know would be very difficult to do as you are not the kind of man to be easily discouraged, but more that there may be no danger of your not having a perfectly clear view of the situation,) I may say that from what I have gathered–all over the country,–misunderstanding your views and ideas, the alumni are by quite a large majority radically opposed to the plan, as *they* understand it.

I presume there will very shortly be a meeting of the Princeton Club here in Pittsburg, and if it is at all practicable, if necessary, I would gladly make a special trip to Princeton to be in position to discuss the matter intelligently here, although I should infinitely prefer that your plans had an abler and more forcible advocate. I am confident that, having thought out and carried to so successful conclusion the many splendid reforms you have made in Princeton, the present Quad plan is not impossible, and can and should be put through.

I can say frankly, however, that, recognizing the tremendous obstacles to its progress, it is only my confidence in you that enables me to take this optimistic view of the situation, and again I may say that the importance of patience and tact on the part of everyone who loves Princeton cannot be over estimated at this time.

I do not anticipate with pleasure the early copies of the Alumni Weekly as it would hurt me to see anything said there which we might all regret. Fortunately, I think Norris is a very level headed fellow and will control those columns pretty effectively.

At the same time it will be suicidal not to allow considerable latitude in the frank, open discussion of these plans.

I am very sorry to hear that you have been so occupied all summer. I fear that you have not secured the rest and strength that is not only so important to you but so vital to Princeton at this time. Very sincerely yours, Lawrence C. Woods

Pray pardon this hurriedly written and rather incoherent letter. Have been unusually busy since my vacation. LCW

TLS (WP, DLC).

Henry Burling Thompson to Cleveland Hoadley Dodge

Dear Cleve: [Wilmington, Del.] 9th Mo., 10th, 1907.

I know I am not to burden you with any discussion concerning "Quads," but believing you are living in the higher atmosphere of Saranac, which rests and stimulates the nerves, I venture to give you the following. It is my duty.

I kept off any serious talk with Wilson until just before leaving; then the necessity arose on account of a talk he had had with Hibben, who was staying with him, and, as Hibben quoted me, I had to substantiate his remarks.

To begin with, Wilson is not in as good physical or mental condition as I should like to see him. This subject has taken such a hold on him, he is nervous and excitable, but keeps all this well under restraint in discussion. This, in itself, is exhausting to his nerve force. His holiday has contained too much work and not enough relaxation. Of course, this is personal criticism,–possibly, irrelevant.

I started in by saying–"From what Hibben tells me, our point of view as to just what the action of the Board meant, differs. My point of view is this: I agree with you absolutely as to the present Club evils, and I advocate immediate reform. I believe in giving you the opportunity of bringing your report before the Princeton college world for full and free discussion; and, if the consensus of opinion is favorable to quads, and the money is forthcoming, I would probably accept the scheme; but I did not feel, in voting for this report, I committed myself absolutely and irrevocably for the idea." He [Wilson] said he interpreted the action of the Board as a *final endorsement of the idea*; whether the scheme could be carried out was contingent on the financial support received.

We then discussed the situation at length. I stated that popular clamor and opposition from the younger Club element would not influence my opinion. The standard of our judgment must be "What good or how much benefit the undergraduate is to receive from any change of systems." At the same time, the question of Alumni and Faculty support was a factor, and if the Alumni opinion is overwhelmingly in opposition to the scheme, and if an influential minority of the Faculty is opposed to it, it would be unwise to press the quad idea too far; but that our status could not be known until after a full and free discussion on the part of all interested was held and all views were obtained. This, of necessity, would be a matter of some months.

Wilson is somewhat inclined to make light of and override Alumni sentiment, on the ground if we are right they must be wrong.

I suggested one plan as a possible compromise, i. e., put all Freshmen and Sophomores in College, and give them separate Refectories and Commons Rooms. This would result in cultivating, in part, the academic spirit and break up Sophomore Clubs. Wilson agrees, in part, with this, in so far as cultivating a partial academic spirit in the two lower classes, but the essential idea of having all classes living on equality with the reflex of the more mature minds of the upper classes working on the lower seems to be his corner stone.

I would, in addition, control the selection, and, in part, the development and management of the Clubs, through Graduate and Faculty supervision.

Van Dyke and Hibben believe this plan to be a better solution of the problem, and likely to accomplish more in the development of the academic spirit than the present quad plan.

Do not understand that I am publicly advocating such a plan. I am, in so far as possible, trying to be loyal to the quad scheme, although not yet convinced it is the proper solution.

Again, I sincerely wish I could feel absolutely in sympathy with Wilson. The more I see of him the more I like him. He appeals to your affections. He is so sincere, so anxious for the promotion of higher ideals in the academic life, and with it all so strong and firm. I am convinced, however, that he is a bit one-sided on this question, due largely, to his incessant thought on the subject. He is discouraged over the attitude of some of the Trustees, for he feels that with their hearty approval and support, his scheme would go through. Now, I told him frankly there would be changes of opinion on the part of some of the Trustees, and that he would run up against opposition at the October meeting, and my advice would be that he should have a full discussion with your Committee before the Board meeting, for the members of that Committee will know unquestionably what constitutes Princeton public opinion, and would know how to advise and decide what the proper course would be before the Board.

It would seem unwise to do anything to injure further discussion on this question, unless some definite compromise could be arranged for in advance.

Pardon the length of this letter. You must acknowledge that I have not quite reached Bayard's [Bayard Henry's] length, as yet.

Very sincerely yours, Henry B Thompson

TLS (Thompson Letterpress Books, NjP); P.S. omitted.

Harold Griffith Murray to Andrew Clerk Imbrie

My dear Andy: New York, Sept. 12th, 1907.

Monday morning I leave for a week's sojourn at Princeton with headquarters at the Nassau Club. As you will not return from your vacation before Monday, I will not see you before leaving.

I have no desire at this time to add to the burden already laid upon you as a Trustee of the University of unraveling the snarl we have all fallen into over the quad system, but would like to present a few facts to you for your earnest consideration.

I am informed from credible sources that Dr. Wilson is counting more on the moral support which your approval of a quad system has given him than on that of any other man. It is natural that this should be so. You have been recently elected an Alumni Trustee from the largest Princeton center. Moreover, you won with a handsome majority the most aggressive and hard-fought campaign for a trustee that has ever been held, and it is right that the President should think that you voice the sentiment of your constituents.

Dr. Wilson has been in the woods all summer and has come in contact with very few Princetonians. He has undoubtedly received many communications on the subject of the quad system. Probably the majority of letters that he has received have been those of commendation. I am well convinced, after a careful canvass of a number of the Alumni in New York City and elsewhere that there is an overwhelming majority opposed to the introduction of the quad system at Princeton at this time or at any other, so far as we can now see. Of course, what the years may bring forth is problematical, and no intelligent man will undertake to judge what system of education would be wise to introduce in a university a score of years from now.

There are, of course, a number of hot-headed enthusiastic Alumni who condemn the quad scheme without giving any careful thought to the matter, or recognizing the fact that the President has made an honest effort to improve the academic and social conditions of the University. Let us count these men out and take only the judgment of men whom we know to be sane and sober in their judgment,–such men, for example as Jos. Shea, '85, Francis Speir, '77, Prof. Hibben, '82, Junius Morgan, '88, Geo. Fraser, '93, Charles Bostwick, '96, etc. I could mention nearly two hundred men with whom I have talked, whose judgment I respect, who are opposed to the quad scheme. I do not think that more than seven per cent of the men I have met or corresponded with, are in favor of Dr. Wilson's innovation.

From a financial standpoint, the quad system is impossible at present. I am positive that if the scheme goes through, the support of the Alumni will be withdrawn from the Committee of Fifty, and we will have to look elsewhere for funds to support the Preceptorial system. We are, at present, dependent on two men[1] to finance the University. Should the death of either of these men occur, it would be a fearful financial blow, outside of the loss of advice and work which each of these men give. We are endeavoring to-day to raise $3,000,000 towards the support of the Preceptorial system. We have raised some $600,-000. towards this amount, with some $400,000 more to go into dormitories, which will increase the revenues to an extent not exceeding $15,000. The $1,400,000. recently given to us has been for specific purposes, and while benefitting the University from a purely academic standpoint, to a very great degree, the gift has made little change in the financial condition.

The expense of maintenance is increasing annually. We have drained the Alumni pretty nearly dry at present, and we are in an extremely unsatisfactory financial condition. Moreover, it would be a breach of faith at this time to start the quad system. We induced Professor West to remain at Princeton agreeing when the Preceptorial system was on its feet, we would take up the graduate school. It seems to me that our duty is to make good this pledge.

I have been unable to collect additional subscriptions since Dr. Wilson's publication of the quad scheme, aggregating more than $300. My cancellations run into the thousands. My work at present is at a standstill and will be until this matter is definitely settled, one way or the other. Should the quad scheme go through, I do not expect to receive the support from the Alumni that we have had heretofore. Personally, as you know, I am opposed to the quad system at Princeton, outside of any financial reasons. I will not discuss this with you in a letter, because I have already done so verbally, and the arguments pro and con you are as familiar with as I am. I believe I am safe in saying that many of the Trustees are opposed to the scheme. Some of them have told me in confidence that they are not in favor of its introduction, and I beg of you, in all sincerity and friendship, to let Dr. Wilson know that a majority of the Alumni are opposed to the scheme.

Mr. Thompson, our Trustee from Wilmington, writes me that he has not met one in favor of the quad scheme. The Philadelphia Club are opposed to it; the Pittsburgh Club are opposed, and Mr. Speir, President of the Orange Club, tells me that he has not met any one in favor of it, and I have received letters from Alumni from various parts of the country, which cause me to think that the various sectional clubs are opposed.

If you are going to be in Princeton next week, I would be glad to make a date to meet you at the Nassau Club at Princeton in the evening, if you care to talk further with me in the matter.

While I should not hesitate to tell Dr. Wilson what I have written you, I should be glad if you will not quote me to him, as I believe it is the duty of the Secretary of the Committee of Fifty to keep out of any arguments of this sort, and it is difficult for me to divorce my official position from the personal one.

I hope that your vacation was a happy one, and that you have come back invigorated and eager to attack the year's work. When you get time, hope that you will come out to Flushing to see us. I will agree to leave the quad system alone on that occasion. Very sincerely, Big

TLS (A. C. Imbrie Coll., NjP).
[1] Moses Taylor Pyne and Cleveland Hoadley Dodge.

From Edmund Bayly Seymour, Jr.[1]

Dear Dr. Wilson, [Philadelphia] September 14, 1907.

At a meeting of the Princeton Club of Philadelphia held in July to discuss "the proposed change from the Club system," "it was moved, seconded and carried that a committee of four be appointed by the President to confer with similar committees of other clubs and with a committee of the Trustees and the President" on the subject under discussion.

In the early part of August the following committee was appointed: Dr. S. S. Stryker '63 chairman, F. V. Lloyd '00, Struthers Burt 04, Coleman P. Brown 06 E. B. Seymour Jr 98.

The committee held a meeting August 8. On account of the summer vacation the meeting adjourned until to-day.

After a very extended discussion, it was decided that if you would be kind enough to give me an appointment I should call upon you some evening during the coming week with a view toward obtaining your views more fully.

I think I may say for the committee that we are convinced that there is something radically wrong with social conditions among the undergraduates. But with the utmost desire to be helpful to the University we find ourselves very much in the dark as to the precise nature of the remedy.

We feel sure that a full discussion with you will be of the greatest assistance in framing the report required from us by the Club in October.

Trusting that you can give me an interview some evening during the coming week, I beg to remain,

Very truly yours E. B. Seymour Jr.

ALS (WP, DLC).

[1] Princeton 1898, Secretary of the Princeton Club of Philadelphia, and lawyer of Philadelphia.

From Lawrence Crane Woods

My dear Dr. Wilson: Pittsburg, September 14, 1907.

I am delighted that we can have the privilege of receiving from you personally full information on the plans so important to Princeton. I have at once taken the matter up and think that you will shortly have an invitation from the Executive Committee of the Princeton Club to address us some evening at the University Club. I should be glad to have your views as to whether the plan strikes you favorably or not. We do not want a dinner because that would mean a cash outlay for any who attended, nor do we wish to give it personally as that would seem like an exclusive private affair. This is a Princeton matter and every man that cares to, has a right to attend. On the other hand, we do not wish to give a smoker as that would attract the very class of people who would not be so deeply interested in an intelligent discussion of such problems, and there would certainly be more or less disorder.

The suggestion, therefore, which will be made to the Executive Committee is that, after receiving your acceptance and fixing a date, an invitation be issued to every member of the Princeton Club to meet you at the new University Club in the East End, which is quiet, absolutely exclusive and retired, for full information and discussion of the plans now under consideration. It will cost no one anything to attend, and naturally only those will attend who really are interested in Princeton and in hearing your views. Incidentally a number of us will make up a list of persons that we particularly wish there, like Judge Macfarlane, Mr. Shea, Mr. Hall[1] and others, and will try to see that as many as possible of these older and wiser heads are there. I shall arrange it so that the Executive Committee shall feel that the initiative in this matter came entirely from them, neither from you nor myself.

Looking forward with the greatest pleasure to meeting you at that time, and trusting that you will permit me to arrange for your accommodations, train reservations, etc., so as to make the trip as comfortable and pleasant as possible for you, believe me, Very sincerely yours, Lawrence C. Woods

TLS (WP, DLC).

[1] Probably William Maclay Hall, Jr., Princeton 1885, lawyer of Pittsburgh.

To Lawrence Crane Woods

My dear Mr. Woods: Princeton, N. J. September 16th, 1907.

Thank you sincerely for your letter of September 14th. The plan that you outline meets with my entire approval. I think it very wise indeed that the Executive Committee of The Princeton Club should act in this matter upon their own judgment as well as upon their own initiative and I will consider myself entirely at their disposal, my only suggestion being that the arrangements be such that reporters will not get wind of it and that every man will feel that he is not only at liberty to come, but is desired to come, for very full and frank conference.[1]

I very much appreciate your kindness and tact in this matter.

With much regard,

Sincerely yours, Woodrow Wilson

TLS (WC, NjP).

[1] As it turned out, Wilson did not go to Pittsburgh until May 2, 1908, when he spoke to the Western Association of Princeton Clubs. See the address printed at that date in Vol. 18.

From Henry Burling Thompson

Wilmington, Del.
Dear President Wilson: 9th Mo., 16th, 1907.

I spent Saturday morning with Mr. Bunn, in an inspection of the summer work in his department.

The usual painting and necessary repairs to the Dormitories, I should assume have been well taken care of, and are up to the usual standard.

I think the removal of the old Gymnasium[1] is a benefit to the appearance of the grounds, and will bring us to a better understanding of the possibilities of the development of the surrounding land.

You will note that there have been two or three maple trees cut down on the Rail Road side of Blair Hall. This was really necessary, as the air and light at this end of the building were absolutely excluded when the trees were in full foliage, and the rooms were rendered partially unsanitary, due to absence of light and air.

The large pine tree at the end of McCosh Hall has also been cut down. This was rendered necessary on account of the grading, as the tree came directly at the entrance of the Hall, and was from two to three feet below the new grade established.

MC COSH HALL:

I hope that you are pleased with Mr. Cram's plan of grading. I think when this is completed, it will add much to the appearance of the building.

While on this subject, I understand from Mr. Bunn that Mr. [Raleigh C.] Gildersleeve is much grieved that Mr. Cram's plan has been substituted for his. I was not aware until Saturday that Mr. Gildersleeve had submitted a plan for this work. I suppose it would have been courtesy, on my part, to him, to have mentioned that the substitution of plans was to have been made; but the harm is done.

The only point in the construction of McCosh Hall that I would criticise is the installation of the registers for ventilation. This work, in most all instances, seems to have been carelessly done. The plaster is more or less blurred; and the face of the registers should have another coat of paint. I called Mr. Bunn's attention to this. It would be just as well, before we receive the building, to see that these faults are corrected. Under present conditions, the work is not up to specifications.

Mr. Bunn has provided only eight chairs for the Preceptorial rooms. Will this number be sufficient?

SUN DIAL:

While I do not know your plans as to the unveiling of the sun dial, I have an impression that you propose to unveil it some time the latter part of October. If this is so, I would suggest that Mr. Bunn proceed immediately with the erection of the dial, for this reason: We may find in the unpacking that certain parts are broken or missing, which would necessitate repairs or replacements. Also, there may be some question of construction, which may mean delay; consequently, if we propose to have it completed and ready for the unveiling the latter part of October, he should start at once on the erection. I gave Mr. Bunn no positive orders on this point, but will leave it to your discretion as to what should be done.

PHYSICAL LABORATORY:

I inspected the staking out of the ground for the new Physical Laboratory, and I am more than ever satisfied—after going over the situation on the ground—that Mr. Cram's plan is the proper one.

I understand that Mr. Palmer's plans and specifications are now in the builder's hands for bids, and assume that the excavation for foundations will begin at an early date.

The only point where Mr. Palmer and the University authorities will come in touch in the construction of this building will be on the question of the sewer and steam pipes of '79 Hall. The sewer will run through the East wing of the Laboratory and the steam pipes through the West wing. Some temporary adjustment will have to be made. I shall see Mr. Palmer in New York on Wednesday, and can arrange with him to leave this entire matter to the adjustment of Mr. Hardenbergh and Mr. Bunn.

GEOLOGICAL AND BIOLOGICAL LABORATORY:

I enclose with this copy of a letter received from Parish & Schroeder. I took the plans of "Scheme C" with me to Princeton, and spent an hour with Professors Libbey and Phillips in going over them. As usual, I found a conflict of opinion between this branch of the Committee[2] and the van Ingen-McClure branch. I will not burden you now with any discussion as to this conflict, for I believe "Scheme C," with certain modifications, will work out to the entire satisfaction of the Committee and the Architects. I think the elevation is unquestionably better than anything the Architects have yet shown.

I have made an appointment with Mr. Schroeder for Wednesday afternoon of this week in order to go over the principal question in dispute, which is the height of the Museum ceiling.

I have asked Libbey, just as soon as their Committee have prepared their report, to turn it over to you with the plans; and I shall be ready at your convenience to go over their report and the drawings.

I received last week a letter from Mr. Cram, in which he says— "We are getting along well with the sketches for '77 Building,[3] and shall have these ready to show you very soon."

Yours very sincerely, Henry B Thompson
Acting Chairman, Grounds & Buildings Committee.

P.S.,—I understand from Mr. Bunn that his fiscal year runs to the first of August. He tells me that he has run about $1,800.00 over the amount appropriated by the Trustees for his Department, but he is very confident, that, during the coming year, his retrenchments will be such, he will make up this deficiency. As yet, I have not posted myself as to the financial details of his Department, but hope to know more about same within the next two or three weeks, as I have requested a detailed statement from him with regard to his prospective budget.

The grading of McCosh Hall is not charged against the Grounds and Buildings Fund. As you will remember, no appropriation having been made by this Committee, I instructed Mr. Bunn to charge it against the building, and notified Cleve Dodge in July that we were doing this. He subsequently told me that this was the proper course to take. H. B. T.

TLS (WP, DLC). Enc.: Parish & Schroeder to H. B. Thompson, Sept. 11, 1907, TCL (WP, DLC).

1 It had stood in the northwestern corner of the campus, just west of Alexander Hall.

2 The committee from the Departments of Biology and Geology which was conferring with the architects about the plans for what would be called Guyot Hall.

3 This dormitory, erected by the Class of 1877 and completed in 1909, was located west of Alexander Hall, almost on the site of the old gymnasium. Designed by Cram, Goodhue and Ferguson in the English collegiate Gothic style, it provided accommodations for sixty men. It was named Campbell Hall in honor of John Alexander Campbell, prominent businessman and civic leader of Trenton, N. J., and President of the Class of 1877.

To Henry Burling Thompson

My dear Thompson: [Princeton, N. J.] September 17th, 1907.

Thank you very much for your letter of the 16th. I feel like again apologizing for having made it necessary for you to write it.

I am very much obliged to you for your full notes about what has been done and is being done. I fear that it was in part my fault that Mr. Gildersleeve's susceptibilities in the matter of the grading were not better taken care of. I knew, but had forgotten, that he had prepared a grading plan. I now remember that so much of it as I saw seemed to me very much less suitable and pleasant to the eye than the one Mr. Cram has devised. I am very sorry that Gildersleeve's feelings have been hurt, but I cannot feel sorry that the thing has been graded as it has been for it seems to me very successful.

I had a conversation with Mr. Bunn yesterday about the sun-dial, and asked him to write to you for your authorization to proceed with its construction. The date for the unveiling has not been fixed yet. We are waiting on Mr. Bryce, who felt quite confident he could fix some date early in November. We have therefore plenty of time to prepare, if we begin at once.

I am happy to believe that we are now nearing the completion of the plans for the geological and biological laboratory. I think the way you have handled the matter is both wise and tactful, and I shall be glad to come in and take a hand at whatever point you may suggest.

Always cordially and faithfully yours,

[Woodrow Wilson]

CCL (WWP, UA, NjP).

From Henry Fairfield Osborn

My dear Wilson, [New York] September 17th 1907.

I hope you have enjoyed a fine rest this summer, and return in your usual good health and spirits.

I also hope you are beginning a most successful and enjoyable year.

After long and prayerful consideration I find myself strongly opposed to the social reorganization plan for the following reasons:

1) Enforced segregation is against the principle of student self-government, and will not attain the end desired—because each larger group will break up into smaller groups on the lines of natural taste and affinity.

2) The expenditure which is envolved, if applied to increasing the number of able and attractive men in the Faculty, will do far more for culture at Princeton.

3) The autocratic manner in which the plan has been proposed has deeply hurt the feelings of the most loyal and devoted body of college alumni in America. It has introduced a wedge and a very strained feeling among a body of men who were all working in the same direction, at the very time when the Com-

mittee of fifty needs the continuous and unanimous support of the alumni. *I have not found a single alumnus* in favor of the plan. On the other hand all are ready and anxious to remove any evils which can be shown to exist.

4) Where would Princeton be today but for *the influence and unbounded generosity of the South-East Club and the Caledonian Club*, organizations which were the forerunners of the present older, Princeton clubs.

5) Are we not making a mistake in invading a sphere of college life which all the world over belongs under the shelter of Academic and University freedom.

6) The alternative plans I have to offer are—

a) the more active participation of the Faculty in the existing club-life.

b) the extension to Sophomore year of membership in certain of the club[s].

c) The institution of a general university club, which shall be open to all members of the university—*who can qualify* by *character, attainments* or *social charm*[—]in other words such qualities as admit men to the *Century* in New in New [*sic*] York.

7) One aspect of the matter which is looming up, is the effect which this plan will have on the men who are considering which *College* they shall enter. Already I have heard from several quarters that this is something which must be taken into account.

8) There is a certain class of men—who have the good fortune to be born with some means and with natural advantages of home culture & refinement. On looking over the rolls of Princeton men, who have achieved something, it is surprising to find what a splendid showing men of this class are making as compared with the class who, through no fault of their own, enter life handicapped for want of means. Another aspect of this subject of parentage entirely overlooked is *that the sons of able men* are *apt to inherit ability*—take the *Dodges* as an as an [*sic*] illustration. Yet our colleges,* (and especially perhaps Princeton,) seem to do little to encourage and attract this class[,] fostering, what I believe to be a scientifically false hope—that the sons of obscure men will constitute her best material in future life.

9. I deeply regret that I cannot follow you in your plan—because of my admiration of the work you have already done, and of my profound faith in your theory of education, and the lead you have taken in establishing it.

I most earnestly hope and pray that the phrase: "*the Clubs*

*** imbued with the American notion that the son of a farmer is better per se than the son of a wealthy man**

must go!" with which the plan was brusquely introduced, will disappear from the discussion of this subject, and the phrase: "*that the President*[,] *the Trustees, the Faculty and the alumni are united in earnest and loyal consideration to discover a plan which will bring about the union of the social and intellectual interests of the University*" will take its place[.] Such an announcement from you will rally all the discordant voices and disorganized forces again under your leadership.

Only the other day, I heard a former President of Ivy say, "If it is for the best interests of Princeton we will burn the club down *but I want to be convinced*, first, that it *is* for the best interests of Princeton."

It is the part of friendship to speak frankly, so I trust you will read this letter as from your warm friend and admirer

Henry Fairfield Osborn

No response is necessary.

ALS (WP, DLC).

From Henry Burling Thompson

Wilmington, Del.

Dear President Wilson: 9th Mo., 17th, 1907.

I have received your letter of the 16th instant, and it was a source of regret to me that I did not have the pleasure of going over the work with you on Saturday, when at Princeton. I quite understood, however, that it was impossible for you to be with me.

Since writing you yesterday, I have received a letter from Mr. Bunn, saying that you think it wise to proceed with the erection of the Sun Dial; consequently, I, as Chairman of the Committee, have authorized him this morning to go ahead.

Yours very sincerely, Henry B Thompson

TLS (WP, DLC).

To Sir William Mather

[Princeton, N. J.]

My dear Sir William: September 18th, 1907.

I have been moving quite constantly from place to place since the receipt of your very kind and interesting letter of August 22nd, and that must be my apology for my delay in reply. I have read the brochure which you purpose publishing with the greatest interest and approval. It will constitute a most interesting memorial of what will always be one of the most interesting gifts that Princeton ever received. I think that everyone will feel a certain enthusiasm in dwelling upon what the gift signifies, and I am peculiarly gratified that Mr. Bryce can make it possible to be present and officiate at the ceremony of presentation. We all wish most heartily that you and Lady Mather could be present again. It would give the occasion a delightful completeness. But I know that you will be present in thought. It is very interesting and appropriate that you should have dated the letter of gift the fourth of July. Our Trustees meet in the latter part of October, and I am sure that they will receive the whole record of the matter with the greatest interest and satisfaction.

Mrs. Wilson and my daughters join me in warmest regards to Lady Mather, your daughters, and yourself, and I am,

Always cordially and faithfully yours,

[Woodrow Wilson]

CCL (WWP, UA, NjP).

From David Benton Jones

My dear Doctor: Chicago September 19, 1907.

Your note of the 16th instant has just come.

It is of the first importance not only that Mr. Pyne should be present at the first meeting of the committee, but that his zeal should not suffer diminution by any appearance of rushing the matter in his absence. Your case is so sound that the longer it is considered, the more certain it is to prevail.

The club system is a cancerous growth, and will not cure itself. It must be removed. While we should avoid using surgical terms in considering the question, we should keep clearly and steadily in mind the essential nature of the malady, and so be better able to judge of such suggestions as are certain to be made looking toward a cure by mere medication or massage. All such suggestions are folly.

The only suggestion that has come to me which seemed to merit attention came from a very able Williams man. He graduated some five or six years ago, and while in college was manager of the strongest of their fraternities. There the fraternities take in members of all four classes, and they eat and sleep in their fraternity houses.

This man frankly admits the evils of the system, and openly advocates the establishment of a common dining hall for all classes and members of the college. He believes this concession would remove some of the difficulty. Fraternity houses would then be merely private dormitories. Fortunately at Princeton the club men even now sleep in the dormitories, and the question is whether we would find it more acceptable and equally effective if one central dining hall were established for all classes, with rooms adjoining for social intercourse and enjoyment.

The club men harp on the term "quad. scheme" as if a quad. were a veritable prison house where they—the elect—would be forced to eat and sleep with the "undesirable" members of the university. They do not avow their vulgarity in quite such bald terms, but that is their meaning.

The further suggestion was made by Mr. Palmer that the present clubs be converted into exclusively graduate clubs. This, of course, would dispose of many of them, as they could not be supported as graduate clubs. I think graduate clubs would be harmless as far as the life of the undergraduates is concerned.

These two are the only serious suggestions that have come to me. The ordinary club man's talk is sheer twaddle—a whimper against being disturbed in the enjoyment of special privileges which he finds very delightful. I do not mean to be contemptuous, but that is the truth. I am using terminology in this letter which I, of course, do not use in discussing the matter with various people, and I am fully in accord with you in feeling that "a little firmness combined with a great deal of tact will in the end bring this matter out to a happy issue."

Since you say Mr. Pyne does not return until the very close of this month, I presume the first meeting will not be called before the 3rd or 4th of October. I shall, however, hold myself in readiness to go east at any time named for the meeting.

Very sincerely yours, David B. Jones.

TLS (WP, DLC).

From William Royal Wilder

My dear Woodrow: New York September 19th, 1907.

. . . Along with my other sins, I have occasionally before me the "Sin of Uzzah."[1] It is needless to state that the Commencement Number of the Alumni Weekly was of thrilling interest.

I appreciate and thoroughly sympathize with your position as regards the clubs. Is it wise, however, to antagonize them and their members, which I fear has been done, and is that your plan? I have personal cognizance of some of their evil effects to an extent that would not make me hesitate to resort to more or less heroic measures[.] Why not, however, start your "Quad System," and take the attitude of Gamaliel[2] towards it? If it proves to be a good thing, it will certainly co-exist with the clubs, and let us hope that it may crowd them out. In the meantime I am heartily in favor of absolutely prohibiting the organization of another club. It is a pity that it was not decided in '95 or '96 to limit them to the half dozen that were then in existence. If I can be of any assistance to you, don't hesitate to command me.

Our classmate Rice[3] and his brother[4] have been with me for the last forty-eight hours, and I have been trying to help them in their still hunt after the right man to organize and start the Rice Institute. He must be a Southerner. Isn't McClenahan a little too young for the job?[5]

Faithfully yours, Wm. R. Wilder

TLS (WP, DLC).

[1] A cart driver in the time of David who handled the Ark too familiarly and was punished by God (I Chronicles 13:9-10).

[2] A Pharisee and doctor of law who counseled against the persecution of the apostles on the grounds that "if this work be of men, it will come to nought, but if it be of God, ye cannot overthrow it; lest haply ye be found to fight against God" (Acts 5:34-39).

[3] William Marsh Rice, nephew of William Marsh Rice, founder of Rice Institute in Houston.

[4] It is impossible to identify him. W. M. Rice '79 had six brothers, at least three of whom were prominent in Houston at this time.

[5] Grover Cleveland had nominated Howard McClenahan to the presidential search committee of Rice Institute. See G. Cleveland to E. Raphael, Jan. 15, 1907, ALS (Rice Institute Papers, TxHR). McClenahan was thirty-four at this time.

A News Report

[Sept. 20, 1907]

OPENING EXERCISES

Held Yesterday Afternoon in Marquand Chapel
New Appointments to the Faculty.

The exercises in connection with the formal opening of the one hundred and sixty-first college year were held yesterday afternoon in Marquand Chapel. The trustees and members of the faculty, in academic costume, formed at the faculty room in Nassau Hall and entered the chapel in a procession.

President Wilson, who presided, opened the exercises with prayer. After reading a portion of the first chapter of Joshua, President Wilson made a short address. He welcomed the incoming students to the comradeship of Princeton, and impressed upon them the fact that this was a comradeship not only of good fellowship and friendship, but also one with fellow students.

He spoke of McCosh Hall, the greater part of which is now ready for use, as a fitting memorial to the man who opened up a larger field of usefulness and did so much for the good of the University. President Wilson also mentioned that presently ground would be broken for some new buildings, which would widen the scope for original research and investigation by the members of the University.

After extending a cordial welcome to the new members of the faculty, the President closed the exercises with a benediction. . . .

Printed in the *Daily Princetonian*, Sept. 20, 1907.

To Melancthon Williams Jacobus

[Princeton, N. J.]

My dear Dr. Jacobus: September 20th, 1907.

I have been in a rush of work and controversy ever since I saw you and have only just now been able to find out about the possibilities for an early committee meeting. I find that Mr. Pyne will not return from Europe until about the twenty-fifth. I am therefore hoping to make an arrangement for a meeting very soon after that date.

I take the liberty of enclosing a copy of a letter that I have just received from Professor H. F. Osborn, which I think you will find illuminating. I need not tell you what I think of it, particularly of the argument for making Princeton a rich man's college.

Please give Mrs. Jacobus my very warm regards. I cannot tell you how keenly I enjoyed the kindness and sympathy and genial hospitality I found with you last week.

Always cordially and faithfully yours,

[Woodrow Wilson]

CCL (RSB Coll., DLC).

From Francis Speir, Jr.[1]

My dear Doctor Wilson: New York. September 20, 1907

I have deemed it expedient to write to you as to your plan for the proposed quad system. I am a man of your time, have known you for over thirty years, and share your interests in the welfare of Princeton.

Since your speech at the alumni dinner in June, and the announcement of the action of the board of trustees of Princeton University on the report of the committee, printed in The Alumni Weekly (which as I understand, was an adoption of the principle and idea of the proposed quads by the trustees), your plan has been more considered and discussed by Princeton men than any other topic. I have personally learned of the views of over a hundred men, of widely distributed classes and from various parts of the country, including trustees of the University and influential members of the faculty. I have failed to find one person who is in favor of the plan, but have found openly-expressed and strongly-worded disapproval of it. The lapse of time since commencement seems only to emphasize this attitude of mind. Many men of good judgment who in June were not prepared to disapprove, are now fixed in disapproval. If you believe that any considerable body of the alumni residing in or about the large cities is with you, you are greatly mistaken. No one knows better than you do that the strength of Princeton is in her alumni. I am afraid that you will find from three fourths to nine tenths of them opposed to you in this new measure.

It seems to me that you, who have successfully instituted the preceptorial system, should hesitate to push through your new plan before ascertaining the real sentiment of the alumni. Such attempt, from what I can learn, would be doomed to failure.

Very sincerely yours, Francis Speir

TLS (WP, DLC).

[1] Princeton 1877, member of the New York law firm of Speir & Bartlett, 52 Wall St.

A News Report of an Address to the Freshman Class

[Sept. 23, 1907]

FRESHMAN RECEPTION

Held in Murray-Dodge Hall
on Saturday Evening.

The annual reception of the Philadelphian Society to the Freshman class was held last Saturday evening at 7.30 o'clock, in Murray-Dodge Hall. After a few introductory remarks, George M. Duff 1907 introduced President Wilson, the first speaker of the evening.

President Wilson first touched upon the advantages that accrue to a college man, but he emphasized the point that unless the college man did his share of the work, the University could do little for him. He went on to say that not only the life in the class rooms fits a man for after life, but also the more intimate intercourse he may get from his professors, if he wishes it, independent of the curriculum. President Wilson next referred to the hold which Princeton very early lays upon every man entering the

University. As a direct outcome of this affection he had found it very hard to change any feature of the college life or customs.

Continuing, he said that in college and in business or professional life a Princeton man was always marked by the conscientiousness which marked his duties as a citizen, and his willingness to take upon himself responsibilities of the more serious kind. It is now characteristic of a Princeton man to study and it is insisted on, for we no longer live in an easy-going way, but in a community where it is necessary to make use of our brains in order to succeed. And so unless the colleges and universities throughout the country trained the young men to use their brains properly, America's supremacy would be in danger of falling. He concluded by saying that we are here to learn the perfect use of our minds and character, and to see that the right shall always conquer, and the wrong be trampled under foot.

Printed in the *Daily Princetonian*, Sept. 23, 1907.

From David Benton Jones

My dear Doctor: Chicago September 23rd, 1907.

Your note of September 20th with copy of Professor Osborne's letter to you is just received. I had a long talk with Professor Osborne on Friday of last week, on his way through Chicago.

Mr. Wilson,[1] whom I think you met some two or three years ago, and who, in my judgment, is the ablest lawyer in the country where legal and business questions are involved, is spending a few days with us while his family linger a little longer in the north.

We have talked Princeton a good deal, but yesterday afternoon he and my brother and myself drifted again on to that subject, and it was late into the night before it was dropped.

Every suggestion was taken up, including Professor Osborne's (as stated verbally to me, which differed somewhat from his written statement to you). Without going into the details of the discussion, which was very thorough and exhaustive, Mr. Wilson's final conclusion and suggestion was:

First: the establishment of a quad., or commons, or club, (the name being immaterial) providing eating and social entertainment for say five hundred students, open to all classes.

Second: the present clubs to continue, but to be compelled to take in members of all four classes; the election of the incoming freshman class to close by say November 1st, and the names of those elected to be reported to the registrar. That after November

1st the clubs would be allowed to take in during freshman year say one-fifth of the number it had elected before November 1st (this to enable them to keep their lists full as they might be impaired by mid-year failures, etc.) If a club, for example, refuse to take in more than five before November 1st, it would add only one more during the year, so that refusal to elect before November 1st would result in the club's extinction as the membership passed out by graduation.

His reasons for such a plan are briefly about as follows:

First: That it conserves and utilizes the great property values involved, which should be kept in mind, while it should not be allowed to impair the principle of your plan, even if it involved the abandonment and ruin of the clubs.

Second: That it allows a certain freedom of choice and selection, which does not defeat the purposes of the plan.

Third: The establishment of a large center free to all classes (in the order of application, the applications of the upper classes receiving preference in case room cannot be found for all) will result in a body of opinion and sentiment which will be found effective in the government of the undregraduate [undergraduate] body, and be a wholesome counterpoise to the elective club sentiment.

This free-for-all eating and social system to be extended with the increase in the University attendance, the clubs to remain as now, unless, in the opinion of the authorities, they demonstrate their usefulness and wholesomeness under the new regime, in which case permission to extend will be favored.

To avoid burdening you with correspondence I wrote to Dean Fine of my interview with Professor Osborne and what I understood from him to be his scheme. I am sending him a carbon copy of this letter.

There are elements in this suggestion evolved by Mr. Wilson which take into account the ends and aims you have in mind, and also which would compell the clubs to come within the operation and effect of the plan.

I am very glad to know that you expect to call the committee together at an early date.

Very sincerely yours, David B. Jones.

TLS (WP, DLC) with WWsh notation on verso: "An organization upon which educational influences can be directly and in a very intimate manner brought to bear."

1 There does not seem to have been at this time a lawyer named Wilson in the Chicago area who had been graduated from Princeton. Jones was probably referring to John P. Wilson, senior partner of the firm of Wilson, Moore & McIlvaine of Chicago.

From Edmund Bayly Seymour, Jr.

Dear Dr Wilson: [Philadelphia] September 23, 1907.

At a meeting of the Conference Committee held this day it was moved, seconded and carried "That Dr Wilson be requested to address the Club at his earliest convenience on the subject of the so-called quad system."

This was in pursuance of the willingness expressed by you to speak to the alumni.

May I ask that I should have at least three full days' notice so as to prepare notices?

Informally the committee instructed me to advise you that on some other occasion at some later date Professor Hibben would be asked to address us on the same subject.

Hoping you can favor us in the near future[1] I beg to remain

Sincerely yours, E B Seymour Jr Secy.

TLS (WP, DLC).

[1] It was not until March 19, 1909, that Wilson next addressed the Philadelphia alumni. See the news report printed at March 20, 1909, Vol. 19.

Comments on the Effects of the Quadrangle Plan

[Sept. 25, 1907]

President Wilson later, in conversation with the editor of The Weekly, added this comment upon the subject-matter of his letter:[1]

"I have been very much surprised at the extraordinary misconception of the character of the proposed quadrangles that has got abroad. I am constantly spoken to about the 'segregation' which will be the result. I am at a real loss to understand what the critics who use this word in objection to the plan can mean. There is to be no more separation between the dormitories when they are grouped into quadrangles than there is now. Now the college dines together in groups of from fifteen to thirty; in the quads they will dine together in groups of from one hundred to one hundred and fifty. That will be the chief, almost the only, difference between the present life of the place and the quad system, so far as the separation of the men is concerned. They will be less segregated then than they are now, and the segregated pieces will not be rivals of one another. There will of course be absolute freedom of intercourse between all parts of the University, greater freedom in fact than there is now. The quads will not be places of confinement, but places of intercourse and freedom."

Printed in the *Princeton Alumni Weekly*, VIII (Sept. 25, 1907), 10.

[1] That is, his letter to Andrew Clerk Imbrie of July 29, 1907, which was printed immediately before these comments.

To Grover Cleveland

Princeton, N. J.

My dear Mr. Cleveland: September 26th, 1907.

I left you this morning without putting in your hands a copy of Professor Osborn's letter which I spoke of. I send it herewith. Pray do not trouble to return the copy.

May I not add for your convenience a brief memorandum of the two principles we spoke of this morning?

First, that the University should have a social organization to which men are not admitted by student election.

Second, it should be a social organization in some way intimately bound up with the teaching organization and susceptible of being dominated by educational influences.

With warm regard,

Always faithfully yours, Woodrow Wilson

TLS (G. Cleveland Papers, DLC). Enc.: H. F. Osborn to WW, Sept. 17, 1907, TCL (G. Cleveland Papers, DLC).

To Robert Garrett

Princeton, N. J.

My dear Mr. Garrett: September 26th, 1907.

I sincerely hope that you have had a very delightful summer, as I am sure you must have had, and that you will not feel it an imposition now to have business thrust upon you. I am writing to ask if it will not be possible for you to attend a meeting of our committee of the Board on the new plans on the evening of Friday, October 4th, at 8 o'clock, in the President's Office in Seventy-Nine Hall, Princeton. I hope that this will be convenient for you. I would have called the committee together earlier, had not Mr. Pyne's return from Europe been so long delayed. It is expected that he will land today.

With warmest regards,

Always cordially and faithfully yours,

Woodrow Wilson

TLS (Selected Corr. of R. Garrett, NjP).

To David Benton Jones

My dear Mr. Jones: [Princeton, N. J.] September 26th, 1907.

I am calling the Committee on the Social Coordination of the University for the evening of Friday, October 4th, at 8 P.M., in the President's Office in Seventy-Nine Hall. Mr. Pyne is expected to land today, and that will give him a week in which to catch up with matters which he must of course feel obliged to give his first attention to upon landing. It is the date suggested in one of your own letters, and I therefore take it for granted that it will be most convenient for you.

I am very much interested in the alternative plans which are now beginning to be suggested, and the one you outline from your conference with Mr. Wilson interests me more than the others. You may remember that I once had the pleasure of meeting Mr. Wilson and got a direct impression of his force and intelligence, and I have long known his reputation as a lawyer.

You will yourself of course have seen the fundamental objection to his plan. As you and I agreed last June, we are not seeking medication for the club evil or alteration of the clubs, but a sound organization upon which the educational influences of Princeton can be directly exercised. A commons of 500 men, or of any number larger than one hundred or one hundred and fifty, would not be susceptible to those influences, and it seems to me inevitable that any associations made up by student election would be as insusceptible to the governing thoughts of the place as are the present clubs. To continue the existence of such organizations would, moreover, inevitably result in dividing the University into two classes, those who were distinctly clubable and those who were not. This shapr [sharp] classification would certainly put the best students of the University at a marked and most undeserved social disadvantage.

As you suggested, Mr. Close, my secretary, has recently been compiling scholarship statistics in connection with the club membership. He finds that during the last four years only 9.3% of club men have won honors, that is, have attained a standing in either of the first two groups of our scholarship classification, while of the non-clubmen 41.7% have been honor men. These are very striking figures. To put it differently, during those four years there have been 1516 clubmen, and 140 of these have been honor men. Of that 140 twenty-one have been first group men and 119 second group men. During those same four years there have been 621 non-clubmen, and of these forty-five have stood in the first group and 215 in the second. Another interesting thing discloses itself in the figures, namely that the number of honor men in any group of clubs varies inversely as the age of that group, the youngest clubs having the largest number of honor men and the oldest clubs the smallest number.

I think that the principle you and I agreed upon at Commencement is absolutely unimpeachable, namely that our object is entirely educational and that the social organization sought shall be intended only to serve that end.

None the less, I feel that we are entirely on the right track in giving to each suggestion, such as that of Professor Osborn and Mr. Wilson, a very careful and detailed discussion, so that we may see just how much of it, if any, is compatible with our principle and can therefore be adopted. The year must be devoted to just such labor as this, to convince both ourselves and those who are most interested outside the Board.

It will be very delightful to talk this matter over with you face to face.

Always cordially and faithfully yours,

[Woodrow Wilson]

CCL (WWP, UA, NjP).

From the Minutes of the Princeton University Faculty

4 p.m. September 26, 1907.

Special Meeting: The Faculty met, the President presiding. . . .

The following resolution was moved by Professor Daniels and seconded by Professor Hunt:

Be it resolved, that in the plan recently sanctioned by the Board of Trustees for the social coördination of the University, this Faculty do concur, and that a committee of seven from this body be appointed to coöperate with the President of the University, the Dean of the Faculty, and the Committee of the Board of Trustees already constituted, to elaborate the plan in question.[1]

The following resolution was moved by Professor Henry van Dyke and seconded by Professors Hibben and McClenahan, as a substitute:

Resolved that we respectfully ask the Board of Trustees of the University that a representative joint Committee be appointed from their Honourable body and from the Faculty which together with the President of the University shall investigate the present social conditions of the University in conjunction with representatives of the Alumni and students and consider the best method of curing the evils which exist and of maintaining and promoting the unity, democracy, and scholarly life of the undergraduate body.

Resolved, that when we adjourn we adjourn to meet on Monday next at 4 p.m. for the discussion of the question raised by these motions. . . .

"Minutes of the University Faculty of Princeton University Beginning in September, 1902 Ending June 1914," bound minute book (UA, NjP).

1 A copy of this resolution in Daniels' handwriting is in WP, DLC.

From the Diary of William Starr Myers

Thurs. Sept. 26 [1907].

The question of the "Social Coordination of the University"—Pres. Wilson's plan to abolish or transform the upper class clubs, was precipitated in faculty meeting this afternoon. Wilson broached it at commencement time, & it has been agitating faculty, students, & alumni since. This afternoon Daniels offered a resolution endorsing the plan & providing for the appointment of a faculty committee to aid the pres. in carrying it out. Seconded by "Granny" Hunt. Henry van Dyke offered another resolution to throw the whole thing to a joint com. of faculty & trustees for investigation, which everyone looks upon as a veiled hit at "Woodrow." Seconded by "Jack" Hibben & McLenahan. The air was electric for a few minutes, but the whole thing has been put over till an adjourned meeting next Monday afternoon. There will be fun then.

Notes for a Speech

Municipal Club, 27 September, 1907.

Present problems of democracy largely city problems because our populations centre there: in this country our undigested foreign population.

The government of a modern city an enormous affair.
The distribution of its population
The distribution and regulation of its industries.
Its health
Its convenience
Its moralization, by art etc.
Its instruction.

The kind of organization we have attempted.
Its false analogies
Its complexity
Its false principle: machinery rather than men

The kind we should attempt, on the basis of choosing and trusting men whom we know and who are so placed and equipped with authority that we can watch them.

The association of unpaid citizens with paid officials in German and other continental cities.

27 Sept., '07.[1]

WWT MS (WP, DLC).
[1] WW's composition date.

A News Item

[Sept. 28, 1907]

MEETING OF MUNICIPAL CLUB.

At a meeting of the Municipal Club held last evening in Dodge Hall, President Woodrow Wilson gave an interesting and instructive talk on "City Government."

Printed in the *Daily Princetonian*, Sept. 28, 1907.

From David Benton Jones

My dear Doctor: Chicago September 28th, 1907.

Your very full and satisfactory statement of September 26th is just received. I have read it with a great deal of interest, and I shall be in Princeton on Friday, October the fourth, to attend the meeting which you have called for that date.

In discussing the club question and such data relating to it as you have tabulated, we should really include only say four clubs: Ivy, Tiger Inn, Cottage, and Cap and Gown. I find upon investigation here that the younger and smaller clubs hold about the same feeling toward these three or four older clubs that the non-club men hold toward the entire club situation. The smaller and younger clubs, as you say, have not grown to be a detrimental influence as yet. They are rather the external manifestation of successive disappointments in failure to make the older and larger clubs. I need not, however, burden you with correspondence, as we can consider the matter next week.

The more I have looked into Mr. Wilson's suggestion, the less I like it, and I am more and more inclined to my original conviction that the elective principle must be eliminated. I think Mr. Wilson's disposition to work out a solution that would conserve the whole situation is the basis of his suggestion, and it does not strike at the root of existing evils.

Very sincerely yours, David B. Jones.

TLS (WP, DLC).

From Cleveland Hoadley Dodge

Camp Nepahwin Upper Saranac

Dear Mr. President Sept 28th, 1907

A hard rainy day & I was just sitting down to write to you when in comes your kind letter of 26th inst[1] . . .

As you suggest, I have had a worrisome Summer with unsatisfactory business & anxiety on account of my dear Mother. Besides all this I was greatly harried during June & July by being jumped on by every Princeton man I met so that Aug. 1st I made a solemn vow not to permit any discussion of Princeton matters until Oct 1st & this vow I have kept so well that even when Bayard Henry spent four days with me in August I would not allow him to mention the subject which was uppermost in his mind.

Nevertheless I have done a lot of thinking & when Harry Thompson dined with me in N. Y. last week I broke my vow & had a good talk with him. I found that quite independently of each other we had reached the same solution of the question which has troubled us all—a solution which I think will satisfy everybody—relieve the unpleasant agitation which has grown up —enable us to cure in the immediate future the evils which have grown into our social life—a modification of your plan which is perfectly consistent with your report & saves your face, and which will enable us gradually & wisely by processes of evolution & not *r*evolution to work out in a few years the full plan which with your long inspired vision you have so prophetically seen. My only hope & prayer is (and I hope I am not speaking too frankly) that you will religiously keep from too much discussion of the subject, and especially refrain from any positive deliverances of your views until the Committee meets & we can agree on some modified plan such as I have referred to.

You may remember that when your report was discussed by the committee last Spring I insisted on the change of the last sentence, so that when the report was accepted by the Trustees, instead of absolutely assenting to all you said, our resolution only meant the general acceptance of your plan with privilege of further consideration,[2] & *now* that the subject has been so well thrashed out will enable us, with perfect consistency[,] to adopt for the immediate future some modified plan which will not be a backdown or a compromise but a step & a big one towards the goal we intend to eventually reach.

It would take me too long now to tell you all that is in my mind & I do trust that no one may further complicate matters by too positive discussion until we can talk it over in Committee & Board.

As to the meeting you propose for Oct. 4th, I would rather have it a week later but if you find that the others can come on the 4th I will be on hand too. If however you cannot get a full meeting then it might be well to try for the 11th.

I have thought a great deal of you this Summer you dear old chap & trust that you have had a good rest & pray that this durned quad business is not going to worry you any more. Your health is more important to Princeton than anything else & I earnestly implore you to have enough faith not only above, but in your old friends to believe that this business is going to work out to the best permanent good of the dear old College we love so well

God bless you old man with much love

Yrs affl'y Cleve

I expect to be at office on Tuesday & shall be obliged if you will drop me a line & let me know what is finally decided as to meeting

ALS (WP, DLC).

[1] It is missing.

[2] The last sentence of Wilson's report (printed at June 6, 1907) had begun: "Your committee, therefore, recommend that the President of the University be authorized to take such steps as may seem wisest for maturing and executing this general plan. . . ." At Dodge's insistence, the words "and executing" were struck out.

From Melancthon Williams Jacobus

My dear President Wilson: Saybrook, Conn., 29 Sept 1907

You may count upon my being present at the Committee meeting, Friday evg at 8 o'clock.

I am surprised at the letter of Osborn, and can account for it, and for other protests, only on the ground of a fundamental misunderstanding of the spirit and purpose of the Board, the removal of which I have every confidence will be effected through frank and open minded conference.

Yours cordially M. W. Jacobus

ALS (WP, DLC).

From David Laurance Chambers[1]

My dear Doctor Wilson, Indianapolis. 29 *September* 1907

There is a rumor afloat that you are coming to this good town in December,—in connection with the Indiana State Teachers Association, I believe.[2] Without waiting to have this agreeable rumor confirmed or denied, I write at once to ask you to save an evening at that time for the Contemporary Club,[3] of which I happen to be Secretary. When this matter was mentioned at a meeting of the Directors, the other day, I was enthusiastically instructed to extend this invitation to you, and I extend it with enthusiasm. You see, every one recalls your previous address with the greatest pleasure.[4] It was the judgment of the Board that the Club wanted you and wanted you *hard*. You can talk to us on anything under the sun, for anything you talk about we know will be "interesting and profitable," and the Club will be glad to pay your usual terms for lectures. Please, good sir, say Yes![5]

Your health, I trust, is completely restored.

The "residential quads" system, as further explained in last week's *Alumni Weekly*, has my heartiest sympathy and the approval of everybody in this community with whom I have talked. The opposition to it, I feel sure, will gradually dwindle away. It is a great and noble program. Good luck to it!

Trusting that I may have a more favorable answer than that I obtained last year when Mr. Porter[6] and I trotted down to Nashville,[7] I am Yours sincerely, Laurance Chambers

ALS (WP, DLC).

1 Princeton 1900, Secretary to the President of the Bobbs-Merrill Co., publishers of Indianapolis.

2 Wilson was to address the Indiana State Teachers' Association. The text of his address is printed at Dec. 27, 1907.

3 About the Contemporary Club of Indianapolis, see WW to May W. Sewall, Sept. 19, 1899, n. 1, Vol. 11.

4 A news report of this address is printed at April 26, 1902, Vol. 12.

5 Wilson did accept. A report of his speech is printed at Dec. 30, 1907.

6 Probably Charles Darwin Porter, husband of the novelist, Gene Stratton Porter.

7 When Wilson spoke there to the Princeton Alumni Association of Tennessee on November 28, 1905. A news report of his address is printed at Nov. 29, 1905, Vol. 16.

From the Minutes of the Princeton University Faculty

4 p.m. September 30, 1907.

Special Meeting. The Faculty met, the President presiding.

The following communication was received from the Princeton Club of Philadelphia: "That in view of the vital importance to the University of the adoption of the so called 'quad' system, and of the general ignorance of its precise nature among the alumni and the very general discussion aroused over the subject, we respectfully request the Faculty and Board of Trustees to take no final action until after conference with representatives of the Alumni, and to that end we request the Faculty and Board of Trustees to appoint Committees of conference."

After debate on the motion offered by Professor Henry van Dyke as recorded in the Minutes of the last meeting, the roll was called, and the motion lost by the following vote:

Ayes: McMillan, Marquand, West, W. F. Magie, McCay, Thompson, Hibben, P. van Dyke, H. van Dyke, Loomis, McClure, Patton, Robbins, Phillips, Neher, Prentice, Butler, McClenahan, Trowbridge, Morgan, Hoskins, Adams, Collins, 23.

Noes: the President, Cornwall, Hunt, Winans, Ormond, Fine, Westcott, Daniels, H. S. S. Smith, Harris, Lovett, W. M. Rankin, Warren, Parrott, Garfield, Vreeland, Axson, Coney, Smyth, Jeans, Richardson, Wyckoff, Dahlgren, Blau, Hulett, Miller, Foster, Robinson, Cooke, Johnson, Jones, Marvin, Sheldon, Spaulding, Adriance, Bogart, Corwin, Dawson, Elliott, McIlwain, Meeker, Myers, Shipman, Spencer, Morey, Tonks, Anderson, Basore, Cameron, Hastings, Kellogg, MacRae, D. Magie, E. M. Rankin, Stuart, Van Hook, Croll, Gerould, Griffin, Long, MacDonald, Miles, Osgood, Root, Spaeth, Beam, Buffum, Critchlow, Gauss, Koren, Moore, Northup, Priest, Thayer, Bliss, Eisenhart, Gillespie, Veblen, Young, Farr, 80.[1]

Resolved that when the Faculty adjourns, it will adjourn to meet at 4 p.m. October 7, and that the motion of Professor Daniels be the first order of business. . . .

[1] There is a WWT analysis of the vote on the van Dyke resolution in WP, DLC.

From the Diary of William Starr Myers

Mon. Sept. 30 [1907]

At faculty meeting. Fine debate of two hours. The opposition voted down 81 to 23. Fine speeches by them—Paul van Dyke calling upon Wilson in a frank sincere speech,—& asking him to deal openly with them, & also with the alumni. This called forth from the President one of the most wonderful speeches I have ever heard. I shall never forget him standing there erect behind the desk, the gavel (mallet head) grasped in his right hand, with the end of the handle occasionally placed firm against the top of the desk as he leaned slightly forward in the earnestness of his plea, and his voice occasionally thrilling with an unusual amount of *visible* emotion (for him)—while he stated his dignified position that the faculty must express its opinion without publicly "investigating," before he could go before the students & alumni in advocacy & explanation of his idea. The whole thing in superb language & diction. A truly wonderful man.

From Henry Burling Thompson

My dear President Wilson: New York, October 1, 1907

A few minutes after leaving you yesterday I found that Mr. Schroeder had made an appointment to meet the Geological and Biological Committee at Prof. Libbey's house, at 8 o'c. last evening. Consequently, I attended the meeting.

I am pleased to say we have finally pinned them down to a unanimous resolution. They approve of plan "C," with the following reservation: they ask for the Museum ceiling to be eighteen feet in height, as opposed to fifteen feet, which is shown on the plan. The object of this is to give them, in the Museum of Mineralogy and Botany, an opportunity to make use of a gallery for their cases, if necessary. Schroeder approves of this suggestion and is inclined to believe it will help, rather than injure, the present elevation of plan "C."

It now rests with you to forward this work. If you approve of plan "C" and the Committee's suggestion, Prof. Libbey can forward the plans to Mr. Schroeder, and he will proceed at once on sketches on that line.

As this is the first time we have got the architect and the Committee to agree, I feel it would be well to clinch it, for McClure is of a temperament that he might want to ask for changes. We have now got him on record, and I would like to hold him there.

Yours very truly Henry B Thompson

TLS (WP, DLC).

From Charles Francis Adams

My dear Mr. President: Boston. Oct. 2, 1907

I was a good deal interested last evening in coming across the communication entitled "Princeton University" in the *New York Evening Post* of Saturday, Sept. 28th.[1] As a Harvard man, though no longer a member of its Board of Overseers, I follow this discussion closely. Your theory of "Quads" seems to me more nearly to meet existing college requirements than anything else which has been advanced. I am sure I sent you, last summer, a copy of my publication entitled "Three Phi Beta Kappa Addresses," in which I reprinted my Columbia Phi Beta Kappa, of fifteen months ago, entitled "Some Modern College Tendencies," with a "Supplementary Note" thereto directed at the existing conditions at Cambridge.[2] If, however, I have not already sent you a copy, I should be only too glad so to do. My own firm conviction is that Eliot, during his long career as President, so far as the college is concerned, has done much to demoralize our youth. At Harvard there is today, so far as I am competent to judge,—and I have made pretty careful enquiry,—no trace of either systematic mental discipline or intelligent intellectual training. It is all a go-as-you-please, on the basis of supposed natural aptitudes, and along the lines of least resistance.

All this, of course, is merely for your private eye. Nevertheless, I cannot but add I consider your vigorous initiative, as head of Princeton, a more intelligent move, in the direction of a most desirable reform, than I am elsewhere aware of.

I should be greatly obliged to you if you would, in this connection, bear me in mind; and, from time to time, send me any publications bearing on the discussion you have started. I, of course, do not see the *Princeton Alumni Weekly*.

I remain, etc, Charles F. Adams

TLS (WP, DLC).

[1] This brief article, with the date line of Princeton, Sept. 27, 1907, and printed in the "News of the College World" pages of the Saturday Supplement of the *Evening Post*, summarized and quoted portions of Wilson's letter to A. C. Imbrie, July 29, 1907, and Henry van Dyke's article of July 10, 1907 (printed in this volume under these dates), as reproduced in the *Princeton Alumni Weekly*, VIII (Sept. 25, 1907), 4-9.

[2] See WW to C. F. Adams, April 11, 1907, ns. 1 and 2.

Henry Burling Thompson to Cleveland Hoadley Dodge

Dear Cleve: [Wilmington, Del.] 10th Mo., 2d, 1907.

. . . I understand your "Quad" Committee meets Wilson on Friday night. I should, without fail, if I were you, see Hibben before going to that meeting.

I met old Mrs. Ricketts[1] on the ferry boat yesterday, and I think, altogether, she is one of the most remarkable old ladies I have ever met. She gave me the result of a conversation she had with Woodrow on Saturday afternoon. It is too long to recite here, but the old lady has grasped the situation, and sized up the various factors controlling Wilson in a way that is nothing less than remarkable. As she talks in epigrams, I will some time recite some of her remarks, which were keen and clever.

Of course, the Faculty community are seething.

Outside of "Quads" everything is in good shape.

Stephen [Palmer] starts into building this week,—the contract having been let to the Fuller Construction Company,—and the work will be pushed rapidly.

Archie and Momo[2] spent the afternoon with me,—going over the summer's work,—and, I think, are satisfied with the way things have been looked after.

Very sincerely yours, Henry B Thompson

TLS (Thompson Letterpress Books, NjP).

[1] Eliza Getty (Mrs. Palmer Chamberlaine, Sr.) Ricketts.

[2] Archibald Douglas Russell and Moses Taylor Pyne.

An Editorial in the *Daily Princetonian* on the Quadrangle Plan

[Oct. 2, 1907]

THE "QUAD" SYSTEM.

The proposed change in the social life of the University has caused endless comment and criticism throughout the entire body of graduates and undergraduates, faculty and friends of Princeton, and its progress is watched on all sides with jealous eyes. Never before has any movement excited such interest. In the past few years the intellectual side of Princeton was practically revolutionized by the institution of the preceptorial system, yet practically no discussion took place in the outside world. This comparison may point to the fact that what endears Princeton to her constituents is the social life and the peculiar weave of the social fabric, not the educational advantages. But after all is not that a natural state of affairs, for the intellectual side of the University is in the hands of men of wide experience whom everyone is willing to trust because of that wide experience. But the social side is peculiarly a possession of the students, built up and maintained by the students, and is it likely that the students would not rise at invasion into their own province? Is it reasonable to expect that the men of the University would be content to resign quickly their control, and surrender the administration of their personal affairs to a committee of the faculty?

We thoroughly appreciate that great benefits would be derived from a closer affiliation of the educational and social sides of Princeton life, but a great doubt reigns in our minds as to whether these benefits would thoroughly justify a change so radical that Princeton as it is to-day would cease to exist and another, a strange and unknown Princeton rise in its place. It is true that present social conditions are a little uneasy but with the wholesome sentiment gathering strength as we believe it is to-day, these conditions should eventually acquire a stability which is typical of the Yale system. Then, to follow another line of thought is not this affiliation between the two sides of undergraduate life being unconsciously accomplished by a slow system of evolution? Several years ago they were distinctly separated as mutually exclusive spheres of existence, but as one follows the underlying influences and appreciates their tendency, can he not see that through the institution of the preceptorial system especially this segregation is being slowly done away with? And if the fundamental object of the new system is being accomplished in this way, would it not be better to expend our energies in perfecting and broadening the preceptorial system rather than instituting a change so radical and so vital to the interests of all that almost universal opposition is offered to it?

We do not wish to discuss the practical operation of the proposed plan, but one phase of it looms up so threateningly that it demands acknowledgement. Should the new system go into effect, quads would be organized and of one or another of these quads, every undergraduate would become a member. The quads would be established in various parts of the campus, and men in crossing what is to-day the *Princeton* campus would pass through —for instance—Blair quad and from there to Little quad and so on through the various divisions into which Princeton would then be divided. In short, instead of having a unified Princeton, strong in its collective strength, we would have a divided Princeton in which petty jealousies between the quads would destroy the unity and democracy of a University not broken up by artificial barriers. *Class* distinctions exist to-day, and experience has long ago taught us the worth of a democracy reconciled with that wholesome aristocracy based on class seniority. But should these sound distinctions be swept away and barriers substituted which would cleave their way through the four classes would not class distinctions become a farce? And if there be no class distinction, what would foster class spirit? And class spirit, we know, is the nursery of that spirit which pervades Princeton and gives impulse to every throb of its life.

But we do not condemn, neither do we advocate. What we ask is that at the first opportunity President Wilson will explain in person to the undergraduates the advantages of the proposed scheme. At present, the men of the University are forced to frame their conclusions in the dark and opinions thus formed are ever unsatisfactory. We desire that a comprehensive understanding may exist on the part of all; Princeton men are always eager for that which will prove to be the best for Princeton and if it be proved that the proposed scheme would accomplish that end, sentiment, we are sure, would favor it. But until such proof be established, is it right to threaten the very life of the University by the adoption of such a radical policy?

Printed in the *Daily Princetonian*, Oct. 2, 1907.

Paul van Dyke to the Editor of the *Princeton Alumni Weekly*

[Oct. 2, 1907]

To the Editor of The Alumni Weekly.

Our honored President has brought forward a plan for the social reorganization of Princeton University. I have given it the long and careful consideration which every plan he proposes ought to receive from all Princeton men. The longer I think of it the more objections to it force themselves upon me. Let me mention a few of these objections.

1. This radical revolution is a remedy for the evils which have gathered round the clubs, more drastic than is necessary. The clubs are more an effect than a cause. The social conditions at Princeton are as good as those of any American university. I believe them to be better than those of most American universities. Surely the gentlest remedies possible are the best for Princeton to use with her own loyal sons.

2. Far worse evils than those which human nature has caused to gather round the clubs would gather round the "quads."

Arbitrary assignment of members to them would drive the social tendencies, now active in every school and college and in every village of America, to seek expression in things to replace the abolished clubs. Some of these new things would be secret. The evils which beset the clubs would beset them. And other evils which no one charges against the clubs might be added.

If play for choice were given in the assignment of inmates to the "quads," a few years would bring about a state of affairs unparalleled in any American university. The "quads" would, by an irresistible process, become ranked in social standing, and the

University would be involved in the situation and responsible for it. Old Princeton and her ancient spirit would be moribund.

3. The beautiful picture of the life of an ideal "quad" seems to be impossible to realize with students as I know them. Such a life they would either run away from or evade. And for those who did not thus escape, there is in the regime sketched, a latent suggestion of a state of tutelage which would not be wholesome for young men between eighteen and twenty-two. Possibly they might gain under it a little more knowledge. My experience constrains me to doubt whether they would have, for the development of strength of character, the same chance they enjoy under a freer and less artificial life.

PAUL VAN DYKE, Class of 1881.

Printed in the *Princeton Alumni Weekly*, VIII (Oct. 2, 1907), 20-21.

From James Bryce

My dear President Intervale N. H Oct. 3/07

Mindful of your request & of Sir W. Mather's, lately renewed to me, I write to ask whether a day between Oct. 29 & Nov. 2 would suit you for the dedication of the Sun Dial. I am as at present advised, arranging to leave this [place] on Oct. 25 in my automobile which, seeing the difficulties of getting it to Washington in any other way (for it was much damaged when I sent it by sea from Baltimore to Boston) I propose to travel in from here to Washington, taking Princeton if possible on the way. Unluckily automobiles are uncertain things, and though I calculate that I ought to reach Princeton on the fifth day from leaving here (giving one day at Lake George to rest the machine & ourselves) still one can't be sure that some delays may not arise on the way[,] therefore it would not be safe to count on my reaching you before Tuesday the 29th, nor could the function be safely fixed for that day. I don't know whether it would be possible for you to postpone it for a day in case I telegraphed to you that some unforeseen difficulty had arisen; but it seems more prudent to fix a later day, say the 30th. However before making any more definite arrangement, will you kindly tell me if 29th or 30th would be a suitable time for us to come. Perhaps you could also say what would be the best route for an automobile from Albany to Princeton, whether down the W. bank of Hudson all the way or down the E. to Poughkeepsie & there cross the Hudson & down through

New Jersey. Among your friends in Princeton there is probably someone who knows all these roads. Believe me

Yours vy truly James Bryce

ALS (WP, DLC).

From William Kelly Prentice

Dear Dr. Wilson Princeton Oct. 3 '07

I called upon you today forgetting that your hours are in the first half of the week. I wanted only to tell you where I stand upon that matter which is agitating our minds, for I do not wish you to misunderstand me.

I am wholly in sympathy with your desire for reform, and, at least in large measure, with your plans as far as I understand them. And I am ready to go even to the length of suppressing the clubs, if this is necessary in order to remove the evils of the present methods of election. I only do not wish to be asked to vote quads or no quads, because I cannot express my judgment by either aye or no on such a motion. It seems to me, whatever is said about it, Daniels motion commits us to quads. Until the last minute before the last meeting I hoped that motion could be amended: then I was told that it could not be amended because Daniels himself meant his motion to commit us to quads. Hence I spoke & voted as I did. I do not wish to vote against the quad plan; but I cannot honestly vote for it now, until we have taken certain preliminary steps, which will be of the nature of experiments

Since the meeting I have been told that Daniels motion does not mean what it seems to mean, and that it can be amended: that you yourself do not wish to commit yourself to a quad scheme yet. Then I shall certainly vote with you & be very happy over it.

The trouble is we have it the other way in print. It is that article in the June Alumni Weekly that has set us all by the ears & made most of us, except the newcomers, genuinely unhappy.

We all want to be loyal and enthusiastic—as least I do. I think all are ready to approve very drastic measures to reform the clubs. I think all think the non-club men should be provided for: that all classes & types should be brought together as far as possible in an academic relationship. It is quite possible that a quad scheme is the only way. If so I think we will all welcome it. But now, on Monday, if we have to vote quads or no quads, I shall feel obliged to vote no quads, and I do not wish to do that, & that is why I did not want Daniels motion to be brought before the faculty in its present form.

If you are already familiar with this point of view, forgive me for troubling you with this long letter.

–I have held this letter for a day, to see if it says what I mean. I think it does, and anyway I think you will understand.

Yours very sincerely William Prentice

ALS (WP, DLC).

From Edwin Grant Conklin[1]

My dear President Wilson: Philadelphia October 3, 1907.

In reflecting upon the proposition which you have made me[2] I find that there are a few matters upon which I desire additional information.

Do you contemplate the appointment of one or more additional men in the Department of Biology? I observe that courses in Botany and Physiology are listed in your Catalogue for which no instructors are named. As I explained to you, these subjects lie outside my field, but it seems to me important for the development of the Biological Department that they should be well represented.

In view of the fact that many anatomical and microscopical preparations would need to be made for my courses would it be possible for me to have an assistant?

There would be immediate need, I think, of about One Thousand Dollars to furnish apparatus and supplies for my work; could such a sum be provided for this purpose?

I wish again to express to you my hearty sympathy with the ideals which you outlined to me on Saturday and to thank you for the courtesy and honor which you have shown me.

Sincerely yours, E. G. Conklin

TLS (WP, DLC).

[1] Professor and Head of the Department of Zoölogy at the University of Pennsylvania.

[2] That is, that he accept a professorship of biology at Princeton.

To Edwin Grant Conklin

Princeton, N. J.

My dear Professor Conklin: October 4th, 1907.

It is our purpose, so soon as our means permit, to appoint one or more additional men in the Department of Biology. I particularly wish to take care of the field of botany, and am only waiting until an existing strain is taken off our budget, to seek ways and means.

I should confidently expect to be able to provide you with an assistant for laboratory work and, while I cannot speak for the Finance Committee, I should expect to find no insuperable difficulty in obtaining the amount of money you speak of, $1000, for furnishing apparatus and supplies for your work.

It was a great pleasure to see you again, and I am hoping that our knowledge of each other may grow more and more intimate.

Always cordially and sincerely yours,

Woodrow Wilson

TLS (E. G. Conklin Papers, NjP).

To Charles Francis Adams

My dear Mr. Adams: Princeton, N. J. October 4th, 1907.

Allow me to thank you very warmly for your kind letter of October 2nd. I will take pleasure in sending you the report which was made by a committee to our Board of Trustees last June with regard to our new plans here, and also a copy of the first number of our Alumni Weekly for this year, which contains some further matter.

I read with a great deal of interest your address on Some Modern College Tendencies, and felt instinctively that you would be in sympathy with what we are trying to do here. I trust that my winter will not be so full of engrossing tasks as to make it impossible for me to come once or twice to the Round Table Club,[1] and I shall hope that some good fortune may bring us together at one of those meetings so that we may have a talk about this and the whole matter of college life which it involves.

In the meantime allow me to express my obligation to you for your thoughtful kindness in writing.

Sincerely yours, Woodrow Wilson

TLS (photostat in RSB Coll., DLC).

1 A private dining club which met monthly in the rooms of the Knickerbocker Club of New York. See WW to C. H. Marshall, Dec. 26, 1902, n. 3, Vol. 14.

To Robert Bridges

My dear Bobby: Princeton, N. J. October 4th, 1907.

If I had not been so engrossed by a score of things, I would have seen you long before this. You may be sure that I will look you up in New York at the earliest possible opportunity, and we can then arrange for the semi-business talk you want.

I hope that your vacation in the woods did you a lot of good and that you are in fine shape every way.

Always faithfully and affectionately yours,

Woodrow Wilson

TLS (WC, NjP).

A Draft of an Announcement[1]

[c. Oct. 4, 1907]

Princeton, 18th Oct. 1907

Some questions having arisen with regard to the exact significance of the action taken by the Board of Trustees last June, we are authorized by the Board to state that it was its purpose to approve the principle of the reform proposed by its Committee in the report already published in the Alumni Weekly; but to leave the question of the exact form of the necessary changes and all questions of practical feasibility for more thorough discussion and subsequent determination.

It recognized the fact that it would not be practicable or desirable to put any plan into execution without the concurrence and approval of the Faculty of the University, and that the counsel of the alumni was of the utmost consequence in determining the question of its wisdom and feasibility; and that, therefore, ample time must be allowed for exhaustive discussion. So great and complex a reform cannot be hastened either in its discussion or in its execution, and the Board never had any thought of hastening it. It very clearly indicated its wish to make the whole process one of common counsel, and it will, through its Committee, take as much time as common cou[n]sel may require before coming to a final conclusion with regard to the practical suggestions of the report.

It will welcome, as an essential part of the discussion, any suggestions that may be made with the purpose of pointing out other ways in which it may achieve the object it has in mind, even though the suggestions made may be radically different from the recommendations of the Committee; and it will give every suggestion its careful consideration. For this reason it wishes to state very clearly the object it has in mind,—the object to which it hopes all suggestions will be directed. Its purpose is not remedial, but constructive. It is seeking to bring the whole social structure of the University under a common organization which will be susceptible of being dominated by educational influences; and it feels that this would have been necessary whether the present disconnection between the life and the studies of the place had produced positive ⟨evils⟩ harm or not. ⟨The evils which have recently so plainly revealed themselves have only emphasized the necessity for a comprehensive reconstruction of university conditions.⟩ The Board hopes, therefore, that all suggestions submitted to it will have this end in view,—that they will suggest a practicable basis of reorganization, and not merely remedies for existing ⟨evils⟩ conditions. ⟨The evils could no doubt be measurably cured without attaining the ends the Board has in mind.⟩

It is the purpose of the Committee of the Board which has this matter in charge to seek conference with representatives of any group or organization of alumni or undergraduates that may be desirous of being heard with regard to it, either to make suggestions or only to urge objections; and all requests for such conferences will meet with as immediate a response as possible. Such requests should be addressed to Mr. M. T. Pyne, the secretary of the Committee.

WWT MS (WP, DLC).

1 Wilson drafted this statement for the approval of the Committee on the Supplementary Report of the President at its meeting during the evening of October 4, and in the expectation that the Board of Trustees would also approve it and authorize its publication on the day after its meeting on October 17. After discussion on October 4, the committee appointed a subcommittee composed of Wilson, Jacobus, and Jones to prepare a new draft statement on the following morning, October 5. It is printed as an Enclosure with M. W. Jacobus to WW, Oct. 8, 1907.

From David Benton Jones

My dear Doctor New York Oct 5 1907

On the train coming to the city today Dr. Jacobus & I felt so confident of the result before the Board that we wondered whether you couldn't say in *substance* to The Faculty what we now have in mind presenting to the Board as our report and which later will appear in an official form—if passed by the Board. This simply by way of inviting debate on the merits or demerits of the plan. This is only a suggestion and you must not act on it unless the wisdom of doing so is clear to you—as we do not know the local situation as you do.

Very Sincerely, David B. Jones.

Please make no reply as I shall be back in Princeton Wednesday afternoon.

ALS (WP, DLC).

Notes for an Address to the Princeton University Faculty

[Oct. 7, 1907]

Faculty Debate. THE QUADS.

Slow gen[e]sis of the plan

Wrongly conceived of as a remedy for evils. It is a necessary sequel to the preceptorial plan, and based upon a definite conception of education, as a process by which educational influences form mind and habit.

Its purpose: to produce a university organization susceptible of being dominated by educational influences.

Present condition of the university world in America. Nowhere any university life either for graduate or for undergraduate students. Everywhere life is separated from intellectual influences and allowed to form itself in complete independence. Resulting fraternity organization.

Our own favourable situation at the moment:

Just at a turning point in numbers, spirit, and development.

Without complete fraternity development and the nexus of intercollegiate organization.

The clubs viewed from the inside.

Unfavourable aspects of our situation:

The clubs viewed from the outside, and their effect on undergsaduate [undergraduate] life.

The Faculty outside
The honormen outside.
The University outside.
THE LOWER CLASSES.

} These not abuses, but illustrations of what is inevitable under the circumstances.

PRINCIPLES.

Study is a mode of life: universities are organisms.

An American college not a place for exclusiveness. Any organization that has the idea of exclusiveness at its foundation is antagonistic to the best training for citizenship in a democratic country. If such organizations exist they must at least be subordinate and not of the very structure of the place.

We have now to make our choice of ideals, whether we wish to invite youngsters to a life which they form altogether for themselves or to a life by which they are to be formed.

METHODS. New units of integration

Units including all elements of the university: faculty, all three classes, hard students and pass men.

Units whose membership shall be determined not by themselves severally, but by some authority representing the university as an organic whole.

THE PLAN ITSELF.

As imagined and misrepresented

As in fact conceived and intended.

Not form, but principle of the essence.

Discussion

Suggestion,

Adoption.

Mems. for Exposition.

Key idea: Present organization cannot be dominated by educational influences.

Study is a mode of life

A college is not a place for exclusiveness, and any organization that has the idea of exclusiveness anywhere embedded in it makes the right training for a democratic country impossible.

Returning to the key idea: The organization proposed will at least be susceptible of being dominated by educational influences. Whether it is or not depends entirely on our characters and capacities, not upon the chance we may have of establishing influential connections with independent organizations.

We have now to make our choice of ideal, whether we wish to invite youngsters to a life which they shall form for themselves or to a life which shall form them, to live near us or to live with us.

WWT MS (WP, DLC).

From the Minutes of the Princeton University Faculty

4 p.m. October 7, 1907

The Faculty met, the President presiding. . . .

The first order of business being the motion offered by Professor Daniels, September 26, by unanimous consent the words "the principle of" were inserted before the words "the plan" in the first paragraph of that motion.

A statement was made by the President introductory to the discussion of the motion. He expressed his opinion as to what constitutes the principle of the plan under discussion by saying in effect that

We are seeking

1. A new unit of organization,

2. Containing representatively all the elements of the University, the Faculty and all four classes of undergraduates.

3. Having a common life and an organization of its own, and

4. With a membership determined by some authority representing the University as a whole.

The Faculty adjourned to meet on Monday at 4 p.m. for the consideration of this pending question. . . .

An Abstract by Andrew Fleming West

October 7, 1907.

ABSTRACT OF PRESIDENT WILSON'S SPEECH TO THE FACULTY

The plan proposed last June before the Trustees is in no sense remedial. I have no quarrel with the Clubs of Princeton University. In fact there is not so wholesome a body of men in any of our American Colleges or Universities as the members of the Princeton Clubs. There is nothing to investigate, only to create.

What is before us is the logical and obvious duty to lift Princeton to the next step of her development.

The Clubs in this connection have never been attacked on account of intrinsic unworthiness.

We are called upon at this time to set the country an example of constructive worth. It is not in our choice to stand still, because Princeton is the natural leader among all the Universities of America. Our problem is their problem, because there is no college or university in America at the present time where there is university life. By university life what do I mean? I mean the relation between teacher and taught which should obtain outside of the classroom through the intimate intercourse which comes only through living together.

No teacher can ever touch the life of the university inside the classroom. Just as a father when he is didactic is offensive and has an influence over his child only when he is his natural companion. So also the relation of the instructor to the student.

What is the situation today in Princeton? Nine-tenths of the Freshmen do not know the names of their instructors (this on the authority of the Dean of the University).

A considerable number of the students do not even know me personally when they meet me on the street.

The members of the Faculty are not related to the students as persons. There is no possible way of their manifesting their personality in the classroom.

The Faculty has no part in the life of the University.

This is practically the situation in all colleges in America. There is, however, a particular opportunity for Princeton at this time.

The advantages which Princeton has in solving this problem. First–Princeton is at the turning point in numbers, spirit and development. Expert educators say that beyond the number of twelve hundred there is an inevitable process of disintegration into units which consist merely of individuals. All spiritual bonds are snapped asunder and forgotten. There must therefore be some organic redintegration of our social life, else the ordinary processes of growth will cause the disintegration of our undergraduate body.

Second advantage–We have organizations already here, namely the club[s], which can be used and transformed into separate colleges. Taken from the inside alone, their organization is admirable, and here I repeat what I have said before that there are no evils to investigate, only something to appreciate. Our only trouble is the bare existence of these clubs, and what that existence brings about. The clubs at the present time constitute in the minds of Princeton graduates the attraction and charm of Princeton. We should not blame them for thinking so because we have allowed them so to think. A criticism of a graduate of Princeton recently will indicate this point of view. He said the characteristic life of Princeton would be destroyed by too much intellectual endeavor. The social life is disconnected now organically from the intellectual life of the University. The characteristic feature of the place is that membership in a club is necessary if a student is to maintain a decent standing among his fellows. The mind of the Freshman is filled with wonder as to whether he will be able to make a club. To wonder is to plan, to plan is to combine and combination results in organized effort. This gives us the entire system of the Sophomore Clubs, and the hat-line followings.

The student cannot devote himself to study without missing social advantages. The honormen are outside of clubs, the Faculty are outside of clubs, the University is outside of the clubs. The clubs therefore estopp any plan for organic reorganization. We must stamp out every principle and practice of exclusiveness, and we ask the clubs to unite with us and become partners in a common undertaking. What is the idea of the organic redintegration of the University according to the Quad plan? It is nothing more or less than Professor West's idea of the Graduate School with its close, dining hall, common room &c. adapted to the undergraduate life. More particularly it may be characterized in the four following respects:

1. It establishes a new unit in which all classes are represented, Freshmen, Sophomores, Juniors, Seniors and Faculty.

2. The unit is given a common life. There is no limitation of social life whatever which may be extended freely to intercourse between members of the several Quads.

3. Membership in the Quad is to be determined by the authorities of the University.

4. Each Quad is to have Preceptors in residence. One is a master, but is the head of the Quad only as a figurehead. Each Quad is to form its own rules of government by a house committee.

In conclusion I am pledged to no specific form of integration. The Imbrie correspondence is to be thrown out of this debate altogether, for I gave at that time my individual views which common counsel with the members of the Board of Trustees may subsequently change. To vote for Professor Danuel's [Daniels'] resolution is to adopt an ideal only.

I BEG OF YOU TO FOLLOW ME IN THIS HAZARDOUS, BUT SPLENDID ADVENTURE.

CC MS (UA, NjP).

From the Diary of William Starr Myers

Mon. Oct. 7 [1907].

Another faculty meeting, mainly taken up by a superb speech of 1½ hours by Pres. Wilson in explanation of his "quad" plan, or "idea" as he prefers to call it. He stated, that of the *Club* men, 9.63% were honor men,–of non-club men, 41.7% were honor men!

From Theodore Whitefield Hunt

Dear Dr Wilson, Princeton University 10 8 1907

I must write you to the effect that it has never been my privilege to hear a more inspiring address on the subject of University Education than that which you gave us yesterday. I went out from the hearing of it feeling more hopeful than I ever have felt with regard to the realization of such an ideal in Princeton. What an exalted ideal it is, and let me say to you that you have done an invaluable service to this institution & to the American college world at large by simply presenting it & insisting upon some approximate exemplification of it. It does one's soul good to hear a college president, in these days of ardent academic rivalry, discard the mere idea of numbers for numbers' sake and urge the primacy of intellectual interests above all else, let it cost what it may.

I wish you signal success in your regenerating work, and it ought to be a source of genuine gratitude to you that your leadership in modern American University Education is already being accorded you.

Cordially Yours T. W. Hunt

ALS (WP, DLC).

From Melancthon Williams Jacobus, with Enclosure

My dear President Wilson: Hartford 8 Oct 1907

I received this morning your request for a Curriculum Com. meeting on Wednesday evening, and have sent out the notices this afternoon.

I enclose herewith the copy of the draft decided upon at our Sub-Committee meeting Saturday forenoon. This has been sent to all members of the Committee by Special Delivery, ensuring its prompt reception by them tomorrow—if not tonight

Mr Jones and I travelled together to New York Saturday and talked over the situation as far as it was possible to do so on the train. His suggestion that you make personal use of the ideas you have embodied in the memorandum during the Faculty debate on the subject Monday ev'g seemed to me to be excellent; since, if it clarified the minds of the Committee, Friday evening, it should help in the same direction with the Faculty.

As these are your personal ideas communicated to the Board for authorized statement as representing their own position, as understood by themselves, there can be no question of your right to embody them in your remarks to the Faculty, as representing your own understanding of the action

I cannot but believe that good humor, patience and a determined hammering away at the principle involved must bring final victory Cordially yours M W Jacobus

ALS (WP, DLC).

ENCLOSURE

An Announcement

Princeton, 18 October, 1907.

Some question having arisen with regard to the exact significance of the action taken by the Board of Trustees last June, I am authorized by the Board to state that it was its purpose to approve the principle of the reform proposed by its Committee in the report already published in the Alumni Weekly; but to leave the question of the exact form of the necessary changes and all questions of practical feasibility for more thorough discussion and subsequent determination.

It recognized the fact that it would not be practicable or desirable to put any plan into execution without the concurrence and approval of the Faculty of the University, and that the counsel of the alumni was of the utmost consequence in determining the question of its wisdom and feasibility; and that, therefore, an ample time must be allowed for exhaustive discussion. So great and complex a reform cannot be hastened either in its discussion or in its execution, and the Board never had any thought of hastening it. It very clearly indicated its wish to make the whole process one of common counsel, and it will, through its Committee, take as much time as common counsel may require before coming to a final conclusion with regard to the practical suggestions of the report.

It will welcome, as an essential part of the discussion, any suggestions that may be made with the purpose of pointing out other ways in which it may achieve the object it has in mind, even though the suggestions made may be radically different from the recommendations of the Committee; and it will give every suggestion its careful consideration. For this reason it wishes to state very clearly the object it has in mind,—the object to which it hopes all suggestions will be directed. Its purpose is not remedial, but constructive. And the principle of the general plan which it has proposed is simply that the whole social structure of the University shall be under a common organization which will be susceptible of being dominated by educational influences. The Board feels that this would have been necessary whether the present disconnection between the life and the studies of the place had produced positive harm or not, and it hopes, therefore, that all suggestions submitted to it will have this end in view,—that they will suggest a practicable basis of reorganization, and not merely remedies for existing conditions.

In other words:

1. What was adopted was a principle expressed in a general plan.
2. This action was based on the conviction that the present conditions are incompatible with the intellectual life of the University.
3. What was sought was a social organization which can be used as a means of intellectual development.
4. The action of the Board was not final as to the particular plan, but with a view to full and free discussion as to the practicableness of the plan.

It is the purpose of the Committee of the Board which has this matter in charge, to seek conferences with representatives of any group or organization of alumni or undergraduates that may be desirous of being heard with regard to it, either to make suggestions or only to urge objections; and all requests for such conferences will meet with as immediate a response as possible. Such requests should be addressed to Mr. M. Taylor Pyne, Princeton, New Jersey, the secretary of the Committee.[1]

T MS (WP, DLC).

[1] It is obvious from Jacobus's further correspondence and Wilson's failure to submit this memorandum to the trustees at their meeting on October 17 that the Committee on the Supplementary Report of the President was not willing to approve this proposed statement. As later documents will also reveal, Pyne had already determined to scuttle the quadrangle plan.

To William Henry Carpenter[1]

My dear Sir: Princeton, N. J. October 9th, 1907.

I spent most of my time this summer writing the lectures which I delivered last spring at Columbia University on the Blumenthal Foundation. The stenographer's notes were of little service to me, and I had practically to write the lectures de novo. I was able, therefore, to complete only six of the eight.

I am hoping, of course, to complete the other two before the Christmas vacation, but the multitude and character of the duties which engross me during term time make it impossible to say with confidence that I can do so.

If you think it worth while, in view of this doubt, to proceed at once to print the six lectures which are ready, I will try to send them to you at an early date, but I must not conceal from you the considerable doubt as to whether the other two can follow them promptly enough to make this desirable.

Awaiting your opinion in the matter,[2]

Very truly yours, Woodrow Wilson

TLS (photostat in RSB Coll., DLC).

[1] Villard Professor of Germanic Philology at Columbia and Secretary of Columbia University Press.

[2] Further correspondence is missing, but Carpenter decided to defer publication until Wilson had completed the last two chapters. These Wilson wrote during his vacation in Bermuda in January and February 1908.

Adrian Hoffman Joline to the Editor of the *Princeton Alumni Weekly*

[Oct. 9, 1907]

To the Princeton Alumni Weekly:

When the plan which, for brevity, may be called "the Quad Plan," was suddenly disclosed to us last summer, many old Princetonians like myself were anxious and perplexed. We recognized the fact that it was revolutionary, and I, for one, was inclined to utter an earnest protest. However, we of advancing years are prone to distrust first impressions. Hence I deemed it wise to wait, to reflect, and to consider the subject carefully before expressing any opinion. I have reflected, and I have not been hasty, but I am confirmed in my original opinion that the adoption of this plan will be the destruction of Princeton. I am in doubt whether it has really been finally adopted or not. The President is not clear on the point. Sometimes he says it is an accomplished fact, and sometimes he invites discussion of it. I am inclined to believe that he regards it as a settled thing, and that only the details are to be considered. If so, a grave mistake has been committed. The great majority of the alumni is against the scheme, and I do not think that he can afford to treat with indifference the views and feelings of the men who represent Princeton in the work of the world.

It is not easy in the limited space which I may venture to occupy in your columns to discuss the matter fully or thoroughly; and it is not necessary for me to go over again the clear and eloquent argument of Doctor van Dyke. I may at least suggest some of the reasons why a loyal and devoted son of Princeton, as I assert myself to be, opposes vigorously this startling effort to efface the honorable traditions of our grand old college and to launch us on an unknown and uncharted sea of useless experiment.

I am told by advocates of the plan that it is necessary because of the "evils of the Clubs." I learn from its distinguished promoter that it is "not primarily or even chiefly social; that it is academic and aims at the best university organization." In other words, it is to appeal to opponents of the Clubs because the Quads are to supplant the Clubs, and to a Club man because it is the best thing for the University. I do not hold any brief for the Clubs; they arose and grew up long after my day. I say nothing about the fact that their foundation and development have for well nigh thirty years been recognized and encouraged by the college authorities. The plainest principles of decency and honor seem to forbid their annihilation now, after large sums have been invested in their properties in reliance upon the good faith of the governors of the University. The "evils" connected with them appear to be of a kind capable of correction. They are not peculiar to Princeton. Wholesale destruction is no remedy. If a patient suffers, to kill him may terminate the suffering, but possibly there are less vigorous ways of relieving him. The only evil I have heard of, which calls for the action of the Trustees, is that they divert the minds of the students from their studies, particularly about election time. But so do athletics and all forms of amusement. If you take away all natural, social life from the Princeton undergraduate you will make Jack a very dull boy indeed. Every one who has had any experience with the world knows that all these things may be made the subject of reasonable regulation. I venture to say that if the task of regulating is too much for the executive officers, I can name at least half a dozen of the Trustees who, if they would give their minds to it, could devise a plan which would settle all the club trouble.

I do not care particularly about the clubs. I am sure that they have many wise and respected graduate members who will be glad to aid in the work of reform. But I do care greatly about dear old Princeton, her traditions, and her spirit. I am proud of an undergraduate body which maintains the honor system,—but whose members we are told cannot be trusted to choose their own friends. Whether you kill the clubs or not, you must deal with Princeton spirit and Princeton independence. You may make all the laws you please, but you can never prevent young men of kindred tastes and kindred feelings from combining in some form and in their own way to maintain their college friendships and associations. You may abolish clubs but you will never be able to abolish human nature. Princeton once prohibited fraternities; but they continued to exist until the clubs were formed. Artificial prohibitions, the product of the pedagogue spirit, will utterly fail, and in the place of dignified and respectable societies you will have secret and illicit combinations which will double and treble the evils of which you complain. Any young man who enters Princeton has a right to choose his friends, to decide for himself with whom he will associate. He ought not to be compelled to submit to dictation about his table-companions. He should not be reduced to the level of a boarding-school boy. If a college education is designed merely to prepare men to be preceptors and pedants I am greatly mistaken; I believe that it is intended to prepare men for an efficient life in any calling.

There is no man who commands more of my admiration than the honored President of our University; but, with becoming humility, I venture to intimate that his habit of the study and the library has tended to conceal from him the real nature of young men, a nature which, guided and directed by wise instructors, has given to Princeton men their reputation as typical college men in this country. A graduate of another college said to me a few days ago, "Princeton is my ideal college." Why? because of the intelligent independence of its men. Fetter that independence by the method proposed, and you ruin the individuality of the lads who are fitting themselves for life. Book-study, class-room drudgery, are well in their way. It is the most natural thing in the world to say that young men go to college to get an education, but that education is not wholly the product of the class-room. The contact of minds, the relations between the men, their little strifes, their debates, their college politics, educate them for the world. I have heard that the President of the University has said that it would be better for Princeton to turn out one man a master of his subject than to have a thousand men in attendance. I doubt it. It is a perversion of the idea of a college. I would rather have Princeton turn out each year one *man*—a man in every sense, in courage, in loyalty, in independence of thought, in originality, than fifty mere scholars. Princeton is not a professional school; it ought to send forth men qualified to deal with the problems of life and not purely closet students, tamed by preceptors or perhaps matrons, launched into the world from the cloisters of a "Quad."

Before we commit ourselves without investigation and at the bidding of a well-beloved, well-meaning, but not infallible personage to a system which is foreign to our traditions and long-established customs; before we go back to the middle ages for our college scheme; may it not be well to inquire into the workings of that system elsewhere? Surely it must be of advantage to examine some competent witnesses as to the effect of it on the English universities, for example. Does it foster democracy there? Does it destroy cliques and associations? Does it help in the educational work of those universities? I am assured that it does not. May I ask why this revolutionary scheme was suddenly and without warning sprung upon Princeton? It may be that the ideas of the Alumni are of little worth; that the graduate body is to be disregarded. I have yet to meet one of our number who is not opposed to the plan. I doubt if it is approved by more than five per cent. of the whole body. I have no time to comment at length upon the President's letter to Mr. Imbrie, but I find it wholly unsatisfactory upon the main points. If occasion arises, I want to be heard further on that exposition. To me, the plan is without a single redeeming feature. ADRIAN H. JOLINE '70.

Printed in the *Princeton Alumni Weekly*, VIII (Oct. 9, 1907), 36-38.

From James Bryce

My dear President Intervale N. H Oct. 12/07

Many thanks for your letter. On further examination of the routes from here to Princeton, and having been pressed by a relative of my wife's to stop for a day with him on the Hudson I think it will be safer to fix the 31st of October rather than the 30th for the function. I hope this will be equally convenient for you and all others concerned. Probably I could reach Princeton by the night of the 29th, but it would be so unfortunate if any collapse of the automobile delayed my arrival that it seems better to run no risks and fix the 31st. I shall of course hope to reach Princeton on the 30th and it will give us great pleasure to stay with you & Mrs. Wilson while we are there.

Thank you for your answer regarding the automobile line of route from Newburgh to Princeton, which you tell me ought to be through Morristown and Somerville. I suppose that from Newburgh to Morristown it runs through Suffern, Pompton Falls, Montclair[,] Caldwell and Denville, so far as I can make out by the Automoble Blue Book. I hope the roads are good, for this will make all the difference to my reaching Princeton in one day from Barrytown on Hudson (near Poughkeepsie)

Will you please tell me at what hour the ceremony will take place? I assumed the afternoon.

Yours very sincerely James Bryce

ALS (WP, DLC).

From Charles August David Burk[1]

[Princeton, N. J.]

My dear President Wilson: Oct. 12, '07.

As a loyal Princetonian I cannot refrain from expressing my unbounded appreciation and commendation of your efforts to insure longevity to *Princeton Spirit* and *Democracy*.

Yours very truly, Charles A. D. Burk.

ALS (WP, DLC).

[1] A member of the Class of 1909, who was not a club member.

To Charles August David Burk

My dear Mr. Burk: Princeton, N. J. October 14th, 1907.

I thank you most sincerely for your letter of October 12th. Our new plans have been very much misunderstood and very ignorantly opposed, and it is very delightful to get an occasional evidence that they are understood and supported.

Sincerely yours, Woodrow Wilson

TLS (WC, NjP).

From the Minutes of the Princeton University Faculty

4 p.m. October 14, 1907.

Special Meeting: The Faculty met, the President presiding.

The discussion of the pending question was postponed to be the first order of business at the next meeting, and the Faculty adjourned to meet at 4 p.m. October 21. . . .

From Melancthon Williams Jacobus

My dear President Wilson: Saybrook, Conn 14 Oct. 1907

This is scribbled in bed, where an acute attack of lumbago placed me yesterday morning

The doctor has done what he could but I confess to having small hopes of being able to get to my feet by Wednesday. Should I be able to do so I will make every effort to get to Princeton for the meeting.[1]

In the meanwhile I submit the following as a possible Committee report by the Board

Resolved: (1) That the Quadrangle Plan presented to the Board in the report of the Committee last June embodied the principle that the existence of the University is dependent upon a guaranteed equality of intellectual and social opportunities to its students and an elimination of any system of special privileges as fatal to its life.

(2) That the Board adopt this principle as its conviction and approve of the plan in which it was embodied—with the understanding that in so approving of the plan it desires full & frank

discussion of it, with a view to assuring itself of its practicableness before final adoption.

You are at liberty of course to do anything with this you choose –or nothing. My only desire is to have some resolution come before the Board that will compel them to definite action.

With kindest regards & the hope that Princeton may yet be saved to her great possibilities

Yours faithfully M W Jacobus

ALS (WP, DLC).

[1] That is, of the Board of Trustees on the following day, Thursday, October 17.

From George Black Stewart

My dear President Wilson: Auburn, N. Y. October 14, 1907.

I learn from the "Alumni Weekly" and other sources that there is developing a serious opposition to the proposed Quad system at Princeton. I merely write to assure you that with my present light I am prepared to stand by you in your effort to improve the existing conditions. My recollection of the action of the Board is that the Board distinctly adopted the Quad system, leaving the matter of ways and means to be wrought out through discussion and effort. It was on this understanding that I voted for the plan. Of course I understood, as I presume all understood, that the plan would involve large expense and that nothing could be done until this expense was satisfactorily provided for, and that there were many details involving Faculty, students, alumni, and clubs, which would have to be wrought out in friendly, frank, and tactful discussion. So far as I am familiar with the opposition to the scheme I am confirmed by it in my original intention cordially to support you in your effort to realize your purpose. I hope to be present at the meeting of the Board on Friday.

I remain, Yours sincerely, Geo B Stewart

P.S. This letter does not need a reply.

TLS (WP, DLC).

Allan Marquand to the Trustees of Princeton University

Dear Sirs, Princeton. Oct. 14 1907

In order to promote in a University the study of the History of Art, it is necessary that its Museum should be provided with a varied and representative collection of original objects, with collections of casts and reproductions and with larger collections of books, photographs and slides. During the last twenty-five years the Museum, out of its meagre resources, has acquired a few representative originals, and by gift collections of pottery and casts of sculpture. I myself during the same period have made a collection of some 4000 books, 30,000 photographs and 7000 slides, selected so as to illustrate the general history of art. Since this collection has been housed in the Museum its usefulness to the University has been greatly increased.

It is my desire that so much of this collection as is required for purposes of reference and study should permanently remain in the Museum. To this end and on condition that you will furnish a suitable librarian to keep it in order and facilitate its usefulness I have great pleasure in presenting it through you to Princeton University. Yours very truly Allan Marquand

ALS (Trustees' Papers, UA, NjP).

From Charles Wood

My dear President, Philadelphia Oct 15/07

Many years of high esteem & admiration for your abilities & character, are the only claim I have to a patient hearing, at this time, on your part. You showed such masterly qualities in conceiving & perfecting the preceptorial system, that the new presentation of the Quad as a substitute for the club on your part, was sufficient to incline me in its favor. Nothing has since ocurred to change my first impression, but it is, I fear impossible to carry out a change so radical at this time, without alienating some of Princetons good friends in the Board of Trustees, & in the Alumni. You will win the unbounded gratitude of every lover of the university, if at this crisis, you can harmonize all diverse elements by consenting to a temporary post-ponement of a triumph, which within a year or two is sure to come

Very cordially yours Charles Wood.

ALS (WP, DLC).

Henry Burling Thompson to Cleveland Hoadley Dodge

Dear Cleve: [Wilmington, Del.] 10th Mo., 15th, 1907.

I shall not come over to New York to-day, as I had expected, for I am still nursing my cold, and I have got to be in shape for the Thursday meeting.

I have received two letters from Momo since Sunday.

Wilson seems absolutely obdurate. Jones showed me a very mild proposition, which, candidly, seems useless, but, at the same time, harmless. I told him that I did not approve of it, but even this proposition, Momo writes me, Wilson refuses to endorse.

I can see only one way out of this situation, with honor to the University, and that is, a manly withdrawal of the scheme by Wilson himself. If we settle this question over his head, his efficiency and prestige for the future must, of necessity, be impaired; but I have decided that it is essential that this question should be settled definitely on Thursday.

I shall be at your house about four o'clock to-morrow afternoon.

Very sincerely yours, Henry B Thompson

P.S. I have stopped worrying about this. What is the use?

TLS (Thompson Letterpress Books, NjP).

Harold Griffith Murray to Cleveland Hoadley Dodge

Dear Sir: New York, October 15th, 1907.

The following is the Financial Report of the Committee of Fifty for the fiscal year ending July 31, 1907.

Month.	*Amount due from subscriptions.*	*Amount cancelled or uncollected.*
1906		
Aug.	$ 2,350.	
Sep.	6,330.	
Oct.	4,895.	$ 125.
Nov.	520.	
Dec.	5,155.	10.
1907.		
Jan.	11,445.	105.
Feb.	27,609.	190.
Mar.	3,816.	760.
Apr.	8,905.	1,105.
May.	15,054.	182.
June	4,264.	285.
July	36,540.	8,450.
TOTAL	$126,883.	$11,212.

TOTAL NET COLLECTIONS $115,671.

Interest earned on money raised by this Committee and paid in to the University for Endowment purposes, is not included in the above statement, although roughly estimated, this sum would approximate Ten Thousand Dollars.

The Endowment Fund has been raised to $605,125., and the books show the total number of subscribers to be 507, of which fourteen are subscribers in the endowment form. These figures do not include the moneys raised by the different Class funds under the auspices of this Committee for the new dormitory. As nearly as I can tabulate, this would amount to approximately $20,000. including the amount being raised by the Classes for Patton Hall during the last year, $21,000. it gives a grand total of $156,671 which the alumni have contributed during the past year toward the support of Princeton, exclusive of the Alumni Fund, and money given by some of the Alumni for specific purposes as Class Dormitories, Laboratories, Halls, etc.

Yours respectfully, H G Murray Secretary.

TLS (Trustees' Papers, UA, NjP).

To Allan Marquand

Princeton, N. J.

My dear Professor Marquand: October 16th, 1907.

I received yesterday your letter to myself,[1] accompanied by a letter to the Board of Trustees presenting your collection of books and photographs and slides to the University, on the condition that a librarian capable of properly caring for them be provided by the University. I know that the Board will regard this as a most generous and valuable gift and that it will seem to them a very delightful evidence of your devotion to the University.

I want especially to thank you for what you so kindly say of your feeling for myself in the personal letter which accompanies the formal gift. I hope that I have not failed to make you realize how highly I appreciate your own character and labors for the University, or how sincerely it is my desire to do everything possible to facilitate the work of the Art Department.

With warmest regard,

Cordially and faithfully yours, Woodrow Wilson

TLS (A. Marquand Papers, NjP).

[1] It is missing.

From Melancthon Williams Jacobus

Saybrook, Conn Oct 16 1907

Sign my name to any committee report embodying essentially the suggested resolution I sent you. In this *momentrous* [momentous] event, I wish to stand with you on unquestioned record before the board. M. W. Jacobus

T telegram (WP, DLC).

From Edwin Grant Conklin

My dear President Wilson, Philadelphia, Oct. 16, 1907.

I have decided to accept the position which you have offered me at Princeton. While my answer has been long delayed, and while I have found it difficult to decide between the several good opportunities which were open to me, now that I have decided I wish you to know that I shall come without hesitation; with full confidence in the situation at Princeton, and with high hopes for the future.[1]

I wrote Professor McClure a few days ago that if I could be granted a sabbatical year while the new building is being completed I should decide at once in favor of Princeton. At the same time I did not wish to make this a condition of my coming. If it would suit you better to have me come to Princeton next year and to grant me leave of absence later for study abroad, this would be satisfactory to me.

In view of the uncertainty of life may I ask you to confirm by letter to me the terms of the offer which you made me and which I have accepted?

With pleasant anticipations of close and helpful associations with you and your colleagues,

I am, Sincerely yours, E. G. Conklin

ALS (WP, DLC).

1 Conklin later recalled that he had accepted the call to Princeton because, after talking with Wilson, he had been "carried away by this [Wilson's] splendid vision of 'the perfect place of learning.'" "When I first met Professor Edward Capps, who had come to Princeton from the University of Chicago," Conklin continued, "he said to me, 'What brought you to Princeton?' I replied: 'Woodrow Wilson, and what brought you here?' 'The same,' he said." William Starr Myers (ed.), *Woodrow Wilson: Some Princeton Memories* (Princeton, N. J., 1946), pp. 58-59.

To Edwin Grant Conklin

Princeton, N. J.
My dear Professor Conklin: October 17th, 1907.

I write at once to express my great gratification that you have decided to come to us. Our Board of Trustees meets today, and I shall submit to them a recommendation to the effect that you be granted a leave of absence for your first year of connection with Princeton, on the same terms upon which you would have enjoyed it at the University of Pennsylvania. I shall hope and expect to write you tomorrow of the adoption of this recommendation. I feel confident that the Trustees will take the same pleasure that I take in arranging for your coming to us under conditions which will be altogether satisfactory to you and which will not disappoint you in your hope to have a year at this time on the other side of the water.

With most cordial regard and very great pleasure at your decision, Sincerely yours, Woodrow Wilson

TLS (E. G. Conklin Papers, NjP).

Henry Burchard Fine to the Board of Trustees' Committee on Morals and Discipline

Gentlemen: PRINCETON UNIVERSITY, OCTOBER 17, 1907.

I beg to submit the following report:

The number of students dropped last June for deficiencies in scholarship was 52 as against 46 in June, 1906. Of these dropped students 8 were Juniors, 21 were Sophomores, 19 were Freshmen, and 4 were Special Students. Of the 48 who were regular students, 16 were A.B. or Litt.B. men, 9 were B.S. men, and 23 were C.E. men.

The total number of new students is 364 as against 358 last year. The following table indicates the number of Freshmen candidates for each of the degrees—A.B., B.S. and Litt.B., and C.E. For purposes of comparison the corresponding figures for last year are also given:

	1907	1906
Freshmen, A.B.	132	138
B.S. and Litt.B	101	92
C.E.	91	95
Total	324	325
Specials and Upperclassmen	40	33
Grand Total	364	358

It should be added that practically all of the 40 students entering this year who are classified above as Specials and Upperclassmen are men who have been admitted from other colleges. Most of them have been given provisional enrolment as Specials in accordance with our present regulations, but are in reality candidates for one of our degrees.

It will be noticed that the number of entering students is practically the same as last year. I regard it as somewhat remarkable that the new rule which went into effect this fall, that students entering the C.E. department must be without conditions in Mathematics, should have so slightly affected the number of such students.

I called attention last fall to the high quality of preparation of the Freshmen as shown by their entrance examinations. I am glad to say that the same thing is to be said of the present Freshmen. Last year 65% of the class were admitted either without conditions or with but one condition; this year 67%.

Of the entering students 42% are Presbyterians and 28% Episcopalians. There are 22 Methodists, 21 Baptists, 15 Catholics, 11 Congregationalists, 8 Lutherans, 7 Jews, 6 Dutch Reformed, 5 Unitarians, 3 Universalists, 3 Christian Scientists, 1 Quaker, and 11 enroll themselves as belonging to no denomination. About one-half of the entering students are communicants of the churches with which they are connected.

The average age of the Freshman class at entrance is eighteen years and nine months.

In May last the Faculty had occasion to suspend 27 students for their connection with a so called keg or beer party, given by one of the Freshmen clubs to celebrate their receiving a hat following. (A full account of the affair is appended to this report.) At the same time we issued a notice that hereafter any one reported as being present at a keg party would be suspended, whether he drank anything or not. We have every reason to believe that our action has put an end to organized affairs of this kind.

Toward the end of the year the Freshmen were notified that the parade on the evening of the Friday before Commencement must be abandoned unless they could give satisfactory assurances that there would be no drinking connected with the affair. The Freshmen met and voted to pledge themselves to no drinking whatsoever that day. The parade was, therefore, permitted, and I am happy to say that so far as our knowledge goes no member of the class violated his pledge.

Since my last report 14 students have been suspended for intoxication, 3 for false chapel registration, and 1 student has been finally dismissed from college for violating the Honor System.

A new Proctor, Wm. Coan, takes the place [of] [John William] Topley, resigned, and thus far is proving to be an efficient officer.

Respectfully submitted, H. B. Fine

THE AFFAIR OF MAY 11, 1907.

On the night of Saturday, May 11, a disorderly and lawless affair occurred on the college campus. Certain students had ordered ten kegs of beer brought to the lower part of the college grounds, and word of this having been passed around, a large number of their fellows gathered to drink it. Early in the afternoon I had learned of what was impending and did what I could to make it known that the beer party was prohibited. I also instructed the Proctor to confiscate the beer. When the beer arrived a considerable body of students had gathered to receive it. The Proctor at once proceeded to carry out my instructions, announcing as he did so that he was acting under the orders of the Faculty, that the beer party was prohibited, and that any interference with him in the discharge of his duty would have very serious consequences. Notwithstanding his repeated warnings, as he was conducting the wagons carrying the beer across the college grounds, the students made an attack on the wagons, wrested the beer from him, and proceeded to drink it.

The names of 27 students were reported to me by the Proctor as being connected with this affair—26 of them at least to the extent of participating in drinking the beer and 1 for being especially disorderly and refusing to go home when told to do so. On examining these students we reached the conclusion that it was impossible to draw distinctions among them, since in the darkness the Proctor was unable to see who had made the attack on the beer wagons. We therefore decided to suspend all 27 of them for the remainder of the term, a period of about three weeks. They were allowed to return to Princeton after Commencement to take their examinations. All, except one who was dropped for deficiency in standing, are back in their classes.

TRS (Trustees' Papers, UA, NjP).

From the Minutes of the Board of Trustees of Princeton University

[Oct. 17, 1907]

The Trustees of Princeton University met in stated session in the Trustees' Room in the Chancellor Green Library, Princeton, New Jersey, at eleven o'clock on Thursday morning, October 17, 1907.

The President of the University in the chair.

The meeting was opened with prayer by Dr. Wood. . . .

On motion of Mr. Henry duly seconded it was

RESOLVED, That the Board of Trustees extend to Professor Marquand their hearty thanks for his generous gift of his collection of books, photographs, and slides, selected to illustrate the general History of Art and that the President of the University be authorized to make whatever arrangements in relation to the care of the collection he shall deem best. . . .

NO REPORT FROM COMMITTEE ON REORGANIZATION OF UNIVERSITY

The President of the University, Chairman of the Committee on the Reorganization of the University, stated that the Committee had no report to offer.

RECONSIDERATION OF ACTION ON REORGANIZATION OF UNIVERSITY

Mr. Pyne offered the following resolutions which were duly seconded:

I. RESOLVED, that the action taken by the Board last June on the recommendation of the Committee on the Supplementary Report of the President be reconsidered.

II. RESOLVED, That the Board do not now deem it wise to adopt the recommendation made last June by the Committee on the Supplementary Report of the President and that the President be requested to withdraw the plan embodied in the Report of that Committee.

III. RESOLVED, That the Committee be discharged.

The first resolution was voted on and adopted.

Chancellor Magie offered an amendment to the second resolution which was duly seconded and a vote having been taken the amendment was lost.

The second resolution was then voted on and adopted.
The third resolution was voted on and adopted.

EXPLANATORY STATEMENT OF ACTION BY BOARD

The following resolution was offered by Mr. Dodge and seconded by Mr. Pyne:

RESOLVED, That the Board adopt the following:

The Board having deemed it wise to reconsider the action, which it took last June on the recommendation of the Committee on the Social Coordination of the University, have requested the President to withdraw the plan, embodied in the report of that Committee, and in compliance with this request, he has withdrawn it. The Board fully recognize the fact that the President's own convictions in the matter have not changed, and have no wish to hinder him in any way in his purpose, to endeavor to convince the members of the Board and Princeton men generally that this plan is the real solution of the problem of coordinating the social and intellectual life of the University.

SUBSTITUTE RESOLUTION

After a discussion of the resolution Mr. Cleveland offered a substitute resolution which was duly seconded and is as follows:

RESOLVED, That the Board of Trustees, recognizing the duty of correcting the evils existing in the social and Academic coordination of the University will speedily cooperate with the President in the performance of such duty–notwithstanding the action this day taken.

SUBSTITUTE RESOLUTION LOST

After a discussion of the substitute resolution a vote was taken and it was declared lost.

ORIGINAL RESOLUTION ADOPTED

The Board then voted on the original resolution offered by Mr. Dodge and it was adopted. . . .

MR. JAMES BRYCE TO BE IN PRINCETON

The President of the University reported that the Right Honorable James Bryce, on whom the Board had voted to confer the Honorary Degree of Doctor of Laws, expected to be in Princeton on October 31st to take part in the exercises in connection with the dedication of the Sun Dial presented to the University by Sir William Mather; and suggested that the degree of Doctor of Laws be conferred on Mr. Bryce at that time.

DEGREE OF LL.D. TO BE CONFERRED ON MR. BRYCE

On motion duly seconded it was

RESOLVED, That the By-Laws be suspended and that the President of the University be authorized to confer the Honorary Degree of Doctor of Laws on the Right Honorable James Bryce on October 31, 1907. . . .

To the Board of Trustees of Princeton University

Gentlemen: [Princeton, N. J., Oct. 17, 1907]

The action you have taken today renders it necessary that I should state to you very frankly my own feeling and purposes.

Last June your special committee on the social coordination of the university suggested to you a plan which you ordered published and authorized me to make ready with the others of the committee for your future consideration in detail and after full consultation with all who would in any way be affected by it. I understood by that action and by the debates and conversations which accompanied it that you had intended to express your approval of the general principle and purpose of the plan, though I, of course, understood that you had in no sense pledged yourselves to its final adoption. I now learn that such was not your own purpose or understanding: that you did not mean to endorse either the plan or its purpose, but merely to authorize its discussion.

It has not yet been discussed. It has only been commented upon and criticized. I had hoped to have the opportunity this winter of explaining it fully to the whole constituency of the university, in order to remove the singularly widespread and diversified impressions which prevail regarding it, and so to bring on and take part in the thorough and intelligent discussion which it needs and deserves. Your action today in effect expresses your disapproval of it in advance of the discussion and of any further report from your committee and makes me aware that if I should push it, I should do so against your wishes.

I of course yield to your decision, congratulating myself that I did not push the matter beyond your wishes before you had had time to correct my misapprehension. But the plan as outlined in the report of your committee seems to me to be, at any rate in all its essential features, absolutely necessary to a realization of all the purposes I have had in mind for the University from the beginning of my administration and for the completion and permanence of the many reforms and changes we have so hopefully

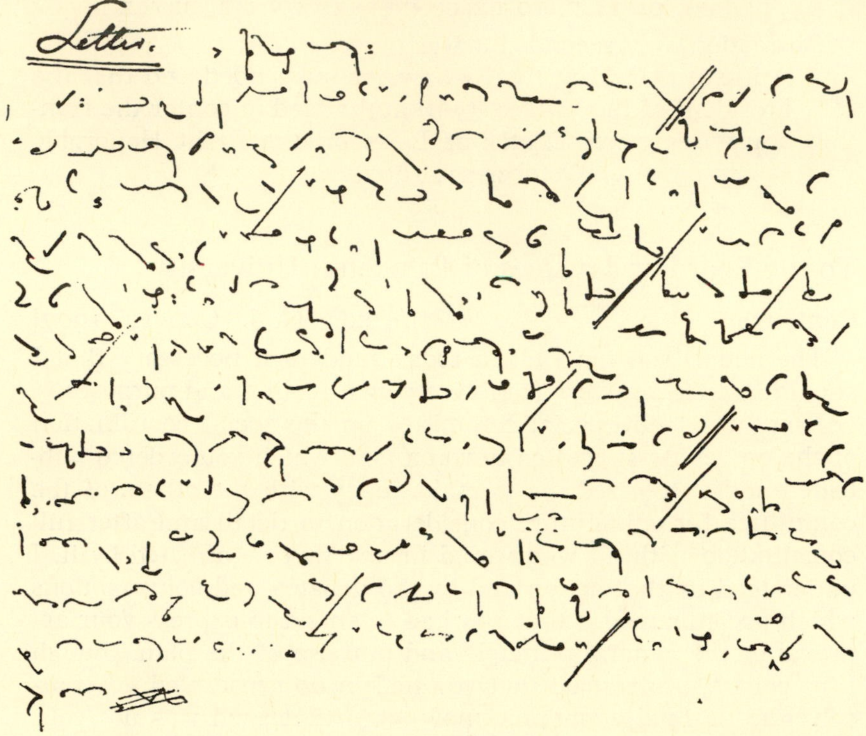

Wilson's shorthand draft of his unfinished letter of resignation.

accomplished. Your rejection of it at the very outset of its consideration makes it plain to me that you will not feel able to support me any further in the only matters in which I feel that I can lead and be of service to you.

I think you already understand how fundamental and necessary the changes proposed by your committee seem to me[1]

Transcript of WWshL (WP, DLC).

[1] Wilson broke off here and did not complete this letter. There is no indication that he ever transcribed this portion of it.

A Report of an Interview

[Oct. 18, 1907]

Princeton's Quad
President Wilson Optimistically
Adheres to His Plan

Princeton, N. J., Oct. 18.—President Woodrow Wilson of Princeton University to-day gave his future plans in regard to the proposed quad system upon which the board of trustees has passed an unfavorable decision. On being asked in what light he viewed the action of the trustees, he said: "I do not consider that the trustees are opposed to the quad system on principle, but merely reversed their former decision on reconsidering the matter, as they thought that the university and alumni were not sufficiently informed or prepared for the new plan. They gave me perfect leave to promote the plan as I thought best by talking to the undergraduates and the alumni; and when I have convinced the graduates and undergraduates of the wisdom of my plan they will immediately sanction the instalment of the quad.

"I expect to outline my plan to the students in the course of a few weeks, and during the winter and spring I will visit the various alumni organizations for the purpose of explaining my plan and getting their support.

"On the whole I consider that the matter stands as it did last June before the vote of approval by the trustees, except that the plan is much better understood now, and, therefore, when I have finished my action this winter I have no doubt of the ultimate acceptance of the system."

Printed in the New York *Evening Sun*, Oct. 18, 1907.

To Edwin Grant Conklin

Princeton, N. J.

My dear Professor Conklin: October 18th, 1907.

I take particular pleasure in writing to say that you were yesterday elected Professor of Biology by our Board of Trustees, your term of service to begin August 1st, 1908, and that the Board voted you leave of absence for the first year of your service with us, on the understanding that it was to be accorded on exactly the same terms which had been offered you by the University of Pennsylvania. Your future colleagues in the Department here requested this action with the greatest cordiality and unanimity, and I took real pleasure in requesting the Board to take it.

Allow me to say again how sincerely gratified I am that we have thus secured the services of a man whom we so highly honor and with whom it is such a pleasure to us to look forward to being associated.

With much regard,

Sincerely yours, Woodrow Wilson

TLS (E. G. Conklin Papers, NjP).

From Edwin Grant Conklin

My dear President Wilson, Philadelphia, October 19, 1907.

I have your very cordial letters of the 17th and 18th of October, the latter notifying me of my election to be Professor of Biology in Princeton University, and I wish to thank you and your Board of Trustees for this great honor.

I accept the position to which I have been elected with a sense of the responsibility which it places upon me and with the resolve to serve to the best of my ability the University which has so highly honored me.

I am particularly pleased by the unusual consideration shown me by the Board in granting me leave of absence for the first year of my service. I express to you and to my future colleagues who requested this action, and to the Trustees who granted it, my hearty thanks for this courtesy. The terms upon which leave of absence would have been granted me, if I had decided to remain here, were not definitely stated, but I assume that I should have received one-half salary, as do other professors in this University who are absent on leave for one year.

In my conversation with you on September 28th I understood the salary offered me to be five thousand dollars per annum. Since this sum was named in conversation only, and in view of the uncertainty of life, I should be glad to have it made a matter of record. May I ask you to confirm by letter my understanding of this matter?

Permit me again to express to you my high appreciation of your confidence and esteem and my great gratification at the prospect of being associated with you and your Faculty in the work of what seems to me to be the ideal cultural University of America.

Cordially yours, E G Conklin

TLS (E. G. Conklin Papers, NjP).

From James Bryce

My dear President Intervale, N. H. Oct. 20. 1907.

Thank you very much for your letter of the 18th Oct. & for the itinerary of the route from Newburgh you have kindly sent. If I succeed in getting to Newburgh with my automobile (for bad weather may make that difficult & it is now snowing here) I shall hope to follow the route indicated. If this is not possible I shall, of course, come on by train. Our plan is to leave here early on the morning of the 24th Oct. & to reach Barrytown on Hudson on the 27th or 28th Oct. where my address will be

c/o John Jay Chapman Esq.
Sylvania
Barrytown on Hudson
N. Y.

The arrangements you propose for the function will suit me very well. I am very grateful for the kindness of the University in proposing to honour me with the degree & I shall have great pleasure in receiving it. We shall be very glad to meet any friends whom you may wish to invite to lunch or dinner, & to remain with you over the night of the 31st unless some sudden official call (which I trust is improbable) should oblige me to return forthwith to Washington. We shall trust to reach you on the 30th October.

Believe me Very sincerely yours James Bryce

ALS (WP, DLC).

From Sir William Mather

[London] October 20th, 1907

Parcel hundred copies brochure[1] shipped today campana for Cunard office New-York addressed your self write office arranging delivery at Princeton for distribution at Ceremony Best wishes, Hearty greetings, Meeting. Mather.

T telegram (WWP, UA, NjP).

[1] A copy of this brochure is in the University Archives, NjP. Untitled and without any indication of place of publication and date, the brochure begins with Mather's letter to Wilson of July 4, 1907 (printed as an Enclosure with W. Mather to WW, Aug. 22, 1907), followed by a detailed description of the sun dial at Corpus Christi College, Oxford. It also includes sketches of the Corpus Christi and Princeton sun dials and a photograph of the one at Corpus Christi.

To Edwin Grant Conklin

Princeton, N. J.

My dear Professor Conklin, 21 October, 1907.

Thank you for your letter of Saturday. It was a real pleasure to get it, and to feel that you are now to all intents and purposes one of us.

It was careless of me to omit, from an official letter, a statement of the salary fixed by the Trustees. It is five thousand dollars a year.

I shall assume, unless I hear to the contrary, that the amount to be allowed you during your year of absence will be twenty-five hundred dollars. If the proportion to be allowed by the University of Pennsylvania should be more, pray let me know.

With warmest regard, and sincere friendship,

Faithfully Yours, Woodrow Wilson

WWTLS (E. G. Conklin Papers, NjP).

From the Minutes of the Princeton University Faculty

4 p.m. October 21, 1907.

The Faculty met, the President presiding. . . .

The pending motion made by Professor Daniels came up as the first order of business. After a statement by the President of the action of the Board of Trustees reconsidering their action on the proposed plan and asking the President to withdraw it and that the plan was withdrawn, by general consent the motion was withdrawn and Professor Daniels gave notice that a motion to approve the principle of the plan in question would be made at the next regular meeting. . . .

From the Diary of William Starr Myers

Mon. Oct. 21 [1907].

Short faculty meeting at four o'clock. As the trustees at their meeting last Wednesday rescinded *their* vote in favor of Woodrow's Quad plan, leaving him permission to go ahead with the agitation of it as an open question, Prof. Daniels gave notice of the withdrawal of his motion of approval, to be resubmitted in another form at the next regular meeting.

From William Royal Wilder

My dear Wilson, New York October 22, 1907.

Since yours of September 21st anent the Rice Institute and Prof. Lovett, I have been in correspondence with our classmate, Dan Rice. In fact I have seen more of him this fall almost, than of any one of our class. He is now back in Houston and is recovering from an attack of malaria. Under date of October 15th he writes as follows, in regard to the gentlemen under consideration to manage the Rice Institute:

> "We have on our list other names fully as well endorsed as Prof. Lovett,–at least in the estimation of some of our Trustees. Personally I feel that President Wilson's unqualified endorsement is satisfactory to me. In fact, if the matter was left to me I would offer the position to Prof. Lovett at once. Now I know you are interested in this matter, and I would like to have you go down to Princeton, talk over the matter with President Wilson, and in an informal way talk over our proposition with Prof. Lovett. You know pretty well what we need in a College President, and you know how necessary it is that we have the right man, and especially at this time when we are beginning a great undertaking and planning for its future. If you will do this for me and write me fully so that if I desire I can read your letter to our Board of Trustees, I would be much obliged. I am calling upon you because I have confidence in your judgment and know that you will be perfectly candid,"

etc. etc.

I realize as fully as you must that frequently a man who is not qualified to either judge or decide, is called upon to do so. This proposition is, however, easy as both Rice and myself are inclined to bank absolutely upon your judgment.

Will Friday evening of this week suit you and Professor Lovett? If so, I will endeavor to come down. If not Friday, please name a couple of nights next week and I will so shape my engagements as to be with you on one of them.

Cordially yours, Wm. R. Wilder

P.S. I do not believe in indulging in morbid curiosity, and I have not as yet found out just how the Trustees justify their action as regards the "Quad System." However, that is another story.

TLS (WP, DLC).

From Robert Bridges

Dear Tommy: New York, October 22nd, 1907.

I had a note from Walter Page this morning asking me to lay particular stress on the preceptorial system in the article which I am to prepare for the *World's Work* in regard to your work.[1] Do you happen to have by you or can you refer me to your best presentation of the system, and is there a report as to its actual workings in the last two years?

And will you also kindly tell me whether the Southern Society printed the address which you made at the dinner last year?[2] I heard the speech and saw summaries of it in the newspapers, but I should like to get hold of the full address if they republished it.

With best wishes always

Faithfully yours Robert Bridges

P.S. Any time that you are here, please come and lunch with me.

TLS (WWP, UA, NjP).

[1] As it turned out, the article was more about Wilson and his educational philosophy than it was about the preceptorial system. See Robert Bridges, "President Woodrow Wilson and College Earnestness," *World's Work*, xv (Jan. 1908), 9792-97.

[2] See WW to R. Bridges, Oct. 25, 1907.

From Edmund Beecher Wilson

My dear Presdt. Wilson: New York, Oct. 22nd, 1907

I have just heard the good news that Conklin is going to Princeton and write to offer you my congratulations—and I shall also heartily congratulate Conklin. I do not know how you could have secured a better man, and I am sure he will be a great acquisition to the university. I learned also of your permission to give him a year's leave of absence, and want to express my appreciation of a policy that is as much to the advantage of the university, I am sure, as it is to him.

I have not yet fully conquered the regret with which I had to give up the prospect of joining you at Princeton—though Columbia has made my position extremely advantageous to my work and has been most generous—but I am sure that Princeton has lost nothing by gaining Conklin in my place. I shall not forget the great kindness and friendliness that you showed me.

I am, with kindest regards to you and Mrs. Wilson

Very sincerely yours Edmund B. Wilson

ALS (WP, DLC).

To Melancthon Williams Jacobus

My dear Friend: Princeton, N. J. 23 October, 1907.

I feel guilty that I have not written to you before about what was done on Thursday last. To tell the mere truth, I have not had the heart to. The action of the Board has, I know, been reported in the papers and you have readily read between the lines. But it seems now that it was not meant by the men who drew the statement which was made public that I should take seriously the part about the Board not wishing in any way to hinder my going forward with my efforts to swing the opinion of Princeton men to the plan. They wish me to be silent; and I have got nothing out of the transaction except complete defeat and mortification. I refrained from resigning because I saw at last that I did not have the right to place the University in danger of going to pieces; and because I felt that the men who were forcing this surrender upon me had made all that I have accomplished financially possible; but I thought that they meant what they said when they offered to leave me free, and am at a loss to understand what my duty is now that I find that most of them did not. I trust that a kind Providence will presently send me some sign of guidance which I shall have sight enough to perceive and to interpret.

One thing I have got out of the whole affair which is deeply precious to me, and which will comfort me and make me deeply thankful for the rest of my life, and that is the splendid proofs of your affection and confidence which every turn of the business has brought me. That is solid profit to have reaped out of deep sorrow; and I want you to know with what warmth and loyalty I have given my ardent friendship and allegiance in return. May God bless you for all that you have given me and may the time come when I can make some adequate return, not as a return, but to satisfy my heart.

I hope with all my heart that the lumbago has entirely left you, and that you are yourself again. Give our warmest regards to all your little household. Mrs. Wilson begs to join me in sending her love.

Faithfully and affectionately yours, Woodrow Wilson

TCL (Charles Scribner's Sons Archives, NjP).

From Shailer Mathews[1]

My dear President Wilson: Chicago, October 23, 1907.

We should like very much to publish in "The World Today" an article on the quadrangle system of Princeton. Personally I am very much interested in the matter, as we have made some attempts at a house system at the University of Chicago.

I should like to illustrate the article with pictures of the various quadrangles of Oxford and Cambridge, if I could get them conveniently. Altogether we should like to make the article of distinct assistance to the scheme. I believe in it myself from my experience at the University, most thoroughly. As you doubtless know, we have undertaken the organization of a number of small colleges within the undergraduate body at large, but we have never undertaken such a thoroughgoing and comprehensive, and from what I know of it, admirable scheme as you propose.

The article ought to be about 2500 or 3000 words long, and while I cannot pay you what I should like, I should be glad to send you a check for $50 for such an article.[2]

Yours very truly, Shailer Mathews Editor.

TLS (WP, DLC).

[1] Editor of *The World Today* and Professor of History and Comparative Theology and Junior Dean of the Divinity School of the University of Chicago.

[2] Wilson did not write the article.

From Lawrence Crane Woods

My dear Dr. Wilson: Pittsburg, Pa. October 23, 1907.

I cannot but feel that the apparent step backward taken by the Board of Trustees last week is in reality the best step forward to the ultimate goal which the more I consider the situation the more I feel will have to be reached by Princeton sooner or later. While I am not prepared to say that I fully appreciate the necessity for all the changes that you are popularly supposed to have advocated, I am in thorough accord and sympathy with the general proposition which you have laid down. The questions of detail, I am sure, can ultimately be worked out, but it must be evolution and not revolution. I hope and believe that, for Princeton's sake as well as your own, you are not disheartened by this temporary reversal of one of your policies.

Every alumnus whom I have talked with, no matter how ardent an opponent of the Quad System he might have been, cheerfully and most gratefully spoke of the magnificent services you have rendered not only to Princeton but to the cause of higher education throughout the world by the brilliant and succesful administration you have given in the face of conditions at the time of your accession which would have appalled a weaker man.

I cannot but feel that you have shown your real greatness in gracefully accepting the real situation and apparently going backward to begin again along the same line. I feel that the entire question is now in a position where it can be sanely and, therefore, more favorably discussed than ever before. I believe that it is most important that we should first fix finally what are the evils or conditions which should be eradicated or improved in Princeton today. With these points clearly in mind and finally crystalized by broad discussion, let us then take up the remedies to be adopted with least injury and most good to the patient.

Let me say in this connection that I feel that the opposition to your plan was at least nine-tenths ignorance of the conditions to be remedied and the nature of the actual remedy you really had in mind. This ignorance was augmented and intensified by the impression that they were being forced into something which they did not know about and, therefore, "viewed with alarm."

I hope that it may be possible, without taxing you too much, to have you here in Pittsburg some time this fall. I believe that it will be a very helpful and profitable thing for Princeton. I think it will do you good and do all of the alumni here good.

With renewed expressions of the deepest appreciation, in which I feel I could voice the sentiments of all real Princeton men for what you have done and are doing for Old Nassau, believe me,

Very sincerely yours, Lawrence C. Woods

TLS (WP, DLC).

Moses Taylor Pyne to Andrew Clerk Imbrie

My dear Andy: New York October 23rd, 1907.

I received your letter on my return from Massachusetts where I have been since the Board meeting. I am leaving for Princeton now and may not be back again this week, but I shall be glad to see you next week.

I was very much surprised on my return to see a most remarkable interview with President Wilson in the Sun of last Friday evening in which he said that "the Board were not opposed to the Quad system on principle, but merely reversed their former decision. On reconsidering the matter they found that the University and the Alumni were not sufficiently informed or prepared for the new plan, and that when he had convinced the Graduates and undergraduates of the practicability of his plan the Trustees would immediately sanction the instalment of the Quad. Also that the matter stood just as it did last June before the vote of the approval of the Trustees."

This is absolutely contrary to the facts, and I cannot understand it and am going over to see him today about it. The Trustees turned down the plan on its merits, or rather on its demerits, as it was absolutely Utopian and could not be carried out under any consideration. It was distinctly understood and I thought he understood it, that this withdrawal was final and could not be changed and that the Trustees had had no intention of changing their vote, nor did they vote because they were not sufficiently well informed in the matter. This is a matter that the President certainly understood and the whole subject was well considered by the Trustees and turned down finally and for good, and the only reason it was not turned down harder was to save the feelings of the President.

I understand that you have told a number of men at the Princeton Club that the matter was not settled but was to come up again. I wish, representing as I know I do, much more than a majority of the Board of Trustees, that it be understood that the matter has been finally disposed of.

Very sincerely yours, M. Taylor Pyne

TLS (A. C. Imbrie Coll., NjP).

Notes for a Religious Talk

Philadelphian Society. 24 Oct., 1907.

Ecclesiastes, XI., 4: "He that observeth the wind shall not sow; and he that regardeth the clouds shall not reap."

The old live in the light of experience; the young must live in the light of counsel, in the light of wisdom, at once benign and rational.

Opportunism one of the subtlest dangers of every career, whether at its outset, at its middle course, or at its culmination

A very different thing from prudence and a regard for opportunity.

The work of the world goes forward by purpose, not by opportunity

The Safeguards, Singleness of mind

Simplicity in the pursuit of duty

Principle held with steadfastness,

Vital, conscious connection with divine Providence.

The long measurements of duty, before lines of success or standards of service can be determined.

The slow, but sure assessments of character,—in the business world, as elsewhere.

24 Oct. '07[1]

WWT MS (WP, DLC).

[1] Wilson's composition date.

A News Report of an Address to the Philadelphian Society

[Oct. 25, 1907]

PRESIDENT WILSON'S ADDRESS

A Strong Talk on "The Importance of Singlemindedness" Given in Murray Hall Last Night.

President Woodrow Wilson addressed the regular meeting of the Philadelphian Society last evening in Murray Hall. His subject was "The Importance of Singlemindedness," taken from the verse in Ecclesiastics xi, 4, "He that observeth the wind shall not sow, and he that regardeth the clouds shall not reap." President Wilson said that often young men lay too much importance on the opinions of other people, and shape their course in accordance with the general trend of thought instead of deciding the question for themselves. The man who is always obsequious, who agrees with the opinions of others, who is always ready to take his cue so as to be on the popular side, will never be of importance in the world. The world is not looking for servants,—there are plenty of these,—but for masters, men who form their purposes and then carry them out, let the consequences be what they may.

The difference between a strong man and a weak one is that the former does not give up after a defeat, but continues the struggle. The greatness of George Washington consisted chiefly in the fact that he never knew when he was beaten. He gained but few victories, but he always fought harder after a defeat. So the work of the world is carried on by the man who lives true to the purpose of his heart, and not to the opinions of other people.

Every college man has to decide what course in life he is to follow, and what kind of person he will make of himself. The great problem is how to keep oneself from doing the easiest things and those nearest at hand. There are various fortifications against this temptation, but the best, although the hardest, is singleness of mind. Almost all men have noble ambitions, but most spend so much time in dreaming about them that they forget the hard work which is necessary to accomplish the desired end. Steady, conscientious work in the long run accomplishes more than spasmodic and uncontinued effort. Such concentration is gained as a result of a singleness of purpose to attach oneself to some great cause, by which one can serve his day and generation to the best of his ability.

In closing President Wilson said: "Let us have some solemn purpose in life, and we will be none the less happy, but will have the satisfaction that comes from the best expenditure of our energies."[1]

Printed in the *Daily Princetonian*, Oct. 25, 1907.

[1] A very similar report of this address appeared in the *Princeton Alumni Weekly*, VIII (Oct. 30, 1907), 89. Whatever may have been the motives of the editor, Edwin M. Norris, the fact remains that this was the first time that the *Alumni Weekly* had ever carried a report of any of Wilson's numerous speeches to the Philadelphian Society.

To Robert Bridges

My dear Bobby: Princeton, N. J. October 25th, 1907.

Mr. Close, my secretary, will send you two of my annual reports containing something about the working of the preceptorial system, and you will find the following articles somewhat systematic in their account of it: The Independent, August 3rd, 1905;[1] The Outlook, June 24th, 1905;[2] and Harper's Weekly[3] for the same date. I wish that I had copies of these latter at hand to send you, but I dare say you can find them in the library of the University Club.

I am asking Mr. Close to send you a copy of the outline of my speech before the Southern Society last year, which I prepared at the time for the press.[4] So far as I know, the society did not print the address in full.

It seems to me a pity that you should be putting yourself to so much trouble about this article, but I am certainly gratified that I am in your hands. I hope it will not be long before I can look in on you and have a chat.

Always affectionately yours, Woodrow Wilson

Did you see my Jamestown address in the Sept. North Am. Rev.?[5]

TLS (WC, NjP).

[1] Woodrow Wilson, "The Princeton Preceptorial System," printed at June 1, 1905, Vol. 16.

[2] "The Preceptor Idea at Princeton," New York *Outlook*, LXXX (June 24, 1905), 465-67, a long editorial.

[3] Woodrow Wilson, "New Plans for Princeton," printed at June 24, 1905, Vol. 16.

[4] A news report of Wilson's speech is printed at Dec. 15, 1906, Vol. 16. A copy of his press release, dated Dec. 14, 1906, is in WC, NjP.

[5] "The Author and Signers of the Declaration of Independence," printed at July 4, 1907.

To Lawrence Crane Woods

My dear Mr. Woods: Princeton, N. J. October 25th, 1907.

Thank you most sincerely for your very kind letter of October 23rd. I think that you have seen into the heart of the situation very truly, and that we are now upon a footing where the gravest and most profitable discussion of the changes we must make here is possible.

I feel that it will be only good taste to delay the active oral discussion of the matter for a little while, but I see no reason why by midwinter it should not be carried forward with the best results.

I cannot tell you how warmly I appreciate all the kind things you say in your letter or how much I value your vital and intelligent interest in the matter.

It may interest you to know that I am about to publish my baccalaureate address of last Commencement through Messrs. Thomas Y. Crowell & Company who will issue it as a little volume, I suppose about the end of the year.[1]

Cordially and sincerely yours, Woodrow Wilson

TLS (WC, NjP).

[1] As has been noted earlier, it appeared as Woodrow Wilson, *The Free Life* (New York, 1908).

To James Hampton Kirkland

Princeton, N. J.

My dear Chancellor Kirkland: October 25th, 1907.

I very much appreciate the kind invitation to address the students of Vanderbilt next month, and particularly appreciate the personal letter[1] with which you urge the matter upon me. I hope you will not think me churlish or unwilling, but my visit to Nashville is to be merely a stop-over call on my brother after some very laborious days which I am to spend in Memphis. I have been peculiarly hard-worked this autumn, and feel that it would be a mere imprudence for me to do all that I am scheduled to do on my visit to Tennessee, without breaking the journey and the labor with one or two days of genuine rest.

I hope that you will express to the other gentlemen who were kind enough to sign with you the formal invitation my very warm appreciation and most unaffected regret that I feel obliged in mere prudence to decline.

With warm regard,

Sincerely yours, Woodrow Wilson

TLS (J. H. Kirkland Papers, TNJ).

[1] It is missing.

From Melancthon Williams Jacobus

My dear Friend: Hartford, Conn., October 25th, 1907.

It needs no assurance from me that yours was a welcome letter, not so much because it contained the first definite information I have had as to the present situation of affairs, for that information was not pleasant reading; but because it brought me an expression of your personal feelings towards me which I shall always treasure as one of the most valued things that has come into my experience.

I had not misunderstood your delay in writing. I knew last Thursday must have been for you a hard and strenuous day, leaving behind a multitude of things to be considered. In good time I knew you would write.

But I must confess I had not expected you would be compelled to write what you did. It is almost beyond thought that self-respecting men should act this way, and yet the issue being the tremendously vital one it is, I must admit it to be possible that no matter how much of a compromise they put into the wording of the public statement,[1] they might put no compromise into their interpretation of it in fact. If so, however, it is the act of desperate men who are championing a desperate cause, and is to be reckoned with from that point of view.

I have no hesitation as to what is your duty in the situation. This is too serious a matter not to be taken seriously by the Board as well as by yourself, for it is being taken most seriously by the great public who are interested in the matter far more deeply than the smart set of the Clubs or the scared set of the Board at present realize. This public and the great body of the alumni of Princeton expect you to do just what the public statement said you were free to do. The appended editorial from the Hartford evening paper of last Friday shows this plainly.[2] I do not know who wrote it. It expresses simply the general opinion consequent upon the action of the Board.[3]

Now, I would act upon this expectation; and if I had to wait for the opportunity to act, I would wait for it with the patience of Job. I would not resign now. I would fight it out. I would take my time, but I would make the scheme and the principle which it embodies so plain to every Alumni Association that the self-respecting spirit of American democracy would rise to the acceptance of them with the instinct of the preservation of our national institutions. You must not think that Princeton is bigger than its President and can survive his withdrawal at the present time. This is not true; and even if it were, you must keep clear before yourself that this principle is bigger than Princeton and she must measure up to it ultimately or lose all moral right to call herself an American institution of learning. And further than this, you must believe us when we say that there is absolutely no one who can lead Princeton to this expression of her best ideals but yourself. Be assured that the plain people of the great body of the alumni and of the educational world outside are with you as surely as the plain people of the nation were with Abraham Lincoln forty-five years ago, or with Theodore Roosevelt today; and in the end you have got to win out.

To come to practical things, you have an invitation from the Alumni Association of Western Pennsylvania, as I understand it, to speak on this Quadrangle plan. Ask the men who drew the public statement whether the action of the Board leaves you free to accept this Pittsburg invitation—as, in fact, you have done. If they say "No," then call your Advisory Committee together, if that Committee be still in existence,[4] for an interpretation of the situation, and let us understand now perfectly where the action of the Board places us; but in any event do not give up nor lose grip on the service Heaven has given you to do for Princeton and for American education.

Yours devotedly, Melancthon W. Jacobus

P.S. I have just received, after writing the above, a letter from Robert Garrett, in answer to an inquiry from me as to what his impression was of the situation in which the action of the Board had placed us, in which he says:

"The way is now open for him [the President][5] to throw all the light upon the subject that he can before the alumni and any other persons who have any connection with the matter; and, as I understand it, he will be perfectly free to broach the subject at a future meeting of the Board whenever it is thought that the time is more ripe than it now is."

It would seem from this that the men who drew the statement and now wish you to be silent have considerable to explain, and I would compell them to make the explanation before the Committee. J.

TLS (WP, DLC).

[1] On October 17, 1907, following the meeting of the Board of Trustees on that day, Charles W. McAlpin gave out the following news release:

"The board, having deemed it wise to reconsider the action which it took last June on the recommendation of the Committee on the Social Co-ordination of the University, requested the President to withdraw the plan embodied in the report of that committee, and in compliance with that request he withdrew it.

"The board fully realizes the fact that the President's own conviction in the matter has not changed, and have no wish to hinder him in any way in his purpose to endeavor to convince the members of the board and Princeton men generally that the plan is the real solution of the problem of co-ordinating the social and intellectual life of the university." See, e. g., the *New York Times*, Oct. 18, 1907.

2 It was a clipping of an editorial, "Princeton's Quad System," *Hartford Times*, Oct. 18, 1907.

3 The editorial said that, now that the turmoil over the quadrangle plan was over, Princeton students would probably be eager to hear Wilson's views, and that "the scheme will for the first time receive the general impartial consideration which is required by its character and is due to its author."

4 There was neither an Advisory Committee nor an Executive Committee of the Board of Trustees during Wilson's tenure as President of the university. Jacobus was probably referring to the Committee on the Supplementary Report of the President, which had been discharged by the Board of Trustees on October 17, 1907.

5 Brackets in the original.

From James Bryce

My dear President Barrytown on Hudson, Oct. 28/07

We have got so far as this in our automobile, tho the roads are not fit for such a vehicle, & we hope, as your N. J. roads are said to be better, to reach you with the car in good time on Wednesday, leaving here if possible at noon to-morrow so as to sleep somewhere, perhaps at Suffern, N. Y., on the way. Anyhow we trust to reach you on Wednesday. There is doubtless a garage in Princeton where the car & chauffeur can find accommodation. We shall also have a manservant with us: if it should not be convenient for you to put him up, may I ask you to be kind enough to arrange for a room somewhere in Princeton to which we can send him?

Should the weather be as bad tomorrow as today, perhaps we may appear on Wednesday by train.

Believe me Very truly yours James Bryce

ALS (WP, DLC).

From Sir William Mather

[London, Oct. 29, 1907]

Hearty greetings to assembly may sundial record day by day through centuries only unbroken attachment between america and Great Britain my grateful thanks to Ambassador Bryce.

Mather London.

T telegram (WWP, UA, NjP).

From Corpus Christi College

[Oxford, Oct. 29, 1907]

Corpus christi College sends you greetings and rejoices at Princeton University having reproduction of Turnbull Dial in its original form.

T telegram (WWP, UA, NjP).

To James Callaway[1]

My dear Sir: [Princeton, N. J.] October 30th, 1907.

Allow me to thank you for your thoughtful kindness in sending me your article contrasting Senator Hill[2] and his views with Mr. Bryan and his advocacy of the initiative and referendum.[3] I agree with you that Senator Hill's position was not only sound, but the only position which a thoughtful and well-informed student of American affairs can legitimately take.

There seems to me to be, moreover, another and entirely conclusive objection to the initiative and referendum, quite apart from their incompatibility with the principles of our system of government. A casual petition by a relatively small number of citizens and a vote by however large a number do not constitute an organic process at all. The only process by which law can be safely and thoughtfully produced is the organic process which brings those who frame it into face to face conference so that the contents of the law will not be made up of the views of a chance combination of persons, but of views beaten out by exchange of thought in actual debate. I quite agree with you, therefore, that it is necessary, in order that the processes of debate should be real, that the proceedure and character of our national House of Representatives should be so changed as to bring back the days of vital and informing exchange of views on the floor within the hearing of the nation.

With much regard,

Sincerely yours, [Woodrow Wilson]

CCL (RSB Coll., DLC).

1 A writer for the *Macon*, Ga., *Telegraph* and father of Margaret (Mrs. Benjamin Palmer) Axson, Mrs. Wilson's first cousin-in-law.

2 Former United States Senator David Bennett Hill of New York.

3 The article presumably appeared in the *Macon Telegraph*. The Editors have been unable to find it.

From the Diary of William Starr Myers

Thurs. Oct 31 [1907].

This morning at 11 o'clock the degree of LLD was conferred on James Bryce the British Ambassador, in the Faculty Room in Nassau Hall, & we then had a faculty pe-rade to the McCosh quadrangle, where has been erected the handsome new sun-dial presented to Princeton Univ. by Sir Wm. Mather, & a copy of the Turnbull dial at Corpus Christi College, Oxford. The formal presentation was made in a fine speech by Mr. Bryce, Pres. Wilson accepting in just as good a vein, & showing up well in the contrast, as he always does. The Ambassador is an alert, vigorous man, with a strong clear voice, wonderful in consideration of his age. A rather small man with bushy eyebrows & beard—almost white. The weather simply magnificent.

A News Report

[Nov. 1, 1907]

SUN-DIAL DEDICATED.

Dedication Speech Delivered by James Bryce,
British Ambassador to the United States.

The degree of Doctor of Laws was conferred upon the Right Honorable James Bryce, the British Ambassador to the United States, yesterday morning in the Faculty Room of Nassau Hall in the presence of the Faculty and Trustees.

Dean West presented Mr. Bryce for the honorary degree of Doctor of Laws in the following words:

"The Right Honorable James Bryce, the British Ambassador to the United States. Long and highly honored elsewhere as here, we seek to honor him anew as an example of truest scholarship, a luminous teacher of the civil law, a leader in education, a master in the art of government and a historian of affluent learning, humane spirit, temperate style and profound insight.

"We welcome him to this home of American history and add his signature to our roll whereon are written the names of Lincoln and Cleveland in our later history and the name of Washington at the beginning. We welcome him in this council hall, familiar to Washington, Adams, Jefferson and Madison, the refuge of Congress in the Revolution, the place whither the official message came overseas, telling the good news of peace concluded with the mother country. We greet in his person a messenger of authority, bearing a new word of peace and good will from beyond that lessening ocean whereby to-day these two Christian peoples are rather joined than severed."

Immediately after the conclusion of these exercises the academic procession marched to the sun-dial. President Wilson introduced Mr. Bryce, who spoke in part as follows:

Mr. President, Ladies and Gentlemen:

I am here to-day to present to you, in behalf of my old and valued friend, Sir William Mather, this sun-dial, which, as you know, is a reproduction of a very ancient dial which stands in the quadrangle of Corpus Christi College, a college in which I have had very many dear friends, and which is separated only by a narrow street from Oriel College, to which I myself belong. Corpus Christi is celebrated for the many illustrious men it has produced and which it produces even down to our own time, of whom I will only mention two. One is well know [known] to you as Dr. Thomas Arnold, who was a scholar of Corpus Christi and afterwards of my own college of Oriel; and one eminent scholar who is a dear friend of mine, and who is known to all of you who pursue classical studies, Henry Nettleship.[1] But I might easily enumerate many men whom Corpus Christi has given to the world and whom I hope you will remember in connection with this dial.

You have very properly thought, Mr. President, that it was not necessary to unveil the dial, because, after all, it is not the dial that does the work; it is the sun that does the work. And the sun has unveiled himself with a brilliance which beats all we could have desired. You have asked me to offer a few remarks, and they must of necessity be few; because, though the sun, as all the poets from Homer down have told us, is unwearied, we are capable of weariness, and most so when we are standing. I need not dilate on the importance and dignity of sun-dials, because some of you may remember an eminent philosopher in the early part of the Nineteenth Century who, in writing a treatise on the sun and the purpose which the sun served in the universe, culminated by saying that the sun runs the sun-dial, and without the sun there would be no sun-dial. That was the teleological view of the sun. Nor need I dilate upon the antiquity of sun-dials—the earliest method of measuring time which, I think, man invented. Herodotus says the sun-dial was invented by the Chaldeans, and we may easily believe him, because it is just the kind of thing that the Chaldeans would have done, and we know from the Scriptures that there was a sun-dial in Jerusalem in the reign of Ahaz. It is hard to realize how man could have made such progress as

[1] Henry Nettleship (1839-93), distinguished Oxford classicist, best known for his work in Latin lexicography and Virgil.

he has made without such aid as the sun-dial affords. At the same time it must be remembered and admitted that the sun-dial is not to be compared with the more modern instruments which man has invented for recording time. The sun-dial was superseded in the Athenian law courts by the water-clock, by which they limited the length of the speeches delivered by the plaintiff and defendant. In England, where we are often not privileged to see the sun for many days at a time, we use in the House of Commons a sand-glass—a comparatively primitive contrivance, but which is in keeping with our conservatism.

It is used to mark when a division is called and when a division is taken. I notice that in Congress you adopt a method of enabling bills to be passed in the last hour of the session which would not be possible if you had to depend on the sun. Someone goes and ostentatiously touches the hands of the clock. You could not get the sun to go back on his dial.

Nor need I dilate on the moral lessons which our ancestors used to draw from the sun-dial. They were lessons of a very sombre character—not much sunshine about them. There are attached to sun-dials mottoes reminding us of the shortness of time and the necessity of using it. I remember one that stands in the quadrangle of All Souls College, Oxford: "Periunt item putantur."[2] But of course that is an idea which the constant passage of the shadows naturally suggests to one that every hour of sunshine is to be used; and it is a reflection which comes back painfully to many of us in the later hours of life, when we think of the many hours, which we might have spent in acquiring knowledge, that we have neglected. I shall not delay upon these melancholy aspects, hoping that every Princeton man uses his time, and that Princeton graduates when they reach the age of sixty or seventy have no such reflections to make.

This dial will, I hope, stand here for many ages. It will stand here when all of us have been forgotten. It will stand here when even our memories will be forgotten, when nothing may be left, though Princeton, I hope, will be even greater, with even a wider range of influence than she has now. Let us hope that it will always be remembered that this dial was the gift of a large-hearted Englishman who loved America as he loves England, and who desired to commemorate, to typify, not only the union of learning and work, but also the union of the heart of the two peoples.

President Wilson then read two cablegrams:

[2] Bryce was probably misquoted by the reporter. The phrase reads "Pereunt et imputantur." It is from Martial and translates as "They perish, and are placed to our account."

"Hearty greeting to the assembly, may the dial record, day by day, through centuries of unbroken attachment between Great Britain and America. Grateful thanks to Ambassador Bryce.

William Mather. London."

"Corpus Christi College sends you greetings and rejoices that Princeton University has a reproduction of the Turnbull sun-dial in original form."

President Wilson concluded the dedication exercises with the following speech:

Ladies and Gentlemen:

It gives me the greatest pleasure, in behalf of the University authorities, to accept this singular and beautiful gift; to express our very deep gratification that it should have been our privilege to receive it through the distinguished ambassador of Great Britain to the United States, . . .[3] to record our admiration for the spirit of a man who thinks of such memorials of good-will, our appreciation of the singularly public-spirited way in which he has felt obliged to lead his life; of the example which he sets, that example not only of service to a single nation but of service to all men everywhere. . . . And we could not think of a more acceptable hand from which to accept so significant a gift.

I want in this public place to request the gratitude of Princeton and the intelligent appreciation of Princeton of the gift which has made it. I want to express the feeling that is in the minds of every one of you, that there could have been no more welcome guest on this occasion than Mr. Bryce. I have said that universities in a certain sense have nothing to do with national bounds, and therefore we have nothing to do with Mr. Bryce as British Ambassador. We have to do with Mr. Bryce as a noble gentleman, a man of learning. We welcome him as what we should like to believe to be the true type of university man. And so it is in your name that I bid him welcome to this place, and thank him for the very handsome and interesting part he has played in this ceremony.[4]

Printed in the *Daily Princetonian*, Nov. 1, 1907.

[3] This elision and the one that follows occur in the original text.

[4] There is a WWhw outline of these remarks in WP, DLC.

To Sir William Mather

[Princeton, N. J.]

My dear Sir William: November 1st, 1907.

Everybody in Princeton wished for you yesterday. The day was wholly brilliant and delightful. A more ideal day for an out-of-door ceremony could not have been imagined. After conferring the degree of Doctor of Laws upon Mr. Bryce in our Faculty Room in the presence of the Faculty and Trustees, we proceeded in academic procession to the dial, which everybody thinks beautifully placed in the space adjoining our new monumental building, McCosh Hall, near the stately avenue of trees which runs by the entrance to Prospect grounds, and there the simple ceremony was performed. Mr. Bryce, speaking of you in terms which all who know you and esteem you would have loved to hear, presented the dial in a speech admirably conceived, and I had the pleasure in reply of paying you the tribute of admiration you deserve for all the public spirit you have shown and all the admirable sentiments of which your life has been an example, and of accepting the beautiful gift in the name of the University. Nothing marred the occasion except that you and Lady Mather and your daughters were not present. Allow me to send you the warmest greetings and renewed assurances of our cordial esteem and lively gratitude.

The books[1] arrived in good time and were very much appreciated. They make an admirable souvenir of an interesting and significant occasion.

Mrs. Wilson and my daughters beg to join me in the most cordial regards to Lady Mather, your daughters, and yourself. I am

Always faithfully and cordially yours,

[Woodrow Wilson]

CCL (WWP, UA, NjP).

[1] That is, the brochures prepared by Sir William. See W. Mather to WW, Oct. 20, 1907, n. 1.

To Andrew Carnegie

Princeton, N. J.

My dear Mr. Carnegie: November 2nd, 1907.

I have learned with real chagrin as well as deep disappointment that your visit to Princeton has been fixed for a date when I am obliged to be in Tennessee to meet important engagements of long standing. The committee in charge of the regatta to be given on the eighth went forward with their arrangements without consulting me at all, and it was only after the whole programme, including your own visit, had been arranged that they informed me of what they had done. It would be so great a pleasure to be here to meet you and it is so great a disappointment to Mrs. Wilson and me that we are not to have the pleasure of entertaining Mrs. Carnegie[1] and you and your daughter,[2] that I must say the disappointment has caused me not a little vexation. I hope sincerely that on some other occasion I may have the pleasure which I am now to miss.

Instead of leaving cordial messages for you, I want to write this letter to say how more than welcome you are to Princeton and how sincerely I hope that the day will bring Mrs. Carnegie and you the fullest measure of enjoyment. Certainly everybody here will regard the day as being made important by your presence and will hope that it may be arranged entirely for your pleasure. I know how well you will be taken care of, but I wish that I might be here to welcome you.

With warmest regard,

Cordially and sincerely yours, Woodrow Wilson

TLS (A. Carnegie Papers, DLC).

[1] Louise Whitfield Carnegie.

[2] Margaret Carnegie.

From the Minutes of the Princeton University Faculty

5 p.m. November 4, 1907.

The Faculty met, the President presiding. . . .

The following resolution was moved by Professor Daniels, seconded by Dean Fine:

Be it Resolved: that the Faculty approve of a plan for the social coordination of the University such as that recently outlined before this Faculty by the President of the University; it being understood that essential to the plan in question is:

1st The creation of a new unit of organization.

2nd That each unit contain representatively all the elements of the University—the Faculty and all four classes of undergraduates.

3d That each unit be of such size and so constituted as to have a common life and an organization of its own, so as to secure the benefits resulting from the opportunity afforded for mutual, informal and friendly relations between its members, both Faculty and undergraduate;

4th That each unit have a student membership to be determined by some authority representing the University as an organic whole, to the end that in essentials the various units shall be similarly constituted, and that the common interests of each unit shall harmonize with those of the other units, and with those of the University as a whole.

The President called the attention of the Faculty to prevailing misconceptions of the proposed plan of social organization and suggested that it might be well for the Faculty to consider the advisability of proceeding at present with the discussion of the motion just made. It was

Resolved, that the motion made by Professor Daniels be laid upon the table. . . .[1]

[1] Although the minutes do not say so, the motion carried, as WW to M. W. Jacobus, Nov. 6, 1907, reveals.

From Melancthon Williams Jacobus

Hartford, Conn.,

My dear President Wilson: November 5th, 1907.

I cannot quite fittingly express my feelings in respect of the information which your letter of the 3rd instant conveys.[1] In fact, I find it hard to realize it. It seems so strange that Pyne should act in this way.[2] But it is one of the things that go to make up the present situation which we must face, but which I am perfectly confident we will, in the end, master.

I shall not take your time with saying to you all I wish to say, though I want to assure you that I never was more convinced than I am today that it is your duty to go ahead and talk plainly, frankly, and with all the force and persuasiveness that you can command in the interests of this scheme which the Board still acknowledges to be the scheme of your conviction. The reduction of the opposition to one man makes it all the clearer to me that the permission given you by the Board to speak should be taken at its full face value and the issue be brought clear before the Princeton men, and the decision made in a fair field upon the frank and honest presentation of the scheme.

I know Mr. Jones feels exactly this way, for he has written to me at length, and I am certain Mr. Garrett would not express himself differently.

But let this rest until we see each other. In the meantime let me say that as soon as you return from the South I am at your disposal, either to meet you in New York for a day's conference or, if it is more convenient to you, I will come to Princeton. But I am going to follow up my words with an invitation for you to come to Hartford. As President of the University Club of Hartford I am going to ask you to speak to them, either before Thanksgiving or after it, on the Quadrangle Scheme at Princeton. We have a membership of 290 College and University men, and I am sure every single one of them will be out to hear what you have to say. It will be an academic audience who will appreciate it, perhaps as a strange question to consider, but as one which, before you get through speaking, they will realize must inevitably come before them for decision. I know the financial stress and strain of these days are pretty fully occupying men's minds and making it less easy to hold their attention to such questions as this one which seems so much to us, but I know you cannot speak to any audience without commanding their attention to what you have to say, and I would not wait for a financial recovery of the country before I presented the issue.

Do not think that you have to accept this invitation. I have said nothing as yet to the Board of Managers, for I wish to leave you perfectly free. But if you would like to do this thing, I am going to give you the chance to do it, and we can have here all the time you wish for talking. The Princeton men, of course, will be there to hear you, but you will reach a larger constituency than the dozen or so of our alumni in this region.

I am hoping this letter will reach you before you leave, and I will be glad of a word from you as to what your convenience will be in this matter of a conference. Do not let the personal element of the invitation cloud your judgment as to what it is best for you physically to do, for I shall be glad to see you wherever you call me to come.

I have quite recovered from my attack, but it did not seem as though I could accomplish the journey to Princeton last Thursday—being compelled to leave here after my work was over—and face the function of the evening, with a return journey on the next day. It was a great disappointment to me not simply because I missed the opportunity of meeting Ambassador Bryce, but for the very reasons that you yourself are kind enough to mention:—I wanted to have a talk with you on this question which so vitally concerns the University that we love.

With kindest remembrances to Mrs. Wilson, believe me, always

Yours faithfully, Melancthon W. Jacobus

TLS (WP, DLC).

[1] It is missing.

[2] As Jacobus soon makes clear, Pyne had advised Wilson to drop all discussion of the quadrangle plan. Moreover, as D. B. Jones to WW, Nov. 12, 1907, discloses, Pyne had also threatened to withdraw his financial support from the university if Wilson resumed his campaign for the quadrangle plan.

To Melancthon Williams Jacobus

Princeton, N. J.
My dear Dr. Jacobus: November 6th, 1907.

Thank you most warmly for your kind letter of November 5th, received this morning by special delivery. It heartens me more than I can say to receive such a letter, and fortifies me in all my resolutions about the serious matter we now have in hand.

I have never for a moment thought of giving the fight up. On the contrary, every indication has convinced me that it is more necessary even than I had thought. Nothing else than such reforms as we have in mind will make Princeton free of the influences which are now allowed to govern her; and if we can bring our Princeton constituency to see the necessity of the reform, it is clearly our duty to do so, no matter how long it takes or how hard the task may prove.

The question in my mind is now wholly one of wise procedure. I am convinced that for a little while, for the sake of quieting the unreasonable and wholly factitious excitement which has been stirred up, there should be healing silence, not among the inner counsellors of the University but among the alumni. For this reason, I would rather not make just yet the address that you suggest before the University Club in Hartford. It would be an ideal audience, but I do not think that it would be wise for me to speak so soon after the action of the Board and after the postponement, which has been thought wise, of the debate in the faculty. One of the things I most wish to talk over with you is the wise plan of campaign, and that cannot be determined until we have thoroughly discussed both the state of opinion in the faculty and the condition of affairs among the alumni. We shall really not be free to do what we deem best at Princeton until we are relieved from the dictation of the men who subscribe to the Committee of Fifty Fund and who can withhold our living from us if we displease them.

Would you be free to come down to New York to spend the afternoon of the 21st or the morning of the 22nd? I am to be in New York on the 20th and 21st, attending the annual meeting of the Trustees of the Carnegie Foundation for the Advancement of Teaching. Perhaps if we could meet there then, you would run down and spend the night with me in Princeton. I should like you to talk matters over, if you will, with such members of the faculty as you feel could give the most assistance, because there has been an extraordinary revelation of the real foundations of opinion amongst us here in Princeton, a revelation wholly satisfactory to me, but which has brought to light certain elements which run out into other important phases of university business.

With warmest regard and gratitude for all your kindness,

Faithfully yours, Woodrow Wilson

Mrs. Wilson joins me in every cordial message.

CCL (RSB Coll., DLC).

From Edwin Grant Conklin

My dear President Wilson, Philadelphia, Nov. 7, 1907.

I have decided to write you that I should like to begin my services at Princeton next year and to postpone until some future time the year's leave of absence which the Trustees have so generously granted me.

My reasons for this are, first of all, the condition of my father's[1] health, and secondly my desire to be at Princeton during the building and equipment of the new laboratory.

I have recently had a visit from my father and mother[2] and I realize, as I had not before, that a year's absence from the country at this time is for me an impossibility.

I am of the opinion also that I may be of service in helping to decide questions which are likely to arise next year, especially in connection with the building of the vivarium and the equipment of the new laboratory, and I think it would be advisable to postpone my year abroad until some less critical time.

I hope that this proposed change in my plans may cause you no inconvenience and that it may meet with your approval.

Allow me once more to express to you my hearty thanks for your kindness in granting me leave of absence for next year and my high appreciation of the generous spirit with which I have been treated by you and your colleagues.

Cordially yours, E. G. Conklin.

ALS (WP, DLC).

[1] Abram V. Conklin.

[2] Maria Hull Conklin.

From Sir William Mather

My dear President Wilson [London] Novr 7th/07

I have to thank you, & I do most warmly, for the several letters & cables you have recently sent me relating to the ceremony of the Sun-dial inauguration.

It gave us all much joy to know that all passed off well under the best of weather. It was a relief to me to know that the pamphlets arrived in time, for I feared the meaning of the whole thing would not be realised without the historic being clearly explained. I hope you had enough copies to go round. I shall look forward to the arrival of Sunday newspaper reports to enable us to enter into the spirit that pervaded the ceremony. I have no doubt Mr Bryce would be happy.

I have duly received the "warmly appreciative thanks" of the Trustees of Princeton University in such choice form & words that I can keep it among my most treasured possessions, & I beg of you to be good enough to assure the Trustees of my deep gratification of their recognition of my simple gift. I loved to do it & feel highly privileged that I was able to show my deep interest in the University in this way.

"All's well that ends well," and though it has required some time & thought on your side & mine to complete the project satisfactorily, with 3000 miles between us, we may be now content.

I should much value a really effective photograph of the Dial in situ with part of McCosh's building showing in the background. I wish to order some copies specially from the photographer if he will send me one copy first to judge by. This need not encroach on your time. The name of the photographer & address will suffice.

I sent all our University Vice-Chancellors a copy of the pamphlet, & all our papers had cables through Reuter announcing the event. Dr. Case of Corpus Christi much wishes a photograph. Now—with heartfelt thanks for all the privileges you have accorded me, & with sincere good wishes to Mrs. Wilson & your daughters Very sincerely yours W. Mather

ALS (WWP, UA, NjP). Enc.: "The Sundial at Corpus Christi College, Oxford, with the Replica at Princeton University which was to be Unveiled by Mr. Bryce yesterday," clipping of a news story from the *Manchester Guardian*, Oct. 31, 1907.

An Interview upon Arrival in Memphis

[Nov. 8, 1907]

DR. WOODROW WILSON IS OPTIMISTIC ABOUT MONEY

Coming to Memphis direct from the East, where he has been in the storm center of the money stringency during the past few weeks,[1] Dr. Woodrow Wilson, president of Princeton college, says the financial situation there appears to be getting better in all ways.

"While I am not a financier, and am not in any sense a business man," he said, "from what I can learn the money situation is improving daily in the East. The sentiment among the people appears to be more optimistic."

Although he did not pass through New York on his way to Memphis, Dr. Wilson said that he had heard much about the conditions of affairs in that city, and all reports were encouraging. "The worst has passed, appears to be the general idea of the situation there, as elsewhere," he said.

Dr. Wilson is in Memphis for his first time, coming to deliver an address at the Goodwyn Institute Friday night on "The Ideals of Public Life."

He will also be the guest of honor at the sessions of the Tennessee Alumni association Saturday. The alumni will give a luncheon Saturday at the Country club in his honor, a boat ride on the Mississippi river in the afternoon and a banquet at the Gayoso [Hotel] Saturday night. He will leave Memphis Sunday afternoon.

Dr. Wilson was met at the train Friday by a delegation of resident Princeton alumni, and is being entertained at the home of R. Brinkley Snowden.[2]

As is well known, Dr. Wilson is a friend of football—that is, a friend of the "reformed game." He believes that the alterations in the rules have made football a better game this year.[3] However, he does not think that the limit in improvement has been reached.

"The game is a better one, but it must be made still better," he said. "I believe, however, that it is following a natural course, and will soon reach the desired high plane."

He has faith in the team that represents Princeton college this year, and here's a tip he inadvertently gave out on the game Saturday afternoon, between the Amherst and Princeton teams: "Predictions are something which are very unreliable, but, if I were to make one, I would say that Princeton is sure to defeat Amherst Saturday."[4]

Printed in the *Memphis News Scimitar*, Nov. 8, 1907; some editorial headings omitted.

1 See C. H. Dodge to WW, March 28, 1907, n. 1.

2 Robert Brinkley Snowden, Princeton 1890, a real estate lawyer in Memphis, and married to Sarah Day Snowden. Wilson was also entertained by David Fentress and his wife, Mabel Kingsbury Fentress. David Fentress was a member of the Princeton Class of 1896 and at this time was practicing law in Bolivar, Tenn., and managing the family estate, "Shandy Plantation," in Bolivar.

3 Thorough reform of the game had been undertaken by the Rules Committee of the Intercollegiate Athletic Association (about the formation of which, see WW to H. M. MacCracken, Dec. 19, 1905, n. 1, Vol. 16) during the spring of 1906. The committee had announced on April 1 of that year a new set of rules governing the conduct of play and the game itself which were designed to make football less dangerous to life and limb and also more open and interesting. The success of the reforms was evident by the end of the football season of 1906. The

change most directly responsible for reduction of injuries and the opening up of action was the creation of the "neutral zone." According to an anonymous article, "Success of the New Football Rules," *New York Times*, November 25, 1906, which reviewed the first season played under the new code, the "neutral zone" was created by the "simple expedient of separating the two rush lines by a space equal to the length of the ball." This change, together with the "absolute prohibition of any interference with another player before the ball is put in play," helped to prevent the immediate clash of opposing lines and the close, grinding scrimmage which frequently led to exhaustion, injury, and little movement of the ball. Moreover, the "neutral zone" enabled officials more easily to detect infringements of the rules.

The Rules Committee added new rules in 1907 and afterward as experience proved them necessary and beneficial. However, football enthusiasts agreed with the writer of the article cited above that it was the Rules Committee's "painstaking and intelligent effort" in 1906 that had saved a great sport from probable abolition.

4 Wilson's prediction was correct. Princeton defeated Amherst 14 to 0 on November 9, 1907.

Two News Reports of Addresses in Memphis

[Nov. 9, 1907]

ADDRESSES AT THREE SCHOOLS

By Dr. Woodrow Wilson

Dr. Woodrow Wilson, president of Princeton University, scholar and statesman, spent yesterday in the city and will be the guest of friends here until Sunday. President Wilson was the guest yesterday of R. Brinkley Snowden. He will be the guest of honor on Saturday at the annual banquet of the Tennessee Alumni of Princeton at the Country Club, and will participate in the other exercises of the annual reunion.

This was Dr. Wilson's first visit to Memphis, and he greatly enjoyed several motor car trips over the city yesterday. During the day he visited several of the private schools, where he made brief addresses, and he also addressed the students of the city high school during the afternoon. Dr. Wilson's published photographs all fail to do him justice. While he would never be classed as a handsome man, the printed likenesses fail to indicate the lighting up of his face as he talks, and he is at the present time considerably stouter than his photographs would indicate.

Dr. Wilson was entertained at luncheon yesterday at the Hotel Gayoso by P. P. Van Vleet.[1] Among the other guests were Gen. Luke E. Wright,[2] Bishop Thomas F[rank]. Gailor of the Episcopal diocese of Tennessee, Mayor James H[enry]. Malone, Hubert Fisher[3] and R. Brinkley Snowden.

Dr. Wilson during the morning addressed the students of St. Mary's School and at the Memphis University School. At the latter institution he spoke briefly on the "Problems of the Future," urging the young gentlemen present to work for the education of both their minds and bodies for the purpose of enabling them to lead useful lives and to do good to others, for in this age no man can live wholly for himself. He alluded to the serious problems which are now beginning to confront the nation, which must be met and settled by the boys who are now students at school and college.

At 3 o'clock in the afternoon Dr. Wilson addressed the students at the city high school. He was introduced by Prof. [Israel C.] McNeill, superintendent of schools, as a man whose great thoughts had made many others think and as one of the greatest of Americans.

Dr. Wilson, who is a fluent and ready speaker, spoke for a few minutes in a semi-humorous strain. He said that after such an introduction great things might be expected of a speaker, but he could prove by the young men, graduates of Princeton, who were following him about over the city, that he never said anything new now, having long ago told over and over again his views on most questions.

"One thing which speaks well for the public schools of the United States," said Dr. Wilson, "is that, in proportion to the numbers enrolled, the students at Princeton who are graduates of the public schools show a higher standard of scholarship than those from private schools. This was shown by tests which were made during a considerable period of time. One reason for this is that in the public schools there is only one purpose among the pupils. You come here for the purpose of studying, and, I hope, of learning.

"We are told by many teachers that their great purpose in teaching is character building. Now, as a matter of fact, in my opinion, character is a by-product. The mere teaching of good manners and gentlemanly deportment does not produce character. If you take pains to do every duty of the hour as it comes to you, your character will take care of itself. You will acquire the best of characters by doing every duty as you see it and doing your best. The public school is like the world also. It makes very little difference if one of you should drop out from his place. You will not be greatly missed, except, of course, in your immediate family circle among those who love you. So in the world, a man is not greatly missed, except in the place he has made for himself by his attention to duty.

"You think doubtless that you have many dry studies in school. But there are absolutely no dry studies. It is your minds that are dry and dusty. A friend of mine once told me that the most discouraging thing about teaching was the almost limitless resources of the human mind in its ability to resist the introduction of knowledge.

"If we coat our minds with a hard varnish of indifference, we will find all subjects dry and without interest. We must open our minds to receive knowledge. It depends upon you what you take from your school life, not upon your teachers. You must be willing and anxious to learn or no one can teach you. You must be interested or no one can interest you. It is one of the most pleasant sensations that one can have to use one's mind, to grasp an idea, to investigate the truth of any subject. In conclusion I want to leave this thought with you, that just in proportion as your work here is [good] will be the knowledge which you will receive and take with you."

Dr. Wilson is a staunch supporter of all college athletic sports and spoke enthusiastically yesterday of the improvement made in college football by the putting into effect of the new rules. He said he thought the game had been greatly improved and that he believed with some other changes which will be worked out the game will be placed upon a higher plane than ever before.

1 Peter Percy Van Vleet, in the wholesale drug business in Memphis. His son, Angus McKay Van Vleet, attended Princeton from 1908 to 1910.

2 Luke Edward Wright, at this time residing in Memphis upon his recent return from service as United States Ambassador to Japan. He became Secretary of War on July 1, 1908, and served in this post until the end of the Roosevelt administration.

3 A lawyer in Memphis.

◇

SOME IDEALS OF PUBLIC LIFE

Woodrow Wilson's Ideas

Before an audience that filled every available foot of space in the auditorium of the Goodwyn Institute and overflowed into the main and the gallery lobbies, Dr. Woodrow Wilson, president of Princeton University, last night delivered an address upon "Ideals of Public Life." Dr. Wilson's reputation as a thinker and statesman attracted a very large audience, and some hundreds, among which were many ladies, stood throughout the lecture. The lecture partook somewhat of the nature of a political address, but on entirely new lines. During the course of his remarks, Dr. Wilson proposed a remedy for the economic ills under which the country is laboring, the social abuses and the wrongs admittedly accomplished by some of the great corporations. His remedy lies in the enactment of laws by which the individuals responsible for the acts of the corporations of which complaint is made, may be located and punished.

Mr. Wilson also pleaded for an enlargement of the conception of public life.

"No man," he said, "in a free country governed by opinion can afford to be a totally private man. It is his duty to enter into public counsel, and in proportion as he enters into counsel he enters into public life. The roll of our public men is not confined to those who occupy or seek public office; all those of whom we take counsel are in the best sense of the word public men. Particularly now, as there seem to be no distinctive party doctrines and when party leaders lead us we know not exactly whither, the country consciously seeks counsel of men who speak definitely and fearlessly and who think close to the facts not only, but also close to definite principles.

"What the country just now needs and wishes more than anything else is distinguished advice and a clearing of counsel. Public life is not merely the transaction of public business; it is also the formation of the public thought, the guidance of the public purposes, the clarification of all programmes and the careful testing of all remedies.

"Our chief political difficulties lie in the field of modern business combinations, and only those who really understand the method and the motives of those combinations will give the public advice which it would be worth its while to follow. Our present tendency is to go almost feverishly in search of strange experimental processes by which to check the things of which we are afraid, and we are apt in such a search to lose the very thing for which we have been distinguished, the only thing for which we have been distinguished among the nations; namely, our clear grasp of principles, our confidence in the operation of the individual freedom, our faith in men rather than in government.

"Many men in public office and who are the accredited leaders of parties, think of these things clearly and act upon definite principle without reward to them. But they need recruiting out of the general ranks of society. Counsel cannot be common counsel if it is confined to accredited political leaders; it must be enriched by the thought and purpose of those whose thought has other foundation and other scope than the interest of parties and the immediate feasibility of particular programmes.

"We need to encourage, as we are already encouraging, the rise of an additional class of public men, intensely practical, intimately acquainted with the facts about which they speak and not afraid of uncovering what is ugly; but not opportunists, not confining their view to what is immediately practicable, but looking forward to the long course which the nation must pursue if it intends to rid itself of economic evils and purify the processes of its life; men determined to lead, but able to lead without being candidates for office, without seeking place, trying to find their leadership in the force of their ideas, not in the force of their ambitions; men with definite programmes, but not tied to parties and not dismayed if parties will not at once take up the measures which they advocate.

"We live in a very confused time. The economic developments which have embarrassed our life are of comparatively recent origin, and our chief trouble is that we do not exactly know what we are about. We have not made a thorough analysis of the facts; we are full of suspicions, but our arguments do not abound in proof. We are eager to touch the springs of action, but have not yet discovered exactly where they lie. We need nothing so much as that public thought should be instructed, purified, invigorated by plain, straightforward, disinterested discussion, not so much of party programmes, as of facts and situations and needs.

"Above all things we need men who, because they are rendered independent by not seeking office or even desiring it, can hold militant ideals for which they are ready to fight in season and out of season, and which they are ready to expound, though no man at first agree with them. If there were a large number of such men, their counsel would presently be heeded, and parties would no longer cast about for popular cries and issues. The public thought would bulk very close to the eyes of all leaders, if formed by non-partisan processes.

"I do not mean that parties can be or should be discredited. I believe that party action is the necessary process of life in a free country governed by opinion. What I mean is that the nation will not get at the real thoughts and purposes, if it take counsel in public matters only of those who are party leaders and who are hampered, as party leaders must always be, by the exigencies of party contests and the necessity of always looking to the major chance at election time. Party leaders are obliged in a great degree to be opportunists. But the country cannot afford to be guided by opportunism alone. It must form its parties by very definitely pursuing its opinions, and opinion may dominate parties instead of merely supplying them with catch words, test candidates for office rather than merely coach them for success.

"Let us insist now for a little while, in this time when new thinking and new purposing is to be done, on thinking outside party formulas and class interests, as the men of our creative period did, when the nation was in process of birth. Let us seek to encourage a class of public men who can make opinion, whom parties must heed and cannot use.

"This is not cynical counsel based upon any pessimistic feeling that party morality is at a low ebb. On the contrary, the action of parties in our day is touched at many points with hopeful signs. Opinion everywhere prefers the process which is righteous and the man who is honest, and parties are as likely now as they ever were to serve the nation creditably and to good purpose. But they must serve the nation and not merely play a game for advantage, and they cannot serve a nation which does not definitely form and declare its thought.

"Nothing is more evident in our day than that the country is confused in its thinking, and needs to look its affairs over very carefully before determining what legal and constitutional changes it will make. In our haste and eagerness to reform manifest abuses, we are inclined to enter upon courses dangerous and unprecedented, I mean unprecedented in America, and quite contrary to the spirit which has hitherto ruled in her affairs. We turn more and more with a sense of individual helplessness to the government, begging that it take care of us because we have forgotten how to take care of ourselves, begging that it will regulate our industries, scrutinize our economic undertakings, supervise our enterprises and keep the men who conduct them within definite bounds of law and morality.

"We no longer know any remedy except to put things in the hands of the government. In such courses we are turning directly away from all the principles which have distinguished America and made her institutions the hope of all men who believe in liberty. Undoubtedly in our own time we must look to government to do a great many things which were once within the power of the individual and are now much beyond it, but it is none the less our duty to see that endeavor is not swallowed up in government.

"We find many things done under forms of corporate organization which are clearly against the public welfare as well as against all principles of private morality, and so we strike at corporations, and, striking at corporations, embarrass the business of the country. There is no such thing as corporate morality or corporate integrity, or corporate responsibility. Every transaction that is against the public welfare or right principle can be traced, if we will but take the pains to trace it, to some individual or body of individuals who are responsible for it, and those individuals should be punished without fear or favor, without checking the courses of the country's business. We must so analyze our new methods of business as to re-discover the individual in them and hold him to his personal responsibility.

"This, and not methods of government supervision, is the task of the enlightened lawyer and legislator, if we would bring back to America her great fame and leadership [in the world of politics and law. It is difficult; it can be accomplished][1] only by the most careful analysis of the facts; but it can be accomplished, and it will set us free alike from individual crime in the field of business and from governmental tutelage in the field of politics. Our two tasks are to break up monopolies and re-discover the individual in all matters of legal responsibility.

"Governmental supervision will not free us or moralize us; it will in the long run enslave us and demoralize us. But individual responsibility and an impartial enforcement of the law against those who are actually responsible will bring us alike freedom and public morals."[2]

Printed in the Memphis *Commercial Appeal*, Nov. 9, 1907; some editorial headings omitted.

[1] This addition is from an undated typed news release of this address, entitled "Ideals of Public Life," in WP, DLC.

[2] There is also a WWT outline of this address in WP, DLC.

An Address in Memphis to the Princeton Alumni Association of Tennessee

[[Nov. 9, 1907]]

Mr. President and Gentlemen:

This is now the sixth speech[1] I have made since I reached Memphis, but I should certainly be very thoroughly exhausted if I could not speak to the toast which I find on the programme,—Princeton University.

I was not bred so far as I know to be a college president. I remember even when I was in the senior class at Princeton, looking with a certain condescension and pity on a member of the faculty and wondering how any man could have so little spirit as to devote himself to such a life. Something, I take it, must have entered into my conclusions at a later time to have changed my point of view, because certainly now it seems to me that there is nothing I would rather do than guide, if I might be so fortunate,

[1] In addition to the four speeches already mentioned in the preceding news reports, he had spoken on November 8 either at a luncheon given him by P. P. Van Vleet or at a dinner given him by Colonel W. H. Carroll and Hubert Fisher at Colonel Carroll's home.

the destinies of young men in respect of the matters which most concern them and which most concern the country.

My duties have been almost exclusively political, and I must say that I find myself generally thinking of a university as a political instrument; I do not mean an instrument for the direct settlement of political questions, but as an instrument for the advancement of the general intelligence and power of the country. I can not think of a university in any more vital way than as a place where men are lifted to the contemplation of those questions which are larger than themselves and larger than any private interest, and which concern them as citizens of the country in which they live.

I was saying the other day at the interesting University School, at which it was my pleasure to be present, that it does seem to me that the younger men and the boys of this country are certain to come to an age more difficult than any which has preceded, and that there never was a time when we could afford less than we can afford it now to narrow our training or preparation for the pushing forward of particular interests. I know that the whole tendency of the time is to train men for particular occupations, and I know also that the danger of the time is that men's minds are confined to particular occupations. If we are to intensify the tendency of our time by preparing our young men only for particular occupations, there will be no properly equipped body of men whose scope of thought will be wider than the particular occupation, and the country will lack the kind of counselors who alone can save it.

The great trouble with this country is, now that we are so busy, we are so immersed in particular interests that we do not think outside the narrow circle of our own particular callings. I meet a great many kinds of men, and I must say that I do not meet many men who can think accurately outside the limits of the things which are daily occupying their attention. And a country governed by opinion is in danger of being misgoverned and misled, if that becomes universally the case. I tell you I would rather have men think superficially, if wisely, than have them think accurately, if narrowly. You know there is a very interesting episode in one of Carlyle's writings in which he speaks in this wise: He is making fun of the whole democratic theory of government, and he says, how is it possible out of a multitude of knaves to make an honest nation?—his thesis being that each individual taken separately is a knave, and hence he questions how, if you please, is it possible by multiplying them to make an honest nation? Well, I think that I can show you how, if we were all knaves, we would all put together be honest. Let us argue the matter on Carlyle's hypothesis: Suppose that we were sitting, as we often sit, and as we more often desire to sit, amongst a great multitude of persons around a football field. The number of persons is so great, the space of the field is so broad, that we can not hear anything that is said unless the tones are inordinately raised upon the field itself; now, then, while you are waiting for the players, two men not in football costume, seeming to be custodians of the field or judges of the contest, emerge and walk out upon the field, and there in the presence of the company presently fall to blows with each other. How instantly we have the impulse to say "It is an outrage! Why are they not arrested?" Now, it may be that if any two of us had been those two, and one of us had said to the other what one of them said to the other, there would have been instant blows. You do not know what one man said to the other, but he did not say it to you, and you are a competent judge of his behavior, because you are not maddened as he has been maddened. Now, if you take a multitude of knaves and divorce most of them from the interest in a particular contest, they will be competent judges of the contest.

Now, I do not admit the hypothesis—I do not admit that we are individually knaves; I might admit that you are, but I won't admit that I am (Laughter) and I feel bound in Christian charity to assume that you are as good as I am. (Laughter.) Now, on the theory that we are not knaves, but honest men, apt to be misled by passion, apt to be prejudiced by interest, we are still better able to judge of the general interest if we take pains to be intelligently informed when particular interests not our own are under discussion, and it seems to me that the particular duty of a university is to give men an intelligent appreciation of the things that they are not going to do. I am not now speaking of technical schools; their business is different; they are to give men a special training, whether of head or hand, which is to make them skillful winners of bread. I am speaking of a university, not a technical school, and I say that the particular business of the university is to give the man a good appreciation of the things he is not going to do.

Most of the best things in this world can not be turned into cash. Well, I won't say that they can not be—they can be; I can turn my health into cash if I want to throw it away on things that are not as enjoyable as it is. I can turn my morals into cash if I think the cash will be more comfortable to live with and to sleep with than my morals. I can turn anything that I have into cash if I am willing to part with it. Now the mistake that some men make is that they cash in their morals and then they find that they have a bad taste in their mouths night and day and that the cash they have for their morals can not buy any adequate substitute, and most of the things in this world that are most enjoyable are the things for which you can not get any cash at all. I know it is not thought so; I know a man thinks he is comfortable in proportion to the shapeliness of his clothes and the conformity of his manners to the standards of the society in which he lives. I know that a man generally thinks himself most comfortable when he takes the advice of Dean Swift when he said, "If you wish to be considered a man of sense, always agree with the man with whom you are conversing." I have known a great many persons to gain the report of being persons of sense by following the Dean's advice, and yet those men are always most careful to have some other companion than themselves, because when they get off by themselves, then they know that they are not men of sense, but that they are gangrene with the insincerity which already paints on them the smell of the grave itself.

I know what the young man's burden of our age is. His burden is not to make a living, because, as our toastmaster has just said,[2] it is easy to make a living if you are diligent and intelligent; if you are willing to work hard and take orders, and to use your brains on what you are doing, you can make a living easily enough. The burden is, our burden is, that we have to carry life as well as a living. The expression that Mr. Granberry used was a very significant expression: we are trying to equip young men for life. Now life is a very much better thing than making a living. Life consists for me of the most part of my neighbors, because I am conditioned in everything that I do by my neighbors. There is an interesting episode in Walter Bagehot's writings, in which he says, "Talk about the tyranny of Nero and Tiberius—the real tyranny is the tyranny of your next door neighbor,"—of having to do everything that he does, and knowing that he is watching you in your exits and entrances and that he is making a note of your whole life; and the worst part is that you are constantly feeling the impingement on your sensitive parts of these picayune comments; and when you widen that situation to the community in which you live and the country in which you live, you know that your life is conditioned by the life of the country with whom you are identified. And therefore intelligent men

[2] William Langley Granbery, Princeton 1885, lawyer of Nashville and President of the Princeton Alumni Association of Tennessee, who had introduced him.

know that they carry the fortunes of their country in their hands, in what they do with them, that they must perforce carry the fortunes of the country.

I was at one time a practitioner of the law. I did not practice it very violently, but I practiced it long enough to know what it felt like, and I practiced it in a place—perhaps some of you may have heard where it was [Atlanta], so I had better not say much about it—where the conditions of practice were wellnigh intolerable. There were men at that bar who lowered the whole tone of legal practice by the things that they did. Some of them, since the time that I remember, have been unjustly rewarded with high office.[3] Those men would condescend to any practice whatever, and they made the life of a man who tried to be decent just as nearly intolerable as possible, because he would not resort to the tricks by which they succeeded, and because they resorted to tricks, clients did not seek him out; and the whole burden of a demoralized bar rested upon every individual practitioner in that place. Now, that is true of every calling, and there is a sense in which every man is bound to carry the burdens of his whole profession and of his whole community.

Last night in an address in this city I said some very disrespectful things about reformers. I do not take them back; on the contrary, I could add a good deal more to them, because your professional reformer is an unmitigated nuisance; but there is a sense in which every man is bound to be a reformer of the particular walk of life in which he himself is thrown. If he has conscience, he has to insist on it that the persons with whom he deals shall themselves exhibit conscience, and if they won't exhibit conscience, he has to say things about them, he has to make it a game of give and take, and say just as disagreeable things about them as they say about him,—and the advantage that the honest man has in abusing other persons is that he can make his abuse consistent, and the dishonest man is apt to make his abuse inconsistent. (Applause.) There is going to be an advantage in the long run on the side of the honest man, because it is going to be found that he is always saying the same thing. If you but widen this situation to modern life, you will see that the man who knows only a particular task is going always to be at the bottom of the heap and carry the greater bulk of the burden, because if you are so narrowly trained that you are necessarily the under dog, being the under dog you have to carry all the dogs that are on top of

[3] Among them was Hoke Smith, Attorney General in Cleveland's second administration and, at this time, Governor of Georgia.

you. The dog that knows where the top of the pile is will sometimes be able to fall on top instead of falling on the bottom.

These are homely and it may be vulgar illustrations of what I am trying to impress upon you. I am trying to impress upon you this circumstance, that universities are not intended to be places where men are trained to make money; they are intended to be places where men are trained to take part in life; and that only in proportion as they give the man the vision which is necessary for the comprehension of life are they valuable. When men come to me, therefore, and say they wish their sons to study those things which will best prepare them for their profession, I ask what their profession is going to be, and then if I am left to advise the boy, I start him just as far off from that profession as I possible [possibly] can in the course of study which he is going to pursue, and I am justified in that by the counsel of the most experienced men in every calling that I know. I have been told by mechanical engineers that they wish that every man who becomes a mechanical engineer should first take a classical course of ancient learning in the university. They can not always tell me why they want it; they simply have found out that the men who have done that first make the best engineers. When you get down to hard pan they will tell you this: the modern engineer does not merely lay out a road or build a bridge or erect a great structure; he is obliged in the modernly conducted organization of labor and of industry to be a captain of men, and it is no more unlikely that he will be sent to build a bridge in India and use coolies as laborers, than he will be sent to build a bridge in New York State and use Italians as laborers. Indeed, a man in the United States is likely to use as many nationalities of laborers as if he traveled all over the globe, and he has to know how to handle men, how to deal like a statesman on a small scale with the great combinations of modern industrial life. And the man who has limbered himself up before he narrows himself down to a particular calling is going to have the biggest and most effective equipment. This world is full of servants and they will always be a drug on the market, and what it needs, what it demands, what it can not dispense with, is masters, and the supply is woefully small.

Some men are born that way; they do not have to be educated into the function, but I notice if they are not educated in the function they always have to be assisted by men who are; that is, practically self-made men always have to use university-bred men to keep the business from breaking down. They could not take it a foot forward unless they had the specially trained servants to employ. They all say so; some of the most conspicuous self-made men in our own time have contributed immense sums of money to universities in the conscience, the declared and admitted conscience, that if they did not do it the enterprises they were engaged in would collapse. Now, I think with Dr. Holmes that a self-made man is a very remarkable creation considering who made him,[4] but every man ought to welcome a certain amount of assistance in what is by nature a very delicate and difficult task, and the universities have it as a task to enable men to discover not the particular qualities they already know they have, but the undisclosed qualities which they do not yet know that they have. When I am told that the right course of education is to let a man do what he wants to do and knows that he can do, I know that I am being told that the object of a university is never to enable a man to be any any [*sic*] broader than he was born, is never to enable a man to discover the covered and covert ore that is in him, is never to enable him to expand his powers, but only to enable him to intensify a particular power. That it is not meant to broaden and diversify the intellectual crops of the world, but merely to exhause [exhaust] the soil by putting in it year after year, season after season, the same crop, which will presently draw every virtue out of the soil. It is practically to tell the South that she ought never to cultivate anything but cotton; to say to a man, you must never cultivate anything in you but what you know you were born with. I knew of a young man once who thought he was born to be a mechanical engineer, because forsooth he was interested in machinery. I should suppose that a man who was interested in horses was meant to be nothing but a hostler. I was interested in horses, but I have risen above the hostler's job, and I remember this young man who thought he was born to be a mechanical engineer, and he turned out to be a metaphysician. He became one of the most profound metaphysicians of his age, and he at least whetted the intellects of his contemporaries by sorely puzzling them with certain things which he did understand and which for the life of them they could not understand; and I believe a man has a certain value if he can do things that nobody else can do and set them wondering what it is all about. Now, you can not imagine anything farther from mechanics than metaphysics; and here was the deepest mind in this fellow undiscovered, until some rude teacher broke the crust away and found this well of knowledge springing up more abundantly than anything else in the boy's nature.

[4] See Oliver Wendell Holmes, *The Autocrat of the Breakfast Table*, Chap. 1.

If I had the educating of a boy and could take him long enough on the assumption that he would have the life of Methuselah, I would confine him exclusively to the study of the things he was not interested in. And when he began to be interested in a thing, I would change the subject on the ground that he would thereby be discovering all the frailties that were in his nature. I believe in my heart that is what the university is for. It is the grand waking up place, where you knock at the doors of a man's mind and say, "Get up, it is morning. The day has come. The world is alive. Get out in the open. You must do the work of the world."

Printed in the *Princeton Alumni Weekly*, VIII (Nov. 20, 1907), 138-41.

From Charles William Kent

Dear Wilson: University of Virginia, November 9, 1907.

To save your time I shall come with directness to the gist of this letter. We are engaged in preparing a Library of Southern Literature,[1] a series which I trust will be worthily edited and just as well printed: we hope for it a large sale and trust that it may be of value in stirring up a more wide spread interest in Southern letters, and in making the next generation better informed about the literary life of their forefathers than the present generation is.

In the first place I take pleasure in saying that you are going to be included and that we have asked Dr. Ballagh of the Johns Hopkins to prepare the brief biographical and critical sketch of you and your work for inclusion as a sort of preface to the selections which we shall reprint from your books.[2] By the way, any help that you night [might] give us as to the selections by which you would prefer to be represented in such a series, would be of direct help.

We are very anxious, however, to include you in another capacity and that is as a direct contributor to this series. In our opinion James Madison was sufficiently literary in his work to be counted a man of letters and to be represented in this series by specimens of his very best style. Mindful of the close connection of Madison with Princeton and his unpremeditated services in linking together your institution and the University of Virginia, I have thought it would be singularly appropriate if the President of Princeton would be willing to furnish the brief biographical and critical sketch of this noted statesman. We would wish the sketch to be about 3000 words; for the rest, you would be the best judge of what it should be.

I feel sure that in the pressure of your many duties you will feel inclined to excuse yourself, but I beg you not to do so, unless it is utterly impossible for you to comply with this request.[3] I might mention, by the way, that my young friend Dr. [Edgar] Dawson, who is now working so loyally and earnestly in your faculty, would I am sure, be glad to do any of the preliminary work that you would desire of him in the preparation of this sketch.

With a hearty welcome for you when you can visit the University and with frequent pleasant memories of our old time association, I am, Cordially yours, Charles W. Kent

TLS (WP, DLC). Enc.: printed announcement concerning the projected *Library of Southern Literature.*

[1] Edwin Anderson Alderman, Joel Chandler Harris, *et al.* (eds.), *Library of Southern Literature* (17 vols., New Orleans, Atlanta, and Dallas, 1907-23). Kent was "literary editor."

[2] James Curtis Ballagh, Associate Professor of History at The Johns Hopkins University. Actually, Stockton Axson contributed the sketch of Wilson printed in *Library of Southern Literature*, XIII, 5881-88. The selections by Wilson printed in *ibid.*, pp. 5888-901, were "The Truth of the Matter," from *Mere Literature and Other Essays*, and "The Spirit of Learning," his Phi Beta Kappa address at Harvard University on July 1, 1909.

[3] Wilson's reply is missing, but see C. W. Kent to WW, Nov. 26, 1907.

A News Report About Wilson's Arrival in Nashville

[Nov. 11, 1907]

DISTINGUISHED ORATOR, EDUCATOR AND PUBLICIST

Dr. Woodrow Wilson, President of Princeton University, Here For Few Days Rest—Will Be Entertained at Smoker at Watauga Club[1] This Evening.

Dr. Woodrow Wilson, President of Princeton University, one of the best-known and most prominent literary and educational figures of the day, is in the city, stopping for a few days at the home of his brother, Mr. Joseph R. Wilson, of the Banner staff, on Fifteenth Avenue, South. Dr. Wilson arrived from Memphis Sunday night in company with Mr. W. L. Granberry of this city, President of the Princeton Alumni Association of this state, after having for the third consecutive time attended the annual meeting of this association. . . .

In view of the arduous exertions of his busy stay in Memphis and the strenuous demands upon his time and energy before returning to Princeton and inasmuch as his local visit was primarily for rest, President Wilson rested the entire morning and could not be seen for publication. He has been compelled to decline with regrets a large number of local engagements sought especially by the city's various educational institutions, and will only appear locally at a smoker given in his honor at the Watagua [Watauga] Club to-night. There is no formal programme for this occasion, the speaker being free to express himself upon any topic of his personal selection. The club management desires to have it understood that in view of the necessarily informal nature of the affair all members of the club are expected to be present, whether notified or not. It will, however, be limited to members of the organization only. President Wilson will probably be in town until Thursday, and hopes to put in all possible time in quiet and rest.

Printed in the *Nashville Banner*, Nov. 11, 1907.

1 Organized on February 23, 1907, by union of the Hermitage and University clubs, the Watauga Club was the leading social organization of Nashville.

An Interview

[Nov. 11, 1907]

THE MAN AND WHAT HE STANDS FOR MAIN QUESTION

President Woodrow Wilson, of Princeton University, Says Section "Cuts Little Ice."

"It doesn't make much difference what section a man hails from; it is what his record has been, what he stands for and the faith of the people in him that must settle the question of the next nominee of [t]he democratic party. The people are looking at men more today than they ever did before and considering the party less." So spoke Dr. Woodrow Wilson, president of Princeton University, last night.

Dr. Wilson is a guest of his brother, Joseph R. Wilson, the well-known political writer of the Nashville Banner, at the latter's home at 1012 Fifteenth avenue, south, and will remain here three or four days to enjoy a quiet rest. . . .

It was in speaking of the movement recently started in Nashville to nominate a southern man for President that Dr. Wilson uttered the words quoted above. "As a southern man, I am in sympathy with the movement," he said, "and I don't think there would be any objection through the north or east to it, but the question of section cuts little ice in choosing the standard bearer. True, the south has not had the representation in the nation's councils it is entitled to, and its voice has been out of all proportion to the electoral votes it casts, but the question upon which nominations for Presidents should be based is who the man is, what has he done and what are his policies, regardless of the section of the country he may live in. I am not acquainted with the purposes of the movement lately started in Tennessee; I have seen allusions to it, and that is all. But I am in hearty sympathy with everything that affects the south's advancement and progress, educationally, politically, and in every way."

Dr. Wilson would not say whom he considered as the most available man for the democratic nomination in 1908 and when asked what he thought of Mr. Bryan in that connection, he laughingly evaded the question: "Oh, now, I can't discuss Mr. Bryan," was all he would say.

"Well, as you are a southern man yourself, Dr. Wilson, and have been frequently mentioned for the nomination, would you take it?" he was asked.

"I am not a politician," he responded with a good-humored laugh. "Some of my friends in various sections of the country have been kind enough to mention my name in that connection, but I have never thought of it myself. I'm not in politics."

He was asked if he thought President Roosevelt would accept a renomination, and replied that he thought not, in view of the President's oft-repeated declarations. He said that Gov. Hughes, of New York, was looming largely on the political horizon in New York, and seemed to be a very strong man. He is very highly regarded among the businessmen of New York.

Dr. Wilson expressed himself as highly gratified with the greatly reduced republican majority in his state last week, and he considers that it gives ground for strong hope of carrying the state next year. For the last three or four years the republican majority in New Jersey has been steadily diminishing. However, he would not venture an opinion on the national outlook for 1908.

Dr. Wilson was asked his opinion of the cause of the financial panic, and replied: "It can hardly be called a panic. Money just got scarce and went in its hole. The failure of the railroads to borrow the money they wanted for improvements no doubt had something to do with it, and their inability to negotiate was doubtless caused, in a measure at least, by the rate regulation, but there were a number of causes, and I don't think any one in particular can be blamed for it. However, the business of the country is good, and I think the worst is over. When I left home the business interests seems to be in a reassured frame of mind." . . .

Dr. Wilson will be the guest of honor at a smoker tonight at 8 o'clock given by the Watauga Club.

Printed in the *Nashville Tennessean*, Nov. 11, 1907.

From Melancthon Williams Jacobus

Hartford, Conn.,
My dear President Wilson: November 11th, 1907.

I shall be very glad indeed to meet you in New York on the afternoon of Friday the 22d, at such hour and place as you may select, and will accept your kind invitation to return with you to Princeton that evening for such conference with members of the Faculty as you may think wise to have.

I do sincerely hope that your trip to the South will not overtax your strength, and that you will not allow the issues involved in the Quadrangle situation to unnecessarily burden you with anxiety.

It is not possible, in my judgment, that principles so profound and interests so large should not ultimately come to right issue. As you counsel, the need at present is patience, in order that, when the time to speak comes, the conditions may be as near what we could ask as possible.

I am glad to say that my own health is greatly improved, as evidence of which is my plan to take Dr. Mackenzie and his son, whose face is already turned towards Princeton,[1] to the game at New Haven on Saturday.[2]

With kind regards,

Yours very sincerely, M. W. Jacobus

TLS (WP, DLC).

[1] The Rev. Dr. William Douglas Mackenzie, President of Hartford Theological Seminary, and Ian Douglas Mackenzie, who entered Princeton in the autumn of 1911 as a freshman.

[2] Yale defeated Princeton in their thirty-third annual football game on November 16 by a score of 12 to 10.

A News Report of an Address in Nashville

[Nov. 12, 1907]

FALSE AND TRUE CONSERVATISM

Subject of Able Address
by Dr. Woodrow Wilson.

Dr. Woodrow Wilson, the eminent President of Princeton University, was the guest last night of the Wautauga [Watauga] Club in an informal smoker and Dutch supper. The invitations were confined to the membership, and something over 100 leading men of the city, representing the commercial and professional circles, gathered to do honor to the visitor.

When Dr. Wilson arrived, shortly after 8 o'clock, he was introduced to the assembled members by Mr. C. C. Slaughter,[1] President of the club, and half an hour was spent in an informal reception in the parlors of the club, after which the guest went to the ball-room, which had been elaborately decorated with Old Gold and Black, colors of Princeton, and trailing Jackson vine. The blending of the colors, old gold and black, and the green of the vines, illuminated with hundreds of incandescent lights, gave a bright, harmonizing effect.

Dr. Wilson was given the seat of honor, beneath a large shield of Princeton's colors.

Mr. C. C. Slaughter was master of ceremonies. Dr. J[ames]. H[ampton]. Kirkland, Chancellor of Vanderbilt University; Mr. W. L. Granbery and Mr. H. M. Suter,[2] Princeton alumni, the former being President of the Princeton Tennessee Alumni Association, accepted seats near Dr. Wilson.

In introducing President Wilson Mr. Slaughter said, in substance: "I am sure I voice the sentiment of every one present when I say how keenly we appreciate the honor of having as our guest this evening the President of Princeton University.

"Princeton has always had a warm place in the hearts of the Southern people before and since the war, and while its memories are entwined around the hearts of many of us, it is but just to say that the tribute we pay to-night is to the man rather than to the university.

"The South is filled with sentiment and ideals, and we admire men more than money. A fact that we are proud of is that our Senators and Representatives in Congress have always returned home poorer than when they went to the nation's capital.

"One great source of pleasure is the achievements of the sons of the South who have cast their lots with sons of the East.

"Dr. Wilson is quoted as saying it does not matter from what section a man hails, it is his record, it is what he stands for that counts.

"We are here this evening to honor our distinguished guest for the record he has made and for the principles which he so ably represents.

"I have the pleasure of introducing to you as our honored guest Dr. Woodrow Wilson."

Dr. Wilson arose amid a storm of applause and gracefully acknowledging the complimentary words spoken by Mr. Slaughter

1 Coleman C. Slaughter, a lawyer in Nashville.

2 Herman Milton Suter, Princeton 1899, publisher and editor of the *Nashville Tennessean.*

he at once entered into a discussion of his subject, "True and False Conservatism." He said that the present condition was one of confusion in political programme and experiment in legislation, and that the danger was that we would form purposes before we got light enough to form them by.

"There are two words," he said, "a great deal used just now, to which it is worth our while to give attention in order that we may use them in their true meaning. These are the words 'conservative' and 'reactionary.' A great many of our public men seem in danger of using the two words as if they meant the same thing. They are, in fact, sharply contrasted in meaning. Reaction is opposed to progress, while progress is often the best instrument of conservatism, and conservative objects can best be served by such changes as constitute real progress. Conservatism is opposed to radicalism, and radicalism itself becomes conservative when it is based upon a real knowledge of conditions and a real appreciation of the remedies which will be efficacious without being destructive. We have allowed the air of our time to be filled with suspicion and we have begun to act while under the influence of suspicion instead of taking the time to look beneath the suspicion to the real condition of affairs.

"No one can doubt that many demoralizing things and many immoral practices have characterized the conduct of business on a great scale in recent years, but it is equally true that the great bulk of our business is sound and honest, and the danger is a danger, illustrated by the present financial anxiety, that we will allow the suspicion to attach to all business instead of confining it to those kinds of business and those particular operations which do strike at the public welfare. Our duty, therefore, is one of candid and searching inquiry, and not of indiscriminate attack. We shall be mere radicals if we attack all along the line, and conservatives if we attack only that which is unsound and untrustworthy. Our first business, therefore, is knowledge, and knowledge is the true conservative force. The country never needed conservative advice more than it does now. Reactionary advice it does not need. That is not conservative, but revolutionary. We must set our processes in order, both moral and economical. We are undertaking to regulate before we have made thorough analysis of the conditions to be rectified. One of the distinguishing characteristics of our time is that our processes of business have ceased to be local and have become national, and one of the most important results of this is that the old contrasts between the different sections of the country are disappearing. I do not think that the North and East any longer feel that the

South stands apart from the rest of the Union in any sort of essential contrast except, of course, that the South is obliged to carry by itself the whole burden of the negro question; and every action of politics will be wholesome which emphasizes this union of sections and [dis]trusts on one side every intimation that the interests of different parts of the country are hostile and rival interests. It is because of this nationalization of conditions, I suppose, that we are more and more inclined to look to the Federal government for the rectification of undesirable conditions; and yet Federal regulation, as contrasted with local, must be of the most general kind; and it must seem clear to every man who has any knowledge of the vast variety of actual conditions in this country that no central management can be satisfactory. Undoubtedly there are many things to be regulated, but regulation may be one of two kinds. It may either be such regulation as practically amounts to managements, or it may be such regulation as only undertakes to prohibit and prevent particular kinds of transactions, to check particular practices, to enforce particular kinds of obligations.

"To put into the hands of the Federal government or any other government the power to practically conduct and control the business of the country or any important part of it is to create a machinery too cumbersome and unmanageable to be desired by any prudent man. It is perfectly practicable, however, for the state and Federal governments to deal with particular transactions and with the persons who are responsible for such transactions. Our grand mistake so far is in trying to deal with men as fractions of corporations. We shall never get at any real remedies until we deal with individuals again as units and hold them separately responsible for the transactions in which they engage. We have lost individuals and allowed them to drop out of the sight of law in all sorts of complex combinations. The immediate duty of lawyers and legislators is to rediscover the individual, to disentangle him from the web of corporate organization in which he has been lost, and to fix upon him once more individual responsibility for business transactions. There is one means by which this can be done. Corporations can be obliged by law to disclose their organization in such way as to make clear which officers, which board, which committee is responsible for each kind of transaction, and then the law can operate in the case of every transaction complained of upon the individuals with whom the transaction originated. This is by no means as simple as it sounds, but it is the only practicable means of reanalyzing our complex machinery of business so as to get at the individual. To punish corporations, unless you mean to dispense with them altogether, is only to interfere with the business of the country and to create a universal feeling of uneasiness which will undoubtedly bring about frequently recurring panics. But to single out the individual is to free the course of business.

"What the country is now desiring is disinterested leadership –leadership by men who do not represent particular interests of any kind, either selfish or revolutionary, and who can be trusted to act only upon knowledge after sufficient investigation to make them definite in their advice and sure of their object. Nothing so unsettles the country as indefinite advice, indiscriminate accusations, the air of fighting everybody instead of fighting somebody in particular. The country will not care from what section such a leader comes, if only they can be sure his purpose is national, and not section[al]; th[a]t his knowledge is not prejudice, but a thing based upon disinterested inquiry. Such a leader it very much desires. It prefers that he should represent a party not committed to any set of vested interests, not looking to any particular section of the community for support, but it is looking for a man rather than for a party. Such a man would be the true conservative, seeking to leave untouched that which is normal and sound, and to give effect to morals in the only field in which morals ever can have effect–the field of individual action."

Dr. Wilson spoke in a conversational tone, but with an emphasis which carried conviction. The speech was frequently interrupted with cordial applause. . . .

Dr. Wilson went to the Hermitage this morning in company with Mr. W. L. Granberry and other friends, returning soon after noon in time to lunch at the home of Judge and Mrs. Robert Ewing[3] on Seventh Avenue, North. He will remain in the city until to-morrow night, when he will leave for Cleveland, O., where he has an engagement to speak, stopping en route at Cincinnati.[4]

Printed in the *Nashville Banner*, Nov. 12, 1907; some editorial headings omitted.

[3] Harriet Hoyt (Mrs. Robert) Ewing was Mrs. Wilson's first cousin.

[4] Wilson may well have visited friends in Cincinnati, but he did not deliver an address there at this time.

From David Benton Jones

My dear Doctor: Chicago November 12th, 1907.

I sent you a telegram saying I would be in Princeton toward the close of this month. At that time you were about to start for the South and I did not follow it up by a letter.

I now expect to be in Princeton Saturday forenoon, November 23d and shall remain until Monday or Tuesday.[1]

I enclose a clipping from last night's Chicago Evening Post. I have not been able to identify the writer as yet, but I more than agree with him. There is no doubt about where the great mass of our Alumni stand on this question and the obstruction narrows itself down to the club men who so largely contribute toward the support of the University. In time even these men will see that the only way in which Princeton can preserve its self-respect is to free itself from dictation from outside, no matter at what cost. It is much better that Princeton should limit its work, even get rid of most of its preceptors and some of its faculty, falling back to what the permanent endowment can take care of and from that to build up again, than that it should become a thing of contempt and a sham institution of learning.

I do not know, of course, what particular things have been done or said since I left Princeton, but nothing can be done or said which will change this opinion and the struggle at Princeton is not one of today or tomorrow, but for the ultimate redemption of the institution from the influences which now seem to threaten its very existence as a serious factor in the university work of this country.

I am convinced that a large majority of the Board will be found unalterable on this side of the question. If Mr. Pyne thinks it best to withdraw his support, I shall be very sorry, but I shall be infinitely more sorry to see the University dominated by the club men of New York, Philadelphia and Pittsburgh.

I did not mean to discuss the situation in this letter, but merely to let you know when I hope to be in Princeton. A note from Dr. Jacobus stated that he would be there some time next week, but I fear it will be too early for me, as I cannot well arrange to reach there before Friday at the earliest.

I do not wish you to infer from what I have said above that I think it is necessary to break with Pyne and those who believe with him at the present time. I only wanted to indicate what I think is the clear path of duty for the Board and especially for the members of the Faculty who believe in a real and not sham institution. You see I do not take into account the possibility of your changing your attitude or your determination. The path of wisdom probably lies in the direction of a carefully planned procedure which will involve a great deal of patience and persistent and determined hard work. This can be carried on in a quiet way which will not involve too great an expenditure of physical and nervous energy on your part.

But I am only anticipating what I am going to Princeton for and that is a quiet talk covering the whole situation.

Very sincerely yours, David B. Jones.

TLS (WP, DLC). Enc.: clipping, "The Woodrow Wilson Plan," *Chicago Evening Post*, Nov. 11, 1907.

[1] For the purpose of Jones's visit, see M. W. Jacobus to WW, Nov. 11, 1907.

An Address to the Annual Dinner of the Cleveland Chamber of Commerce[1]

[[Nov. 16, 1907]]

THE IDEALS OF PUBLIC LIFE

Mr. President and Gentlemen: I wish that these noble speakers who preceded me might have gone on forever. It was very much more enjoyable to hear them talk than to hear myself talk. I feel, in one sense, as if I came here as a stranger, and yet I have been often enough in your city not to feel altogether a stranger. And I feel a certain peculiar acquaintance with the Cleveland Chamber of Commerce, because it has been my privilege and pleasure for the last four years to be associated with a man who knew a great deal about you and whom I have learned to love, as I know you learned to love him—I mean Harry Garfield.

And then, there is something familiar about the cut of your jibs. I feel very much as an acquaintance of mine did who was something of a wag. He was sitting at his club, when there came in one of those men who make themselves too suddenly familiar, and slapped him on the shoulder and said, "Well, Ollie, old boy, how are you?" And with some shrinking from the blow he looked up at him coldly and said, "I don't know you; I don't know your name; but your manners are very familiar." And I think I can say that of you—I don't know you all, but your manners are pretty familiar.

And then there is another thing that makes me feel as if I had some connection with you. There are dotted about among you Princeton men, and my very familiarity with them causes me some embarrassment. It is very difficult to play a great role before persons who know you well. I feel that my disguise, in trying to be the handsome things which I have been said to be, will be exceedingly transparent.

[1] The banquet was held in the Chamber of Commerce Hall. The other speakers were James Bryce, British Ambassador to the United States, and Curtis Guild, Jr., Governor of Massachusetts. Lyman Hambright Treadway, General Manager of Peck, Stow and Wilcox Co., manufacturers of hardware and tools, and President of the Cleveland Chamber of Commerce for 1907, presided.

And yet, gentlemen, I believe that there is something in what your president so kindly said. I believe that this country does sincerely desire disinterested counsel. And it is one very great responsibility now cast upon college men—I mean men engaged in the administration of colleges—to attempt to give such counsel, at the invitation of their fellow citizens. Sometimes those invitations are very exacting. I was asked to speak to the bankers of New York city on the "Elasticity of the Currency," and I told them it was obvious that they had chosen me as an impartial witness, because it was obvious that a man living on a salary knew nothing about the elasticity of the currency; therefore I was at least competent to testify not as an interested party.[2]

I have been very much interested, and I hope I will not be misunderstood when I say surprised, at the way in which the other two speakers of the evening have apologized for offering you ideals, and for the apparent contrast which exists in their minds between that which is practical and that which is ideal. They have said to you: "Gentlemen, we know that you are practical men, but perhaps you will excuse us for offering you ideals." Now, if I know anything about the history of this country it has been distinguished by nothing so much as declining to draw any distinction between what was practical and what was ideal. This is the country which has purposed, at any rate, to put principles into practice. And therefore in offering you standards of action, I am offering you pieces out of the imaginative conception that America has had of her destiny in the world. This is the one country which has founded its polity upon dreams, which has seen and told the world that it saw visions that were to come to pass through its instrumentality. If we have not dreamed dreams and struggled forward to their realization, we have had no distinguished role in the world; we have been as all other peoples have been, trying to make our daily bread, to patch together a polity which would at any rate serve for our day and hour. There is no excuse due any American audience that remembers American history, for offering it ideals, though it be never so practical in the objects which it seeks.

I would, if I could, get you to think of ideals as intensely practical things. And for my part it does not seem to me that anything not practical ought to be talked about in serious company in this year of grace. For if ever we came upon difficult times we have come upon them now. I pray God they may not grow more difficult; but they will grow more difficult unless we take stock of

2 See the news report of Wilson's remarks to the New York State Bankers' Association printed at Dec. 19, 1902, Vol. 14.

our purposes now and make certain of what it is we are about. It is very delightful, it is very easy to state general propositions to ourselves; but in asking leave to speak to you on "The Ideals of Public Life," I have been most interested to draw your attention to the fact that public life does not consist merely of the transaction of public business. It consists of the formation of public opinion, of the guidance of public purpose, of the promoting of progress and of the criticising of remedies. And the greater part of this is the task of the citizen and not the task of the politician. There is not public opinion enough in this country, and that is what is the matter with it. For by public opinion I do not mean the aggregate of the unspoken opinion of individuals, but that compound which comes from the agreement of minds and is the result of compared and expressed opinion. The opinion of classes is not public opinion. The opinion of men in particular occupations is not public opinion. Public opinion is that part of opinion which is comprehended by all, and nothing less is public opinion. If therefore you do not feel that public opinion contains enough understanding of your occupation, you are the only persons to blame for its not doing so. How is it going to contain a comprehensive view of your calling, unless you explain your calling?

Now, I have heard a great many complain of public legislation that embarrassed their business, but those very men will not talk to me, even privately, candidly about their business. If you don't take the American people into your confidence, they are not going to understand your business. I have had corporation lawyers complain to me—and I am a lawyer myself—that the way in which legislation was handling corporate matters was an ignorant way. Very well, these gentlemen who represent corporations know the way that would not be ignorant. Have they ever suggested it? Have they come on public platforms and into public prints and explained these things in a way which the public could understand? Possibly the public does not understand these things, but they never will understand them unless you come and explain them.

Now, I want to plead here tonight for the recognition of the fact that there is a very much bigger public life than is comprehended in party contests. I want to plead for the creation of a body of public men whose action will be independent of party contests. Mark you, I am not saying anything to the detriment of parties, for I believe, with Governor Guild, that it is absolutely necessary that a country governed by public opinion should be governed by organized movements such as are exhibited in the action of parties. But I do believe that parties must have a great substance, a body of opinion to draw from, which is not made by the spokesmen of the party. That is what I mean. I mean that we must have a body of men just as practical as the politicians, but not opportunists. Don't let me be misunderstood. A politician, a man engaged in party contests, must be an opportunist. Let us give up saying that word as if it contained a slur. If you want to win in party action, I take it for granted you want to lure the majority to your side. I never heard of any man in his senses who was fishing for a minority. Now, if you want to win, you have got to fish for the majority, and the only majority you can get is the majority that is ready. You can't wait for the majority of tomorrow, if you want a majority today. You have got to take the opportunity as you find it, and work on that, and that is opportunism, that is politics, and it is perfectly legitimate. But in order that there may be an interesting tomorrow, in order that the opportunism of the next election may be different from the opportunism of this election, there ought to be a body of practical thinkers, of practical talkers, who don't have to win—just as practical as the politicians, but with a longer time to wait, not particularly caring whether those who believe what they say are at present a minority, if they believe so intensely in what they preach that they believe that five, ten, twenty years from now there will be a tremendous majority agreeing with them. Unless you have men of this sort, who belong to a party that does not have to be elected, you are not going to have the moving force of public opinion; public opinion is going to be a plaything and not a master; politicians are going to manipulate it and not be governed by it.

This is a government by public opinion. It is not a game by public opinion, and therefore you must insist that men who are not talking for the sake of getting elected, who would if they could, avoid being elected, are nevertheless going to run the risk of being elected twenty years from now. That is the kind of thing that I mean by the ideals of public life—the ideals which make you realize that in a country like this nobody can afford to be a private individual, and that therefore every man who says of himself, I am not a public man, is declaring that he is declining the responsibilities of his citizenship. The number of men who in this country can talk sense and don't talk at all, is the most astonishing phenomenon of our life, and if you complain that the number of men who do talk are the men, chiefly, who have nothing to say, then you are yourselves to blame if you think you have something to say. Hire a hall and get as many of your fellow-citizens together as will come, and if the first experiment is successful, more will come next time, and next time you will be able to say something that will attract attention. If you have a friend whom you consider particularly foolish, encourage him to hire a hall, because there is nothing that kills nonsense so much as exposure to the air. That is the great point which politicians were so many centuries in learning, that the very way in which to make folly look like sense is to box it up and not let it get out; and that the very way to explode foolish ideas is to give them room to explode in, and then nothing will be hoisted by the explosion. We have not talk enough in this country; we have not discussion enough by men who are talking by the card, not discussion enough by men who know what they are talking about.

Now, do you know at present what we are talking about? The thing that we are trying to handle now is a complicated economic situation. There are men living who understand parts of it. How many men are there now living who understand all of it? I must tell you frankly that I don't know one. This complicated economic situation of ours has come into existence within the last fifteen years, and we are trying to deal with it before we have so much as successfully begun to analyze it. We are trying to deal with it in the bulk before we know it in its parts. And the men who know it in its parts are not contributing to the general enlightenment that will enable us to know it as a whole. Every man is lying low and minding his own business, and the consequence is that we are forcing the legislators of this country to mind our business for us, because if you don't let them know the right way to manage it, they are going to manage it the wrong way, because it is going to be managed.

Another thing—most of you here present, at any rate, I take it for granted, are honest men. Now, large bodies of your fellow-citizens suspect that most of you here present are dishonest men. They suspect that of every Chamber of Commerce—I am not picking out The Cleveland Chamber of Commerce. They suspect that of every body of men that control the industries and the commerce and the distribution of the money of the country. Now, the reason they suspect that you are dishonest is that you have never enabled them to pick out the dishonest men and trust the honest men. The discredit that now lies upon the business of this country has proceeded from a few men, and in abusing them we have abused everybody, because we have not named them. Now, I think it is time that we named them. I think it is time we had a list. I think it is time that we put the aspersion upon the persons upon whom it ought to be put, and lift it from the persons from whom it should be lifted.

Let us take the railway situation. The railways of this country are supposed—I mean by the large body of the populace of the country—are supposed to be dishonestly and selfishly managed. Now, anybody who knows anything about railroad management, knows that in almost every case the actual administration of the road—I mean the actual executive management of it—is perfectly straight and honest. The dishonest part comes out in the manipulation of the securities of that road. And yet the discredit has fallen upon the men who actually carry the tremendous task of managing the roads as a daily operative business. Now is it not about time we divided our blame, we discriminated our blame, and put it upon the men who are embarrassing the administration of the railways of the country by their manipulation of the securities of those railways? We know the names of some of them, and yet we are told that nothing is going to be done to them. They have reached some high plane of immunity which I should like to reach myself, but am all too humble to attain to. I am held responsible for what I do; they are not held responsible for what they do. I know what they do, much better than they know what I do, because I have not yet been investigated, I have not yet testified before a commission. There are many things that might be found out about me, but haven't yet been found out. These gentlemen have been found out, and we know their names. Now, I would not like to name them in a public place. They named themselves in a public place, but I think it would be discourteous on my part to follow their example. I simply want to make a moral without naming names. The moral is this, gentlemen: We have lost individuality in our present organization. And I want to call your attention to the fact that all the distinction that America has is based upon our belief in the responsibility and the liberty of the individual. The distinction of America is not based upon belief in the power of the government but upon belief in the integrity of the individual.

Now, if we don't rediscover the individual, somebody will have, some day, to rediscover America, for with the submergence of the individual, America, in respect to everything distinctive attached to her name, is submerged. We have got to rediscover the individual. There is no such thing as corporate morals, there is no such thing as corporate integrity; there is no morals, there is no integrity, except that of the individual. It is a saying as old as the law itself, that a corporation has no body to be kicked or soul to be damned. The bodies that are to be kicked are the bodies of persons and the souls that are to be damned are the souls of persons, and the program is going to be carried out.

Now, America believes in this more fundamentally than she believes in anything else, if she believes in anything at all. And my program is to rediscover the individual. I will tell you one way in which it can be done; not an easy way, an infinitely difficult way. But no matter how difficult it is, it has got to be attempted. We have got to find the individual in the corporation. We have thrown individuals together in heaps; now we have got to dissect the heap and discover the individual again. And we have got to do it with the assistance of the corporations themselves. For my part, I don't believe that fining corporations is of the least use for the ends we seek. If you fine a corporation twenty-nine million dollars,[3] what happens is that you take twenty-nine million dollars, if you get it—it has not been paid yet—but if you get it you put it into the public treasury and take it out of the business of the country, and the same thing will be done the next day that was done the day before and was the antecedent of the fine. We have lost our minds. If a chauffeur goes too fast, I have heard some of my fellow-citizens propose that we lock up the machine. I had a great deal rather lock up the chauffeur. I suppose that if a railway accident occurs you will lock up the locomotive presently—you will lock up our tools, because we do not have sense enough or humanity enough to use them properly. Corporations, these imaginary persons, are our tools; they are not ourselves. And the responsibility is not to rest upon them to the incommoding of the whole business development of the country, but is to rest upon the individuals who are misusing them.

Suppose that we obliged corporations to analyze themselves for the advantage of the district attorney, and to say that such and such of their transactions were authorized and ordered by the executive committee of their board of directors, that such

[3] On August 3, 1907, following an earlier verdict of guilty by a trial jury, Kenesaw Mountain Landis, Judge of the United States District Court for the Northern District of Illinois, fined the Standard Oil Company of Indiana $29,-240,000, assessing the maximum penalty of $20,000 for each of 1,462 counts, based on that number of carloads of oil shipped between Whiting, Ind., and East St. Louis, Ill., on which the company was alleged to have accepted rebates from the Chicago and Alton Railroad Company in violation of the Elkins Act of 1903. Since the Standard of Indiana did not possess assets equal to the fine, Landis ruled that the holding company, the Standard Oil Company of New Jersey, would have to pay. This fine made Landis famous overnight and stirred great controversy throughout the country. Upon appeal, Peter Stenger Grosscup, Presiding Judge of the United States Circuit Court of Appeals, 7th Circuit, reversed the decision of the lower court on July 22, 1908, calling Landis's fine an "abuse of judicial discretion." The case was later retried, but Grosscup's decision was upheld.

and such things were done by the whole board, that such transactions were ordered by the president, such by the general manager, and so on down through the major transactions of the corporations, and then we should return to the only sound basis of law, which denounces certain transactions; and when those transactions were indulged in, we should go to this analysis and find out the person said to be responsible for that transaction, and then should put him in the penitentiary, the thing would stop; the thing would stop but the business of the country would not. Now, you say if we did that the corporations would put up dummies. Not more than once. You cannot hire a man to go to the penitentiary, and the dummy would not work more than once; and for my part I am willing to have one or two dummies in the penitentiary in order to have some genuine men there afterwards. Mind you, gentlemen, the thing that faces us is to save the business of the country and yet moralize it. The way we are going now we are not going to save the business, and we are not going to moralize it. There is nothing that pulls transactions up like pulling transactors up, and if a man could not hide behind his corporation, he would walk as straight as a string. You know that there is an old problem, propounded by Thomas Carlyle, who did not believe much in human nature, believed that almost every man was naturally a rogue—at least he believed it when his digestion was wrong; he said the problem was, how, out of a multitude of rogues, to make an honest nation. Now, let us suppose that every man is a rogue and see how it works. Let us suppose—this is a painful subject for me today—but let us suppose that we are one of a great body of persons collected around a football field. The stands are big and crowded with people, and they are so far apart that they cannot communicate with each other. In the center lies the open field. The players have not yet come on, and two men, it may be officials about to act in the game, meet in the middle of this vacant arena and fall to blows. There is an instant outcry from the people collected around, "What an outrage, why aren't they arrested? How indecent to fight here in this open place. They have no respect for us." Now, if you and I had been those two men we might have fought. We don't know what intolerable thing one said to the other. Our blood is as hot as theirs; the same thing might have happened to us. But it happens that it did not happen to us, and we are the cool self-collected audience, and if we are not interested we are more moral than the persons who are. And the way in which you make an honest nation out of a multitude of rogues is by having most of the rogues not interested in the particular transaction that made the others dishonest.

Now, I don't believe that the nation is a multitude of rogues, but on that hypothesis you can see how the cool nation is more moral than the hot individual; and public opinion is never so tickled as when it can fix itself upon the individual, and the individual is never so careful as when he knows he cannot escape public opinion. In the state where I live all judges are appointed by the governor. We have had governors who did not do anything respectable except make good appointments to the bench, and that was because that was the only thing in which they could not hide behind anybody else. Nobody, under the laws of the state, could be regarded as responsible for these appointments but themselves, and therefore New Jersey is celebrated for its good judges. I am informed that the city of Galveston, in Texas, vested its government recently, at least for a great many purposes, in the hands of a commission of five persons, all of whom had been ward politicians, suspected of all sorts of things; and that since then they have done nothing which has not met with the universal approbation of their fellow-citizens. Now, this is the only moralizing process, the fixing of the fine upon the individual. Gentlemen, it concerns us very deeply whether we are going to depart from the immemorial practices of America or not. We founded this government upon principles, and the center of those principles was faith in the individual rather than in the government. The way we are going, we are apt to vest everything, every function that we despair of performing ourselves, in a government, when we are, in the same act, in the same day, saying to ourselves that we do not know how to constitute our government, because we do not succeed in choosing the persons we would prefer. At the very time when we are least satisfied with the make-up of our government, we are putting more in their hands than we ever put in their hands before. And you know how our governments are constituted. Why, in the little borough of Princeton, I have to vote so long a ticket that I literally have not time to find out about all the men I vote for, and if I don't know the characters of the men in the borough of Princeton, how am I to know about the multitude of persons that I vote for for innumerable other offices, state and national? And how am I to know that the business which is supervised by them will be any better than the business which is conducted by men who at least are checked by the old laws of self-interest? As Ambassador Bryce says, ours is a very different society from that of thirty or forty years ago. There are a great many things which are now in the rightful sphere of government, which then were not in existence at all, or on so small a scale that it was not necessary to control them; and it is not necessary to add to the inevitable increase of government functions things which can easily be avoided. I wish to see America not give up the attempt to found her government upon individual responsibility, until she has made it. She is not now making it. We are now like little children, who, finding themselves puzzled, turn to the government and say, "Will you help us?" There is nothing American in that. We never before went to the government to make us honest; and the government will not make us honest. If God did not make us honest, the government cannot make us over again. You know old Doctor Holmes's quip about the self-made man, that he was a remarkable creation, considering who made him; and our feeling about our business is that it is remarkably good, considering how badly we have conducted it and how badly we have regulated it.

In speaking, therefore, gentlemen, of the ideals of public life, I am indeed speaking of ideals, but of very practical things. We have come again to a constructive period in our history, and we must look to it that we have that comprehensive grasp of the things we are attempting, which will enable us to be successfully constructive. You remember that fine passage in De Tocqueville where, speaking of the calm way in which we were able to put our affairs in order after the disorderly time of the Confederation, he speaks of the singular spectacle of a nation turning its eye upon itself and correcting abuses which had been about to corrupt the body politic, and reconstructing a government without having drawn a tear or a drop of blood from mankind? Shall we repeat the process? Our affairs are in some respects as disordered now, and as full of threat of a fatal change, as they were in 1784. Are we going to turn a critical eye upon ourselves and reconstruct our affairs without drawing a tear or a drop of blood from mankind? Or are we going to repeat that round of fatal experiment, of governmental regulation, which has brought every other government in the world to grief, and so pass out of history having lost that dearest thing of all, our birthright, the thing with which we first arrested the attention of the world—the power to understand and to control and to correct ourselves?

Printed in *The Cleveland Chamber of Commerce Annual 1908* (n.p., 1908), pp. 218-30.

To Edwin Grant Conklin

Princeton, N. J.
My dear Professor Conklin: November 18th, 1907.

I am sorry that my absence from home has delayed so long my reply to your letter of November 7th.

I agree with great pleasure to your proposed change of plans. We will welcome you here next year with the greatest satisfaction, and the leave of absence can be postponed to some other time when you feel free to leave the country.

I am very sorry that your father's health should be infirm and that you should have any cause of anxiety on that score.

I agree with you that it would be of real advantage that you should be here during the construction of the laboratory and museum. I only hope that we can arrange matters so that you will not be too much inconvenienced in your work, pending the erection of the new building.

With much regard,

Cordially and sincerely yours, Woodrow Wilson

TLS (E. G. Conklin Papers, NjP).

From Lyman Hambright Treadway

My dear Sir: [Cleveland] November 18th, 1907.

Upon your return to Princeton I wish you to find this reassurance of our sincere appreciation of the honor you accorded us in attending our annual dinner, and of the interest and pleasure of our members in your eloquent and potential address on that occasion. You have greatly increased the cordial feeling already existing in this city toward yourself and the great university of which you are the head.

I am sure that the idle and silly newspaper despatches sent from Cleveland, I regret to say, to New York newspapers, intimating that Mayor [Tom Loftin] Johnson had not treated you with entire courtesy,[1] will not affect recollections of an event that otherwise must be pleasant to you. His Honor, the Mayor, arriving late, came to the platform, on my request, between two speeches; he was naturally anxious to take his seat as soon as he could, in order to cause as little interruption in the proceedings as possible, and I therefore presented him only to the guests sitting nearest him at the table. No discourtesy on his part was intended, and indeed none could be intended for that would imply that I had intended discourtesy to you in not presenting the Mayor to you, and that, as you know, is absurd.

I believe it is the intention of His Honor, the Mayor to write to you himself on this subject, but I feel certain that neither his letter, nor mine is needed to give you assurance that the Mayor of Cleveland would not show discourtesy to any guest of The Cleveland Chamber of Commerce, and least of all to the honored president of Princeton University.

Very truly yours, Lyman H. Treadway

TLS (WP, DLC).

[1] These reports must have appeared in editions of the New York newspapers of November 17, 1907, which are no longer extant. The Editors have been unable to find them. The Cleveland *Leader*, Nov. 18, 1907, printed the following item:

"Induced by the publication in New York newspapers Sunday morning of a story that he had refused to shake the hand of Woodrow Wilson, president of Princeton College, and had slighted Congressman Theodore E. Burton at the Chamber of Commerce dinner Saturday evening, Mayor Tom L. Johnson yesterday asked that a denial and explanation be given publicity.

" 'I shall write President Wilson at once explaining the incident and assuring him that the story as published had no foundation in fact. I was called to the speakers' table while Ambassador Bryce was speaking, by President Treadway, of the chamber. I greeted those at the end of the table at which I was seated. As I took my seat I noticed Mr. Burton, and expressed to my neighbor surprise that he was present, saying I did not know he was in the city.

" 'President Wilson, seated next to Mr. Burton at the far end of the table, had scarcely finished his address when President Treadway permitted me to leave, after I had asked that I be excused, if possible, because of an engagement with guests from whom I had come, late, to the dinner. I did not recognize Mr. Wilson when I came in, and could not have shaken hands with those at his end of the table without interrupting the addresses in any event. I shook hands with Governor Guild and asked and was given an introduction to Ambassador Bryce, as he resumed his seat after his address.

" 'It is far from my nature to snub anyone, and the story as published in New York was not founded on fact.' "

From Tom Loftin Johnson

My dear Sir, Cleveland Nov. 18, 1907.

The fact that some New York newspapers published a sensational item charging me with intentional discourtesy to you is my excuse for writing.

Confirming Mr. Lyman H. Treadway's letter to you, of which he kindly sent me a copy, permit me to add that I had no other intention than to show you the courtesy and respect I feel for you personally and for your office.

I had an engagement which I begged off from long enough to hear the three addresses delivered at the banquet. When you were about closing your remarks I left the platform so as to avoid the rush and save as much time as I could. This was a matter of so much regret on my part that I explained it to President Treadway while you were speaking and told him how much it grieved me.

Immediately after shaking hands with Ambassador Bryce I returned, if you will remember, to my seat, and it was only then that I discovered for the first time Mr. Burton's[1] presence on the platform for up to that time I did not even know that he was in the City.

I am now exceedingly sorry that I did not ask Mr. Treadway to be presented to you and to have extended to Mr. Burton the courtesy due him.

I regret it as a great misfortune that I had not an opportunity to at least shake hands with you and tell you how much I enjoyed your address, for I regard it as one of the ablest addresses I ever listened to. While I did not quite agree with your conclusion I was charmed with the manner of presentation and the logical way in which you dealt with your subject.

On my next visit to Trenton I propose to give myself the pleasure of a personal call, as I am deeply interested in the institution and you personally.

Yours sincerely, Tom L. Johnson

TLS (WP, DLC).

1 Theodore Elijah Burton, Representative from the twenty-first Ohio congressional district, which included part of Cleveland.

From Sir William Mather

My dear President Wilson [London] Novr 18th./07

Your delightful letter of the 1st Inst. gave us all the greatest pleasure. I thank you most sincerely for the trouble you so cheerfully took to make the dedication ceremony in every way a perfect success. There seemed to be a sort of occult collusion between you & the sun to render the scene memorable for its glowing beauty, of which so many have written me. I am especially indebted to you for giving me so realistic a description of Mr. Bryce's admirable treatment of the occasion & of the impression he made on the assembled Faculty & under-graduates. I was anxious that he should feel happy amid you all & say something inspiring to the young men.

I fear too much was said of the Donor, but on reading such reports of the speeches as have reached me it is evident that Mr Bryce was felicitous[,] eloquent[,] humorous & wise in describing the Corpus Dial & what the re-production stood for at Princeton.

I cannot tell you how grateful I am for the great care you have bestowed to make my humble gift a symbol of the great fact that America & Gt. Britain are truly in accord as well as akin.

My friend Dr. Macalister of Philadelphia[1] has written me fully of your speeches & bearing on the occasion. Nothing could have added to the effect produced by all you said & did. If I had made the *halls* instead of merely sending you this piece of stone (albeit with a sermon in it)[2] you could not have shown greater appreciation. My children & their children will have occasion to regard Princeton with reverence & gratitude for the kindness shown to me. I wonder whether you would mind a bronze tablet being inserted in one of the small panels of the plinth, recording Mr Bryce's visit.[3] As he is the British Ambassador & now a member of Princeton, the visit in long years to come would be of interest were it recalled by a simple tablet such as I would send out for insertion. Mr Bunn very kindly sent me some photographs which are really beautiful. What a noble building is McCosh Hall! The quad & surroundings will eventually be a glorified Corpus Christi college.

My wife & daughters send their love to you all & join with me very heartily in thanks for all your aid to make our project a perfect success. Ever your grateful friend W. Mather

ALS (WWP, UA, NjP).

[1] James MacAlister, President of the Drexel Institute of Technology in Philadelphia.

[2] He referred to the inscription carved on the base of the sun dial, which reads: "This Reproduction of the Turnbull Sun Dial of Corpus Christi College, Oxford, was presented by Sir William Mather, LL.D., to be a lasting memorial of the Friendship between the people of the Old Country and of the New. A.D. 1907."

[3] No such plaque was attached to the sun dial.

To Henry Smith Pritchett

Princeton, N. J.
My dear President Pritchett: November 19th, 1907.

I have just returned from a round-about journey of twelve days, which seems to have seriously upset me in some way, and I have been obliged to go to bed. This cuts me out of the pleasure of dining with you this evening not only, but I fear makes it unlikely that I can attend the meeting of the Board tomorrow.

I the more deeply regret this because I know the important question which is to come before the Board for decision, and I should very much value the privilege of speaking upon it. It seems to me we should be entering upon very uncertain ground indeed if we were to determine to grant retiring allowances to the members of the faculties of such State universities as could assure us that their legislatures would at the end of a particular period themselves provide a system of pensions. No legislature can give any such promise in any legally binding form, and the very fact that some legislatures would be willing to make the promise shows that the pressure upon them to provide a system of pensions is already bringing them to terms and can be counted upon to do the very thing we have anticipated and hoped for. One of the most hopeful things in the whole situation, to my mind, has been this likelihood of bringing the State Legislatures to see their duty with regard to the pensioning of teachers, and I think that action on our part such as is requested would be particularly unwise at this time. It is too soon to judge what the outcome will be, and action on our part might indefinitely postpone, if it did not prevent, the outcome which we desire.

I shall make a special effort tomorrow morning to get over to New York, but if it turns out to be impossible for me to come, I hope that you will present my excuses to the Board and my great regret that illness has prevented my attending.

Always cordially and faithfully yours,

[Woodrow Wilson]

CCL (WWP, UA, NjP).

From Henry Smith Pritchett

Personal

My dear Mr. Wilson, New York November 21 1907

Inasmuch as I did not get a chance to chat with you at the meeting of the Executive Committee or the Trustees I venture to send you a friendly enquiry by pen.

In the proof of my annual report which I sent you[1] I have expressed a doubt as to whether the change of name of Princeton in 1896 was justified. Also in the discussion of the Association of American Universities I have made a comparison between Johns Hopkins & Princeton as to their college and university characteristics. In both cases I have said what seemed to me on the whole worth saying as well as the truth as I know it. I am sure you know me me [*sic*] well enough by this time to know that I have no wish to say the sharp thing for its own sake. Perhaps I was led to be a little more specific in the case of Princeton because it is an accepted list and you are my colleague. It is easy to criticise the weak college. Princeton is big and strong and can afford a friendly whack. I may be mistaken in my estimate. It has seemed to me your own work as President has been most wise because it has tended toward the betterment of the American college rather than to imposing a graduate school on what seems to me, on the whole, the greatest of our American colleges.

Now with this preface let me add that I will be sorry to print a thing which is simply sharp without carrying any result; most of all will I be sorry to print a thing which is unfair. The report still stands in proof. Be good enough to tell me if it is open, in these two matters or any others, to either of these objections.

Yours faithfully, Henry S. Pritchett

ALS (WWP, UA, NjP).

1 This document is missing in the various Wilson collections.

From James Jackson Forstall[1]

Dear President Wilson, Chicago November 23, 1907.

I have been wanting for some time to write to tell you how sorry I am that the "residential quad" system plan has been given up. My four years at Princeton convince me that such a step would be a great one in advance; and the arguments of the opposition impressed me very little. But I appreciate what a terrific task it would be to secure the adoption of such a plan in view of the strong hold that the upper-class clubs have already secured—and yet I have not given up hope that it may come later.

During the short time I was at Princeton I witnessed a great improvement in the scholarship standards, and I have every reason to believe that on the educational side Princeton has now the best possible system. I regret that a majority of the trustees has not been won over to the plan which seems to give the long looked-for solution of the social problem, and which at the same time would add the best atmosphere for scholarship.

But in spite of her failure to take this further step in advance Princeton has certainly come up to the front among our colleges, and this independent of its athletic prowess; and for a great part of this advance I feel that the credit is wholly yours, and that we all owe you a deep debt of gratitude.

Please excuse my rather involved sentences, as I am too tired to think very clearly; and please do not take the trouble to acknowledge this note.

With best wishes for you and yours and everything that is Princeton's.

Very sincerely yours, James J. Forstall 1904.

ALS (WP, DLC).

1 Princeton 1904, at this time Assistant Attorney of the Legal Aid Society of Chicago. During the summer of 1907, he was affiliated with the Hull House Branch of the Legal Aid Society. As a student at Princeton, he had done secretarial work for Wilson, Henry van Dyke, and others and had not been a member of a club. Later a strong supporter of the League of Nations, in 1929 he purchased a large estate, La Pelouze, outside Geneva and donated it to the League, which used it as its temporary headquarters.

An Interview in the *New York Times*

[Nov. 24, 1907]

DR. WOODROW WILSON DEFINES MATERIAL ISSUES

Scathing Arraignment of Political and Industrial Conditions Which Have Made Possible the Recent Panic in Financial Circles.

Radical Reform in Our National Politics Suggested through the Appointment of a Common Council Selected from College Men.

"Our currency system is almost the poorest in the world."

"Political opinions must be stripped of their political intentions, to meet the present demands of the public."

"Gov. Hughes has given the public an impression of political integrity, but he generalizes where his knowledge could exemplify facts."

"Corporations should be compelled to file, with the District Attorney, a copy of the minutes of their Directors' meetings."

"Mr. Roosevelt's plan for Government control is only depriving the people of their right to operate the business of the country."

"If corporation lawyers would only explain the transactions of their clients the public would not have so dangerous an opinion of corporations."

"I am told that as soon as Mr. Roosevelt thinks he talks, a simultaneous miracle that is not, according to our education, the customary way of forming an opinion."

"I charge the present financial panic to the aggressive attitude of legislation toward the railroads, that made it impossible for them to borrow money."

"The corporation problem resembles a society of burglars, legally organized to plunder, against whom criminal proceedings result only in an indictment, or a fine, which the plundered themselves must pay."

These are a few of the fruitful parables that Dr. Woodrow Wilson, President of Princeton College, volunteered during a review of certain obviously National issues. The political system by which they are continously being resurrected in more or less partisan molds, is not their ideal formation, not even a fruitful representation, Dr. Wilson thinks.

It is not so very far from the babel of Wall Street to the remote, tree-lined avenues of Princeton, but, in the pleasant lamplight of the collegian's study, within the inclosure of a place devoted to the making of moral standards, one seems to have left a world of delirium for a world of normal vision. The contrast is very vivid, and if public opinion could be admitted to the council chamber of such men as the President of Princeton College it would throw off the present fever of its large body and acquire health, vigor, and, above all, a temperate judgment.

"Morality is a tremendous force in the impetus of American prosperity, and it is due to this impulse of the American people that we are passing through a crisis, a struggle for its supremacy in the affairs of the Nation," said Dr. Wilson, as he sat in his office chair, erect, alert, alive in every degree of a man's best conception of republican ideals.

A lawyer by profession, a college man in all the precise advantages that college discipline of theories provides, Dr. Wilson, now in the prime of life, has been mentioned quite often for public office in politics. He objects to this, because, in his observation of contemporary politics, he has the interest of constitutional ideals too much at heart to become entangled in the embarrassments of political promises. The political promise must be kept, somehow, in a year or so, whereas Dr. Wilson plans for political ideals that may not be fulfilled for twenty years. What does it matter so long as they are seen and we pursue them loyally?

"Political opinions must be stripped of their political intentions," he says, before they can accomplish the public benefits to which they aspire.

"I think, perhaps," said Dr. Wilson, "that I am not fanciful in the supposition that the public demands enlightenment from the opinion of men whose position in the world is sufficiently remote from political activity to make them disinterested, quite apart from personal advantage. The impressions of such men, upon matters of National issue, are now being sought by the public, because they have lost confidence in the political spellbinder, in the private responsibility of the banker, in the legerdemain of the corporation or the business man, not that I have lost faith in the business man, because I am sure there are many honest, temperate men doing business in a straightforward way in this country, but I mean that as a figure in the contemporary history of affairs in our land the public turns for advice to the men whose notch in life is on the stairway that leads up or down the structural framework of National morals.

"We are a people with the gift of foresight, but we have fallen into a bad habit of making rash promises, not because we make these promises fraudulently, but because we have a mania for quick results.

"It is not just to suspect the politician who fails to mature his promise in the short time his profession allows him. Sometimes he fulfills it, sometimes he doesn't, but his chief mistake is the impossibility of defining just what he will do, clearly enough to verify his promise to public expectation.

"Men in my position of life, circumstantially removed from the necessity of immediate result to a promise, are able to make plans upon which our National architecture may be improved, at leisure, by a building process of fixed calculation. I can afford to wait for the maturity of time to develop any value there may be in my premises, because I have no individual issues at stake beyond my relation as an American to the ultimate improvement of citizenship and public morals."

"There is a moral force in our National issues, you think?"

"Undoubtedly there is a great moral force at work in the public at large, which keeps it in restless sway against the oppression of trusts. It has reached an opinion about politics that the Scotchman expressed when he was asked how he liked his claret, 'It leaves you just where you were,' he said.

"I believe that men who in their station give the public an impression of unbiased, non-partisan interest in the National welfare should speak out, should volunteer their plans, because we need to-day, more than ever, a common council for the people that shall unselfishly and seriously express views of legislative relief, but the trouble is, that no sooner does a man submit his political opinions than they are deprived of their true value by the suspicion that he is himself a political candidate. For this reason, I have repeatedly declined to discuss politics or National affairs."

"The politician's appeal to the public is not as sincere as it ought to be?"

"It seems to me that the politician has a bad habit of generalizing and that he avoids definitions in specified fact. Gov. Hughes, for instance, has given the public a universal impression of political integrity, and I believe that this impression is made sincerely, but I cannot help thinking that his vast private knowledge of political and business transactions would enable him to be more specific in his speeches, to define more clearly to the public, than he does, the exact means of political integrity. I remember, last Summer, being scheduled to speak on the same platform with Gov. Hughes, and after hearing him I felt obliged to alter the entire plan of my address. I said publicly then, that while the Governor had generalized political ideals, that he had in his pocket, or if not in his pocket, at any rate somewhere within his reach, a list of the names of the men implicated in the insurance frauds, and that with such knowledge at his command it would have justified the purpose of political integrity if he had told us clearly what such transactions were and how they could be avoided in the future. The Governor turned red in the face, but, of course, nothing more was said about it.[1]

"I am afraid the ignorance of the public is something it admits in the very clamor of its demands, and the politician can best serve his cause by making his knowledge define rather than generalize his promises. He must be specific, above board, without timid reservations, or expedient phrases.

"There are specific objections that I could point out in Bryan, political propositions in his platform that I consider absurd, and could never indorse, but what use would it serve any one if I named them? No matter how humble my prospects, I should still be accused of political intention if I went into these matters. If I specify his political mistakes they lose the force of their intention."

"But we need a common council."

"The zest of the times is the opportunity for the individual, of course, the chance to speak plainly, with ethical motive. I believe in the individual, and I object to corporate power in its present indefinable authority."

"Are the corporations within the law?"

"Certainly; and that is the legislative embarrassment of the State Legislatures in dealing with them. A corporation or trust, to my mind, is exactly in the position of a group of burglars who meet in a room and incorporate themselves to pursue the business of plundering.

"The law proceeds against 'it,' the corporation, not against any specific individual. The dilemma of the law is to find 'it,' to bring 'it' before the Judges, and finally to incarcerate 'it' in jail. Of course you cannot put a finger on 'it,' there is no coat collar for the policeman to hold 'it' by, and there is no 'it' that the Judge can see tangibly enough to sentence to jail.

"The result is a fine against 'it.'

"It stands to reason that if 'it' should be a corporation of burglars the fine must be paid by the plundered out of the plunder they have provided for the purpose. Corporations seem to be

[1] Wilson seems to have been exaggerating at this point, if he was quoted accurately. He certainly did not alter the "entire plan" of his address, "The Author and Signers of the Declaration of Independence," at the Jamestown Exposition on July 4, 1907. Contemporary news reports make it clear that he used the text of this address substantially as it is printed at July 4, 1907. For the question that Wilson actually put to Governor Charles Evans Hughes of New York, and for Hughes's reaction and that of the audience, see the news report printed at July 4, 1907.

conducted by a predatory state of mind duly adapted to evade the innermost intention of the law."

"Criminal proceedings against corporations cannot be effective?"

"It is next to impossible to imprison any man of influence in this country. The fault is not with the Judges, whom I believe are essentially honest and above criticism, but with our system of juries. A jury is susceptible, and frequently unable to understand the ethics of law. Of course the difficulty of obtaining a clear definition of anything so complex as the transactions of corporate power is very great, but I believe if the corporations would explain their business methods to the public that a different impression would ensue. At present there is only a mild clamor against the predatory instinct of the trusts, without any definite knowledge of just how these tremendous operations are possible."

"The corporation lawyers are obviously unable to enlighten us?"

"My view of the attitude of the corporation lawyers, standing as they do at present between public opinion and the private transactions of their clients, is that, by insisting upon a passive indifference to the public demand for information, they seriously injure their clients' cases. The reason that there is just now, and there will be to a much larger extent, an almost universal aggressive legislation against trusts is because the people are kept in ignorance of their business affairs. It is quite possible that there are corporations conducting business on lines that are the legitimately competitive issues in trade, and that if the public were informed in detail of these transactions the impression would be less violent against them than it is.

"My advice to corporation lawyers has been to influence legislation toward a ruling that will make the business of the corporations a matter of public record.

"I believe a statute could be drawn up compelling the officers of corporations to file in the office of the people's executive officer of the State a complete report of their Directors' meetings. Such a rule would make stock transactions a matter of official record for the people, and with a law governing the limit of such competitive incidents of corporation business as came up, any violation of that law would entail the imprisonment of the executive officer of the corporation. Of course the obvious remedy for the trust against such a law would be dummy Directors' meetings, but that would only occur once, because while you can hire men to do almost anything, you cannot hire a man to go to the penitentiary. He simply declines at any price."

"Could such a statute be drawn up under the conflict of existing laws?"

"I am proposing, of course, a colossal idea; but I have consulted the most eminent lawyers about it, and they have told me that it could be done. I would myself undertake to draw up such a statute, with the assistance of lawyers whose experience in the practice of corporation law would crystallige [crystallize] the terms.

"The corporation lawyers frequently assume an air of indifference to public opinion, and so imperil their clients to an attack from State Legislatures that will ruin them. They only cast the corporation into a deeper shadow of suspicion, instead of openly informing us of their grounds of defense. It is quite often said by the corporations that the 'public is crazy.' Well, if it is, we demand a lunacy commission competent to establish the fact. The public is not crazy, it is merely emerging into a better sense of its rights to the American sense of fair play and just exchange of value for value. The recent law passed by the Legislature of the State of Texas forbidding the sale of any goods manufactured by a trust has driven the trusts out of that State.[2] Of course for a time perhaps they will suffer through the loss of manufacturing interests in their State, but imagine if the Legislatures of all the States were to do the same, what would become of the trusts?"

"Are they violating the Constitution?"

"There is nothing in the Constitution that forbids the accumulation of business; on the contrary, it demands protection for life, limb, and property, but behind the enormous growth of corporate power is the American social spirit that insists upon a moral basis of human life, as distinguished from a selfish, inhuman greed."

"Government control will not solve the problem?"

"Mr. Roosevelt seems to be set on that idea, but I see no solution of the predatory conditions in such a method. It would merely mean taking the power away from the people and putting it into the hands of political discontent. I cannot believe that the

[2] In making this remark, Wilson was either exaggerating or badly misinformed, again if he was correctly quoted. The Texas legislature in its session of 1907 had passed a number of new acts regulating corporations, but it did not enact any law of the kind described by Wilson. He may have had in mind a number of Texas antitrust suits under older laws, notably the famous Waters-Pierce case involving the Standard Oil Company, which drove some of the "trusts" out of the state or at least forced them to take a less open role in the economic life of the state.

President, when he really is brought face to face with the actual transaction of business in that way, would indorse it. I have not seen much of Mr. Roosevelt since he became President, but I am told that he no sooner thinks than he talks, which is a miracle not wholly in accord with an educational theory of forming an opinion."

"We are in no danger of becoming an empire?"

"Such a scheme would end in a big laugh. In any event, before the time arrived when Mr. Roosevelt could be declared Emperor he would have brought everything for himself to an end. But it is surprising what a following the President has in Congress and at the White House."

"The Presidential election will be exciting?"

"Yes; I believe it will pull the biggest free vote ever known in the history of the country. There is really no offense to the public in the fact that corporations contribute campaign funds to a candidate's election if he would only fulfill his promises, give the people what they want, whether it is good for them or not."

Dr. Wilson had just returned from a trip South and West, and he described the impression he had received.

"I feel as though I had witnessed a farce," he said, "when I recall the extraordinary state of mind in which this financial crisis has effected [affected] the people."

"For instance, in Memphis a young reporter came to me.

" 'What is the financial situation?' he asked, and I confessed I didn't know any more than he did actually. Then he asked me what the feeling was in the East when I left, and I told him that there were appearances of restored confidence. The next morning the newspaper headlines announced my opinion,[3] and then came the farcical situation. A leading business man in Memphis came and shook me by the hand, thanking me for having restored the financial situation in his town. Now, that is on a par with the entire source of this financial trouble.

"A panic has been described as a state of mind, and it seems to proceed from the ignorance of the public with the business conditions. I found myself next to a very intelligent man at the theatre, and we got into conversation about the financial situation. I found that he was under the impression that Mr. Morgan had actually put up the cash in millions that he was reported to have done. When I told him that he had merely loaned his credit to that amount he could scarcely believe it.[4]

"There seems to be an impression in the public mind that the

[3] See the interview printed at Nov. 8, 1907.
[4] See C. H. Dodge to WW, March 28, 1907, n. 1.

millionaire keeps his millions in a cash stocking, a steel stocking, I suppose."

"The Federal Government has no control over the financial situation?"

"None whatever, the Treasury has done all that it can.

"The rate legislation against railroads,[5] I consider, which made it impossible for the railroads to borrow any more money, precipitated the panic. The abominable currency system under which we are staggering, and have been for years, is responsible for the present tightness of money. The American Bankers' Association has repeatedly submitted plans for a new currency law, but Congress has paid no attention whatever to it.

"The European currency system is far better than our own, but they are better able to adopt calculations than we are, because they have had more time to arrive at a fixed basis of resource. Doubtless Congress will have to take up the currency question."

"I am glad to see that in the midst of all this turmoil of undefined wickedness, Mr. Morgan's name has not been among the celebrities. He seems to have kept his hands clean and his reputation clear of any dishonor."

"He would make a good Chairman for a common council of the people?"

"He is a man of brains, and would make a good leader. What we need is the frank opinion of men who are superior to the manner of contest that exists in the political arena, a common council, a sort of people's forum, there is so much that needs defining in the complex whirl of modern events."

"A better balance of power?"

"Yes, some condition that will make it impossible for one man to control a railroad, to the oblivion of the money invested by smaller stockholders. Such a thing as one man controlling the stock of a railroad in England is unheard of. There is no law, as I understand, forbidding it, but Europe has reached a stage of definite calculations, whereas American prosperity is incalculable.

"We are divided into three personalities of opinion on National issues—the conservative, the reactionary, and the revolutionary. All these are really aiming at moral preferment, but along different ways.

"The conservative demands what he wants, but in the sequence of precedent that proves his values, with a calculation that does not annihilate while it builds.

[5] That is, the Hepburn Act of 1906, which greatly strengthened the powers of the Interstate Commerce Commission.

"The reactionary demands also what he wants, but by measures that are mere impulse of intolerance without discreet reasons.

"The revolutionary demands what he wants by certain semi-picturesque and fanciful ways that are unavailable and wild."

Dr. Wilson had carefully, sharply pierced the armor of our National standard. If he had not made any absolutely new holes in the structure, he had defined their causes, and, in some instances, proposed a soldering process by new legislation.

It was clear that we needed definitions, that the public was under the impression they were being denied to them, and that the forthcoming Presidential election would show "an enormous free vote."

Believing mostly in the chances of Gov. Hughes for President, he did not dispose of Mr. Roosevelt's popularity, but he epitomized him by referring to a cartoon of the President that had appeared in an English paper.

"It hit the nail on the head," said Dr. Wilson. "It was aimed at the reform spelling episode of Mr. Roosevelt's career. A huge tree represented the English language. Down near the roots a small nick had been made, and the President was depicted standing near with the axe in his hand. Uncle Sam asks him what he is doing, and he tells him that he is cutting down the tree.

" 'Ah! well,' says Jonathan, 'boys will be boys!' " and, laughing heartily, Mr. Wilson went with me to the door.

"It seems quiet and restful here after the noise of the town," I said.

"Yes, it seems so, but it is sequestered, that is all." And so are the 10 per cent. of thoughtful Americans from whom Dr. Wilson has made a request for a committee of common council.

Printed in the *New York Times*, magazine section, Nov. 24, 1907; editorial subheadings omitted.

To the Editor of the *New York Times*

My dear Sir: Princeton, N. J. November 24th, 1907.

I have made it a rule never to take exception to newspaper interviews or to attempt to correct the impressions that may have been made by them. But, knowing the character of your paper and being sure of your desire to do justice, I take the liberty of protesting against the color given to a recent interview with me in your issue of Sunday, the 24th of November.

Concerning the body of the interview I have little to complain of. It seems, indeed, singularly to heighten the color of the views that I expressed; all the way through makes me feel inclined to dissent from what are represented to be my own views, and several things which it contains I did not say. I would not be so foolish as to suggest, for example, that the corporations of the country file with a public official the minutes of their Directors' meetings. Neither was I conscious of taking the tone of superiority with regard to the wisdom of college men which the language of the interview seems to attribute to me. But on the whole, the interviewer represented what I had said, I am sure, with the most honest intention of reproducing what he had heard.

It does, indeed, seem quite incredible to me that the reporter should have so fundamentally misunderstood me as he seems to have done in the passage which he imagines me to have uttered, comparing our corporations to bodies of burglars. I used a playful illustration to show how burglars might, under the law of corporations, escape with nothing but a fine on the corporation itself, but I certainly did not say, because I do not think, that our regular corporations are conceived or conducted in a predatory spirit. It is a matter of very deep regret with me that my real opinions, which are not only moderate but hopeful, in regard to our industrial situation, should have been given a color which they never bore in my own mind. I have used the passage just spoken of as an illustration of how the interviewer has allowed himself latitude not justified by what I actually said.

It is chiefly, however, of the headlines that I think I have a right to complain. I certainly did not indulge in a "scathing arraignment" of our present political and industrial conditions. It is just such scathing arraignments as have got us into our present state of mind and brought about the present very dangerous condition of our business. The whole interview was meant to suggest only this: that we must refrain from scathing arraignment and general denunciation, and that the business men of the country must assist the law-makers to make such a correct analysis of our present business methods as would enable us to check questionable and immoral transactions, and bring the persons responsible for them to book, without deranging the whole business of the country as it is now being deranged. I believe that our present methods of attacking the question are blundering and unintelligent.

Neither did I say anything that would justify the statement of the headlines which says that I suggested the appointment of a common council selected from college men. How such a council could be appointed or what use it would serve I cannot imagine. What I suggested was simply common counsel.

I beg, my dear sir, that you will do me the favor of giving a prominent place to this letter, for the sake of correcting, so far as they may be corrected, the false impressions certain to be created by the manner in which the interview was presented.

Very truly yours, [Woodrow Wilson][1]

CCL (RSB Coll., DLC).

[1] The *New York Times* did not print this letter. Instead, it sent a reporter to interview Wilson and permit him to make a statement (printed at Nov. 27, 1907) correcting the alleged misrepresentations and inaccuracies in the report of the first interview.

To Mabel Kingsbury Fentress

Princeton, N. J.
My dear Mrs. Fentress, 26 November, 1907.

I hope that you will pardon a writer who has worn out his pen hand for using this mose [more] elaborate pen, the typewriter. I can only plead that the letter is not dictated.

But more particularly I beg that you will pardon my long delay in writing. I did not reach home until the eighteenth, and then I went almost at once to bed with an illness, no doubt induced by fatigue and dining car fare, which lasted the better part of a week.

I look back to my visit to Memphis with the greatest pleasure, and to your great kindness with sincere gratitude. It was delightful to have your cordial greeting and to get at least a glimpse of you and yours in your home.

Please remember me most cordially to your grandmother,[1] and give my warmest regards and thanks to Mr. Fentress, whose kindness I shall not soon forget.

With warmest appreciation,

Most sincerely Yours, Woodrow Wilson

WWTLS (WC, NjP).

[1] Mary Ridgly Talbot (Mrs. Pitser) Miller, who lived in the Fentress home.

From Charles William Kent

Dear Wilson: University of Virginia, November 26, 1907

I am very sorry that you cannot yourself prepare the sketch of President Madison, but I am not at all surprised that you cannot find the time to do so I knew, of course, that you were very busy, but it would have been most agreeable to us to have had you contribute something to our book[1]

We shall probably reprint about 7500 words of your writings I trust this will be sufficient to print one of your things in full and then significant extracts from several others I am very glad that you are going to aid Dr. Ballagh in the preparation of the sketch of you

With very kindest regards to Mrs. Wilson, and my very best wishes to yourself, I am,

Sincerely yours, Charles W. Kent

TLS (WP, DLC).

[1] Edgar Dawson wrote the sketch of James Madison in *Library of Southern Literature*, VIII, 3283-288.

A Statement in the *New York Times*

[Nov. 27, 1907]

WOODROW WILSON PLEADS FOR LIGHT

We Must Find Out Exact Corporate Evils and Seek a Remedy, He Says.

BRING INDIVIDUALS TO BOOK

Fining Corporations Hurts Only the Public–Abuse No Remedy–It's a Time for Moderation.

Dr. Woodrow Wilson, President of Princeton University, made this statement yesterday to a TIMES reporter, in further elucidation of the views expressed by him in an interview published in last Sunday's TIMES, which Dr. Wilson felt hardly represented his views with sufficient accuracy and clearness:

" 'Scathing indictments' of our present industrial and political conditions are exactly what we are suffering from at the present moment, and they are to be offset not by other 'scathing indictments,' but by a very calm and self-possessed examination of the actual condition of things. What we need at present is not heat, but light. A just view of the existing situation would not, of course, excuse any of the gross evils which have sprung up in our business management, or rather in our manipulations of industrial enterprise.

"It would, on the contrary, seek to discover just what those evils are and just what the best remedy for them is. At the moment we are suffering quite as much from the blundering and unintelligent methods by which our Governments, State and Federal, and public opinion throughout the country, have been attempting to remedy these evils, as from the evils themselves.

"Indiscriminate abuse is clearly no remedy and does not create the state of mind in which a remedy is possible. We need, above all things else at present, moderation in counsel and a careful discrimination of the good from the evil. The vast bulk of our business is sound; the vast majority of our business men are upright and honest.

"It would be deeply unjust to say that our great corporations are 'predatory' in their intentions or in their methods. No doubt there are individuals who scruple at nothing in the accumulation of wealth and who use the wealth they have accumulated without regard to the laws either of public justice or of private morals. But these men impair the business of the country more than they assist it, and it is in the interest of all concerned that they should be singled out and separated from those who are carrying forward the legitimate undertakings of the country.

"Indeed, upon a close view of the matter it is quite evident that there are two very different sets of persons dealing with our business at present: one set actually administers the business, gives it its efficiency and success; the other set trades in the values thus created and devotes itself to the game of controlling the securities listed on the stock market, so that a power which is not administrative, but speculative, manipulative, rather, may fall to it.

"Through their influence, the business of the country has come to be touched at a score of points by questionable practices and methods which are clearly opposed both to private morals and to the public welfare. Just what those practices and methods are and how they can be remedied can be ascertained only by the frankest common counsel; and that common counsel rather than scathing arraignments and hastily conceived remedies, is the business of the hour.

"The only sound method of law is to seek out and prohibit particular transactions, and when those transactions occur, to bring not corporations but individuals to book for them. Those corporation lawyers who insist upon standing between the public and the corporations which they represent, in order to shield the corporations from close scrutiny and to prevent the intervention of legal remedy, are really doing the interests they represent the deepest possible injury.

"It is a duty which it is to be hoped they will see very soon, and not after it is too late, to come forward with the frankest disclosures, not divulging confidential matters, not attacking the reputations of individuals, but frankly informing the public as to the actual methods of corporate business, and showing where those methods can be squared with the best rules of justice, without impairing either the efficiency of corporate action or the prosperity of the country. I do not know from whom else such counsel can come, and if it does not come from them, we are in danger of seeing the present tendencies outstrip all reason, and the corporations which they are seeking to defend fatally injured to the detriment of the whole National future.

"Clearly, the object of existing remedial legislation is to strike at the corporations themselves. They cannot be imprisoned; they can only be dissolved or fined. If they are fined, it is clear that the result is that just so much money is taken out of the business of the country, that it comes from the pockets not of those who have originated the questionable practices complained of, but of the stockholders and of those who buy what the corporation produces, and that the money goes into the public Treasury, where it is not needed, and where, under our singularly belated currency system, it can be of no use to anybody. Corporations cannot be moralized. Morals belong to individuals, and a law which strikes at corporate action itself will be entirely ineffectual unless it reaches the individuals who originate that action and are truly responsible for it.

"A great deal has been said about giving entire publicity to everything that corporations do. This is clearly out of the question for many practical reasons; but it is not out of the question that each corporation should so disclose the exact methods of its business that the officers of the law may know who is responsible for each class of its transactions; whether certain things that it has done or authorized have been voted by its Directors as a board, or ordered by the Executive Committee of its Directors, or originated by its President or by its Treasurer or by some other officer whom it would be equally easy to name by title. And it would be perfectly possible to base upon such self-analyses direct personal responsibility for every transaction which transgresses the law. This would not disclose the business of the corporation to its rivals, but would analyze its make-up for the benefit of the officers of the law.

"I think a great deal of allowance should be made for the mistakes which politicians and legislators have been making. They have been driven forward by public opinion, but they have not been assisted by the candid advice of business men and of the lawyers of the country who are most intimate with its business.

Nothing is so much needed as that the range of our consultation in public affairs should be extended, and that the sense of public duty and of the obligation to give public advice should be extended to those who now stand outside politics and criticise those who are trying to conduct it. We have had enough of speech-making in general terms, and ought now to get down to the actual business of putting our affairs rationally in order."[1]

Printed in the *New York Times*, Nov. 27, 1907; editorial sub-headings omitted.

[1] There is a WWsh outline of this statement in WP, DLC, and a typed copy in WC, NjP with minor differences from the one printed above.

To Henry Smith Pritchett

[Princeton, N. J.]

My dear Mr. Pritchett: November 27th, 1907.

I am very much obliged to you for calling my attention to the passages in the advance copy of your report, touching Princeton's title of University.

I did not myself feel in '96 any particular enthusiasm for the assumption of the new name, but at the same time I feel that your intimations that Princeton is less entitled to the name than some others who have long borne it without question is not justified. As you know, we are struggling amidst a great confusion of standards in respect of this matter as in respect of almost every other in our educational system. Some of our universities are universities in the German sense and some are not, but it does not seem to me that that single standard, introduced virtually by the Johns Hopkins, should settle the question in the face of innumerable historical circumstances. Princeton has been doing very serious graduate work for a long time, not in all departments, but in many departments, and since '96 has steadily increased her claim to the title even on German grounds. I feel that it is an unnecessary shadow thrown upon her claims, to speak of them as if they were wholly artificial and adventitious. I shall insist some day on having you down here to find out what we are really doing.

I was extremely sorry to miss the meeting of the Trustees of the Foundation, particularly after I heard that they had been playing with a proposition which I think it would be most unwise to close with. But I shall hope to have a very full and frank discussion of this matter with you when the Executive Committee meets again.

Always cordially and faithfully yours

[Woodrow Wilson]

CCL (WWP, UA, NjP).

A Response to an Address of Welcome to the Association of Colleges and Preparatory Schools of the Middle States and Maryland[1]

[[Nov. 29, 1907]]

PROCEEDINGS

of the

Twenty-first Annual Convention

FIRST SESSION.

Friday, November 29th, at 10.30 A. M.
President Woodrow Wilson Presiding.

After a few words of welcome by President [John Huston] Finley, of the College of the City of New York, President Wilson said:

President Finley, I am very happy to acknowledge, with gratitude for the Association, the words of welcome that you have just uttered.

President Finley has been kind enough and prudent enough to say that I was going to deliver an admirable address this evening. I say prudent enough because it is always more prudent to praise an address before you have heard it than after; and therefore I shall not say more this morning than that it is a very pleasant circumstance, indeed, to find ourselves in this beautiful place.

It is true that this place stands in some senses at the gate of the continent, and yet it is not true that these buildings stand near the actual gate; and therefore it may often require some special errand to bring us this far uptown. We are very glad to have been drawn so far uptown to see this noble group of buildings, but more particularly to feel the warmth that inhabits them in the hearts and minds of the men who are conducting this institution.

You know that at Princeton we are now engaged in that new industry, the production of college presidents. We will devote a special chair to it. I mean that we expect the occupants of the chair to supply the now exigent demand for this kind of material. Our chair of politics has been occupied so far by only two persons—by President Finley and by the gentleman who will presently become President Garfield of Williams College. I am now seeking a suitable third person, to be for a little while Professor of Politics and afterward president of some institution. I therefore feel the pleasure in listening to President Finley that one feels in listening to a home voice. It is very delightful to have known him so long and intimately as we did, and I cannot help feeling that there is in my breast some family sense of welcome here, of being welcomed to a place where at any rate a very beloved friend of ours has come to preside, and I am sure that all of you who know President Finley will share with me the feeling of personal regard and of personal gratification at the association with him. It is therefore in many ways grateful to be welcomed to this place, and I am sure that we shall feel the hospitality of it grow in warmth as the sessions continue in length.

I am now going to give myself the pleasure of proceeding with the programme of the morning, and I hope that if the speakers of the morning are both present they will be kind enough to come to the platform—Dr. Balliet and Mr. Myers.[2]

The topic is "The Influence of the Present Methods of Graduate Instruction upon the Teaching in the Secondary School," and I shall ask Dean Thomas M. Balliet, of New York University, to introduce the discussion.

Printed in *Proceedings of the Twenty-first Annual Convention of the Association of Colleges and Preparatory Schools of the Middle States and Maryland* (n.p., 1908), pp. 7-8.

1 Which met in Townsend Harris Hall of the College of the City of New York.

2 Thomas Minard Balliet, Professor of the Science of Education and Dean of the School of Pedagogy, New York University; and George William Myers, Professor of the Teaching of Mathematics and Astronomy and Mathematics Supervisor at the School of Education, the University of Chicago.

A Presidential Address to the Association of Colleges and Preparatory Schools of the Middle States and Maryland

[[Nov. 29, 1907]]

SCHOOL AND COLLEGE.

There is no one to introduce the speaker of the evening except myself. I would fain commend my friend to your indulgent hearing. He is essentially a modest man, but he is accustomed to utter certain ideas for the pleasure of intellectual adventure. There is no way in which to avoid life's falling dull unless you propose things which at least arouse discussion; and he professes to have found, in his brief experience as a college president, that no one is more serviceable to you than the men who oppose your ideas. My friend tells me that his ideas have been more perfected by those who have opposed them than by himself. They have enabled him to see the points at which they needed adjustment, the points at which they needed to be guarded, the points which would make them efficacious in execution. It is such a person, so disposed to learn, so new in learning in his present position, whom I have the pleasure of introducing to you this evening.

The topic I have chosen is one which allows me plenty of sea room. Speaking on "School and College," one can give himself leave to say almost anything about education that it pleases him to say; and I think that one of the greatest interests that attaches to our generation is, that almost everything regarding education has to be said over again.

We have just passed through a period in education when everything seemed in process of dissolution, when all standards were removed, when there was a universal dispersion of every established conception; when men did not hold themselves to plans, but opened the whole field, as if you drew a river out of its courses and invited it to spread abroad over the countryside. For there was a time in the generation which preceded our own, when education was confined within very narrow courses, when it did not sufficiently fertilize the great areas of educational interest—of intellectual interests; and it was the task of that particular generation to see that the waters were no longer confined to a little territory, but were allowed to spread abroad over a great new land.

To come out of my figure, we have just passed through a period when the whole domain of knowledge has been added to by subject after subject, and when it was absolutely necessary that the boundaries should be constantly enlarged in order that we might include the new things that had come to engage the human mind.

It does not make very much difference how you define the features of the period through which we have passed. The term under which we generally designate it is "the elective system of studies." I received a catalogue from a college the other day, a college not ancient in its foundation, in which it was stated that the institution was ready to offer 365 courses, and would offer any others upon the demand of as many as five students. In other words, this institution, like its elders and betters, had undertaken to put upon its curriculum almost every known subject of study, and had put all those subjects of study upon its curriculum upon an equal footing, not presuming to suggest to the student which were the greater subjects and which the minor; not presuming to point out to him what was the natural point of entrance and the natural point of exit, but inviting him to enter anywhere and go any whither in his search for knowledge throughout a vast and various field.

This is what I have called the period of dispersion, the period of the dissolution of standards, when we do not undertake to say that one study is more worth while than another study, but say to every student: "Judge for yourself, by your own tastes to begin with, which studies are most worth while for you; and sit you down to a free feast!"

Not only so, but we have just passed through a period abounding in pedagogical theories. We have been doing nothing else than make reckless experiments upon lads and youths, upon girls and maidens, for the purpose of testing newfangled notions which we put forth out of intellectual curiosity more than out of deep conviction. I was talking not long ago to a very interesting lady, who was trying to expound to me some of the new theories of education, finding me to be a very ignorant person; and she was talking to me about the individual child, and the sociologic child, and various other kinds of children until I became confused; and I said, "I beg your pardon, but I am afraid I don't know what you are talking about"; and she said, "Perhaps it is the terms I am using." "No," I replied; "I am afraid it is the ideas you are using." She was representing each child as having a sort of section here and there in its intellectual biology which made it necessary to treat one section of the child after one chemistry of development and another layer of the child after another chemistry of development. I had never met children so sectionalized; I had never been aware that I had myself developed out of such an incomplete and un-united series of sections; and so I was confused not by her terminology (for I understood what the words meant), but by her ideas, for I was unable to grasp them.

And yet she was perfectly serious; she was very capable; and she was subjecting the children whom she dealt with to experimentation upon the basis of these theories. You know perfectly well what the result has been; you know that the children of the past two or three decades in our schools have not been educated. You know that the pupils in the colleges in the last several decades have not been educated. You know that with all our teaching we train nobody; you know that with all our instructing we educate nobody. I say you know this–not meaning that you will admit it in a public discussion, but that when you are alone upon your knees at night you would feel obliged to confess it.

I have had the experience (which I am sure is common to modern teachers) of feeling that I was bending all my efforts to do a thing which was not susceptible of being done, and that the teaching that I professed to do was as if done in a vacuum, as if done without a transmitting medium, as if done without an atmosphere in which the forces could be transmitted. I am not indicting other persons any more than I am indicting myself. I have been teaching now for nearly twenty years; I have been conducting classroom exercises for nearly twenty years; and I don't think I have been teaching any appreciable portion of that time. I have been delivering lectures which I meant to be interesting; I have been saying things some of which I knew; I have been repeating other things—many other things—which I have heard; I have been putting together views of knowledge much more systematic than my own investigations warranted me in putting together; and the result has been that my pupils have for the most part remembered my stories and forgotten my lectures. Because it is one of the privileges of a teacher, I think, to be bored, himself, with his own lecture and to allow himself to depart once and again from the course of the lecture in order to tell a story which has more or less connection with what he is saying.

I wish to state these things, if need be, in an extravagant form, in order to have you realize that we are upon the eve of a period of reconstruction. We are upon the eve of a period when we are going to set up standards. We are upon the eve of a period of synthesis, when, tired of this dispersion and standardless analysis, we are going to put things together into something like a connected and thought-out scheme of endeavor. It is inevitable; I never attend any gathering of this kind that I do not hear the frankest admissions that we are in search of the fundamental principles of the thing that we are trying to do.

It is certainly a most favorable state of mind in which to enter a new age. No man who knows the history of knowledge would think of impeaching the men who have been responsible for the dissolution of standards, because until the old narrow curricula were shattered it was impossible to include in our conception of learning all those great new bodies of knowledge which have arisen almost within the lifetime of men now living. It is only since about 1850 that the great bodies of science which we now teach have come into existence in teachable form; and it is only within that time that science has won its place among the great disciplines of the human mind; it is only within that period that we have taken the physical universe within the boundaries of our comprehension and have tried to make men acquainted, not merely with the things which proceed out of their own consciousness, but also with the things which proceed out of their own environment. It was necessary that the old hard-and-fast bodies of study should be broken in upon like antiquated fortresses, a new garrison put in, and all knowledge given leave at any rate to be brought into the synthe[s]is which we were subsequently to attempt.

You will notice that whenever we have a serious discussion, such as the discussions which have characterized the sessions of this Association to-day, we find ourselves confused, because we are talking about several different things at the same time, and are sometimes misled into supposing that we are talking about one and the same thing. We are not often enough aware that in speaking of education—present-day education—we are really speaking of two things and not of one thing. We must discriminate the two things of which the modern age stands in need. It stands in need, in the first place, of technical training: the great majority of our young people must be made mechanics. I do not mean *merely* mechanics of the hand, but mechanics *also* of the mind. They must be given some skilled capacity to accomplish certain definite and narrow tasks—must be given technical training—all those things which lead up to skill in particular material occupations and which are more neccessary in our age than they ever were in any preceding age. There is almost no limit to the number of expert intellectual or manual mechanics which this age needs. The number of technical things there are to be understood, the number of technical things there are to be done, the number of technical things there are to be combined is almost beyond calculation. The majority of our youth must be given an exact and thorough technical training. That is one of the things this age needs; and if you count heads, it is the main thing that this age needs.

But in education we don't count heads: that is to say, we don't count the outsides of them. There is another sort of education which this age needs, and needs more than any preceding age: that kind which for many ages has borne amongst us the name of liberal education. If ever an age stood in need of men capable of seeing the invisible things, it is the age in which we live. If ever an age stood in need of the statesmanship of mind, this is that age; if ever an age stood in need of men lifted a little above their fellows in their point of view, who can see the significance of knowledge and of affairs, this is the age. If our great army of workers is to be left to work with their gaze concentrated upon the task, and there is no one to see visions, no one to order the field, no one to organize the great functions of mind and of organized effort of which we stand in need every day—why, then, we shall stumble upon immediate disaster. We are in need as no age ever was of liberal education; there are so many things to coordinate in our thinking that we sadly stand in need of thinkers. When I speak of education, therefore, I mean a liberal education as distinguished from technical training, for it is to that theme I wish to confine myself this evening.

I am speaking of something which we too often leave out of our reckoning when we are thinking of our schools and colleges. I don't need to tell this company that information is not education; and I need only point out to you that in the great bulk of the work that we do in our schools and colleges, we are seeking nothing more than to impart information. We are seeking to communicate bodies of fact. Now, bodies of fact do not educate. Information is not an education. Information may clog the powers of the mind instead of drawing them forth. Information, unless the mind has the scope and grasp to digest and order it, is merely an impediment to the action of the mind. My father was in the habit of using very explicit English; and one of the things I remember him saying to me in one of the very early stages of my own education was this: "My son," he said, "the mind is not a prolix gut to be stuffed."

Now, when you think of the prolixity of the gut which is stretched back from the day of college graduation to the day of entering upon the primary school and think of the systematic stuffing it has undergone ever since the process was begun, you don't need to be told that there has been no process of digestion whatever. The figure is coarse only because we regard one of the words in it as coarse. It is true—as true as any material figure can be to a spiritual fact. It behooves us, therefore, to see what we are going to choose as our ideal standards in education. I mean, what we are going to understand education to be, let me again say, as distinguished from technical training, which I am not disparaging, but which I am now seeking to discriminate from this other thing.

It seems to me that the idea of education involves three things: it involves in the first place enlightenment. I read a very whimsical essay the other day by that delightful newer essayist of ours, Mr. Crothers, entitled "The Anglo-Saxon School of Polite Unlearning."[1] Mr. Crothers pretends to have discovered in an out-of-

[1] Samuel McChord Crothers, "The Anglo-American School of Polite Unlearning," *Atlantic Monthly*, c (Sept. 1907), 408-19. Crothers, Princeton 1874, had been pastor of the First Unitarian Church of Cambridge, Mass., since 1894.

the-way part of London a school whose object is to dispossess persons of their erroneous prepossessions, acting upon the principle that the trouble with us is the number of things that we know that we [know] are not so; and one of the most interesting pupils represented to be in this school was an Oxford graduate, who was contemplating an early visit to the United States. They had there undertaken to unload him of his misinformation about the United States of America. One of the exercises they gave him was this: they gave him an extract from a San Francisco newspaper saying that O'Brien, the well-known pugilist,[2] was now devoting himself to literary studies and, under the guidance of a tutor, was reading Homer, Dante, and Milton, expecting, after he retired from the ring, to devote himself to literary pursuits. The Oxford man was directed to write an essay upon this extract showing how characteristic it was of a crude country to suppose that anybody was ready to study anything; "and then," said his teacher, "after satisfying yourself by proving that you with your classical education are much better able to appreciate Homer than O'Brien is, ask yourself which Homer would have appreciated more–you or O'Brien." It is so obvious that Homer would have preferred O'Brien! A stroke of insight and wit like that seems to strip away all the false paraphernalia with which we have surrounded classical learning and to set the Iliad up before us as an epic of the natural human being.

A great deal of perception is to be got by thus unloading most of the unilluminated information which we have conveyed to our pupils, by stripping away ruthlessly all those adornments of careful, painstaking scholarship which have obscured the storied facts of human existence; and one flash of the perception that Homer would have loved O'Brien is more illuminating than all the Oxford training with regard to the classics in that particular specimen of the Oxford outlook. It at least renders Homer as he probably was. That is what I call enlightenment; it is letting in that very rare thing in college and school classrooms–illuminating perception of what the thing means.

We are so punctilious about form in our teaching; we are so careful not to use gross words like the word gut; we are so careful to avoid the real facts of the case; we are so careful to obscure knowledge by interposing between the pupil and knowledge that great, thick, impenetrable body that we call information, the enormous, incalculable mass of irrelevant facts: facts irrelevant to the spiritual intent of the thing itself! It is a great deal better

[2] Joseph Francis Aloysius Hogan, who went by the name of Philadelphia Jack O'Brien.

to see one thing than merely to look at a thousand; it is a great deal better to penetrate to the heart of some one mystery than to idly speculate about a score of mysteries. And so it is better to conduct the student to the interior *penetralia* of some great subject than to take him on an excursion "Seeing Greater Knowledge."

Then there is another object in education; and that is what we have latterly grown into the habit of calling orientation—a word carrying certainly a very beautiful figurative meaning—that is to say, showing, with regard to some one thing perceived, how it stands related to the other things which the mind is capable of perceiving. There was a very interesting suggestion made in one of the discussions this forenoon when it was shown that our universities in their attempt to train teachers did not train the kind of teachers that would be most serviceable in the secondary schools because they did not train teachers who saw the relations of the particular things they taught to the larger bodies of knowledge to which they belonged. One of the speakers suggested that every university should have some one whose object it should be by some stimulating form of lecture to bring the students of pedagogical method to perceive that in handling any one subject they were moving in a particular part of the great domain of knowledge. It has always been a favorite idea of mine that every university should have a professor of things in general—that every university should have some one who would take the entering class and show them, as if upon a map, the great extending fields of knowledge: "Here lies biology, but close neighbor to it, so that you can hardly draw the frontiers, lies chemistry; and there close to chemistry (with boundaries again obscured) lies physics; and there alongside physics (again without scientific frontier) lies mathematics; and there, surrounding all this territory of related subjects, lie the great and sometimes shadowy territories of philosophy, our conception of what the human mind is capable of, of what the brain perceives, what the mind comprehends and what it is possible to establish by reason, the demonstrable, the undemonstrable, the purely speculative, the knowable. You are ever upon a continent of knowledge; you cannot look far abroad without seeing into other great territories of study. And all this territory has had an ancient and honorable history; up and down these great plains and upon these great slopes have moved the great armies of human thinkers."

In the old ages, when they knew little of the history of thought, they went about among shadows, went about subject to many strange superstitions, which overcame them when they went out upon their expeditions to learn; but by slow degrees the mind's conquests of arms were pushed forward; men went first into this *terra incognita*, and there lies before us the map of the known world of knowledge.

It seems to me that it would be possible for the youngster to find himself in any one subject by knowing how it stands related to its great neighbor subjects, and never after that feel that he was in contact with a mere body of information, but know that he was in the territory of a great kingdom where vital forces were afield and where any day some new flash of light might come to make the way plainer and the day broader.

And so this business of orientation, of showing the youngster where he is, is one of the chief businesses of education. It is not necessary for the teacher alone; it is necessary also for the pupil, that he should know where he is. I cannot refrain from returning to a favorite illustration of mine (which I am sure some of my friends present have heard). When a man loses his way in a strange country you say that he has lost himself, and yet, in fact, that is the only thing he has *not* lost: *he* is *there*. That is demonstrable, and he knows it. But *he has lost all the rest of the world.* If he knew where any fixed point was, he could steer by it; but he doesn't know any fixed point, and therefore he has lost all the rest of the world.

Now, if you take a human mind and put it in a strange country and leave it, it is there, but it hasn't the least notion where it is; it is lost in the strictest sense of the word. That is, so far as its consciousness is concerned; it is nowhere at all. It has no relations to anything else. And you get the figure of orientation by knowing that if you only give that mind the notion of where the East is, it is easy after that to find the West and the North and the South and to box the whole compass; but not until some point of the compass is known.

But there is another object of education. We have talked a great deal in our day about enlightenment and about orientation; but we have stopped talking about *discipline.* The chief object of education is discipline. There is an old and trite illustration which must always be used, because it is the best illustration; that is, the illustration of the gymnasium. I have never heard of any youngster who went into the gymnasium because he expected to do the double trapeze with his partner in business when he graduated. I have never seen anything done in the gymnasium which was practical, in the sense in which we are now inclined to use that word with regard to the subject of education. All that the youngster in the gymnasium is trying to do is to get his muscles in such shape and the red corpuscles of his blood in such heart that he can do anything with himself physically that he wishes afterward; can stand the strains and be ready for all the sudden exertions of life; so that his heart will be used to having a strain put upon it and can pump, with slow and persistent complacency, when the utmost strains of life are put upon it at last.

That is discipline of the body; and anything that can discipline the body is serviceable for the uses of our physical life. Similarly, anything—it is sometimes a matter of indifference what—that can discipline the mind is serviceable for our life intellectual; and what does not discipline the mind is not serviceable.

If you accept that principle, then you cannot put all subjects of study upon an equality. Some things discipline the mind, and some do not. Some things are difficult and some things easy; and nothing so disciplines the mind as that which is difficult. I think the ideal method of discipline intellectually would be to give young people the things hardest for them to do, and then as soon as they begun [began] to be easy, stop them and give them something else that was hard, so that they might presently get accustomed to the constant strain of fibre which would make anything after that easy of accomplishment. There is an old adage: "Beware of the man of one book!" By which is not meant beware of him because he is narrow, but beware of him because he knows something, and if you get in his track with regard to that thing you are going to get run over. If every man was a man of one book, of one subject, your only right strategy in life would be to feel tenderly around when you got in conversation with him until you found what his one subject of conversation was, and then avoid that. The athleticism of perfection in that one thing would make him a dangerous and ugly customer to handle.

When you come to look over the exceedingly various fields of modern knowledge, how many elements are there? Not how many subjects—they are innumerable—but how many *elements*? I do not see more than these: science (by which I mean pure science), literature, philosophy, history. Of course, in speaking of literature I include language, which is the vehicle of literature; of course, in speaking of history, I include politics, which concerns itself with many of the chief transactions of history; but, if we make the proper inclusions of these terms, what else is there besides pure science, pure philosophy, pure literature, and history and politics?

There are four bodies of discipline. There is the body of discipline which we call science; and inasmuch as almost all sciences have the same method and involve the same processes of observation and generalization, they can be regarded as alike in disciplinary effect. Not all of them are alike in the degree in which they discipline; but all of them are alike in the kind of discipline to which they subject the human mind.

Then there is the great body of philosophical thinking: by which I do not mean vague speculation as to the human mind, but the rational putting together of the experiences of the human mind.

And then there is pure literature, that product of thought and of fancy and of form which springs almost (it would sometimes seem in the case of great national literatures) out of the common consciousness, where the most exquisite voices are, the voices which most perfectly express the general and common impulse, where your most authentic spokesman is the poet, who can demonstrate nothing, but who feels and perceives everything. And for the hearing of this authentic voice you must be master of its instrument, of the speech which it uses.

Then there are all the transactions of the human race which we call its history and politics.

Now, in seeking a process of enlightenment, of discipline, and of orientation amidst these great bodies of knowledge, *how* are we going to seek them? It seems to me, ladies and gentlemen, that we shall never accomplish anything in our attempt at educational reorganization until we get rid of the idea which too much pervades an association, like this—the idea that our relations to each other as schoolmen and collegemen is that the one set of us are preparing youngsters for the other set of us to teach. Until we realize that the school and the college are doing the same thing exactly, we shall not get anywhere. Until we realize that, it is neither here nor there with regard to the kind of thing we are doing whether the boy or girl is going beyond the school course or going to stop at the end of it. It is only a question of how far you carry them in a process which is the same from beginning to end; and if there were any process, such as the process of certification that we were discussing this afternoon, which could make us unaware that we were crossing a bridge when we were leaving the school and entering the college; if there were some common method of life for the schoolboy and the collegeman which should make him feel less sharply than he does that when he leaves the school and enters the college he has entered a new kind of world, it would be worth while to make all the changes necessary in order to adopt it—in order to make the boy feel that he is not going from one thing to another, but that he is simply going on to prosecute a little further the fair journey upon which he had set out.

We ought to realize that the school is not preparing the boy for the college, but that school and college are alike endeavoring, so far as time and opportunity permit, to educate the boy; and therefore it is just as important for the school to make up its mind what its method of enlightening, of discipline and of orientation is to be, as for the college.

We are all of one family; we are all engaged upon the same thing; and we cannot do it in two ways. We must do it in one way. If we do it in two ways we shall miss connection. Therefore, it seems to me that you must set your technical training schools apart from your other schools; your technical colleges apart from your other colleges. I do not mean geographically apart from them. I think they ought to have a spiritual relationship, which is best preserved when they are in close geographical juxtaposition; but I mean that you must not confuse the aims and processes of the one with the aims and processes of the other, must not try to do two things at once with the same pupils. I am asking you to consider liberal education to-night as a task of the school as well as a task of the college.

Now, if I have been speaking the truth, what is the proper method of liberal education? I have spoken of its object, namely, enlightenment, discipline, orientation; I have spoken of its elements: pure science, pure philosophy, pure literature, history and politics. Now, what of its method? Well, in the first place, it seems to me that you must choose a particular body of studies; you must choose a particular sequence of studies; you must choose a particular systematization and relation of studies; not the same for all men, for all pupils, but some one consistent thing for each pupil. Let me illustrate. I am not going to make practical suggestions. The suggestions I am going to make are merely by way of illustration and are unpractical, because for the moment impracticable. I am simply trying to point you forward to a time which may come, but which I do not know whether we shall ever see.

Suppose that you were to make up your mind to find your liberal education in the schools in this way: to give every pupil the fundamental science; that is to say, mathematics; to give every pupil one language—let him choose any one he pleases besides Latin. It happens that Latin is the medium, so to say the background—almost the substance—of so many modern languages that it is in a sense indispensable. Let him choose one language besides the Latin—let it be Greek or let it be Spanish; it does not make any difference whether it is a modern language or an ancient language, but one language besides Latin—let him swim from first to last in the atmosphere of Latin, and then let him choose one language besides Latin. Then give up the attempt to teach English literature. You can teach English literature as a science, which it is not; or as an art, which in your hands it cannot be; but whichever way you choose to attempt to teach it you will fail, if you regard it as a thing to be objectively imparted. You cannot pedagogically impart the song of a bird; you cannot pedagogically impart the appreciation of a landscape; you cannot pedagogically impart even the nice appreciation of idioms. The only way you will ever appreciate the idiom is by hearing it often; the idiom you hear most of you will most appreciate. I judge that the modern young college man and the modern young college woman most appreciate the idiom we call slang, for I don't hear them use anything else with gusto. The other idioms which they use they use as if they were on dress parade and knew that they were talking to a college professor. For them the only possible appreciation is the appreciation of slang, which in certain instances I very much appreciate myself. I admit that there are exigencies in one's life when nothing else will serve.

English, I believe, will some day come to have its proper place, both in our schools and in our colleges. It will be, what it is not to-day—the medium of all instruction. If you hold yourselves to the rule that nothing is taught by you correctly that is not taught in the best English you can command, and if you accustom the pupil to realize the fact that nothing is acceptable from him or her by way of reply that is not couched in the best English within their reach, you won't have to teach English as a language in any other way. The only way to learn English and to appreciate it is to use it. That is the law with regard to every fact. The only way to feel its power, the only way to find its thrill communicable to you, is to get into electric connection with it by appropriating its power and making it think your thoughts, making it the vehicle of your messages from mind to mind.

I have sometimes wondered what would happen to a college class if every examination paper were rejected which did not contain correct English. There wouldn't be any school certified then, because everybody would fail. And the excuse is, that they had to be so rapidly written; in other words, we know so little English that we need time and deliberation to use it. That is because from our childhood up we have not been brought to book and made to use it. We have been told stories in the crudest form, instead of being carried to the exquisite fountains of English in which all our older stories are to be found—instead of having been reared, from the time we were born until now, upon the sweet musical sound of a language richer than any other in cadence and sweetness, we have been given the rough phrases of the street ever since we can remember; and we cannot be taught English literature on those terms. If you ever teach English in your schools or colleges it will be because English is the atmosphere in your schools and colleges, the vehicle of their thoughts.

And then it is perfectly possible in every school to give the pupils a sense of the movement of affairs in the world in the past and at the present time. I think the impression I got when I was a boy of history was that it was something that had happened long ago, but wasn't happening now. I certainly got the impression that almost every schoolboy gets, that Cæsar's Commentaries were written for a schoolbook. If I had ever been allowed to realize the fact that this book was written by a famous general of what he did himself I think I would have sat up nights and taken notice; but none of these things were communicated to me. I was simply asked: "In what case is that noun?"

You will say that this is reducing education to very simple terms. Yes, very simple terms. But suppose you had a thorough grasp on the fundamental principles of mathematics; suppose that you thoroughly knew Latin and were thoroughly grounded in some one other language; suppose that you could really read the English language and love its finer forms; suppose that you had a conception of the reality of history—don't you think you will be fairly educated? And how many of your pupils has any one of those things? I am not blaming you; you have been caught in a ridiculous system, where we are trying to teach a student everything and don't teach him anything. When we come down to the real education of school children and undergraduates, we are going to come down to some basis like this.

When you pass over into the college, what are you going to do? You are going to make the pupil take one science besides his mathematics, in which he is already grounded and which he will need in almost any science that he takes. Mathematics is, so to say, science relieved of the embarrassments of physical environment. It is science which is free of the trammels of time and space, and reasons about everything with its feet off the ground for the most part, so that it may reason without impediment, but which reasons with the strictest fidelity from the premises to the conclusion, and will not allow itself to leap in the process or diverge from the direct line of inference. So that it is the fundamental discipline of all scientific thinking. If your youngster really has got his mind habituated to that kind of fidelity in the treatment of his premises, then put him in some one science and give him four years of it. Let him continue the one language besides Latin whose grammar and vocabulary you grounded him in in school, and let him take that four years so that when he comes out he can read anything in that language and can speak it and write it with ease. Subject him during those four years also to the principal processes of philosophical training: logic, the main conceptions of psychology, the main items of the history of human thought, the conceptions men have had of the universe and of their relation to it, and of their own processes of thinking; and you will incidentally have done everything that I have been suggesting with regard to the school. You will have saturated him in two literatures: in the literature of the language which he is adding to Latin and in the literature of his own language, because it will be a constant medium for everything that he thinks.

And then, at last, because in the school he has learned the reality of history and of political action, you can take him out upon the great field of the systematic study of history for four years.

Four subjects pursued for four years will have a remarkable effect upon him when he graduates. Where are we now amidst a miscellany of studies? It is said that the quantity of our entrance examinations is too great; of course it is too great; but it is not too great simply because we add a little piece here to mathematics and another over there in Latin and piece out the subjects; but because we have an enormous variety of subjects which every school is obliged to prepare its pupils in if they are going to enter college. There will be, after we have made our changes, as many subjects for the school, but not as many subjects for any one student. He will be examined (if I may recur to my illustration again) in his mathematics, in his Latin, in the one language which he has qualified to follow, and in practically nothing else; and when he comes out, he will have had enlightenment and discipline and orientation. I sympathized so deeply with Dr. Sihler[3] this morning when he said that we shall be obliged to reduce our education for each person—not for all, but

[3] Ernest Gottlieb Sihler, Professor of Latin and Lecturer in the Graduate School, New York University.

for each person,—to a small body of great subjects; and until we have done that, we will not have returned to the true process of education.

Now, ladies and gentlemen, you will say: "You have attempted to deliver to us a very dogmatic and far-reaching lecture on education; and you have called it 'School and College.'" What else could I call it? For the central idea I wish to leave with you is, that in purpose and method there is no difference between school and college. We have neglected the union and organization of forces. We have divided our learning as if we had done away with our union of States and had dissolved the federal government into a body of local principalities; and so we have neglected the very genius of our race, which is the genius of organization. The only way in which the American people have not yet shown a supreme genius in organization is that they have not yet shown a genius for simplification.

The very genius of organization is simplification. That man has not a genius for executive duty or for organization who multiplies means of action. He is the true genius who unites and simplifies; and so our real task for the immediate future is to discover the essential elements of education, whether they be those that are found catalogued here or not, and then with the utmost courage and with profound simplicity bring them together into a great *organum* which we shall be able after that to use as the lasting standard of the things we are trying to do.

We have enlarged our territories of knowledge, and we are at the same stage of mind that the Supreme Court is in: it says that Porto Rico is foreign territory and the Philippines are not: I have forgotten whether it is that way or the other way; it doesn't make any difference; but for some purposes they are foreign countries and for other purposes they are domestic countries, and we have not found the method of law by which to tie them unto ourselves and digest them into our political system.[4] So with our

[4] Wilson's confusion was understandable in view of the complexity of this subject. Since the so-called Insular Cases of 1901, the Supreme Court had generally ruled that Puerto Rico was not "foreign" territory and that the Philippine Islands were "foreign" territory. It had also decided that the Constitution did not "follow the flag" either to Puerto Rico or the Philippines so long as they were unincorporated territories. This meant in effect that the United States could hold and govern colonial possessions without extending American citizenship and all the benefits and protection of the Constitution to their inhabitants. Decisions concerning internal government and the economic relationships between the colonies and the United States lay with Congress. On the other hand, the Court had also said that Puerto Ricans and Filipinos did enjoy the protection of certain fundamental rights guaranteed in the Constitution. "The Court," one authority has written, "has never produced a full list of the . . . fundamental provisions. *Obiter dicta* it has mentioned as fundamental: freedom of religion, freedom of speech and the press, immunity from unreasonable searches and seizures and

knowledge: we have annexed territories and not known how to govern and unite them to those that are older and more established in their forms of instruction. What I plead for is, not agreement with the specific things that I have made this discourse up of, but agreement with the great thesis that I have endeavored, by all sorts of excursions and illustrations, to illustrate, namely: that we have missed the meaning of education; we have forgotten to assemble the elements of education; and we have forgotten to concentrate and simplify its methods.[5]

---

from cruel and unusual punishments, free access to the courts, and the protection against deprivation of life, liberty, or property without due process of law." Julius W. Pratt, *America's Colonial Experiment* (New York, 1951), p. 162.

[5] There is an undated WWsh outline, an undated T outline, and a WWT outline, dated Nov. 25, 1907, of this address in WP, DLC.

Printed in *Proceedings of the Twenty-first Annual Convention of the Association of Colleges and Preparatory Schools of the Middle States and Maryland* (n.p., 1908), pp. 73-89.

From Henry Smith Pritchett

My dear Mr. Wilson: New York, Nov. 29, 1907.

Thank you very much for your kind note of the 27th November. I think I shall let my language stand with a slight modification.[1] The great confusion of standards with respect to this matter is, as you say, most evident. This is the occasion for my remarks. My own conviction is that it is important that the American college as such should continue to exist. The best type we have of this to-day, from my point of view, is Princeton. The point at which I would differ from you probably is in accepting a graduate school on top of such a college as constituting a sufficient reason for calling the institution so formed a university.

The state university matter has proved a longer and more difficult fight than I had anticipated, but I am personally ready to go to any length to let the representatives of the state universities understand our friendly attitude toward their work and our appreciation of the place of the state university. I have, therefore, agreed to meet the state university representatives in Chicago on the 23rd January to hear the presentation of their proposed compromise. This compromise simply puts forward the plea that we carry the retiring allowance system in these institutions for a period of years. The compromise has, in my judgment, no merit, but when we have heard it patiently through, I hope that our trustees and the executive committee will be willing to act promptly so that this matter may be put out of the way at an early date. Faithfully yours, Henry S. Pritchett

TLS (WP, DLC).

[1] Pritchett's comments appeared in *The Carnegie Foundation for the Advancement of Teaching: Second Annual Report of the President and Treasurer* (New York, 1907).

In connection with the use of the term "university" in the United States, Pritchett discussed briefly the history of Princeton, concluding with the following statement (p. 83): "On October 22, 1896, the college celebrated in a formal manner the 150th anniversary of the signing of the first charter, and on that occasion adopted the title Princeton University. The reasons for this step are not entirely clear."

Further on, in a section on the Association of American Universities, Pritchett compared Princeton and The Johns Hopkins University as follows (p. 91): "For example, Johns Hopkins and Princeton are both noble institutions, both are centers of intellectual and moral influence, but one is in its spirit, its methods, its atmosphere essentially a university, the other a great college. To bring together in an 'Association of American Universities' institutions differing so widely in their essential characteristics means agreement only on generalities, a process which is not likely to raise the standards of weaker institutions."

From Salomé Machado Warren[1]

My dear Mr. Wilson, Cambridge [Mass.], Dec. 3, 1907.

I little thought when I had to forego the pleasure of dining with you last Spring at Prof. J. B. Clarke's,[2] that when I next saw you—if ever—the sun would be darkened for me forever. You have heard of my husband's death which came without a note of warning. Aside from my personal loss, it is hard to be reconciled, for he had just attained the maturity of his powers; had just published a brilliant piece of work regarded by epigraphists as his best;[3] and had not yet found leisure to finish his edition of Terence for which scholars on both sides of the water have long been anxiously waiting, as in this field he is regarded the supreme authority.

He was looking forward too with such joy to spending his last years abroad, devoting himself entirely to original work for which he was so evidently created. The classical scholars of America all combined last spring to appoint him Director of a large scheme which Carnegie was to be asked to back financially. This failing, my husband hoped after the children were educated to retire on a pension and work abroad on his own lines, being sure of eager publishers. The past year and the next five or six were to be our hardest financially for my son[4] has only had a year in college and my daughter[5] has her education before her (she is sixteen) It has been very evident for some time that Minton has felt the strain not only of unremitting toil but of straitened means. His own health has been threatened for eight years and the children have had many illnesses at home & in our sabbatical year abroad, when Minton was working so hard on MSS. I too had a very dangerous illness over there & came home a wreck. So that I had to be banished from a Northern climate for two winters practically. In this way our little savings have been ruthlessly dissipated, so that in spite of his life of austere simplicity of habits and the exercise of heroic self-abnegation and devotion to the highest, in which I have truly tried to be a faithful helpmeet, I am left to face life without resources and with two children to educate. There is a life insurance of $2,000. only and two small investments. What little is in the bank will at once be eaten up doubtless by unpaid bills and current expenses.

I write you thus frankly because Pres. Eliot thinks the Carnegie committee on pensions may be willing to give Minton's widow one half of the pension due to him. They did so in the case of Mrs. Shaler who had no children to educate.[6]

Seeing so many workers dropping in the harness here and the fearful strain of life, I have long foreseen the possibility of this sad day and hoped to be able to teach, in such a case, as I am fitted to do by my Smith College training; but I am now quite frail and of late my hearing is impaired so my friends and Pres. Eliot seem to think it out of the question.

I am facing the future with the calmness either of despair or of courage–I hardly know which–but it is plain I must be a very practical and strong woman to meet it. So I have written to you thus frankly and fully, for the Carnegie pensions are in the nature of prizes awarded for faithful service so that I can regard the matter impersonally in a way, and feel no delicacy in asking whether such a distinguished, devoted, untiring laborer is not worthy of a part of his hire at least, even after death, through the hands of his desolate wife and destitute children!

Minton has devoted and powerful friends who might have approached you in my behalf but you have always been so friendly to us–you and your wife–that I was moved to write directly to you. It is not easy to tell people one's private affairs, but you *had* to know mine in order to make your decision and so it seemed simpler and wiser for me to state them, as I know them better than any one else.

I shall not however write to any others of the committee. I don't know them well enough. With warmest remembrances to Mrs. Wilson, I am

Always most sincerely yours,

Salomé Machado Warren

It is not customary to pension the widows of deceased professors unless they have attained especial eminence.

You must know that my husband has for years been regarded the first Latinist in America[.] Of his eminence abroad you may not know so much, but you can easily find out how he is regarded in Germany, England, France, Sweden, Italy. I myself have a wonderful book of letters about his work[—]letters written in many languages, showing how his work was esteemed by all scholars as early as 1887. And he has grown very much since then with his Italian experience. Those letters were written without his knowledge to Columbia in 1887 and I begged them of Pres. [Frederick Augustus Porter] Barnard when Minton broke down at the Hopkins with that terrible illness of the brain—the first great tragedy in my life which however ended happily.

Pardon the length of this but my brain has given way under two recent shocks. A dear brother was drowned recently.

ALS (WP, DLC).

1 Widow of Minton Warren, an old friend of Wilson's who had died on November 26, 1907. Warren had taught Latin at The Johns Hopkins University from 1879 to 1899 and at Harvard since 1899, becoming Pope Professor of Latin in 1905. Wilson's friendship with him dated from their association at the Hopkins.

2 She was probably referring to John Bates Clark, Professor of Political Economy at Columbia University.

3 Minton Warren, "The Stele Inscription in the Roman Forum," *American Journal of Philology*, XXVIII (1907), 249-72, 373-400.

4 Minton Machado Warren, a member of the Class of 1910 at Harvard.

5 Francisca Machado Warren.

6 Sophia Penn Page Shaler, widow of Nathaniel Southgate Shaler, Professor of Geology at Harvard, who had died on April 10, 1906. Her two daughters were grown and married.

To Salomé Machado Warren

[Princeton, N. J.]

My dear Mrs. Warren: December 6th, 1907.

I cannot tell you with what sorrow we were stricken or with what deep sympathy, when we heard of Professor Warren's sudden death. It was indeed a terrible and irreparable thing to lose such a man, and for you of course the loss is overwhelming.

I need not tell you how I appreciate the confidence of your letter of December 3rd or how glad it will make me if I can be of any service in securing what the Carnegie Foundation should certainly in such a case grant—some part of the allowance for yourself which the Trustees would certainly have voted for Professor Warren himself. Under our rules there is no obligation, I am sorry to say, to make grants of this kind, but I know that the Executive Committee feels it a moral obligation to do so, whenever it is possible, and I think that you may be sure that they will give this case their most favorable and sympathetic consideration.

I hope that you will let me add for Mrs. Wilson and myself the most heartfelt sympathy. There is nothing adequate that can be said in such circumstances, but I hope that it will be some slight comfort to you to know with how warm and affectionate sympathy our hearts go out to you in this hour of tremendous trial and utter darkness. With warmest regard and the hope that the years may yet bring you in the furtunes [fortunes] of your children and in the later fortunes of your own life a return of cheer and happiness,

Cordially and sincerely yours, [Woodrow Wilson]

CCL (WWP, UA, NjP).

To Henry Smith Pritchett

[Princeton, N. J.]

My dear President Pritchett: December 6th, 1907.

This seems almost too intimate a letter to be handing about as a business document, but I know that you will understand my motive in sending it to you as the best possible statement of a most distressing case. I am sure you do not need to be told anything of Professor Warren's eminence, and I hope with all my heart that it will be possible for us to make a liberal grant for Mrs. Warren's relief. A more singularly and completely distressing case I have not in many a year come upon, and it gives me not a little pleasure to think that our precedents make it possible for us to grant relief on such an occasion. I would be very much obliged if, after you have read the letter and made a note of the case for the action of the Committee, you will be kind enough to return Mrs. Warren's letter to me.

Always cordially yours, [Woodrow Wilson]

CCL (WWP, UA, NjP).

From Moses Taylor Pyne

My dear Woodrow: New York December 6th, 1907.

I had expected to get in to see you before I left and was much disappointed that I did not find time, as I had a number of people stopping with me and could not get away.

I was very sorry to learn from Mrs. Fine, who spent Monday night [December 2] with us in New York, that you were suffering from an attack of Neuritis.[1] I hope it was not serious and that you are entirely recovered.

What I wanted to ask you was what your views are as to the new Alumni Dormitory.[2] It looks as if we should have over $80,000 in cash by the middle of the summer and as the subscribers are beginning to ask when the building is to be started, it is getting a little difficult to put them off much longer. My own opinion is that it would be injudicious to start next spring, but that possibly later in the summer we might make a start if we see our way clear, but I do not wish to put a heavy financial charge upon the University unless it is absolutely necessary.

The most important question before us now is the site. Mr. Cram seems to think that the building should not be carried as far down the Elm Drive as it was laid out by [Benjamin Wistar] Morris, but that the lower part of it should be cut off. I do not know whether this would cut into the Brokaw Field or not. If it were not for the complication with the Class of '84 regarding their tower,[3] I should be inclined myself to put it parallel with the '77 Dormitory on the other side of the proposed road from University Place to Alexander Hall,[4] but I should be glad to hear your views in the matter.

With kind regards, and hoping you are entirely recovered, believe me, as ever,

Yours very sincerely, M Taylor Pyne

TLS (WP, DLC).

[1] In fact, Wilson had unquestionably suffered a slight stroke. It caused numbness and pain in his right arm until at least the autumn of 1908.

[2] That is, the proposed extension of Patton Hall. The extension was never constructed.

[3] The Class of 1884 had pledged $50,000 for the tower of the Patton Hall extension. See the *Princeton Alumni Weekly*, VII (Feb. 9, 1907), 300. It, too, was never constructed.

[4] About this dormitory, later named Campbell Hall, see H. B. Thompson to WW, Sept. 16, 1907, n. 3.

From John Huston Finley

My dear Wilson: [New York] December 6, 1907.

There are two men whom you may wish to consider for your chair of politics: one to whom I called your attention four years or more ago (who so nobly put forward Garfield), Frederick Howe,[1] and one who has been recommended to me, Samuel P. Orth, also of Cleveland. I do not need to give you further information concerning Howe. He is better known to you through Garfield. Of Orth a friend of mine writes: "He is a graduate of Oberlin, served for a time as Professor in Buchtel College, meanwhile fitting himself for the legal profession. He came to this city as a stranger and in eighteen months was the President of the Board of Education. He is now the Assistant District Attorney. (This was written in September). He has won some distinction already as an author in addition to being one of the most remarkable public speakers that I know."[2] I suppose that Garfield knows him well. I feel under compulsion of this advice to send it on to you.

Sincerely yours, John H. Finley

TLS (WWP, UA, NjP).

[1] Frederic Clemson Howe, at this time practicing law in Cleveland as a member of the firm of Garfield, Garfield and Howe, and a member of the Ohio State Senate.

[2] Samuel Peter Orth became Professor of Political Science at Cornell in 1912.

To Charles Richard Van Hise

Princeton, N. J.

My dear President Van Hise: December 7th, 1907.

It is a real disappointment to me that I must again decline your cordial invitation to visit the University of Wisconsin, but the fact of the matter is that I have not been very well this winter, and it seems really necessary that after the meeting of our Board of Trustees in January I should go for several weeks to Bermuda. At any rate, I am keeping the month of February free of engagements with a view to a plan of that kind.

I have a genuine admiration for the work you are doing at the University of Wisconsin and could look forward to meeting many valued friends there, so that it is a genuine disappointment to me to be obliged to decline your invitation for the twenty-second of February. Pray accept my warmest assurances of appreciation and regret. Faithfully yours, Woodrow Wilson

TLS (Presidents' File, WU).

To Edmund Janes James[1]

Princeton, N. J.

My dear President James: December 7th, 1907.

I am sincerely complimented by your kind invitation to make the address at your approaching University Convocation, but I am sorry to say that at the time of Lincoln's Birthday I am expecting to be in Bermuda. Immediately after the meeting of our own Board of Trustees in January, I am hoping to get away for a brief vacation.

Pray express to the faculty of the University and to all concerned my very warm appreciation and sincere regret.

Very truly yours, Woodrow Wilson

TLS (Archives, IU).

[1] President of the University of Illinois since 1904.

Gilbert Fairchild Close to Moses Taylor Pyne

My dear Mr. Pyne: [Princeton, N. J.] December 7th, 1907.

President Wilson asked me to say that he has received your letter of the 6th, and that he will take it up at the earliest possible moment. He is still suffering very much with a severe attack of neuritis in his right arm and shoulder, and business seems out of the question for him at present. The trouble seems to be hanging on very stubbornly, but he is hoping every day to be better.

Very sincerely yours, [Gilbert F. Close]
Sec'y to the President.

CCL (WWP, UA, NjP).

To Henry Burchard Fine, with Enclosure

My dear Harry: [Princeton, N. J.] December 9th, 1907.

My thoughts have got running, the last day or two, on the important matter of reorganization which we discussed, and I have dictated the enclosed as memoranda of the chief points. The thing, if carried out, will eventually have to be formulated for the by-laws of the Board of Trustees, but probably it would not be good form for us to send the recommendations to the Board in that shape. I therefore send them to you in a more general form which might serve as the subject matter for the faculty's action.

Always affectionately yours, [Woodrow Wilson]

CCL (WWP, UA, NjP).

E N C L O S U R E

Memorandum. Princeton, December 9th, 1907.

Resolved, that the University Faculty recommend to the Board of Trustees the following changes in the administrative organization of the University:

1st. That the academic and scientific faculties be abolished as administrative bodies, and that they be retained as merely nominal bodies for the purpose of distinguishing the two sets of studies in the arrangement of the catalogue upon the model long established.

2nd. That there be created a faculty of graduate studies, to consist of the President of the University, the Deans, and all those Professors, Assistant Professors and Preceptors who are actually engaged in giving graduate instruction of a non-technical and non-professional character.

3rd. That the faculty of graduate studies be charged with the administration and oversight of the whole body of graduate courses of a non-technical and non-professional character given in the University, as well as the oversight of all graduate students and fellows, and be constituted the responsible administrative organ of the University for the administration of all matters affecting graduate study.

4th. That the Dean of the Graduate School be made the executive officer of the faculty of graduate studies, as the Dean of the faculty is the executive officer of the University Faculty in respect of all matters covering his field of duty, and that it be made the duty of the Dean of the Graduate School to present to the University Faculty an annual report showing the conditions and progress of graduate studies in the University for the preceding year.

5th. That the faculty of graduate studies be authorized to commit such parts of its routine administrative functions as it may deem wise to an Executive Committee of seven full professors selected in such wise as it may direct, provided that the Dean of the Graduate School shall be ex-officio a member of that Executive Committee.[1]

CC T memorandum (WWP, UA, NjP).

1 These and similar proposals for administrative reorganization were to undergo much discussion in 1908, but no action was taken on them until early 1909. Actually, the Academic and Scientific faculties (about the establishment of which, see the Minutes of the Princeton University Faculty printed at Sept. 21, 1898, Vol. 11) met as separate groups for the last time on December 12, 1905, and November 28, 1904, respectively. At these last meetings, it was agreed that the separate faculties would meet only on the call of the President or at the request of any member. They ceased to exist by common consent, as it were, without being formally abolished by the Board of Trustees. However, the trustees on January 14, 1909, approved a plan of reorganization which included the creation of the office of Dean of the Departments of Science, to have administrative oversight of the departments of instruction in pure and applied science, it being understood that Henry Burchard Fine would be the first incumbent. On April 8, 1909, the trustees also approved creation of a Faculty Graduate School Committee which, in effect, was to take over a large measure of the administrative control of the Graduate School, heretofore almost completely in the hands of Dean West. There will be much discussion of these matters in Vols. 18 and 19 of this series.

From Henry Smith Pritchett

My dear President Wilson: New York, December 9, 1907.

I thank you for sending me Mrs. Warren's letter. I knew both Warren and his wife quite well and was greatly grieved to hear of his sudden death.

Harvard College has applied for a pension for Mrs. Warren. The only question was whether his service as associate in Johns Hopkins was equivalent to the rank of assistant professor. I have just learned from Johns Hopkins that this service, which covered a period of five years, was really of important professorial rank, so that Mrs. Warren is entitled to a retiring allowance of $1200, if computed at the ordinary rate. It may be that we shall feel like dealing more generously by her than this and I hope that if you think well of our doing so, you may urge it upon us. It is certainly one of the cases in which Mr. Carnegie's great gift comes in as fitly as any which I have ever known.

I think it would be pleasant if you would let Mrs. Warren know of the fact that a retiring allowance will be granted, as it may relieve her of anxiety to some extent and it will come much better from you than from me.

Very sincerely yours, Henry S. Pritchett

TLS (WP, DLC).

To Salomé Machado Warren

[Princeton, N. J.]

My dear Mrs. Warren: December 10th, 1907.

It gives me peculiar pleasure to say that after a little correspondence with President Pritchett of the Carnegie Foundation for the Advancement of Teaching, I think that there is practically no doubt of the Foundation's being able to make you a small allowance. The Executive Committee of the Foundation does not meet until next week, but I have taken the liberty of saying this now in order that you may know that things are in course to do as much as it is possible to do under the rules of the Foundation. It is a matter of the sincerest gratification to me, as I need not tell you, to have the privilege of having some part in this business.[1]

With warmest regard and sympathy,

Always sincerely yours, [Woodrow Wilson]

CCL (WWP, UA, NjP).

[1] An "allowance" was granted to Mrs. Warren in December 1907. However, the *Annual Reports* of the Carnegie Foundation for the Advancement of Teaching do not state the amounts of pensions.

From Henry Jones Ford

My dear Sir: Baltimore, Dec. 10. 1907

I am advised that there may be an opening on your staff from the changes consequent upon the departure of Professor Garfield, and if so I beg that you will consider me in connection therewith.

My specialty, in which I am qualified to give instruction, is as regards the working of political institutions, or practical politics.

Throughout the last academic year I lectured once a week at the University of Pennsylvania, and also at Johns Hopkins, on the "Theory and Practice of Politics." This year I am lecturing once a week at Johns Hopkins on "Institutions of Popular Government." As to my capability in class-room work, I beg to refer to Dr. James T. Young, Director of the Wharton School, Dr. Leo S. Rowe of the same School, University of Pennsylvania, and Professor W. W. Willoughby of the Johns Hopkins University.[1]

I could come on for a personal conference on short notice, if one should be desired.

With my best respects, I am,

Very sincerely yours Henry J. Ford

ALS (WP, DLC). Enc.: CC MS, "Publications in Political Science."

[1] James Thomas Young, Director of the Wharton School of Finance and Commerce of the University of Pennsylvania; Leo Stanton Rowe, Professor and Head of the Department of Political Science, University of Pennsylvania; and Westel Woodbury Willoughby, Professor of Political Science at The Johns Hopkins University.

To the Board of Trustees of Princeton University

[Princeton, N. J.]
December 13th, 1907.

GENTLEMEN OF THE BOARD OF TRUSTEES:

I have the honor to submit my annual report for the year 1906-1907.

Since my last report we have had the pleasure of receiving the following additions to the teaching staff of the University:

Professor Edward Capps, Professor of Classics, who graduated with the degree of Bachelor of Arts from Illinois College in 1887 and who was Instructor in Greek and Latin in his alma mater, 1887-1888; who pursued graduate studies in Greek, Latin and Sanskrit at Yale University from 1888 to 1891, and who received from that institution in 1891 the degree of Doctor of Philosophy. Mr. Capps was Instructor in Latin in Yale, 1890-1891; Tutor in Latin in the same institution, 1891-1892; Assistant Professor of Greek at the University of Chicago, 1892-1896; studied in the

American School for Classical Studies at Athens, and at the Universities of Berlin, Munich, and Halle from 1893 to 1895; became Associate Professor of Greek at the University of Chicago in 1896, and Professor of Greek in the same institution in 1900, the chair which he occupied until coming to us. He was Lecturer on Greek Comedy and the Greek Theatre at Harvard University during the first half year, 1904-1905, and was Managing Editor of *Classical Philology* from 1906 to 1907. He is at present President of the Classical Association of the Middle West and South. Professor Capps' reputation as a classical scholar has placed him in the front rank of the students of the classical languages, and it is with especial pleasure that we welcome him to Princeton, where the faith in the disciplinary and illuminating power of those languages still continues vivid and effectual.

Mr. LeRoy Carr Barret, Preceptor in Classics, was graduated from Washington and Lee University with the degree of Bachelor of Arts in 1897 and received the degree of Master of Arts from the same university in the following year. From 1900 to 1903 he was a student of Sanskrit, Latin, and Greek at Johns Hopkins University, where for two years he held the Fellowship in Sanskrit. From 1903 to 1907 he served as Instructor in Latin in Johns Hopkins University.

Mr. Austin Morris Harmon, Preceptor in Classics, was graduated from Williams College with the degree of Bachelor of Arts in 1902. In 1903, after a year of graduate study at Yale University, he received from that institution the degree of Master of Arts. During the year 1903-1904 he continued his classical studies at Yale, and from 1904 to 1907 was a student at the American School of Classical Studies in Rome, where for two years he was a Fellow of the school and during the third year Carnegie Fellow in Classical Archæology.

Mr. Régis Michaud, who joins the staff of the University as Preceptor in Modern Languages, was graduated Bachelier ès lettres from the University of Lyons, France, in 1898, and in 1905 received the degree of Licencié ès lettres from the University of Paris. From 1903 to 1906 he was a student of Romance Philology at the Ecole des Hautes Etudes and Collège de France. From 1904 to 1906 he was Professor of French Literature at the Guilde Internationale in Paris. In 1906 he accepted a place on the teaching staff of the Rosemary Hall School at Greenwich, Connecticut, from which school he was called to Princeton.

The following have received appointments as Instructors or Assistants in the University: *In Philosophy*, George Washington Tapley Whitney, Ph.B., University of Vermont, 1897, A.M. 1902,

Ph.D. Cornell University, 1903; and Clement Leslie Vaughan, A.B. Harvard University 1903, Ph.D. 1905. *In History and Politics*, Benjamin Marsden Price, A.B. Princeton, 1904, B.C.L. Oxford University, 1907; Edwin William Pahlow, B.L. Wisconsin University, 1899, M.L., 1900, M.A. Harvard University, 1901; and Ivory Victor Iles, A.B. University of Kansas, 1904, A.M., 1905. *In Classics*, William Alexander Fleet, A.B. and A.M. University of Virginia, 1904; Paul Nixon, B.A. Wesleyan University, 1904, and M.A., 1905; Harry Brown Van Deventer, A.B. Yale University, 1903, A.M., 1904, Ph.D., 1907; and Herbert Pierrepont Houghton, A.B. Amherst College, 1901, A.M., 1904, Ph.D., Johns Hopkins University, 1907. *In Mathematics*, Elijah Swift, A.B., Harvard University, 1903, A.M., 1904, Ph.D., University of Göttingen, 1907. *In Chemistry*, William Richey Hulsizer, A.B. Princeton, 1907, and Isaac Ripple Schumaker, A.B. Princeton, 1907. *In Civil Engineering*, Nathaniel Dain, C.E. Princeton, 1907, Harry Newton Clark, C.E. Princeton, 1907, and William Earle Cory, C.E. Princeton, 1907. Mr. Price, Mr. Fleet and Mr. Nixon have for three years been Rhodes Scholars at the University of Oxford, Mr. Price at Wadham College, Mr. Fleet at Magdalen College, and Mr. Nixon at Balliol.

Dr. Duane Reed Stuart, last year Preceptor in Classics, has been advanced to the rank of Professor of Classics; and Mr. Christian Gauss, last year Preceptor in Modern Languages, has been advanced to the rank of Professor of Modern Languages.

Three Preceptors of last year's staff have resigned: Dr. Hiram Bingham, of History and Politics, to pursue studies in the history of South America which made long periods of residence in the field of his studies necessary; Dr. Henry Russell Spencer, of History and Politics, to accept the headship of a department at the University of Ohio; and Mr. Fred LeRoy Hutson, of the Department of Classics, to pursue further studies in his chosen field, which he had long had in contemplation.

Nothing specially calling for report has marked the progress of the year. It was a season passed in a quiet adjustment of the work of the class-room and preceptorial conference to the new plans and methods of study which have been instituted during the last five years of the administration of the University. I think that I can say that we have become still more deeply convinced by reason of the quiet and substantial success of our new plans that we have passed the period of experiment and are entering a period of satisfactory fruition. I think that my colleagues of the faculty would agree with me in saying that the work of the year was more solidly done and was lifted to a higher level than the work of any previous year that we remember. We feel that we have reason to congratulate ourselves upon the way in which the new course of study and the new methods of instruction have stood the test of use and experience. No modifications of any consequence have been necessary since the outset, and we hope that further experience will only confirm our success.

The comfort and convenience of class-room work and of preceptorial conferences have been immeasurably increased by the completion of McCosh Hall, a building which has in use confirmed in every way our anticipation of what it would be. It has increased our class-room space sufficiently to relieve entirely the old congestion, and it has added to the old rooms rooms of delightful proportion and unusual beauty and dignity. The building is a remarkable monument alike to the generosity and to the good taste of the donors, and the architect is deserving of very warm praise for the care and success with which he has worked out its spacious and convenient arrangements.

On the thirty-first of October last we had the pleasure of unveiling a beautiful sun-dial presented to the University by the generosity of Sir William Mather. The dial is an exact reproduction of the historic sun-dial constructed in 1551 by Charles Turnbull, that stands in the quadrangle of Corpus Christi College at Oxford. It is monumental in character, standing upon a broad base and lifting its shaft with the emblematic pelican borne upon its top to a height of more than twenty feet. It is placed just north of McCosh Hall in the newly graded portion of the ground which will constitute the court of the quadrangle of buildings which we have planned sooner or later to draw about the space behind Marquand Chapel. The unveiling of the sun-dial was rendered a very notable ceremony by the presence of the Right Honorable James Bryce, the British Ambassador to the United States, who, as a friend of Sir William Mather's, as a representative by long and distinguished connection of Oxford University, and as the spokesman of good will between the two nations, presented this singular and significant gift to the University in the name of the donor in a way which all who were present will long remember. It is pleasant to add that this interesting gift was made by Sir William Mather with the very cordial consent and good wishes of the authorities of Corpus Christi College.

Work has begun and is being rapidly pushed forward on the foundations of the new Physical Laboratory which it is hoped will be completed by the beginning of the academic year 1908-1909. This laboratory has been planned upon the most liberal scale and will be one of the most notable additions ever made to the teaching facilities of the University in the field of science.

The total number of graduate students, which was last year 112, is this year 113. Of this number 46 are devoting themselves exclusively to graduate study as against 38 last year, and 67 are combining graduate study in the University with work in Princeton Theological Seminary. Of the 46 regular graduate students, ten are in residence at Merwick and sixteen take their meals there.

The following table shows the number admitted to the University as undergraduates this year as compared with last:

	1906	1907
Freshmen without conditions	146	128
Freshmen with conditions	202	230
Specials	13	21
Seniors	2	3
Juniors	4	2
Sophomores	11	16
Totals	378	400

Of the students admitted upon examination in 1906, twenty-six for one reason or another did not come. Of those admitted this year, thirty did not come. So that the corrected figures for the two years are: 1906, 352; 1907, 370. The number of freshmen who entered the University in 1906 was 322, in 1907, 328, a gain of six in the entrance figures of this year as compared with those of last year. To these statistics the following should, for the full information of the Board, be added:

	1906	1907
Examined but not admitted	72	80
Preliminary and partial examinations	455	485

There was thus a gain of thirty in the number of preliminary and partial examinations this year as compared with a gain of eighteen last year and a loss of forty-eight the year preceding.

The total undergraduate enrollment of the University is 1188 and was last year 1235, a decrease of forty-seven. The figures of last year showed a decrease of forty-four as compared with the preceding year.

Respectfully submitted, WOODROW WILSON.[1]

Printed report (WP, DLC).

1 There is a TS copy of this report in WP, DLC.

From Paul Lendrum Blakely[1]

Dear Sir, St. Louis, December 14th, 1907.

Under the heading, "The Meaning of Education Missed," the Literary Digest for Dec. 14th[2] comments upon an address given by you to the Association of Colleges and Preparatory Schools, in New York on Nov. 29th. I do not know if you have been correctly reported, but as a teacher of the classics I would thoroughly agree with you that much of our high school and college work is anything but educational; and I would add that most of our American school programmes seem to have been devised by men who held the direct opposite of the belief so tersely enunciated by your father. The theories of one American University President—let him be unsung[3]—have done much to ruin real education in the United States. I sincerely trust that yours is the influence which is to lead our teachers as well as the public back to sanity in matters educational.

I should esteem it a great favour if you will let me know where I can obtain your address. The fragments gathered by the Literary Digest incite me to call like Oliver for more.

Believe me, Yours very sincerely, Paul L. Blakely.

TLS (WP, DLC).

1 Professor of Literature at St. Louis University.

2 "The Meaning of Education Missed," *Literary Digest*, xxxv (Dec. 14, 1907), 915-16.

3 He referred undoubtedly to Charles William Eliot.

To Moses Taylor Pyne

My dear Momo: Princeton, N. J. December 16th, 1907.

I am glad to say I am beginning to be well enough to take up a little business, and turn at once to your letter of the 6th.

I am clearly of the opinion that it would not be wise to involve the University, in the present state of our finances, in any such obligations as it undertook in connection with Patton Hall. My own judgment would be that the wiser course would be to wait until the classes concerned have either collected the whole of their subscriptions or are able to anticipate in some way the balances that they lack.

In the meantime I would suggest (and would be obliged to you if you would see that the suggestion is carried out) that upon his next visit to New York Mr. Cram have a conference with Mr. Morris with regard to the whole question of the continuation of the buildings along Brokaw Field or the possible substitution of dormitories upon the higher part of the campus. My own preference just now would of course be to have a dormitory erected parallel with Seventy-Seven Hall as Mr. Cram's plans contemplate, parallel, I mean, on the North with the road which Mr. Cram has planned intervening. It may be that in conference with Mr. Morris, Mr. Cram and he can make some suggestion of such a tower or mass connected with a building at that place as would meet the views and ambitions of the Class of '84. We could then be guided, as I think we must be in the circumstances, by the choice of that class. We definitely offered them the opportunity to erect the tower by Brokaw Field and cannot now withdraw that choice. But it may be that Mr. Morris and Mr. Cram can suggest an arrangement which would be equally satisfactory to them and meet the objections of those members of the class who in the first place desired to make a gift to the University which would yield more income than the meager accommodations of the Magdalen Tower would yield.

I was sincerely sorry that you got away without my seeing you.

Hoping that you are all well,

Always faithfully yours, [Woodrow Wilson]

CCL (WWP, UA, NjP).

From Edwin Grant Conklin

My dear President Wilson, Philadelphia, Dec. 16, 1907.

Your kind and cordial letter, in which you approve of my coming to Princeton next year, should have been answered long ago, but I have been waiting until I could report to you some of the proposed plans for my work at Princeton.

I have had several conferences with Professors McClure, Rankin and Dahlgren, and as a result it has seemed advisable that I should take charge of the work in Junior Biology. In order that the course may be made as effective as possible I should be glad to associate with me, in certain portions of the work, other members of the biological staff. This is the plan which is followed at Columbia and at Pennsylvania, and it not only makes the course more instructive and interesting but it also serves to make the students acquainted with the instructors in the department, at the beginning of their work in biology.

I shall expect also to take part in the graduate work and to assist in any other work of the department where I can be of service.

Laboratory room for myself and an assistant can probably be provided without much trouble or expense in the room on the third floor of the School of Science Hall in which the collection of birds is now stored.

I shall send you soon, for your approval, a list of apparatus and supplies which I shall need, and I hope within a few months to be able to nominate a good man to serve as my assistant.

Cordially yours, E. G. Conklin.

ALS (WWP, UA, NjP).

From Moses Taylor Pyne

My dear Woodrow: New York December 17th, 1907.

I am glad to hear that you are commencing to improve and trust that you will not try to take up any business now, but let things go and devote your attention to getting entirely well and strong. It is "A stitch in time that saves nine" and there is no use of your trying to take up matters before you are entirely recovered only to break down again, while by going off and taking a long, sensible and proper vacation you can bring yourself up to concert pitch again.

My own belief is that you should leave as soon as possible and go to the South of Europe or some place where you will be out of touch with Princeton matters, and at the same time, where you will have a chance to travel and amuse yourself and study and devote your whole time to getting well.

I am glad to hear what you say about the building of the Patton Hall Extension this spring. I agree with you that it would be very foolish to undertake it. I had a short talk with Mr. Cram the other day and am sending that part of your letter referring to the new dormitory, which Morris has been preparing, to Mr. Cram to take up with Morris. I agree with you that, if possible, we must keep it away from the Brokaw Field and put it up near the '77 building.

With best wishes of the season and the earnest hope that you will devote your time this winter to taking care of yourself, leaving the University affairs to be administered by your lieutenants, who are perfectly competent men and only anxious to carry out your wishes, believe me, as ever,

Very sincerely yours, M. Taylor Pyne

TLS (WP, DLC).

From Westel Woodbury Willoughby

Baltimore, Md.
My dear President Wilson: December 17, 1907.

Replying to your inquiry of December 16 I would say that though I know Mr. Ford well, and admire him, and though he last year gave a one-hour-a-week lecture course in my department, and is giving another one this year, I do not feel confident of my ability to judge regarding his ability to give systematic instruction to college students. Mr. Ford is certainly an acute thinker, he is widely read in certain parts of political literature, and he writes well. His conversation is almost always suggestive and stimulating and I have no doubt that his lectures have the same qualities. I have not myself heard him lecture, but understand that he lectures in a conversational and rather informal manner. His lectures have been to graduate students, and have served as a sort of *hors-d'oeuvre* to the more systematic instruction which I give or am supposed to give. Mr. Ford has not, I am inclined to think, paid much attention to the legal phases of political science, or to analytical political theory, his reading having been more largely, if not exclusively, in the sociological and what I suppose you would call the "merely literary" fields.

I do not wish to be understood to assert that Mr. Ford has not ability to give satisfactory systematic courses in politics to undergraduate students, but only to say that I have no actual knowledge regarding it. Speaking with absolute frankness, I myself if I should be called upon to take action, would hesitate to assume that he has the ability, though it may easily be that in so doing I would do Mr. Ford an injustice. I shall be glad to give any further information that you may desire and which I am able to give.

Very sincerely yours, W. W. Willoughby

TLS (WP, DLC).

From Cleveland Hoadley Dodge

Dear Tommie New York Dec 18th 1907

Thanks awfully for your two lovely letters.[1]

My heart goes out to you & I long to have you get thoroughly well.

If a good solid rest is the best thing for you, you must take the medicine, not only because we love you but because we love Princeton & you are it's best & biggest asset.

God bless you, old chap. With warmest Xmas greetings

Ever affly Cleve

ALS (WP, DLC).

[1] They are missing.

From Henry Burling Thompson

Wilmington, Del.

My dear President Wilson: 12th Mo., 18th, 1907.

I sincerely hope that you are in better health than when I was last in Princeton. I came up the day of the Yale debate,[1] but did not call to see you, for I concluded, from my conversation with Dean Fine, I would only bother you.

I have received a letter this morning from Parish & Schroeder, in which they say they have prepared a set of water color sketches of the Geological and Biological Building, which they want the Grounds & Buildings Committee to view and approve. I have requested them to forward these plans by express to Mr. Bunn's care, and have written to Bunn that he had better submit them to you previous to the meeting of our Committee.

I spent about an hour with Professor McClure on the sketch plans of the various floors of the building, and, as far as I know, with some minor changes, the plans are satisfactory to the Biological and Geological Faculty.

The suggestion that Professor McClure and I have made to Mr. Schroeder is that we have probably overdone the ventilating system. From my investigation of some of the more recent buildings, I find that the ventilating systems are more elaborate than necessary; in fact, I believe the system installed in the Gymnasium, which is a most expensive system, has never been used.

I have asked Schroeder to make a careful investigation of this point, for I believe we can save some money, which we will need for the Vivarium, for the Vivarium, as originally planned, does not meet the views of Professors Conklin and McClure, and it is necessary to save $6,000.00 somewhere in the building in order to give them what they want.

You will note that I am writing to you in reference to this matter, in place of Mr. Russell, the Chairman of the Committee, but at his request, I have relieved him of the charge of this particular building, and propose to look after it until its completion.

Yours very sincerely, Henry B. Thompson

TLS (WP, DLC).

[1] December 6, 1907, when Princeton won the debate with Yale held in Alexander Hall.

From Salomé Machado Warren

My dear Mr. Wilson, Cambridge, Mass Dec. 18, 1907

Thank you with all my heart for your sympathy with me and my children in our irreparable loss, and for the tribute you have paid him not only in what you say of him as man and scholar but in the trouble you have taken to secure for us a material token that he was most faithful to his high calling and that he achieved.

The Carnegie pension is a godsend to us, as you can well understand, but it is more than a means of keeping the wolf from the door. I prize it as a recognition of my husband's eminence.

Give my warmest regards to Mrs. Wilson and thank her for her sympathy. Wishing I might serve you or yours some day in little or great ways, believe me

Yours faithfully, Salomé Machado Warren

I wonder if the first reward of the faithful after death, is a full consciousness of the good he has done and the inspiration he has supplied on earth. If so, judging from the hundreds of wonderful letters from everywhere, my husband's spirit must be having one great source of joy.

ALS (WP, DLC).

To Louis Wiley[1]

My dear Mr. Wiley: Princeton, N. J. December 20th, 1907.

Allow me to thank you most sincerely for your kind letter of December 19th and to express my very great regret that absence from the country will prevent my attending the annual dinner of the Society of the Genesee on the evening of February 8th next. I am expecting to go to Bermuda the latter part of January for a stay of some four or five weeks.

Pray express to the committee of the society my warm appreciation and sincere regret.

Very truly yours, Woodrow Wilson

TLS (L. Wiley Papers, NRU).

1 Business Manager of the *New York Times*.

From George Lansing Raymond[1]

My dear Doctor, Washington. D. C. Dec. 20, 1907

I have been reading with much pleasure, for which I wish to thank you, your remarks on education as reported in last week's

Literary Digest. They are somewhat in the line of what I said myself several years ago—to tell the truth—because I was troubled about the situation at Princeton, & did not know what to do except to appeal in a general way to public sentiment. It is wonderful how much a position like that which you have enables a man to do, & it is equally wonderful how much you yourself in a very little time have done as a fact. Dr. [Alfred Ernest] Stearns, Principal of Phillips Academy Andover, told me, the other day, that he considers Princeton to rank, now, at the head of all the institutions of our country in doing good & effective educational work. If you had lived in New England & associated with New Englanders as much as I have, you would appreciate, perhaps, better than you now do what such a remark from such a man means! You ought, at least, to know of it. To tell you of it is really a sufficient reason for writing you. I am sorry that the Trustees have not sustained you—fully at least—in your position with reference to the clubs. I hoped that by making graduate club-men members of quads &c you might meet their objections. Of course you are eternally right in your main propositions. The clubs would be a social, undemocratic nuisance, even if they did not kill—as I fear they will do eventually—the Halls.[2] I don't suppose, however, that every evil in the world can be righted, but it is too bad to find acknowledged evils encouraged by those who should be governed by the highest motives.

Meantime, you have re-made Princeton as an educational institution. This is something that, as an outsider, I can tell you now is acknowledged, apparently, by everybody.

I will send you the paper to which I referred in my opening.[3] Wishing yourself, Mrs. Wilson & all the family a Merry Christmas believe me Very sincerely, Geo. L. Raymond

ALS (WP, DLC).

[1] Former Professor of Aesthetics at Princeton, at this time he held a similar position at George Washington University.

[2] That is, the American Whig and Cliosophic Societies.

[3] It is missing in the various Wilson collections.

From Ralph Adams Cram

Dear Dr. Wilson: Boston, December 23, 1907.

Mr. Pyne has sent me an extract from your letter with regard to the probable tower offered by the class of 84. I shall be only too glad to take this matter up with Mr. Morris.

The general scheme that I have submitted permits the erection of this "Magdalen" tower on Brokaw Field, more or less where it was indicated by Mr. Morris, but you will remember that my suggestion was that, instead of prolonging dormitories to the south and so across the southerly end of the field, the group be terminated much nearer the position of the Gymnasium and continued north until it joins onto this same Gymnasium. I quite feel that while this tower might still be built at this place, it would not be a particularly effective position, nor do I feel that this is a good place for it, even were the tentative scheme submitted by Mr. Morris to be carried out, for there doesn't seem to be much sense in building a very lofty tower, which depends for its effect on its height, on the lowest land available; rather should this tower be placed on high land. The ideal position for it would be over the northerly entrance to the future freshman quad, which I hope may ultimately take the place of the present University Hall. This position, however, will not be available for a long time, as I don't conceive that you have any idea of tearing down University Hall for some years. I cannot see that any good and convincing position for this proposed tower offers itself on the southerly side of this proposed group of dormitories: on the other hand, I wholly coincide with you in believing that the very next group of dormitories to be constructed should, as you say, parallel the proposed 77 Hall on the other side of the proposed carriage entrance to the campus from University Road. This new dormitory could be built perfectly well at this time and without interfering in any degree with University Hall itself, which might remain indefinitely; still, no opportunity offers itself here for such a tower as the Class of '84 has in mind. There is another good place for this tower, which would be adjoining West Hall immediately to the south and closing the vista west from the present chapel. If you look at the large scale plan, a copy of which is in Mr. Bunn's possession, you will see this position I indicate.

Since writing the above, I have considered still further the question of the '84 tower, on the line of Nassau Street, and find that it can perfectly well be built at this time without conflicting with University Hall. If you look at this same plan to which I have referred above, you will see that I have shown, by vaulting lines, a future tower on Nassau Street, and about on the line of the face of University Hall. This would be the great entrance to the future group of freshman quads. This position occupies the site of the house next east from University Hall. I understand that all these houses, between the latter building and the Presbyterian Church, are now owned by the University and may soon be removed. Now if this is true, then here is unquestionably the place for the 84 tower, and if you can obtain enough money to build some portion of the dormitories connected with this tower, at the time the tower itself is built, then, by all means, let us induce the class of '84 to accept this position for its proposed building. The site is infinitely to be preferred to the one on Brokaw Field, since it occupies the highest land and lies full on Nassau Street. It would be a very great thing if at this time we could begin the construction of the great line of buildings along Nassau Street, which ultimately is to cover the entire northwest corner of the University grounds.

If you will kindly look over the general plan in Mr. Bunn's office, and let me know what your ideas are as to the best site for the 84 tower, I will take the matter up with Mr. Morris at once, but my recommendation is, first; the Nassau Street site, second; the West Hall site, third; the Brokaw Field site.

Very respectfully yours, R A Cram.
Supervising Architect.

TLS (WP, DLC).

From Moses Taylor Pyne

My dear Woodrow: New York December 24th, 1907.

Mr. Cram, in answer to my letter, has sent me a copy of a letter which he has written you, which more or less covers the ground. It is a difficult question to answer as we cannot foresee exactly what shall be done with the Guyot House,[1] especially as there still remains a mortgage on the property, but, fortunately, we do not have to take this matter up immediately as I think there is no chance of our building this spring.

I understand from C. C.[2] that you go to Bermuda immediately after the Board meeting. I wish I could persuade you to go sooner, as I feel that it is of vital importance to the University that you get well and strong again and every day you remain in Princeton is postponing your cure.

C. C. also tells me that you are thinking of going to Indianapolis on the 25th. As one of your warmest friends please allow me to protest against this. It is not fair to you and you are taking great chances in making this long railroad journey and undertaking this strain. You have a perfectly satisfactory excuse in the fact that your health will not permit you to do so, and I do beg of you not to take this risk and undergo the strain of the journey.

I had hoped to see you before now but it has been impossible for me to get to Princeton, as I have been so pressed with work, but I cannot urge too strongly that you postpone this trip.

With my kindest regards to Mrs. Wilson, and the best wishes for a Merry Christmas and a Happy New Year, believe me, as ever, Yours very sincerely, M Taylor Pyne

TLS (WP, DLC).

1 The former residence of Arnold Henry Guyot, Professor of Geology and Physical Geography at Princeton, 1854-84, which was located at 31 Nassau Street, just east of University Hall; it was moved to Greenholm in 1909.

2 Cornelius Cuyler Cuyler.

An Address in Indianapolis to the Indiana State Teachers' Association[1]

[Dec. 27, 1907]

Mr. Chairman, Mr. President, Ladies and Gentlemen: I was very much interested to hear Mr. Williams[2] say that this was the fifty-fourth annual convention of this Association. Ever since three years before I was born you have been self-disciplining, have been giving yourselves the catholicity of taste and patience to hear me this afternoon. I can only imagine how many addresses you must have listened to, and I shall be able to judge before I get through how well you have endured them. It is a great pleasure to me to feel that this is not an ordinary audience, that this is a body of persons whose interest centers in a great particular influential profession. There are many things it might be necessary for me to say to a mixed audience that it is not necessary for me to say to you.

I am not the extraordinary person Mr. Williams described. I could listen to that description with the greatest and sincerest approbation, because I regarded it as a work of art. I am simply an ordinary person with a habit of saying what he thinks, and I have come here this afternoon to ask you to bear with me while I say what I think. You know perfectly well when a man prefaces his remarks that way what you will get—you will get something which will be exaggerated. When a man prepares himself consciously and with unusual fervor to speak the truth, he generally overleaps the mark and says something more than the truth; and, inasmuch as I do not intend to speak to you for an inordinate length of time, it will be very convenient if you will allow me to

1 Delivered in Tomlinson Hall in Indianapolis.

2 Charles Richard Williams, Princeton 1875, editor of the *Indianapolis News*.

do that this afternoon; because if you try to draw in vivid colors only one phase of a great subject you will certainly obscure and belittle the other. I beg you to believe that the things I omit to say I do not omit out of malice, but only because of my keen interest in the few things I do intend to say.

I want to speak to you about some of the utilities of education. This is a utilitarian country. We are proud that we know what is useful and what is useless. We are proud that we are a practical people who do not waste their time upon matters of mere fancy which do not set their lives forward. America is a very vast and complex whole. It is, I dare say, impossible for the intelligence of any one man to grasp it as a whole. For America is no one thing. When I am asked by foreigners, "Is not so and so true of America?" I invariably reply, "What part of America?" Nothing is true of all of America. You cannot sum up the various life of a great people like this in any single generalization. It is folly, therefore, to try to make standards which will fit all the conditions of this country, whether of education or of anything else. The size of this country is something we are apt to be proud of; but I think we ought to be very careful not to be proud of it unless we are as big as it is. A little man cannot afford to be proud of a large country, because it is so obvious he is an insignificant and negligible part of it. We have been laughed at by foreigners for boasting of the size, the physical size of America. "As if," they say, "you made it." Well, we did not make America, but we took possession of it; and I suppose a man is as big as the thing he conquers, and a race as great as the task it accomplishes. And when you think of the great physical and political task this nation has accomplished in getting the great continent of America under the plow, under the walls of the factory, under the dominance of government, you will know that there is something in the size of America of which we can afford to be proud, because we have possessed it. But the task of possession, the initial task of development, is a comparatively simple thing with the thing that is immediately ahead of us in our generation.

It was once a tolerably easy thing to serve America. The mere stroke of the axe in the frontier forest rang some of that tune of conquest which was going forward as we beat our way over the eastern mountains, and trod our way across the medial plain, and the[n] breasted the great mountains of the Pacific slope. Every physical task accomplished was part of the great patriotic duty of making America subject to the will of the American people. But all that is done now. You know that until the census of 1890 was taken the census takers, when they drew their maps, were always able to draw a frontier somewhere between the Atlantic and the Pacific. But in 1890 it became impossible any longer to draw a continuous line at any rate which marked any frontier within this country. It is a significant thing that so soon as we found that out we provided ourselves with a frontier on the other side of the Pacific. The fact that the frontier on the continent of America has disappeared means that our task is no longer extensive, but intensive. The unsettled places are filling in thicker, thicker, thicker. We are beginning to send great canals and irrigation across the deserts of the western part of the country in order that there may be room for this thickening population and sustenance for a great people.

And so, turning from this crude task we had in the beginning, we have to finish the work. Now we must turn about and give them their artistic touches of completion. And there are a great many things that we find we did very crudely indeed. We have boasted hitherto of nothing so much as our form of government, and yet we have suddenly found there was one form of government, namely, city government, which we have made abominably ill, and that there is not another civilized country in the world that can show as many ill governed cities as America. And so we talk about the Grand Rapids plan of city government, and about the Galveston plan,[3] and are beginning all over again, and asking men, north, east, west and south, "How are you going to govern your cities?" knowing it is something we have yet to learn. We have yet to learn how to govern! Why, we have supposed that is what we have been teaching the world! It will not do us any harm to have some of the boastfulness taken out of it. Hereafter we have got to get down to business and saw wood. That is the reason hifalutin oratory is going out. We have an uncomfortable feeling that it lacks substantial foundation. Even to build an air castle you have to have some footing to start upon, I dare say.

And those self-gratulatory addresses about our political success, to which we used to listen with self-indulgence, now causes [cause] a deep uneasiness because we wonder after all if we are warranted in the self-indulgence.

And it is for this age of difficulty and of reconstruction that we teachers have to furnish a systematic education. And the first thing we have to admit to ourselves is that we haven't any system

3 The Galveston plan was of course the commission plan of government instituted in that city in 1901, which had spread widely across the country by 1907. The Grand Rapids plan was a variation on the Galveston plan. It provided for a city government by four general managers appointed by the mayor, each in charge of a single department. This plan was rejected by the voters of Grand Rapids, Michigan. See Benjamin P. De Witt, *The Progressive Movement* (New York, 1915), pp. 300-309.

of education. We have a great deal of education, but it is very much like what is illustrated in a story I heard the other day. Some one asked another if he did not think Miss So and So had a great deal of taste. "Yes," he said, "a great deal, and some of it is good." We have a great deal of education, and some of it is good. But it is a miscellaneous mass; there is no system in it. What living man or woman could describe our education in less than a month's time? Under what categories will you sum it up? You can not sum anything up which is not founded upon plain and recognized principles. And the proposition I begin with is that we have no system of education. We have all sorts of education, good, bad and indifferent; and we have some things called education that are not education at all. We are serving a material and a utilitarian people. How do we try to serve them? By putting everything into the curriculum of our schools and colleges that anybody suggests. I got the catalogue of a college the other day which said that that college was offering two hundred and fifty different courses, and would offer any other not there mentioned upon the request of five pupils. If you don't see what you want, ask for it! It does not make any difference how young you are, it does not make any difference how ignorant you are, it does not make any difference how self-indulgent you are, why, if we haven't got what you want, my dear boy, we will get it for you if you can find four other persons who have the same desire! In every educational journal, in every educational discussion I hear, I find somebody complaining that their particular interest is not included in the school and college curricula, and our present school and college curricula have become real curiosities in the miscellany of their contents. I was urging something like this the other day and a young gentleman, one of those terribly earnest young persons whose brows are always knitting, came up to me and said, "You seem to base what you said on the theory that one subject is of greater educational value than another." "Why, certainly, I did," I said, "I am a sane man." He looked a little hurt at that, and I said, "Don't you think one subject is more educationally valuable than another?" "Certainly not," he said. "Then," I said, "We had better not discuss this matter any further, because it would take us all the time it would require to unmake our personalities and make them over to come to an agreement." I cannot discuss education with a man that believes that shorthand is of as great educational value as Sanskrit. I cannot, because I am made that way. I mean I am given some knowledge of what the different bodies of studies are and of what their mastery involves, and having been given that I cannot base an argument upon what is not a fact. I say I am constituted that way, because that is the way my mind works. And if my neighbor's mind does not work that way we will have to adjourn the discussion. My father used to say there is no use trying to reason out of a man's mind what reason did not put into it. You have got to be a homeopathist in this business, you cannot be an allopath. You cannot administer reason to extract what reason did not establish. If any considerable number of this audience think that all subjects are of equal educational value, I am willing to stop while they retire, because I will do nothing but offend them from this point out, and I do not wish to offend anyone.

I believe that we have got into an almost inextricable confusion in our education in this country by not stopping to think what it is we would be at. In the first place, there are two kinds of education which we have been constantly confusing. There is the practical education whose object is to give the pupil some particular skill, to prepare him immediately for some particular occupation. Let me, for the sake of brevity and convenience, call that technical education. And let me say further that technical education is what we must provide for the vast majority of the young people of this country. In what I am going to say this afternoon I am not only not disparaging technical education, I am trying to save technical education by giving it a distinct standing of its own that belongs to it, so that it will not be confounded with that other and more general kind of education which is my particular theme this afternoon. Let me say it is our business to make most of the young people in this country skilled mechanics. I do not use the word "mechanic" in any narrow sense. There are mechanics of the mind as well as mechanics of the hand. It is our business to give to the vast majority of the young people of this country a technical knowledge and a technical skill which will equip this country as it is not now equipped in the great physical undertakings upon which its material power and its fame among the nations in large part rests. The fact that the label, "Made in Germany," commends wares on our markets, whether it be truly put upon the wares or not, is in itself a condemnation of our methods of education. There ought to be nothing made in Germany better than it is made in America; and if there is anything better made in Germany than it is made in America it is because Germany recognizes the distinction between the technical education which must be given to a large majority of the young people and the liberal education which only a small minority of the children can get. Let us be done, then, once and for all, with the futile effort of trying to combine the two theories.

One object of education, as Mr. Williams said, which belongs to both kinds is discipline. Now you cannot get discipline in little pieces; you have got to get it in long, connected pieces of work. You cannot get discipline in a dozen things at once; you must concentrate, concentrate, concentrate in order to get discipline. Information is not education. I was reading a very interesting article not long ago about teaching agriculture in our schools. How are you going to teach agriculture in schools? Only by giving the pupils information about what they have no opportunity to do. Now you can teach the chemistry underlying agriculture—you can teach it badly, but you can teach it. Most of the pupils are not mature enough for it yet. You can teach it, if you wish to try; you can describe the grains and their habits, you can describe soils; you can describe all the conditions which constitute the information underlying agriculture, and after you have imparted all that information you will not have taught agriculture. You cannot teach agriculture inside a house, whether that house be a schoolhouse or any other kind. And there is no discipline in information. Some of the best informed men I ever met could not reason at all. You know what you mean by an extraordinarily well informed man. You mean a man who always has some fact at his command to trip you up; and you will generally find that all this man can do is to throw little chunks of fact in the way so you will stumble on them and make yourself ridiculous. And if you say, "Very well, please be kind enough to generalize on this matter," you will find he can not do it. Information is not education. Information is the raw material of education, but it is not education. You could inform your pupils, supposing it were possible, with regard to everything in the world, and inform them accurately, and leave them uneducated, provided you did not subject them to the discipline or uniting the facts you had given them in some system of thought. The things that I possess are not mine unless I can use them in any intellectual sense of the term. I have one of my own books in a Japanese translation,[4] and it does not belong to me, I don't know what is in it. The fact is I have forgotten the information in the original. I would have to go to the English version to find out the things I once knew. I wrote that book twenty years ago and I am a very much better educated man than I was when I knew all the things in it, because there are things in it I can now disprove. I know now enough to know that they are not so. And I don't care whether a man faces me with the statement in a book of my own or not; I am a free American citizen

[4] See Midori Komatz to WW, Nov. 10, 1895, n. 2, Vol. 9.

and I am going to believe what I know now, not what I knew when I wrote the book.

The modern system of education is a process of contenting the student with what the textbook contains, and any pupil who is contented with what the textbook contains is not educated. He is just like a little bird on a branch with his mouth open waiting to have things put in it. My father, who was addicted to strong terms, once said to me, "The mind is not a prolix gut to be stuffed; it is a digestive organ, it is an assimilating organ, and what it does not assimilate it rejects and gets no profit from." And if you treat the mind, as you do treat the mind of the present young American, as a prolix gut to be stuffed, why, the young American when he gets to be an old American is going to be a useless American, unless in spite of you he learns how to use his mind. Now when I say "in spite of you," I am including myself. I do not recognize any difference in questions of education between the primary school and the university. It does not make any difference what stage of education you are talking about, the same things are true of all of them. Let us make up our minds that we will not go on attempting a miscellany of information, but that we will divide our teaching according to its objects; that if the object is technical we are going to stick to the technical processes until they are mastered as a discipline, and if we are going to extend the education to those things not technical we are going to stick to a few of those things until something like a mastery of them has been established by the student.

If I had my way I would take every child and keep him on the same track, in the same regions of endeavor, from the time he left the elementary school until he graduated from the university, with the certainty that, being master of a few things, he could make conquests of as many more as he chose. Now I do not mean to say we can go back to the old single curriculum, because the modern body of knowledge is too great and various; but I do mean to say that for each pupil we can lay down a definite and simple line of study. Keeping each student to a definite and simple line of study we shall discipline, whereas, if we do not confine him to such a line we shall never discipline him. If you try to teach him many things you will teach him nothing. It does not make any difference to me whether you accept that proposition or not, nature is going to enforce it against you in a generation. You are at perfect liberty to try to teach each child of America everything, and you will only teach him nothing. It is not my funeral; it is his funeral. But I do take the liberty of saying that you do not understand what education is for unless you begin to raise the banner now before worse things come, and unless written upon it are these two words "Simplification," "Concentration."

You cannot effect a miscellaneous discipline; you must effect a concentrated discipline, and unless you effect a concentrated discipline you have effected no discipline at all. Now, that is the ground that belongs to all kind of education, liberal and technical. What do I mean by liberal education? The matter with American [America] socially and politically is that so many men's minds are immersed, caught hard and fast in particular occupations. The trouble with America is that so many men are thinking in the terms of the things they are doing, that they cannot think in the terms of what other men are doing, and therefore cannot think in national terms of what the nation is doing. That is the reason that the progress of America depends upon a liberal education for as many persons as can afford it. It is not that one kind of child needs a technical education and another a liberal education. It is that most children are not going to have a chance to get a liberal education, but as many of them as can afford it ought to have it; not for their own sakes merely, for I suppose for a man's own sake a liberal education is a sort of indulgence, but for the sake of the nation. Liberal training is part of the training of the statesmanship of mind for most people; it is a process of lifting men's minds above the level of their daily tasks and giving them a glimpse of the map of the world, so that statesmen may be checked by thinking of the people to whom they speak, and so that out of the ranks of the people there may constantly arise those who have knowledge of their day and generation and can speak to their people like prophets of things to come.

It is for this reason we must give as many minds as possible a liberal education. There is no richer reservoir of supply than a great democratic people. You do not call this lad or that maiden out to the privileges of a liberal education because of his family or her lineage, or his money or her privilege; but because every American citizen who is economically at liberty should seek the highest things in the gift of the nation, and so give back to the nation those high things of which it stands in need. That is the argument for a liberal education. And by a liberal education I mean an education which does not concentrate its attention upon particular individual interests; but seeks to acquaint the mind with those great bodies of thought which are meant for the enlightenment of the world. For while discipline inheres in all education, enlightenment is the particular word of a liberal education. Discipline, of course, for without discipline education is of no avail, but also enlightenment, light thrown upon life, light thrown upon the phenomena of the universe, light thrown upon the course of human history, light, always light, so that men and women who stand in it can see the road they travel and know the bearing their lives have upon the lives of mankind along steadily rising heights up which man is struggling with sweat and blood.

Now I take it a liberal education has four necessary elements. Everybody seeking a liberal education should master some one great science; but only one, only one. If you disperse your energies within the time goven [given] for such a one you will not master the one. It is also necessary that every pupil seeking a liberal education should have some knowledge, some sufficient and considerable knoweldge [knowledge], of the great body of philosophy. By philosophy I do not mean figments of the mind; I do not mean the subtelties [subtleties] woven by men who interest themselves in those things that are distant from the common experience of men. By philosophy I mean some knowledge of the secrets of the human mind, some knoweldge [knowledge] of the roads that human thought has traveled, some guiding acquaintance with the things that men have attempted and have succeeded at or failed at.

I had a colleague that had not traveled the broad paths of philosophy. He did not know what men had attempted to do and failed. He spent five good years of his life writing a book which fortunately before he published he submitted to another colleague who had traveled these high roads. The friend said, "Why, my dear fellow, you have spent five years trying to establish what has been exploded ever since Aristotle!" The experiences of the human mind, the things that are fancied to be true and are not true. If you do not travel these roads you will be like the American people in regard to their currency question. Once every generation the American people has to find out it had better not coin silver free. I state that as a historical fact that every generation has had to find out. Every generation has found it out, fortunately, but it seems a great waste of time for each generation to forget [what] the preceding generation knew. We have been learning that lesson ever since the days of the old confederation which made the present government of the United States necessary in order to take the nonsense out of it. I often think that those persons who think education should only be concerned with the things of the present day must be in favor of the free coinage of silver. Now those people who believe only in the things of the present day, who believe you can establish an intellectual coinage independent of the intellectual attainments of another day, I believe always vote for the free coinage of silver. One country cannot establish a coinage independent of all other nations unless it wishes to stop trading with all other nations. You can try it, of course. You cannot stop trading intellectually with other generations, and therefore there is no way in which you can establish a standard of intellectual values which belong only to this generation. The history of thought is indispensible to every liberally trained man.

Then he has got to know something about some one language. Most of us do not know our own language, to judge by the way we use it. The American systematically avoids the use of his own language by using slang. That is a deliberate and cowardly device for avoiding the difficulties of English grammar and vocabulary. And I take it that if a man really masters some one language he will have got into him something that is of the essence of science. The best teacher I ever had[5] used to say to me, "When you frame a sentence don't do it as if you were loading a shotgun, but as if you were loading a rifle. Don't fire in such a way and with such a load that while you hit the thing you aim at you will hit a lot of things in the neighborhood besides; but shoot with a single bullet and hit that one thing alone." The studious and collected use of language is an act of precision; it is the process of eliminating surplusage and embodying only those things which are of the substance of the statement itself. It is an attempt always to fire for the one thing, and in the use of language we ought to be like the Boers in South Africa, who when they go out intending to bring back one piece of game carry only one bullet. Now when you get loaded with language after that fashion you will find nobody is anxious to get into a controversy with you about anything.

One of the most noteworthy things about Abraham Lincoln was that when he was a mere lad he realized that one of the instruments by which to make conquests of your fellow men was the instrument of speech, and he trained himself from boyhood to manhood in such a use of the English language as would compel his fellow citizens to know exactly what he meant to say. For the purpose of my present argument it matters not whether it be French, English, or Greek, or Latin, or German, if you have mastered the language you have made all intellectual conquests comparatively easy.

Then I take it that everybody must exhibit to his mind some at any rate of the processes of history and politics. No person can

[5] He meant his father.

be said to be liberally trained who does not know the greater events and tendencies of history and the greater principles and practices of politics. And when I have said that I have merely said that simplification should not be carried so far as not to include in all liberal training these elements, scientific thinking, philosophical comprehension, precision of statement, mastery of language and a knowledge of human experience. If you teach every lad four subjects, and teach them to him from the time he enters the grammar school until he graduates from college, look out for him after that! He is going to make an impression on his generation, or the laws of nature are going to be reversed. But if you try to teach him a dozen subjects every day in twenty or forty minute periods he will dissolve in thin air and become part of the armosphere [atmosphere] of his generation.

Now what are you going to do as to the method? Why, several things seem plain to me. You must first think out your body of studies; you must first make up your mind that some things do not train as much as you would like to train; that there are some things that do not enlighten; that there are some things that do not sufficiently educate to make it worth your while to undertake to get them. Eliminate. The real courage we need as teachers is the courage to eliminate, not the cowardice to add to our present curriculum. We should have the courage to eliminate and say, "This thing does not train as thoroughly as that does; therefore we will not have this and we will have that. You ask us to add this thing. We will not do it; we cannot teach it in such a way as to give enlightenment; therefore we will not teach it." A thoroughly weeded, discriminating, brought-out body of studies is what we need in each stage of our education. Then we need something we have never given ourselves in this generation in college until some very recent years, and that is a systematic sequence of studies. You would think from some of our college curricula it did not make any different [difference] whether you came in the front door or back door. Fortunately you cannot study mathematics backward. You can study philosophy backward if you are fool enough; you can study science backward if you have the temerity, and you can study history upside down. You can learn so much you will know no history at all. You can follow your taste in our colleges, or in some of them, but the lines of taste are not always the lines of intelligence. In all the education I have anything personal to do with I take the liberty of going upon the presumption that, having been connected with education longer than the various young gentlemen who come under my instruction, I know more about it, and therefore I say, "My dear young fellow, you have got to begin here. After you have chosen your body of studies you have got to go in here, and if you don't want to you have got to go somewhere else." Nobody is admitted by any window, nobody is admitted by any cellar door, nobody is admitted first by the attic. A systematic sequence of study, and then a systematic combination of studies. All of these things are necessary for a liberal training. We are trying a great many experiments, and it does not do knowledge any harm. Doctor Holmes used to say the truth was no invalid; no matter how roughly you treated her her constitution would stand it. But we are treating the truth very roughly these days, and one thing I feel like protesting against to the Society for the Prevention of Cruelty to Animals, and that is basing our teaching of children upon what is called "child psychology." I know two gentlemen who have written books on child psychology. To my certain knowledge one of them never knew more than three children—his own—and is not trusted for advice upon any particular subject whatever. I can tell you the names of dozens of schools that are training the poor little creatures that attend them in accordance with the theories of that man. I protest against it in the name of humanity. One of the interesting singularities of that kind of teaching is that we teach the children always as if we were bent upon keeping them children. They will grow up in spite of us, and the object of education is to prepare them to become mature. I tell you plainly I think most of the teaching that is done in the schools attended by the younger children seems to be meant to see to it that the children should remain children as long as they live. All the studying is done by the teacher, all the work is done by the teacher; the dear little children must not be allowed to do one stroke of work out of school for fear they might strengthen their minds. Their minds must be carried upon pillows and coddled by all kinds of indulgences; we must see to it that they must not experience a single throe of effort. They will grow up with flabby minds. One of the things our schools are devoting themselves to now is the development of character; and they develop character so singularly the boys they send to college cannot do any work. I don't believe anybody can deliberately develop his own character without making a prig of himself. Character is a by-product, and if you attend to business your character will attend to itself. If you do your duty you need not stay awake at nights wondering what will become of your character.

Some years ago we were foolish enough to permit an evangelist to come to the college just three weeks before the mid year examinations, and he upset everything. In the midst of the excitement one of the undergraduates fastened his door and put this notice on the outside, "I am a Christian and studying for examination." I have always told our undergraduates I regarded that as an absolutely logical sequence of ideas. That was a very practical notion of what Christianity is—it is attending to the highest and nearest duties so far as our lives are concerned. Now, I do not find many schoolboys getting that idea of life. Their idea of life is if they are well mannered, if they are clean in their personal habits, it does not make very much difference whether they know anything or not. A gentleman came to me at the beginning of a college year and said, "You are making a mistake not to admit Young So and So. He was the leader of his class in everything that was fine." I said, "I am very sorry, he did not pass the entrance examination." "Oh," he said, "you do not understand," and he went over the explanation again. I said, "It is you who do not understand. He did not pass the entrance examination." While it is not likely, if the Angel Gabriel should apply for admission to Princeton University he would have to pass the entrance examination. There is a moral behind that, because if he didn't he would be wasting his time and he would get dropped at the mid year. I would not put the fraud upon the boy's parents of admitting him into the University when he would be dropped at mid year. One of the wisest things I ever heard was said by a college president.[6] An anxious mother brought a son to him and he said, "Very well, madam, we will guarantee satisfaction or return the boy." Don't you think we are setting a very self-indulgent pace for the pupil? We are seeking every means to sugarcoat everything he takes, and insuring bad digestion thereby. We are seeking to do his tasks for him.

Two or three years ago we stopped that at Princeton, and the consequence is every graduate I meet of recent years thanks his stars he graduated before that began. In a university where life smiles and is gracious we are compelling men to shut themselves up in a room and actually study. The beauty of it is that when a boy once tries it he likes it. Really it is an indulgence to use your mind, if you happen to have one, and the minute a boy finds out the zest of using his mind, something we try to conceal from him as long as we can, he begins to feel the blood of real energy springing in his veins.

The future, ladies and gentlemen, is going to be strenuous. If we have not looked to our education and made it systematic and made it produce muscle of mind and of spirit, the condemnation

[6] James McCosh.

of those who follow us will be upon us and it will be said, "They labored, but they labored ignorantly; they knew nothing of the statesmanship of the mind."

CC T transcript (WP, DLC).

From Melancthon Williams Jacobus

My dear President Wilson: [Hartford] Dec. 29th 1907

I take for granted that a meeting of the Committee on Instruction[1] should be called and am writing to ask you for the day and hour which would be most convenient to you.

The enclosed report of a discussion at the University Club last Friday night[2] is interesting among other things in the confession made by Mayor Landers as to the influence of "societies" at Yale on the University life.[3] The real democracy of that life lies but in one direction.

Has the matter of the Graduate Dep't been discussed yet by the Faculty?

Yours cordially, with best wishes for the New Year

Melancthon W. Jacobus

ALS (WP, DLC).

1 That is, the Committee on the Curriculum.

2 A clipping from the *Hartford Courant*, Dec. 28, 1907, of a report of a meeting of the University Club of Hartford, of which Jacobus was president, on December 27. The subject of the discussion was "The College Man in Politics."

3 George M. Landers, Yale 1891, Mayor of New Britain, Conn., who in the course of his remarks said: "The trouble lies in the fact that we are started wrong in the universities. Young men of fine character and the best of intention find themselves drawn away by social lines from others less fortunately situated. They drift apart. The men in societies cling together, seeing not enough of the outsiders, and thereby narrowing their view of life instead of widening it. The seriousness of this question no thinking man will dispute. At Princeton we have the president recommending radical changes in the club system. At New Haven, last year, the 'Sheff' [Sheffield Scientific School] men outside societies revolted and combined against the society ticket."

A News Report of an Address in Indianapolis

[Dec. 30, 1907]

WOODROW WILSON TALKS ON PUBLIC LIFE IDEALS

The meeting of the Contemporary Club was addressed on "Ideals of Public Life" by Woodrow Wilson, president of Princeton University, Saturday evening [December 28] at the Propylaeum. President Wilson spoke in a genial, straightforward fashion, frequently reinforcing his pithy sayings with his index finger—a gesture which is characteristic of the speaker. The members of the Irvington Athenaeum were guests of the club.

Dr. Wilson spoke in favor of an intelligent and independent class of citizens, free from party and party prejudices, who will devote their entire life to politics. He rebuked the more intelligent class of citizens for their lack of interest in the Government, leaving the work to the party politicians and professional reformers, men for whom he expressed little admiration.

The speaker dwelt at considerable length on the affairs of the corporations, referring in particular to the Standard Oil Company and the recent fine imposed on that company by Judge Landis, of Chicago. "The fine has not been paid," he said, "and when it is we shall be worse off than we are now. In this present financial stringency we do not want $29,000,000 taken out of circulation and locked up in the public treasury, where there is already a surplus."

"Now you know we must uncover the individual," he continued. "The Government can not regulate the great corporations of the country wisely or prudently. The commissioners of no single State would wisely administer the business of the common carrier in that State. There are no two roads on which it would be well to impose the same flat rate, and we have not the commissioners with courage anywhere to make one rate for one road and another for its competitor. And unless they do there is no administering the roads properly, with a view to fairness and progress. We must leave the development of the business to the knowledge and self-interest of the people engaged in it, respecting at the same time the rights of the individual. You can make certain kinds of business entered into on their part illegal. You can do the only thing the law has ever done successfully—you can define the acts and things which you do not wish to permit.

"I believe the great business of this country is honest. The curse is, because some men have done wrong, every man is suspected, and because some corporations have been corrupt, every corporation is supposed to be corrupt. Now, this is not true, and I appeal for the protection of the honest men in the country by appealing for the detection of the dishonest men of the country. Why, we know who some of the men are. We know their names an[d] initials, and what their initials stand for, but we take pains to promise them immunity beforehand. What we are after is the thing itself. Now, the law never locks up the thing itself. The only way you can do is to lock up the vessel which contains the thing itself.

"One of our papers says, suppose in the present crisis all of the burglars of the country should go together and form a corporation, and when you find burglary is going on you know it is going on under the instrumentality of this corporation, so you fine the corporation. You know it is some particular expert burglar, but you do not go out to him. You say the corporation may need him and so leave him to help pay the fine.

"This is a ridiculous comparison, but it illustrates the point. I should as lief have a man break into my house as to break into my safety deposit vault and decrease the value of my securities. This is burglary. We are fining the incorporated burglar and not even attempting to hunt for the expert burglar himself.

"A great political party is trying to fool the people of the United States by a perfectly futile program.[1] The other party not only has equally weak suggestions, but has none at all.

"The Interstate Commerce Commission has done about as much to impede interstate commerce as to improve it, going so far as to show the laws under which it was acting were bad laws. For example, the laws against pooling—finding it necessary to amend the laws, so as to permit certain kinds of pooling.

"I have said that the corporation magnates must come out into the open. If the corporation lawyers of this country insist on silence they are going to bring the mob to the door of the office of the corporation. We must be told what we are about by the men who know the secrets of the inside of these things.

"I do not expect the corporation lawyers to do it. Being a lawyer myself, I know how stubborn lawyers are. They are going to continue on in their stupid reticence until some calamity falls upon them. And I will not be sorry for them. They know what they are bringing on and after they have brought it on, they need not cry.

"We are embarking on experimental legislation which may cost this country the supremacy of the modern world, but yet you do not go and tell them and offer them intelligent counsel. Have we lost our sense of honesty? Then there is no use talking about the ideals of public lives."

After the address a reception was held in the parlors of the Propylaeum. President Wilson left for the East last night at 7 o'clock.

Printed in the *Indianapolis News*, Dec. 30, 1907; some editorial headings omitted.

[1] He was referring to President Theodore Roosevelt's earlier success in strengthening the regulatory powers of the Interstate Commerce Commission with the passage of the Hepburn Act in 1906, as well as to Roosevelt's suggestions, made in his Annual Message of December 3, 1907, that the Interstate Commerce Commission's powers be further enlarged, that corporations engaged in interstate commerce be required to take out federal charters, and that some form of federal commission be established to supervise the day-to-day operations of large corporations.

From Ralph Adams Cram

Dear Dr. Wilson: Boston, December 31, 1907.

I am sending you today three prints[1] showing what seemed to me the three possible positions for the '84 tower, as indicated in my recent letter. Before taking the matter up with Mr. Morris, I should like from you an expression of opinion as to which, if any, of these schemes appeals to you most strongly. I hope it may be the Nassau Street site, but I am not quite clear in my own mind as to whether you control the buildings next University Hall or not. I know that you have acquired the property, but one or two of the houses, I believe, must remain for a year or two before they can be removed. I, personally, do not like the Brokaw Field site at all, for the reasons I gave you last week, but if it were necessary, '84 Hall could go there perfectly well, if it were crowded up against Patten [Patton] Hall as indicated.

Very sincerely yours, R A Cram
Supervising Architect.

TLS (WP, DLC).

[1] They are missing.

From Melancthon Williams Jacobus

Hartford,
My dear President Wilson: New Year's Day, 1908.

I have just learned today of the long and severe illness through which you have been passing, and write to express my sympathy for you in your suffering and to urge you not to impose upon yourself any unnecessary Committee work in connection with the meeting of the Board next week. If any such work is really required, please allow us to do it as far as possible without your personal attendance.

It is clear that you need a rest such as cannot be secured even in the quiet of Prospect. I do hope you may be persuaded to go away for the remainder of the winter to some comfortable climate and let things take care of themselves until you are strong again. This is a good time for good resolutions

Yours with cordial greetings of the Season
Melancthon W. Jacobus

ALS (WP, DLC).

From Edgar Odell Lovett

Princeton, New Jersey
My dear President Wilson: 3rd January, 1908.

It is with very great regret that I am writing to ask you to receive and present to the Trustees of the University my resignation of the professorship which I have had the honour to hold at Princeton, the resignation to take effect at the close of the current academic year. I am making this request in order that I may be free to accept an administrative appointment[1] which you have generously brought to my door, and which seems to offer unusual opportunity to translate into action the inspiration received in this place under your leadership and the tutelage of those who have been associated with you in shaping the policy and directing the destiny of this institution.

I grew into Princeton from the Faculty side, but the best of the formative years of my manhood have been lived here, and I am leaving Princeton a Princeton man firmly believing that whatever training I may have achieved here can be devoted to the interests of the University in no better way than in an effort to bring to realization in another environment those spiritual and intellectual ideals and traditions which have made Princeton conspicuous in the Nation's service, and which, in terms of your own far-reaching plans for the development of the University, are now making Princeton the most interesting educational center on the continent.

I have been trying to make this letter a formal one, and to keep my feelings out of it, but I am unwilling to bring it to a close without saying to you again that my roots here are long and deep; I cannot tell you how hard it is for me to break them.

With great respect and affectionate regards I have the honour to remain,

Most faithfully yours, Edgar Odell Lovett

TLS (WP, DLC).

[1] The presidency of Rice Institute.

From W. F. Keohan[1]

Dear Sir: New York. Jan. 7, 08.

Would you kindly favor me with your views on the Democratic party at the present time, if not in the United States, as to how the party in New Jersey appeals to you. I would greatly esteem it to hear from you as one whose Democracy is not confined to our little state of New Jersey.

Coming in contact as I do with many prominent New Jersey Democrats, I find little sentiment in favor of the nomination of Mr. Bryan, many whom I have met declaring that you were their choice for the nomination and quite a few deploring the fact that the nomination of Mr. Bryan was likely to be brought about unless steps were quickly taken to prevent it. Hoping to hear from you, I am, sincerely W. F. Keohan

ALS (WP, DLC).

[1] All that can be discovered about him is that he was the New Jersey editor of the *New York Tribune.*

A News Item

[Jan. 8, 1908]

President Wilson '79 . . . has been suffering for several weeks from a severe attack of neuritis, from which, we are very glad to be able to announce, he has now almost entirely recovered. This attack prevented Dr. Wilson from filling an engagement to speak at the annual dinner of the Southern Society of New York.

Printed in the *Princeton Alumni Weekly*, VIII (Jan. 8, 1908), 219.

From Edward Capps

My dear President Wilson: Princeton, Jan. 8, 1908

But for your absence from the city today, and the knowledge that you are very busy just now, I should have tried to see you in person about the following matter, which Professor Westcott and Dean West thought of sufficient importance to be brought to your attention.

While in New Haven last week at the funeral of Professor Seymour[1] I learned that the Faculty committee appointed to select a successor to Dean Wright,[2] of which Professor Seymour was chairman, was disposed to nominate Professor F. F. Abbott of Chicago. They have long desired to secure him as Professor of Latin, and by adding the office of Dean of the College Faculty I suppose they feel they could attract him from Chicago. I learned there also that he is looked upon at Harvard as the best man to fill the place of the late Professor Warren. It is my opinion that a Professorship of Classics at Princeton would, in the present circumstances, be more attractive to him than the professorship plus the deanship at Yale, and that he would not accept a call from here, if he were once here, to Harvard.

The situation in the classical faculties in the large institutions in the country at the present time offers to Princeton a unique opportunity to assume the leadership in graduate studies in that field. The death of Professor Warren at Harvard and the recent retirement of Professors Goodwin and Smith[3] and the early retirement of Professors White and Wright[4] will soon work a complete change in the personnel of the classical faculty which has given Harvard the primacy in classical studies during the past decade, and President Eliot has not built up the department from below with younger men who seem likely to maintain the old traditions. Similarly at Yale, the loss of Professor Seymour, for 25 years their ablest man and widely known throughout the country, and the retirement this year of Professor Peck[5] and next year of Professor Wright, leaves their classical department weaker than at any time in fifteen years. Professor Hendrickson of Chicago[6] will ably fill Professor Peck's place, but the loss of Seymour cannot be made good. With Abbott, however, the Latin side would be the best in the country. At Hopkins there has been a perceptible decline for some time, and when Professor [Basil Lanneau] Gildersleeve retires—he is now 75—there will be a yawning void that cannot be filled. In a recent talk with Professor Hale[7] of Chicago, the senior member of the classical faculty there, I learned that he did not hope for an aggressive policy on the part of the present administration. He expects to lose Abbott to Harvard, Yale, or Princeton, and believes that the places of Hendrickson and myself will be filled by the appointment of instructors or assistant professors—and he does not know where to find them. And Cornell also is failing to hold her own in classics at present, and just for the lack of able teachers and scholars.

With the addition of one Latin professor of the standing of Professor Abbott, Princeton, I feel convinced, would at once take the lead among all these institutions and would hold it for many years, with the splendid department we have to build upon. I presume that the question is primarily financial, but I believe that it would pay us, if necessary, to save the necessary money by enlarging somewhat the preceptorial divisions to say five or six instead of four. Professor Westcott, I understand, regards this as feasible and, in the circumstances, desirable—though you doubtless know his views better than I do. At any rate, I have thought it would do no harm to lay the situation before you in this way, as I see the situation, in accordance with Professor Westcott's suggestion.

It is a great pleasure to know that you are well again, and I take this opportunity of wishing you a Happy New Year.

Sincerely yours, Edward Capps

TLS (WWP, UA, NjP).

1 Thomas Day Seymour, Hillhouse Professor of the Greek Language and Literature at Yale, 1880-1907.

2 Henry Parks Wright, Dunham Professor of the Latin Language and Literature and Dean of Yale College, who retired in 1909.

3 William Watson Goodwin, Eliot Professor of Greek at Harvard, 1860-1901; and Clement Lawrence Smith, Professor of Latin, 1883-1901, and Pope Professor of Latin, 1901-1904.

4 John Williams White, Professor of Greek, 1884-1909; and John Henry Wright, Professor of Greek, 1887-1908, and Dean of the Graduate School of Arts and Sciences, 1895-1908.

5 Tracy Peck, Professor of the Latin Language and Literature, 1880-1908.

6 George Lincoln Hendrickson, at this time Professor of Latin at the University of Chicago, who became Professor of the Latin Language and Literature at Yale in 1908.

7 William Gardner Hale, Professor and Head of the Department of Latin at the University of Chicago.

Notes for Remarks to the Board of Trustees of Princeton University

9 January, 1908.

The purpose of the Board in October was to throw the question of the establishment of quadrangles open to discussion without prejudice.

The effect of the action taken, as generally interpreted, just the opposite, namely, to force discussion underground.

This has produced a situation in the University wholly abnormal and very dangerous. Likely to deepen rather than to remove misunderstandings and differences of opinion.

The question one whose discussion cannot now be checked or silenced, for we have raised it, and it is not a domestic question peculiar to Princeton but a general question common alike to schools and colleges throughout the United States.

Has attracted as much attention and as much hopeful and favorable comment as the Preceptorial System prior to its actual inauguration.

The difficulty throughout the country is that the organization of their own life, independently of the college or school, engrosses the attention and the ambition of students and makes study necessarily secondary, absorbing energy and particularly engrossing men of initiative.

This, rather than athletics, the real diverting and absorbing interest of undergraduates.

Until action and discussion in this all-important matter were driven under cover, Princeton was advancing by enormous strides to national leadership in educational matters, both of substance and of organization, and I, as her spokesman, was being turned to on every hand for guiding advice. That is now visibly checked, and the doubt is evidently wide spread whether we shall have the courage and conviction to go on.

These are very serious matters, which the Board should take under consideration, not with a view to immediate constructive action, because it is acknowledged on all hands that constructive action must await further discussion and the pecuniary means necessary for an outlay upon a great scale, but with a view to clearing up Princeton's purpose and reputation and releasing her influence from doubt and entanglement.

T MS (WP, DLC).

To the Board of Trustees of Princeton University

GENTLEMEN: [Princeton, N. J.] 9 January, 1908.

I am sure you have heard with interest Dean West's views upon the question of the choice of a site for the Graduate College and that you have been struck, as I have been, by the force of the arguments which he has presented for placing the college at a distance from the present grounds of the University, in the very beautiful park now occupied by Merwick.[1] I do not wonder that two years of residence at Merwick have created a deep attachment to the place. Its charm justifies the attachment. If I could agree with the ideals of academic seclusion presented by Professor West and could separate the Graduate College from the organic problems of the University as a whole, I could easily be convinced by the interesting reasons which he has advanced for retaining the site of Merwick as the place of residence for our graduate students.

But I cannot separate this question in consideration from the

[1] Wilson probably prepared this report in the anticipation that Moses Taylor Pyne, acting for the ailing Grover Cleveland, chairman of the trustees' Committee on the Graduate School, would present Dean West's views favoring Merwick as the permanent site of the Graduate College at the meeting of the Board of Trustees on January 9, 1908. As it turned out, since it had proved impracticable to hold the regular meeting of the Committee on the Graduate School before the trustees met, Pyne presented to the Board only a summary report on Graduate School enrollment, courses offered, and the expenses of Merwick for the preceding year, together with a brief discussion of the Swann bequest. The Minutes of the Board of Trustees do not indicate whether Wilson presented his report, but in the circumstances it seems unlikely that he did so.

life of the University as a whole. Perhaps it is not reasonable to expect any but the President and Trustees of the University, whose responsibility is whole and indivisible, to look at its parts only as parts and at none singly and for its own sake, and I do not wonder that with his natural concentration upon the interests of the school he has conceived Dean West should have formed wrong impressions. But geographical separation from the body of the University has already created in the Graduate School a sense of administrative as well as social seclusion which has already begun to be felt by the teaching body of the University and which, slight as it is and probably unconscious, is of course undesirable. It could, perhaps, by special effort, be overcome, but, because it is natural from the situation of the place, it would have to be overcome by conscious effort. It is the inevitable consciousness of separateness, and that is a consciousness which would naturally grow as the Graduate College itself grew to proportions which would give it a great and complex individuality of its own. Separation is not a question of distances in a town so small as Princeton and so definitely constituted in its life and prepossessions. It is a question of situation entirely. Sites very near the university campus are psychologically separated from the University as sharply as if they lay remote by Lovers' Lane or Stony Brook. To turn into Mercer Street or into Bayard Lane, or even into Chambers Street, is to leave the vicinity of the University. Undergraduates will pay high prices for rooms on University Place while better rooms at half the price go a'begging a stone's throw off in Mercer Street. I would not deprive the Graduate College of seclusion. I know that a certain degree of seclusion is of its essence as we have conceived it. But seclusion is not a matter of geographical separation; it is a matter of construction, a matter of privacy, as every college in Oxford attests. A quadrangle that opens upon a crowded street may be as secluded as if it were flanked by the spaces of a park set upon the outskirts of a town, provided that in its structure it be really separated, its interior really private and reserved for a special body of persons. It is the common comment of every visitor to Oxford that the seclusion of the several colleges is in some subtle way enhanced and emphasized, given an additional charm, a stronger hold on the imagination, by the fact that just without the wall is the thronging thoroughfare. The gardens that lie beyond, to be reached only through quiet quads and lying safe within sheltering walls, have an air of privacy and of privileged enjoyment which you will never find in any country garden which has only the privacy of remoteness.

The effect of this imaginative seclusion upon the mind and fancy of the undergraduate,—the effect of passing every day by secluded places which he seems almost to touch and yet is expected neither to invade nor to use uninvited,—would be incomparably deeper than that of any seclusion he took casual note of on his walks abroad or conducted friends to the edge of the village to wonder at. Dean West is mistaken in his psychology.

I have, therefore, the gratification of knowing that in leading the Board to a very different conclusion with regard to its site, I am not in danger of taking away from the Graduate School even so much as an added element of charm; that I am, on the contrary, proposing to give it the true charm and seclusion of a guarded and cloistered place rather than that commoner charm of a gentleman's country residence with its open park and pleasure grounds, and that I am, moreover, recalling Dean West to his own original and better conception of this great instrumentality of our intellectual growth when I declare it to be my clear and mature conviction that it should be placed upon some portion of the University property which lies near the actual geographical heart of the University as at present constructed. The site I propose and would very earnestly urge upon you for approval is that which lies upon the nearer corner of the very beautiful field, with its incomparable opportunities for development, which lies just across Washington Road from the great laboratories which we are just now constructing.

I should do this even if it were at the expense of some of the ideals of a separate life which Professor West so persuasively urges. For this is not merely a question of taste and preference or merely a question concerning the development of the Graduate College. It has wider and more important aspects than appear in any representations that have yet been made to you. It concerns the whole development of the University.

The Graduate School, as originally conceived, affords an unequalled means of vitalizing the whole intellectual life of the University, if we take care that it shall be actually associated with that life in some intimate and constant way. It is the history of every great graduate school developed out of an older foundation such as that which exists at Princeton that it has received its first, its greatest, and its most persistent vitalization from students drawn into it out of the ranks of the undergraduates of the institution itself. Only after its initial self-vitalization has attracted the attention of the country does it tend to draw any considerable number of students from other institutions. Not only is its best authentication the fact that undergraduates of its own stimulation crowd into it, but it can hardly be an acceptable place of study to those who come to it from a distance if it exist in an atmosphere unsympathetic with it and in the midst of activities which do not work towards it, but away from it. It would indeed be necessary to place the Graduate School at a distance from the rest of the University, should it prove true that the rest of the University is in any sense hostile or even indifferent to it.

In my opinion it would be one of the most serious and far-reaching mistakes that we could make, to regard the Graduate School as anything but a vital completion and outgrowth of the general development of the University as a whole. Our preparation for supplying such courses and facilities of study as attract serious graduate students are now advanced to the stage when it will certainly be possible, if we take the right measures, to make the graduate college a means and example whereby the undergraduates of the University may be constantly stimulated. But we cannot do this unless that college is so placed as to be in constant, visible, conscious contact with the stirring daily life of the place. To hide its exterior, its walls and portals, away from the common view and the common passing to and fro which constitutes the stir and life of the place would be to deprive ourselves of one of the chief instrumentalities we can hope for by which to permeate the University as a whole with a consciousness of the higher occupations and ideals of scholarship. Placed at a distance, the Graduate College might indeed have a pleasant and attractive, even an alluring, life of its own, but it would be a life which did not react upon the body of the University and which did not constitute one of the moving forces by which its ideals are to be raised and its impulses guided.

In the minds of all the teachers of the University who have looked at this matter as a general university question, these considerations are the conclusive considerations of the whole matter. I know that I am speaking their judgment as well as my own when I say that it would not be for the real and lasting benefit of the Graduate College, and that it would be to the deep and permanent loss of the University as a whole, if the Graduate College should be placed at any point where it would be, either actually or psychologically, separated from the daily goings and comings of the university body. Its interior seclusion may be counted on to give it the greater charm because of its obvious exterior presence and beauty, and the life which it holds may easily be made in the course of a few fortunate years a governing force in the life of many an undergraduate as well as in the daily experience of the teaching body of the University.

Let me add that this conception of the position and influence of the Graduate College is the conception originally presented by Professor West, originally accepted by the Trustees of the University and by myself upon my inauguration as President, originally embodied in the plans which at the outset of my administration I sketched for the development of Princeton and during all the years of my presidency cherished by my colleagues of the faculty and by me as the crowning hope of the things to which we were looking forward and toward which we were constantly striving. The separation of the Graduate College from the body of the University puts a different character upon it and leads in a direction in which it would, in my opinion, be folly to advance. [Woodrow Wilson]

TR (V. L. Collins Coll., UA, NjP).

From the Minutes of the Board of Trustees of Princeton University

[Jan. 9, 1908]

The Trustees of Princeton University met in stated session in the Trustees' Room in the Chancellor Green Library, Princeton, New Jersey, at eleven o'clock on Thursday morning January 9, 1908.

The President of the University in the chair.

The meeting was opened with prayer by Dr. Frazer. . . .

Supplementing his printed report the President of the University spoke on the action taken by the Board at the October meeting and on the question of the Social Organization of the University in general. . . .

On motion of Mr. John A. Stewart seconded by Mr. Green it was

> RESOLVED, That the Committee on the Graduate School be and are hereby respectfully requested to report at the next meeting of this Board upon the selection of a suitable site for said school. . . .[1]

On motion of Mr. Henry duly seconded it was

> RESOLVED, That a committee of three, composed of members of the Board residing in New Jersey, be appointed to take into consideration the advisability of asking an annual appropriation from the State of New Jersey in return for which a certain number of scholarships could be given.

In accordance with this resolution the President of the University appointed the following Committee: Archibald D. Russell, Chairman, M. Taylor Pyne, Henry W. Green.[2]

COMMITTEE TO CONFER WITH COMMITTEE OF ALUMNI

The following resolution was offered by Mr. Pyne and seconded by Mr. Green:

> WHEREAS certain of the alumni represented by Messrs. Junius S. Morgan, George C. Fraser, Franklin Murphy, Jr., William W. Phillips, and Charles B. Bostwick, recognizing the evils connected with the Upper Class Clubs as presented by the Committee on the Supplementary Report of the President and believing that the said evils can and should be remedied have asked the Board to appoint a Committee to confer with them regarding the correction and elimination of said evils; now therefore be it
>
> RESOLVED, That a committee of three be appointed by the President to confer with said committee and to report back to the Board at the April meeting.

DISCUSSION OF RESOLUTION

After a discussion of the resolution an amendment was offered by Dr. Dixon and duly seconded. After further discussion Dr. Wood offered the following amendment which was seconded by Dr. Jacobus:

> RESOLVED, That a committee of seven be appointed to consider the Social Organization of the University and that the President appoint three of the members of the said committee to confer with representative alumni who have asked for such conference.

Dr. Dixon withdrew his amendment by consent.

After further discussion a rising vote was taken on Dr. Wood's amendment and it was declared lost.

RESOLUTION ADOPTED

A standing vote on the original resolution of Mr. Pyne was taken and it was declared adopted.

COMMITTEE TO CONFER WITH ALUMNI APPOINTED

The President of the University appointed the following Committee to confer with a Committee of the Alumni: Henry B. Thompson, Chairman, Edward W. Sheldon, Andrew C. Imbrie.[3]

GENERAL DISCUSSION

A general discussion of the question of the Social Organization of the University followed.

RESOLUTION OFFERED BY DR. WOOD

The following resolution was offered by Dr. Wood and seconded by Mr. Garrett:

RESOLVED, That a committee of seven be appointed to consider the Social Organization of the University.

ACTION ON DR. WOOD'S RESOLUTION POSTPONED

On motion of Dr. McPherson duly seconded the following resolution was adopted:

RESOLVED, That action on the resolution offered by Dr. Wood be postponed to the meeting of the Board in April next and that such action be taken after the Board receives the report of the committee on conference with alumni.

MR. GARRETT'S RESOLUTION ABOUT PROFESSOR ABBOTT

On motion of Mr. Garrett duly seconded the following resolution was adopted:

RESOLVED, That the President be empowered to approach Professor Abbott with a view to extending to him an invitation to become a member of the Classical Department, if after consultation with the Finance Committee and others who may be able to assist in the matter, he finds that it is feasible and proper to do so.

ADJOURNMENT

After prayer by Dr. Wood the Board adjourned to meet at eleven o'clock on Thursday morning April 9, 1909 [1908].

C W McAlpin Secretary of the University.

[1] For the report, see E. W. Sheldon to the Board of Trustees, April 9, 1908, Vol. 18.

[2] See the extract from the Minutes of the Board of Trustees printed at April 9, 1908, Vol. 18.

[3] For this committee's report, see H. B. Thompson *et al.* to the Board of Trustees, April 8, 1908, Vol. 18.

To Edward Capps

Princeton, N. J.

My dear Professor Capps: January 10th, 1908.

I am extremely obliged to you for your letter of January 8th. It was not possible to lay it before any committee of the Board, the Board meeting being immediately at hand, but I took the liberty of reading it to the Board itself, in the desperate hope that even in this year of extreme difficulty in financial matters I might be encouraged to hope for Professor Abbott.

I need not tell you that there was a universal desire to have him, but the most that the Board felt it could do, in view of the state of the funds of the University, was to sanction a motion made by one of the members, that I be authorized to approach Professor Abbott provided I obtain the approval of the Finance Committee or of any others who might feel inclined to guarantee a certain amount of money.

My hope is that this vague and apparently discouraging motion means that the member of the Board who moved it is willing to put his hand in his own pocket and to organize some effort to obtain a guarantee of the money we should need, at any rate long enough to tide us over the present time of stringency.

May I take the liberty of asking a very intimate question? Can you tell me how much you think it would be necessary to offer Professor Abbott in order to make the call seem to him one of sufficient dignity and worth his consideration? You will understand why, in the circumstances, I ask this direct question. It is not as if I were bargaining, but rises out of my earnest desire to obtain the money.

It is very delightful to me to have your counsel in matters of this sort, and you may be sure that I will make every effort possible. I hope that Professor Abbott is not likely to receive or consider calls elsewhere immediately.

I must say that my own judgment is against curtailing the preceptorial force in order to obtain the money. It would not only involve the dropping from our list of several men who at least deserve longer notice, but it would also probably mean that the amount of work to divide up among the force in the department would be so great that Professor Abbott himself would probably be caught in the net of undergraduate work entirely and left too little free for the graduate teaching we should hope to give him an opportunity to do.

With warmest regard,

Sincerely yours, [Woodrow Wilson]

CCL (WWP, UA, NjP).

From Melancthon Williams Jacobus

My dear President Wilson: New York, Jany 10, 1908

It was a great regret to me that I could not remain longer yesterday afternoon and not only assure you of my loyal adherence to the great principles which constitute our struggle—of which loyalty, however, I do not believe you need assurance—but also extend to you a word of courage and cheer in view of the events and happenings of the day.

The issue is simply coming closer to its ultimate joining. On this joining if we win, the future is sure—if we lose, the future is clear and plain for several of us besides yourself.

I am glad to know from Mr. Jones that you are going to address the Chicago Association and the Association at Pittsburgh.[1] If others approach you, I hope you will accept their invitations and in all your addresses make clear not only the issue which is joined, but the money spirit of the opposition! The present day is not propitious for the tyranny of wealth, and if the plain people of our alumni are at one with you on the Quads as against the Clubs, they will be a hundred fold more so on freedom against the dictation of dollars. I do not believe Osborne can be elected against the protest of an insulted alumni.[2]

In the meanwhile whatever it costs accept the situation until the April meeting, when, if the Conference Committee reports, Dr Woods resolution for the larger Committee can be called up for action, and if it does not report—or whether it does or not, and Dr. Woods resolution is again postponed—you will at least have the satisfaction of knowing that in the meanwhile you have laid the issues before the Alumni Associations and that they know and appreciate the fight that is on.

Action on your part can not come until Dr Woods resolution is called up in a free and fair field, and the Board forced to record itself for or against—at least it can not come with any lasting and effective force—and it is too tremendous an action to take without making it tell for all it is worth.

I wish for you a time of rest and recuperation in Bermuda. If there is any service, small though it may be, which I can render you or the cause at issue I can count it only a pleasure to render it.

With kind regards to Mrs. Wilson

Yours cordially Melancthon W Jacobus

ALS (WP, DLC).

[1] See Wilson's address to the Princeton Club of Chicago printed at March 12, 1908, and his address to the Western Association of Princeton Clubs at Pittsburgh printed at May 2, 1908, both in Vol. 18.

[2] Henry Fairfield Osborn. However, if he was considering running for election as Alumni Trustee to replace David Benton Jones, who had announced that he would not again be a candidate, he soon dropped the idea. As it turned out, there were only two official candidates for the post—William Brown McIlvaine, Princeton 1885, prominent lawyer of Chicago and President of the Western Association of Princeton Clubs, and Wilson Farrand, Princeton 1886, Headmaster of Newark Academy. When it became known that many western alumni felt strongly that Jones's replacement should come from the area west of the Alleghenies, Farrand withdrew, leaving McIlvaine the only candidate.

To Melancthon Williams Jacobus

My dear Dr. Jacobus: [Princeton, N. J.] January 11th, 1908.

Allow me to thank you most warmly for your letter of January tenth written from New York. It has done not a little to cheer me.

I know of nothing that gives me greater satisfaction than the kind of support you have been generous enough to give me and the warm and friendly way in which you have rendered it. I entirely agree with your conclusions as to the wise course for me to pursue. Indeed I think we must now regard the fight as definitely on, not in any usual or unpleasant sense of the word fight, but with the deep conviction that we must now by every wise means available discover whether the University is to be left or put into the hands of those who will certainly mar its usefulness almost hopelessly, and that it is our duty to stick to our posts and maintain the fight until it is evidently ended and we are either entirely successful or evidently and permanently defeated.

I need not tell you that I feel no bitterness in this matter, but only a very solemn and deep conviction and purpose. I hope with all my heart that we may be given not only the wisdom but the patience and the endurance which we shall now need. Certainly I will take every means to make the issue clear without making it exasperating. Again let me thank you with all my heart for your letter. Faithfully yours, [Woodrow Wilson]

CCL (RSB Coll., DLC).

To Andrew Carnegie

My dear Mr. Carnegie, [New York, Jan. 12, 1908]

Would you be generous enough to give me about an hour of your valuable time some day next week? I am ordered to Bermuda to get rid of my neuritis and sail next Saturday, the 18th; but I am very anxious to discuss with you before I go an educational question which I am sure you will think of national importance.[1]

I do not know when more of the sources of pleasure have been touched in me than were touched last night[2]

Always faithfully yours, Woodrow Wilson

ALS (A. Carnegie Papers, DLC).

1 He hoped to persuade Carnegie to provide the money to implement the quadrangle plan.

2 At a dinner party at the Carnegies' in New York.

To Harry Augustus Garfield

Princeton, N. J.
My dear Professor Garfield: January 13th, 1908.

I am anxious, before going to Bermuda, to hold a conference of Heads of Departments. Would it not be possible for you to come to my office in Seventy-Nine Hall on Wednesday evening, the 15th, at 8.30?

Hoping that this will entirely suit your convenience,

Always faithfully yours, Woodrow Wilson

TLS (H. A. Garfield Papers, DLC).

From Moses Taylor Pyne and Archibald Douglas Russell

My dear Mr. President: New York January 13th, 1908.

The undersigned have just received the notice of their appointment on the Committee to take into consideration the advisability of procuring an appropriation from the State of New Jersey, in return for Scholarships, and we both feel, with such eminent and distinguished men on the Board of Trustees as Mr. Grover Cleveland and Chancellor Magie, not to mention yourself, that the University is losing a great deal in not appointing these men on the Committee in place of ourselves, and hope that if you agree with us that you will not consider us at all in the matter, as we believe the other gentlemen to be far superior to us in every particular.

You will appreciate that the time is very limited. The Legislature will meet this week and probably adjourn in March, and what is to be done should be done at once. Mr. Cleveland informs us that he is not going away at present.

Very truly yours, M. Taylor Pyne
Arch D. Russell

TLS (WP, DLC).

From Edward Capps

My dear President Wilson: Princeton, Jan. 13, 1908

I am glad that my letter reached you in time to be of some service, and that you found the suggestion worth bringing to the attention of the Board. In the circumstances it seems to me that the action of the Board was very generous, as well as wise.

Professor Abbott is very generally regarded as the strongest and most successful teacher of graduate students in Latin in the country, and his ideals of scholarship as shown in the dissertations written under his direction seem to me to be precisely those which you desire shall characterize our graduate work at Princeton. We shall be fortunate if you are enabled to carry out the plan.

Perhaps the best way of answering your question would be to tell you just what Professor Abbott's present position is. A few years ago, when he had declined a call to Yale, President Harper made a special arrangement for him whereby he normally teaches six months of each year at a salary of $3500: the other six months he spends in study at his place in Connecticut. If the Department needs his services during the whole academic year, he receives either two-thirds pro rata additional salary or full pro rata additional vacation. The normal salary of $3500 is thus based upon an hypothetical salary of $5000 (really a little more), but if he teaches nine months for salary and not vacation he receives in cash, by the peculiar system of the University of Chicago, about $4700.

Apart from the positive advantages of a similar position in Princeton, there are three considerations, in my opinion, which would at the present time be likely to influence Professor Abbott to leave Chicago, in whose upbuilding he has been a large factor: first, the fact that Chicago is not a beneficiary of the Carnegie Foundation, second, the attraction of the East for an eastern-bred man, and third, the very general discontent that seems to prevail in the faculty there.

You will see that I do not regard it likely that Professor Abbott would accept a position elsewhere at a salary less than $5000, but it is quite possible that a proposal such as Professor Westcott had in mind last spring would attract him, and at the same time be somewhat easier to arrange, viz. that he should teach here during the first term only next year, at a salary of say $3000, his full salary and service to begin the year following. I understand that he is planning to spend a part of next year abroad anyway. And we need additional advanced Latin courses here mainly in the first term at present.

I wish I could be of some practical service to you in this matter, or that in some way I might serve you, for I believe most heartily in the things you are trying to achieve for Princeton.

Very sincerely yours, Edward Capps

TLS (WWP, UA, NjP).

To Moses Taylor Pyne

My dear Momo: [Princeton, N. J.] January 14th, 1908.

The action taken by the Board of Trustees the other day did not contemplate our approaching the Legislature of the State at this time to ask for a grant of money. It merely directed that a committee should be appointed to consider the advisability of making such an application, and I think that the committee appointed is in every way better than the one that you suggest. Neither Mr. Cleveland nor Chancellor Magie would have time to do more than play a formal part in such conferences as we might finally determine to have with a committee or committees of the Legislature. In the meantime, it is very desirable that a committee composed of active members of the Board should consider very carefully the whole lay of the land and advise the Board as to whether in their opinion such a move at the present time is desirable.

Thank you very much for the information enclosed in your letter about the grants made in other States in aid of education.[1] Always faithfully yours, [Woodrow Wilson]

CCL (WWP, UA, NjP).

[1] This enclosure is missing.

To Edgar Odell Lovett

Princeton, N. J.

My dear Professor Lovett: January 14th, 1908.

I read your letter of resignation to the Board at its meeting last week, and it was voted to accept the resignation with the greatest regret.

I was instructed to express to you the Board's deep sense of the distinguished services you have rendered in the faculty and its very cordial hope that you would have the most abundant success in the new work which you are undertaking.

I wish you might have been present to hear what was said, for you would know that these assurances which I now convey were in no sense perfunctory, but sprung from the warmest feeling and from a real knowledge of your work and worth. I need not tell you that it gives me peculiar pleasure to be the medium of such messages of warm appreciation and heartfelt God-speed.

Always faithfully and cordially yours,

Woodrow Wilson

TLS (E. O. Lovett Papers, TxHR).

From Cleveland Hoadley Dodge

Dear Woodrow: New York January 14, 1908.

You were awfully good to write me such a lovely letter.[1]

I was broken hearted not to get to the Trustees' meeting, but for the first time in my life I had a genuine attack of illness, and although my pneumonia was very slight, it necessitates my taking good care of myself.

I have to go west to the mines sometime this spring, and will probably kill two birds with one stone and start a little earlier to spend three or four weeks in southern California, so I am afraid I will not be able to get to Princeton much this winter; but hope, if you are in town during the next two or three weeks, before I go, that I may have a chance of seeing you.

With warm regards,

Very affectionately yours, C. H. Dodge

TLS (WP, DLC).

[1] It is missing.

From Lawrence Crane Woods

Pittsburg, Penna.

My dear Doctor Wilson: January 15, 1908.

It is mortifying to me that I have not been able to secure the information regarding Mr. Ford, about which you have written to me. I have not only found it an exceedingly difficult task as he seems to be comparatively unknown in this community outside of a few newspaper men, and even they do not seem to know very much about him aside from his editorial writings, but I have not been able to give the attention to it which I propose to owing to business and personal conditions with which I need not trouble you. I hope to be able, however, shortly to give you more favorable information than I have yet been able to secure.

I am glad to see from the Alumni Weekly that you have recovered from your attack of neuritis. I enjoyed very much reading your Indianapolis speech on the 28th.[1] In fact, I never hear or read anything of yours that I do not enjoy and profit by.

Regretting the unavoidable delay in securing you the information you desire, believe me,

Very truly yours, Lawrence C Woods

TLS (WWP, UA, NjP).

[1] Woods had probably just read the extracts of Wilson's speech to the Indiana State Teachers' Association on December 27, 1907, printed in the *Princeton Alumni Weekly*, VIII (Jan. 8, 1908), 224-25.

To Ralph Adams Cram

My dear Mr. Cram: [Princeton, N. J.] January 16, 1908.

Allow me to thank you for your letters concerning a possible change in the site of the Magdalen tower, and to apologize for my delay in replying. That delay has been due chiefly to my illness from an attack of neuritis.

Unfortunately, too, this is not a pressing question, because it is not likely that sufficient money will be available within the next twelve-month to make it necessary for us to decide this question and push the plans forward.

I must say that my own mind is a good deal at a balance. I think the choice clearly lies between the site on Nassau Street which you suggest and the site first selected beside Brokaw Field. I feel that any line of buildings we may draw down beside or around that field will need some point of emphasis such as the Magdalen tower would so beautifully supply. The location chosen for it by Mr. Morris was selected as the result of my own observations in the many walks I have taken on that side of the college. I found that my eye always sought for some feature of special height and beauty at that point as I tried to conceive of lines of buildings running in that direction.

I am sailing for Bermuda on Saturday and shall be back by about the 27th of February. If you can find it convenient some time in the spring to come down here and take a walk or two with me, we can come to a final conclusion which I think will be best arrived at on the ground. You will find me quite open to conviction.

With warm regard,

Always cordially yours, [Woodrow Wilson]

CCL (WWP, UA, NjP).

To Moses Taylor Pyne

My dear Momo: [Princeton, N. J.] January 16th, 1908.

You will remember that when we were negotiating with Professor Conklin we promised him an assistant and the absolutely necessary apparatus for carrying on his work. I requested him to ask for no apparatus which would not be absolutely necessary and which would not constitute a part of the necessary equipment of the new Biological Laboratory. The list which I enclose is the list which he has submitted to me. It comes in the total to some $1200, whereas $1000 was the sum he originally guessed at. He tells me that it is not absolutely necessary to order at once the items below the pencil mark which I have drawn above the last paragraphs on the list, and the items above that pencil mark aggregate $1066.

It is necessary to take this matter up at this time, because everything in the list has to be ordered from abroad and cannot be counted upon for use next year unless ordered by the middle of February, that is, before the probable date of my return from Bermuda.

This, you understand, is a list of things which would in any case be necessary for the new Biological Laboratory.

Will you not be kind enough to return this list, not to me, but to Professor McClure, authorizing him to put in the necessary orders and telling him whether in your judgment the articles below the pencil mark should be ordered now or later. I dare say that in any case we should have to pay the bills at about the same time.

I am glad to say that most of the business which seems necessary between this and my return has, so far as I can foresee, been attended to, and I go off with a comparatively clean slate.

Hoping that I will find you all well when I come back,

Always faithfully yours, [Woodrow Wilson]

CCL (WWP, UA, NjP).

To William Henry Carpenter

My dear Mr. Carpenter: Princeton, N. J. January 16th, 1908.

I have your letter of January 15th, and am sincerely sorry that any mistake should have arisen as to the title of my lectures on the Blumenthal Foundation. I fear there has been some mistake from the first. It was not with my approval that the lectures were announced as on Party Government in the United States. Indeed, I did not see the circular announcing that title until it was printed and issued and the lectures were about to begin. I did not think it worth while then to make a point of the change.

But it seems to me that the change is absolutely necessary, because the subject of the lectures is not Party Government in the United States. That is the subject of only one of the lectures. The rest concern constitutional arrangements looked at from every side. I should be sorry, in order to find a more attractive title, to give the book so misleading a description.

You will see, therefore, why it seems to me necessary to insist in [on] the word "Constitutional" instead of the word "Party" in the title of the volume.

With much appreciation of the kind terms of your letter,[1]

Very sincerely yours, Woodrow Wilson

TLS (photostat in RSB Coll., DLC).

[1] It is missing.

To Mary Allen Hulbert Peck

Hotel Hamilton
My dear Mrs. Peck, Hamilton, Bermuda [c. Jan. 25, 1908]

You are very thoughtful of my pleasure. Of course I will come, and shall be glad when one o'clock arrives.

With warm regard,

Sincerely Yours, Woodrow Wilson

ALS (WP, DLC).

To Ellen Axson Wilson

My precious, precious darling, Bermuda, 26 January, 1908.

The boat has come and brought me the longed for letter.[1] Ah! how many times I kissed it! I love you beyond expression, my true, my delightful darling, and in this far away place, where my thoughts are my own and nothing invades them uninvited except when I am tired, I spend hours luxuriating in the consciousness of it, the very pain of separation seeming to enhance the joy of knowing that my darling is mine and I am hers. You are all the world to me, my Eileen, and your sweet letter seemed to me a part of yourself!

It made me deeply uneasy to hear that you and Stock. had started South in a raging blizzard.[2] Even here we heard by cable (everything disagreeable that happens in or to the United States is cabled all over the British Empire) how it was flinging itself southward along the coast. But I should have heard before this if anything untoward happened to you; and ere this you are certainly out of it and among those who will take care of you.

There must have been a sad rush of work just before you left, my poor dear; but you will have time to rest now, thank goodness. It makes my heart much lighter to think of you where you are among the dear southern kinsfolk. Give them all my warmest love.

The boat brought me a sweet little letter from dear Margaret,[3] and I am sending her a little epistle in reply with this.[4] She wrote in the midst of the gathering storm, a little lonely and sick at heart but very brave and sweet.

I am perfectly well, and have settled to a quiet round which takes me back to last winter. I was lazy and did not begin my writing until Saturday, and, since to-day must be a day of letters, will not return to it until to-morrow, Tuesday; but it began rather easily and I feel sure that I am going to enjoy it. I hope to get the two lectures[5] finished in a couple of weeks and then the arrangement of the essays will be mere amusement with which to fill in the remaining two weeks. I will linger over it to make it last.

I have seen Mrs. Peck twice, and really she is very fine. You must know her. She lives at Pittsfield, Massachusetts, and insists that when we go up to Garfield's inauguration we shall go down to visit her. I feel that we must manage it if possible, for I know that you would like her, despite her free western manner. I went to one o'clock dinner at her house yesterday and they kept me all afternoon, a most engaging household: her mother,[6] a stately old lady who may herself once have been beautiful; her son by her first marriage,[7] an interesting boy kept down here because of weak lungs; her stepdaughter, a charming little piece of about sixteen;[8] two other boys whom she seems to have half adopted, at any rate for the winter; and, dominating all, herself, any age by turns, and overflowing with spirits. Every young person seems at once devoted to her. The young officers of the garrison began dropping in as the afternoon advanced, and all seemed equally at home,—not as our boys do, but with a quieter, more sedate enjoyment and delightful manners. It was all very pretty, and just such a scene as this place of quiet and of leisurely moods and open hearts seemed to itself create. I am sure you would have liked to see me in the midst of it all, rather soothed and thawed out than excited. Mrs. Peck showed me a charming letter from a young fellow ordered away from here last year to South Africa which began "My dear Mother." That is the way they seem to regard her. It was a new and wholly delightful light in which to see her. Before I had known only how interesting her mind was and how frank and open her disposition.

Now I am cut out by Mark Twain! He arrived on the boat this morning, and Mrs. Peck at once took possession of him. They are old friends. Indeed, she seems to know everybody that is worth knowing. She has been coming down here a great many winters, and everybody turns up here sooner or later, it would seem.

I have not yet found out where Mr. Clemons [Clemens] is staying. I hoped he was coming to the [Hotel] Hamilton, but he went off in another direction.[9] I did not get a chance to speak to him, and do not know whether he would remember me or not.[10]

I spend very pleasant evenings with Major and Mrs. Meyer,[11] fellow boarders, from Montclair, whom I met last year. He is an old army officer and student of engineering, whose only fault is that he has no light talk and is always bent upon canvassing serious matters,—which for me is a *very* serious matter. There is no one in the hotel who is very remarkable, but a sufficient number of pleasant people to form an enjoyable circle. Young and gay people for the most part go to the other hotel:[12] this one is the favourite resort of sedate middle-aged persons like myself. I feel *very* sedate and middle-aged at this remove from my field of battle, and look upon myself with a sort of half sad amusement.

Are there any rumbles of Democratic party politics in the Savannah circle? I am entirely cut off here from such news.

Give me your itinerary, with dates, as nearly as you can, my dear one, for my guidance in writing. I want my letters to go to you direct and without delay if possible, for fear some sort of anxiety should visit my darling.

Give yourself up to enjoyment, my sweet pet. I do so long to think of you as free from care and in the midst of people who love you and whom you can enjoy!

Give my love to Stock. I am so sorry to hear of what he had to suffer at the hands of the dentist. I hope it did not in any way prostrate him or permanently upset his nerves.

I love you! I love you! My heart sings it all the time. Ah! if I had only not been fool enough to leave you behind! My darling! My precious, precious little wife! It nearly broke my heart to shut that door at the Collingwood!

With a heart full to overflowing with tender love,

Your own Woodrow

WWTLS (WC, NjP).

1 This and all following letters from Mrs. Wilson during this separation are missing.

2 Mrs. Wilson had just left for a visit to relatives in Savannah and Atlanta.

3 It is missing.

4 It is also missing.

5 That is, the last two chapters of *Constitutional Government in the United States.*

6 Anjenett Holcomb (Mrs. Charles Sterling) Allen.

7 Allen Schoolcraft Hulbert, born in 1888.

8 Harriet Roberts Peck, who was, as WW to EAW, Feb. 4, 1908, discloses, actually twenty-two.

9 Clemens was staying at the Princess Hotel during this visit to the colony.

10 He had been a luncheon guest of Wilson's at the time of his inauguration as President of Princeton University.

11 Henry Coddington Meyer, consulting engineer with offices in New York, and his wife, Charlotte English Seaman Meyer. Meyer had been an officer in the Union army during the Civil War.

12 The Princess Hotel.

To Oswald Garrison Villard[1]

My dear Mr. Villard, Bermuda, 26 January, 1908.

I hope that you will not think that I forgot, or that I did not appreciate, your kind invitation to come in and talk over the Democratic situation. When I saw you at Mr. Carnegie's I had already engaged passage for Bermuda for the following Saturday, and in the days intervening the many things I had to attend to before breaking away for my mid-winter vacation so disposed themselves that it was literally impossible for me to find a free space for calling at your office. I hope that I shall have better luck when I return.

Do you never seek this haven of rest for a few weeks detachment? I am to be here till the latter part of February, and always return from such a stay more sane about everything.

With much regard,

Sincerely Yours, Woodrow Wilson

WWTLS (O. G. Villard Papers, MH).

1 Grandson of William Lloyd Garrison, the abolitionist, and son of Henry and Fanny Garrison Villard, he was at this time editorial writer for and Vice President of the New York *Evening Post*.

A Petition

[c. Feb. 1, 1908]

We, the undersigned, visitors to Bermuda, venture respectfully to express the opinion that the admission of automobiles to the island would alter the whole character of the place, in a way which would seem to us very serious indeed.

The island now attracts visitors in considerable numbers because of the quiet and dignified simplicity of its life. It derives its principal charm from its utter detachment from the world of strenuous business and feverish pleasure in which most of us are obliged to spend the greater part of our time. If it should lose that charm, the character of the visitors who resort to it would undoubtedly change, and the class substituted would, we feel sure, be neither so numerous, nor so acceptable to the residents of the Colony as those whom they now so hospitably welcome.

We do not feel qualified to form or justified in expressing an opinion with regard to the domestic use of motor cars on the island. What its business needs may demand or the convenience of its residents render desirable we are not in a position to judge; but we are confident that the free introduction of such vehicles, especially by visitors, would in the mind of every one capable of appreciating the natural and wholesome pleasures of the place make it a place to shun rather than to resort to.

Our own experience in the use of motor cars convinces us that their use in Bermuda would be especially dangerous. Not only are the roads narrow and winding, but the hills are many and abrupt and sweep through curves around which motor cars could be driven only with the greatest difficulty. When these curving hills are wet it would be practically impossible to prevent even a light car from "skidding" and becoming unmanageable, and it is easy to see that the lives of pedestrians would be almost as much in danger from them as the lives of those riding or driving.

It has everywhere proved impossible to enforce a speed limit without the use of a very numerous and widely dispersed constabulary. Moreover, the enforcement of a speed limit in Bermuda would be peculiarly difficult. It is necessary on such hilly roads as these to drive a machine at a very considerable rate of speed to avoid repeated stalling.

The danger to be apprehended is chiefly from reckless tourists who would care nothing for local opinion or for the convenience and safety of others. This is one of the last refuges now left in the world to which one can come to escape such persons. It would, in our opinion, be a fatal error to attract to Bermuda the extravagant and sporting set who have made so many other places of pleasure entirely intolerable to persons of taste and cultivation.[1]

Henry C Meyer Montclair, N J
Woodrow Wilson Princeton, N J. . . .[2]

Printed in the Hamilton, Bermuda, *Royal Gazette*, Feb. 1, 1908.

[1] The tradition that Wilson was the author of this petition (e. g., Hudson Strode, *The Story of Bermuda*, pp. 146-47) is correct. There is a WWsh draft of the petition in WP, DLC.

[2] All told, there were 111 signers of this petition—107 Americans (including Samuel L. Clemens) and four Canadians. They were all staying at the Hotel Hamilton and the Princess Hotel.

The petition was published just at the moment when a movement to ban automobiles altogether from Bermuda was gathering momentum, and when the pro-automobile forces were also rallying for battle. On March 6, 1908, Clarence Peniston introduced in the House of Assembly a bill entitled the Motor Car Act, 1908, which would have virtually prohibited motor traffic within the limits of the colony. Amended to prohibit all motor cars, it was approved by the House of Assembly by a vote of fifteen to fourteen on April 13 and by the Legislative Council (the upper house of the Bermuda legislature) by a vote of five to three on May 8, 1908. Hamilton, Bermuda, *Royal Gazette*, March 10 and 21, April 4 and 14, and May 9, 1908. The ban on automobiles was not lifted until August 1946, with the passage of the Motor Car Act, 1946, authorizing the operation of motor vehicles under certain restrictions. *Ibid.*, Aug. 5, 1946.

A Salutation

[Hamilton, Bermuda, c. Feb. 1, 1908]

My precious one, my beloved Mary,

Transcript of WWsh written on verso of the WWsh draft of the petition printed above.

To Ellen Axson Wilson

My precious darling, Bermuda, 4 February, 1908.

I have to write to-day before I even know whether I have a letter from you or not. The boat is to stay only a few hours, and the mail that is to go out on her may be closed before that which came in on her is distributed, this post office being manned by the slowest and dullest persons obtainable on the island. The boat should have been in yesterday, but she encountered a disabled vessel and had to lie by her all one night in order to take off her crew in the morning, the we[a]ther being too heavy to attempt it at night. To-day is her regular sailing day and she must turn back at once.

I am very well, my sweetheart, and having a very good time indeed. The weather is not quite so genial as it was a year ago: we have been having a good deal of cold rain and heavy wind. And I have been a good deal hampered in my out-door pleasures by a bad knee. On the ship coming down I was careless enough to fall and twist my left knee rather badly. It was just the day before we arrived and I saw an excellent doctor here within an hour after we landed; and of course I have been following his advice religiously; but it has not yielded to treatment as promptly as I had hoped,—partly, I dare say, because it is my left leg and, being "fleabitten,"[1] has a little less vigour of circulation. But at most it is a small matter, affecting nothing but my out-of-door exercise. It is steadily getting well, but is provokingly slow about it. It is now two weeks since I wrenched it, and that ought to have sufficed it.

But, notwithstanding weather and knees, I am all right and am enjoying my stay here immensely. My work prospers. I was lazy and did not get at it until a week had gone by, but when I did settle down to it it went very well indeed. One of the two lectures is finished and the other is on the stocks, to be launched, I confidently expect, before I write you another letter, that is, by next Saturday or Monday. I find that, though, as usual, it is hard work, drawing blood as all my writing does, I am enjoying it and getting real mental strength and spiritual relief out of it. Bermuda is certainly the best place in the world in which to forget Princeton, at least Princeton as an organization and a problem; it would in any case afford me the most soothing rest; but a bit of work is tonic added. It keeps the blood moving aggressively. And, inasmuch as my knee keeps me from taking much exercise out of the house, this piece of business inside the house is all the more wholesome and opportune.

My social duties have begun. I did not realize how many people I had met here last year until the calling began and the calls had to be returned. And now there are luncheons and dinners. Mark Twain has been down here between boats, and I have seen a good deal of him. He seems to like being with me. Yesterday Mrs. Peck gave him a lunch at her house and gathered a most interesting little group of garrison people to meet him. He was in great form and delighted everybody.

Of course I am seeing a great deal of Mrs. Peck. She is fine and dear. But I am remembering your injunction. There is quite a household, all of whom I enjoy: her mother, a fine old lady with the breeziness of the West about her, her step-daughter, a perfectly charming young person of twenty-two of whom she has had charge since she was four, and who is enough like her to be her own daughter, her son by her first marriage, for the sake of whose throat and lungs she stays down here, the tutor who is preparing him for college (for which he is a good deal belated), a very attractive young product of sober college training, and another youngster who is her son's most intimate friend and whose modesty and good sense prove her son's good taste in choosing chums. This youngster, too, is studying with the tutor. It is a lively and most engaging household, in which one can never be alone, and in the midst of which your husband is as young and gay as the youngest member, never, unless expressly challenged to it, saying a single serious word. They are nearly out of the woods: they have heard nearly all my stories! I brought two pictures of you with me: a small copy of the drawing and the photograph which I keep in an oval frame, and Mrs. Peck is so charmed with them that she insists upon keeping one of them on the mantelpiece in her drawing room, so that it sometimes seems almost as if my darling were there. You can imagine how delightful it is for me to have such a young and jolly circle to resort to. They are a thoroughly wholesome lot.

The man I like best is the chief justice,[2] a man a little younger than myself, I judge, though it is hard, with his peculiar, faded out colouring, to tell, and full of what one may call the vivacity of knowledge and of thoughtfulness. I have seldom known a man who responds more quickly to your thought. It [His] mother is a Portug[u]ese: perhaps he has a little of the Latin liveliness in him to which he is entitled as her son but would hardly be entitled as a mere Englishman.

To-morrow evening I dine at the officers' mess at the barracks, as the guest of a captain Rendell[3] who has been so kind as to invite me, after a fifteen minute's talk with me at Mrs. Peck's one afternoon.

There are just enough attractive people in the hotel to make my evenings pleasant and interesting.

And all the while my thoughts follow my darling. How lonely I feel when I realize that I do not know exactly where you are or what you are doing. I love to be with you *in detail*, and it hurts me not to be. But it is delightful to know that you are away from troublesome Princeton and among those whom you have loved and trusted from of old. How hungrily I shall devour the letter now in that stupid post office, with its news of your visit to Savannah! Ah! my pet, how intensely, how passionately, how constantly I love you, and with how intimate a love. It is in my breath, in my life. If you were not there to think of and to return to, how flat and empty everything I now enjoy would be! I love you, I love you, I love you! My heart cries out with a mixture of pain and joy in the words and I am always and altogether

Your own Woodrow

Thank you for the lovely letter from Savannah just rec'd.

WWTLS (WC, NjP).

1 Because he had had phlebitis in this leg in December 1904-January 1905, about which see WW to R. Bridges, Dec. 9, 1904, n. 1, Vol. 15.

2 Henry Cowper Gollan.

3 Captain F. H. Rendall, 2nd Battalion, the Duke of Cornwall's Light Infantry, a veteran of the Boer War, 1899-1902.

From John Howell Westcott

Dear Woodrow: Princeton, N. J. Feb. 6, 1908

First, many thanks for your kind letter, which gave much pleasure to Miss Bate[1] as well as to me[.] The satisfaction expressed by all our best friends is a great element in our happiness.

My own thankfulness I cannot express. With this beautiful and brave woman beside me, I can face life again with normal courage, and do my duty with some pleasure, & not merely be-[cause] I must.

I have been thinking a good deal, lately, of the situation in the department. Abbott will be here tomorrow, & we hope his visit will lead to his acceptance of the call.[2] We shall then be in a fair way to plan out a satisfactory scheme of advanced courses to be offered. With our fine Seminary equipment, and with such teachers, we need only a fair number of graduate scholarships & fellowships to put us in the front rank.

I, as well as the other men, realize that our department has been most generously treated by you & the Trustees. I realize also that the annual expense is very heavy, and I do not wish to lose sight of the need of due economy. When I took the chairmanship at your desire, it was with the understanding that the preceptorial method was to be applied strictly to all courses in classics. I therefore urged the necessity of having men enough to do it, without undue taxing of each man—that is, so that each man should have neither too many pupils at once nor too many hours of teaching. And my demands were all met. During the term just closed we had in these two particulars exactly what seemed desirable—as the number of freshmen was a little smaller than last year. This coming term, owing to the loss which always occurs at this time, and the fact that none are taking one or two of the advanced courses, the men are actually not called on to do quite as much as we could reasonably ask. This is no disaster, for many of them have been a little overworked once or twice, & it may encourage them to more study, & to the development of material for advanced courses, such as we hope to enable some of them to offer soon. So far, I am sure you will agree with me. Upon this basis, & with the tendency of the numbers in Greek to diminish rather than increase, it might be safe to drop off one or two of our instructors at the end of this year—with the understanding that if the next class is decidedly larger, we should try to get additional teachers.

As to the next point I am not sure whether you will agree with me. Many of the men in the department feel that the preceptorial method does not apply very well to some of the courses—that it is unnecessarily expensive of time and money, & that there is a chance for a wise economy just here. I am rather non-committal about it, until I know your views. I wish to do nothing that will in any way impair the efficiency or the prestige of the system, which is of the utmost value. But a merely "academic" application of it, in an *a priori* spirit is not very wise. Are you willing to consider some modification in its application, even if some important courses should not seem to be "preceptorial" in the sense in which you have expounded the idea. You can never quite realize the actual conditions of the problem, in any department, where you do not personally teach. I think you had better call the professors of classics together when you come home, & go into this matter & hear all views. If there were no bill to pay, it would not be so important, but I am very anxious that the system, especially in our department, shall not be open to the charge of extravagance, & that we may be as economical as we can be without loss of efficiency.

Ever yours faithfully J. H. Westcott

ALS (WWP, UA, NjP).

[1] His fiancée, Marian Bate, of Salisbury Mills, N. Y., and Princeton, sometime assistant in the university Art Museum. They were married on March 25, 1908.

[2] He did accept Princeton's call. See F. F. Abbott to H. B. Fine, March 2, 1908, printed as an Enclosure with H. B. Fine to WW, March 4, 1908, Vol. 18.

To Cyrus Hall McCormick

My dear Cyrus, Bermuda, 10 February, 1908.

Your letter of January thirtieth has been forwarded to me here.[1]

It will give me the greatest pleasure to be your guest when I come on for the alumni banquet.[2] My secretary writes me that March twelfth has been chosen.

I will also gladly attend the Y.M.C.A. dinner of which you write as planned for the twenty-seventh of April. I think that you are probably engaging too many speakers, but I at least can be brief.[3]

Thank you most warmly for what you say about the April meeting of the Board. Things will certainly have to be very wisely and very courageously handled at Princeton; but I have an abiding faith, in the face of all mortifications, that they will be.

Please give Mrs. McCormick my warmest regards and believe me

Always

Faithfully and cordially Yours, Woodrow Wilson

WWTLS (WP, DLC).

[1] It is missing.

[2] Wilson's address to the Princeton Club of Chicago is printed at March 12, 1908, Vol. 18.

[3] A news report of Wilson's remarks at the semi-centennial celebration of the Chicago Y.M.C.A. is printed at April 28, 1908, Vol. 18.

An Announcement

[Feb. 15, 1908]

Lecture.

We understand that Dr. Woodrow Wilson, President of Princeton University, will lecture, probably in the Princess Hotel, on Monday evening next.[1] The proceeds will be donated to the Bermuda Natural History Society.

Printed in the Hamilton, Bermuda, *Royal Gazette*, Feb. 15, 1908.

[1] The Hamilton *Royal Gazette* did not print a report of this lecture, if, indeed, Wilson delivered it.

To William Henry Carpenter

Hamilton, Bermuda.

My dear Mr. Carpenter, 17 February, 1908.

I am glad to tell you that I have been able here to write out at last the last two lectures of my Blumenthal course. So soon as I get home I will have my secretary copy them and forward them to the printers.

At the same time I will send a brief prefatory note.

I am expecting to sail next week, and to reach Princeton on the twenty-seventh of this month.

Very sincerely Yours, Woodrow Wilson

WWTLS (photostat in RSB Coll., DLC).

From Lawrence Crane Woods

Personal & Confidential

Pittsburg, Penna.

My dear Dr. Wilson: February 19, 1908

It has been difficult for me to secure the information which you desire regarding Mr. Henry Jones Ford as it was of such an intimate personal character that I had to proceed most carefully, as of course it was impossible for me to say why I desired the information. I think I have secured all the information it is possible for me to secure, and I shall answer your questions categorically.

1. "What impression of him was formed by his colleagues in the newspaper business, and why did he give up his position with the newspaper?"

Mr. Ford was editor of the Pittsburg "Gazette Times." Mr. George T. Oliver, the proprietor of this paper, is one of the millionaires who have purchased and consolidated a number of

Pittsburg papers, principally to increase his own political influence. He is politically allied with Senator [Boies] Penrose and is supposed to be one of the principal powers in Pennsylvania politics. No one on his newspapers has a right to any opinions of his own, and apparently morals are not considered, at least as far as politics are concerned. In the editorial work of his newspaper, as far as I can judge, it is creditable to Mr. Ford that such a position was uncongenial to him. Aside from this, his wife was from Baltimore and preferred residence in the East, especially if it could be at her old home. The opinion of his colleagues is, I think, covered by the enclosed statement,[1] which comes to me from a source in which I have thoro confidence.

2. "Did he exercise any personal influence outside of the newspaper office of any kind to show personal force, etc?"

I think I am safe in answering this question No. Mr. Ford was of a scholarly, rather retiring type personally and seems to have hardly been known in Pittsburg in spite of the fact that he lived in the East End and Sewickley for a number of years, altho, of course, from the very nature of his position under Mr. Oliver it would have been impossible for him to have shown any gifts of leadership or stimulation.

3. "Of whom does his family consist, and what in general are his wife and children like?"

Mrs. Ford was a Miss Bertha Batory, daughter, I am given to understand, of a wealthy Hungarian wholesale fruit dealer of Baltimore. Her father died some years ago, leaving her personally some $30,000. By Hungarian, of course I mean a high type of this nationality. Mrs. Ford when she lived in Sewickley was quite active in the Women's Club and in the Episcopal Church. My sister tells me that she played one of Beethoven's most difficult Sonatas before you made your first address in Edgeworth Club, Sewickley, some years ago. The fact that a woman forty-five years of age, mother of four children almost grown, had not only the original talent to do this but had maintained it thru all her married life shows that she is a woman of more than ordinary force of character. In appearance she is slightly foreign, of the type of Southern Europe. While she moved in the best circles of Sewickley society and was president of the Southern Society of Pittsburg, the intimation is that she was slightly of the "climber" type in perhaps the best sense of that expression—ambitious for her own and more particularly for her children's social position, and perhaps not quite as sure of it as she might have been. Her only daughter, Miss Dorothy Ford, was quite popular among the young people of Sewickley, her name appearing almost continuously in the society columns, and you will notice from the attached memorandum that she is reported to be engaged to one of the Carrolls of Carrollton.

The picture that our Mr. Duff gave me, and which I sent to you last summer,[2] of their somewhat Bohemian housekeeping will probably give you some clue to a correct answer to this question. There were three sons, John Howard, Albert and Franklin. I am under the impression that one of them has since died.

On the whole, the impression conveyed to me is that his family relationship would not be any bar to a professorship in Princeton. At the same time, I do not believe they would be peculiarly congenial and exceptionally helpful to him in Princeton circles. Perhaps neutral is the best word to apply to this phase of the question. Personally, Mr. Ford impressed me as a charming personality, combining a traveled mind with broad human ideals and the highest standards for political and business life, but perhaps a little too much inclined to a theoretical, scholarly study of such questions rather than to a forceful application with a view to helping such conditions and leading in any forward, constructive work.

I am frankly and as intelligently as the means at my disposal permit answering your inquiries. At the same time, however, I must confess that I do not feel that I have secured a close enough contact with the whole matter to feel that it would be just either to Princeton or to Mr. Ford to regard my findings as conclusive. Might it not be well to institute some inquiries thru Baltimore? If anyone were going down there it would be an easy matter to secure a much truer picture of the man and his family. At the same time, I have a number of friends in Baltimore and if you would like to have me continue my inquiries by correspondence there, I think I could properly and quietly do so. Meanwhile, should I hear anything further which I think would throw further light on the whole subject, I shall promptly advise you.

Trusting that you have had a very delightful and refreshing rest, with very kindest regards, believe me,

Most cordially yours, Lawrence C. Woods

TLS (WP, DLC).

[1] A one-page typed statement about Henry Jones Ford and his family, dated Jan. 17, 1908, and initialed "O. M. S."

[2] See L. C. Woods to WW, Aug. 24, 1907, n. 1.

From Leo Stanton Rowe

My dear President Wilson: Philadelphia Feb. 24, 1908.

You may remember that some time ago I wrote to you with reference to the work in political science of Mr. Henry Jones Ford. I then mentioned the fact that I considered him one of the most advanced thinkers in this field and that his book on "The Rise and Growth of American Politics" is one of the most suggestive of recent works in this field.

I know that Mr. Ford is extremely anxious for a permanent academic post, and that the matter of salary is rather a secondary consideration. He is anxious to be in a position to devote all his time to teaching and research in political science.

During my absence in South America Mr. Ford gave two courses at the University of Pennsylvania, and his work was very satisfactory.

I feel quite certain that if he is placed in a position to devote himself exclusively to his special interests he will publish some most important investigations in the development of political institutions.

I am, Very cordially yours, L S Rowe

TLS (WP, DLC).

A News Item

[Feb. 29, 1908]

PRESIDENT WILSON'S RETURN. . . .

President Woodrow Wilson landed in New York Thursday morning [February 27] from Bermuda after a four weeks rest, and came to Princeton that afternoon, arriving here on the 2 o'clock train.

Printed in the *Daily Princetonian*, Feb. 29, 1908.

ADDENDA

To Henry Mills Alden

My dear Mr. Alden, Princeton, New Jersey, 4 August, 1895.

Can you beg, borrow, or steal for me a copy of the "History of the Dividing Line and other tracts, from the papers of William Byrd of Westover," commonly called the Westover Manuscripts? One edition was published in Petersburg, Va., 1844,[1] but a much better in Richmond in 1866, under the editorship of Thomas H. Wynne.[2] I have tried all the second hand book men at all likely to know where to get it, have asked the loan of it in vain of one or two public libraries, and now at last turn to you, in the hope you may know how to get it. I am sorry to trouble you, but time flies.

My first essay[3] is well under way; and I have little fear of not having it ready by the first of September. I should like to keep it much longer, and work it over to suit my standards better; but that process is no doubt endless.

What decision have you reached about illustration? I should suppose that illustration would be almost necessary if special prominence or emphasis is to be given this series.[4]

With warm regard,

Sincerely Yours, Woodrow Wilson

WWTLS (WC, NjP).

1 Edmund Ruffin (ed.), *The Westover Manuscripts* (Petersburg, Va., 1841).

2 Thomas H. Wynne (ed.), *History of the Dividing Line, and Other Tracts . . .* (Richmond, Va., 1866).

3 Of his biography of Washington, to be serialized in *Harper's Magazine*.

4 See H. M. Alden to WW, Aug. 10, 20, and 23, 1895, Vol. 9.

Three Letters to John Raleigh Mott

My dear Mr. Mott: Princeton, N. J. March 15, 1905.

I need not tell you with what force your kind invitation[1] to speak at the Conference next Summer, comes to me, but as you know, I have only recently undergone a surgical operation and the doctor tells me very imperatively that I really must avoid undertaking any duties which do not lie directly in my official path, so that the summer's rest may intervene before I give rein to my energies again.

I feel perfectly well, and am of course fulfilling the engagements made before I knew the trouble I was to get into, but I am sure you will understand how necessary it is for me to obey orders.

Cordially and sincerely yours, Woodrow Wilson

TLS (J. R. Mott Coll., CtY-D).
[1] It is missing.

My dear Mr. Mott: Princeton, N. J. 25 October, 1905.

I have thought about your invitation[1] over night and see very clearly that I must accept. I do so with a great deal of misgiving as to my ability to do well the thing which you wish me to do, but I promise you to do my best.

I will ask you to give me full information as to particulars as soon as your program and arrangements are made.

With warm regards,

Sincerely yours, Woodrow Wilson

TLS (J. R. Mott Coll., CtY-D).
[1] Mott's letter is missing, but it was an invitation to Wilson to speak at the Inter-Church Conference on Federation in New York on November 19, 1905, about which see n. 2 to the notes for an address printed at Nov. 19, 1905, and the news reports of Wilson's address printed at Nov. 20, 1905, all in Vol. 16.

My dear Mr. Mott: Princeton, N. J. 1 November, 1905.

I have found myself very much at a loss to devise a title for the address I am to make on the afternoon of November 19th. The best I can think of is very vague. What would you think of this as a title—"The Function and Mediation of Youth in Christian Progress"?

If you do not like that, please frankly say so and I will try for something more simple. This title, abstract as it sounds, really describes what I am going to speak about. Perhaps it would be as well to leave out the word "Function" and simply make the title —"The Mediation of Youth in Christian Progress," but I shall welcome any suggestion you may wish to make.[1]

Cordially and sincerely yours, Woodrow Wilson

TLS (J. R. Mott Coll. CtY-D).
[1] Wilson used the title, "The Mediation of Youth in Christian Progress."

From John Raleigh Mott

My dear President Wilson: [New York] November 20th, 1905.

Once more let me express to you my deepest appreciation of the address you gave yesterday afternoon. If you could hear what has come to my attention today from so many quarters regarding your message you would be impressed by the Providential character of your visit.

If you will kindly let me have an item of your total expenses I shall see that the amount is remitted to you promptly. I regret that the Committee on the Inter-church Conference have not been able to arrange to provide more than the expenses of speakers.

With sincere regard, believe me,

Faithfully yours, John R. Mott.

CCL (J. R. Mott Coll., CtY-D).

To John Raleigh Mott

My dear Mr. Mott: Princeton, N. J. 21 November, 1905.

Allow me to thank you for your kind letter of November 20th. It is very delightful to me to think that I was of some real service to you at the meeting on Sunday afternoon.

My expenses were only $7.30.

With warm regard,

Sincerely yours, Woodrow Wilson

TLS (J. R. MOTT Coll., CtY-D).

INDEX

NOTE ON THE INDEX

THE alphabetically arranged analytical table of contents at the front of the volume eliminates duplication, in both contents and index, of references to certain documents, such as letters. Letters are listed in the contents alphabetically by name, and chronologically within each name by page. The subject matter of all letters is, of course, indexed. The Editorial Notes and Wilson's writings are listed in the contents chronologically by page. In addition, the subject matter of both categories is indexed. The index covers all references to books and articles mentioned in text or notes. Footnotes are indexed. Page references to footnotes which place a comma between the page number and "n" cite both text and footnote, thus: "624,n3." On the other hand, absence of the comma indicates reference to the footnote only, thus: "55n2"—the page number denoting where the footnote appears. The letter "n" without a following digit signifies an unnumbered descriptive-location note.

An asterisk before an index reference designates identification or other particular information. Re-identification and repetitive annotation have been minimized to encourage use of these starred references. Where the identification appears in an earlier volume, it is indicated thus: "*1:212,n3." Therefore a page reference standing without a preceding volume number is invariably a reference to the present volume. The index supplies the fullest known forms of names, and, for the Wilson and Axson families, relationships as far down as cousins. Persons referred to in the text by nicknames or shortened forms of names can be identified by reference to entries for these forms of the names.

A sampling of the opinions and comments of Wilson and Ellen Axson Wilson covers their more personal views, while broad, general headings in the main body of the index cover impersonal subjects. Occasionally opinions expressed by a correspondent are indexed where these appear to supplement or to reflect views expressed by Wilson or by Ellen Axson Wilson in documents which are missing.

INDEX

PRINCETON UNIVERSITY

See also Wilson, Woodrow, PRESIDENT OF PRINCETON

WOODROW WILSON

APPEARANCE

FAMILY LIFE AND DOMESTIC AFFAIRS

HEALTH